GLEIM® | Aviation

2021 EDITION

FUNDAMENTALS OF INSTRUCTING
FAA Knowledge Test Prep

for the FAA Computer-Based Pilot Knowledge Test

by
Irvin N. Gleim, Ph.D., CFII, and Garrett W. Gleim, CFII

Gleim Publications, Inc.
PO Box 12848
Gainesville, Florida 32604

(352) 375-0772
(800) 87-GLEIM or (800) 874-5346
www.GleimAviation.com
aviationteam@gleim.com

For updates to the first printing of the 2021 edition of
Fundamentals of Instructing
FAA Knowledge Test Prep

Go To: www.GleimAviation.com/updates

Or: Email update@gleim.com with **FOI 2021-1** in the subject line. You will receive our current update as a reply.

Updates are available until the next edition is published.

ISSN 1553-6890
ISBN 978-1-61854-327-1

Let Us Know!

This 2021 edition is designed specifically for pilots who aspire to obtain the flight instructor certificate and/or ground instructor certificate. Please send any corrections and suggestions for subsequent editions to us via the feedback links within the online components or using the form at www.GleimAviation.com/questions.

A companion volume, ***Flight/Ground Instructor FAA Knowledge Test Prep***, is available, as is ***Flight Instructor Flight Maneuvers and Practical Test Prep***, which focuses on the FAA practical test, just as this book focuses on the FAA knowledge test. Save time, money, and frustration--order online at www.GleimAviation.com today! Please bring these books to the attention of flight instructors, fixed-base operators, and others with a potential interest in acquiring their flight instructor certificates. Wide distribution of these books and increased interest in flying depend on your assistance and good word. Thank you.

Environmental Statement -- This book is printed on recyclable paper sourced from suppliers certified using sustainable forestry management processes and is produced either TCF (Totally Chlorine-Free) or ECF (Elementally Chlorine-Free).

Our answers have been carefully researched and reviewed. Inevitably, there will be differences with competitors' books and even the FAA. If necessary, we will develop an UPDATE for ***Fundamentals of Instructing FAA Knowledge Test Prep***. Visit our website or email update@gleim.com for the latest updates. Updates for this 2021 edition will be available until the next edition is published. To continue providing our customers with first-rate service, we request that technical questions about our materials be sent to us via the feedback links within the online components. We will give each question thorough consideration and a prompt response. Questions concerning orders, prices, shipments, or payments will be handled via telephone by our competent and courteous customer service staff.

ABOUT THE AUTHORS

Irvin N. Gleim earned his private pilot certificate in 1965 from the Institute of Aviation at the University of Illinois, where he subsequently received his Ph.D. He is a commercial pilot and flight instructor (instrument) with multi-engine and seaplane ratings and is a member of the Aircraft Owners and Pilots Association, American Bonanza Society, Civil Air Patrol, Experimental Aircraft Association, National Association of Flight Instructors, and Seaplane Pilots Association. He is the author of flight maneuvers and practical test prep books for the sport, private, instrument, commercial, and flight instructor certificates/ratings and the author of study guides for the remote, sport, private/recreational, instrument, commercial, flight/ground instructor, fundamentals of instructing, airline transport pilot, and flight engineer FAA knowledge tests. Three additional pilot training books are *Pilot Handbook*, *Aviation Weather and Weather Services*, and *FAR/AIM*.

Dr. Gleim has also written articles for professional accounting and business law journals and is the author of widely used review manuals for the CIA (Certified Internal Auditor) exam, the CMA (Certified Management Accountant) exam, the CPA (Certified Public Accountant) exam, and the EA (IRS Enrolled Agent) exam. He is Professor Emeritus, Fisher School of Accounting, University of Florida, and is a CFM, CIA, CMA, and CPA.

Garrett W. Gleim earned his private pilot certificate in 1997 in a Piper Super Cub. He is a commercial pilot (single- and multi-engine), ground instructor (advanced and instrument), and flight instructor (instrument and multi-engine), and he is a member of the Aircraft Owners and Pilots Association, the National Association of Flight Instructors, and the Society of Aviation and Flight Educators. He is the author of study guides for the remote, sport, private/recreational, instrument, commercial, flight/ground instructor, fundamentals of instructing, and airline transport pilot FAA knowledge tests. He received a Bachelor of Science in Economics from The Wharton School, University of Pennsylvania. Mr. Gleim is also a CPA.

REVIEWERS AND CONTRIBUTORS

Paul Duty, CFII, MEI, AGI, Remote Pilot, is a graduate of Embry-Riddle Aeronautical University with a Master of Business Administration-Aviation degree. He is our aviation product manager and the Gleim Part 141 Chief Ground Instructor. Mr. Duty is an active flight instructor, commercial pilot, and remote pilot. He researched questions, wrote and edited answer explanations, and incorporated revisions into the text.

Clayton Gamber, ATP, A&P, IA, is a graduate of Virginia Tech with over 40 years experience in operations and maintenance for commercial aviation. He researched questions, wrote and edited answer explanations, and incorporated revisions into the text.

Ryan Jeff, CFI, AGI, Remote Pilot, graduated summa cum laude from Embry-Riddle Aeronautical University with a degree in Aeronautics and a minor in Applied Meteorology. He researched questions, wrote and edited answer explanations, and incorporated revisions into the text.

Karl Winters, CFII, AGI, IGI, Remote Pilot, is a graduate of Purdue University and is a 141 check airman and a flight instructor in the School of Aeronautics at Liberty University. Mr. Winters is also the Gleim Part 141 Assistant Chief Ground Instructor and one of our aviation editors. He researched questions, wrote and edited answer explanations, and incorporated revisions into the text.

The CFIs who have worked with us throughout the years to develop and improve our pilot training materials.

The many FAA employees who helped, in person or by telephone, primarily in Gainesville; Orlando; Oklahoma City; and Washington, DC.

The many pilots who have provided comments and suggestions about *Fundamentals of Instructing FAA Knowledge Test Prep* during the past several decades.

A PERSONAL THANKS

This manual would not have been possible without the extraordinary effort and dedication of Jacob Bennett, Julie Cutlip, Ethan Good, Doug Green, Fernanda Martinez, Bree Rodriguez, Teresa Soard, Justin Stephenson, Joanne Strong, Elmer Tucker, Candace Van Doren, and Ryan Van Tress, who typed the entire manuscript and all revisions and drafted and laid out the diagrams, illustrations, and cover for this book.

The authors also appreciate the production and editorial assistance of Sirene Dagher, Michaela Giampaolo, Jessica Hatker, Sonora Hospital-Medina, Katie Larson, Michael Lupi, Bryce Owen, Shane Rapp, and Alyssa Thomas.

The authors also appreciate the video production expertise of Gary Brook, Philip Brubaker, and Matthew Church, who helped produce and edit all Gleim Aviation videos.

Finally, we appreciate the encouragement, support, and tolerance of our families throughout this project.

TABLE OF CONTENTS

NOTE: The FAA does not release its complete database of test questions to the public. Instead, sample questions are released on the practice exam page of the PSI website. These questions are similar to the actual test questions, but they are not exact matches.

Gleim utilizes customer feedback and FAA publications to create additional sample questions that closely represent the topical coverage of each FAA knowledge test. In order to do well on the knowledge test, you must study the Gleim outlines in this book, answer all the questions under exam conditions (i.e., without looking at the answers first), and develop an understanding of the topics addressed. You should not simply memorize questions and answers. This will not prepare you for your FAA knowledge test, and it will not help you develop the knowledge you need to competently teach someone how to fly.

Always refer to the Gleim update service (www.GleimAviation.com/updates) to ensure you have the latest information that is available. If you see topics covered on your FAA knowledge test that are not contained in this book, please contact us at www.GleimAviation.com/questions to report your experience and help us fine-tune our test preparation materials.

Thank you!

PREFACE

This book has three purposes:

1. To provide you with the easiest and fastest means of passing the Fundamentals of Instructing (FOI) Knowledge Test

2. To help experienced and inexperienced aviation instructors improve instruction techniques

3. To assist flight and/or ground instructors in organizing and presenting aviation ground schools that prepare individuals to pass the FAA pilot knowledge tests

FOI Knowledge Test

Successful completion of the FOI knowledge test is required by the FAA for those seeking the flight instructor or ground instructor certificates. The introduction of this book (beginning on the next page) contains a discussion of the requirements to obtain the flight instructor and ground instructor certificates and a description of the FOI knowledge test, how to prepare for it and take it, and how to maximize your score with minimum effort. Study Units 1 through 6 contain outlines of what you need to know to answer the FAA knowledge test questions, as well as all of the previously released FAA test questions and our own similar questions, each accompanied by a comprehensive explanation.

NOTE: Appendix A contains a practice test, consisting of 50 questions from this book, that reflects the subject matter composition of the FAA knowledge test.

Improving Instruction Methods

The FAA publishes *Aviation Instructor's Handbook* (FAA-H-8083-9B), which explains the basic principles and processes of teaching and learning. This is the subject matter of the FOI knowledge test. This material is more easily presented and studied in outline format, as it appears in Study Units 1 through 6 of this book. Both experienced and inexperienced aviation instructors will find the study of these outlines very useful in improving their instruction methods.

Appendix B of this book (226 pages in length) is a reprint of the *Aviation Instructor's Handbook*. It is useful reading and a valuable periodic review for CFIs; thus, we include it in this Gleim book. The FAA text consists of 10 chapters and 4 appendixes:

1. Risk Management and Single-Pilot Resource Management
2. Human Behavior
3. The Learning Process
4. Effective Communication
5. The Teaching Process
6. Assessment
7. Planning Instructional Activity
8. Aviation Instructor Responsibilities and Professionalism
9. Techniques of Flight Instruction
10. Teaching Practical Risk Management during Flight Instruction
Appendix A: References
Appendix B: Developing a Test Item Bank
Appendix C: Certificates, Ratings, and Endorsements
Appendix D: Personal Minimums Checklist

Ground School Course Suggestions

Many aviation instructors would like to increase the general public's interest in learning to fly. These instructors also enjoy teaching. Appendix C of this book consists of suggestions on how to find (or become) a sponsor for a ground school. It also contains suggestions on course organization, lecture outlines, and class presentation.

Enjoy Flying Safely!

Irvin N. Gleim
Garrett W. Gleim

August 2020

INTRODUCTION: THE FAA PILOT KNOWLEDGE TEST

This introduction explains how to obtain a flight instructor certificate, including a sport pilot rating. The ground instructor certificate is also addressed. It explains the content and procedures of the relevant Federal Aviation Administration (FAA) knowledge tests, including how to take a test at a computer testing center. The remainder of this introduction discusses and illustrates the Gleim **Online Ground School** and **FAA Test Prep Online**. Achieving an instructor certificate is fun. Begin today!

Fundamentals of Instructing FAA Knowledge Test Prep is one of four related books for obtaining your flight and/or ground instructor certificate. The other three books are

1. *Flight/Ground Instructor FAA Knowledge Test Prep*
2. *Flight Instructor Flight Maneuvers and Practical Test Prep*
3. *Pilot Handbook*

Flight/Ground Instructor FAA Knowledge Test Prep prepares you to pass the FAA's flight and/or ground instructor knowledge test. If you are planning to obtain both the flight and ground instructor certificates, you only need to pass the Fundamentals of Instructing (FOI) test once.

Flight Instructor Flight Maneuvers and Practical Test Prep is a comprehensive, carefully organized presentation of everything you need to know to prepare for your flight training and for your flight instructor practical (flight) test. It integrates material from FAA publications and other sources.

Pilot Handbook is a complete pilot reference book that combines over 100 FAA books and documents, including *AIM*, Federal Aviation Regulations, ACs, and much more. Aerodynamics, airplane systems, airspace, and navigation are among the topics explained in *Pilot Handbook*.

While the following books are not included in the list above, you may want to purchase them if you do not already have them:

FAR/AIM is an essential part of every instructor's library. The Gleim *FAR/AIM* is an easy-to-read reference book containing all of the Federal Aviation Regulations applicable to general aviation flying, plus the full text of the FAA's *Aeronautical Information Manual (AIM)*.

The Gleim *Aviation Weather and Weather Services* book combines all of the information from the FAA's *Aviation Weather* (AC 00-6), *Aviation Weather Services* (AC 00-45), and numerous FAA publications into one easy-to-understand reference book.

WHAT IS A FLIGHT INSTRUCTOR CERTIFICATE?

A flight instructor certificate is similar in appearance to your commercial pilot certificate and will allow you to give flight and ground instruction. The certificate is sent to you by the FAA upon satisfactory completion of your training program, two knowledge tests, and a practical test. It expires at the end of the 24th month after issue. A new certificate is sent to you by the FAA upon renewal. A sample flight instructor certificate is reproduced below.

REQUIREMENTS TO OBTAIN A FLIGHT INSTRUCTOR CERTIFICATE

1. Be at least 18 years of age.

2. Be able to read, write, speak, and understand the English language (certificates with operating limitations may be available for medically related deficiencies).

3. Hold a commercial or airline transport pilot (ATP) certificate with an aircraft rating appropriate to the flight instructor rating sought (e.g., airplane, glider).

    a. You must also hold an instrument rating to be a flight instructor in an airplane.

4. Study this book, ***Flight Instructor FAA Knowledge Test Prep***, ***Flight Instructor Flight Maneuvers and Practical Test Prep***, ***FAR/AIM***, ***Aviation Weather and Weather Services***, and ***Pilot Handbook*** or use the Gleim Online Ground School to learn

    a. Fundamentals of instructing

    b. All other subject areas in which ground training is required for recreational, private, and commercial pilot certificates

5. Pass both the FOI and the flight instructor knowledge tests with scores of 70% or better.

    a. All FAA knowledge tests are administered at FAA-designated computer testing centers.

        1) Page 12 contains additional details.

    b. The FOI and flight instructor tests consist of 50 and 100 multiple-choice questions, respectively, selected from the airplane-related questions in the FAA's flight and ground instructor knowledge test bank.

    c. Questions similar to those you will see on the knowledge test are reproduced in this book with complete explanations.

    d. You are not required to take the FOI knowledge test if you

        1) Hold an FAA flight or ground instructor certificate,

        2) Hold a current teacher's certificate authorizing you to teach at an educational level of the 7th grade or higher, or

        3) Are employed as a teacher at an accredited college or university.

6.　Demonstrate flight proficiency (14 CFR 61.187).

    a.　You must receive and log flight and ground training and obtain a logbook endorsement from an authorized instructor on the following areas of operations for an airplane category rating with a single-engine or multi-engine class rating:

        1)　Fundamentals of instructing

        2)　Technical subject areas

        3)　Preflight preparation

        4)　Preflight lesson on a maneuver to be performed in flight

        5)　Preflight procedures

        6)　Airport and seaplane base operations

        7)　Takeoffs, landings, and go-arounds

        8)　Fundamentals of flight

        9)　Performance maneuvers

        10)　Ground reference maneuvers

        11)　Slow flight, stalls, and spins (single-engine only)

            a)　Slow flight and stalls (multi-engine only)

        12)　Basic instrument maneuvers

        13)　Emergency operations

        14)　Multi-engine operations (multi-engine only)

        15)　Postflight procedures

    b.　A CFI who provides training to an initial applicant for a flight instructor certificate must have held a flight instructor certificate for at least 24 months and have given at least 200 hr. of flight training as a CFI.

    c.　You must also obtain a logbook endorsement by an appropriately certificated and rated flight instructor who has provided you with spin entry, spin, and spin recovery training in an airplane that is certificated for spins and who has found you instructionally competent and proficient in those training areas, i.e., so you can teach spin recovery.

7.　Alternatively, enroll in an FAA-certificated pilot school that has an approved flight instructor certification course (airplane).

    a.　These are known as Part 141 schools or Part 142 training centers because they are authorized by Part 141 or Part 142 of the Federal Aviation Regulations.

        1)　All other regulations concerning the certification of pilots are found in Part 61 of the Federal Aviation Regulations.

    b.　The Part 141 course must consist of at least 40 hr. of ground instruction and 25 hr. of flight instructor training.

8.　Successfully complete a practical (flight) test, which will be given as a final exam by an FAA inspector or designated pilot examiner. The practical test will be conducted as specified in the FAA's Flight Instructor Practical Test Standards (FAA-S-8081-6).

    a.　FAA inspectors are FAA employees and do not charge for their services.

    b.　FAA-designated pilot examiners are proficient, experienced flight instructors and pilots who are authorized by the FAA to conduct flight tests. They do charge a fee.

 The FAA's Flight Instructor Practical Test Standards are outlined and reprinted in the Gleim *Flight Instructor Flight Maneuvers and Practical Test Prep* book.

REQUIREMENTS TO OBTAIN A GROUND INSTRUCTOR CERTIFICATE

1.   To be eligible for a ground instructor certificate, you must

    a.   Be at least 18 years of age.

    b.   Be able to read, write, speak, and understand the English language (certificates with operating limitations may be available for medically related deficiencies).

    c.   Exhibit theoretical knowledge by passing the FOI and the appropriate ground instructor knowledge tests.

        1)   Item 5.d. on page 2 discusses when the FOI knowledge test is not required.

2.   Ground instructor certificates cover three levels of certification:

    a.   Basic ground instructor (BGI) may provide

        1)   Ground training in the aeronautical knowledge areas required for a sport, recreational, or private pilot certificate

        2)   Ground training required for a sport, recreational, or private pilot flight review

        3)   A recommendation for the sport, recreational, or private pilot knowledge test

    b.   Advanced ground instructor (AGI) may provide

        1)   Ground training in the aeronautical knowledge areas required for any certificate or rating (except for an instrument rating) issued under Part 61

        2)   Ground training required for any flight review, but not for an instrument proficiency check (IPC)

        3)   A recommendation for a knowledge test required for any certificate issued under Part 61 except for the instrument rating knowledge test

    c.   Instrument ground instructor (IGI) may provide

        1)   Ground training in the aeronautical knowledge areas required for an instrument rating to a pilot or instructor certificate

        2)   Ground training required for an instrument proficiency check

        3)   A recommendation for the instrument rating knowledge test for a pilot or instructor certificate

    NOTE: The Gleim *Instrument Pilot FAA Knowledge Test Prep* covers the IGI knowledge test, which consists of 50 questions with a 2.5 hr. time limit.

3.   If you are not a CFI, the Federal Aviation Regulations require you to have a ground instructor certificate to teach ground school or to sign off applicants for the appropriate pilot knowledge test.

Recall that this book has its primary focus on flight instructor -- airplane. Your BGI or AGI knowledge test may have a few non-airplane questions. Use the knowledge you have acquired to take your best guess at these questions without worry. There is no need to study all of the extra questions unless you are going to teach subjects related to rotorcraft, gliders, or lighter-than-air aircraft.

REQUIREMENTS TO OBTAIN A FLIGHT INSTRUCTOR CERTIFICATE WITH A SPORT PILOT RATING

1. To obtain a flight instructor certificate with a sport pilot rating, you must pass both practical and knowledge tests.

    a. To take the knowledge tests for both the fundamentals of instructing and the aeronautical knowledge areas for a sport pilot certificate, you must receive a logbook endorsement from an authorized instructor who trained you or evaluated your home-study course on the materials. This certifies that you are prepared for the tests.

FAA PILOT KNOWLEDGE TEST AND TESTING SUPPLEMENT

1. This book is designed to help you prepare for and pass the FAA FOI knowledge test for the flight and/or ground instructor certificate, which consists of 50 questions and has a time limit of 1.5 hours.

    a. The remainder of this introduction explains the FAA test procedures.

2. The FAA has one FOI figure contained in a book titled *Airman Knowledge Testing Supplement for Flight Instructor, Ground Instructor, and Sport Pilot Instructor*, which you will be given to use at the time of your test.

    a. For the purpose of test preparation, we have reproduced the figure on page 131 in this book.

3. In an effort to develop better questions, the FAA frequently **pretests** questions on knowledge tests by adding up to five "pretest" questions. The pretest questions will not be graded.

    a. You will **not** know which questions are real and which are pretest, so you must attempt to answer all questions correctly.

    b. When you notice a question **not** covered by Gleim, it might be a pretest question.

        1) We want to know about each pretest question you see.

        2) Please contact us at www.GleimAviation.com/questions or call 800-874-5346 with your recollection of any possible pretest questions so we may improve our efforts to prepare future instructors.

FAA'S KNOWLEDGE TESTS: CHEATING OR UNAUTHORIZED CONDUCT POLICY

The following is taken verbatim from an FAA knowledge test. It is reproduced here to remind all test takers about the FAA's policy against cheating and unauthorized conduct, a policy that Gleim consistently supports and upholds. Test takers must click "Yes" to proceed from this page into the actual knowledge test.

14 CFR part 61, section 61.37 Knowledge tests: Cheating or other unauthorized conduct

(a) An applicant for a knowledge test may not:
(1) Copy or intentionally remove any knowledge test;
(2) Give to another applicant or receive from another applicant any part or copy of a knowledge test;
(3) Give assistance on, or receive assistance on, a knowledge test during the period that test is being given;
(4) Take any part of a knowledge test on behalf of another person;
(5) Be represented by, or represent, another person for a knowledge test;
(6) Use any material or aid during the period that the test is being given, unless specifically authorized to do so by the Administrator; and
(7) Intentionally cause, assist, or participate in any act prohibited by this paragraph.

(b) An applicant who the Administrator finds has committed an act prohibited by paragraph (a) of this section is prohibited, for 1 year after the date of committing that act, from:
(1) Applying for any certificate, rating, or authorization issued under this chapter; and
(2) Applying for and taking any test under this chapter.

(c) Any certificate or rating held by an applicant may be suspended or revoked if the Administrator finds that person has committed an act prohibited by paragraph (a) of this section.

FAA PILOT KNOWLEDGE TEST QUESTION BANK

In an effort to keep applicants from simply memorizing test questions, the FAA does not disclose all the questions you might see on your FAA knowledge test. We encourage you to take the time to fully learn and understand the concepts explained in the knowledge transfer outlines contained in this book. Memorization greatly reduces the amount of information you will actually learn during your study.

Using this book or other Gleim test preparation material to merely memorize the questions and answers is unwise and unproductive, and it will not ensure your success on your FAA knowledge test.

The questions and answers provided in this book include all previously released FAA questions in addition to questions developed from current FAA reference materials that closely approximate the types of questions you should see on your knowledge test. We are confident that by studying our knowledge transfer outlines, answering our questions under exam conditions, and not relying on rote memorization, you will be able to successfully pass your FAA knowledge test and begin learning to become a safe and competent instructor.

FAA QUESTIONS WITH TYPOGRAPHICAL ERRORS

Occasionally, FAA test questions contain typographical errors such that there is no correct answer. The FAA test development process involves many steps and people and, as you would expect, glitches occur in the system that are beyond the control of any one person. We indicate "best" rather than correct answers for some questions. Use these best answers for the indicated questions.

Note that the FAA corrects (rewrites) defective questions as they are discovered; these changes are explained in our updates (discussed on page ii). However, problems due to faulty or out-of-date figures printed in the FAA Airman Knowledge Testing Supplements are expensive to correct. Thus, it is important to carefully study questions that are noted to have a best answer in this book. Even though the best answer may not be completely correct, you should select it when taking your test.

REORGANIZATION OF FAA QUESTIONS

1. Questions previously released by the FAA were **not** grouped together by topic; i.e., they appeared to be presented randomly.

    a. We have reorganized and renumbered the questions into study units and subunits.

2. Pages 409 through 412 contain a list of all the questions in FAA learning statement code order, with cross-references to the study units and question numbers in this book.

    a. For example, question 3-18 is assigned the code PLT230, which means it is found in Study Unit 3 as question 18 in this book and is covered under the FAA learning statement, "Recall FOI techniques - responsibilities."

HOW TO PREPARE FOR THE FAA PILOT KNOWLEDGE TEST

1. Begin by carefully reading the rest of this introduction. You need to have a complete understanding of the examination process prior to initiating your study. This knowledge will make your studying more efficient.

2. After you have spent an hour analyzing this introduction, set up a study schedule, including a target date for taking your knowledge test.

    a. Do not let the study process drag on and become discouraging; i.e., the quicker, the better.

    b. Consider enrolling in an organized ground school course, like the Gleim **Online Ground School**, or one held at your local FBO, community college, etc.

    c. Determine where and when you are going to take your knowledge test.

3.   Work through Study Units 1 through 6.

   a.   All previously released questions in the FAA's flight and ground instructor knowledge test question bank that are applicable to fundamentals of instructing have been grouped into the following six categories, which are the titles of Study Units 1 through 6:

   Study Unit 1 -- The Learning Process
   Study Unit 2 -- Barriers to Learning
   Study Unit 3 -- Factors Affecting Learning
   Study Unit 4 -- Teaching Methods
   Study Unit 5 -- Planning Instructional Activity
   Study Unit 6 -- Critique and Evaluation

   b.   Within each of the study units listed, questions relating to the same subtopic are grouped together to facilitate your study program. Each subtopic is called a subunit.

   c.   To the right of each question, we present

      1)   The correct answer

      2)   The appropriate source document for the answer explanation (e.g., *FAA-H-8083-9B Chap 1* means *Aviation Instructor's Handbook*, Chapter 1)

      3)   A comprehensive answer explanation, including

         a)   A discussion of the correct answer or concept

         b)   An explanation of why the other two answer choices are incorrect

4.   Each study unit begins with a list of its subunit titles. The number after each title is the number of questions that cover the information in that subunit. The two numbers following the number of questions are the page numbers on which the outline and the questions for that particular subunit begin, respectively.

5.   Begin by studying the outlines slowly and carefully. The outlines in this part of the book are very brief and have only one purpose: to help you pass the FAA knowledge test.

   a.   **CAUTION:** The **sole purpose** of this book is to expedite your passing the FAA knowledge test for the fundamentals of instructing certificate. Accordingly, all extraneous material (i.e., topics or regulations not directly tested on the FAA knowledge test) is omitted, even though much more knowledge is necessary to be an instructor. This additional material is presented in three related Gleim books: ***Flight/Ground Instructor FAA Knowledge Test Prep***, ***Flight Instructor Flight Maneuvers and Practical Test Prep***, and ***Pilot Handbook***.

6.   Next, answer the questions under exam conditions. Cover the answer explanations on the right side of each page with a piece of paper while you answer the questions.

 Remember, it is very important to the learning (and understanding) process that you honestly commit to an answer. If you are wrong, your memory will be reinforced by having discovered your error. Therefore, it is crucial to make an honest attempt to answer the question before reading the answer.

---

   a.   Study the answer explanation for each question that you answer incorrectly, do not understand, or have difficulty with.

   b.   Use our **Online Ground School** or **FAA Test Prep Online** to ensure that you do not refer to answers before committing to one AND to simulate actual computer testing center exam conditions.

7. Note that this test book contains questions grouped by topic. Thus, some questions may appear repetitive, while others may be duplicates or near-duplicates. Accordingly, do not work question after question (i.e., waste time and effort) if you are already conversant with a topic and the type of questions asked.

8. As you move through study units, you may need further explanation or clarification of certain topics. You may wish to obtain and use the following Gleim books described on page 1:

    a. *Flight Instructor Flight Maneuvers and Practical Test Prep*
    b. *Pilot Handbook*
    c. *Aviation Weather and Weather Services*

9. Keep track of your work. As you complete a subunit, grade yourself with an A, B, C, or ? (use a ? if you need help on the subject) next to the subunit title at the front of the respective study unit.

    a. The A, B, C, or ? is your self-evaluation of your comprehension of the material in that subunit and your ability to answer the questions.

    - A   means a good understanding.
    - B   means a fair understanding.
    - C   means a shaky understanding.
    - ?   means to ask your CFI or others about the material and/or questions, and read the pertinent sections in *Flight Instructor Flight Maneuvers and Practical Test Prep* and/or *Pilot Handbook*.

    b. This procedure will provide you with the ability to quickly see (by looking at the first page of each study unit) how much studying you have done (and how much remains) and how well you have done.

    c. This procedure will also facilitate review. You can spend more time on the subunits that were more difficult for you.

    d. **FAA Test Prep Online** provides you with your historical performance data.

Follow the suggestions given throughout this introduction and you will have no trouble passing the FAA knowledge test the first time you take it.

With this overview of exam requirements, you are ready to begin the easy-to-study outlines and rearranged questions with answers to build your knowledge and confidence and **pass the FAA's fundamentals of instructing knowledge test**.

The feedback we receive from users indicates that our materials reduce anxiety, improve FAA test scores, and build knowledge. Studying for each test becomes a useful step toward advanced certificates and ratings.

MULTIPLE-CHOICE QUESTION-ANSWERING TECHNIQUE

Because the FOI knowledge test has a set number of questions (50) and a set time limit (1.5 hours), you can plan your test-taking session to ensure that you leave yourself enough time to answer each question with relative certainty. The following steps will help you move through the knowledge test efficiently and produce better test results.

1. **Budget your time.** We make this point with emphasis. Just as you would fill up your gas tank prior to reaching empty, so too should you finish your exam before time expires.

   a. If you utilize the entire time limit for the test, you will have about 1.8 minutes per question.

   b. If you are adequately prepared for the test, you should finish it well within the time limit.

      1) Use any extra time you have to review questions that you are not sure about and similar questions in your exam that may help you answer other questions.

   c. Time yourself when completing study sessions in this book and/or review your time investment reports from the Gleim **FAA Test Prep Online** to track your progress and adherence to the time limit and your own personal time allocation budget.

2. **Answer the questions in consecutive order.**

   a. Do **not** agonize over any one item. Stay within your time budget.

   b. Mark any questions you are unsure of and return to them later as time allows.

      1) Once you initiate test grading, you will no longer be able to review/change any answers.

   c. Never leave a multiple-choice question unanswered. Make your best educated guess in the time allowed. Remember, your score is based on the number of correct responses. You will not be penalized for guessing incorrectly.

3. **For each multiple-choice question,**

   a. **Try to ignore the answer choices.** Do not allow the answer choices to affect your reading of the question.

      1) If three answer choices are presented, two of them are incorrect. These choices are called **distractors** for good reason. Often, distractors are written to appear correct at first glance until further analysis.

      2) In computational items, the distractors are carefully calculated such that they are the result of making common mistakes. Be careful, and double-check your computations if time permits.

   b. **Read the question carefully** to determine the precise requirement.

      1) Focusing on what is required enables you to ignore extraneous information, to focus on the relevant facts, and to proceed directly to determining the correct answer.

         a) Be especially careful to note when the requirement is an **exception**; e.g., "Which of the following is **not** a type of hypoxia?"

   c. **Determine the correct answer** before looking at the answer choices.

   d. **Read the answer choices carefully.**

      1) Even if the first answer appears to be the correct choice, do **not** skip the remaining answer choices. Questions often require the "best" answer of the choices provided. Thus, each choice requires your consideration.

      2) Treat each answer choice as a true/false question as you analyze it.

    e.   **Click on the best answer.**

        1)   You have a 33% chance of answering the question correctly by blindly guessing; improve your odds with educated guessing.

        2)   For many multiple-choice questions, at least one answer choice can be eliminated with minimal effort, thereby increasing your educated guess to a 50-50 proposition.

4.   After you have been through all the questions in the test, consult the question status list to determine which questions are unanswered and which are marked for review.

    a.   Go back to the marked questions and finalize your answer choices.

    b.   Verify that all questions have been answered.

EDUCATED GUESSING

 The FAA knowledge test sometimes includes questions that are poorly worded or confusing. Expect the unexpected and move forward. Do not let confusing questions affect your concentration or take up too much time; make your best guess and move on.

1.   If you don't know the answer, make an educated guess as follows:

    a.   Rule out answers that you think are incorrect.

    b.   Speculate on what the FAA is looking for and/or the rationale behind the question.

    c.   Select the best answer or guess between equally appealing answers. Your first guess is usually the most intuitive. If you cannot make an educated guess, re-read the stem and each answer choice and pick the most intuitive answer. It's just a guess!

2.   Avoid lingering on any question for too long. Remember your time budget and the overall test time limit.

SIMULATED FAA PRACTICE TEST

Appendix A, "Fundamentals of Instructing Practice Test," beginning on page 163, allows you to practice taking the FAA knowledge test without the answers next to the questions. This test has 50 questions randomly selected from the questions in our fundamentals of instructing knowledge test bank. Topical coverage in the practice test is similar to that of the FAA knowledge test.

It is very important that you answer all 50 questions in one sitting. You should not consult the answers, especially when being referred to figures (charts, tables, etc.) throughout this book where the questions are answered and explained. Analyze your performance based on the answer key that follows the practice test.

It is even better to practice with Test Sessions in the Gleim **FAA Test Prep Online**. These simulate actual computer testing conditions, including the screen layouts, instructions, etc., for PSI.

More information on the Gleim **FAA Test Prep Online** is available on pages 17 and 18.

AUTHORIZATION TO TAKE THE FAA PILOT KNOWLEDGE TEST

The FAA does not require an instructor endorsement for your initial attempt of the FOI. The flight instructor knowledge test also does not require an endorsement, except for sport pilot instructor applicants.

If you fail the knowledge test, you will need an instructor endorsement before you can retake the exam.

WHEN TO TAKE THE FAA PILOT KNOWLEDGE TEST

1.   You must be at least 16 years of age to take the FOI knowledge test.

2.   Take the FAA knowledge test within 30 days of beginning your study.

    a.   Complete the knowledge test early in your training so you can focus your effort toward building your skills through aeronautical experience.

3.   You must obtain your flight or ground instructor certificate within 24 months.

    a.   Otherwise, you will have to retake your knowledge test.

WHAT TO TAKE TO THE FAA PILOT KNOWLEDGE TEST

1.   Picture identification of yourself (e.g., valid driver's license)
2.   Proof of age

COMPUTER TESTING CENTERS

The FAA has contracted with a computer testing service (PSI) to administer FAA knowledge tests. PSI has testing centers throughout the country. To register for the knowledge test, call (844) 704-1487 or visit PSI's website at https://faa.psiexams.com/FAA/login. More information can be found at www.GleimAviation.com/testingcenters.

COMPUTER TESTING PROCEDURES

When you arrive at the testing center, you will be required to provide positive proof of identification and documentary evidence of your age. The identification must include your photograph, signature, and actual residential address if different from the mailing address. This information may be presented in more than one form of identification.

Next, you will sign in on the testing center's daily log. Your signature on the logsheet certifies that, if this is a retest, you meet the applicable requirements (discussed in "Failure on the FAA Pilot Knowledge Test" on page 15) and that you have not passed this test in the past 2 years.

You will be taken into the testing room and seated at a computer terminal. A person from the testing center will assist you in logging onto the system, and you will be asked to confirm your personal data (e.g., name, Social Security number, etc.).

Then you will be given an online introduction to the computer testing system, and you will take a sample test. If you have used our **FAA Test Prep Online**, you will be conversant with the computer testing methodology and environment and will breeze through the sample test.

When you have completed your test, an Airman Knowledge Test Report will be printed out, validated, and given to you by a person from the testing center. Before you leave, you will be required to sign out on the testing center's daily log.

YOUR FAA AIRMAN KNOWLEDGE TEST REPORT

1. You will receive your FAA Airman Knowledge Test Report upon completion of the test. An example test report is reproduced below.

    a. Note that you will receive only one grade as illustrated.

    b. The expiration date is the date by which you must take your FAA practical test.

    c. The report lists the FAA learning statement codes of the questions you missed so you can review the topics you missed prior to your practical test.

U.S. DEPARTMENT OF TRANSPORTATION
Federal Aviation Administration
Airman Knowledge Test Report

NAME:

FAA TRACKING NUMBER (FTN):   **EXAM ID:**

EXAM: Fundamentals of Instructing (FOI)

EXAM DATE: 10/08/2020   **EXAM SITE:**

SCORE: 96   **GRADE:** Pass   **TAKE:** 1

Learning statement codes listed below represent incorrectly answered questions. Learning statement codes and their associated statements can be found at **www.faa.gov/training_testing/testing/airmen**.

Reference material associated with the learning statement codes can be found in the appropriate knowledge test guide at **www.faa.gov/training_testing/testing/airmen/test_guides**.

A single code may represent more than one incorrect response.

PLT229   PLT306

EXPIRATION DATE: 10/31/2022

DO NOT LOSE THIS REPORT

AUTHORIZED INSTRUCTOR'S STATEMENT: (if applicable)

On _____ (date) I gave the above named applicant _____ hours of additional instruction, covering each subject area shown to be deficient, and consider the applicant competent to pass the knowledge test.

Name _____

Cert. No. _____ *(print clearly)*

Type of instructor certificate _____

Signature _____

FRAUDULENT ALTERATION OF THIS FORM BY ANY PERSON IS A BASIS FOR SUSPENSION OR REVOCATION OF ANY CERTIFICATES OR RATINGS HELD BY THAT PERSON.
ISSUED BY: PSI Services LLC
FEDERAL AVIATION ADMINISTRATION

THIS INFORMATION IS PROTECTED BY THE PRIVACY ACT. FOR OFFICIAL USE ONLY.

2.   Use the FAA Listing of Learning Statement Codes listed below to determine which topics you had difficulty with.

PLT022 Define Aeronautical Decision Making (ADM)
PLT103 Recall Aeronautical Decision Making (ADM) - hazardous attitudes
PLT204 Recall effective communication - basic elements
PLT211 Recall evaluation testing characteristics
PLT227 Recall FOI techniques - integrated flight instruction
PLT228 Recall FOI techniques - lesson plans
PLT229 Recall FOI techniques - professionalism
PLT230 Recall FOI techniques - responsibilities
PLT231 Recall FOI techniques / human behavior - anxiety / fear / stress
PLT232 Recall FOI techniques / human behavior - dangerous tendencies
PLT233 Recall FOI techniques / human behavior - defense mechanisms
PLT270 Recall human behavior - social / self fulfillment / physical
PLT271 Recall human factors (ADM) - judgment
PLT272 Recall human factors - stress management
PLT295 Recall instructor techniques - obstacles / planning / activities / outcome

PLT306 Recall learning process - levels of learning / transfer of learning / incidental learning
PLT307 Recall learning process - memory / fact / recall
PLT308 Recall learning process - laws of learning elements
PLT481 Recall student evaluation - learning process
PLT482 Recall student evaluation - written tests / oral quiz / critiques
PLT487 Recall teaching methods - demonstration / performance
PLT488 Recall teaching methods - group / guided discussion / lecture
PLT489 Recall teaching methods - known to unknown
PLT490 Recall teaching methods - motivation / student feelings of insecurity
PLT491 Recall teaching methods - organizing material / course of training
PLT504 Recall use of training aids - types / function / purpose
PLT505 Recall use of training aids - usefulness / simplicity / compatibility

a.   Look them over and review them with your CFI so (s)he can certify that (s)he reviewed the deficient areas and found you competent in them when you take your practical test. Have your CFI sign off your deficiencies on the FAA Airman Knowledge Test Report.

3.   Keep your FAA Airman Knowledge Test Report in a safe place because you must submit it to the FAA evaluator when you take your practical test.

APPLYING FOR YOUR GROUND INSTRUCTOR CERTIFICATE

Flight instructor applicants will take their FAA Airman Knowledge Test Reports to their FAA practical tests. A ground instructor applicant (BGI, AGI, or IGI) does not, however, have to take an FAA practical test.

You must take your FAA Airman Knowledge Test Report and a completed Airman Certificate and/or Rating Application (FAA Form 8710-1) to your local Flight Standards office or an FAA-designated examiner where you will be issued an appropriate temporary ground instructor certificate. Also, on FAA Form 8710-1, the Instructor's Recommendation block does not require an instructor's signature.

Your permanent ground instructor certificate will be mailed to you from the FAA in Oklahoma City.

FAILURE ON THE FAA PILOT KNOWLEDGE TEST

1. If you fail (score less than 70%) the knowledge test (which is virtually impossible if you follow the Gleim system), you may retake it after your instructor endorses the bottom of your FAA Airman Knowledge Test Report certifying that you have received the necessary ground training to retake the test.

2. Upon retaking the test, you will find that the procedure is the same except that you must also submit your FAA Airman Knowledge Test Report indicating the previous failure to the computer testing center.

3. Note that the pass rate on the FOI knowledge test is about 96%; i.e., fewer than 1 out of 10 fail the test initially. Reasons for failure include

    a. Failure to study the material tested and mere memorization of correct answers. (Relevant study material is contained in the outlines at the beginning of Study Units 1 through 6 of this book.)

    b. Failure to practice working through the questions under test conditions. (All of the previously released FAA questions appear in Study Units 1 through 6 of this book.)

    c. Poor examination technique, such as misreading questions and not understanding the requirements.

This Gleim Knowledge Test book will prepare you to pass the FAA knowledge test on your first attempt! In addition, the Gleim *Flight Instructor Flight Maneuvers and Practical Test Prep* book will save you time and frustration as you prepare for the FAA practical test.

Just as this book organizes and explains the knowledge needed to pass your FAA knowledge test, *Flight Instructor Flight Maneuvers and Practical Test Prep* will assist you in developing the competence and confidence to pass your FAA practical test.

Also, flight maneuvers are quickly perfected when you understand exactly what to expect before you get into an airplane to practice the flight maneuvers. You must be ahead of (not behind) your CFI and your airplane. Our flight maneuvers books explain and illustrate all flight maneuvers so the maneuvers and their execution are intuitively appealing to you. Visit www.GleimAviation.com or call (800) 874-5346 and order today!

GLEIM ONLINE GROUND SCHOOL

1. Gleim **Online Ground School (OGS)** course content is based on the Gleim Knowledge Test Prep books, **FAA Test Prep Online**, FAA publications, and Gleim reference books.

    a. Online Ground School courses are available for

        1) Sport Pilot
        2) Private Pilot
        3) Instrument Pilot
        4) Commercial Pilot
        5) Flight/Ground Instructor
        6) Fundamentals of Instructing
        7) Airline Transport Pilot
        8) Flight Engineer
        9) Canadian Certificate Conversion

    b. OGS courses are airplane-only and have lessons that correspond to the study units in the Gleim FAA Knowledge Test Prep books.

    c. Each course contains study outlines that automatically reference current FAA publications, the appropriate knowledge test questions, FAA figures, and Gleim answer explanations.

    d. OGS is always up to date.

    e. Users achieve very high knowledge test scores and a near-100% pass rate.

    f. **Gleim Online Ground School is the most flexible course available!** Access your OGS personal classroom from any computer with Internet access 24 hours a day, 7 days a week. Your virtual classroom is never closed!

    g. **Save time and study only the material you need to know!** Gleim **Online Ground School** Certificate Selection will provide you with a customized study plan. You save time because unnecessary questions will be automatically eliminated.

    h. **We are truly interactive. We help you focus on any weaker areas.** Answer explanations for wrong choices help you learn from your mistakes.

Register for Gleim Online Ground School today:
www.GleimAviation.com/OGS

or

Demo Study Unit 1 for FREE at
www.GleimAviation.com/Demos

GLEIM FAA TEST PREP ONLINE

Computer testing is consistent with aviation's use of computers (e.g., flight simulators, computerized flight decks, etc.). All FAA knowledge tests are administered by computer.

Computer testing is natural after computer study, and computer-assisted instruction is a very efficient and effective method of study. The Gleim **FAA Test Prep Online** is designed to prepare you for computer testing because our software simulates PSI. We make you comfortable with computer testing!

FAA Test Prep Online contains all of the questions in this book, context-sensitive outline material, and on-screen charts and figures. It allows you to choose either Study Mode or Test Mode.

In Study Mode, the software provides you with an explanation of each answer you choose (correct or incorrect). You design each Study Session:

- Topic(s) and/or FAA learning statement codes you wish to cover
- Number of questions
- Order of questions -- FAA, Gleim, or random
- Order of answers to each question -- Gleim or random
- Questions marked and/or missed from last session -- test, study, or both
- Questions marked and/or missed from all sessions -- test, study, or both
- Questions never seen, answered, or answered correctly

In Test Mode, the software emulates the operation of the FAA-approved PSI computer testing centers. When you finish your test, you can and should study the questions missed and access answer explanations. Thus, you have a complete understanding of how to take an FAA knowledge test and know exactly what to expect before you go to a computer testing center.

The Gleim **FAA Test Prep Online** is an all-in-one program designed to help anyone with a computer, Internet access, and an interest in flying pass the FAA knowledge tests.

Study Sessions and Test Sessions

Study Sessions give you immediate feedback on why your answer selection for a particular question is correct or incorrect and allow you to access the context-sensitive outline material that helps to explain concepts related to the question.

Choose from several different question sources: all questions available for that library; questions from a certain topic (Gleim study units and subunits); questions that you missed or marked in the last sessions you created; questions that you have never seen, answered, or answered correctly; questions from certain FAA codes; etc. You can mix up the questions by selecting to randomize the question and/or answer order so that you do not memorize answer letters.

You may then grade your study sessions and track your study progress using the performance analysis charts and graphs. The Performance Analysis information helps you to focus on areas where you need the most improvement, saving you time in the overall study process. You may then want to go back and study questions that you missed in a previous session, or you may want to create a Study Session of questions that you marked in the previous session. All of these options are made easy with **FAA Test Prep Online**'s Study Sessions.

After studying the outlines and questions in a Study Session, you can further test your skills with a Test Session. These sessions allow you to answer questions under actual testing conditions. In a Test Session, you will not know which questions you have answered correctly until the session is graded.

Recommended Study Program

1. Start with Study Unit 1 and proceed through study units in chronological order. Follow the three-step process below.

    a. First, carefully study the Gleim Outline.

    b. Second, create a Study Session of all questions in the study unit. Answer and study all questions in the Study Session.

    c. Third, create a Test Session of all questions in the study unit. Answer all questions in the Test Session.

2. After each Study Session and Test Session, create a new Study Session from questions answered incorrectly. This is of critical importance to allow you to learn from your mistakes.

Practice Test

Take an exam in the actual testing environment of the PSI testing centers. **FAA Test Prep Online** simulates the testing formats of these testing centers, making it easy for you to study questions under actual exam conditions. After studying with **FAA Test Prep Online**, you will know exactly what to expect when you go in to take your pilot knowledge test.

On-Screen Charts and Figures

One of the most convenient features of **FAA Test Prep Online** is the easily accessible on-screen charts and figures. Several of the questions refer to drawings, maps, charts, and other pictures that provide information to help answer the question. In **FAA Test Prep Online**, you can pull up any of these figures with the click of a button. You can increase or decrease the size of the images, and you may also use our drawing feature to calculate the true course between two given points (required only on the private pilot knowledge test).

Order FAA Test Prep Online today
(800) 874-5346 or www.GleimAviation.com

or

Demo Study Unit 1 for FREE at
www.GleimAviation.com/Demos

FREE UPDATES AND TECHNICAL SUPPORT

Gleim offers FREE technical support to all users of the current versions. Fill out the technical support request form online (www.GleimAviation.com/contact), send an email to support@gleim.com, or call (800) 874-5346. Additionally, Gleim **FAA Test Prep Online** is always up to date. The program is automatically updated when any changes are made, so you can be confident that Gleim will prepare you for your knowledge test. More information on our email update service for books is on page ii.

STUDY UNIT ONE

THE LEARNING PROCESS

(8 pages of outline)

1.1 CHARACTERISTICS OF LEARNING

1. Learning can be defined as a change in behavior as a result of experience.

   a. The behavior change can be physical and overt (a better glide path, for instance), or psychological and attitudinal (better motivation, more acute perceptions, insights).

2. The learning process may include any (or all) of the following elements: verbal, conceptual, perceptual, motor skills, emotional, and problem solving.

3. While learning the subject at hand, the learner may be learning other useful things as well. This learning is called incidental and can have a significant impact on the learner's total development.

1.2 THE PRINCIPLES OF LEARNING

1. Educational psychology professor Edward L. Thorndike has suggested several "principles of learning" that apply to the learning process. While these principles are not absolute, they do give important insight into effective teaching.

2. The **principle of readiness** states that if a learner is ready to learn, and has a strong purpose, clear objective, and well-fixed reason for learning, (s)he will make more progress than if (s)he lacks motivation. Readiness implies single-mindedness.

3. The **principle of exercise** states that those things most often repeated are best remembered or performed.

   a. The basis of the principle is to provide opportunities for a learner to practice and then direct this process towards a goal.

4. The **principle of effect** relates to the emotional reaction of the learner:

   a. Learning is strengthened when accompanied by a pleasant or satisfying feeling.
   b. Learning is weakened when associated with an unpleasant feeling.

5. The **principle of primacy** states that those things learned first often create a strong, almost unshakable impression.

   a. This principle means that bad habits learned early are hard to break. Instructors must thus insist on correct performance from the outset of maneuvers.

6. The **principle of intensity** states that a vivid, dramatic, or exciting experience teaches more than a routine or boring experience.

    a. The principle of intensity thus implies that a learner will learn more from the real thing than from a substitute.

7. The **principle of recency** states that the things most recently learned are best remembered.

    a. Instructors recognize the principle of recency when they determine the sequence of lectures within a course of instruction.

1.3 PERCEPTION AND INSIGHT

1. Perceiving involves more than the reception of stimuli from the five senses. Perceptions result when the person gives meaning to sensations being experienced.

    a. Thus, perceptions are the basis of all learning.

2. It takes time and opportunity to perceive.

    a. A properly planned training syllabus allows sufficient time and opportunity for key perceptions to occur.

3. A person's basic need is to maintain, enhance, preserve, and perpetuate the organized self.

    a. Thus, all perceptions are affected by this basic need.

4. Self-concept, or self-image, has a great influence on the total perceptual process.

5. Fear or the element of threat narrows the learner's perceptual field.

    a. The resulting anxiety may limit a person's ability to learn from perceptions.

6. Insight occurs when associated perceptions are grouped into meaningful wholes, i.e., when one "gets the whole picture."

    a. Evoking insights is the instructor's major responsibility.

    b. Instruction speeds the learning process by teaching the relationship of perceptions as they occur, thus promoting the development of insights by learners.

    c. An instructor can help develop learner insights by providing a secure and nonthreatening environment in which to learn.

1.4 MEMORY

1. Memory is an integral part of the learning process. It includes three parts: the sensory register, the short-term or working memory, and the long-term memory.

    a. The **sensory register** receives input from the environment and quickly processes it according to the individual's preconceived concept of what is important. This occurs on a subconscious level.

        1) **Precoding** is the selective process by which the sensory register recognizes certain stimuli and immediately transmits them to the working memory for action.

            a) Irrelevant stimuli are discarded by the sensory register.

b.   The **short-term memory** (or working memory) is the receptacle of the information deemed important by the sensory register.

1)   The information may temporarily remain in the short-term memory, or it may rapidly fade.

a)   Retention of information by the short-term memory is aided when the information is initially categorized into systematic chunks in a process known as **coding**.

b)   Retention is also aided by repetition or rehearsal of the information (rote learning).

2)   Information remains in the short-term memory for longer periods when it can be related to an individual's previous knowledge or experiences through a process known as recoding.

a)   **Recoding** may be described as a process of relating incoming information to concepts or knowledge already in memory.

b)   Methods of recoding vary with the subject matter, but they typically involve some type of association, such as mnemonics.

i)   Mnemonics include, but are not limited to, acronyms, acrostics, rhymes, and chaining.

ii)   A mnemonic uses a pattern of letters, ideas, images, or associations to assist in remembering information.

iii)   The use of associations such as rhymes and mnemonics is best suited to the short-term memory.

c)   Short-term memory is the part of the memory system where information is stored for roughly 30 seconds, after which it may rapidly fade or be consolidated into long-term memory, depending on the individual's priorities. Several common steps help retention in short-term memory. These include rehearsal or repetition of the information and sorting or categorization into systematic chunks.

i)   The short-term memory is not only time limited; it also has limited capacity, usually about seven bits or chunks of information at a time. A seven-digit telephone number is an example.

d)   The ability to retrieve knowledge or skills from memory is primarily related to two things: (1) how often that knowledge has been used in the past and (2) how recently the knowledge has been used.

i)   These two factors are called frequency and recency of use. Frequency and recency can be present individually or in combination.

c.   The **long-term memory** is where information is stored for future use.

1)   For the stored information to be useful, some special effort must have been expended during the recoding process.

2)   It should be noted that the long-term memory is a reconstruction, not a pure recall of information or events.

1.5 FORGETTING AND RETENTION

1.   The following are three theories of forgetting:

    a.   The **theory of fading** states that a person forgets information that is not used for an extended period of time. Learners are saddened by the small amount of actual data retained several years after graduation.

    b.   The **theory of interference** suggests that people forget something because a certain experience has overshadowed it or the learning of similar things has intervened.

        1)   This theory might explain how the range of experiences after graduation from school causes a person to forget or lose knowledge. In other words, new events displace many things that had been learned.

        2)   From experiments, at least two conclusions about interference may be drawn. First, similar material seems to interfere with memory more than dissimilar material; second, material not well learned suffers most from interference.

    c.   The **theory of repression or suppression** states that memories are pushed out of reach because the individual does not want to remember the feelings associated with them. Unpleasant or anxiety-producing material is forgotten by the individual.

        1)   **Repression** is an unconscious form of forgetting and is unintentional.
        2)   **Suppression** is conscious and intentional.

2.   Responses that produce a pleasurable return are called praise.

    a.   Praise stimulates remembering because responses that give a pleasurable return tend to be repeated.

1.6 TRANSFER OF LEARNING

1.   The learner may be either aided or hindered by things learned previously. This process is called transfer of learning.

    a.   Positive transfer occurs when the learning of one maneuver aids in learning another.

        1)   EXAMPLE: Flying rectangular patterns to aid in flying traffic patterns.

    b.   Negative transfer occurs when a performance of a maneuver interferes with the learning of another maneuver.

        1)   EXAMPLE: Trying to steer a taxiing plane with the control yoke the way one drives a car.

        2)   Negative transfer thus agrees with the interference theory of forgetting.

2.   By making certain the learner understands that what is learned can be applied to other situations, the instructor helps facilitate a positive transfer of learning.

    a.   This is the basic reason for the building-block technique of instruction in which each simple task is performed acceptably and correctly before the next learning task is introduced.

    b.   The introduction of instruction in more advanced and complex operations before the initial instruction has been mastered leads to the development of poor habit patterns in the elements of performance.

1.7 LEVELS OF LEARNING

1. Learning may be accomplished at any of four levels.

    a. The lowest level, **rote learning**, is the ability to repeat back what one has been taught without necessarily understanding or being able to apply what has been learned.

        1) EXAMPLE: Being able to cite the design maneuvering speed of an airplane.

        2) Many learners use commercially-developed training material to memorize FAA testing concepts, which is another example of rote learning.

            a) While test preparation materials may be effective in preparing learners for FAA tests, the danger is that learners may learn to pass a given test but fail to learn other critical information essential to safe piloting and maintenance practices.

            b) FAA inspectors and designated examiners have found that learner applicants often exhibit a lack of knowledge during oral questioning, even though many have easily passed the FAA knowledge test.

            c) Because test preparation materials emphasize rote learning, instructors should stress that these materials are not designed as stand-alone learning tools. They should be considered as a supplement to instructor-led training.

    b. At the **understanding** level, the learner not only can repeat what has been taught but also comprehends the principles and theory behind the knowledge.

        1) EXAMPLE: Being able to explain how gross weight affects design maneuvering speed.

        2) Being able to explain (not demonstrate) is the understanding level.

    c. At the **application** level, the learner not only understands the theory but also can apply what has been learned and perform in accordance with that knowledge.

        1) The learner understands the procedure, has had the procedure demonstrated, and has practiced the procedure to a point that it can be performed with consistency.

        2) This is the level of learning at which most instructors stop teaching.

    d. At the **correlation** level, the learner is able to associate various learned elements with other segments or blocks of learning or accomplishment.

        1) EXAMPLE: Know what to do if, during the flight portion of the practical test, the examiner closes the throttle and announces "simulated engine failure."

1.8 DOMAINS OF LEARNING

1. In addition to the four basic levels of learning discussed in Subunit 1.7, learning can be categorized in other ways.

2. Three **domains of learning** have been identified based on what is learned:

    a. The **cognitive domain** deals with knowledge (e.g., facts, concepts, or relationships).

    b. The **affective domain** relates to attitudes, beliefs, and values.

    c. The **psychomotor domain** concerns physical skills. These skills involve physical movement, coordination, and the use of motor skills.

3. Each of the domains of learning has a hierarchy of educational objectives.

    a. A listing of the hierarchy of objectives is often referred to as a taxonomy.

        1) A **taxonomy of educational objectives** is a systematic classification scheme for sorting possible learning outcomes into the three domains of learning and ranking them in a developmental hierarchy from least complex to most complex.

            a) Each of the three domains of learning has several distinct learning outcomes. These outcomes are equivalent to the educational objective levels.

        2) The following are hierarchical taxonomies for the three domains of learning:

    b. The educational objectives/learning outcomes become more complex from bottom to top.

1.9 LEARNING SKILLS AND THE LEARNING CURVE

1.   The best way to prepare a learner to perform a task is to provide a clear, step-by-step example. Learners need a clear picture of what they are to do and how they are to do it.

2.   Learning typically follows a pattern that, if shown on a graph, would be called the learning curve. The first part of the curve indicates rapid early improvement. Then the curve levels off. This leveling-off of an individual's learning rate is called a **learning plateau**.

   a.   Learning plateaus are a normal part of the learning process and tend to be temporary, but instructors and learners should be prepared for them.

      1)   Keep in mind that the apparent lack of increasing proficiency does not necessarily mean that learning has ceased.

   b.   A learning plateau may signify any number of conditions. For example, the learner may

      1)   Have reached capability limits.
      2)   Be consolidating levels of skill.
      3)   Have lost interest.
      4)   Need a more efficient method for increasing progress.

   c.   Instructors themselves can bring on a learning plateau by overpractice.

      1)   After repeating any task three or four times, give it a break to avoid causing a learning plateau.

   d.   The instructor should prepare the learner for the likelihood of learning plateaus during training to avert discouragement.

   e.   Instructors can help learners who fall into a learning plateau by moving them to a different place in the curriculum and giving the plateaued task a break.

3.   The development of any skill acquisition has three characteristic stages: cognitive, associative, and automatic. An instructor must learn to recognize each stage in learner performance in order to assess learner progress.

   a.   The **cognitive stage** of learning has a basis in factual knowledge. Since the learner has no prior knowledge of flying, the instructor first introduces him or her to a basic skill.

      1)   The learner memorizes the steps required to perform the skill.

      2)   As the learner carries out these memorized steps, (s)he is often unaware of progress or may fixate on one aspect of performance.

      3)   Performing the skill at this stage typically requires all the learner's attention; distractions introduced by an instructor often cause performance to deteriorate or stop.

   b.   The **associative stage** of learning involves the storage of a skill via practice.

      1)   As practice continues, the learner learns to associate individual steps in performance with likely outcomes.

      2)   The learner no longer performs a series of memorized steps but is able to assess his or her progress along the way and make adjustments in performance.

      3)   Performing the skill still requires deliberate attention, but the learner is better able to deal with distractions.

    c.   The **automatic response stage** of learning produces automaticity, which is one of the by-products of continued practice.

        1)   As procedures become automatic, less attention is required to carry them out, so it is possible to do other things simultaneously, or at least do other things more comfortably.

        2)   By this stage, learner performance of the skill is rapid and smooth. The learner devotes much less deliberate attention to performance and may be able to carry on a conversation or perform other tasks while performing the skill.

        3)   The learner makes far fewer adjustments during his or her performance, and these adjustments tend to be small.

        4)   The learner may no longer be able to remember the individual steps in the procedure or explain how to perform the skill.

        5)   An example of a learner who has reached the automatic response stage is a learner who can fly an ILS approach while simultaneously handling the radio communications.

4.   There are three types of practice, each of which yields particular results in acquiring skills.

    a.   During **deliberate practice**, the learner practices specific areas for improvement and receives specific feedback after practice.

        1)   Studies of skill learning suggest a learner achieves better results if distractions are avoided during deliberate practice.

        2)   When feedback is needed to correct learner performance, it should be brief and explicit.

    b.   **Blocked practice** is practicing the same drill until the movement becomes automatic.

        1)   Doing the same task over and over leads to better short-term performance but poorer long-term learning.

        2)   It tends to fool not only the learner but also the instructor into thinking the skills have been well learned.

    c.   **Random practice** mixes the skills to be acquired throughout the practice session.

        1)   This type of practice leads to better retention because, by performing a series of separate skills in a random order, the learner starts to recognize the similarities and differences of each skill, which makes the practice more meaningful.

        2)   The learner also is able to store the skill more effectively in the long-term memory.

QUESTIONS AND ANSWER EXPLANATIONS: All of the Fundamentals of Instructing knowledge test questions chosen by the FAA for release as well as additional questions selected by Gleim relating to the material in the previous outlines are provided on the following pages. These questions have been organized into the same subunits as the outlines. To the immediate right of each question are the correct answer and answer explanations. You should cover these answers and answer explanations while responding to the questions. Refer to the general discussion in the Introduction on how to take the FAA knowledge test.

Remember that the questions from the FAA knowledge test bank have been reordered by topic and organized into a meaningful sequence. Also, the first line of the answer explanation gives the citation of the authoritative source for the answer.

QUESTIONS

1.1 Characteristics of Learning

1. A change in behavior as a result of experience can be defined as

    A. learning.

    B. knowledge.

    C. understanding.

Answer (A) is correct. (FAA-H-8083-9B Chap 3)
    DISCUSSION: Learning can be defined as a change in behavior as a result of experience.
    Answer (B) is incorrect. Knowledge is awareness as a result of experience but not necessarily a change in behavior. **Answer (C) is incorrect.** Understanding is only one of the four levels of learning.

2. The learning process may include some elements such as verbal, conceptual, and

    A. habitual.

    B. experiential.

    C. problem solving.

Answer (C) is correct. (FAA-H-8083-9B Chap 3)
    DISCUSSION: The learning process involves many elements. Verbal, conceptual, perceptual, motor skill, problem solving, and emotional elements may be used at the same time.
    Answer (A) is incorrect. Habits are the customary or usual way of doing things and can be changed by the learning process. **Answer (B) is incorrect.** All learning is by experience, but it takes place in different forms in different people.

3. While learning the material being taught, learners may be learning other things as well. This additional learning is called

    A. residual.

    B. conceptual.

    C. incidental.

Answer (C) is correct. (FAA-H-8083-9B Chap 3)
    DISCUSSION: While learning the subject at hand, learners may be learning other things as well. They may be developing attitudes (good or bad) about aviation depending on what they experience. This learning is called incidental, but it may have a great impact on the total development of the learner.
    Answer (A) is incorrect. Residual is not a term used to define any type of learning. **Answer (B) is incorrect.** Conceptual learning is an element of learning the subject at hand, not other incidental things.

1.2 The Principles of Learning

4. Individuals make more progress learning if they have a clear objective. This is one feature of the principle of

- A. primacy.
- B. readiness.
- C. willingness.

Answer (B) is correct. (FAA-H-8083-9B Chap 3)
DISCUSSION: One feature of the principle of readiness is that when a learner has a strong purpose, a clear objective, and a well-fixed reason to learn something, (s)he will make more progress than if (s)he lacks motivation.
Answer (A) is incorrect. The principle of primacy states that first experiences create a strong, almost unshakable impression. **Answer (C) is incorrect.** There is no principle of willingness.

5. Things most often repeated are best remembered because of which principle of learning?

- A. Principle of effect.
- B. Principle of recency.
- C. Principle of exercise.

Answer (C) is correct. (FAA-H-8083-9B Chap 3)
DISCUSSION: The principle of exercise states that those things most often repeated are best remembered. This is the basis of practice and drill.
Answer (A) is incorrect. The principle of effect relates to the learner's emotional reaction to the learning experience. **Answer (B) is incorrect.** The principle of recency states that things most recently learned are best remembered.

6. Providing opportunities for a learner to practice and then directing this process towards a goal is the basis of the principle of

- A. exercise.
- B. learning.
- C. readiness.

Answer (A) is correct. (FAA-H-8083-9B Chap 3)
DISCUSSION: The principle of exercise states that those things most often repeated are best remembered. You must provide opportunities for your learner to practice and then direct this process towards a goal.
Answer (B) is incorrect. Learning is a change in behavior as a result of experience. The principle of exercise is part of the learning process. **Answer (C) is incorrect.** The principle of readiness states that individuals learn best when they are ready to learn, not practicing a task.

7. The principle that is based on the emotional reaction of the learner is the principle of

- A. effect.
- B. primacy.
- C. intensity.

Answer (A) is correct. (FAA-H-8083-9B Chap 3)
DISCUSSION: The principle of effect is the one which directly relates to the learner's emotional reaction. Pleasant experiences strengthen the learning process, whereas unpleasant experiences tend to weaken it.
Answer (B) is incorrect. The principle of primacy states that a strong, almost unshakable impression is created by first experiences. **Answer (C) is incorrect.** The principle of intensity states that dramatic or exciting experiences teach more than routine experiences.

8. Which principle of learning often creates a strong impression?

- A. Principle of primacy.
- B. Principle of intensity.
- C. Principle of readiness.

Answer (A) is correct. (FAA-H-8083-9B Chap 3)
DISCUSSION: Primacy, the state of being first, often creates a strong, almost unshakable impression. For the instructor, this means that what is taught must be right the first time. The first experience should be positive and functional and should lay the foundation for all that is to follow.
Answer (B) is incorrect. The principle of intensity means that a learner will learn more from the real thing than from a substitute. **Answer (C) is incorrect.** The principle of readiness means that a learner must be willing and eager to learn.

9. Which principle of learning implies that a learner will learn more from the real thing than from a substitute?

   A. Principle of effect.

   B. Principle of primacy.

   C. Principle of intensity.

Answer (C) is correct. (FAA-H-8083-9B Chap 3)
   DISCUSSION: The principle of intensity states that a vivid, dramatic, or exciting learning experience teaches more than a routine or boring experience. Thus, the principle of intensity implies that a learner will learn more from a real thing than from a substitute.
   Answer (A) is incorrect. The principle of effect is based on the emotional reaction of the learner. Thus, pleasant experiences strengthen the learning, while unpleasant experiences weaken the learning. These may be experienced by learning from either the real thing or a substitute. **Answer (B) is incorrect.** The principle of primacy states that a strong, almost unshakable impression is created by first experiences. These experiences may be from either a real thing or a substitute.

10. Which principle of learning often determines the sequence of lectures within a course of instruction?

   A. Principle of primacy.

   B. Principle of recency.

   C. Principle of intensity.

Answer (B) is correct. (FAA-H-8083-9B Chap 3)
   DISCUSSION: The principle of recency states that the things most recently learned are best remembered. The further a learner is removed time-wise from a new fact or understanding, the more difficult it is to remember it. The principle of recency often determines the sequence of lectures within a course of instruction.
   Answer (A) is incorrect. The principle of primacy means to the instructor that what is taught must be right the first time. **Answer (C) is incorrect.** The principle of intensity means that a learner will learn more from the real experience than a substitute.

1.3 Perception and Insight

11. What is the basis of all learning?

   A. Perception.

   B. Motivation.

   C. Positive self-concept.

Answer (A) is correct. (FAA-H-8083-9B Chap 3)
   DISCUSSION: Initially, all learning comes from perceptions that are directed to the brain by one or more of the five senses. Perceptions result when a person gives meaning to sensations.
   Answer (B) is incorrect. Motivation is the dominant force that governs a learner's progress and ability to learn, not the basis for all learning. **Answer (C) is incorrect.** Positive self-concept is a factor that affects an individual's ability to learn, not the basis of all learning.

12. Perceptions result when a person

   A. gives meaning to sensations being experienced.

   B. is able to discern items of useful information.

   C. responds to visual cues first, then aural cues, and relates these cues to ones previously learned.

Answer (A) is correct. (FAA-H-8083-9B Chap 3)
   DISCUSSION: Perceptions occur when a person gives meaning to sensations being experienced. This is the difference between just seeing something and understanding what is seen.
   Answer (B) is incorrect. A person who is able to discern items of useful information has learned, not just perceived. **Answer (C) is incorrect.** It describes the rote level of learning, i.e., memorization without concern for meaning.

13. A basic need that affects all of a person's perceptions is the need to

   A. maintain and enhance the organized self.

   B. accomplish a higher level of satisfaction.

   C. avoid areas that pose a threat to success.

Answer (A) is correct. (FAA-H-8083-9B Chap 3)
   DISCUSSION: A person's basic need is to maintain and enhance the organized self. The self is a person's past, present, and future and is both physical and psychological. A person's most fundamental need is to preserve and perpetuate this self. Thus, all perceptions are affected by this need.
   Answer (B) is incorrect. Accomplishing a higher level of satisfaction is a goal, not a basic need. **Answer (C) is incorrect.** Avoiding areas that are a threat to success is a defense mechanism, not a basic need that affects perceptions.

14. Which factor affecting perception has a great influence on the total perceptual process?

    A. Self-concept.

    B. Goals and values.

    C. Time and opportunity.

Answer (A) is correct. (FAA-H-8083-9B Chap 3)
    DISCUSSION: A learner's self-concept (or self-image) has a great influence on the total perceptual process. Negative self-concepts inhibit the perceptual process by introducing psychological barriers, which tend to keep a learner from perceiving. Positive self-concepts allow the learner to be less defensive and more ready to digest experiences by assimilating all of the instructions and demonstrations offered.
    Answer (B) is incorrect. Perceptions depend on one's goals and values in that every experience is colored by the individual's own beliefs and value structures, but they do not have a great influence on the total perceptual process. **Answer (C) is incorrect.** It takes time and opportunity to perceive, but it is not a great influence on the total perceptual process.

15. Which factor affecting perceptions is based on the effectiveness of the use of a properly planned training syllabus?

    A. Basic need.

    B. Time and opportunity.

    C. Goals and values.

Answer (B) is correct. (FAA-H-8083-9B Chap 3)
    DISCUSSION: It takes time and opportunity to perceive. Learning some things depends on other perceptions that have preceded these learnings and on the availability of time to sense and relate these new things to the earlier perceptions. Thus, sequence and time are necessary to learn; a properly planned training syllabus facilitates sequencing and timing. The effectiveness of using a properly planned training syllabus is proportional to the consideration given by the instructor to the need for sufficient time and opportunity for perception to occur.
    Answer (A) is incorrect. A person's basic need is to maintain and enhance the organized self, which does not relate to a properly planned training syllabus. **Answer (C) is incorrect.** Goals and values are the basis for perceptions. Every experience and sensation that gets funneled into one's central nervous system is colored by the individual's beliefs and value structures, which do not relate to a properly planned training syllabus.

16. In the learning process, fear or the element of threat will

    A. narrow the learner's perceptual field.

    B. decrease the rate of associative reactions.

    C. cause a learner to focus on several areas of perception.

Answer (A) is correct. (FAA-H-8083-9B Chap 3)
    DISCUSSION: Fear or the element of threat will impair the learner's perceptual field. This is because one tends to limit attention to the threatening object or condition rather than to what should be learned.
    Answer (B) is incorrect. The element of threat causes stress and anxiety; the mind tends to race, often irrationally, thereby increasing, not decreasing, the rate of associative reactions. **Answer (C) is incorrect.** Fear or the element of threat will cause a learner to focus only on the threatening object or condition, not on several areas of perception.

17. Which is one of the ways in which anxiety will affect a learner?

    A. Anxiety may limit the learner's ability to learn from perceptions.

    B. Anxiety will speed up the learning process for the learner if properly controlled and directed by the instructor.

    C. Anxiety causes dispersal of the learner's attention over such a wide range of matters as to interfere with normal reactions.

Answer (A) is correct. (FAA-H-8083-9B Chap 2)
    DISCUSSION: Anxiety is a state of mental uneasiness arising from fear of anything, real or imagined, which threatens the person who experiences it. Anxiety may have a potent effect on actions and on the ability to learn from perceptions.
    Answer (B) is incorrect. Perceptions blocked by anxiety will tend to slow, not speed up, the learning process. **Answer (C) is incorrect.** Anxiety narrows, not disperses, a learner's attention.

18. The mental grouping of affiliated perceptions is called

    A. insights.

    B. association.

    C. conceptualization.

Answer (A) is correct. (FAA-H-8083-9B Chap 3)
    DISCUSSION: Many principles, theories, and learned tasks can be treated as pieces relating to other pieces in the overall pattern of the task to be learned. This mental relating or grouping of associated perceptions is called insight.
    Answer (B) is incorrect. Association is not the final, completed mental picture, although it is a necessary process to connect the affiliated perceptions. **Answer (C) is incorrect.** It refers only to the formation of individual ideas.

19. Insights, as applied to learning, involve a person's

    A. association of learning with change.

    B. grouping of associated perceptions into meaningful wholes.

    C. ability to recognize the reason for learning a procedure.

Answer (B) is correct. (FAA-H-8083-9B Chap 3)
    DISCUSSION: Insights, as applied to learning, involve a person's grouping of associated perceptions into meaningful wholes. As perceptions increase in number and are grouped to become insights by the learner, learning becomes more meaningful and permanent.
    Answer (A) is incorrect. Insights involve the grouping of perceptions into meaningful wholes, not the association of learning with change. **Answer (C) is incorrect.** The ability to recognize the reason for learning a procedure is a feature of the principle of readiness, not insight.

20. Instruction, as opposed to the trial and error method of learning, is desirable because competent instruction speeds the learning process by

    A. motivating the learner to a better performance.

    B. emphasizing only the important points of training.

    C. teaching the relationship of perceptions as they occur.

Answer (C) is correct. (FAA-H-8083-9B Chap 3)
    DISCUSSION: Competent instruction speeds the learning process by teaching the relationship of perceptions as they occur, thus promoting the development of insights by the learner.
    Answer (A) is incorrect. Motivating a learner to a better performance is just one element of instruction. **Answer (B) is incorrect.** Instructors must emphasize all points of training, not just the major, important points.

21. Name one way an instructor can help develop learner insights.

    A. Provide a secure and nonthreatening environment in which to learn.

    B. Point out various items to avoid during the learning process.

    C. Keep learning blocks small so they are easier to understand.

Answer (A) is correct. (FAA-H-8083-9B Chap 3)
    DISCUSSION: Pointing out the relationships of perceptions as they occur, providing a secure and nonthreatening environment in which to learn, and helping the learner acquire and maintain a favorable self-concept are most important in fostering the development of insights.
    Answer (B) is incorrect. The instructor should point out the relationships of perceptions as they occur, not point out various items to avoid during the learning process. **Answer (C) is incorrect.** Insights develop when a learner's perceptions increase in number and are assembled into larger, not smaller, blocks of learning.

1.4 Memory

22. The use or association of rhymes or word patterns to aid in remembering is called

    A. acronyms.

    B. mnemonics.

    C. coding.

Answer (B) is correct. (FAA-H-8083-9B Chap 3)
    DISCUSSION: A mnemonic uses a pattern of letters, ideas, images, or associations to assist in remembering information. It is a memory-enhancing strategy that involves teaching learners to link new information to information they already know.
    Answer (A) is incorrect. Mnemonics may include acronyms but are not necessarily acronyms themselves.
    Answer (C) is incorrect. Coding is a sorting process. It is not designed for remembering information.

23. Which memory system processes input from the environment?

    A. Working.

    B. Long-term.

    C. Sensory register.

Answer (C) is correct. (FAA-H-8083-9B Chap 3)
    DISCUSSION: The sensory register receives input from the environment and quickly processes it according to the individual's preconceived concept of what is important (i.e., it recognizes certain stimuli as significant). The sensory register processes inputs or stimuli from the environment within seconds, discards what is considered extraneous, and processes what is considered by the individual to be relevant.
    Answer (A) is incorrect. The working, or short-term, memory is the receptacle for the information determined to be relevant by the sensory register. Once in the short-term memory, the information may temporarily remain for immediate use, or it may fade rapidly. **Answer (B) is incorrect.** The long-term memory is where information is stored for future use.

24. While short-term memory is time-limited, it also has a capacity limit of

    A. usually 5 bits or chunks of information.

    B. usually 7 bits or chunks of information.

    C. usually 9 bits or chunks of information.

Answer (B) is correct. (FAA-H-8083-9B Chap 3)
    DISCUSSION: The short-term memory is not only time limited; it also has limited capacity, usually about seven bits or chunks of information at a time. A seven-digit telephone number is an example.
    Answer (A) is incorrect. The short-term memory is not only time limited; it also has limited capacity, usually about seven, not five, bits or chunks of information at a time. **Answer (C) is incorrect.** The short-term memory is not only time limited; it also has limited capacity, usually about seven, not nine, bits or chunks of information at a time.

25. The use of some type of association, such as rhymes or mnemonics is best suited to which memory system?

    A. Short-term.

    B. Sensory.

    C. Long-term.

Answer (A) is correct. (FAA-H-8083-9B Chap 3)
    DISCUSSION: For information to remain in the short-term memory for a significant amount of time, it must be categorized in some way. The information is initially grouped into systematic chunks in a process called coding. It must then be related to concepts or knowledge already in memory in a process called recoding. The use of some type of association, such as rhymes or mnemonic devices, is well suited to this task.
    Answer (B) is incorrect. The sensory register detects and processes stimuli on a subconscious level. They are then discarded or transferred to the short-term memory according to the individual's preconceived concept of what is important. **Answer (C) is incorrect.** In order for information stored in long-term memory to be useful, some special effort must have been expended during the recoding process while the information was in short-term memory.

26. How can recoding be described?

    A. The relating of incoming information to concepts or knowledge already in memory.

    B. The initial storage of information in short-term memory.

    C. The selective process where the sensory register is set to recognize certain stimuli.

Answer (A) is correct. (FAA-H-8083-9B Chap 3)
    DISCUSSION: Recoding takes place in the short-term memory, when new information is adjusted to individual experiences. Recoding may be described as a process of relating incoming information to concepts or knowledge already in memory.
    Answer (B) is incorrect. The initial storage of information in short-term memory is coding, not recoding. **Answer (C) is incorrect.** The selective process where the sensory register is set to recognize certain stimuli is precoding, not recoding.

27. Which of the following memory systems would be enhanced with practice and repetition?

    A. Long-term.

    B. Short-term.

    C. Perception.

Answer (B) is correct. (FAA-H-8083-9B Chap 3)
    DISCUSSION: Short-term memory is the part of the memory system where information is stored for roughly 30 seconds, after which it may rapidly fade or be consolidated into long-term memory, depending on the individual's priorities. Several common steps help retention in short-term memory. These include rehearsal or repetition of the information and sorting or categorization into systematic chunks. The sorting process is usually called coding or chunking.
    Answer (A) is incorrect. Practice and repetition enhance short-term memory, with the hope that these memories will become long-term memories. **Answer (C) is incorrect.** Learner perceptions are unrelated to short-term memory.

28. Which of the following statements about long-term memory is true?

    A. Long-term memory is a reconstruction, not a pure recall of information or events.

    B. Long-term memory is not subject to limitations such as time, biases, and, in many cases, personal inaccuracies.

    C. Initial encoding is not related to long-term memory.

Answer (A) is correct. (FAA-H-8083-9B Chap 3)
    DISCUSSION: Long-term memory is a reconstruction, not a pure recall of information or events.
    Answer (B) is incorrect. Long-term memory is in fact subject to limitations, such as time, biases, and, in many cases, personal inaccuracies. **Answer (C) is incorrect.** If initial encoding is not properly accomplished, recall is distorted and may be impossible.

29. Where is information for future use stored?

    A. Short-term memory.

    B. Sensory register.

    C. Long-term memory.

Answer (C) is correct. (FAA-H-8083-9B Chap 3)
    DISCUSSION: Information for future use is stored in the long-term memory.
    Answer (A) is incorrect. Short-term memory is where information is temporarily stored, not stored for future use, after the sensory register deems it to be significant. **Answer (B) is incorrect.** The sensory register processes stimuli from the environment according to the individual's preconception of what is important. Significant information is sent to the short-term memory for immediate, not future, use.

30. The selective process by which the sensory register discards and transmits certain stimuli to the working memory is called

    A. recoding.

    B. coding.

    C. precoding.

Answer (C) is correct. (FAA-H-8083-9B Chap 3)
    DISCUSSION: Precoding is the selective process by which the sensory register recognizes certain stimuli and immediately transmits them to the working memory for action.
    Answer (A) is incorrect. Recoding is the process of relating incoming information to concepts already in memory. **Answer (B) is incorrect.** Coding is the initial sorting or categorization of information into systematic chunks in the short-term memory to aid in retention.

31. The ability to retrieve knowledge or skills from memory is primarily related to

    A. absence of interference.

    B. how often that knowledge has been used in the past.

    C. the practice of "information chunking."

Answer (B) is correct. (FAA-H-8083-9B Chap 3)
    DISCUSSION: The ability to retrieve knowledge or skills from memory is primarily related to how often and how recently the knowledge has been used in the past. These two factors are called frequency and recency of use. Frequency and recency can be present individually or in combination.
    Answer (A) is incorrect. The absence of interference is not the primary factor in the ability to retrieve knowledge. **Answer (C) is incorrect.** Chunking is one of the steps that helps retention of short-term memory. After rehearsal or repetition of the information, it is sorted or categorized into systematic chunks. The sorting process is usually called coding or chunking.

1.5 Forgetting and Retention

32. The phenomenon of information not used for an extended period of time becoming harder to recall is termed

    A. fading.

    B. forgetting.

    C. retrieval failure.

Answer (A) is correct. (FAA-H-8083-9B Chap 3)
    DISCUSSION: The theory of fading, or decay, suggests that a person forgets information that is not used for an extended period of time. It has been suggested that humans are physiologically pre-programmed to eventually erase data that no longer appears pertinent.
    Answer (B) is incorrect. Forgetting typically involves a failure in memory retrieval. **Answer (C) is incorrect.** Retrieval failure is simply the inability to retrieve information, for example, the "tip-of-the-tongue" phenomenon when a person knows the meaning of a word or the answer to a question but cannot retrieve it.

33. When a person has difficulty recalling facts after several years, this is known as

    A. repression.

    B. fading.

    C. retrieval failure.

Answer (B) is correct. (FAA-H-8083-9B Chap 3)
    DISCUSSION: The theory of fading or decay suggests that a person forgets information that is not used for an extended period of time.
    Answer (A) is incorrect. Repression is the practice of submerging an unpleasant experience into the subconscious. **Answer (C) is incorrect.** Retrieval failure is simply the inability to retrieve information. Some would call it the "tip-of-the-tongue" phenomenon when a person knows the answer to a question but cannot retrieve it.

34. When the learning of similar things overshadows other learning experiences, it is called

    A. suppression.

    B. correlation.

    C. interference.

Answer (C) is correct. (FAA-H-8083-9B Chap 3)
    DISCUSSION: The theory of interference states that new or similar events can often replace previously learned facts. Most susceptible to this replacement by interference are closely similar materials and materials not well learned to begin with.
    Answer (A) is incorrect. Suppression is not a consideration (or theory) as to why a person forgets. **Answer (B) is incorrect.** Correlation is the highest level of learning, which means that it is resistant to forgetting.

35. According to one theory, some forgetting is due to the unconscious practice of submerging an unpleasant experience into the subconscious. This is called

    A. suppression.

    B. immersion.

    C. repression.

Answer (C) is correct. (FAA-H-8083-9B Chap 3)
    DISCUSSION: Repression is the unconscious form of forgetting where memories are pushed out of reach because the individual does not want to remember the feelings associated with them.
    Answer (A) is incorrect. Suppression is a conscious, not unconscious, form of forgetting. **Answer (B) is incorrect.** Immersion is not discussed in the *Aviation Instructor's Handbook* and is a nonsense answer in this context.

36. Responses that produce a pleasurable return are called

    A. reward.

    B. praise.

    C. positive feedback.

Answer (B) is correct. (FAA-H-8083-9B Chap 3)
    DISCUSSION: Responses that give a pleasurable return, called praise, tend to be repeated, thus stimulating and encouraging retention.
    Answer (A) is incorrect. Rewards are motivators and are not usually responses (e.g., praise); that is, they are normally financial, self-interest, or public recognition. **Answer (C) is incorrect.** Positive feedback (e.g., constructive criticism) is part of the learning, not retention, process. Positive feedback teaches a learner how to capitalize on things done well and to use them to compensate for lesser accomplishments.

37. The act of consciously pushing a memory out of reach due to feelings associated with remembering it is

    A. avoidance.

    B. suppression.

    C. repression.

Answer (B) is correct. (FAA-H-8083-9B Chap 3)
    DISCUSSION: Suppression is a conscious form of forgetting where the learner intentionally forces memories that are unpleasant or anxiety-producing into the subconscious.
    Answer (A) is incorrect. Avoidance is not a theory of forgetting and is not discussed in the *Aviation Instructor's Handbook*. **Answer (C) is incorrect.** Repression is an unconscious, not conscious, form of forgetting.

38. When a new experience displaces memories or information that had been previously learned, it is called

    A. fading.

    B. retrieval failure.

    C. interference.

Answer (C) is correct. (FAA-H-8083-9B Chap 3)
    DISCUSSION: Interference theory suggests that people forget something because a certain experience has overshadowed it or the learning of similar things has intervened. In other words, new events displace many things that had been learned.
    Answer (A) is incorrect. The theory of fading suggests that a person forgets information that is not used for an extended period of time. **Answer (B) is incorrect.** Retrieval failure is simply the inability to retrieve information, for example, the "tip-of-the-tongue" phenomenon when a person knows the meaning of a word or the answer to a question but cannot retrieve it.

1.6 Transfer of Learning

39. The performance of rectangular patterns helps a learner fly traffic patterns. What type transfer of learning is this?

    A. Lateral.

    B. Positive.

    C. Deliberate.

Answer (B) is correct. (FAA-H-8083-9B Chap 3)
    DISCUSSION: Transfers of learning can be negative or positive. Since the learning of Task A (flying rectangular patterns) helps in the learning of Task B (flying traffic patterns), it is advantageous and therefore a positive transfer of learning.
    Answer (A) is incorrect. There is no lateral transfer of learning, only positive or negative. **Answer (C) is incorrect.** There is no deliberate transfer of learning, only positive or negative.

40. Which transfer of learning occurs when the performance of a maneuver interferes with the learning of another maneuver?

    A. Adverse.

    B. Positive.

    C. Negative.

Answer (C) is correct. (FAA-H-8083-9B Chap 3)
    DISCUSSION: Transfers of learning can be negative or positive. If the learning of Task A helps in the learning of Task B, the transfer of learning is deemed to be positive. If, on the other hand, Task A interferes with Task B, the transfer is a hindrance to learning and is thus negative.
    Answer (A) is incorrect. There is no adverse transfer of learning, only positive or negative. **Answer (B) is incorrect.** The transfer of learning is a hindrance and is thus negative.

41. To ensure proper habits and correct techniques during training, an instructor should

    A. use the building block technique of instruction.

    B. repeat subject matter the learner has already learned.

    C. introduce challenging material to continually motivate the learner.

Answer (A) is correct. (FAA-H-8083-9B Chap 3)
    DISCUSSION: The building-block technique of teaching insists that each simple task be performed correctly before the next is introduced. This technique fosters thorough and meaningful performance and good habits, which will be carried over into future learning.
    Answer (B) is incorrect. Too much repetition can lead to boredom. The instructor must mix teaching methods to sustain interest and promote learning. **Answer (C) is incorrect.** Complex or difficult tasks introduced before simpler ones are mastered can be frustrating, not motivating, for the learner. This approach will not ensure proper habits; the learner will likely develop bad habits from trying to perform tasks not completely understood.

1.7 Levels of Learning

42. What level of knowledge is being tested if asked, "What is the maneuvering speed of the aircraft listed in the owner's manual?"

    A. Rote.

    B. Application.

    C. Understanding.

Answer (A) is correct. *(FAA-H-8083-9B Chap 3)*
    DISCUSSION: The lowest level, rote learning, is the ability to repeat something back that one has been taught without understanding or being able to apply what has been learned. An example of rote learning is to be able to cite the maneuvering speed of the aircraft listed in the owner's manual.
    Answer (B) is incorrect. Application is the ability of a learner to apply what has been taught. This is the third level of learning and is achieved after the learner understands, has practiced, and can consistently perform a task. **Answer (C) is incorrect.** The second level of learning is understanding, which has been achieved when a learner can put together a block of learning and develop an insight into the performance of a task.

43. Once a learner understands a procedure, has had the procedure demonstrated, and has practiced the procedure until it can be performed with consistency, the learner has demonstrated what level of learning?

    A. Application.

    B. Rote.

    C. Duplication.

Answer (A) is correct. *(FAA-H-8083-9B Chap 3)*
    DISCUSSION: Application is a basic level of learning at which the learner puts something to use that has been learned and understood.
    Answer (B) is incorrect. Rote learning is simple memorization without necessarily gaining an understanding of what has been memorized. **Answer (C) is incorrect.** Duplication is not a level of learning.

44. Learners who use test preparation materials in preparing for FAA tests may commit which of the following adverse actions?

    A. Focusing on test-taking skills rather than critical information essential for safe piloting.

    B. Excelling in the oral exam portion of practical tests.

    C. Focusing on correlation level learning.

Answer (A) is correct. *(FAA-H-8083-9B Chap 5)*
    DISCUSSION: By relying on test preparation materials as a source of learning, learners may learn to pass a given test but fail to learn other critical information essential to safe piloting and maintenance practices.
    Answer (B) is incorrect. FAA inspectors and designated examiners have found that learner applicants often exhibit a lack of knowledge during oral questioning, even though many have easily passed the FAA knowledge test. **Answer (C) is incorrect.** Test preparation materials often encourage rote-level learning, not correlation.

45. Commercially-developed test preparation material

    A. teaches higher-order thinking skills.

    B. replaces instructor-led training.

    C. places emphasis on rote learning rather than more advanced learning levels.

Answer (C) is correct. *(FAA-H-8083-9B Chap 5)*
    DISCUSSION: While commercially-developed training material is a great study aid, it emphasizes rote learning rather than higher levels of learning that promote increased understanding. Commercially-developed training material should be used as a supplement to instructor-led, comprehensive training, not as a replacement for it. Gleim supports and encourages the view that learners should strive for a level of understanding beyond rote memorization. That is why, for 30+ years, all of our knowledge test preparation materials have included both multiple-choice questions and Knowledge Transfer Outlines. These detailed outlines help learners conceptualize why the correct answers are correct and the incorrect answers are incorrect. We also provide additional outline material for learners' practical training in our Flight Maneuvers and Oral Exam Guide books. These texts prepare Gleim learners for the higher-level thinking demanded of these future pilots.
    Answer (A) is incorrect. Higher-order thinking skills involve decision-making principles. Commercially-developed training material emphasizes rote learning rather than higher levels of learning that promote increased understanding. For this reason, instructor-led training is essential for the learner to develop higher-order thinking skills. **Answer (B) is incorrect.** While commercially-developed training material is a great study aid, it cannot be used as a replacement to instructor-led training because it focuses on rote learning rather than higher levels of learning.

46. A disadvantage of using commercially-developed test preparation material is that

    A. the emphasis is on correlation learning.

    B. learners may learn to pass a given test.

    C. learners often exhibit a lack of knowledge during oral questioning.

Answer (C) is correct. (FAA-H-8083-9B Chap 5)
    DISCUSSION: FAA inspectors and designated examiners have found that learners often exhibit a lack of knowledge during oral questioning, even though many have easily passed the FAA knowledge test. This is most often the result of learner memorization rather than true concept understanding. The emphasis of test preparation materials is on rote learning rather than higher levels of learning that promote increased understanding. Gleim supports and encourages the view that learners should strive for a level of understanding beyond rote memorization. That is why, for 30+ years, all of our knowledge test preparation materials have included both multiple-choice questions and Knowledge Transfer Outlines. These detailed outlines help learners conceptualize why the correct answers are correct and the incorrect answers are incorrect. We also provide additional outline material for learners' practical training in our Flight Maneuvers and Oral Exam Guide books. These texts prepare Gleim learners for the higher-level thinking demanded of these future pilots.
    Answer (A) is incorrect. While commercially-developed training material is a great study aid, it emphasizes rote learning rather than higher levels of learning, such as correlation, that promote increased understanding. **Answer (B) is incorrect.** Commercially-developed training material is incredibly useful at helping learners pass FAA tests. This is only a disadvantage if the learner memorizes the material and fails to develop understanding of the covered topics.

47. During the flight portion of a practical test, the examiner simulates complete loss of engine power by closing the throttle and announcing "simulated engine failure." What level of learning is being tested?

    A. Application.

    B. Correlation.

    C. Understanding.

Answer (B) is correct. (FAA-H-8083-9B Chap 3)
    DISCUSSION: When the examiner simulates complete loss of engine power by closing the throttle and announcing "simulated engine failure," the examiner is testing at the correlation level of learning. The applicant must be able to correlate (associate) the engine failure with the requirements to perform the elements of an emergency approach and landing; e.g., establish best-glide speed, select a field, perform restart checklist, plan a flight pattern to the selected field, complete all appropriate checklists, etc.
    Answer (A) is incorrect. The application level of learning is tested when the examiner closes the throttle and tells the applicant to perform an emergency approach and landing. **Answer (C) is incorrect.** The understanding level of learning is tested when the examiner asks the applicant to explain the elements of an emergency approach and landing.

48. When asking a learner to explain how gross weight affects maneuvering speed, what level of learning is being tested?

    A. Application.

    B. Correlation.

    C. Understanding.

Answer (C) is correct. (FAA-H-8083-9B Chap 3)
    DISCUSSION: At the understanding level of learning, a learner will be able to explain how gross weight affects maneuvering speed (V_A). Understanding is the next level after rote memorization and the level before acquiring the skill to apply knowledge, which is application (correlation is the fourth and highest level of learning). Being able to explain (not demonstrate) is the understanding level of learning, not the application or correlation level.
    Answer (A) is incorrect. At the application level, a learner will be able to apply the knowledge that gross weight affects maneuvering speed when determining the appropriate airspeed for entering turbulent air or maneuvers that require an airspeed at or below V_A. **Answer (B) is incorrect.** At the correlation level, a learner has developed the ability to correlate the elements of maneuvering speed with other concepts, such as gust loads, accelerated stalls, load factors, acceleration forces in the aircraft, etc.

49. At which level of learning do most instructors stop teaching?

    A. Application.

    B. Correlation.

    C. Understanding.

Answer (A) is correct. (FAA-H-8083-9B Chap 3)
    DISCUSSION: Most instructors stop teaching at the application level of learning. Discontinuing instruction on an element at this point and directing subsequent instruction exclusively to other elements is characteristic of piecemeal instruction, which is usually inefficient. It violates the building block concept of instruction by failing to apply what has been learned to future learning tasks.
    Answer (B) is incorrect. Correlation is the highest level of learning and should be the goal of each instructor. Instructors all too often stop at the application level. **Answer (C) is incorrect.** Understanding is the second level of learning, and at this point, a learner understands a task but may not be able to do it. Instructors will usually continue teaching to the next level, which is application.

1.8 Domains of Learning

50. Which domain of learning deals with knowledge?

    A. Affective.

    B. Cognitive.

    C. Psychomotor.

Answer (B) is correct. (FAA-H-8083-9B Chap 3)
    DISCUSSION: Domains of learning are classified based on what is to be learned. The cognitive domain of learning deals with knowledge (e.g., facts, concepts, or relationships).
    Answer (A) is incorrect. The affective domain deals with attitudes, beliefs, and values, not knowledge. **Answer (C) is incorrect.** The psychomotor domain deals with physical skills, not knowledge.

51. Affective domain relates to

    A. physical skills.

    B. knowledge.

    C. attitudes, beliefs, and values.

Answer (C) is correct. (FAA-H-8083-9B Chap 3)
    DISCUSSION: Domains of learning are classified based on what is to be learned. The affective domain relates to attitudes, beliefs, and values.
    Answer (A) is incorrect. The psychomotor domain, not the affective domain, relates to physical skills. **Answer (B) is incorrect.** The cognitive domain, not the affective domain, relates to knowledge.

52. The educational objective levels for the cognitive domain are

    A. receiving, responding, valuing, organization, and characterization.

    B. perception, set, guided response mechanism, complex overt response, adaptation, and origination.

    C. knowledge, comprehension, application, analysis, synthesis, and evaluation.

Answer (C) is correct. (FAA-H-8083-9B Chap 3)
    DISCUSSION: Each domain of learning has multiple educational objective levels. The six educational objective levels of the cognitive domain are knowledge, comprehension, application, analysis, synthesis, and evaluation.
    Answer (A) is incorrect. Receiving, responding, valuing, organization, and characterization are the five educational objective levels of the affective, not cognitive, domain. **Answer (B) is incorrect.** Perception, set, guided response mechanism, complex overt response, adaptation, and origination are the seven educational objective levels of the psychomotor, not cognitive, domain.

53. The most complex outcome in the affective domain is

    A. organization.

    B. characterization.

    C. valuing.

Answer (B) is correct. (FAA-H-8083-9B Chap 3)
    DISCUSSION: A taxonomy of educational objectives is a systematic classification scheme for sorting learning outcomes into the three domains of learning (cognitive, affective, and psychomotor) and ranking the desired outcomes in a developmental hierarchy from least complex to most complex. The most complex learning outcome in the affective domain is characterization in which the learner incorporates a value or attitude into his or her life.
    Answer (A) is incorrect. Organization (in which the learner rearranges his or her value system to accommodate a new value or attitude) is the second-most-complex, not the most complex, learning outcome in the affective domain. **Answer (C) is incorrect.** Valuing (in which the learner accepts a new value or attitude) is the third-most-complex, not the most complex, learning outcome in the affective domain.

54. The listing of the hierarchy of objectives is often referred to as a

    A. taxonomy.

    B. skill.

    C. domain.

Answer (A) is correct. *(FAA-H-8083-9B Chap 3)*
    DISCUSSION: Each of the domains of learning has a hierarchy of educational objectives. The listing of the hierarchy of objectives is often called a taxonomy.
    Answer (B) is incorrect. A skill is what is learned in the psychomotor domain of learning. It is not a hierarchy of educational objectives. **Answer (C) is incorrect.** Domains of learning contain, but are not, hierarchies of educational objectives.

55. Learning objectives can be sorted in a system known as a

    A. taxonomy.

    B. database.

    C. schema.

Answer (A) is correct. *(FAA-H-8083-9B Chap 2)*
    DISCUSSION: The hierarchy of learning objectives is known as a taxonomy. Taxonomy is the systematic classification of learning outcomes into one of the three broad categories or domains of learning (cognitive, affective, and psychomotor).
    Answer (B) is incorrect. A database is an interconnected group of data elements. **Answer (C) is incorrect.** "Schema" is a term used in information technology to refer to the layout of a database.

56. The least complex outcome in the psychomotor domain is

    A. adaptation.

    B. mechanism.

    C. perception.

Answer (C) is correct. *(FAA-H-8083-9B Chap 3)*
    DISCUSSION: A taxonomy of educational objectives is a systematic classification scheme for sorting learning outcomes into the three domains of learning (cognitive, affective, and psychomotor) and ranking the desired outcomes in a developmental hierarchy from least complex to most complex. The least complex learning outcome in the psychomotor domain is perception in which the learner has awareness of sensory stimuli.
    Answer (A) is incorrect. Adaptation (in which the learner modifies his or her performance of a skill for special problems) is the second-most-complex, not the least complex, learning outcome in the psychomotor domain. **Answer (B) is incorrect.** Mechanism (in which the learner performs simple acts well) is the fourth-least-complex, not the least complex, learning outcome in the psychomotor domain.

57. Which of the following domains relates a grouping of levels of learning associated with a person's attitudes?

    A. Affective.

    B. Cognitive.

    C. Psychomotor.

Answer (A) is correct. *(FAA-H-8083-9B Chap 3)*
    DISCUSSION: The affective domain is a grouping of levels of learning associated with a person's attitudes, personal beliefs, and values, which range from receiving through responding, valuing, and organization to characterization.
    Answer (B) is incorrect. The cognitive domain is a grouping of levels of learning associated with mental activity. In order of increasing complexity, the domains are knowledge, comprehension, application, analysis, synthesis, and evaluation. **Answer (C) is incorrect.** The psychomotor domain is a grouping of levels of learning associated with physical skill levels, which range from perception through set, guided response, mechanism, complex overt response, and adaptation to origination.

58. An example of a skill involving the cognitive domain would be

    A. Understanding how the flight controls should be positioned during a turn.

    B. A positive reception for learning new skills.

    C. Performing a short-field approach and landing to Practical Test Standards/Airman Certification.

Answer (A) is correct. *(FAA-H-8083-9B Chap 3)*
    DISCUSSION: The cognitive domain includes remembering specific facts (content knowledge) and concepts that help develop intellectual abilities and skills, such as understanding how and why the flight controls should be positioned in a certain way.
    Answer (B) is incorrect. This answer choice best describes the affective domain. The affective domain addresses a learner's emotions toward the learning experience. It includes feelings, values, enthusiasms, motivations, and attitudes. **Answer (C) is incorrect.** This answer choice best describes the psychomotor domain. The psychomotor domain is skill-based and includes physical movement, coordination, and use of the motor-skill areas.

59. An example of a skill involving the psychomotor domain would be

   A. Responsiveness to an instructor's demonstration of steep turns.

   B. Applying back pressure to maintain altitude during a steep turn.

   C. Correlating pitch control inputs during a medium-bank with those of a steep turn.

Answer (B) is correct. (FAA-H-8083-9B Chap 3)

DISCUSSION: The psychomotor domain is skill-based and includes physical movement, coordination, and use of the motor-skill areas, such as physically manipulating the flight controls during a steep turn.

Answer (A) is incorrect. This answer choice best describes the affective domain. The affective domain addresses a learner's emotions toward the learning experience. It includes feelings, values, enthusiasms, motivations, and attitudes.

Answer (C) is incorrect. This answer choice best describes the cognitive domain. The cognitive domain includes remembering specific facts (content knowledge) and concepts that help develop intellectual abilities and skills.

60. Which of the following would be an example of a skill involving the psychomotor domain?

   A. Memorizing aircraft V-speeds.

   B. Computing takeoff distance over a 50 foot obstacle.

   C. Programming a Global Positioning System (GPS) receiver.

Answer (C) is correct. (FAA-H-8083-9B Chap 3)

DISCUSSION: The psychomotor domain is skill-based and includes physical movement, coordination, and use of the motor-skill areas. Development of these skills requires repetitive practice and is measured in terms of speed, precision, distance, and techniques. Skills involving the psychomotor domain include learning to fly a precision instrument approach procedure, programming a global positioning system (GPS) receiver, or using sophisticated maintenance equipment.

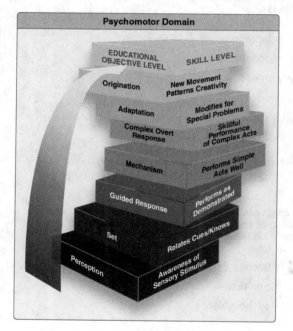

Figure 3-12.

Answer (A) is incorrect. Skills in the psychomotor domain involve physical movement, coordination, and use of the motor-skill areas. Memorization is only the cognitive domain and does not encompass all seven educational objective levels.

Answer (B) is incorrect. Skills in the psychomotor domain involve physical movement, coordination, and use of the motor-skill areas. Computing a takeoff distance does not require physical movement or coordination and, therefore, does not require all seven education objective levels.

61. An example of a skill involving the affective domain would be

    A. Responding to an instructor's question.

    B. Recalling the information needed to answer an instructor's question.

    C. Practicing the conditions of an instructor's question to determine an answer.

Answer (A) is correct. (FAA-H-8083-9B Chap 3)
    DISCUSSION: The affective domain addresses a learner's emotions toward the learning experience. It includes feelings, values, enthusiasms, motivations, and attitudes, including responsiveness to instructor inquiries.
    Answer (B) is incorrect. This answer choice best describes the cognitive domain. The cognitive domain includes remembering specific facts (content knowledge) and concepts that help develop intellectual abilities and skills. **Answer (C) is incorrect.** This answer choice best describes the psychomotor domain. The psychomotor domain is skill-based and includes physical movement, coordination, and use of the motor-skill areas.

62. Which domain of learning includes physical movement and coordination?

    A. Affective.

    B. Cognitive.

    C. Psychomotor.

Answer (C) is correct. (FAA-H-8083-9B Chap 3)
    DISCUSSION: Domains of learning are classified based on what is to be learned. The psychomotor domain concerns physical skills (e.g., movement and coordination).
    Answer (A) is incorrect. The affective domain relates to attitudes, beliefs, and values, not physical skills. **Answer (B) is incorrect.** The cognitive domain deals with knowledge (e.g., facts, concepts, or relationships), not physical skills.

63. The educational objective levels; receiving, responding, valuing, organization, and characterization; are a part of which domain of learning?

    A. Psychomotor.

    B. Affective.

    C. Cognitive.

Answer (B) is correct. (FAA-H-8083-9B Chap 3)
    DISCUSSION: Each domain of learning has multiple educational objective levels that start with the least complex and end with the most complex. Receiving, responding, valuing, organization, and characterization are the five educational objective levels of the affective domain.
    Answer (A) is incorrect. The educational objective levels of the psychomotor domain are perception, set, guided response, mechanism, complex overt response, adaptation, and origination. **Answer (C) is incorrect.** The educational objective levels of the cognitive domain are knowledge, comprehension, application, analysis, synthesis, and evaluation.

64. The educational objective level of the psychomotor domain at which a learner's skill demonstrates new movement patterns and creativity is

    A. origination.

    B. complex overt response.

    C. adaptation.

Answer (A) is correct. (FAA-H-8083-9B Chap 3)
    DISCUSSION: Each educational objective level of the domains of learning has a distinct learning outcome. The learning outcome where a learner's skill demonstrates new movement patterns and creativity is equivalent to the origination educational objective level of the psychomotor domain.
    Answer (B) is incorrect. At the complex overt response educational objective level, the learner would demonstrate skillful performance of complex acts, not new movement patterns and creativity. **Answer (C) is incorrect.** At the adaptation educational objective level, the learner would demonstrate modifiers for special problems, not new movement patterns and creativity.

65. The least complex outcome in the cognitive domain is

    A. synthesis.

    B. knowledge.

    C. comprehension.

Answer (B) is correct. (FAA-H-8083-9B Chap 3)
    DISCUSSION: A taxonomy of educational objectives is a systematic classification scheme for sorting learning outcomes into three domains of learning (cognitive, affective, and psychomotor) and ranking the desired outcomes in a developmental hierarchy from least complex to most complex. The least complex learning outcome in the cognitive domain is knowledge where the learner has the capacity to recall and recognize facts, concepts, or relationships.
    Answer (A) is incorrect. Synthesis (in which the learner has the capacity to create new relationships) is the fifth most complex, not the least complex, learning outcome in the cognitive domain. **Answer (C) is incorrect.** Comprehension (in which the learner has the capacity to translate, interpret, and extrapolate) is the second most complex, not the least complex, learning outcome in the cognitive domain.

1.9 Learning Skills and the Learning Curve

66. The best way to prepare a learner to perform a task is to

    A. explain the purpose of the task.

    B. provide a clear, step-by-step example.

    C. give the learner an outline of the task.

Answer (B) is correct. (FAA-H-8083-9B Chap 3)
    DISCUSSION: The best way to prepare a learner to perform a task is to provide a clear, step-by-step example. Having a model to follow permits a learner to get a clear picture of each step in the sequence (e.g., what it is, how to do it).
    Answer (A) is incorrect. While a learner should know the purpose of a task, (s)he must be provided with a clear, step-by-step example showing how to perform the task. **Answer (C) is incorrect.** An outline is not as useful as a clear, step-by-step example.

67. During learning, a leveling-off process or plateau is

    A. normal and should be expected after an initial period of rapid improvement.

    B. normal and can be overcome with more practice.

    C. not normal and requires that the instructor reteach the lesson in a different format to ensure learner learning and retention.

Answer (A) is correct. (FAA-H-8083-9B Chap 3)
    DISCUSSION: Learning plateaus are normal and should be expected after an initial period of rapid improvement.
    Answer (B) is incorrect. Instructors should also be aware that they can bring on a learning plateau by over-practice. After repeating any task three or four times, give it a break to avoid causing a learning plateau. **Answer (C) is incorrect.** Learning plateaus are normal and can sometimes be alleviated by the instructor better explaining the lesson, the reason for the lesson, and how it applies to the learner. Reteaching lesson content is not necessary in the event of a learning plateau.

68. A learning plateau may be defined as the

    A. leveling-off in learning at the point which a learner has reached the highest competence of a particular subject.

    B. gradual decrease in learning almost to the point where it appears to have ceased before it resumes and proficiency increases.

    C. point in the learning curve at which skill proficiency retrogresses.

Answer (B) is correct. (FAA-H-8083-9B Chap 3)
    DISCUSSION: A learning plateau may be defined as the gradual decrease in learning rate. This is normal and should be expected by the instructor and learner after an initial period of rapid improvement. Note that the apparent lack of increasing proficiency does not necessarily mean that learning has ceased.
    Answer (A) is incorrect. A learning plateau is the leveling-off of an individual's rate of learning, usually after a period of rapid improvement, not after reaching the highest competence of a particular subject. **Answer (C) is incorrect.** A learning plateau is a gradual decrease in learning rate almost to the point where it appears to have ceased before it resumes and proficiency increases, not retrogresses.

69. Which is true concerning "learning plateaus"?

    A. Learning plateaus are the direct result of poor instruction.

    B. Learning plateaus are a normal part of the learning process and tend to be temporary.

    C. Learning plateaus are caused by under-practice.

Answer (B) is correct. (FAA-H-8083-9B Chap 3)
    DISCUSSION: Learning plateaus are a normal part of the learning process and tend to be temporary, but instructors and learners should be prepared for them to avoid discouragement.
    Answer (A) is incorrect. Learning plateaus are normal, even in quality instruction. They often occur after a period of rapid improvement on the part of the learner. **Answer (C) is incorrect.** Learning plateaus can be caused by over-practice, not under-practice. After repeating any task three or four times, give it a break to avoid causing a learning plateau. Keep in mind that the apparent lack of increasing proficiency does not necessarily mean that learning has ceased.

70. Instructors can help learners who arrive at a learning plateau by

    A. Continuing practice to help the learner move past it.

    B. Assuming that the plateau represents the learner's maximum skill achievement.

    C. Moving the learner to a different place in the curriculum.

Answer (C) is correct. (FAA-H-8083-9B Chap 3)
    DISCUSSION: Instructors can help learners who fall into a learning plateau by moving them to a different place in the curriculum and giving the current task a break. Learning plateau problems can sometimes also be alleviated by the instructor better explaining the lesson, the reason for the lesson, and how it applies to the learner.
    Answer (A) is incorrect. Rather than treating a learning plateau, overpractice can actually create one. After repeating any task three or four times, give it a break to avoid causing a learning plateau. **Answer (B) is incorrect.** Keep in mind that the apparent lack of increasing proficiency does not necessarily mean that learning has ceased. The point is that, in learning motor skills, a leveling-off process, or plateau, is normal and should be expected after an initial period of rapid improvement.

71. The three stages of skill acquisition are

  A. cognitive, associative, and automatic.

  B. cognitive, understanding, and automatic.

  C. cognitive, additional, and automatic.

Answer (A) is correct. (FAA-H-8083-9B Chap 3)
  DISCUSSION: The three stages of skill acquisition are cognitive, associative, and automatic.
  Answer (B) is incorrect. Understanding is not one of the three stages of skill acquisition. **Answer (C) is incorrect.** The three stages of skill acquisition are cognitive, associative, and automatic.

72. Which stage of skill acquisition is characterized by the ability to perform a procedure rapidly and smoothly while devoting little deliberate attention to performance and simultaneously performing other tasks?

  A. Cognitive stage.

  B. Associative stage.

  C. Automatic response stage.

Answer (C) is correct. (FAA-H-8083-9B Chap 3)
  DISCUSSION: By the automatic response stage, learner performance of the skill is rapid and smooth. The learner devotes much less deliberate attention to performance and may be able to carry on a conversation or perform other tasks while performing the skill.
  Answer (A) is incorrect. There is a lack of understanding of the skill in the cognitive stage; thus, there can be no automatic performance of the skill by the learner. **Answer (B) is incorrect.** At the associative stage, the learner no longer performs a series of memorized steps but is able to assess his or her progress along the way and make adjustments in performance. There is, however, no smooth or rapid skill performance associated with this stage.

73. Which stage of skill acquisition may be characterized by learner ability to assess personal progress and make adjustments in performance?

  A. Cognitive stage.

  B. Associative stage.

  C. Automatic response stage.

Answer (B) is correct. (FAA-H-8083-9B Chap 3)
  DISCUSSION: As the storage of a skill continues due to practice, the learner learns to associate individual steps in performance with likely outcomes. The learner no longer performs a series of memorized steps but is able to assess his or her progress along the way and make adjustments in performance.
  Answer (A) is incorrect. Cognitive learning has a basis in factual knowledge. Since the learner has no prior knowledge of flying, the instructor first introduces him or her to a basic skill. The learner then memorizes the steps required to perform the skill. As the learner carries out these memorized steps, (s)he is often unaware of progress or may fixate on one aspect of performance. **Answer (C) is incorrect.** While learner performance assessment certainly exists in the automatic response stage, it is not the characterizing trait of the stage. Rather, the characterizing trait of the automatic response stage is that a learner performs automatically, even instinctively, to flight tasks. The learner devotes far less deliberate attention to performing the task.

74. Distractions can be used as a valuable learning tool, but they should be avoided during

  A. deliberate practice.

  B. blocked practice.

  C. random practice.

Answer (A) is correct. (FAA-H-8083-9B Chap 3)
  DISCUSSION: In order for a learner to gain skill knowledge and learn how to perform the skill on the automatic level, a learner must engage in deliberate practice. Studies of skill learning suggest a learner achieves better results if distractions are avoided during deliberate practice. When feedback is needed to correct learner performance, it should be brief and explicit.
  Answer (B) is incorrect. Blocked practice is practicing the same drill until the movement becomes automatic. The *Aviation Instructor's Handbook* does not specifically state distractions should be avoided during blocked practice. **Answer (C) is incorrect.** Random practice mixes up the skills to be acquired throughout the practice session. The *Aviation Instructor's Handbook* does not specifically state distractions should be avoided during random practice.

75. If a learner can fly an ILS while communicating with ATC at the same time, (s)he has reached which stage of skill acquisition?

   A. Associative stage.

   B. Automatic response stage.

   C. Psychomotor stage.

Answer (B) is correct. (FAA-H-8083-9B Chap 3)
   DISCUSSION: As procedures become automatic, less attention is required to carry them out, so it is possible to do other things simultaneously, or at least do other things more comfortably. By the automatic response stage, learner performance of the skill is rapid and smooth.
   Answer (A) is incorrect. Even demonstrating how to do something does not result in the learner learning the skill. Practice is necessary in order for the learner to learn how to coordinate muscles with visual and tactile senses. Learning to perform various aircraft maintenance skills or flight maneuvers requires practice. Another benefit of practice is that as the learner gains proficiency in a skill, verbal instructions become more meaningful. A long, detailed explanation is confusing before the learner begins performing, whereas specific comments are more meaningful and useful after the skill has been partially mastered. **Answer (C) is incorrect.** As the storage of a skill via practice continues, the learner learns to associate individual steps in performance with likely outcomes. The learner no longer performs a series of memorized steps but is able to assess his or her progress along the way and make adjustments in performance. Performing the skill still requires deliberate attention, but the learner is better able to deal with distractions.

76. Studies of skill learning suggest that a learner achieves better results if distractions are avoided during what type of practice?

   A. Deliberate practice.

   B. Blocked practice.

   C. Random practice.

Answer (A) is correct. (FAA-H-8083-9B Chap 3)
   DISCUSSION: During deliberate practice, the learner practices specific areas for improvement and receives specific feedback after practice. Studies of skill learning suggest a learner achieves better results if distractions are avoided during deliberate practice. When feedback is needed to correct learner performance, it should be brief and explicit.
   Answer (B) is incorrect. Using distractions during blocked practice can actually be helpful in preventing learner and instructor from falsely determining that repeated skills have been well learned. **Answer (C) is incorrect.** Random practice relies heavily on the incorporation of distractions to mix up the skills to be acquired throughout the practice session. This type of practice leads to better retention because performing a series of separate skills in a random order helps the learner recognize the similarities and differences of each skill.

77. What type of practice is repeating the same drill or doing the same task again and again until the movement becomes automatic?

   A. Deliberate.

   B. Blocked.

   C. Random.

Answer (B) is correct. (FAA-H-8083-9B Chap 3)
   DISCUSSION: Blocked practice is practicing the same drill until the movement becomes automatic. Doing the same task over and over leads to better short-term performance but poorer long-term learning.
   Answer (A) is incorrect. In order for a learner to gain skill knowledge and learn how to perform the skill on the automatic level, a learner must engage in deliberate practice. However, this type of practice in and of itself does not produce the ability to perform skills automatically. **Answer (C) is incorrect.** Random practice mixes up the skills to be acquired throughout the practice session to increase long-term skill retention. This practice type is not effective at producing automatic responses, but rather more meaningful ones.

78. Which stage of skill acquisition may be characterized by performing memorized steps unaware of progress?

    A. Cognitive stage.

    B. Associative stage.

    C. Automatic response stage.

Answer (A) is correct. (FAA-H-8083-9B Chap 3)
    DISCUSSION: In the cognitive stage, learning has a basis in factual knowledge. Since the learner has no prior knowledge of flying, the instructor first introduces him or her to a basic skill. The learner then memorizes the steps required to perform the skill. As the learner carries out these memorized steps, (s)he is often unaware of progress or may fixate on one aspect of performance. Performance is deliberate and often characterized by the learner making many abrupt control inputs.
    Answer (B) is incorrect. At the associative stage, the learner no longer performs a series of memorized steps but is able to assess his or her progress along the way and make adjustments in performance. **Answer (C) is incorrect.** By the automatic response stage, learner performance of the skill is rapid and smooth. The learner devotes much less deliberate attention to performance and may be able to carry on a conversation or perform other tasks while performing a skill.

79. Distractions interjected by instructors during training may help

    A. learners learn to ignore distractions.

    B. learners determine whether or not a distraction warrants further attention or action on their part.

    C. learners learn more effective multitasking techniques.

Answer (B) is correct. (FAA-H-8083-9B Chap 3)
    DISCUSSION: A distraction is an unexpected event that causes the learner's attention to be momentarily diverted. Learners must learn to decide whether or not a distraction warrants further attention or action on their part. Once this has been decided, the learners must either turn their attention back to what they were doing or act on the distraction.
    Answer (A) is incorrect. Not all in-flight distractions should be ignored. Some require immediate action on the part of the pilot. **Answer (C) is incorrect.** Multitasking is not a strategy for identifying and prioritizing distractions during flight.

STUDY UNIT TWO

BARRIERS TO LEARNING

(5 pages of outline)

2.1 SELF-CONCEPT

1. Self-concept is how one pictures oneself.

    a. Self-concept or self-image can be described in terms such as "confident" or "insecure."

        1) "Confident" denotes a favorable view of self, or positive self-concept.
        2) "Insecure" denotes an unfavorable view of self, or negative self-concept.

    b. This is a powerful determinant in learning.

    c. Self-concept has a great influence on the total perceptual process.

2. If a learner's experiences tend to support a favorable self-image, the learner tends to remain receptive to subsequent experiences. These learners are less defensive and more receptive to new experiences, instructions, and demonstrations.

3. Negative self-concept contributes most to a learner's failure to remain receptive to new experiences and creates a tendency to reject additional training.

4. Instructors must be able to detect negative self-image in their learners and strive to prevent these feelings from undermining the instructional process.

    a. An instructor can foster the development of insights by helping the learner acquire and maintain a favorable self-concept.

        1) The way instructors conduct themselves, their own positive attitudes, and the manner in which they instruct can help their learners achieve this positive view.

            a) EXAMPLE: During an introductory flight with a potential flight learner, the instructor does not focus on emergency procedures or potential hazards to flight, but instead emphasizes how smooth, efficient, and enjoyable the flight was.

2.2 DEFENSE MECHANISMS

1. Certain behavior patterns are called defense mechanisms because they are subconscious defenses against the reality of unpleasant situations.

    a. People use these defenses to soften feelings of failure, alleviate feelings of guilt, and protect feelings of personal worth and adequacy.

2. Although defense mechanisms can serve a useful purpose, they can involve some degree of self-deception and distortion of reality.

    a. They alleviate symptoms, not causes.

3. Common defense mechanisms:

    a. **Repression** – A person places uncomfortable thoughts into inaccessible areas of the unconscious mind. For example, a learner pilot may have a repressed fear of flying that inhibits his or her ability to learn how to fly.

        1) Things a person is unable to cope with at present are pushed away to be dealt with at another time, or hopefully never to be dealt with because they faded away on their own accord.

        2) The level of repression can vary from temporarily forgetting an uncomfortable thought to amnesia, where the events that triggered the anxiety are deeply buried.

        3) Repressed memories do not disappear and may reappear in dreams or slips of the tongue ("Freudian slips").

    b. **Denial** – Refusal to accept external reality because it is too threatening. It is the refusal to acknowledge what has happened, is happening, or will happen.

        1) Denial is a form of repression through which stressful thoughts are banned from memory.

        2) Related to denial is minimization. When a person minimizes something, (s)he accepts what happened, but in a diluted form, usually justifying the event because "nothing bad happened."

    c. **Compensation** – Process of psychologically counterbalancing perceived weaknesses by emphasizing strength in other areas.

        1) Learners often attempt to disguise the presence of a weak or undesirable quality by emphasizing a more positive one.

        2) Compensation involves substituting success in a realm of life other than the realm in which the person suffers a weakness.

d.   **Projection** – An individual places his or her own unacceptable impulses onto someone else. A person relegates the blame for personal shortcomings, mistakes, and transgressions to others.

   1)   A learner pilot who fails a flight exam and says, "I failed because I had a poor examiner" believes the failure was not due to a lack of personal skill or knowledge.

   2)   This learner projects blame onto an "unfair" examiner.

e.   **Rationalization** – When a person cannot accept the real reasons for his or her own behavior, this device permits the substitution of excuses for reasons. Rationalization is a subconscious technique for justifying actions that otherwise would be unacceptable.

f.   **Reaction formation** – A person fakes a belief opposite to his or her true belief because the true belief causes anxiety. The person feels an urge to do or say something and then actually does or says something that is the opposite of what (s)he really wants.

g.   **Fantasy** – Occurs when a learner engages in daydreams about how things should be rather than doing anything about how things are. The learner uses his or her imagination to escape from reality into a fictitious world–a world of success or pleasure.

   1)   Fantasy provides a simple and satisfying escape from problems, but if a learner gets sufficient satisfaction from daydreaming, (s)he may stop trying to achieve goals altogether.

   2)   Lost in the fantasy, the learner spends more time dreaming about being a successful pilot than working toward the goal.

   3)   When carried to extremes, the worlds of fantasy and reality can become so confused that the dreamer cannot distinguish one from the other.

h.   **Displacement** – Results in an unconscious shift of emotion, affect, or desire from the original object to a more acceptable, less threatening substitute.

   1)   Displacement avoids the risk associated with feeling unpleasant emotions and puts them somewhere other than where they belong, similar to repression.

2.3 STRESS, ANXIETY, AND FATIGUE

1. Normal individuals react to stress by responding rapidly and exactly, often automatically, within their experience and training.

    a. This underlines the need for proper training prior to emergency situations.

    b. The effective individual thinks rapidly, acts rapidly, and is extremely sensitive to his or her surroundings.

2. Abnormal reactions to stress may result in inadequate, illogical, or random responses. These may include

    a. Inappropriate reactions, such as extreme overcooperation, painstaking self-control, inappropriate laughter or singing, and very rapid changes in emotion

    b. Marked changes in mood (e.g., high spirits followed by deep depression)

    c. Severe, unreasonable anger toward the flight instructor, service personnel, or others

3. Anxiety is probably the most significant psychological barrier affecting flight instruction. It is the extreme worry brought on by stressful situations (e.g., an emergency, an exam, etc.). Anxiety can be countered by

    a. Treating fears as a normal reaction rather than ignoring them,
    b. Reinforcing the learner's enjoyment of flying, and
    c. Teaching learners to cope with fears.

4. Fatigue is one of the most treacherous hazards to flight safety as it may not be apparent to a pilot until serious errors are made. Fatigue can be either acute (short-term) or chronic (long-term).

    a. **Acute fatigue**, a normal occurrence of everyday living, is the tiredness felt after long periods of physical and mental strain, including strenuous muscular effort, immobility, heavy mental workload, strong emotional pressure, monotony, and lack of sleep.

        1) A CFI who is familiar with the signs indicative of acute fatigue will be more aware if the learner is experiencing them as the signs of acute fatigue are often apparent to others before the individual notices any signs of fatigue.

        2) Acute fatigue is characterized by

            a) Inattention
            b) Distractibility
            c) Errors in timing
            d) Neglect of secondary tasks
            e) Loss of accuracy and control
            f) Lack of awareness of error accumulation
            g) Irritability

b. **Chronic fatigue** is a combination of both physiological problems and psychological issues and occurs when there is not enough time for a full recovery from repeated episodes of acute fatigue.

    1) Without resolution, human performance continues to fall off, judgment becomes impaired, and unwarranted risks may be taken.

    2) Recovery from chronic fatigue requires a prolonged and deliberate solution.

        a) Chronic fatigue's underlying cause is generally not "rest-related" and may have deeper points of origin. Therefore, rest alone may not resolve chronic fatigue.

            i) Chronic fatigue is a combination of both physiological problems and psychological issues. Psychological problems such as financial, home life, or job-related stresses cause a lack of quality rest that is only solved by mitigating the underlying problems before the fatigue is solved.

2.4 THE OVERCONFIDENT OR IMPATIENT LEARNER

1. Because they make few mistakes, those who are fast learners may assume that the correction of errors is unimportant.

    a. This overconfidence soon results in faulty performance.

    b. For apt learners, a good instructor will constantly raise the standard of performance for each lesson, demanding greater effort.

2. Impatience is a greater deterrent to learning pilot skills than is generally recognized. For example, a learner may have a strong desire to make an early solo flight.

    a. The impatient learner fails to understand the need for preliminary training. (S)he seeks only the final objective without considering the means necessary to reach it.

    b. Instructors can correct impatience by presenting the necessary preliminary training one step at a time, with clearly stated goals for each step.

        1) Instructors should emphasize that it is necessary to master the basics if the entire task is to be performed competently and safely.

    c. Impatience can result from instruction set at the pace of a slow learner when it is applied to a motivated, fast learner.

        1) It is important that an instructor analyze each learner's ability and adapt lessons accordingly to counteract this trait.

QUESTIONS AND ANSWER EXPLANATIONS: All of the Fundamentals of Instructing knowledge test questions chosen by the FAA for release as well as additional questions selected by Gleim relating to the material in the previous outlines are provided on the following pages. These questions have been organized into the same subunits as the outlines. To the immediate right of each question are the correct answer and answer explanations. You should cover these answers and answer explanations while responding to the questions. Refer to the general discussion in the Introduction on how to take the FAA knowledge test.

Remember that the questions from the FAA knowledge test bank have been reordered by topic and organized into a meaningful sequence. Also, the first line of the answer explanation gives the citation of the authoritative source for the answer.

QUESTIONS

2.1 Self-Concept

1. The factor which contributes most to a learner's failure to remain receptive to new experiences and which creates a tendency to reject additional training is

A. basic needs.

B. element of threat.

C. negative self-concept.

Answer (C) is correct. (FAA-H-8083-9B Chap 3)
   DISCUSSION: A learner with a negative self-concept is resistant to new experiences and may reject additional training. People tend to avoid experiences that contradict their self-concept.
   Answer (A) is incorrect. A learner's basic needs can be used by the instructor to promote learning. For instance, personal safety is one of the most important basic needs, and aviation training heavily emphasizes this need. **Answer (B) is incorrect.** An element of threat will cause a learner to limit his or her attention to the threatening object or condition. Once this is removed, the learner will be able to learn.

2. An instructor may foster the development of insights by

A. helping the learner acquire and maintain a favorable self-concept.

B. pointing out the attractive features of the activity to be learned.

C. keeping the rate of learning consistent so that it is predictable.

Answer (A) is correct. (FAA-H-8083-9B Chap 3)
   DISCUSSION: Especially in a field such as aviation training, the instructor can foster the development of insights by helping the learner acquire and maintain a favorable self-concept. The learner who feels sure of his or her knowledge, skills, and judgments learned in class will also feel better about actual performance and his or her own ability to fly.
   Answer (B) is incorrect. The attractive features in a learning situation tend to increase motivation rather than insight. **Answer (C) is incorrect.** Learning rates will vary, not stay constant, with each training lesson.

3. What is an outcome of a learner showing a favorable self-concept?

A. A more receptive attitude to experiences.

B. Failure to remain open to new learning experiences.

C. A positive attitude on the part of the flight instructor.

Answer (A) is correct. (FAA-H-8083-9B Chap 3)
   DISCUSSION: Learners with a favorable self-concept will be more receptive to subsequent experiences. Learners who show favorable self-concept are less defensive and more receptive to new experiences, instructions, and demonstrations.
   Answer (B) is incorrect. Failure to remain open to new learning experiences is a result of an unfavorable view of self, or negative self-concept. **Answer (C) is incorrect.** An outcome of a learner's favorable self-concept will not guarantee that a positive attitude will be shown by the instructor. However, the way in which instructors conduct themselves, and their own positive attitudes, can help their learners achieve this same positive view.

4. Which term denotes a favorable view of self?

A. Insecure.

B. Unassured.

C. Confident.

Answer (C) is correct. (FAA-H-8083-9B Chap 3)
   DISCUSSION: Being confident denotes a favorable view of self, or positive self-concept.
   Answer (A) is incorrect. The term "insecure" denotes an unfavorable view of self, or negative self-concept. **Answer (B) is incorrect.** The term "unassured" is similar to the term "insecure" and portrays a negative view of self.

2.2 Defense Mechanisms

5. Defense mechanisms

A. are subject to the learner's normal behavioral processes.

B. are related to the conscious domain.

C. involve some degree of self-deception and distortion of reality.

Answer (C) is correct. (FAA-H-8083-9B Chap 2)
DISCUSSION: Defense mechanisms involve some degree of self-deception and distortion of reality. They alleviate the symptoms but not the causes. Defense mechanisms do not solve problems. Moreover, because defense mechanisms operate on an unconscious level, they are not subject to normal conscious checks and balances.
Answer (A) is incorrect. Defense mechanisms occur on a subconscious level and are thus not subject to the learner's normal behavioral processes. **Answer (B) is incorrect.** Defense mechanisms are not related to the conscious domain.

6. Although defense mechanisms can serve a useful purpose, they can

A. provide feelings of adequacy.

B. alleviate the cause of problems.

C. involve some degree of self-deception and distortion of reality.

Answer (C) is correct. (FAA-H-8083-9B Chap 2)
DISCUSSION: Although defense mechanisms can serve a useful purpose, they can also be hindrances. Because they involve some self-deception and distortion of reality, defense mechanisms do not solve problems.
Answer (A) is incorrect. Defense mechanisms mask and protect feelings of adequacy rather than provide them. **Answer (B) is incorrect.** Defense mechanisms alleviate symptoms, not causes, of problems.

7. If an instructor has a learner with a hidden fear of flying that inhibits learning, the learner is most likely displaying which defense mechanism?

A. Reaction formation.

B. Repression.

C. Projection.

Answer (B) is correct. (FAA-H-8083-9B Chap 2)
DISCUSSION: Repression is the defense mechanism whereby a person places uncomfortable thoughts into inaccessible areas of the unconscious mind.
Answer (A) is incorrect. In reaction formation, a person fakes a belief opposite to the true belief because the true belief causes anxiety. **Answer (C) is incorrect.** Through projection, an individual places his or her own unacceptable impulses onto someone else.

8. When a learner uses excuses to justify inadequate performance, it is an indication of the defense mechanism known as

A. fantasy.

B. displacement.

C. rationalization.

Answer (C) is correct. (FAA-H-8083-9B Chap 2)
DISCUSSION: Rationalization is a subconscious technique for justifying unacceptable actions or performance. This allows a learner to substitute excuses for reasons and make those excuses plausible and acceptable to themselves.
Answer (A) is incorrect. Fantasy is the defense mechanism in which the learner escapes (either physically or mentally) from a frustrating experience. **Answer (B) is incorrect.** Displacement is the defense mechanism in which the learner shifts emotion, affect, or desire from the original object to a more acceptable, less threatening substitute.

9. Fantasy is a defense mechanism learners use when they

A. want to escape from frustrating situations.

B. cannot accept the real reasons for their behavior.

C. place blame on someone or something other than themselves.

Answer (A) is correct. (FAA-H-8083-9B Chap 2)
DISCUSSION: The defense mechanism of flight allows a learner to escape from a frustrating situation. This escape can be physical flight (absenteeism, illness, etc.) or mental flight (daydreaming).
Answer (B) is incorrect. If a learner cannot accept the real reasons for his or her behavior, (s)he may rationalize, not take flight. **Answer (C) is incorrect.** Learners who place blame on someone or something other than themselves are displaying the defense mechanism of projection.

10. Learners may display the defense mechanism called denial, which is revealed by the learner's

A. hostility.

B. attempts to minimize the situation.

C. attempts at rationalization.

Answer (B) is correct. (FAA-H-8083-9B Chap 2)
DISCUSSION: Minimization is related to denial. When a person minimizes something, (s)he accepts what happened but in a diluted form.
Answer (A) is incorrect. Aggression is not associated with the defense mechanism of denial. **Answer (C) is incorrect.** Rationalization is the process of justifying a course of action, not denying it.

11. When learners subconsciously use the defense mechanism called rationalization, they

    A. use excuses to justify acceptable behavior.

    B. cannot accept the real reasons for their behavior.

    C. fake a belief opposite to their true belief because the true belief causes anxiety.

Answer (B) is correct. *(FAA-H-8083-9B Chap 2)*
    DISCUSSION: Rationalization is a subconscious technique for justifying unacceptable actions or performance. This allows learners to substitute excuses for reasons and make those excuses plausible and acceptable to themselves.
    Answer (A) is incorrect. In rationalization, excuses are used to justify unacceptable, not acceptable, behavior. **Answer (C) is incorrect.** When learners fake a belief opposite to their true belief, they are displaying the defense mechanism of reaction formation. This is done because their true belief causes them anxiety.

12. When a learner engages in daydreaming, it is the defense mechanism of

    A. compensation.

    B. fantasy.

    C. denial.

Answer (B) is correct. *(FAA-H-8083-9B Chap 2)*
    DISCUSSION: A learner engaging in daydreaming is an example of fantasy or mental escape.
    Answer (A) is incorrect. Through compensation, learners often attempt to disguise the presence of a weak or undesirable quality by emphasizing a more positive one. **Answer (C) is incorrect.** Denial is a refusal to accept external reality because it is too threatening. It is the refusal to acknowledge what has happened, is happening, or will happen.

13. When learners display the defense mechanism called repression, they

    A. refuse to accept reality.

    B. place uncomfortable thoughts into inaccessible areas of the unconscious mind.

    C. attempt to justify actions by asking numerous questions.

Answer (B) is correct. *(FAA-H-8083-9B Chap 2)*
    DISCUSSION: In repression, things a person is unable to cope with in the present are pushed away to be dealt with at another time, or hopefully never to be dealt with at all because they faded away on their own accord.
    Answer (A) is incorrect. When learners refuse to accept reality, they are exhibiting the defense mechanism of denial. **Answer (C) is incorrect.** Attempting to justify actions is an example of rationalization.

14. When a learner presents a belief opposite to what (s)he truly believes, it usually is an indication of the defense mechanism known as

    A. fantasy.

    B. reaction formation.

    C. displacement.

Answer (B) is correct. *(FAA-H-8083-9B Chap 2)*
    DISCUSSION: In reaction formation, a person fakes a belief opposite to his or her true belief because the true belief causes anxiety.
    Answer (A) is incorrect. Fantasy is the defense mechanism when a person mentally removes himself or herself from a frustrating situation. **Answer (C) is incorrect.** Displacement is the defense mechanism in which the learner shifts emotion, affect, or desire from the original object to a more acceptable, less threatening substitute.

15. When a learner attempts to disguise the presence of a weak or undesirable quality by emphasizing a more positive one, the defense mechanism is usually in the form of

    A. projection.

    B. compensation.

    C. rationalization.

Answer (B) is correct. *(FAA-H-8083-9B Chap 2)*
    DISCUSSION: Compensation is a process of psychologically counterbalancing perceived weaknesses by emphasizing strength in other areas.
    Answer (A) is incorrect. Through projection, an individual places blame for his or her own unacceptable impulses onto someone else. **Answer (C) is incorrect.** Rationalization is a process of making excuses for unacceptable behavior.

16. A learner pilot who fails a practical test and attributes the failure to an "unfair" evaluation by the examiner may be demonstrating a defense mechanism known as

    A. Rationalization.

    B. Projection.

    C. Denial.

Answer (B) is correct. *(FAA-H-8083-9B Chap 2)*
    DISCUSSION: Through projection, an individual places his or her own unacceptable impulses onto someone else. A person relegates the blame for personal shortcomings, mistakes, and transgressions to others.
    Answer (A) is incorrect. Rationalization is a subconscious technique for justifying actions that otherwise would be unacceptable. It does not involve the placement of blame on any other party. **Answer (C) is incorrect.** Denial is a refusal to accept external reality because it is too threatening. It does not involve the placement of blame on any other party.

2.3 Stress, Anxiety, and Fatigue

17. When under stress, normal individuals usually react

    A. by showing excellent morale followed by deep depression.

    B. by responding rapidly and exactly, often automatically, within the limits of their experience and training.

    C. inappropriately such as extreme overcooperation, painstaking self-control, and inappropriate laughing or singing.

Answer (B) is correct. (FAA-H-8083-9B Chap 2)
    DISCUSSION: When under stress, normal individuals begin to respond rapidly and exactly, within the limits of their experience and training. Many responses are automatic, which indicates the need for proper training in emergency operations prior to an actual emergency.
    Answer (A) is incorrect. Marked changes in mood, e.g., excellent morale followed by deep depression is an abnormal, not a normal, reaction to stress. **Answer (C) is incorrect.** Inappropriate reactions, such as extreme overcooperation, painstaking self-control, and inappropriate laughter or singing, are abnormal, not normal, reactions to stress.

18. A learner reacting abnormally to stress is most likely to display which of the following indications?

    A. The learner is using automatic responses.

    B. The learner has a rapid and exacting response.

    C. The learner is using inadequate, illogical, random responses or no response at all.

Answer (C) is correct. (FAA-H-8083-9B Chap 2)
    DISCUSSION: The following learner reactions are indicative of abnormal reactions to stress. None of them provides an absolute indication, but the presence of any of them under conditions of stress is reason for careful instructor evaluation. Instructors should look for inappropriate reactions, such as extreme over-cooperation, painstaking self-control, inappropriate laughter or singing, and very rapid changes in emotions. Marked changes in mood on different lessons, such as excellent morale followed by deep depression and severe anger directed toward the flight instructor, service personnel, and others are warning signs of unusual reactions to stress.
    Answer (A) is incorrect. A learner using automatic responses is a normal reaction to stress. **Answer (B) is incorrect.** A rapid and exacting response is a normal reaction to stress.

19. Which would most likely be an indication that a learner is reacting abnormally to stress?

    A. Slow learning.

    B. Inappropriate laughter or singing.

    C. Automatic response to a given situation.

Answer (B) is correct. (FAA-H-8083-9B Chap 2)
    DISCUSSION: Inappropriate laughter or singing is an abnormal reaction to stress. The instructor should be alert for other inappropriate (and possibly dangerous) reactions.
    Answer (A) is incorrect. Slow learning is a normal, not an abnormal, reaction to stress. **Answer (C) is incorrect.** Automatic response to a given situation is a normal, not an abnormal, reaction to stress.

20. One possible indication of a learner's abnormal reaction to stress would be

    A. a hesitancy to act.

    B. extreme overcooperation.

    C. a noticeable lack of self-control.

Answer (B) is correct. (FAA-H-8083-9B Chap 2)
    DISCUSSION: Extreme overcooperation is an indication that a learner is reacting abnormally to stress. The abnormally tense or anxious learner may be noticeably over-agreeable.
    Answer (A) is incorrect. A hesitancy to act is an indication of anxiety, not an abnormal reaction to stress. **Answer (C) is incorrect.** Painstaking self-control, not a lack thereof, is an indication of an abnormal reaction to stress.

21. The instructor can counteract anxiety in a learner by

    A. treating the learner's fears as a normal reaction.

    B. discontinuing instruction in tasks that cause anxiety.

    C. allowing the learner to decide when he or she is ready for a new maneuver to be introduced.

Answer (A) is correct. (FAA-H-8083-9B Chap 2)
    DISCUSSION: Psychologists tell us that a learner's fear is a normal reaction and should be treated as such by an instructor. Treating fear as normal will help in counteracting anxiety.
    Answer (B) is incorrect. Discontinuing instruction in stressful tasks will not help the learner to overcome the anxiety. Perhaps a different approach to the task is necessary. **Answer (C) is incorrect.** It describes an example of negative motivation, which would tend to contribute to the learner's anxiety.

22. Which of the following is required to recover from chronic fatigue?

   A. Mitigating the underlying physiological and psychological causes.

   B. A break in instruction and practice.

   C. Proper rest and time to "clear your thoughts."

Answer (A) is correct. (FAA-H-8083-9B Chap 2)
   DISCUSSION: The underlying cause of chronic fatigue is generally not rest-related and may have deeper points of origin. Psychological problems such as financial, home life, or job-related stresses are some examples. Mitigating the underlying problems is essential before the fatigue issue can be solved.
   Answer (B) is incorrect. Chronic fatigue is only solved by mitigating the underlying problems that are causing the fatigue. **Answer (C) is incorrect.** Chronic fatigue is only solved by mitigating the underlying problems that are causing the fatigue.

23. The principal reason why fatigue is one of the most treacherous hazards to flight safety is that

   A. fatigue can overtake even a physically robust person.

   B. it is usually impossible for a CFI to detect learner fatigue early in a lesson.

   C. it may not be apparent to a pilot until serious errors are made.

Answer (C) is correct. (FAA-H-8083-9B Chap 2)
   DISCUSSION: Fatigue is one of the most treacherous hazards to flight safety because it may not be apparent to a pilot until serious errors are made.
   Answer (A) is incorrect. Although it is true that fatigue can overtake even a physically robust person, this is not the principal reason why it is such a treacherous hazard. **Answer (B) is incorrect.** It is important for a CFI to be able to detect fatigue, both in assessing a learner's substandard performance early in a lesson and in recognizing the deterioration of performance.

24. Chronic fatigue

   A. Occurs when there is not enough time for a full recovery from repeated episodes of acute fatigue.

   B. Is the tiredness felt after long periods of physical and mental strain and lack of sleep.

   C. Impairs personal performance and ability but not pilot judgment.

Answer (A) is correct. (FAA-H-8083-9B Chap 2)
   DISCUSSION: Prolonged exposure to acute fatigue without adequate time for recovery can result in chronic fatigue.
   Answer (B) is incorrect. This describes acute, not chronic, fatigue. Chronic fatigue's underlying cause is generally not "rest-related" and may have deeper points of origin. **Answer (C) is incorrect.** Unless preventive measures are taken, chronic fatigue will certainly impact both personal performance and pilot judgment.

25. Chronic fatigue may best be described as a

   A. combination of both physiological problems and psychological issues.

   B. cluster of specific symptoms such as errors in timing and neglect of secondary tasks.

   C. result of over-application of a learning task.

Answer (A) is correct. (FAA-H-8083-9B Chap 2)
   DISCUSSION: Chronic fatigue is a combination of both physiological problems and psychological issues.
   Answer (B) is incorrect. Errors in timing and neglect of secondary tasks are symptoms of acute, not chronic, fatigue. **Answer (C) is incorrect.** Acute fatigue occurs as a result of the over-application of a learning task. To prevent this, the learner should be given a break in instruction and practice.

26. Chronic fatigue as a result of physiological problems and/or psychological issues may be evidenced by a learner pilot's apparent

   A. Increase in knowledge and skill retention.

   B. Need for sleep.

   C. Acceptance of unwarranted risks.

Answer (C) is correct. (FAA-H-8083-9B Chap 2)
   DISCUSSION: Without resolving the underlying causes of chronic fatigue, human performance gradually falls off, judgment becomes impaired, and unwarranted risks may be taken.
   Answer (A) is incorrect. Chronic fatigue brings about a decrease, not an increase, in a learner's knowledge and skill retention. **Answer (B) is incorrect.** Chronic fatigue's underlying cause is generally not "rest-related" and may have deeper points of origin. Therefore, rest alone may not resolve chronic fatigue.

27. Acute fatigue symptoms may include

   A. error accumulation, inattention, and distractibility.

   B. dizziness, weakness, nausea, tingling of hands and feet, abdominal cramps, and extreme thirst.

   C. unwarranted risk taking.

Answer (A) is correct. (FAA-H-8083-9B Chap 2)
   DISCUSSION: Acute fatigue is characterized by, among other things, inattention, distractibility, and errors in timing.
   Answer (B) is incorrect. Dizziness, weakness, nausea, tingling of hands and feet, abdominal cramps, and extreme thirst are symptoms of dehydration, not acute fatigue. **Answer (C) is incorrect.** Unwarranted risk taking is a symptom of chronic fatigue, not acute fatigue.

28. A sign that a learner may be experiencing acute fatigue is

   A. Acceptance of unwarranted risks.

   B. Neglect of secondary tasks.

   C. Increased attention to detail.

Answer (B) is correct. (FAA-H-8083-9B Chap 2)
   DISCUSSION: A CFI who is familiar with the signs indicative of acute fatigue will be more aware if the learner is experiencing them. One common sign of acute fatigue is the neglect of secondary tasks. Because the mind's resources are limited, secondary or non-essential tasks are often overlooked.
   Answer (A) is incorrect. Acceptance of unwarranted risks is a common indicator of chronic, not acute, fatigue. Pilot judgment as it relates to safety decisions is not typically compromised in acute fatigue, but this would be a common deficiency in someone suffering from chronic fatigue.
   Answer (C) is incorrect. Inattention, not increased attention, to detail is a common sign of acute fatigue.

29. Acute fatigue is

   A. a function of physical robustness or mental acuity.

   B. a combination of both physiological problems and psychological issues.

   C. observable by performance deficiencies that are apparent to others before the individual notices any physical signs of fatigue.

Answer (C) is correct. (FAA-H-8083-9B Chap 2)
   DISCUSSION: Acute fatigue may be observed by performance deficiencies that are apparent to others before the individual notices any physical signs of fatigue. One of the main characteristics of acute fatigue is lack of awareness of error accumulation. Third parties can, therefore, notice errors before you.
   Answer (A) is incorrect. Acute fatigue is not necessarily a function of physical robustness or mental acuity. **Answer (B) is incorrect.** Chronic fatigue, not acute fatigue, is a combination of both physiological problems and psychological issues.

30. Which of the following is a sign of acute fatigue?

   A. Error accumulation.

   B. Nausea.

   C. Acuteness of vision.

Answer (A) is correct. (FAA-H-8083-9B Chap 2)
   DISCUSSION: Acute fatigue is characterized by such symptoms as inattention, distractibility, errors in timing, and neglect of secondary tasks. Error accumulation is a result of these types of symptoms.
   Answer (B) is incorrect. Nausea is a symptom of dehydration, not acute fatigue. **Answer (C) is incorrect.** Acuteness of vision is a possible symptom of a minor illness, such as a cold, not acute fatigue.

31. Acute fatigue may be evident by a learner's apparent

   A. desire to take unwarranted risks.

   B. dizziness, weakness, and nausea.

   C. errors in timing.

Answer (C) is correct. (FAA-H-8083-9B Chap 2)
   DISCUSSION: Acute fatigue is characterized by such symptoms as inattention, distractibility, and errors in timing.
   Answer (A) is incorrect. The desire to take unwarranted risks is a symptom of chronic, not acute, fatigue. **Answer (B) is incorrect.** Dizziness, weakness, and nausea are symptoms of dehydration and heat stroke.

32. Which would most likely be an indication that a learner is reacting normally to stress?

   A. Slow learning.

   B. Inappropriate laughter or singing.

   C. Automatic response to a given situation.

Answer (C) is correct. (FAA-H-8083-9B Chap 2)
   DISCUSSION: When under stress, normal individuals begin to respond rapidly and exactly, within the limits of their experience and training. Many responses are automatic, which indicates the need for proper training in emergency operations prior to an actual emergency.
   Answer (A) is incorrect. While slow learning can be a normal reaction to stress, it could also be the result of a learning plateau. This choice is not the best answer to the question because it could just as likely be the result of something else as the result of an abnormal reaction to stress. **Answer (B) is incorrect.** Inappropriate laughter or singing is an abnormal, not a normal, reaction to stress.

2.4   The Overconfident or Impatient Learner

33. Learners who grow impatient when learning the basic elements of a task are those who

- A.   are less easily discouraged than the unaggressive learners.
- B.   should have the preliminary training presented one step at a time with clearly stated goals for each step.
- C.   should be advanced to the next higher level of learning and not held back by insisting that the immediate goal be reached before they proceed to the next level.

Answer (B) is correct. (FAA-H-8083-9B Chap 2)
   DISCUSSION: Impatient learners fail to see why they must learn one step thoroughly before they move to the next. Presenting the preliminary training with clearly stated goals for each step will minimize learner impatience.
   Answer (A) is incorrect. Impatient learners are often aggressive and more easily discouraged than unaggressive learners. **Answer (C) is incorrect.** It is necessary to hold a learner until (s)he masters the basics if the whole task is to be performed competently and safely. This is the basis of the building block technique of instruction.

34. Which obstacle to learning is a greater deterrent to learning pilot skills than is generally recognized?

- A.   Anxiety.
- B.   Impatience.
- C.   Physical discomfort.

Answer (B) is correct. (FAA-H-8083-9B Chap 2)
   DISCUSSION: Failing to understand the need for preliminary training, the impatient learner can only see the ultimate objective of flying an airplane. This impatience can be detrimental to the usual, careful acquisition of pilot skills.
   Answer (A) is incorrect. Although anxiety may be detrimental to the learning process, it is generally recognized as such, whereas impatience has an equal effect and is not widely recognized. **Answer (C) is incorrect.** Although physical discomfort may be detrimental to the learning process, it is generally recognized as such, whereas impatience has an equal effect and is not widely recognized.

35. Should an instructor be concerned about an apt learner who makes very few mistakes?

- A.   No. Some learners have an innate, natural aptitude for flight.
- B.   Yes. The learner may assume that the correction of errors is unimportant.
- C.   Yes. The learner will lose confidence in the instructor if the instructor does not invent deficiencies in the learner's performance.

Answer (B) is correct. (FAA-H-8083-9B Chap 8)
   DISCUSSION: Because apt learners make few mistakes, they may assume that the correction of errors is not important. Such overconfidence soon results in faulty performance. For such learners, a good instructor will constantly raise the standard of performance for each lesson, demanding greater effort.
   Answer (A) is incorrect. Regardless of natural gift, apt learners may assume that the correction of errors is not important. Such overconfidence soon results in faulty performance. **Answer (C) is incorrect.** The instructor should not invent deficiencies in order to diminish a learner's confidence. On the contrary, a good instructor will constantly raise the standard of performance for each lesson, demanding greater effort.

36. What should an instructor do with a learner who assumes that correction of errors is not important?

- A.   Divide complex flight maneuvers into elements.
- B.   Try to reduce the learner's overconfidence to reduce the chance of an accident.
- C.   Raise the standard of performance for each lesson, demanding greater effort.

Answer (C) is correct. (FAA-H-8083-9B Chap 8)
   DISCUSSION: Because apt learners make few mistakes, they may assume that the correction of errors is not important. Such overconfidence soon results in faulty performance. For such learners, a good instructor will constantly raise the standard of performance for each lesson, demanding greater effort.
   Answer (A) is incorrect. Dividing complex tasks into simpler elements should be done with learners whose slow progress is due to a lack of confidence, not apt learners. **Answer (B) is incorrect.** Reducing learners' overconfidence would be inefficient for properly motivating the apt learner. After realizing the impatience of such learners comes only from improperly paced instruction, instructors should give them challenges fitting their abilities.

37. The overconfidence of fast learners should be corrected by

    A. high praise when no errors are made.

    B. raising the standard of performance for each lesson.

    C. providing strong, negative evaluation at the end of each lesson.

Answer (B) is correct. (FAA-H-8083-9B Chap 8)
    DISCUSSION: Because apt learners make few mistakes, they may assume that the correction of errors is not important. Such overconfidence soon results in faulty performance. For such learners, a good instructor will constantly raise the standard of performance for each lesson, demanding greater effort.
    Answer (A) is incorrect. High praise will only lead the learner to become more overconfident. **Answer (C) is incorrect.** A strong, negative evaluation should not be used to diminish a learner's confidence. On the contrary, a good instructor will constantly raise the standard of performance for each lesson, demanding greater effort.

38. Faulty performance due to learner overconfidence should be corrected by

    A. increasing the standard of performance for each lesson.

    B. praising the learner only when the performance is perfect.

    C. providing strong, negative evaluation at the end of each lesson.

Answer (A) is correct. (FAA-H-8083-9B Chap 8)
    DISCUSSION: Because apt learners make few mistakes, they may assume that the correction of errors is not important. Such overconfidence soon results in faulty performance. For such learners, a good instructor will constantly raise the standard of performance for each lesson, demanding greater effort.
    Answer (B) is incorrect. Learners need consistent, fair critique of every performance, perfect or not. Overly high standards also frustrate learners by making them work too hard without reward (and for an unrealistic goal). **Answer (C) is incorrect.** The principle of effect states that learning is weakened when associated with an unpleasant feeling. Aside from being unfair, the continual negative evaluations will also increasingly frustrate learners.

39. A method for correcting learner impatience is for the instructor to

    A. Present the necessary preliminary training one step at a time, with clearly stated goals for each step.

    B. Key the instruction to utilize the interests and enthusiasm learners bring with them.

    C. Avoid assigning impossible or unreasonable goals for the learner to accomplish.

Answer (A) is correct. (FAA-H-8083-9B Chap 2)
    DISCUSSION: With every complex human endeavor, it is necessary to master the basics if the whole task is to be performed competently and safely. The instructor can correct learner impatience by presenting the necessary preliminary training one step at a time, with clearly stated goals for each step.
    Answer (B) is incorrect. This solution is appropriate for combating worry or lack of interest on the part of the learner, not impatience. **Answer (C) is incorrect.** This solution is appropriate for combating a learner's feelings of unfair treatment during flight instruction, not impatience.

40. What is an example of a learner showing impatience?

    A. A learner not wanting to fly without an instructor on board.

    B. A learner desiring to conduct a cross-country flight before the basic elements of flight have been learned.

    C. A learner wishing to solo an aircraft.

Answer (B) is correct. (FAA-H-8083-9B Chap 2)
    DISCUSSION: An impatient learner wants to undertake tasks before (s)he is ready or competent. An impatient learner seeks only the final objective without considering the means necessary to reach it.
    Answer (A) is incorrect. An example of a learner not wanting to fly solo would show worry, not impatience. **Answer (C) is incorrect.** There is nothing wrong with a learner desiring to accomplish a task such as flying an aircraft solo. An impatient learner, however, would want to solo before (s)he is properly prepared and competent.

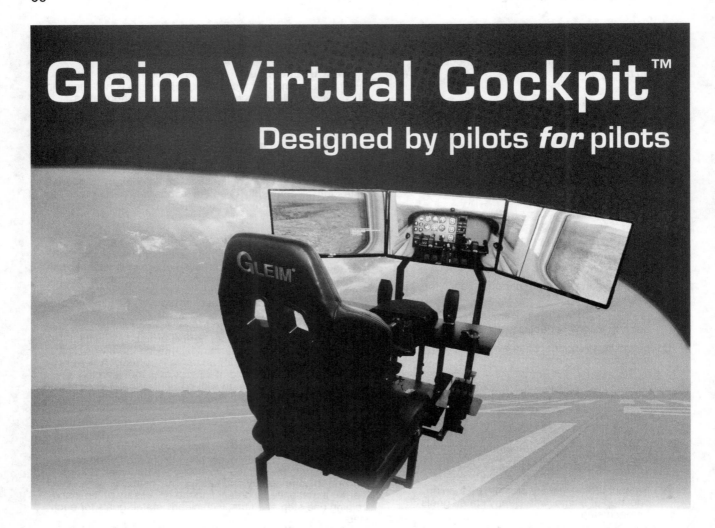

STUDY UNIT THREE

FACTORS AFFECTING LEARNING

(14 pages of outline)

Study Units 1 and 2 cover the learning process and barriers to learning, respectively. This study unit discusses human behavior, communication skills, and instructor professionalism. Understanding all three of these topics will help you become an exemplary instructor.

1) You need to understand human behavior and how to guide your learners to be safe and responsible pilots.

   a) The subunit on Aeronautical Decision Making and Risk Management will help you correct the negative behaviors your learners may have.

2) Possessing knowledge of what it takes to be a safe and proficient pilot is but one important element of being a competent instructor.

   a) You must also have effective communication skills so you can pass this knowledge to your learners.

3) Being an instructor is a significant responsibility. Pilots and others in the aviation community hold Flight Instructors and Ground Instructors in the highest esteem, and your daily actions must reflect professionalism.

   a) It is imperative that you model your behavior as a standard-setter and be professional at all times.

3.1 HUMAN NEEDS

1. Human needs can be organized into a series of levels. The "pyramid of human needs" has been suggested by Abraham Maslow.

    a. For instance, physical needs must be satisfied before so-called "higher" needs can be used as motivators.

    b. Maslow suggests that needs must be satisfied in an ascending order.

2. However, multiple psychological studies have since shown that humans can experience higher levels of motivation before their lower basic needs are met.

    a. These studies show that lower needs do not have to be completely fulfilled before people are able to achieve higher needs.

    b. What matters is that parts of each level have been met, which allows the learner to focus on the instructions given.

    c. The order in which needs are met does not matter. Instructors should verify that most of the learner's needs have been met (law of readiness) and then focus the learner's perception on the lesson.

3. **Physiological needs** are biological needs.

    a. They consist of the need for air, food, water, and maintenance of the human body.

    b. Unless the biological needs are met, a person cannot concentrate fully on learning, self-expression, or any other tasks.

    c. Instructors should monitor their learners to make sure that their basic physical needs have been met. A hungry or tired learner may not be able to perform as expected.

4. **Safety and security needs** become essential after the basic biological needs are met.

    a. Security needs are about keeping oneself from harm.

    b. The aviation instructor who stresses flight safety during training mitigates feelings of insecurity.

5. **Love and belonging needs** are social needs that people pursue to overcome feelings of loneliness and alienation.

    a. Aviation learners are usually out of their normal surroundings during training, and their need for association and belonging is more pronounced.

    b. Instructors should make every effort to help new learners feel at ease and to reinforce their decision to pursue a career or hobby in aviation.

6. **Esteem needs** are about feeling good about oneself.

   a. Humans have a need for a stable, firmly based, high level of self-respect and respect from others.

   b. Humans get esteem in two ways: internally or externally.

      1) Internally, a person judges himself or herself worthy by personally defined standards.

         a) High self-esteem results in self-confidence, independence, achievement, competence, and knowledge.

      2) Most people, however, seek external esteem through social approval and esteem from other people, judging themselves by what others think of them.

         a) External self-esteem relates to one's reputation, such as status, recognition, appreciation, and respect of associates.

   c. When esteem needs are satisfied, a person feels self-confident and valuable as a person in the world.

      1) When these needs are frustrated, the person feels inferior, weak, helpless, and worthless.

      2) Esteem needs not only have a strong influence on the learner-instructor relationship but also may be the main reason for a learner's interest in aviation training.

7. **Cognitive and aesthetic needs** include the need to know and understand and the emotional results of achievement.

   a. Humans have a deep need to understand what is going on around them. If a person understands what is going on, (s)he can either control the situation or make informed choices about what steps might be taken next.

   b. The brain even reinforces this need by giving humans a rush of dopamine whenever something is learned, which accounts for that satisfying "eureka!" moment, such as when a learner completes his or her first solo flight.

   c. Aesthetic needs (e.g., how well something is liked) can factor into the learner-instructor relationship. If an instructor does not "like" a learner, this subtle feeling may affect the instructor's ability to teach that learner, and vice versa.

8. **Self-actualization needs** include a person's need to be and do what the person was "born to do."

   a. These needs are only triggered when all underlying needs are met.

   b. Self-actualized people realize their potential, seek to develop themselves further, and think creatively.

   c. Self-actualized people are characterized by

      1) Being problem-focused
      2) Incorporating an ongoing freshness of appreciation of life
      3) A concern about personal growth
      4) The ability to have peak experiences

   d. Helping a learner achieve his or her individual potential in aviation training offers the greatest challenge as well as the greatest reward to the instructor.

3.2 MOTIVATION

1. Motivation is the reason one acts or behaves in a certain way and lies at the heart of goals.

    a. Motivation is probably the dominant force governing the learner's progress and ability to learn.

    b. Slumps in learning are often due to declining motivation.

2. **Positive motivation** is essential to true learning, is provided by the promise or achievement of rewards, and is generally the more effective way to properly motivate learners.

    a. Such rewards may involve financial gain, satisfaction of the self-concept, personal gain, or public recognition.

        1) Intangible positive motivations may include the desire for personal comfort and security, group approval, and the achievement of a favorable self image.

        2) Tangible positive motivation may include rewards that involve financial gain or public recognition.

3. **Negative motivations** are those that cause a learner to react with fear and anxiety.

    a. Negative motivations in the form of reproof and threats should be avoided with all but the most overconfident and impulsive learners.

4. Motivations may be

    a. Positive or negative
    b. Tangible or intangible
    c. Obvious or subtle and difficult to identify

5. Sources of motivation vary, but all offer some type of reward in exchange for performing work. It is important for an instructor to make the learner aware that a particular lesson can help him or her reach an important goal.

    a. When learners are unable to see the benefits or purpose of a lesson, they will be less motivated.

    b. Confusion, disinterest, and uneasiness on the part of the learner could happen as a result of not knowing the objective of each period of instruction.

    c. If motivation is to be effective, learners must believe that their efforts will be suitably rewarded in a definite, tangible manner.

6. To maintain motivation, an instructor must reward success by frequently presenting positive feedback.

    a. EXAMPLE: Praising incremental successes during training, relating daily accomplishments to lesson objectives, and commenting favorably on learner progress.

7. Learner anxiety can be minimized throughout training by emphasizing the benefits and pleasurable experiences that can be derived from flying, rather than by continuously citing the unhappy consequences of faulty performances.

8. Both drops in motivation and learning plateaus, which are a common source of frustration, are normal and can be overcome by reminding learners of their own goals and reassuring them that there will be rewards for their continued efforts.

3.3 AERONAUTICAL DECISION MAKING AND RISK MANAGEMENT

1. **Aeronautical decision making (ADM)** can be defined as a systematic approach to the mental process used by pilots to consistently determine the best course of action in response to a given set of circumstances.

2. One step in the ADM process for good decision making is to identify personal attitudes hazardous to safe flight.

    a. Examples of classical behavioral traps that experienced pilots may fall into are the compulsion to complete a flight as planned, the desire to please passengers, the pressure to meet schedules, and the determination to get the job done.

    b. At some time, many experienced pilots have fallen prey to dangerous tendencies or behavior problems that must be identified and eliminated, including

        1) Peer pressure
        2) Scud running
        3) Loss of positional or situational awareness
        4) Operating without adequate fuel reserves

    c. In order to gain a realistic perspective on your attitude toward flying, you should take a Self-Assessment Hazardous Attitude Inventory Test.

    d. ADM addresses the following five hazardous attitudes:

        1) **Antiauthority** – "Do not tell me what to do!"

            a) EXAMPLE: During a stall recovery, the CFI allows the learner to exceed maneuvering speed. An antiauthority attitude expressed by the CFI would be "The aircraft can handle a lot more than the maneuvering speed."

        2) **Impulsivity** – "Do something quickly!"

            a) EXAMPLE: On short final, the CFI realizes his learner has forgotten to lower the flaps and immediately adds full flaps. The impulsivity attitude expressed by the CFI would be "I have to extend the flaps to get this aircraft down."

        3) **Invulnerability** – "It will not happen to me."

            a) EXAMPLE: Before a flight, the CFI does not check to verify a learner has completed a pre-flight inspection. The invulnerability attitude expressed by the CFI would be "Nothing bad will happen on this flight."

        4) **Macho** – "I can do it."

            a) EXAMPLE: A pilot is on an instrument approach in which the aircraft in front of him have had to go around yet continues instead of diverting to an alternate. The macho attitude expressed by the pilot would be "I am better than others and can make it."

        5) **Resignation** – "What is the use?"

            a) EXAMPLE: A non-instrument-rated pilot continues into an area of known low visibility. The resignation attitude expressed by the pilot would be "What can I do about the weather conditions?"

3. In the ADM process, the first step in neutralizing a hazardous attitude is recognizing it.

    a. When you recognize a hazardous thought, you should label it as hazardous; then correct the attitude by stating the corresponding antidote.

    b. Hazardous attitudes, which contribute to poor pilot judgment, can be effectively counteracted by the appropriate antidote, as listed below.

        1) Antiauthority -- "Follow the rules. They are usually right."
        2) Impulsivity -- "Not so fast. Think first."
        3) Invulnerability -- "It could happen to me."
        4) Macho -- "Taking chances is foolish."
        5) Resignation -- "I am not helpless. I can make a difference."

4. **Stress** describes the body's response to a set of circumstances that induces a change in an individual's current physiological and/or psychological patterns of functioning, forcing the individual to adapt to these changes.

    a. Success in reducing stress associated with crisis management on the flight deck begins by making a personal assessment of stress in all areas of your life.

    b. To help manage flight deck stress, you should try to relax and think rationally at the first sign of stress.

5. The DECIDE process consists of six elements to help provide a pilot a logical way of approaching ADM. These elements are to

    a. **D**etect
    b. **E**stimate
    c. **C**hoose
    d. **I**dentify
    e. **D**o
    f. **E**valuate

    These elements represent a continuous loop decision process that can be used to assist a pilot in the decision-making process when faced with a change in a situation that requires a judgment.

6. A flight instructor should begin teaching ADM when the learner has the ability to control the airplane confidently during the most basic maneuvers.

7. **Risk management** is a decision-making process designed to systematically identify hazards, assess the degree of risk, and determine the best course of action associated with each flight. This process relies on situational awareness, problem identification, and good judgment to reduce the risks associated with each flight.

   a. **Situational awareness** is defined as the accurate perception and understanding of all the factors and conditions within the four fundamental risk elements that affect safety before, during, and after the flight.

   b. The four fundamental risk elements in the ADM process that comprise any given aviation situation are the

      1) **Pilot (PIC)** – The pilot's fitness to fly must be evaluated, including competency in the aircraft, currency, and flight experience.

      2) **Aircraft** – The aircraft performance, limitations, equipment, and airworthiness must be determined.

      3) **Environment** – Factors such as weather and airport conditions must be examined.

      4) **External pressures** – The purpose of the flight is a factor that influences the pilot's decision to begin or continue the flight.

   c. Risk management involves two broad steps: risk assessment and risk mitigation.

      1) Every flight has hazards and some level of risk associated with it. It is critical that pilots and especially learners are able to differentiate in advance between a low-risk flight and a high-risk flight and then establish a review process and develop risk mitigation strategies to address flights throughout that range.

      2) All identified risks should be addressed in proper risk management. Risks must be either accepted or mitigated in some way.

         a) Common mitigation strategies include taking along a more experienced pilot or flight instructor, delaying the flight, or canceling the flight altogether.

3.4 EFFECTIVE COMMUNICATION

1. The process of communication is composed of three dynamically interrelated elements:

    a. A source (instructor)
    b. The symbols used in composing and transmitting the message (e.g., words)
    c. The receiver (learner)

2. Communication takes place when one person transmits ideas or feelings to another person or to a group of people.

    a. The effectiveness of communication is measured by the similarity between the idea transmitted and the idea received.

    b. Effective communication has taken place when, and only when, the receivers react with understanding and change their behavior accordingly.

    c. Instruction has taken place when a procedure has been explained and the desired learner response has occurred.

3. The effectiveness of persons acting in the role of communicators is related to at least three basic factors.

    a. First, their ability to select symbols that are meaningful to the listener.

    b. Second, communicators consciously or unconsciously reveal attitudes toward themselves, toward the ideas they are trying to transmit, and toward their receivers.

        1) Thus, to communicate effectively, instructors must reveal a positive attitude while delivering their message.

    c. Third, to be more likely to communicate effectively, communicators should speak or write from a broad background of accurate, up-to-date, stimulating material.

4. **Symbols** are oral and visual codes used to communicate.

    a. Ideas are communicated only when symbols are combined into meaningful wholes (e.g., sentences, paragraphs, chapters, etc.).

    b. Symbols are perceived through three sensory channels: visual, auditory, or kinesthetic (touching, doing, etc.).

        1) Instructors will be more successful in gaining and retaining learner attention by using a variety of these channels.

    c. The feedback an instructor gets from a learner needs to be monitored constantly in order to modify the symbols, as required, to optimize communication.

5. To understand the process of communication, at least three characteristics of receivers must be understood.

    a. First, they exercise their ability to question and comprehend the ideas that have been transmitted.

    b. Second, the receiver's attitude may be one of resistance, willingness, or of passive neutrality. Communicators must gain the receiver's attention and then retain it.

        1) The communicator will be more successful in this area by using a varied communicative approach.

    c. Third, the receiver's background, experience, and education frame the target at which communications must aim.

3.5 BARRIERS TO EFFECTIVE COMMUNICATION

1. Probably the greatest single barrier to effective communication is the lack of a common core of experience between communicator and receiver.

   a. A receiver's past experience with the words and things to which they refer determine how the receiver responds to what the communicator says.

   b. A communicator's words cannot communicate the desired meaning to another person unless the listener or reader has had some experience with the objects or concepts to which these words refer.

   c. In order for communication to be effective, the learner's understanding of the meaning of the words needs to be the same as the instructor's understanding and desired thought.

2. Confusion between the symbol (word or sign) and the symbolized object results when a word is confused with what it is meant to represent.

   a. Words and symbols do not always represent the same thing to each person.

   b. To communicate effectively, speakers and instructors should be aware of these differences and choose words or symbols that represent what is intended.

3. Overuse of abstractions should be avoided.

   a. **Concrete words** refer to objects that human beings can experience directly.

   b. **Abstract words** stand for ideas that cannot be directly experienced or things that do not call forth specific mental images.

      1) Abstractions thus serve as shorthand symbols that sum up large areas of experience.

   c. The danger with using abstract words is that they may not evoke in the listener's mind the specific items of experience the communicator intends.

   d. By using concrete words, the communicator narrows (and gains better control of) the image produced in the minds of the listeners and readers.

4. **External factors** may prevent a process or activity from being carried out properly and are composed of factors outside the control of the instructor yet may be overcome.

   a. **Physiological external factors** are any biological problem that may inhibit reception.

      1) EXAMPLE: Hearing loss, injury, or physical illness.

   b. **Environmental external factors** are caused by external physical conditions.

      1) EXAMPLE: Aircraft noise or vibration or lighting conditions.

   c. **Psychological external factors** are a product of how the instructor and learner feel at the time the communication process is occurring.

      1) EXAMPLE: If either the instructor or learner is not committed to the communication process, communication is impaired.

   d. The instructor must recognize when external factors are present and adapt the presentation to allow the learner to be more receptive to new ideas.

3.6 INSTRUCTOR RESPONSIBILITIES

1. Flight instructors are responsible for producing the safest pilots possible with the overall focus on education and learning. There are five main responsibilities of aviation instructors.

    a. Helping Learners

        1) The use of standards, and measurement against standards, is key to helping learners learn.

        2) Knowing the objective of each period of instruction gives meaning and provides interest to learner and instructor.

    b. Providing Adequate Instruction

        1) Flight instructors should analyze the learner's personality, thinking, and ability to tailor their teaching technique to the learner.

    c. Demanding Adequate Standards of Performance

        1) Evaluation of demonstrated ability during flight instruction must be based upon established standards of performance, suitably modified to apply to the learner's experience and stage of development as a pilot.

        2) In evaluating learner demonstrations of piloting ability, it is important for the flight instructor to keep the learner informed of his or her progress.

            a) EXAMPLE: This may be done as each procedure/maneuver is completed or summarized during postflight critiques.

    d. Emphasizing the Positive

        1) Emphasize the positive because positive instruction results in positive learning.

    e. Ensuring Aviation Safety

        1) The safety practices aviation instructors emphasize have a long-lasting effect on learners.

        2) Emphasizing safety by example is one of the best actions an instructor can take to ensure aviation safety.

2. Additional responsibilities of flight instructors include

    a. Evaluation of learner piloting ability

        1) In evaluating learner demonstrations of ability, it is important for the aviation instructor to keep the learner informed of progress. This may be done as each procedure or maneuver is completed or summarized during a postflight or class critique.

    b. Pilot supervision

    c. Practical test recommendations

    d. Flight instructor endorsements

        1) Examples of all common endorsements can be found in the current issue of AC 61-65, Appendix A.

    e. Additional training and endorsements

    f. Pilot proficiency

    g. See and avoid responsibility

    h. Learner's pre-solo flight thought process

3. It is a flight instructor's responsibility to teach the learner how to take charge during a flight. A pilot in command (PIC) must know when to tell any passengers, even a designated pilot examiner (DPE), when the PIC finds actions in the aircraft that distract and interfere with the safe conduct of the flight.

   a. Instructor responsibilities include teaching the learner to divide his or her attention between the distracting task and maintaining control of the aircraft.

   b. Properly interjected distractions may help learners learn to determine whether a distraction warrants further attention or action on their part.

4. Flight instructors have a particular responsibility to provide guidance and restraint regarding the solo operations of their learners.

   a. Before receiving an instructor endorsement for solo flight, a learner should be required to demonstrate the consistent ability to perform all of the fundamental maneuvers without the need of instructor assistance.

   b. The learner should also be capable of handling ordinary problems that might occur, such as traffic pattern congestion, a change in the active runway, or unexpected crosswinds.

5. **Minimizing Learner Frustrations**

   a. Motivate Learners

      1) More can be gained from wanting to learn than from being forced to learn.

      2) Too often, learners do not realize how a particular lesson or course can help them reach an important goal.

      3) When learners can see the benefits and purpose of the lesson or course, their enjoyment and efforts increase.

   b. Keep Learners Informed

      1) Learners feel insecure when they do not know what is expected of them or what is going to happen to them.

      2) Instructors can minimize feelings of insecurity by telling learners what is expected of them and what they can expect in return.

      3) Instructors keep learners informed in various ways, including giving them an overview of the course, keeping them posted on their progress, and giving them adequate notice of examinations, assignments, or other requirements.

   c. Approach Learners as Individuals

      1) When instructors limit their thinking to a group mentality without considering the individuals who make up that group, their efforts are directed at an average personality that really fits no one.

      2) Each learner group has its own personality that stems from the characteristics and interactions of its members, but each individual within the group has a unique personality to constantly be considered.

   d. Give Credit When Due

      1) When learners do something extremely well, they normally expect their abilities and efforts to be noticed. Otherwise, they may become frustrated.

      2) Praise or credit from the instructor is usually ample reward and provides an incentive to do even better. Praise pays dividends in learner effort and achievement when deserved, but when given too freely, it becomes valueless.

e.   Criticize Constructively

1)   Although it is important to give praise and credit when deserved, it is equally important to identify mistakes and failures. It does not help to tell learners they have made errors and not provide explanations.

2)   If a learner has made an earnest effort but is told that the work is unsatisfactory, with no other explanation, frustration occurs.

3)   Errors cannot be corrected if they are not identified, and if they are not identified, they will probably be perpetuated through faulty practice. On the other hand, if the learner is briefed on the errors and is told how to correct them, progress can be made.

f.   Be Consistent

1)   Learners want to please their instructor—the same desire that influences much of the behavior of subordinates toward their superiors in industry and business.

2)   Naturally, learners have a keen interest in knowing what is required to please the instructor. If the same thing is acceptable one day and unacceptable the next, the learner becomes confused. The instructor's philosophy and actions must be consistent.

g.   Admit Errors

1)   No one, including learners, expects an instructor to be perfect. The instructor can win the respect of learners by honestly acknowledging mistakes.

2)   If the instructor tries to cover up or bluff, learners are quick to sense it. Such behavior tends to destroy learner confidence in the instructor.

3)   If in doubt about some point, the instructor should admit it.

h.   Assign Goals

1)   Goals the learner considers difficult but possible usually provide a challenge and promote learning.

2)   In a typical flight lesson, reasonable goals are listed in the lesson objectives and the desired levels of proficiency for the goals are included in statements that contain completion standards.

i.   Learners will remain engaged if they are aware of the progress they are making.

1)   One way to make learners aware of their progress is to repeat a demonstration or example and to show them the standards their performance must ultimately meet.

3.7 INSTRUCTOR PROFESSIONALISM

1. Although the term professionalism is widely used, it is rarely defined. In fact, no single definition can encompass all of the qualifications and considerations of true professionalism. The following are some of the major considerations:

    a. Professionals must be able to reason logically and accurately.

    b. Professionalism requires good decision-making ability.

        1) Professionals cannot limit actions and decisions to standard patterns and practice.
        2) Professionals commit themselves to continuous learning and development.

    c. Professionalism demands a code of ethics.

2. The professional flight instructor should be straightforward and honest.

    a. Anything less than a sincere performance is quickly detected and immediately destroys instructor effectiveness.

    b. Learner confidence tends to be destroyed if instructors bluff when in doubt.

    c. The well-prepared instructor instills not only confidence but good habits, since preparing well for a flight is a basic requirement for safe flying. Learners quickly become apathetic when they recognize that the flight instructor is inadequately prepared.

3. The attitude, movements, and general demeanor of the flight instructor contribute a great deal to his or her professional image.

    a. The instructor should avoid erratic movements, distracting speech habits, and capricious changes in mood. The professional image requires development of a calm, pleasant, thoughtful manner that puts the learner at ease.

4. The professional relationship between the instructor and the learner should be based on a mutual acknowledgment that both the learner and the instructor are important to each other and that both are working toward the same objective.

    a. Accepting lower-than-normal standards to please a learner will **NOT** help the learner-instructor relationship.

    b. Reasonable standards strictly enforced are not resented by an earnest learner.

    c. Learners must be treated with respect, regardless of whether they are quick to learn or require more time to absorb certain concepts.

5. The professional flight instructor should accept learners as they are with all of their faults and problems.

    a. However, (s)he should also build learner self-confidence, set challenges, and generally create an atmosphere for learning.

6. A flight instructor who is not completely familiar with current pilot certification and rating requirements cannot do a competent job of flight instruction.

    a. Flight instructors must strive to maintain the highest level of knowledge, training, and currency in their field.

    b. For a professional performance as a flight instructor, it is essential that the instructor maintain current copies of

        1) The Federal Aviation Regulations, especially Parts 1, 61, and 91;
        2) The *Aeronautical Information Manual*;
        3) Practical Test Standards or Airman Certification Standards; and
        4) Appropriate pilot training manuals.

    c. True performance as a professional is based on study and research.

7. Flight instructors fail to provide competent instruction when they permit learners to partially learn an important item of knowledge or skill.

    a. More importantly, such deficiencies may in themselves allow hazardous inadequacies to develop in the learner's ongoing piloting performance.

8. Aviation instructors should be constantly alert for ways to improve the services they provide to their learners, their effectiveness, and their qualifications.

QUESTIONS AND ANSWER EXPLANATIONS: All of the Fundamentals of Instructing knowledge test questions chosen by the FAA for release as well as additional questions selected by Gleim relating to the material in the previous outlines are provided on the following pages. These questions have been organized into the same subunits as the outlines. To the immediate right of each question are the correct answer and answer explanations. You should cover these answers and answer explanations while responding to the questions. Refer to the general discussion in the Introduction on how to take the FAA knowledge test.

Remember that the questions from the FAA knowledge test bank have been reordered by topic and organized into a meaningful sequence. Also, the first line of the answer explanation gives the citation of the authoritative source for the answer.

QUESTIONS

3.1 Human Needs

1. Before a learner can concentrate on learning, which human needs must be satisfied?

    A. Security.

    B. Biological.

    C. Psychological.

Answer (B) is correct. (FAA-H-8083-9B Chap 2)
    DISCUSSION: Physiological, or biological, needs consist of the need for air, food, water, and maintenance of the human body. Unless the biological needs are met, a person cannot concentrate fully on learning, self-expression, or any other tasks.
    Answer (A) is incorrect. The need for security is only a driving force once all of the physiological needs are met.
    Answer (C) is incorrect. Psychological needs, such as belonging and esteem, are only important after the basic biological and security needs are met.

2. After individuals are physically comfortable and have no fear for their safety, which human needs become the prime influence on their behavior?

    A. Esteem.

    B. Self-Actualization.

    C. Belonging.

Answer (C) is correct. (FAA-H-8083-9B Chap 2)
    DISCUSSION: When individuals are physically comfortable and do not feel threatened, they seek to satisfy their social needs of belonging, that is, to overcome feelings of loneliness and alienation.
    Answer (A) is incorrect. The need of esteem follows after the need of belonging. Generally speaking, a person must feel accepted by peers to develop stable, positive self-esteem.
    Answer (B) is incorrect. The needs of self-actualization are only applicable after all other human needs have been met.

3. Which of the learner's human needs offer the greatest challenge to an instructor?

    A. Physiological.

    B. Psychological.

    C. Self-Actualization.

Answer (C) is correct. (FAA-H-8083-9B Chap 2)
    DISCUSSION: When all of the foregoing needs are satisfied, the needs for self-actualization are activated. Self-actualization is a person's need to be and do what the person was "born to do." Helping a learner achieve his or her individual potential in aviation training offers the greatest challenge as well as reward to the instructor.
    Answer (A) is incorrect. Physiological needs are needs that the instructor has no direct impact on. These basic biological needs include the need for air, food, water, and maintenance of the human body. **Answer (B) is incorrect.** Psychological needs include the learner's need to belong, have positive self-esteem, cognitively know and understand, and emotionally be drawn to learning. While difficult to develop, these needs are not as difficult to encourage as self-actualization.

4. The need for realizing one's own potentialities, for continued development, and for being creative is defined as a(n)

    A. esteem need.

    B. social need.

    C. self-actualization need.

Answer (C) is correct. (FAA-H-8083-9B Chap 2)
    DISCUSSION: Self-actualization needs are the needs for realizing one's own potentialities, for continued development, and for being creative.
    Answer (A) is incorrect. Esteem needs relate to feeling good about one's self. **Answer (B) is incorrect.** Social needs are the needs to belong and to associate with other people.

3.2 Motivation

5. Which is generally the more effective way for an instructor to properly motivate learners?

    A. Maintain pleasant personal relationships with learners.

    B. Provide positive motivations by the promise or achievement of rewards.

    C. Reinforce their self-confidence by requiring no tasks beyond their ability to perform.

Answer (B) is correct. (FAA-H-8083-9B Chap 2)
    DISCUSSION: Providing positive motivation is generally considered the most effective way to properly motivate people. Positive motivations are provided by the promise or achievement of rewards.
    Answer (A) is incorrect. Maintaining pleasant personal relationships with learners (while desirable) is not the more effective way for an instructor to properly motivate learners. **Answer (C) is incorrect.** A learner who is not required to perform a task beyond present abilities will neither be motivated nor make any progress.

6. How can an instructor help a learner cope with fear and anxiety?

    A. By emphasizing the benefits and pleasurable experiences from flying.

    B. By minimizing fear by teaching the learner advanced maneuvers.

    C. By keeping the learner focused on achieving Practical Test Standards (PTS).

Answer (A) is correct. (FAA-H-8083-9B Chap 2)
    DISCUSSION: Learner anxiety can be minimized throughout training by emphasizing the benefits and pleasurable experiences that can be derived from flying, rather than by continuously citing the unhappy consequences of faulty performances.
    Answer (B) is incorrect. Anxiety for learners is usually associated with certain types of flight operations and maneuvers. Instructors should introduce these maneuvers with care so that learners know what to expect and what their reactions should be. **Answer (C) is incorrect.** The PTS should not be introduced to the learner prior to the last 3 hours of training prior to the practical test.

7. Motivations in the form of reproof and threats should be avoided with all but the learner who is

    A. overconfident and impulsive.

    B. avidly seeking group approval.

    C. experiencing a learning plateau.

Answer (A) is correct. (FAA-H-8083-9B Chap 2)
    DISCUSSION: Educational experts have shown that negative motivation is useful only for a learner who is overconfident and impulsive. Otherwise, negative motivation in the form of reproof and threats tends to discourage learner behavior.
    Answer (B) is incorrect. Group approval is a strong motivating force. Use of reproofs and threats with a learner seeking group approval would only alienate him or her from the group. **Answer (C) is incorrect.** One of the reasons a learner has reached a learning plateau is due to a lack of motivation. Use of reproofs and threats would only cause a learner to remain at the plateau longer.

8. Confusion, disinterest, and uneasiness on the part of the learner could happen as a result of not knowing the

    A. importance of each period of instruction.

    B. objective of each period of instruction.

    C. subject of each period of instruction.

Answer (B) is correct. (FAA-H-8083-9B Chap 8)
    DISCUSSION: Knowing the objective of each period of instruction gives meaning and interest to the learner as well as the instructor. Not knowing the objective of the lesson often leads to confusion, disinterest, and uneasiness on the part of the learner.
    Answer (A) is incorrect. Confusion, disinterest, and uneasiness on the part of the learner could happen as a result of not knowing the objective of each period of instruction, not its importance. **Answer (C) is incorrect.** Confusion, disinterest, and uneasiness on the part of the learner could happen as a result of not knowing the objective of each period of instruction, not its subject. The subject of the instructional period will be obvious if it has been planned appropriately.

9. Which statement is true regarding sources of motivation?

    A. A desire for monetary gain is the main source of motivation for each individual.

    B. All sources of motivation offer some type of reward in exchange for performing work.

    C. Sources of motivation are normal and can be overcome by reminding learners of their own goals.

Answer (B) is correct. (FAA-H-8083-9B Chap 2)
    DISCUSSION: Sources of motivation vary, but all offer some type of reward in exchange for performing work.
    Answer (A) is incorrect. While the desire for monetary gain is a source of motivation to some, there are many different sources of motivation, and each individual may have a different one. Sources of motivation all offer some type of reward in exchange for performing work. **Answer (C) is incorrect.** Drops in motivation, not sources of motivation, can be overcome by reminding learners of their own goals. Sources of motivation all offer some type of reward in exchange for performing work.

10. Motivations that cause a learner to react with fear and anxiety are

   A. tangible.

   B. negative.

   C. difficult to identify.

Answer (B) is correct. (FAA-H-8083-9B Chap 2)
   DISCUSSION: Negative motivations may produce fears and may thus be seen by learners as threats. Negative motivation generally intimidates learners and should be avoided.
   Answer (A) is incorrect. Motivations, whether tangible or intangible, can be either positive or negative. **Answer (C) is incorrect.** Motivations, whether very subtle or difficult to identify, can be either positive or negative.

11. When learners are unable to see the benefits or purpose of a lesson, they will

   A. be less motivated.

   B. not learn as quickly.

   C. be expected to increase their efforts.

Answer (A) is correct. (FAA-H-8083-9B Chap 2)
   DISCUSSION: Learners will be less motivated if they are unable to see the benefits or purpose of a lesson. It is important for the instructor to make the learner aware that a particular lesson can help him or her reach an important goal.
   Answer (B) is incorrect. While a learner may not learn as quickly when (s)he is unable to see the benefits or purpose of a lesson, (s)he will become less motivated. **Answer (C) is incorrect.** The frustration of working without a known goal will likely decrease, not increase, their efforts.

12. Which statement is true concerning motivations?

   A. Motivations must be tangible to be effective.

   B. Motivations may be very subtle and difficult to identify.

   C. Negative motivations often are as effective as positive motivations.

Answer (B) is correct. (FAA-H-8083-9B Chap 2)
   DISCUSSION: Motivations may be subtle, subconscious, and difficult to identify. A learner may be motivated without even being aware (s)he is being influenced.
   Answer (A) is incorrect. Intangible motivations can be as effective (or even more effective) than tangible motivations. Rewards such as accomplishment, fame, and peer acceptance are intangible, but they are among the best positive motivators. **Answer (C) is incorrect.** Negative motivation tends to discourage the learner.

13. For a motivation to be effective, learners must believe their efforts will be rewarded in a definite manner. This type of motivation is

   A. subtle.

   B. negative.

   C. tangible.

Answer (C) is correct. (FAA-H-8083-9B Chap 2)
   DISCUSSION: Learners, like any worker, need and want tangible returns for their efforts. These rewards must be constantly apparent to the learner during instruction.
   Answer (A) is incorrect. The learner is often unaware of the application of subtle motivation and thus feels unrewarded for his or her effort. **Answer (B) is incorrect.** Negative motivations are not as effective as positive motivations, as they tend to intimidate learners and cause unpleasant experiences.

14. An instructor can most effectively maintain a high level of learner motivation by

   A. making each lesson a pleasurable experience.

   B. relaxing the standards of performance required during the early phase of training.

   C. continually challenging the learner to meet the highest objectives of training that can be established.

Answer (A) is correct. (FAA-H-8083-9B Chap 2)
   DISCUSSION: An instructor can most effectively maintain a high level of motivation by making each lesson a pleasant experience for a learner. People avoid negative experiences, but they will seek out and want to repeat positive experiences.
   Answer (B) is incorrect. Relaxing the standards of performance required during the early phase of training may actually reduce a learner's motivation. Reasonable standards strictly enforced are not resented by an earnest learner. **Answer (C) is incorrect.** Performance standards should be set to the learner's potential and not his or her current ability or to unrealistically high objectives. Improvement must be fostered.

15. How can drops in motivation be overcome?

   A. By reminding learners of their own goals and reassuring them there will be rewards for their continued efforts.

   B. By praising incremental successes during training, relating daily accomplishments to lesson objectives, and commenting favorably on learner progress.

   C. By making each lesson a pleasurable experience.

Answer (A) is correct. (FAA-H-8083-9B Chap 2)
   DISCUSSION: Drops in motivation, which are a common source of frustration, are normal and can be overcome by reminding learners of their own goals and reassuring them that there will be rewards for their continued efforts.
   Answer (B) is incorrect. Praising incremental successes during training, relating daily accomplishments to lesson objectives, and commenting favorably on learner progress are ways to maintain motivation, not to overcome a drop in motivation. **Answer (C) is incorrect.** While an instructor should strive to make each lesson a pleasurable experience, this will not guarantee that learners will not experience a drop in motivation.

16. Examples of tangible positive motivation may include

    A.   rewards such as accomplishment, personal comfort, and peer acceptance.

    B.   penalties in the form of reproof and threats.

    C.   rewards that involve financial gain or public recognition.

Answer (C) is correct. (FAA-H-8083-9B Chap 2)
    DISCUSSION: Examples of positive motivations that are tangible may involve financial gain or public recognition.
    Answer (A) is incorrect. Rewards such as accomplishment, personal comfort, and peer acceptance, while positive, are types of intangible motivators. **Answer (B) is incorrect.** Motivations in the form of reproof and threats are defined as negative motivations.

3.3 Aeronautical Decision Making and Risk Management

17. What is the systematic approach to the mental process used by pilots to determine the best course of action in response to a given set of circumstances?

    A.   Pilot Judgment Chain.

    B.   Aeronautical Decision Making.

    C.   Crew Resource Management.

Answer (B) is correct. (FAA-H-8083-9B Chap 1)
    DISCUSSION: Aeronautical Decision Making is defined as the systematic approach to the mental process used by pilots to determine the best course of action in response to a given set of circumstances.
    Answer (A) is incorrect. This approach is the definition of Aeronautical Decision Making, not the Pilot Judgment Chain. **Answer (C) is incorrect.** Crew Resource Management pertains to team management concepts on the flight deck, as well as those that affect flight attendants, maintenance personnel, and others. This question describes Aeronautical Decision Making.

18. Which of the following identifies accurate perception of the aircraft and environmental factors that affect the aircraft and passengers during a specific period of time?

    A.   CRM.

    B.   Situational Awareness.

    C.   ADM.

Answer (B) is correct. (FAA-H-8083-9B Chap 1)
    DISCUSSION: Situational awareness is defined as an accurate perception and understanding of all the factors and conditions within the four fundamental risk elements that affect safety before, during, and after the flight.
    Answer (A) is incorrect. Crew Resource Management (CRM) refers to the application of team management concepts on the flight deck environment, including cabin crew, maintenance personnel, and others. It is situational awareness that involves the accurate perception and understanding of all the factors and conditions within the four fundamental risk elements that affect safety before, during, and after the flight. **Answer (C) is incorrect.** Aeronautical Decision Making (ADM) is defined as the systematic approach to the mental process used by pilots to determine the best course of action in response to a given set of circumstances. It is situational awareness that involves the accurate perception and understanding of all the factors and conditions within the four fundamental risk elements that affect safety before, during, and after the flight.

19. One of the risk elements in the Aeronautical Decision Making process is?

    A.   Fuel on board.

    B.   Passengers.

    C.   Aircraft.

Answer (C) is correct. (FAA-H-8083-9B Chap 1)
    DISCUSSION: The four fundamental risk elements incorporated into aeronautical decision making are the pilot, the aircraft, the environment, and the type of operation that comprises any given aviation situation.
    Answer (A) is incorrect. Fuel on board is not one of the risk elements included in the aeronautical decision making process. The pilot, the aircraft, the environment, and the type of operation are the four fundamental risk elements included in ADM. **Answer (B) is incorrect.** The passengers are not considered to be one of the risk elements included in aeronautical decision making. The pilot, the aircraft, the environment, and the type of operation are the four fundamental risk elements included in ADM.

20. Risk management, as part of the aeronautical decision making (ADM) process, relies on which features to reduce the risks associated with each flight?

    A. Application of stress management and risk element procedures.

    B. The mental process of analyzing all information in a particular situation and making a timely decision on what action to take.

    C. Situational awareness, problem recognition, and good judgment.

Answer (C) is correct. (AC 60-22)

    DISCUSSION: Risk management is that part of the ADM process which relies on situational awareness, problem recognition, and good judgment to reduce risks associated with each flight.

    Answer (A) is incorrect. Risk management relies on situational awareness, problem recognition, and good judgment, not the application of stress management and risk-element procedures, to reduce the risks associated with each flight. **Answer (B) is incorrect.** Judgment, not risk management, is the mental process of analyzing all information in a particular situation and making a timely decision on what action to take.

21. The aeronautical decision making (ADM) process identifies several steps involved in good decision making. One of these steps is

    A. making a rational evaluation of the required actions.

    B. identifying personal attitudes hazardous to safe flight.

    C. developing a "can do" attitude.

Answer (B) is correct. (AC 60-22)

    DISCUSSION: The ADM process addresses all aspects of decision making on the flight deck and identifies several steps involved in good decision making. One of these steps is to identify personal attitudes hazardous to safe flight.

    Answer (A) is incorrect. Making a rational evaluation of the required actions is a step in good judgment, not a step in good decision making. **Answer (C) is incorrect.** The "can do," or macho, attitude is one of the personal hazardous attitudes to identify in the steps involved in good decision making.

22. Examples of classic behavioral traps that experienced pilots may fall into are to

    A. promote situational awareness and then necessary changes in behavior.

    B. complete a flight as planned, please passengers, meet schedules, and "get the job done."

    C. assume additional responsibilities and assert PIC authority.

Answer (B) is correct. (AC 60-22)

    DISCUSSION: Pilots have been known to fall into a number of classic behavioral traps. Pilots, particularly those with considerable experience, as a rule always try to complete a flight as planned, please passengers, meet schedules, and do what it takes to "get the job done."

    Answer (A) is incorrect. To promote situational awareness and then to make necessary changes in behavior are part of learning good decision making, not classical behavioral traps. **Answer (C) is incorrect.** Assuming additional responsibilities and asserting PIC authority are not examples of classical behavioral traps.

23. Hazardous attitudes occur to every pilot to some degree at some time. What are some of these hazardous attitudes?

    A. Antiauthority, impulsivity, macho, resignation, and invulnerability.

    B. Poor situational awareness, snap judgments, and lack of a decision making process.

    C. Poor risk management and lack of stress management.

Answer (A) is correct. (AC 60-22)

    DISCUSSION: The five hazardous attitudes addressed in the ADM process are antiauthority, impulsivity, invulnerability, macho, and resignation.

    Answer (B) is incorrect. Poor situational awareness and snap judgments are indications of the lack of a decision-making process, not hazardous attitudes. **Answer (C) is incorrect.** Poor risk management and lack of stress management lead to poor ADM and are not considered hazardous attitudes.

24. In the aeronautical decision making (ADM) process, what is the first step in neutralizing a hazardous attitude?

    A. Recognizing hazardous thoughts.

    B. Recognizing the invulnerability of the situation.

    C. Making a rational judgment.

Answer (A) is correct. (AC 60-22)

    DISCUSSION: Hazardous attitudes, which contribute to poor pilot judgment, can be effectively counteracted by redirecting that hazardous attitude so that appropriate action can be taken. Recognition of hazardous thoughts is the first step in neutralizing them in the ADM process.

    Answer (B) is incorrect. Invulnerability is a hazardous attitude. The first step in neutralizing a hazardous attitude is to recognize it. **Answer (C) is incorrect.** Before a rational judgment can be made, the hazardous attitude must be recognized then redirected so that appropriate action can be taken.

25. Success in reducing stress associated with a crisis on the flight deck begins with

   A. eliminating the more serious life and flight deck stress issues.

   B. knowing the exact cause of the stress.

   C. assessing stress areas in one's personal life.

Answer (C) is correct. (AC 60-22)
   DISCUSSION: If you hope to succeed in reducing stress associated with crisis management on the flight deck, it is essential to begin by making a personal assessment of stress in all areas of your life.
   Answer (A) is incorrect. In order to eliminate the more serious life and flight deck stress issues, you must first make an assessment of stress in all areas of your life to identify those stressors. **Answer (B) is incorrect.** In order to know the exact cause of the stress, you must first make an assessment of stress in all areas of your life to identify stressors and the causes of them.

26. The DECIDE process consists of six elements to help provide a pilot a logical way of approaching aeronautical decision making. These elements are to

   A. estimate, determine, choose, identify, detect, and evaluate.

   B. determine, evaluate, choose, identify, do, and eliminate.

   C. detect, estimate, choose, identify, do, and evaluate.

Answer (C) is correct. (AC 60-22)
   DISCUSSION: The DECIDE model, comprised of six elements, is intended to provide a pilot with a logical way of approaching decision making. These six elements, using the acronym DECIDE, are detect, estimate, choose, identify, do, and evaluate.
   Answer (A) is incorrect. One of the elements of the DECIDE process is "do," not "determine." **Answer (B) is incorrect.** Two of the elements of the DECIDE process are "detect," not "determine," and "estimate," not "eliminate."

27. If a pilot wanted to mitigate risk during a cross-country flight in MVFR conditions, the pilot could

   A. Take a pilot who is IFR-rated.

   B. Continue the flight as planned.

   C. Stay out of controlled airspace.

Answer (A) is correct. (FAA-H-8083-9B Chap 1)
   DISCUSSION: Risk assessment is only part of the risk management equation. After determining the level of risk, the pilot needs to mitigate, or reduce, the risk. In this example, the pilot could reduce the risk by taking a qualified IFR-rated pilot along on the trip in case the weather deteriorated below VFR minimums.
   Answer (B) is incorrect. Continuing the flight as planned is acceptance, not mitigation, of the risk of flying in MVFR conditions. **Answer (C) is incorrect.** Deciding to stay out of controlled airspace should be an immediate red flag, as it signals that the pilot may try to push his or her limits and continue into weather that could present additional hazards. Risk mitigation is about reducing total risk, not adding additional potential risks to the planned flight.

28. A pilot's inexperience in direct crosswinds greater than 10 knots is an example of which of the fundamental risk elements?

   A. The pilot in command.

   B. The aircraft.

   C. The external pressures.

Answer (A) is correct. (FAA-H-8083-9B Chap 1)
   DISCUSSION: The pilot is one of the risk factors in a flight. The pilot must ask, "Am I ready for this trip?" in terms of experience, currency, and physical and emotional condition. If the pilot has experience with 10 knots of direct crosswind, it could be unsafe to exceed a 10-knot crosswind component without additional training. Therefore, the crosswind experience level is that pilot's personal limitation until additional training with a CFI provides the pilot with additional experience for flying in crosswinds that exceed 10 knots.
   Answer (B) is incorrect. The pilot's lack of experience level in crosswinds that exceed 10 knots is a personal limitation and risk factor, not one having to do with the aircraft itself. **Answer (C) is incorrect.** The pilot's lack of experience level in crosswinds that exceed 10 knots is a personal limitation and risk factor, not one having to do with external pressures associated with a planned flight.

29. The antidote for the antiauthority hazardous attitude is

   A. "Follow the rules. They are usually right."

   B. "It could happen to me."

   C. "I am not helpless. I can make a difference."

Answer (A) is correct. (FAA-H-8083-9B Chap 1)
   DISCUSSION: The antidote for the antiauthority hazardous attitude is "Follow the rules. They are usually right."
   Answer (B) is incorrect. "It could happen to me" is the antidote for the invulnerability hazardous attitude. **Answer (C) is incorrect.** "I am not helpless. I can make a difference" is the antidote for the resignation hazardous attitude.

30. Which of the following aircraft risks can be mitigated during the preflight inspection?

    A. Urgency of completing the flight.

    B. Weather en-route.

    C. Fuel quantity.

Answer (C) is correct. *(FAA-H-8083-9B Chap 1)*
    DISCUSSION: As part of a preflight inspection, the pilot in command should check the fuel quantity to ensure that the amount is accurate compared with what was ordered and what was planned for during the preflight planning phase.
    Answer (A) is incorrect. The urgency of completing the flight is a risk factor associated with external pressures, not the aircraft. This risk factor should be dealt with during the pilot's evaluation of the planned flight, not during the preflight inspection. **Answer (B) is incorrect.** The weather en-route for a planned flight is an environmental risk factor, not one associated with the aircraft. This risk factor should be dealt with during the preflight planning phase rather than during the preflight inspection.

31. The macho attitude can be described by which of the following statements?

    A. "Do something quickly!"

    B. "I can do it."

    C. "Do not tell me what to do!"

Answer (B) is correct. *(AC 60-22)*
    DISCUSSION: "I can do it" is an example of a macho attitude. It is characteristic of an individual who thinks (s)he is superior to others.
    Answer (A) is incorrect. The impulsivity attitude is expressed by taking action quickly with little thought for the consequences. A macho attitude is displayed by someone who thinks "I can do it." **Answer (C) is incorrect.** "Do not tell me what to do!" is the thought had by one who displays the antiauthority attitude. A macho attitude is displayed by someone who thinks "I can do it."

32. During a stall recovery, the instructor allows the learner to exceed maneuvering speed. Which best illustrates an 'anti-authority' reaction by the instructor?

    A. There has not been a problem doing this in the past.

    B. The aircraft can handle a lot more than the maneuvering speed.

    C. The learner should know how to recover from a stall by this time.

Answer (B) is correct. *(AC 60-22)*
    DISCUSSION: An example of the antiauthority ("Don't tell me what to do!") attitude would be an instructor allowing a learner to exceed maneuvering speed during a stall recovery. The specific antiauthority attitude expressed by the instructor is "The aircraft can handle a lot more than the maneuvering speed."
    Answer (A) is incorrect. This attitude falls closer to the hazardous attitude of invulnerability ("It won't happen to me"). There might not have been a problem in the past, but it could happen. **Answer (C) is incorrect.** The hazardous attitude in this answer selection is resignation ("What's the use?"). The instructor in this case should instead ask himself or herself "How can I teach this learner how and when to recover from a stall?"

33. The body's response to a set of circumstances that induces a change in an individual's current physiological and/or psychological patterns of functioning forcing the individual to adapt to these changes is

    A. risk management.

    B. aeronautical decision making.

    C. stress.

Answer (C) is correct. *(AC 60-22)*
    DISCUSSION: Stress describes the body's response to a set of circumstances that induces a change in an individual's current physiological and/or psychological patterns of functioning, forcing the individual to adapt to these changes.
    Answer (A) is incorrect. Risk management is the part of the decision-making process that relies on situational awareness, problem recognition, and good judgment to reduce risks associated with each flight, not stress. **Answer (B) is incorrect.** Aeronautical decision making is a systematic approach to the mental process used by pilots to consistently determine the best course of action in response to a given set of circumstances. Stress describes the body's response to a set of circumstances that induces a change in an individual's current physiological and/or psychological patterns of functioning, forcing the individual to adapt to these changes.

34. What is the antidote to the hazardous attitude of invulnerability?

    A. "It could happen to me."

    B. "Not so fast. Think first."

    C. "Taking chances is foolish."

Answer (A) is correct. *(AC 60-22)*
    DISCUSSION: To properly counteract the attitude of invulnerability, the antidote is thinking or saying "It could happen to me."
    Answer (B) is incorrect. "Not so fast. Think first." describes the antidote to the hazardous attitude of impulsivity. **Answer (C) is incorrect.** A macho attitude can be neutralized by thinking "Taking chances is foolish."

35. To help manage flight deck stress, you should

    A. evaluate the effect(s) of the action taken to counter the change.

    B. recall the antidote "I am not helpless. I can make a difference."

    C. try to relax and think rationally at the first sign of stress.

Answer (C) is correct. (AC 60-22)
    DISCUSSION: To help manage flight deck stress, you should try to relax and think rationally at the first sign of stress.
    Answer (A) is incorrect. Evaluating the effect(s) of the action taken to counter the change describes the sixth element of the DECIDE model, evaluate. **Answer (B) is incorrect.** The antidote "I am not helpless. I can make a difference" will not help reduce stress, but instead will help counteract the tendency to display an attitude of resignation.

36. The likely cause of a pilot ignoring the requirements for minimum fuel reserve is most likely overconfidence, disregard for applicable regulations, or

    A. lack of flight planning.

    B. acute fatigue.

    C. learning plateau.

Answer (A) is correct. (FAA-H-8083-9B Chap 1)
    DISCUSSION: Operating without adequate fuel reserves or ignoring minimum fuel reserve requirements is generally the result of overconfidence, lack of flight planning, or disregarding applicable regulations.
    Answer (B) is incorrect. Acute fatigue, a normal occurrence of everyday living, is the tiredness felt after long periods of physical and mental strain, including strenuous muscular effort, immobility, heavy mental workload, strong emotional pressure, monotony, and lack of sleep. **Answer (C) is incorrect.** A learning plateau is a phenomenon where progress appears to cease or slow down for a significant period of time before once again increasing.

3.4 Effective Communication

37. The effectiveness of communication between instructor and learner is measured by the

    A. degree of dynamic, interrelated elements.

    B. similarity between the idea transmitted and the idea received.

    C. relationship between communicative and dynamic elements.

Answer (B) is correct. (FAA-H-8083-9B Chap 4)
    DISCUSSION: Communication takes place when one person transmits ideas or feelings to another person or group of people. Its effectiveness is measured by the similarity between the idea transmitted and the idea received.
    Answer (A) is incorrect. The process, not the effectiveness, of communication is composed of three dynamic, interrelated elements -- the source, the symbols, and the receiver. **Answer (C) is incorrect.** The relationship between the communicative elements (source, symbols, and receiver) is dynamic. There are no dynamic elements.

38. Effective communication has taken place when, and only when, the

    A. information is transmitted and received.

    B. receivers react with understanding and change their behavior accordingly.

    C. receivers have the ability to question and comprehend ideas that have been transmitted.

Answer (B) is correct. (FAA-H-8083-9B Chap 4)
    DISCUSSION: The rule of thumb among communicators is that communication succeeds only in relation to the reaction of the receiver. Effective communication has taken place only when the receivers react with understanding and change their behavior.
    Answer (A) is incorrect. Information may be transmitted and received without effective communication. Only when the receiver reacts to the information being transmitted and received with understanding, and changes his or her behavior accordingly, has effective communication taken place. **Answer (C) is incorrect.** The ability to question and comprehend ideas that have been transmitted is only one characteristic of a receiver.

39. When has instruction taken place?

A. When a procedure has been explained, and the desired learner response has occurred.

B. When the learner hears what is presented.

C. When all the required material has been presented.

Answer (A) is correct. (FAA-H-8083-9B Chap 4)

DISCUSSION: Instruction has taken place when the instructor has explained a particular procedure and subsequently determined that the desired learner response has occurred.

Answer (B) is incorrect. Instruction has taken place when the instructor has explained a particular procedure and subsequently determined that the desired learner response has occurred, not only when the learner hears what is presented. **Answer (C) is incorrect.** Instruction has taken place when the instructor has explained a particular procedure and subsequently determined that the desired learner response has occurred, not only when all the required material has been presented.

40. To communicate effectively, instructors must

A. recognize the level of comprehension.

B. provide an atmosphere which encourages questioning.

C. reveal a positive attitude while delivering their message.

Answer (C) is correct. (FAA-H-8083-9B Chap 4)

DISCUSSION: Communicators consciously or unconsciously reveal attitudes toward themselves, the ideas they are trying to transmit, and their receivers. These attitudes must be positive if the communicators are to communicate effectively.

Answer (A) is incorrect. An instructor can recognize the level of a learner's comprehension in the application step of the teaching process, not during the communication process. **Answer (B) is incorrect.** While an instructor should provide an atmosphere that encourages questioning, the learner must exercise his or her ability to ask questions to communicate effectively.

41. To be more likely to communicate effectively, an instructor should speak or write from a background of

A. technical expertise.

B. knowing the ideas presented.

C. up-to-date, stimulating material.

Answer (C) is correct. (FAA-H-8083-9B Chap 4)

DISCUSSION: A basic factor of a communicator's effectiveness is the ability to speak or write from a broad background of accurate, up-to-date, and stimulating material.

Answer (A) is incorrect. A speaker or writer with technical expertise may depend on technical jargon. Reliance on technical language can impede effective communication, especially when the receiver lacks a similar background. **Answer (B) is incorrect.** Just knowing the ideas presented does not ensure that effective communication will take place. A communicator must be able to make the receiver react with understanding and change his or her behavior accordingly.

42. In the communication process, the communicator will be more successful in gaining and retaining the receiver's attention by

A. being friendly and informative.

B. using a varied communicative approach.

C. using a variety of audiovisual aids in class.

Answer (B) is correct. (FAA-H-8083-9B Chap 4)

DISCUSSION: The most successful communicator will use the variety of channels that best communicates the necessary ideas and techniques, i.e., a varied communicative approach.

Answer (A) is incorrect. Effective, engaging communication is more complex than merely being friendly. The source, the symbols, and the receiver are all interrelated in the communication process. **Answer (C) is incorrect.** Audiovisual aids can often further the learning, not the communication, process by supporting, supplementing, or reinforcing important ideas. By presenting the material in a new manner, instructional aids can even improve communication between instructor and learner.

43. Communication takes place when

A. one person transmits ideas or feelings to another person or to a group of people.

B. symbols are used to transmit messages.

C. the instructor takes into account the learner's background, experience, and education.

Answer (A) is correct. (FAA-H-8083-9B Chap 4)

DISCUSSION: Communication takes place when one person transmits ideas or feelings to another person or to a group of people.

Answer (B) is incorrect. While symbols are used to transmit messages, the receiver has to have the same understanding of the symbol as the communicator for communication to take place. **Answer (C) is incorrect.** Knowledge of the learner's background does not guarantee communication will take place. Communication takes place when one person transmits ideas or feelings to another person or to a group of people.

44. The three dynamically interrelated elements that compose the process of communication are

A. Visual, auditory, and kinesthetic.

B. Source, symbol, and receiver.

C. Background, experience, and education.

Answer (B) is correct. (FAA-H-8083-9B Chap 4)

DISCUSSION: The process of communication is composed of a source, the symbols used in transmitting the message, and the receiver.

Answer (A) is incorrect. The three sensory channels through which symbols are perceived are the visual, auditory, and kinesthetic channels. The process of communication, however, is composed of a source, the symbols used in transmitting the message, and the receiver. **Answer (C) is incorrect.** The process of communication is composed of a source, the symbols used in transmitting the message, and the receiver.

45. What is true of symbols?

A. Ideas can be communicated by presenting individual symbols.

B. The three sensory channels that symbols are perceived through are words, signs, visual aids.

C. Instructors should use a variety of sensory channels to be more successful in gaining and retaining learner attention.

Answer (C) is correct. (FAA-H-8083-9B Chap 4)

DISCUSSION: Instructors will be more successful in gaining and retaining learner attention by using a variety of sensory channels.

Answer (A) is incorrect. Ideas are communicated only when symbols are combined into meaningful wholes (e.g., sentences, paragraphs, chapters, etc.). Instructors will be more successful in gaining and retaining learner attention by using a variety of sensory channels. **Answer (B) is incorrect.** Symbols are perceived through three sensory channels: visual, auditory, or kinesthetic, not words, signs, or visual aids.

46. Oral and visual codes used to communicate are called what?

A. Signals.

B. Sensory channels.

C. Symbols.

Answer (C) is correct. (FAA-H-8083-9B Chap 4)

DISCUSSION: Symbols are defined as oral and visual codes used to communicate.

Answer (A) is incorrect. Symbols, not signals, are defined as oral and visual codes used to communicate. **Answer (B) is incorrect.** Sensory channels are ways through which symbols are perceived. Oral and visual codes used to communicate are symbols.

3.5 Barriers to Effective Communication

47. Probably the greatest single barrier to effective communication in the teaching process is a lack of

A. respect for the instructor.

B. personality harmony between instructor and learner.

C. a common experience level between instructor and learner.

Answer (C) is correct. (FAA-H-8083-9B Chap 4)

DISCUSSION: The greatest single barrier to effective communication is the lack of common experience between the communicator and the receiver. Those with the least in common usually find it difficult to communicate.

Answer (A) is incorrect. While lack of respect for the instructor is a barrier to communication, it is not as great and as prevalent as a lack of common experience between the communicator and the receiver. **Answer (B) is incorrect.** While lack of personality harmony is a barrier to communication, it is not as great and as prevalent as a lack of common experience between the communicator and the receiver.

48. A communicator's words cannot communicate the desired meaning to another person unless the

A. words have meaningful referents.

B. words give the meaning that is in the mind of the receiver.

C. listener or reader has had some experience with the objects or concepts to which these words refer.

Answer (C) is correct. (FAA-H-8083-9B Chap 4)

DISCUSSION: Since a common core of experience is basic to effective communication, a communicator's words cannot communicate the desired meaning to another person unless the listener or the reader has had some experience with the objects or concepts to which these words refer.

Answer (A) is incorrect. The words must have not only meaningful referents, but the exact same meaningful referents in order for the communicator and the receiver to share a desired meaning. **Answer (B) is incorrect.** Words only arouse desired meanings if the communicator generates the desired response in the mind of the receiver. The nature of this response is determined by the receiver's past experiences with the words and the concepts to which they refer.

49. Which of the following is an example of a problem with using abstract words?

A. They may stand for ideas that cannot be directly experienced by the learner.

B. They tend to confuse the listener between the symbol and the symbolized object.

C. They reduce the effectiveness of role-playing methods.

Answer (A) is correct. (FAA-H-8083-9B Chap 4)
DISCUSSION: Abstract words stand for ideas that cannot be directly experienced; i.e., they do not call forth the specific mental image in the mind of the learner that the instructor intends. The word "aircraft" is an abstract word. It does not call to mind a specific aircraft in the imaginations of various learners.
Answer (B) is incorrect. Confusion between the symbol and the symbolized object is a barrier to communication separate and distinct from the use of abstract words. **Answer (C) is incorrect.** Reducing the effectiveness of role-playing methods is not among the problems of using abstract words.

50. The danger in using abstract words is that they

A. sum up vast areas of experience.

B. call forth different mental images in the minds of the receivers.

C. will not evoke the specific items of experience in the listener's mind that the communicator intends.

Answer (C) is correct. (FAA-H-8083-9B Chap 4)
DISCUSSION: The purpose of abstract words is not to bring forth specific ideas in the mind of the receiver but to serve as shorthand symbols that sum up vast areas of experience. The danger in using abstract words is that they will not evoke the specific items in the listener's mind that the communicator intends.
Answer (A) is incorrect. The purpose, not the danger, of using abstract words is to use them as shorthand symbols that sum up vast areas of experience. **Answer (B) is incorrect.** Abstract words do not call forth mental images; on the contrary, they stand for ideas that cannot be directly experienced.

51. By using abstractions in the communication process, the communicator will

A. bring forth specific items of experience in the minds of the receivers.

B. be using words which refer to objects or ideas that human beings can experience directly.

C. not evoke in the listener's or reader's mind the specific items of experience the communicator intends.

Answer (C) is correct. (FAA-H-8083-9B Chap 4)
DISCUSSION: Abstract words are necessary and useful. Their purpose is not to bring forth specific items of experience in the minds of receivers but to serve as shorthand symbols that refer to thoughts or ideas. The danger is that an abstract term might not evoke in the listener's mind the specific item of experience the communicator intended.
Answer (A) is incorrect. Abstract words are not used to bring forth specific items of experience in the minds of the receivers. **Answer (B) is incorrect.** Concrete, not abstract, words refer to objects or ideas that human beings can experience directly.

52. What is required for communication to be effective?

A. The learner's past experience needs to be the same as the instructor's.

B. The learner's understanding of the meaning of symbols needs to be the same as the instructor's intended meaning.

C. The instructor should explain technical terms that he uses in speech.

Answer (B) is correct. (FAA-H-8083-9B Chap 4)
DISCUSSION: A learner's understanding of the meaning of words and symbols needs to be the same as the instructor's understanding of the words and symbols. This requires the instructor to spend time making sure the learners understand that terminology and the correct or intended use.
Answer (A) is incorrect. A learner and instructor will never have exactly the same experiences in life. Because past experience varies greatly among each individual, the learner's understanding of the meaning of the words needs to be the same as the instructor's understanding. **Answer (C) is incorrect.** While an instructor should explain technical terms (s)he uses, the learner still needs to understand what they mean and how and when they apply to a given situation.

53. What is the term for when a symbol is different from the intended meaning?

A. External factors.

B. Confusion.

C. Abstraction.

Answer (B) is correct. (FAA-H-8083-9B Chap 4)
DISCUSSION: Confusion between the symbol and the symbolized object results when a word is confused with what it is meant to represent.
Answer (A) is incorrect. External factors may prevent a process or activity from being carried out properly and are composed of factors outside the control of the instructor. **Answer (C) is incorrect.** Abstractions serve as shorthand symbols that sum up large areas of experience.

54. Because words and symbols do not always represent the same thing to each person, speakers and instructors should

    A. use technical terms to accurately explain the subject being covered.

    B. employ words and symbols that are concrete to narrow the image being produced in the listener's mind.

    C. choose words and symbols that represent what is intended.

Answer (C) is correct. (FAA-H-8083-9B Chap 4)
    DISCUSSION: To communicate effectively, speakers and instructors should choose words and symbols that represent what is intended. Thus, confusion will be avoided.
    Answer (A) is incorrect. Technical terms do not necessarily accurately explain the subject being covered. This requires the listener to have background knowledge of what is being presented. **Answer (B) is incorrect.** Concrete words and symbols, while narrowing the images produced in the mind of a listener, can still confuse a learner if they do not represent what is intended.

55. External factors may prevent a process or activity from being carried out properly and are composed of what three factors outside the control of the instructor?

    A. Physiological, Psychological, Environmental.

    B. Psychological, Physiological, Biological.

    C. Physical, Environmental, Psychological.

Answer (A) is correct. (FAA-H-8083-9B Chap 4)
    DISCUSSION: The three factors that compose external factors are physiological, environmental, and psychological.
    Answer (B) is incorrect. Any biological problem that may inhibit symbol reception is known as a physiological external factor. The three factors that compose external factors are physiological, environmental, and psychological. **Answer (C) is incorrect.** Any physical problem, such as hearing loss, injury, or illness, is a type of a physiological external factor. The three factors that compose external factors are physiological, environmental, and psychological.

56. Physiological external factors are defined as

    A. the product of how the instructor and learner feel at the time the communication process is occurring.

    B. external factors caused by external physical conditions.

    C. external factors resulting from any biological problem.

Answer (C) is correct. (FAA-H-8083-9B Chap 4)
    DISCUSSION: Physiological external factors are defined as any biological problem that may inhibit reception.
    Answer (A) is incorrect. Physiological external factors are defined as any biological problem that may inhibit reception. Psychological external factors are a product of how the instructor and learner feel at the time the communication process is occurring. **Answer (B) is incorrect.** Physiological external factors are defined as any biological problem that may inhibit reception. External factors caused by external physical conditions are defined as environmental external factors.

57. Aircraft noise, vibration, or lighting conditions are what type of external factors?

    A. Environmental.

    B. Physiological.

    C. Psychological.

Answer (A) is correct. (FAA-H-8083-9B Chap 4)
    DISCUSSION: Environmental factors could include aircraft noise, vibration, or lighting conditions.
    Answer (B) is incorrect. Physiological factors could include hearing loss, injury, or physical illness. **Answer (C) is incorrect.** If either the instructor or learner is not committed to the communication process, communication is impaired.

58. Which type of external factor is displayed in the example of a learner who is not actively engaged in the learning process and seems distracted?

    A. Physiological.

    B. Psychological.

    C. Environmental.

Answer (B) is correct. (FAA-H-8083-9B Chap 4)
    DISCUSSION: If the learner is not committed to the communication process, as demonstrated by seeming distracted or not engaged, communication is impaired. This type of external factor is a psychological factor.
    Answer (A) is incorrect. Examples of physiological external factors could include hearing loss, injury, or physical illness. **Answer (C) is incorrect.** Examples of environmental external factors could include aircraft noise, vibration, or lighting conditions.

3.6 Instructor Responsibilities

59. Evaluation of demonstrated ability during flight instruction must be based upon

A. the progress of the learner.

B. the instructor's opinion concerning the maneuver(s).

C. established standards of performance.

Answer (C) is correct. (FAA-H-8083-9B Chap 8)
DISCUSSION: Evaluation of demonstrated learner ability during flight instruction must be based upon established standards of performance, suitably modified to apply to the learner's experience and stage of development as a pilot. **Answer (A) is incorrect.** Evaluation must be based on established standards of performance, not the progress of the learner. **Answer (B) is incorrect.** Evaluation must be based on established standards of performance, not on the instructor's opinion.

60. Evaluation of demonstrated ability during flight instruction must be based upon

A. the instructor's background and experience relating to learner pilots at this stage of training.

B. the progress of the learner, considering the time and experience attained since beginning training.

C. established standards of performance, suitably modified to apply to the learner's experience.

Answer (C) is correct. (FAA-H-8083-9B Chap 8)
DISCUSSION: Evaluation of demonstrated learner ability during flight instruction must be based upon established standards of performance, suitably modified to apply to the learner's experience and stage of development as a pilot. **Answer (A) is incorrect.** Evaluation should be based on established standards of performance and modified based on the learner's experience, not the instructor's experience. **Answer (B) is incorrect.** Evaluation should be based on established standards of performance, not the learner's progress since beginning training, modified based on the learner's experience.

61. It is important that an instructor enhance a learner's acceptance of further instruction by

A. keeping the learner informed of the progress made.

B. constantly reminding the learner of the learning objectives that lie ahead.

C. setting standards beyond the learner's abilities.

Answer (A) is correct. (FAA-H-8083-9B Chap 8)
DISCUSSION: In assessing piloting ability, it is important for the flight instructor to keep the learner informed of progress. This may be done as each procedure or maneuver is completed or summarized during post-flight critiques. Post-flight critiques should be in a written format such as notes to aid the flight instructor in covering all areas that were noticed during the flight or lesson. **Answer (B) is incorrect.** Keeping a learner informed of progress made to date is a more effective motivator than drawing attention to the tasks that the learner has not yet addressed. **Answer (C) is incorrect.** Performance standards should be realistic and achievable.

62. In evaluating learner demonstrations of piloting ability, it is important for the flight instructor to

A. remain silent and observe.

B. keep the learner informed of progress.

C. explain errors in performance immediately.

Answer (B) is correct. (FAA-H-8083-9B Chap 8)
DISCUSSION: In evaluating learner demonstrations of piloting ability, it is important for the flight instructor to keep the learner informed of his or her progress. This may be done as each procedure/maneuver is completed or summarized during post-flight critiques. **Answer (A) is incorrect.** In evaluating learner demonstrations of piloting ability, it is important for the flight instructor to keep the learner informed of his or her progress, not remain silent and observe. **Answer (C) is incorrect.** Learners should be allowed to make mistakes and correct them on their own; errors should not be pointed out immediately because learners learn by correcting their mistakes. The error can be explained at the completion of the procedure/maneuver or during a post-flight critique.

63. Goals learners consider difficult, but possible, tend to

A. provide a challenge and promote learning.

B. cause frustration and lead to failure.

C. be appropriate only for learners lacking motivation.

Answer (A) is correct. (FAA-H-8083-9B Chap 2)
DISCUSSION: Assignment of goals the learner considers difficult, but possible, usually provides a challenge and promotes learning. Motivation also declines when a learner believes the instructor is making unreasonable demands for performance and progress. **Answer (B) is incorrect.** The assignment of impossible or unreasonable goals discourages the learner, diminishes effort, and retards the learning process. **Answer (C) is incorrect.** All learners will benefit from the assignment of reasonable goals that offer a challenge to complete.

64. The use of distractions by a flight instructor

A. will teach the learner to divide his or her attention between the distracting task and maintaining control of the aircraft.

B. will be of little value to more experienced learners.

C. will allow learners to develop concentration skills so they can ignore distracting passengers.

Answer (A) is correct. (FAA-H-8083-9B Chap 9)
DISCUSSION: Instructor responsibilities include teaching the learner to divide his or her attention between the distracting task and maintaining control of the aircraft.
Answer (B) is incorrect. Pilots at all skill levels should be aware of the increased risk of entering into an inadvertent stall or spin while performing tasks that are secondary to controlling the aircraft. **Answer (C) is incorrect.** The proper use of distractions will not develop concentration skills that allow learners to ignore distracting passengers.

65. Examples of all common endorsements can be found in the current issue of

A. AC 61-67, Appendix A.

B. AC 91-67, Appendix A.

C. AC 61-65, Appendix A.

Answer (C) is correct. (FAA-H-8083-9B Chap 9)
DISCUSSION: Examples of all common endorsements can be found in the current issue of AC 61-65, Appendix A.
Answer (A) is incorrect. Examples of all common endorsements can be found in the current issue of AC 61-65, not AC 61-67, Appendix A. **Answer (B) is incorrect.** Examples of all common endorsements can be found in the current issue of AC 61-65, not AC 91-67, Appendix A.

66. Before endorsing a learner for solo flight, the instructor should require the learner to demonstrate consistent ability to perform

A. all maneuvers specified in the Student Pilot Guide.

B. all of the fundamental maneuvers.

C. slow flight, stalls, emergency landings, takeoffs and landings, and go-arounds.

Answer (B) is correct. (FAA-H-8083-9B Chap 9)
DISCUSSION: Before endorsing a learner for solo flight, the instructor should require the learner to demonstrate the consistent ability to perform all of the fundamental maneuvers.
Answer (A) is incorrect. Before endorsing a learner for solo flight, the instructor should require the learner to demonstrate the consistent ability to perform all of the fundamental maneuvers, not all maneuvers specified in the Student Pilot Guide (which contains no maneuvers). **Answer (C) is incorrect.** Before endorsing a learner for solo flight, the instructor should require the learner to demonstrate the consistent ability to perform all of the fundamental maneuvers, not just slow flight, stalls, emergency landings, takeoffs, landings, and go-arounds.

67. The learner should be capable of handling problems that might occur, such as traffic pattern congestion, change in active runway, or unexpected crosswinds prior to

A. the first solo cross-country flight.

B. initial solo.

C. being recommended for a Recreational or Private Pilot Certificate.

Answer (B) is correct. (FAA-H-8083-9B Chap 9)
DISCUSSION: Flight instructors have a responsibility to provide guidance and restraint regarding the solo operations of their learners. Before receiving an instructor endorsement for solo flight, a learner should be required to demonstrate the consistent ability to perform all of the fundamental maneuvers and should be capable of handling ordinary problems that might occur, such as traffic pattern congestion, a change in the active runway, or unexpected crosswinds.
Answer (A) is incorrect. The learner should be capable of handling problems that might occur prior to initial solo, not the first solo cross-country flight. **Answer (C) is incorrect.** The learner should be capable of handling problems that might occur prior to initial solo, not being recommended for a recreational or private pilot certificate.

68. What is one of the best actions an instructor can take to emphasize aviation safety?

A. By setting the example.

B. By informing the learner of his or her progress as each procedure is completed.

C. By analyzing the learner's personality, thinking, and ability to tailor his or her teaching technique to the learner.

Answer (A) is correct. (FAA-H-8083-9B Chap 8)
DISCUSSION: Emphasizing safety by example is one of the best actions an instructor can take to ensure aviation safety.
Answer (B) is incorrect. Informing the learner of his or her progress as each procedure is completed is an example of evaluating the learner's piloting ability. Emphasizing safety by example is one of the best actions an instructor can take to ensure aviation safety. **Answer (C) is incorrect.** Analyzing a learner's personality, thinking, and ability and then tailoring a teaching technique to fit the learner is an example of providing adequate instruction.

69. What are the five main responsibilities of aviation instructors?

A. Helping learners, providing adequate instruction, emphasizing the positive, providing pilot endorsements, and ensuring aviation safety.

B. Helping learners, providing adequate instruction, demanding adequate standards of performance, emphasizing the positive, and ensuring aviation safety.

C. Helping learners, providing adequate instruction, emphasizing the positive, practical test recommendations, and ensuring aviation safety.

Answer (B) is correct. (FAA-H-8083-9B Chap 8)
DISCUSSION: The five main responsibilities of aviation instructors include helping learners, providing adequate instruction, demanding adequate standards of performance, emphasizing the positive, and ensuring aviation safety.
Answer (A) is incorrect. Providing pilot endorsements, while a responsibility of an aviation instructor, is not one of the five main responsibilities. **Answer (C) is incorrect.** Practical test recommendations, while a responsibility of an aviation instructor, is not one of the five main responsibilities.

70. The use of standards, and measurement against those standards, is key to

A. ensuring aviation safety.

B. pilot supervision.

C. helping learners.

Answer (C) is correct. (FAA-H-8083-9B Chap 8)
DISCUSSION: The use of standards, and measurement against standards, is key to helping learners.
Answer (A) is incorrect. The use of standards, and measurement against standards, is key to helping learners, not to ensuring aviation safety. **Answer (B) is incorrect.** The use of standards, and measurement against standards, is key to helping learners, not pilot supervision.

71. Which would more likely result in learners becoming frustrated?

A. Giving the learners meaningless praise.

B. Telling learners their work is unsatisfactory with no explanation.

C. An instructor freely admitting mistakes causing lack of trust.

Answer (B) is correct. (FAA-H-8083-9B Chap 8)
DISCUSSION: It does not help to tell learners they have made errors and not provide explanations. If a learner has made an earnest effort but is told that the work is unsatisfactory, with no other explanation, frustration occurs. Errors cannot be corrected if they are not identified, and if they are not identified, they will probably be perpetuated through faulty practice. On the other hand, if the learner is briefed on the errors and is told how to correct them, progress can be made.
Answer (A) is incorrect. While you are not providing effective instruction by offering a learner meaningless praise, you are also not creating frustration on the part of the learner. This instructional error offers many other negative consequences, though, and should be avoided. **Answer (C) is incorrect.** While failing to admit your own errors might frustrate a learner pilot, freely acknowledging your mistakes to the learner is more likely to increase rather than decrease trust on the part of the learner. You are also acting as a good example to the learner pilot by acknowledging and talking through your errors.

72. What is one method of keeping learners aware of their progress?

A. Learners should keep attempting a maneuver even if they are making the same mistake.

B. Repeating a demonstration, showing the learners the standard their performance must ultimately meet.

C. Learners are usually aware of their progress without instructor intervention.

Answer (B) is correct. (FAA-H-8083-9B Chap 3)
DISCUSSION: One way to make learners aware of their progress is to repeat a demonstration or example and to show them the standards their performance must ultimately meet.
Answer (A) is incorrect. They should be told as soon after the performance as possible and should not be allowed to practice mistakes. It is more difficult to unlearn a mistake, and then learn the skill correctly, than to learn correctly in the first place. **Answer (C) is incorrect.** Mistakes are not always apparent. A learner may know that something is wrong but not know how to correct it. In any case, the instructor provides a helpful and often critical function in making certain that the learners are aware of their progress.

3.7 Instructor Professionalism

73. Which statement is true regarding true professionalism as an instructor?

   A. Anything less than sincere performance destroys the effectiveness of the professional instructor.

   B. To achieve professionalism, actions and decisions must be limited to standard patterns and practices.

   C. A single definition of professionalism would encompass all of the qualifications and considerations which must be present.

Answer (A) is correct. (FAA-H-8083-9B Chap 8)
   DISCUSSION: Professionalism demands a code of ethics. Professionals must be true to themselves and to those they serve. Anything less than sincere performance will be detected by learners and immediately destroy instructor effectiveness.
   Answer (B) is incorrect. Professionalism requires good judgment. Professionals cannot limit their actions and decisions to standard patterns and practice. **Answer (C) is incorrect.** Professionalism is so multi-dimensional that no single definition can encompass all of the qualifications and considerations.

74. Aviation instructors should be constantly alert for ways to improve the services they provide to their learners, their effectiveness, and their

   A. appearance.

   B. qualifications.

   C. demeanor.

Answer (B) is correct. (FAA-H-8083-9B Chap 8)
   DISCUSSION: Professional aviation instructors must never become complacent or satisfied with their own qualifications and abilities. Aviation instructors should be constantly alert for ways to improve the services they provide to their learners, their effectiveness, and their qualifications.
   Answer (A) is incorrect. While an instructor's personal appearance is important to maintaining a professional image, aviation instructors should be constantly alert for ways to improve the services they provide to their learners, their effectiveness, and their qualifications. **Answer (C) is incorrect.** While an instructor's demeanor is important to maintaining a professional image, aviation instructors should be constantly alert for ways to improve the services they provide to their learners, their effectiveness, and their qualifications.

75. Learner confidence tends to be destroyed if instructors

   A. bluff whenever in doubt about some point.

   B. continually identify learner errors and failures.

   C. direct and control the learner's actions and behavior.

Answer (A) is correct. (FAA-H-8083-9B Chap 8)
   DISCUSSION: No one, including learners, expects an instructor to be perfect. An instructor can gain the respect of learners by honestly acknowledging mistakes. If the instructor tries to cover up or bluff, learners will be quick to sense it and lose their confidence in the instructor.
   Answer (B) is incorrect. Identifying the learner's errors and failures helps the learner to progress and gain confidence. **Answer (C) is incorrect.** Directing the learner's actions and behavior is a basic responsibility of the flight instructor.

76. Learners quickly become apathetic when they

   A. realize material is being withheld by the instructor.

   B. understand the objectives toward which they are working.

   C. recognize that the instructor is not adequately prepared.

Answer (C) is correct. (FAA-H-8083-9B Chap 2)
   DISCUSSION: Learners become apathetic when they recognize that the instructor has made inadequate preparations for the instruction being given or when the instruction appears to be deficient, contradictory, or insincere.
   Answer (A) is incorrect. Learners will lose respect for the instructor (not become apathetic) when they realize material is being withheld by the instructor. **Answer (B) is incorrect.** It is optimal that both the learner and instructor understand the objectives so that they may work cooperatively toward them.

77. Which is true regarding professionalism as an instructor?

   A. Professionalism demands a code of ethics.

   B. To achieve professionalism, actions and decisions must be limited to standard patterns and practices.

   C. Professionalism does not require extended training and preparation.

Answer (A) is correct. (FAA-H-8083-9B Chap 8)
   DISCUSSION: Professionalism demands a code of ethics. Professionals must be true to themselves and to those they serve. Anything less than a sincere performance will be detected by learners and immediately destroy instructor effectiveness.
   Answer (B) is incorrect. Professionalism requires good judgment. Professionals cannot limit their actions and decisions to standard patterns and practices. **Answer (C) is incorrect.** Professionalism is achieved only after extended training and preparation.

78. Which statement is true regarding the achievement of an adequate standard of performance?

    A. A flight instructor should devote major effort and attention to the continuous evaluation of learner performance.

    B. Flight instructors can affect a genuine improvement in the learner-instructor relationship by not strictly enforcing standards.

    C. Flight instructors fail to provide competent instruction when they permit learners to partially learn an important item of knowledge or skill.

Answer (C) is correct. (FAA-H-8083-9B Chap 8)
    DISCUSSION: Flight instructors fail to provide competent instruction when they permit their learners to partially learn an important item of knowledge or skill. More importantly, such deficiencies may in themselves allow hazardous inadequacies in the learner's later piloting performance.
    Answer (A) is incorrect. A flight instructor should devote major effort and attention to all areas of the teaching process, not only to the evaluation of learner performance. **Answer (B) is incorrect.** It is a fallacy to believe that a flight instructor can affect a genuine improvement in the learner-instructor relationship by not strictly enforcing standards. Reasonable standards strictly enforced are not resented by an earnest learner.

79. True performance as a professional is based on study and

    A. perseverance.

    B. research.

    C. attitude.

Answer (B) is correct. (FAA-H-8083-9B Chap 8)
    DISCUSSION: True performance as a professional is based on study and research.
    Answer (A) is incorrect. True performance as a professional is based on study and research, not perseverance. **Answer (C) is incorrect.** True performance as a professional is based on study and research, not attitude.

80. The professional relationship between the instructor and the learner should be based on what?

    A. A predetermined code of ethics.

    B. A mutual acknowledgment that both the learner and the instructor are working toward the same objective.

    C. The knowledge that the instructor will maintain the highest level of knowledge, training, and currency during training.

Answer (B) is correct. (FAA-H-8083-9B Chap 8)
    DISCUSSION: The professional relationship between the instructor and the learner should be based on a mutual acknowledgment that both the learner and the instructor are important to each other and that both are working toward the same objective.
    Answer (A) is incorrect. While professionalism demands a code of ethics, this is not what a professional relationship is based on. **Answer (C) is incorrect.** A relationship is two-sided and does not rest solely on the instructor to be knowledgeable and prepared. The professional relationship between the instructor and the learner should be based on a mutual acknowledgment that both the learner and the instructor are working toward the same objective.

STUDY UNIT FOUR

TEACHING METHODS

(10 pages of outline)

4.1 LECTURE METHOD

1. The lecture is used primarily for

    a. Introducing learners to new subject material,
    b. Summarizing ideas,
    c. Showing relationships between theory and practice, and
    d. Reemphasizing main points.

2. There are four types of lectures:

    a. The illustrated talk, in which the speaker relies heavily on visual aids to convey his or her ideas to the listeners;

    b. The briefing, in which the speaker presents a concise array of facts to the listeners, who do not expect elaboration or supporting material;

    c. The formal speech, in which the speaker's purpose is to inform, persuade, or entertain; and

    d. The teaching lecture, for which the instructor must plan and deliver an oral presentation in a manner that helps the learners reach the desired learning outcomes.

3. One advantage of a teaching lecture is that the instructor can present many ideas in a relatively short time. Facts and ideas that have been logically organized can be concisely presented in rapid sequence.

    a. Thus, a teaching lecture is the most economical of all teaching methods in terms of the time required to present a given amount of material.

4. One disadvantage of a teaching lecture is that the instructor does not receive a direct reaction (either words or actions) from the learners.

    a. Thus, the instructor must develop a keen perception for subtle responses from the class and must be able to interpret the meaning of these indirect reactions and adjust the lesson accordingly.

        1) These reactions could be in the form of facial expressions, manner of taking notes, and apparent interest or lack of interest in the lesson.

    b. The instructor must recognize that the lecture method is least useful for evaluating learner performance.

5.   The following four steps should be followed in preparing a lecture:

   a.   Establish the objective and desired outcomes,

   b.   Research the subject,

   c.   Organize the material, and

   d.   Plan productive classroom activities.

6.   The teaching lecture is best delivered extemporaneously–but from a written outline.

   a.   Because the exact words used to express an idea are chosen at the moment of delivery, the lecture can be personalized or suited to the moment more easily than one that is read or spoken from memory.

7.   In the teaching lecture, use simple rather than complex words whenever possible.

   a.   Picturesque slang and colloquialisms, if they suit the subject, can add variety and vividness to a teaching lecture.

   b.   Errors in grammar and use of vulgarisms detract from an instructor's dignity and reflect upon the intelligence of the learners.

4.2   COOPERATIVE OR GROUP LEARNING METHOD

1.   Cooperative group learning is an instructional strategy used to organize learners into small groups so that they can work together to maximize their own and each other's learning.

   a.   The most significant characteristic of group learning is that it continually requires active participation of the learner.

   b.   The main reason that learners are put in cooperative learning groups is so they can individually achieve greater success than if they were to study alone.

   c.   Learners in cooperative learning groups tend to interact and achieve in ways and at levels that are rarely found with other instructional strategies.

2.   Instructor planning is key to achieving meaningful learning.

   a.   Instructors must determine and outline clear lesson objectives and completion standards. Evidence of mastery of targeted content and skills must be stated to inform learners of the intended results.

3.   Instructors should organize small heterogeneous groups of learners who have different academic abilities, ethnic backgrounds, race, and gender.

   a.   The main advantage of heterogeneous groups is that learners tend to interact and achieve in ways and at levels that are rarely found with other instructional strategies.

   b.   Heterogeneous groups lead learners to learn to work together, to seek more support for opinions, to tolerate each other's viewpoints, and to consider viewpoints dissimilar to their own.

4.3 GUIDED DISCUSSION METHOD

1. Fundamentally, the guided discussion method of teaching is the reverse of the lecture method. The instructor uses questions to guide and stimulate discussion among learners. The instructor does not present new ideas.

2. In the guided discussion, learning is achieved through the skillful use of questions.

    a. Questions facilitate discussion, which in turn develops an understanding of the subject.

3. Questions used in a guided discussion can be broken into several types, each with its usefulness in the guided discussion:

    a. **Overhead** -- directed to the entire group to stimulate thought and response from each group member.

    b. **Rhetorical** -- also stimulates thought, but the instructor will answer it himself or herself. This is normally used in a lecture, not a guided discussion.

    c. **Direct** -- question addressed to an individual for a response.

    d. **Reverse** -- The instructor answers a learner's question by redirecting the question for that learner to provide the answer.

    e. **Relay** -- The reverse question is addressed to the entire group, not the individual.

4. In preparing questions, the instructor should remember that the purpose is to bring about discussion, not merely to get answers.

    a. Leadoff questions should be open-ended; i.e., they should start with "how" or "why."

    b. Avoid questions that begin with "what," "when," or "does" because they only require short, categorical answers such as "yes," "no," "green," "one," etc.

5. Each question, in order to be effective, should

    a. Have a specific purpose,
    b. Be clear in meaning,
    c. Contain a single idea,
    d. Stimulate thought,
    e. Require definite answers, and
    f. Relate to previously taught information.

6. When it appears the learners have adequately discussed the ideas that support a particular part of the lesson, the instructor should summarize what they have accomplished.

    a. This interim summary is one of the most effective tools available to the instructor.

        1) This summary can be made immediately after the discussion of each learning outcome.

        2) It consolidates what learners learned, emphasizes how much they know already, and points out any aspects they missed.

7. Unless the learners have some knowledge to exchange with each other, they cannot reach the desired learning outcomes.

    a. Learners without some background in a subject should not be asked to discuss that subject.

4.4 DEMONSTRATION/PERFORMANCE METHOD

1.   The demonstration/performance method is based on the principle that we learn by doing.

   a.   It is the most commonly used teaching method of flight instructors.

   b.   This is the ideal method for teaching a skill that requires practice, such as using a flight computer or performing crosswind landings.

2.   The demonstration/performance method of instruction has five essential steps:

   a.   **Explanation** -- the instructor must clearly explain the objectives of the particular lesson to the learner.

      1)   Additionally, the precise steps to be completed and the desired end result should be explained.

      2)   Learners should be given the opportunity to ask questions to understand the requirements fully.

      3)   EXAMPLE: An instructor describes the steps (power settings, flap configurations, etc.) needed to successfully perform a short-field landing. Using the Practical Test Standards (PTS)/Airman Certification Standards (ACS) as a guide, the instructor explains what the completion requirements are.

   b.   **Demonstration** -- the instructor must show the learner how to perform a skill.

      1)   Demonstrations not closely representing the explanation should be immediately acknowledged and explained so learners do not replicate improper techniques.

      2)   EXAMPLE: An instructor demonstrates and completes a short-field landing within the given tolerances.

   c.   **Learner performance** -- the learner must act and do.

      1)   To learn skills, learners must practice.

      2)   Through doing, learners learn to follow correct procedures and to reach established goals.

      3)   EXAMPLE: A learner practices short-field landings under the supervision of an instructor.

   d.   **Instructor supervision** -- the instructor coaches, as necessary, the learner's practice.

      1)   Both learner performance and instructor supervision are performed concurrently.

      2)   EXAMPLE: During a short-field landing by the learner, the instructor follows along on the controls during the demonstration of the maneuver and coaches as needed.

   e.   **Evaluation** -- the instructor judges the learner performance.

      1)   From the measurement of learner achievement, the instructor determines the effectiveness of the instruction.

      2)   EXAMPLE: During a post-flight debriefing, the instructor explains the learner's performance.

3. The **telling and doing technique** is a form of the demonstration/performance method of instruction that includes specific variations for flight instruction.

    a. This technique consists of performing several steps in proper order.

        1) Instructor tells -- instructor does/shows
        2) Learner tells -- instructor does/shows
        3) Learner tells -- learner does/shows
        4) Learner does/shows -- instructor evaluates

4. The telling and doing technique should be followed by the drill and practice method, which is based on the learning principle (Thorndike's Law) of exercise. Connections are strengthened with practice. It promotes learning through repetition because those things most often repeated are best remembered.

    a. The human mind rarely retains, evaluates, and applies new concepts or practices after a single exposure. Learners do not learn to perform crosswind landings during one instructional flight. They learn by applying what they have been told and shown.

    b. Every time practice occurs, learning continues.

4.5 PROBLEM-BASED LEARNING

1. Problem-Based Learning (PBL) describes a type of learning environment in which lessons are structured to confront learners with problems encountered in real life that force them to reach real-world solutions.

    a. A characteristic of PBL is that there is no single solution to the given problem.

        1) These types of "authentic" problems allow the learner to "make meaning" of the information based on past experience and personal interpretation.

    b. Benefits of PBL include helping the learner gain a deeper understanding of the information. Learners will also improve their ability to recall information in this type of learning.

    c. Effective PBL problems

        1) Relate to the real world, stimulating learner desire to solve them
        2) Require learners to make decisions
        3) Are open ended and not limited to one correct answer
        4) Are connected both to previously learned and new knowledge
        5) Reflect the lesson objective(s)
        6) Challenge the learner to think critically

    d. The three types of PBL instruction are **scenario-based training**, the **collaborative problem-solving method**, and the **case study method**.

2.   **Scenario-Based Training Method (SBT)**

   a.   SBT is a realistic situation that allows the learner to rehearse mentally for a situation and requires practical application of various pieces of knowledge.

   b.   SBT scenarios challenge learners to manage available resources, exercise sound judgment, and make timely decisions with the goal of reducing accidents. The overall learning objective is for the learner to be more prepared to make good decisions based on a variety of real-world situations.

   c.   SBT is a powerful tool because the future is unpredictable and there is no way to train a pilot for every combination of events that may happen in the future.

   d.   A good scenario

      1)   Is not a test,

      2)   Will not have only one correct answer,

      3)   Does not offer an obvious answer,

      4)   Should not promote errors,

      5)   Should promote situational awareness and opportunities for decision making, and

      6)   Usually tells a story that begins with a reason to fly, because a pilot's decisions will differ depending on the motivation to fly.

         a)   EXAMPLE: "A newly rated private pilot is heading out on a cross-country flight to see his son graduate from college. He has already gotten a late start because of poor weather at his home field. Halfway through his flight he encounters low visibility and increased turbulence. ATC and AWOS both confirm the weather is IMC at his destination airport and several others nearby. What will he do now?"

3.   **Collaborative Problem-Solving Method**

   a.   The collaborative problem-solving method combines collaboration with problem solving when the instructor provides a problem to a group of two or more people working together who then solve the problem.

   b.   This type of instruction is similar to SBT in that it includes open ended "what if" questions.

4.   **Case Study Method**

   a.   This method uses a written or oral account of a real-world situation that contains an educational message for the learner.

   b.   The instructor presents the case to the learners who then analyze it, reach conclusions, and offer possible solutions. Case studies require learners to use critical thinking skills.

   c.   A good resource for source material for the creation of case studies can be found at the National Transportation Safety Board's (NTSB) website.

      1)   The flight instructor will have the learner analyze the information and suggest possible reasons for the accident. This analysis will both reinforce positive decision-making skills and provide the learner with the consequences of improper decision making.

5.   Operational pitfalls are classic behavioral traps that can ensnare the unwary pilot. Pilots, particularly those with considerable experience, try to complete a flight as planned, please passengers, and meet schedules. This basic drive to demonstrate achievements can have an adverse effect on safety.

   a.   These tendencies ultimately may lead to practices that are dangerous and sometimes illegal.

      1)   Learners develop awareness and learn to avoid many of these operational pitfalls through effective ADM training. The scenarios and examples provided by instructors during ADM instruction should involve these pitfalls.

   b.   Lack of effective ADM training may lead to overconfidence, disregard for applicable regulations, or disregard of flight planning.

      1)   An overconfident pilot may not properly plan for minimum fuel reserves during preflight planning or may neglect the preflight planning altogether.

4.6   ELECTRONIC LEARNING (E-LEARNING)

1.   Electronic learning (e-learning) is defined as any type of education that involves an electronic component (e.g., Internet, stand-alone software, simulators, etc.).

   a.   Advantages of e-learning include less time spent on instruction and higher levels of mastery and retention.

      1)   E-learning often seems more enjoyable from the learner standpoint because it allows learners to feel as if they are in control of what they are learning and at a rate that is comfortable for them.

   b.   **Distance learning**, the use of electronic media to deliver instruction when the instructor and learner are separated, is another advantage of e-learning.

   c.   Improper or excessive use of e-learning should be avoided. It will always be the responsibility of the instructor to monitor and oversee learner progress and to intervene when necessary.

   d.   Limitations of e-learning include

      1)   Lack of peer interaction and personal feedback,
      2)   Lack of instructor control and oversight, and
      3)   Costs associated with equipment/programs.

2. **Computer-Assisted Learning (CAL)** is a specific form of e-learning that integrates a personal computer with multimedia software to create a training device.

   a. The major advantage of CAL is that it is interactive in that the computer will respond in different ways depending on learner input.

      1) Some of the more advanced CAL applications allow learners to progress through a series of interactive segments in which the presentation varies as a result of their responses.

         a) CAL responds quickly to learner input.

         b) When CAL is combined with multimedia, learners can control the pace of instruction.

   b. Other advantages of CAL include the fact that learners can progress at a rate that is comfortable for them and are often able to access material at locations and times convenient to them.

   c. Both initial and recurrent training can be accomplished with CAL.

      1) Aviation companies that incorporate CAL reduce the amount of manpower, and associated costs, needed to train employees.

   d. CAL can be used to test a learner's achievement, compare results with past performance, and indicate a learner's weak or strong areas.

      1) EXAMPLE: In preparing for an FAA knowledge test, learners may use test prep software to practice tests, evaluate scores, and review missed questions.

   e. CAL should be thought of and used as a reference aid, not as the sole means of accomplishing a training program.

   f. Instructors should remain actively involved with the learners by using close supervision, questions, exams, or guided discussions to constantly assess learner progress.

3. Simulation, role playing, and video gaming are other forms of e-learning that, while not thought of as primary means of instruction, are still valuable tools for aviation training.

   a. Many flight schools incorporate flight simulation into a learner's training regimen to have them practice scenarios that would otherwise be unwise or unsafe to perform in an actual aircraft.

   b. Depending on the type of device, use of flight simulators can be credited for actual flight time.

4.7 INTEGRATED METHOD OF FLIGHT INSTRUCTION

1. Integrated flight instruction is flight instruction during which learners are taught to perform flight maneuvers, both by outside visual references and by inside reference to flight instruments for the same operations. As an instructor, your primary goal is safety. You must develop the habit of constantly monitoring the learner's performance and the aircraft's performance while maintaining an appropriate scan for traffic.

    a. For this type of instruction to be fully effective, the use of instrument references should begin the first time each new maneuver is introduced.

    b. It is also important for the learner to learn the feel of the aircraft while conducting maneuvers.

        1) EXAMPLE: Determining, by feeling, that the aircraft is out of trim or in an unusual attitude.

    c. Learners who have been taught by means of integrated flight instruction will develop the habit of continuously monitoring both their own performance and that of the aircraft.

2. The habitual attention to instrument indications leads to improved pilot competency, operating efficiency of the aircraft, and an overall increase in safety.

    a. EXAMPLE: Landings will be improved due to more precise airspeed control, and average cruising flight performance increases by holding precise headings and altitudes.

    b. The ability to fly in instrument meteorological conditions (IMC) is not the objective of this type of primary training yet will provide a good foundation for later training for an instrument rating.

3. During the conduct of integrated flight instruction, you are responsible for collision avoidance while the learner is flying by simulated instruments, i.e., under the hood.

    a. You must guard against diverting your attention to the learner's performance for extended periods.

4. At the same time, you must be sure that the learner develops, from the first lesson, the habit of looking for other traffic when (s)he is not operating under simulated instrument conditions.

    a. Any observed tendency of a learner to enter a maneuver without clearing the area must be corrected immediately.

4.8 THE POSITIVE APPROACH IN FLIGHT INSTRUCTION

1.   In flight instruction, an effective positive approach will point out the pleasurable features of flying before the unpleasant possibilities are discussed.

2.   EXAMPLE of a positive first flight lesson:

    a.   A preflight inspection familiarizing the learner with the airplane and its components

    b.   A perfectly normal flight to a nearby airport and back

       1)   The instructor calls the learner's attention to how easy the trip was in comparison with other ways to travel and the fact that no critical incidents were encountered or expected.

3.   EXAMPLE of a negative first flight lesson:

    a.   An exhaustive indoctrination on preflight procedures with emphasis on the potential for disastrous mechanical failures in flight.

    b.   Instructions on the dangers of taxiing an airplane too fast.

    c.   A series of stalls with emphasis on the difficulties in recovering from them. (The side effect of this performance is likely to be airsickness.)

    d.   A series of simulated forced landings, stating that every pilot should always be prepared to cope with an engine failure.

4.9 TESTING THE LIMITS OF LEARNER KNOWLEDGE

1.   Presenting learners with problems that require them to make a decision to test the limits of their understanding is an effective way to help them acquire knowledge. Some examples may include the following:

    a.   Ask learners to recite or practice newly acquired knowledge.

    b.   Ask questions that probe learner understanding and prompt them to think about what they have learned in different ways.

    c.   Present opportunities for learners to apply what they know to solving problems or making decisions.

    d.   Demonstrate the benefits of understanding and being able to apply knowledge.

    e.   Introduce new topics that support the objectives of the lesson whenever possible.

2.   Fatigue is one of the most treacherous hazards to flight safety as it may not be apparent to a pilot until serious errors are made.

    a.   The amount of training any learner can absorb without incurring debilitating fatigue varies.

    b.   Complex operations tend to induce fatigue more rapidly than simpler procedures do, regardless of the physical effort involved.

    c.   Fatigue is the primary consideration in determining the length and frequency of flight instruction periods, and flight instruction should be continued only as long as the learner is alert, receptive to instruction, and performing at a level consistent with experience.

QUESTIONS AND ANSWER EXPLANATIONS: All of the Fundamentals of Instructing knowledge test questions chosen by the FAA for release as well as additional questions selected by Gleim relating to the material in the previous outlines are provided on the following pages. These questions have been organized into the same subunits as the outlines. To the immediate right of each question are the correct answer and answer explanations. You should cover these answers and answer explanations while responding to the questions. Refer to the general discussion in the Introduction on how to take the FAA knowledge test.

Remember that the questions from the FAA knowledge test bank have been reordered by topic and organized into a meaningful sequence. Also, the first line of the answer explanation gives the citation of the authoritative source for the answer.

QUESTIONS

4.1 Lecture Method

1. In the teaching process, which method of presentation is suitable for presenting new material, for summarizing ideas, and for showing relationships between theory and practice?

    A. Lecture method.

    B. Integrated instruction method.

    C. Demonstration/performance method.

Answer (A) is correct. (FAA-H-8083-9B Chap 5)
    DISCUSSION: The lecture is used primarily to introduce learners to new material. It is also valuable for summarizing ideas, showing relationships between theory and practice, and reemphasizing main points. The lecture is the most efficient teaching method in terms of time and scale, if not in other ways.
    Answer (B) is incorrect. The integrated method of flight instruction is designed to teach learners to perform maneuvers both by outside visual references and by reference to flight instruments. **Answer (C) is incorrect.** The demonstration/performance method is better suited to teaching a skill (i.e., flight instruction).

2. What is one advantage of a lecture?

    A. A lecture is effective in showing relationships between theory and practice.

    B. Excellent when additional research is required.

    C. Allows for maximum attainment of certain types of learning outcomes.

Answer (A) is correct. (FAA-H-8083-9B Chap 5)
    DISCUSSION: In a lecture, the instructor can present many ideas in a relatively short time. Facts and ideas that have been logically organized can be concisely presented in rapid sequence. Lecturing is unquestionably the most economical of all teaching methods in terms of time required to present a given amount of material.
    Answer (B) is incorrect. One advantage of the lecture is that it can be used to present information without requiring learners to do additional research. **Answer (C) is incorrect.** A disadvantage, not an advantage, of a lecture is that the lecture does not enable the instructor to estimate the learner's progress; thus, learning may not be maximized.

3. When an instructor is teaching in a lecture environment (s)he should

    A. maintain a consistent tone of voice and pace of speaking.

    B. try to use simple rather than complex words.

    C. move from the unknown to the known.

Answer (B) is correct. (FAA-H-8083-9B Chap 5)
    DISCUSSION: In the teaching lecture, simple rather than complex words should be used whenever possible. The instructor should not, however, use substandard English. Errors in grammar and vulgarisms detract from an instructor's dignity and insult the intelligence of the learners.
    Answer (A) is incorrect. Instructors should attempt to add life to the lecture by varying the tone of voice and pace of speaking. **Answer (C) is incorrect.** Instructors should always move from the known to the unknown.

4. During a teaching lecture, what would detract from an instructor's dignity and reflect upon the learner's intelligence?

    A. Use of figurative language.

    B. Errors in grammar and use of vulgarisms.

    C. Using picturesque slang and colloquialisms.

Answer (B) is correct. (FAA-H-8083-9B Chap 5)
    DISCUSSION: During a teaching lecture, errors in grammar and the use of vulgarisms detract from an instructor's dignity and reflect upon the learner's intelligence.
    Answer (A) is incorrect. Figurative language, when used properly, can add interest and color to a lecture. **Answer (C) is incorrect.** Picturesque slang and colloquialisms, if they suit the subject, can add variety and vividness to a lecture.

5. Which teaching method is most economical in terms of the time required to present a given amount of material?

   A.   Briefing.

   B.   Teaching lecture.

   C.   Demonstration/performance.

Answer (B) is correct. (FAA-H-8083-9B Chap 5)
   DISCUSSION: The teaching lecture is unquestionably the most economical of all teaching methods in terms of the time required to present a given amount of material. The instructor can concisely present many ideas that have been logically organized in rapid sequence.
   Answer (A) is incorrect. Although a briefing is a type of lecture, it is used to present a concise array of facts to the listeners who do not expect elaboration or supporting material. **Answer (C) is incorrect.** The demonstration/performance method is the least, not the most, economical in terms of time required to present a given amount of material.

6. Which is a true statement regarding the teaching lecture?

   A.   Delivering the lecture in an extemporaneous manner is not recommended.

   B.   Instructor receives direct feedback from learners which is easy to interpret.

   C.   Instructor must develop a keen perception for subtle responses and be able to interpret the meaning of these reactions.

Answer (C) is correct. (FAA-H-8083-9B Chap 5)
   DISCUSSION: In the teaching lecture, the instructor must develop a keen perception for subtle responses from the class (e.g., facial expressions, manner of taking notes, and apparent interest or lack of interest in the lesson), and must be able to interpret the meaning of these reactions and adjust the lesson accordingly.
   Answer (A) is incorrect. The lecture is best delivered extemporaneously but from a written outline. The lecture can thus be personalized to suit different audience moods. **Answer (B) is incorrect.** In the teaching lecture, the instructor's feedback is not as direct as other teaching methods and therefore is harder, not easier, to interpret.

7. The first step in preparing a lecture is to

   A.   research the subject.

   B.   develop the main ideas or key points.

   C.   establish the objective and desired outcome.

Answer (C) is correct. (FAA-H-8083-9B Chap 5)
   DISCUSSION: The following four steps, in order, should be used in preparing a lecture:

1. Establish the objectives and desired outcomes.
2. Research the subject.
3. Organize the material.
4. Plan productive classroom activities.

   Answer (A) is incorrect. Researching the subject is the second, not the first, step in preparing a lecture. **Answer (B) is incorrect.** Developing the main ideas or key points is the third, not the first, step in preparing a lecture.

8. The distinguishing characteristic of an informal lecture is the

   A.   use of visual aids.

   B.   learner's participation.

   C.   requirement for informal notes.

Answer (B) is correct. (FAA-H-8083-9B Chap 5)
   DISCUSSION: The distinguishing characteristic of an informal lecture is the active learner participation. A formal lecture does not include learner participation.
   Answer (A) is incorrect. Visual aids can be used in either the formal or informal lecture. **Answer (C) is incorrect.** The requirement for informal notes is not the distinguishing characteristic of an informal lecture. Notes may or may not be used in the formal or informal lecture.

9. An instructor can inspire active learner participation during informal lectures through the use of

   A.   questions.

   B.   visual aids.

   C.   encouragement.

Answer (A) is correct. (FAA-H-8083-9B Chap 5)
   DISCUSSION: An instructor can inspire learner participation during informal lectures through the use of questions. In this way, the learners are encouraged to make contributions that supplement the lecture.
   Answer (B) is incorrect. Visual aids emphasize and enhance the lecture but do not help get the learners actively involved. **Answer (C) is incorrect.** Encouragement aids learning in all situations, not just participation during lectures.

4.2 Cooperative or Group Learning Method

10. An instructional strategy which organizes learners into small groups so that they can work together to maximize their own and each other's learning is called

    A. workshop learning.

    B. heterogeneous group learning.

    C. cooperative or group learning.

Answer (C) is correct. (FAA-H-8083-9B Chap 5)
    DISCUSSION: Cooperative group learning is an instructional strategy that organizes learners into small groups so that they can work together to maximize their own and each other's learning.
    Answer (A) is incorrect. Workshop learning may take place individually; it does not necessarily involve groups.
    Answer (B) is incorrect. Cooperative group learning is an instructional strategy that organizes learners into small groups so that they can work together to maximize their own and each other's learning. Heterogeneous groups are recommended for effective cooperative group learning.

11. The most significant characteristic of group learning is that learners tend to

    A. actively participate in the learning process.

    B. allow the instructor to actively engage the group.

    C. passively participate in the learning process.

Answer (A) is correct. (FAA-H-8083-9B Chap 5)
    DISCUSSION: Many positive characteristics have been attributed to group learning, the most significant of which is that it continually requires active participation in the learning process by the learner.
    Answer (B) is incorrect. The most significant characteristic of group learning is that it continually requires active participation of the learner, not the instructor. The instructor must allow groups to work by themselves if the learners are to maximize each other's learning. **Answer (C) is incorrect.** Group learning requires active, not passive, participation of the learner.

12. The main reason that learners are put in cooperative learning groups is so they

    A. learn and help each other.

    B. can individually achieve greater success than if they were to study alone.

    C. learn that teamwork is essential if all members are to learn equally well.

Answer (B) is correct. (FAA-H-8083-9B Chap 5)
    DISCUSSION: The main reason that learners are put in cooperative learning groups is so they can individually achieve greater success than if they were to study alone.
    Answer (A) is incorrect. While learners do learn and help each other, the main reason that learners are put in cooperative learning groups is so they can individually achieve greater success than if they were to study alone. **Answer (C) is incorrect.** While teamwork is essential to group learning, it is unlikely that all members will learn equally well. Learners are put in cooperative learning groups so they can individually achieve greater success than if they were to study alone.

13. The main advantage(s) with heterogeneous groups are that learners tend to

    A. think for themselves since they are in a group of dissimilar learners.

    B. interact and achieve in ways and at levels that are rarely found with other instructional strategies.

    C. interact and achieve since they are in a group of similar learners.

Answer (B) is correct. (FAA-H-8083-9B Chap 5)
    DISCUSSION: Instructors should organize small heterogeneous groups of learners who have different academic abilities, ethnic backgrounds, race, and gender. The main advantage of heterogeneous groups is that learners tend to interact and achieve in ways and at levels that are rarely found with other instructional strategies.
    Answer (A) is incorrect. Heterogeneous groups lead learners to learn to work together, to seek more support for opinions, and to tolerate each other's viewpoints, not to think for themselves. **Answer (C) is incorrect.** Heterogeneous groups contain dissimilar, not similar, learners.

14. To achieve meaningful learning on the part of all in a group, instructors must

    A. interact with individuals in the group so as to ensure lesson objectives are being met.

    B. determine and outline clearly what the lesson objectives and completion standards are.

    C. consider the background abilities of learners.

Answer (B) is correct. (FAA-H-8083-9B Chap 5)
    DISCUSSION: To achieve meaningful learning, instructors must determine and outline clear lesson objectives and completion standards.
    Answer (A) is incorrect. Interaction with individuals in a group does not guarantee lesson objectives are being met. By providing clear lesson objectives and explaining the completion standards, meaningful learning can be achieved. **Answer (C) is incorrect.** The background of the learner is not a factor in group learning as all individuals will be sharing ideas and potentially new thoughts. To achieve meaningful learning, instructors must determine and outline clear lesson objectives and completion standards.

4.3 Guided Discussion Method

15. In a guided discussion, learning is achieved through the

    A. skillful use of questions.

    B. use of questions, each of which contains several ideas.

    C. use of reverse questions directed to the class as a whole.

Answer (A) is correct. (FAA-H-8083-9B Chap 5)
DISCUSSION: The guided discussion method relies on the learners to provide ideas, experiences, opinions, and information. The instructor guides the discussion by use of questions aimed at drawing out what the learners know. Thus, learning is achieved through the skillful use of questions.
    Answer (B) is incorrect. In a guided discussion, each question used should contain only one, not several, ideas.
    Answer (C) is incorrect. A relay, not reverse, question is redirected to the class as a whole.

16. A question directed to an entire group to stimulate thought and response from each group member is identified as

    A. Relay.

    B. Overhead.

    C. Rhetorical.

Answer (B) is correct. (FAA-H-8083-9B Chap 5)
DISCUSSION: In the guided discussion, learning is produced through skillful use of questions. To begin a guided discussion, the instructor should use an overhead question. This type of question is directed to the entire group to stimulate thought and response from each learner.
    Answer (A) is incorrect. A relay question responds to a learner's question by redirecting it back to the rest of the group.
    Answer (C) is incorrect. A rhetorical question is similar in nature to an overhead question, but the instructor answers the question. This is more commonly used in lecturing than in guided discussion.

17. In a guided discussion, leadoff questions should usually begin with

    A. why.

    B. what.

    C. when.

Answer (A) is correct. (FAA-H-8083-9B Chap 5)
DISCUSSION: In preparing questions, the instructor should remember that the purpose is to bring about discussion, not merely to get only short categorical answers (e.g., yes, no, one, etc.). Thus, leadoff questions should usually begin with "how" or "why."
    Answer (B) is incorrect. A question beginning with "what" usually requires only a short categorical answer and will not encourage a discussion. **Answer (C) is incorrect.** A question beginning with "when" usually requires a short answer and will not encourage a discussion.

18. To begin a guided discussion, instructors should ask a leadoff question that begins with

    A. who or when.

    B. what.

    C. why or how.

Answer (C) is correct. (FAA-H-8083-9B Chap 5)
DISCUSSION: Leadoff questions should usually begin with "how" or "why." For example, it is better to ask "Why does an aircraft normally require a longer takeoff run at Denver than at New Orleans?" than "Would you expect an aircraft to require a longer takeoff run at Denver or at New Orleans?" Learners can answer the second question by merely saying "Denver," but the first question is likely to start a discussion of air density, engine efficiency, and the effect of temperature on performance.
    Answer (A) is incorrect. Leadoff questions should contain "why" or "how," not "who" or "when." The former type of question creates a chance for deeper thought on the part of the learner, which can stimulate a more productive discussion. **Answer (B) is incorrect.** Leadoff questions should contain "why" or "how," not "what." The former type of question creates a chance for deeper thought on the part of the learner, which can stimulate a more productive discussion.

19. Which question would be best as a leadoff question for a guided discussion on the subject of torque?

  A. Does torque affect an airplane?

  B. How does torque affect an airplane?

  C. What effect does torque have on an airplane in a turn?

Answer (B) is correct. (FAA-H-8083-9B Chap 5)
  DISCUSSION: In preparing questions to lead off a guided discussion, the instructor should remember that the purpose is to bring about discussion, not merely answers. Avoid questions that require only short, categorical (i.e., yes or no) answers. Leadoff questions should usually begin with "how" or "why."
  Answer (A) is incorrect. A question beginning with "does" only requires a yes or no answer and will not encourage a discussion. **Answer (C) is incorrect.** A question beginning with "what" only requires a short, categorical answer and will not encourage a discussion.

20. When it appears learners have adequately discussed the ideas presented during a guided discussion, one of the most valuable tools an instructor can use is

  A. a session of verbal testing.

  B. a written test on the subject discussed.

  C. an interim summary of what the learners accomplished.

Answer (C) is correct. (FAA-H-8083-9B Chap 5)
  DISCUSSION: When it appears the learners have discussed the ideas that support a particular part of the lesson, the instructor should summarize what the learners have accomplished. This interim summary is one of the most effective tools available to the instructor in a guided discussion. To bring ideas together and help in transition, an interim summary should be made after the discussion of each desired learning outcome.
  Answer (A) is incorrect. A session of verbal testing goes against the intention of the guided discussion, where the instructor aims to "draw out" what the learners know in a structured but personable manner. **Answer (B) is incorrect.** A written test on the subject without an instructor summary would be testing learner opinions and experiences rather than facts.

21. Which statement about the guided discussion method of teaching is true?

  A. The lesson objective becomes apparent at the application level of learning.

  B. Learners without a background in the subject can also be included in the discussion.

  C. Unless the learners have some knowledge to exchange with each other, they cannot reach the desired learning outcomes.

Answer (C) is correct. (FAA-H-8083-9B Chap 5)
  DISCUSSION: Throughout the time the instructor prepares the learners for their discussion (e.g., early lectures, homework assignments), the learners should be made aware of the lesson objectives. This gives them the background for a fruitful guided discussion. Learners without some background in a subject should not be asked to discuss that subject.
  Answer (A) is incorrect. The lesson objective should be known while the learners are preparing for the guided discussion, or at least during the introduction, not afterward at the application level of learning. **Answer (B) is incorrect.** Learners with no background in the subject will not be able to contribute to an effective discussion.

4.4 Demonstration/Performance Method

22. The drill and practice method of instruction is based on which of the following learning principles (Thorndike's Laws)?

A. Primary.

B. Effect.

C. Exercise.

Answer (C) is correct. (FAA-H-8083-9B Chap 5)
DISCUSSION: The drill and practice method is based on Thorndike's Law of exercise, which holds that connections are strengthened with continued practice. It promotes learning through repetition because those things most often repeated are best remembered.
Answer (A) is incorrect. Primacy, the state of being first, is an important learning principle, but it is not the basis of the drill and practice method. Primacy often creates a strong, almost unshakable impression and underlies the reason an instructor must teach correctly the first time and the learner must learn correctly the first time. For example, a learner learns a faulty technique. Now the instructor must correct the bad habit and reteach the correct technique. Relearning is more difficult than initial learning. **Answer (B) is incorrect.** Effect is an important learning principle, but it is not the basis of the drill and practice method. All learning involves the formation of connections, and connections are strengthened or weakened according to the law of effect. Responses to a situation that are followed by satisfaction are strengthened, while responses followed by discomfort are weakened, either strengthening or weakening the connection of learning, respectively. Thus, learning is strengthened when accompanied by a pleasant or satisfying feeling and weakened when associated with an unpleasant feeling.

23. Which method of presentation is desirable for teaching a skill such as ground school lesson on the flight computer?

A. Lecture/application.

B. Presentation/practice.

C. Demonstration/performance.

Answer (C) is correct. (FAA-H-8083-9B Chap 5)
DISCUSSION: The demonstration/performance method of teaching is based on the principle that you learn by doing. Learners learn physical or mental skills best by actually performing them under supervision. Learning to use a flight computer is an ideal application of this teaching method.
Answer (A) is incorrect. The lecture method is not suitable to teach flight computer use because the lecture does not provide for learner participation and, as a consequence, lets the instructor do all the work. **Answer (B) is incorrect.** Presentation/practice is not a method of presentation.

24. Learners should be given the opportunity to ask questions during which step of the demonstration/ performance method?

A. Instructor supervision.

B. Evaluation.

C. Explanation.

Answer (C) is correct. (FAA-H-8083-9B Chap 5)
DISCUSSION: Learners should be given the opportunity to ask questions so as to understand the requirements fully during the explanation stage.
Answer (A) is incorrect. Instructor supervision occurs when the instructor watches learner performance and coaches as necessary. **Answer (B) is incorrect.** Evaluation occurs at the end of a task, and any questions relating to the desired outcome of the task should have already been asked.

25. What are the essential steps in the demonstration/performance method of teaching?

A. Demonstration, practice, and evaluation.

B. Demonstration, learner performance, and evaluation.

C. Explanation, demonstration, learner performance, instructor supervision, and evaluation.

Answer (C) is correct. (FAA-H-8083-9B Chap 5)
DISCUSSION: The demonstration/performance method of teaching is based on the principle that we learn by doing. Thus, it is used by flight instructors in teaching procedures and maneuvers. The five essential steps are

1. Explanation
2. Demonstration
3. Learner performance
4. Instructor supervision
5. Evaluation

Answer (A) is incorrect. The five, not three, essential steps in the demonstration/performance method of teaching are explanation, demonstration, learner performance (not practice), instructor supervision, and evaluation. **Answer (B) is incorrect.** The five, not three, essential steps in the demonstration/performance method of teaching are explanation, demonstration, learner performance, instructor supervision, and evaluation.

26. What is the last step in the demonstration/performance method?

    A. Summary.

    B. Evaluation.

    C. Learner performance.

Answer (B) is correct. (FAA-H-8083-9B Chap 5)

    DISCUSSION: The demonstration/performance method of teaching is based on the principle that we learn by doing. Thus, it is used by flight instructors in teaching procedures and maneuvers. The five essential steps are

1. Explanation
2. Demonstration
3. Learner performance
4. Instructor supervision
5. Evaluation

    Answer (A) is incorrect. Summary is not a step in the demonstration/performance method. **Answer (C) is incorrect.** Learner performance is the third, not last, step in the demonstration/performance method.

27. The basic demonstration/performance method of instruction consists of several steps in proper order. They are

    A. instructor tells--learner does; learner tells--learner does; learner does--instructor evaluates.

    B. instructor tells--instructor does; learner tells--instructor does; learner does--instructor evaluates.

    C. instructor tells--instructor does; learner tells--instructor does; learner tells--learner does; learner does--instructor evaluates.

Answer (C) is correct. (FAA-H-8083-9B Chap 9)

    DISCUSSION: The telling and doing technique of flight instruction (basically the demonstration/performance method) is very effective and valuable in teaching procedures and maneuvers. First, the instructor explains, then demonstrates. Then the learner performs, first by explaining as the instructor does, then by explaining and doing it him/herself while the instructor supervises. Finally, the instructor evaluates how the learner performs.

    Answer (A) is incorrect. It omits the first step, which is instructor tells--instructor does. The second step is learner tells--instructor does, not vice versa. **Answer (B) is incorrect.** It omits the third step of learner tells--learner does.

28. A post-flight debriefing is an example of which step in the demonstration/performance method?

    A. Instructor supervision.

    B. Evaluation.

    C. Explanation.

Answer (B) is correct. (FAA-H-8083-9B Chap 5)

    DISCUSSION: During a post-flight debriefing, the instructor explains the learner's performance. This is known as evaluation.

    Answer (A) is incorrect. Instructor supervision occurs when the instructor watches learner performance and coaches as necessary. **Answer (C) is incorrect.** Explanation is the first step in the demonstration/performance method and occurs before a task is performed. A post-flight debriefing would not occur during this step.

29. The telling and doing technique promotes learning because

    A. learners learn more by passively watching a task rather than engaging in it themselves.

    B. things that are most often repeated are best remembered.

    C. it consists of one simple step to remember; that of the instructor telling and doing.

Answer (B) is correct. (FAA-H-8083-9B Chap 9)

    DISCUSSION: The telling and doing technique promotes learning through repetition because those things most often repeated are best remembered.

    Answer (A) is incorrect. Learners do not learn better by passively watching. An engaged learner with proper supervision and who gets evaluated learns better; this happens in the telling and doing technique. **Answer (C) is incorrect.** The telling and doing technique consists of four steps, not one. They are as follows: instructor tells--instructor does/shows, learner tells--instructor does/shows, learner tells--learner does/shows, and learner does/shows--instructor evaluates. The telling and doing technique promotes learning through repetition because those things most often repeated are best remembered.

30. In the demonstration/performance method of instruction, which two separate actions are performed concurrently?

    A. Instructor explanation and demonstration.

    B. Learner performance and instructor supervision.

    C. Instructor explanation and learner demonstration.

Answer (B) is correct. (FAA-H-8083-9B Chap 5)

    DISCUSSION: In the demonstration/performance method of instruction, learner performance and instructor supervision are performed concurrently. As the learner practices, the instructor supervises and coaches as necessary.

    Answer (A) is incorrect. During the explanation phase, the instructor explains to the learner the actions they are to perform. This is accomplished during the preflight discussion. The demonstration is done in the airplane as the instructor shows the learner how to perform a maneuver. **Answer (C) is incorrect.** Instructor supervision, not explanation, and learner performance, not demonstration, are performed concurrently.

4.5 Problem-Based Learning

31. The overall learning objective of scenario-based training (SBT) is

    A. that learners will improve their ability to recall previously learned information.

    B. for the learner to be more prepared to make good decisions based on a variety of real world situations.

    C. to promote situational awareness and opportunities for decision making.

Answer (B) is correct. (FAA-H-8083-9B Chap 5)
    DISCUSSION: The overall learning objective of scenario-based training is for the learner to be more prepared to make good decisions based on a variety of real-world situations.
    Answer (A) is incorrect. A benefit of problem-based learning is that learners will improve their ability to recall information. **Answer (C) is incorrect.** A good scenario should promote situational awareness and opportunities for decision making.

32. The three types of problem-based learning instruction are:

    A. Scenario-based training, the collaborative problem-solving method, and the case study method.

    B. Scenario-based training, the critical thinking method, and the case study method.

    C. Scenario-based training, the cooperative problem-solving method, and the case study method.

Answer (A) is correct. (FAA-H-8083-9B Chap 5)
    DISCUSSION: The three types of PBL instruction are scenario-based training, the collaborative problem-solving method, and the case study method.
    Answer (B) is incorrect. The critical thinking method is not a type of problem-based learning. **Answer (C) is incorrect.** The collaborative problem-solving method, not the cooperative problem-solving method, is one of the three types of problem-based learning.

33. What is a characteristic of an effective scenario?

    A. It should not promote errors.

    B. It should be in the form of a test.

    C. It should include an account of a real world situation that contains an educational message.

Answer (A) is correct. (FAA-H-8083-9B Chap 5)
    DISCUSSION: A effective scenario should not promote errors.
    Answer (B) is incorrect. A good scenario should not be in the form of a test. **Answer (C) is incorrect.** An account of a real-world situation that contains an educational message is a case study method.

34. "A type of learning environment in which lessons are structured to confront learners with problems encountered in real life that force them to reach real world solutions" is the definition of what?

A. Problem-Based Learning.

B. Case Study Method.

C. Collaborative Problem-Solving Method.

Answer (A) is correct. (FAA-H-8083-9B Chap 5)
DISCUSSION: Problem-Based Learning (PBL) describes a type of learning environment in which lessons are structured to confront learners with problems encountered in real life that force them to reach real-world solutions.
Answer (B) is incorrect. A written or oral account of a real-world situation that contains an educational message is the definition of the case study method. **Answer (C) is incorrect.** The collaborative problem-solving method combines collaboration with problem solving when the instructor provides a problem to a group of two or more people working together who then solve the problem.

35. Which of the following is true concerning effective problem-based learning?

A. Effective PBL problems are open ended and not limited to one correct answer.

B. Effective PBL problems are only connected to previously learned information.

C. Effective PBL problems begin with a reason to fly because a pilot's decisions will differ depending on the motivation.

Answer (A) is correct. (FAA-H-8083-9B Chap 5)
DISCUSSION: Effective PBL problems are open ended and not limited to one correct answer.
Answer (B) is incorrect. Effective PBL problems are connected both to previously learned and new knowledge.
Answer (C) is incorrect. A good scenario usually tells a story that begins with a reason to fly because a pilot's decisions will differ depending on the motivation to fly.

36. A written or oral account of a real world situation that contains an educational message for the learner describes what?

A. The Collaborative Problem-Solving Method.

B. The Scenario-Based Training Method.

C. The Case Study Method.

Answer (C) is correct. (FAA-H-8083-9B Chap 5)
DISCUSSION: The case study method is a written or oral account of a real-world situation that contains an educational message for the learner.
Answer (A) is incorrect. The collaborative problem-solving method combines collaboration with problem solving when the instructor provides a problem to a group of two or more people working together who then solve the problem. **Answer (B) is incorrect.** The scenario-based training method is a realistic situation that allows the learner to rehearse mentally for a situation and requires practical application of various pieces of knowledge.

4.6 Electronic Learning (E-Learning)

37. Which statement is true regarding e-learning?

A. The instructor need not be actively involved with the learner when using a form of e-learning.

B. E-learning can be used as the sole means of instruction for a learner.

C. An advantage of e-learning includes higher levels of mastery and retention.

Answer (C) is correct. (FAA-H-8083-9B Chap 5)
DISCUSSION: Advantages of e-learning include less time spent on instruction and higher levels of mastery and retention.
Answer (A) is incorrect. Instructors should still be actively involved with learners using e-learning so as to monitor and oversee learner progress. **Answer (B) is incorrect.** E-learning, while having many advantages, should not be solely relied upon to ensure proper knowledge transfer has taken place.

38. What is one reason why flight schools use flight simulation in training learners?

A. All flight simulation time can be credited for actual flight time.

B. Learners can practice scenarios that would be unwise or unsafe to perform in real-life.

C. Instructor oversight is not required when learners perform maneuvers on a flight simulator.

Answer (B) is correct. (FAA-H-8083-9B Chap 5)
DISCUSSION: Many flight schools incorporate flight simulation into a learner's training regimen to have them practice scenarios that would otherwise be unwise or unsafe to perform in an actual aircraft.
Answer (A) is incorrect. Not all time spent on a simulator may be credited toward actual flight time. Credit toward logging actual flight time also depends on the type of device being used for simulation. **Answer (C) is incorrect.** Instructors should still be on hand to oversee all types of e-learning, including that of flight simulation.

39. The capabilities of the most recently developed computer-based training (CBT) systems allow the presentation to be customized based on the user's

A. responses.

B. previous experience.

C. wants and desires.

Answer (A) is correct. (FAA-H-8083-9B Chap 5)
DISCUSSION: Some of the more recent CBT applications allow learners to progress through a series of interactive segments where the presentation varies as a result of their responses.
Answer (B) is incorrect. The presentation can be varied based on the user's responses, not his or her previous experience. **Answer (C) is incorrect.** The presentation can be varied by the user's responses, not his or her wants and desires.

40. Which method allows a learner to control the pace of instruction?

A. Simulation.

B. Role playing games.

C. Computer-assisted learning (CAL).

Answer (C) is correct. (FAA-H-8083-9B Chap 5)
DISCUSSION: Real interactivity with CAL means the learner is fully engaged with the instruction by doing something meaningful, which makes the subject of study come alive. For example, the learner controls the pace of instruction, reviews previous material, jumps forward, and receives instant feedback.
Answer (A) is incorrect. Simulation gives the learner a stake in the outcome, placing him or her in the shoes of a character in a real-world scenario. This valuable teaching method does not offer a learner direct control over the pace of instruction. **Answer (B) is incorrect.** Role playing games give the learner a stake in the outcome, placing him or her in the shoes of a character in a real-world scenario. This valuable teaching method does not offer a learner direct control over the pace of instruction.

41. Among the many advantages of computer-based training (CBT) over other forms of instruction is that the computer can respond in different ways depending on the learner's

    A. age.

    B. mathematical ability.

    C. input.

Answer (C) is correct. (FAA-H-8083-9B Chap 5)
    DISCUSSION: The major advantage of CBT is that it is interactive—the computer responds in different ways, depending on learner input. When using CBT, the instructor should remain actively involved with the learners by using close supervision, questions, examinations, quizzes, or guided discussions on the subject matter to constantly assess learner progress.
    Answer (A) is incorrect. The learner's age is not a factor used by the computer to determine a response. **Answer (B) is incorrect.** The learner's mathematical ability is not a factor used by the computer to determine a response.

42. Which statement is true regarding e-learning?

    A. A major limitation of e-learning is that it can be conducted from alternate locations.

    B. Improper or excessive use of e-learning should be avoided.

    C. E-learning requires a learner to learn at the pace provided by the monitoring instructor.

Answer (B) is correct. (FAA-H-8083-9B Chap 5)
    DISCUSSION: Improper or excessive use of e-learning should be avoided. It will always be the responsibility of the instructor to monitor and oversee learner progress and to intervene when necessary.
    Answer (A) is incorrect. A major advantage, not limitation, of e-learning is that users can be in alternate locations from an instructor. This is termed distance learning. **Answer (C) is incorrect.** E-learning allows learners to feel as if they are in control of what they are learning and at a rate that is comfortable for them, not at a pace required by an instructor.

43. Which statement is true regarding Computer-Assisted Learning, or CAL?

    A. CAL will not be able to indicate a learner's weak or strong areas.

    B. CAL is used by flight schools so learners can practice scenarios that are unwise to perform in an actual aircraft.

    C. The learner controls the pace and content of instruction.

Answer (C) is correct. (FAA-H-8083-9B Chap 5)
    DISCUSSION: With CAL, the learner controls the pace and content of the instruction.
    Answer (A) is incorrect. Many CAL programs can and will indicate a learner's weak or strong areas. An example of this is software used in preparing for an FAA knowledge test. **Answer (B) is incorrect.** Flight simulation, not CAL, is used to practice scenarios that are unwise or unsafe to perform in an actual aircraft.

44. The major advantage of Computer-Assisted Learning (CAL) is that it is interactive; the computer will respond in different ways depending on learner

    A. background.

    B. input.

    C. training.

Answer (B) is correct. (FAA-H-8083-9B Chap 5)
    DISCUSSION: The major advantage of CAL is that it is interactive in that the computer will respond in different ways depending on learner input.
    Answer (A) is incorrect. The computer responds based on the learner's input, not background. The choice of CAL training may depend on the learner's academic or experimental background. **Answer (C) is incorrect.** The computer responds based on the learner's input, not training.

4.7   Integrated Method of Flight Instruction

45. Which of the following is the primary objective of integrated flight instruction?

   A. To develop the learner's habit of constantly monitoring both his or her performance and the aircraft's performance.

   B. To develop a proper scan while relating the instrument indications to the horizon.

   C. To develop multitasking skills.

Answer (A) is correct. (FAA-H-8083-9B Chap 9)
DISCUSSION: It is important for the learner to establish the habit of observing and relying on flight instruments from the beginning of flight training. It is equally important for the learner to learn the feel of the airplane while conducting maneuvers, such as being able to feel when the airplane is out of trim or in a nose-high or nose-low attitude. Learners who have been required to perform all normal flight maneuvers by reference to instruments, as well as by outside references, develop from the start the habit of continuously monitoring their own and the aircraft's performance.
Answer (B) is incorrect. The primary objective of integrated flight instruction is to develop the habit of constantly monitoring the pilot's own performance and the aircraft's performance. **Answer (C) is incorrect.** The primary objective of integrated flight instruction is to develop the habit of constantly monitoring the pilot's own performance and the aircraft's performance.

46. During integrated flight instruction, the instructor must be sure the learner

   A. develops the habit of looking for other traffic.

   B. is able to control the aircraft for extended periods under IMC.

   C. can depend on the flight instruments when maneuvering by outside references.

Answer (A) is correct. (FAA-H-8083-9B Chap 9)
DISCUSSION: If learners are allowed to believe that the instructor assumes all responsibility for avoiding other traffic, they cannot develop the habit of keeping a constant watch, which is essential to safety. Any observed tendency of a learner to enter flight maneuvers without first making a careful check for other possible air traffic must be corrected immediately.
Answer (B) is incorrect. The ability to control the aircraft for extended periods under IMC is not the objective of integrated flight instruction. **Answer (C) is incorrect.** The instructor must be sure not to let the learner focus his attention on the instruments at the expense of looking for other traffic.

47. What is integrated flight instruction?

   A. Flight instruction during which the learner learns by sole reference to the flight instruments.

   B. Flight instruction that combines the use of flight simulation with actual flight.

   C. Flight instruction during which learners are taught to perform flight maneuvers by outside visual references and reference to flight instruments.

Answer (C) is correct. (FAA-H-8083-9B Chap 9)
DISCUSSION: Integrated flight instruction is flight instruction during which learners are taught to perform flight maneuvers, both by outside visual references and by inside reference to flight instruments for the same operations.
Answer (A) is incorrect. Integrated flight instruction is not accomplished by sole reference to the flight instruments. It also includes outside visual references for the same operations or maneuvers. **Answer (B) is incorrect.** Simulation, not integrated flight instruction, uses flight simulators in conjunction with actual flight to train learners.

48. For integrated flight instruction to be fully effective, what must take place?

   A. A learner must rely on the instructor for collision avoidance.

   B. The use of instrument references should begin the first time each new maneuver is introduced.

   C. Learners must already have learned the feel of the aircraft while conducting maneuvers.

Answer (B) is correct. (FAA-H-8083-9B Chap 9)
DISCUSSION: For integrated flight instruction to be fully effective, the use of instrument references should begin the first time each new maneuver is introduced.
Answer (A) is incorrect. A learner should develop the habit of scanning for other traffic from the first flight lesson. The learner will rely on the instructor to ensure adequate collision avoidance while flying by simulated instruments, but this is not a factor in effectively conducting integrated flight instruction. **Answer (C) is incorrect.** Feel for the aircraft during a maneuver is learned during integrated flight training and is not necessary for effective integrated flight training.

49. Foremost among the objectives of integrated flight instruction is

A. encouraging habit patterns for observing and referencing the flight instruments.

B. developing the learner's ability to operate in IMC.

C. ensuring the learner is completely dependent on the instruments during VFR flight.

Answer (A) is correct. (FAA-H-8083-9B Chap 9)
DISCUSSION: The early establishment of proper habits of instrument cross-check, instrument interpretation, and aircraft control are highly useful to the learner. The habitual attention to instrument indications leads to improved landings because of more precise airspeed control. Effective use of instruments also results in superior cross-country navigation, better coordination of the aircraft, and generally a better overall pilot competency level.
Answer (B) is incorrect. The habits formed during integrated flight instruction provide a firm foundation for later training for an instrument rating but are not intended to provide the skills required to operate in IMC. **Answer (C) is incorrect.** Integrated flight instruction ensures the learner is able to operate the aircraft using visual references as well as the flight instruments.

50. Which of the following statements about integrated flight instruction is true?

A. Devote certain training lessons entirely to instrument or visual flight.

B. Instruction in the control of an aircraft by outside visual references is integrated with instruction in the use of flight instrument indications for the same operations.

C. Introduce maneuvers using visual references, then repeat the maneuvers using only the instruments.

Answer (B) is correct. (FAA-H-8083-9B Chap 9)
DISCUSSION: Integrated flight instruction is flight instruction during which learners are taught to perform flight maneuvers both by outside visual references and by reference to flight instruments. For this type of instruction to be fully effective, the use of instrument references should begin the first time each new maneuver is introduced. No distinction in the pilot's operation of the flight controls is permitted, regardless of whether outside references or instrument indications are used for the performance of the maneuver. When this training technique is used, instruction in the control of an aircraft by outside visual references is integrated with instruction in the use of flight instrument indications for the same operations.
Answer (A) is incorrect. In integrated flight instruction, learners must learn to use both the visual references and flight instruments simultaneously. **Answer (C) is incorrect.** In integrated flight instruction, learners must learn to use both the visual references and flight instruments simultaneously.

51. What is a benefit of learning to habitually give attention to instrument indications during primary training?

A. Cruising performance will increase by holding precise headings and altitudes.

B. Learners will be completely prepared for their instrument checkride.

C. Learners will be more likely to watch for other traffic.

Answer (A) is correct. (FAA-H-8083-9B Chap 9)
DISCUSSION: A benefit of habitually giving attention to instrument indications is better cruising performance because a learner will hold more precise headings and altitudes.
Answer (B) is incorrect. Additional training on the specifics of flying solely by reference to flight instruments will be needed. Giving habitual attention to instrument indications during primary flight training will, however, provide a basis for future training for an instrument rating. **Answer (C) is incorrect.** Instructors must be careful that learners develop the habit of looking for other traffic when operating by reference to instruments, even during VFR conditions. It can actually be a disadvantage if a learner focuses solely on an aircraft's instruments during primary flight training.

4.8   The Positive Approach in Flight Instruction

52. Which is an example of a positive approach in the first flight lesson of a learner with no previous aviation experience?

    A. Conducting a thorough preflight.

    B. A normal flight to a nearby airport and return.

    C. Instruction in the care which must be taken when taxiing an airplane.

Answer (B) is correct. (FAA-H-8083-9B Chap 8)
    DISCUSSION: A normal flight to a nearby airport and back shows the learner some of the pleasant aspects of aviation. Such an introductory lesson leaves a positive impression in the new learner's mind. Positive teaching results in positive learning.
    Answer (A) is incorrect. In the first flight lesson of a learner with no aviation experience, conducting a thorough, exhaustive preflight is an example of a negative, not a positive, approach. The learner may question whether learning to fly is a good idea or not. **Answer (C) is incorrect.** In the first flight lesson of a learner with no aviation experience, instruction in the care that must be taken when taxiing an airplane is an example of a negative, not a positive, approach. The learner may question whether learning to fly is a good idea or not.

53. Which statement is true regarding positive or negative approaches in aviation instructional techniques?

    A. A learner with normal abilities should not be affected by an instructor who emphasizes emergency procedures early in training.

    B. A positive approach, to be effective, will point out the pleasurable features of aviation before the unpleasant possibilities are discussed.

    C. The introduction of emergency procedures before the learner is acquainted with normal operations is likely to be neither discouraging nor affect learning.

Answer (B) is correct. (FAA-H-8083-9B Chap 8)
    DISCUSSION: Flight instructor success depends, in large measure, on the ability to frame instructions so that learners develop a positive image of flying. A positive approach, to be effective, will point out the pleasurable features of aviation before the unpleasant possibilities are discussed. A negative approach generally results in negative learning because the learner's perceptual process would be adversely affected by fear.
    Answer (A) is incorrect. An instructor who emphasizes emergency procedures early in training will most likely have a negative effect on the learning process regardless of a learner's abilities. The learner new to aviation is still quite impressionable. **Answer (C) is incorrect.** The introduction of emergency procedures before the learner is acquainted with normal operations most likely will be discouraging or threatening and will adversely affect learning.

4.9   Testing the Limits of Learner Knowledge

54. Which of the following is the primary consideration when determining the length and frequency of flight instruction periods?

    A. Inattention.

    B. Fatigue.

    C. Distractibility.

Answer (B) is correct. (FAA-H-8083-9B Chap 2)
    DISCUSSION: Fatigue is the primary consideration in determining the length and frequency of flight instruction periods. Flight instruction should be continued only as long as the learner is alert, receptive to instruction, and performing at a level consistent with experience.
    Answer (A) is incorrect. Inattention is one of the symptoms of fatigue; it is not the same as fatigue. **Answer (C) is incorrect.** Distractibility is one of the symptoms of fatigue; it is not the same as fatigue.

55. Asking learners about problems or decisions that test the limits of their knowledge is

    A. ineffective, only promoting rote level learning.

    B. beneficial to gauge understanding and determines that the learner is able to apply the knowledge.

    C. an effective method to help learners acquire knowledge.

Answer (C) is correct. (FAA-H-8083-9B Chap 3)
    DISCUSSION: To help learners acquire knowledge, the instructor should ask learners questions about problems or decisions that test the limits of their knowledge.
    Answer (A) is incorrect. For learners to fully understand a task or concept, instructors must push the limits of the learners' knowledge. This technique encourages learning beyond merely the rote level of learning. **Answer (B) is incorrect.** Asking questions about problems or decisions to test the limits of a learner's knowledge is beneficial to gauge understanding but is not a determination that the learner has the ability to apply the knowledge.

STUDY UNIT FIVE

PLANNING INSTRUCTIONAL ACTIVITY

(8 pages of outline)

5.1 COURSE DEVELOPMENT

1. A course of training is a complete series of studies leading to attainment of a goal, such as a certificate of completion, graduation, etc.

2. A determination of objectives and standards is necessary before any important instruction can be presented. Any instructional activity must be competently planned and organized if it is to achieve the desired learning outcomes.

   a. The broad overall objective of any pilot training is to qualify the learner to be a competent, efficient, safe pilot.

   b. There are two types of objectives in aviation: performance-based objectives and decision-based objectives.

3. **Performance-based objectives** are used to set measurable, reasonable standards that describe the required learner performance.

   a. They provide a way of stating what performance level is desired of a learner before progressing to the next stage of instruction.

   b. Written objectives are clear, measurable, and repeatable.

   c. These objectives consist of three elements: description of the skill or behavior, conditions, and criteria.

      1) **Description of the skill or behavior:** desired outcome of training stated in concrete terms that can be measured.

         a) EXAMPLE: "The learner should be able to repeat the steps to a proper engine start."

      2) **Conditions:** used to explain the rules under which the skill or behavior is to be demonstrated.

         a) EXAMPLE: "Using an approved airplane checklist and referencing the Pilot's Operating Handbook (POH), perform a normal engine start."

      3) **Criteria:** the standards used to measure the accomplishment of the objective. The performance-based objectives must fit the desired outcome for a particular lesson, and the criteria should be stated so that there is no question whether the objective has been met.

         a) EXAMPLE: "Using an approved airplane checklist and referencing the POH, perform a normal engine start. Engine power should be reduced to below 1000 RPM after the engine is engaged, and fuel pump adjustments should be made as required in the POH."

   d. Practical Test Standards (PTS)/Airman Certification Standards (ACS) provide specific performance-based objectives based on the standards that must be met for the issuance of a particular aviation certificate or rating.

4. **Decision-based objectives** allow for a more dynamic training environment and are designed to develop pilot judgment and ADM skills.

    a. Combined with traditional task and maneuver training, decision-based objectives facilitate a higher level of learning and application and thus reduce improper pilot decision making and increase overall flight safety.

5. Instructors must identify the blocks of learning that make up the necessary parts of the total objective.

    a. You must ensure that each block of learning identified is truly an integral part of the overall objective.

        1) Extraneous blocks of instruction are expensive frills, especially in flight instruction, and detract from the completion of the final objective.

    b. The blocks of learning must be developed and arranged in their proper sequence.

        1) In this way, a learner can master the segments of the overall pilot performance requirements individually and can progressively combine these with other related segments until their sum meets the final objective.

    c. Learners will master segments of blocks individually and can progressively combine these with other related segments until the overall training objectives are reached.

        1) EXAMPLE: Flight training may be divided into the following major blocks: achievement of the knowledge and skills necessary for solo flight, achievement of the knowledge and skills necessary for solo cross-country flight, and achievement of the knowledge and skills appropriate for achieving a private pilot certificate.

    d. Using this approach provides the learner with a boost of self-confidence as each block is successfully completed.

6. A training syllabus is an abstract or digest of the course of training. It consists of the blocks of learning to be completed in the most efficient order.

    a. All syllabi should stress well-defined objectives and standards for each lesson.

    b. The order of training can and should be altered when necessary to suit the progress of the learner and the demands of special circumstances, such as weather conditions.

        1) However, it is often preferable to skip to a completely different part of the syllabus when the conduct of a scheduled lesson is impossible, rather than proceeding to the next lesson, which may be predicated completely on skills to be developed during the lesson being postponed.

        2) EXAMPLE: If a learner is having a difficult time with normal approach and landings, it might be wise for the instructor to skip the next proposed lesson on short field landings and instead review another area of training. This would enable the learner to gain confidence and reinforce skills needed to perform normal landings.

5.2 ORGANIZATION OF TRAINING MATERIAL

1. Once a determination of objectives and standards has been made, an instructor must formulate a plan of action to lead learners through the course in a logical manner toward the desired goal. One effective way to organize a lesson is by introduction, development, and conclusion.

   a. The **introduction** sets the stage for everything to come. The introduction can be divided into three subparts:

      1) **Attention** -- The instructor must gain each learner's attention and focus it on the subject.

         a) EXAMPLE: Stories, video clips, questions, or jokes can be used to gain learner attention.

      2) **Motivation** -- The instructor should offer specific reasons why they need to learn the material. This motivation should appeal to each learner personally and accentuate the desire to learn.

         a) EXAMPLE: The instructor may talk about where the knowledge in the lesson was or will be applied in real life or remind learners of an upcoming test on the material.

      3) **Overview** -- Each lesson introduction should contain an overview that tells the learner(s) what is to be covered during the period.

         a) The overview is presented as a clear, concise presentation of the objective.

   b. The **development** is the main part of the lesson during which the instructor organizes the explanations and demonstrations in a manner that helps the learners achieve the desired learning outcomes.

      1) The instructor must logically organize the material to show the relationships of the main points to each other. This is done by developing the main points in one of the following ways:

         a) Chronologically; from past to present or present to past

         b) From simple to complex

         c) From known to unknown (i.e., using a learner's previous experiences and knowledge to acquire new concepts)

         d) From most frequently used (most familiar) to least frequently used

   c. The **conclusion** retraces the important elements of the lesson and relates them to the objective.

      1) This reinforces learning and improves retention of what has been learned.

      2) New ideas should not be introduced in the conclusion because doing so at this point in the lesson will only confuse learners.

5.3 LESSON PLAN

1. Each lesson of the training syllabus includes an objective, content, and completion standards.

2. A lesson plan is an organized outline that is developed for a single instructional period.

   a. A properly constructed lesson plan will provide an outline that tells the instructor what to do, in what order to do it, and what teaching procedure to use.

   b. The lesson plan must be appropriate for the particular learner.

      1) Standard lesson plans may not be effective for learners requiring a different approach.

      2) Therefore, the main concern in developing a lesson plan is the learner.

3. A lesson plan should be prepared in writing for each instructional period to show what specific knowledge and/or skills will be taught during a lesson.

   a. A so-called mental outline is not a lesson plan.

   b. Another instructor should be able to take the lesson plan and know what to do in conducting the same period of instruction.

4. Lesson plans are designed to ensure that each learner receives the best possible instruction under existing circumstances. Lesson plans help instructors keep a constant check on their own activity, as well as that of learners.

5. Steps to ensuring a quality lesson:

   a. Determine the objective of the lesson,
   b. Instructor research,
   c. Determine the method of instruction,
   d. Identify the lesson planning format,
   e. Decide how to organize the lesson and supporting material,
   f. Assemble training aids, and
   g. Write the lesson plan outline.

6. A characteristic of a well-planned lesson is that it should contain new material that is related to the lesson previously presented.

   a. In flight training, a short review of earlier lessons is usually necessary.

   b. Each lesson should also fall logically into the four steps of the teaching process: preparation, presentation, application, and review/evaluation.

   c. An adequate lesson plan, when properly developed, should

      1) Assure a wise selection of material and the elimination of unimportant details.

      2) Make certain that due consideration is given to each part of the lesson.

      3) Aid the instructor in presenting the material in a suitable sequence for efficient learning.

      4) Provide an outline of the teaching procedure to be used.

      5) Serve as a means of relating the lesson to the objectives of the course of training.

      6) Give the inexperienced instructor confidence.

      7) Promote uniformity of instruction regardless of the instructor or the date on which the lesson is given.

7. Each lesson plan should contain the following items: lesson objective, content, schedule, equipment, instructor's actions, learner's actions, and completion standards. The illustration below is an example.

LESSON	Ground reference maneuvers	LEARNER		DATE	/ /

OBJECTIVE
To develop the learner's skill in planning and following a pattern over the ground compensating for wind drift at varying angles.

CONTENT
Use of ground references to control path
Observation and control of wind effect
Control of airplane attitude, altitude, and heading

SCHEDULE
Preflight discussion   :10
Instructor demonstrations   :25
Learner practice   :45
Postflight critique   :10

EQUIPMENT
Chalkboard for preflight discussion
IFR visor for maneuvers reviewed

INSTRUCTOR'S ACTIONS
Preflight—discuss lesson objective. Diagram "S" turns, eight along a road, and rectangular course on a chalkboard.

Inflight—demonstrate elements.
Demonstrate following a road, "S" turns, eights along a road, and rectangular course, coach learner practice.

Postflight—critique learner performance and make study assignment.

LEARNER'S ACTIONS
Preflight—discuss lesson objective and resolve questions.

Inflight—review previous maneuvers including power-off stalls and flight at minimum controllable airspeed. Perform each new maneuver as directed.

Postflight—ask pertinent questions.

COMPLETION STANDARDS
Learner should demonstrate competency in maintaining orientation, airspeed within 10 knots, altitude within 100 feet, and headings within 10 degrees, and in making proper correction for wind drift.

8.   Figure 1A below is an example of a ground lesson plan.

LESSON PLAN

Introduction (3 minutes)

A _____   Relate aircraft accident in which a multi-engine ran off the end of the runway. This could have been avoided by correctly computing the landing distance. Relate similar personal experience of the same type of mishap.

B _____   Tell learners how landing distance can affect them (any aircraft, plus future application).

C _____   Explain what will be learned. Explain how the lesson will proceed. Define landing distance and explain the normal landing distance chart. Then, demonstrate how to solve for landing distance. The learners will practice the procedure at least once with supervision and at least once with as little help as possible. Next, the learners will be evaluated according to the standards. Finally, the lesson will conclude with questions and answers, followed by a brief summary.

Body (29 minutes)

D _____   Define landing distance. Explain the normal landing distance chart to include the scale and interpolation. Ensure learners can see demonstrations and encourage questions. Demonstrate the procedure using °C with a headwind and °F with a tailwind. Show the normal landing distance chart with given data in the following order:
1. temperature
2. pressure altitude
3. gross weight
4. headwind-tailwind component
5. read ground roll distance from graph

E _____   Review standards. Hand out chart and practice problems. Remind learners to use a pencil, to make small tick marks, and to work as accurately as possible. Explain that they should follow the procedure on the chart to work the practice problems. Encourage learners to ask questions. Check progress of each learner continually so they develop skill proficiency within acceptable standards. Reteach any area(s) of difficulty to the class as they go along.

F _____   Review procedure again from the chart. Reemphasize standards of acceptable performance including time available. Prepare area for evaluation by removing the task step chart and practice problem sheets, and by handing out the evaluation problems. Ask learners to work the three problems according to conditions and standards specified. Terminate evaluation after 6 minutes. Evaluate each learner's performance and tactfully reveal results. Record results for use in reteaching any area(s) of difficulty in the summary.

Conclusion (3 minutes)

G _____   Review lessons with emphasis on any weak area(s).

H _____   Remind learners that landing distance will be an important consideration in any aircraft they fly.

I _____   Advise learners that this lesson will be used as a starting point for the next lesson. Assign study materials for the next lesson.

Figure 1A. Lesson Plan (not in supplement).

Figure 1A above is a sample ground lesson plan in contrast to the sample flight lesson plan on the previous page.

NOTE: Figure 1A has been omitted from the testing supplement since the one released by the FAA in June 2016. We left it in our materials because we believe it will help you to better understand ground lesson plans.

9. The objectives of each lesson, content to support these objectives, and completion standards should be clearly stated.

    a. The objective is the reason for the lesson -- what the learner is expected to know or be able to do at the end of the lesson.

    b. Keeping the learner informed of lesson objectives and completion standards minimizes the learner's insecurity.

10. When planning time for learner performance, a primary consideration is the length of the practice session.

    a. A beginning learner reaches a point where additional practice is not only unproductive but may be harmful. As a learner gains experience, longer periods of practice become profitable.

        1) **Overlearning** is the continued study of a skill after initial proficiency has been achieved. Practice proceeds beyond the point at which the act can be performed with the required degree of excellence.

        2) One common effect of overlearning is the development of automated routines rather than development of concept application skills.

    b. As a learner gains experience, longer periods of practice are profitable.

11. A blank lesson plan is provided on page 413 so you may make copies for your use.

5.4 INSTRUCTIONAL AIDS AND TRAINING TECHNOLOGY

1. Instructional aids are useful tools that emphasize, support, supplement, or reinforce the key points or concepts in a lesson and assist an instructor in the teaching-learning process.

    a. Instructional aids include models, chalkboards, charts, and projected material (e.g., videotapes, movies, slides, etc.).

2. Reasons for using instructional aids include the following:

    a. Helping learners remember important information,

    b. Gaining and holding learner attention,

    c. Clarifying the relationship between material objects and concepts, and

    d. Giving support when topics involve the use of more senses (i.e., sight, hearing, or a combination of others).

3. The following four-step procedure should be used to determine if and when instructional aids are necessary:

    a. Clearly establish the lesson objective, being certain what must be communicated.

    b. Gather the necessary data by researching for support material.

    c. Organize the material into an outline or lesson plan. The outline should include all key points to be presented.

    d. Finally, determine what ideas should be supported with instructional aids.

        1) They should be compatible with the learning outcomes to be achieved.
        2) They should be designed to cover the key points in a lesson.

4. Instructional aids used in the teaching/learning process should not be used as a crutch by the instructor.

5. Interactive video is a type of computer software that responds quickly to certain choices and commands by the user.

    a. The questions or directions are programmed using a branching technique, which provides several possible courses of action for the user to choose in order to move from one sequence to another.

QUESTIONS AND ANSWER EXPLANATIONS: All of the Fundamentals of Instructing knowledge test questions chosen by the FAA for release as well as additional questions selected by Gleim relating to the material in the previous outlines are provided on the following pages. These questions have been organized into the same subunits as the outlines. To the immediate right of each question are the correct answer and answer explanations. You should cover these answers and answer explanations while responding to the questions. Refer to the general discussion in the Introduction on how to take the FAA knowledge test.

Remember that the questions from the FAA knowledge test bank have been reordered by topic and organized into a meaningful sequence. Also, the first line of the answer explanation gives the citation of the authoritative source for the answer.

QUESTIONS

5.1 Course Development

1. In planning any instructional activity, the first consideration should be to

A. determine the overall objectives and standards.

B. establish common ground between the instructor and learner.

C. identify the blocks of learning which make up the overall objective.

Answer (A) is correct. *(FAA-H-8083-9B Chap 7)*
DISCUSSION: The first step in planning any instructional activity is to determine the overall objectives and standards. If the instructor does not have a logical view of what is to be achieved, then the learners will not.
Answer (B) is incorrect. Establishing a common ground between the instructor and learner is the purpose of a lesson introduction, not the first step in planning instructional activity. **Answer (C) is incorrect.** The second, not the first, consideration in planning for any instructional activity is to identify the blocks of learning that make up the overall objective.

2. Which statement is true concerning extraneous blocks of instruction during a course of training?

A. They are usually necessary parts of the total objective.

B. They detract from the completion of the final objective.

C. They assist in the attainment of the lesson's objective.

Answer (B) is correct. *(FAA-H-8083-9B Chap 7)*
DISCUSSION: While identifying the blocks of learning to be used in the course, the instructor must examine each carefully to see that it is truly an integral part of the structure. Extraneous blocks of instruction can detract from, rather than assist, in the completion of the final objective.
Answer (A) is incorrect. Extraneous blocks of instruction are unnecessary parts of the total objective. **Answer (C) is incorrect.** Extraneous blocks of instruction detract, not assist, in the attainment of the lesson's objective.

3. When it is impossible to conduct a scheduled lesson, it is preferable for the instructor to

A. review and possibly revise the training syllabus.

B. proceed to the next scheduled lesson, or if this is not practical, cancel the lesson.

C. conduct a lesson that is not predicated completely on skills to be developed during the lesson which was postponed.

Answer (C) is correct. *(FAA-H-8083-9B Chap 7)*
DISCUSSION: It is preferable for the instructor to skip to a completely different part of the syllabus when it is impossible to conduct a scheduled lesson, rather than proceeding to the next lesson, which may be predicated completely on skills to be developed during the lesson that was postponed.
Answer (A) is incorrect. An instructor should review and possibly revise the training syllabus when there is an applicable change to the Federal Aviation Regulations or PTSs/ACSs, not because a lesson had to be postponed. **Answer (B) is incorrect.** The next lesson may need skills that were to be learned in the postponed lesson.

4. Performance-based objectives consist of which three elements?

A. Flight training scenarios, judgment assessment, and maneuver assessment.

B. Cognitive skills, affective skills, and psychomotor skills.

C. Description of the skill or behavior, conditions, and criteria.

Answer (C) is correct. *(FAA-H-8083-9B Chap 5)*
DISCUSSION: Performance-based objectives are used to set measurable, reasonable standards that describe the desired performance of the learner. Performance-based objectives consist of three elements: description of the skill or behavior, conditions, and criteria.
Answer (A) is incorrect. This answer choice describes elements of decision-based, not performance-based, objectives. **Answer (B) is incorrect.** This answer choice describes the three domains of learning, not the elements of performance-based objectives.

5. Development and assembly of blocks of learning in their proper relationship will provide a means for

A. both the instructor and learner to easily correct faulty habit patterns.

B. challenging the learner by progressively increasing the units of learning.

C. allowing the learner to master the segments of the overall pilot performance requirements individually and combining these with other related segments.

Answer (C) is correct. *(FAA-H-8083-9B Chap 7)*
DISCUSSION: Training for a skill as complicated and involved as piloting an aircraft requires the development and assembly, in their appropriate sequence, of many segments or blocks of learning. In this way, a learner can master the segments of the overall pilot performance requirements individually and can progressively combine these with other related segments until (s)he learns to fly, which is the final objective.
Answer (A) is incorrect. Organizing the appropriate blocks of learning in their proper relationship should prevent the formation of bad habits. This is the basic reason for the building block technique of instruction. **Answer (B) is incorrect.** The challenge presented to the learner is one way to test for a useful size of a minimum block of learning, but progressively increasing the blocks of learning may deter the learner's progress.

6. As an instructor you should write performance-based objectives that

- A. fit the desired outcome of a particular lesson.
- B. do not require the consideration of conditions.
- C. must be open to interpretation by knowledgeable readers.

Answer (A) is correct. (FAA-H-8083-9B Chap 5)
DISCUSSION: An instructor should write performance-based objectives to fit the desired outcome of the lesson. **Answer (B) is incorrect.** Conditions are necessary to specifically explain the rules under which the skill or behavior is demonstrated. If a desired capability is to navigate from point A to point B, the objective as stated is not specific enough for all learners to do it in the same way. Information such as equipment, tools, reference material, and limiting parameters should be included. **Answer (C) is incorrect.** Performance-based objectives must be clear, measurable, and repeatable. In other words, they must mean the same thing to any knowledgeable reader.

7. A series of studies leading to an attainment of a goal is

- A. a determination of objective.
- B. a course of training.
- C. a decision based objective.

Answer (B) is correct. (FAA-H-8083-9B Chap 5)
DISCUSSION: A course of training is a complete series of studies leading to attainment of a goal, such as a certificate of completion, graduation, etc.
Answer (A) is incorrect. A determination of objectives and standards is necessary before any important instruction can be presented. **Answer (C) is incorrect.** Decision-based objectives are a type of objective designed to develop pilot judgment and ADM skills.

8. What is the overall objective of any pilot training?

- A. To make sure all objectives are clear, measurable, and repeatable.
- B. To facilitate a higher level of learning and application.
- C. To qualify the learner to be a competent, efficient, safe pilot.

Answer (C) is correct. (FAA-H-8083-9B Chap 5)
DISCUSSION: The broad overall objective of any pilot training is to qualify the learner to be a competent, efficient, safe pilot.
Answer (A) is incorrect. Making sure written objectives are clear, measurable, and repeatable is an element of a performance-based objective. **Answer (B) is incorrect.** Decision-based objectives facilitate a higher level of learning and application and thus reduce improper pilot decision making and increase overall flight safety.

9. Which is not a type of objective used in aviation training?

- A. Performance-based objectives.
- B. Decision-based objectives.
- C. Description-based objectives.

Answer (C) is correct. (FAA-H-8083-9B Chap 5)
DISCUSSION: A description-based objective is not a type of objective in aviation training.
Answer (A) is incorrect. There are two types of objectives in aviation: performance-based objectives and decision-based objectives. Performance-based objectives are used to set measurable, reasonable standards that describe the required learner performance. **Answer (B) is incorrect.** There are two types of objectives in aviation: performance-based objectives and decision-based objectives. Decision-based objectives allow for a more dynamic training environment and are designed to develop pilot judgment and ADM skills.

10. Which element of a performance-based objective explains the standards used to measure the accomplishment of the objective?

- A. Description of the skill or behavior.
- B. Conditions.
- C. Criteria.

Answer (C) is correct. (FAA-H-8083-9B Chap 5)
DISCUSSION: Criteria are the standards used to measure the accomplishment of the objective.
Answer (A) is incorrect. The description of the skill or behavior is the desired outcome of training stated in concrete terms that can be measured. **Answer (B) is incorrect.** Conditions are used to explain the rules under which the skill or behavior is to be demonstrated.

11. After the instructor establishes the overall training objectives, his or her next step is

- A. the identification of the blocks of learning which constitute the necessary parts of the total objective.
- B. create a lesson plan for the unit of instruction.
- C. create a syllabus for the training objective.

Answer (A) is correct. (FAA-H-8083-9B Chap 7)
DISCUSSION: After the overall training objectives have been established, the next step is the identification of the blocks of learning which constitute the necessary parts of the total objective.
Answer (B) is incorrect. A lesson plan cannot be developed until the appropriate blocks of learning have been identified. **Answer (C) is incorrect.** A syllabus cannot be developed until the appropriate blocks of learning have been identified.

12. What is true of all syllabi?

    A. The order of training should not be altered as this will detract from the completion of the final objective.

    B. All syllabi should stress well-defined objectives and standards for each lesson.

    C. Common ground between the learner and instructor will be established by using a syllabus.

Answer (B) is correct. (FAA-H-8083-9B Chap 7)
    DISCUSSION: All syllabi should stress well-defined objectives and standards for each lesson.
    Answer (A) is incorrect. The order of training can and should be altered when necessary to suit the progress of the learner and the demands of special circumstances, such as weather conditions. **Answer (C) is incorrect.** Establishing a common ground between the instructor and learner is the purpose of a lesson introduction and is not dependent on a syllabus.

5.2 Organization of Training Material

13. The method of arranging lesson material from the simple to complex, past to present, and known to unknown, is one that

    A. creates learner thought pattern departures.

    B. shows the relationships of the main points of the lesson.

    C. requires learners to actively participate in the lesson.

Answer (B) is correct. (FAA-H-8083-9B Chap 5)
    DISCUSSION: An instructor must logically organize the lesson material to show the relationships of the main points. This can be done by arranging the material from the simple to the complex, past to present, known to unknown, and from the most frequently used to the least frequently used.
    Answer (A) is incorrect. By arranging lesson material from the simple to complex, past to present, and known to unknown, the instructor will make meaningful transitions from one point to another and thus keep the learners oriented, not create thought pattern departures. **Answer (C) is incorrect.** The objective of each lesson, not the method of arranging material, should require learners to actively participate (either directly or indirectly) in the lesson in order to achieve the desired learning outcomes.

14. In organizing lesson material, which step sets the stage for everything to come?

    A. Overview.

    B. Conclusion.

    C. Introduction.

Answer (C) is correct. (FAA-H-8083-9B Chap 5)
    DISCUSSION: The introduction to a lesson should set the stage for everything to come. The introduction is made up of three elements: attention, motivation, and overview.
    Answer (A) is incorrect. The overview is included in the introduction and tells the group what is to be covered during the period of instruction, not how it relates to the entire course. **Answer (B) is incorrect.** The conclusion retraces the important elements of the lesson and relates them to the lesson objective. It does not set the stage for everything to come because it is at the end of a lesson.

15. In developing a lesson, the instructor should organize explanations and demonstrations to help the learner

    A. achieve the desired learning outcome.

    B. acquire a thorough understanding of the material presented.

    C. acquire new concepts, generally progressing from the known to the unknown.

Answer (A) is correct. (FAA-H-8083-9B Chap 5)
    DISCUSSION: In developing a lesson, the instructor should organize the subject matter (explanations and demonstrations) in a manner that helps the learner achieve the desired learning outcome.
    Answer (B) is incorrect. The learner's ability to acquire a thorough understanding of the material is dependent on more than an instructor's organized presentation, e.g., motivation, needs, etc. **Answer (C) is incorrect.** Progressing from the known to the unknown is a way of logically organizing the lesson material to show the relationships of the main points, not the intent of developing a lesson, which is to help the learner achieve the desired learning outcome.

16. When teaching from the known to the unknown, an instructor is using the learner's

    A. current knowledge of the subject.

    B. previous experiences and knowledge.

    C. previously held opinions, both valid and invalid.

Answer (B) is correct. (FAA-H-8083-9B Chap 5)
    DISCUSSION: Teaching from the known to the unknown allows the instructor to use the learner's previous experience and knowledge as the point of departure from which to lead into new ideas and concepts.
    Answer (A) is incorrect. When teaching from the known to the unknown, an instructor is using a learner's knowledge of related subjects, not the subject at hand. **Answer (C) is incorrect.** Organizing lessons using the known to the unknown pattern requires learners' previous knowledge, not their previously held opinions.

17. The proper sequence for the subparts of an introduction is

   A. attention, motivation, and overview.

   B. attention, development, and overview.

   C. overview, motivation, and conclusion.

Answer (A) is correct. (FAA-H-8083-9B Chap 5)
DISCUSSION: The proper sequence for the subparts of an introduction is attention, motivation, and overview. First, the instructor must gain the learner's attention and focus it on the subject at hand. Second, the introduction should offer the learners specific reasons for needing to be familiar with, to know, to understand, to apply, or to be able to perform whatever they are about to learn. This motivation should appeal to each learner personally and accentuate the desire to learn. Third, every lesson introduction should contain an overview that tells the group what is to be covered during the period.
    Answer (B) is incorrect. Development is the main part of the lesson, not a subpart of the introduction. **Answer (C) is incorrect.** Conclusion is the review portion of the lesson, not a subpart of the introduction.

18. Instructors should utilize the proper sequence for the subparts of an introduction. These are

   A. attention, motivation, and overview.

   B. application, correlation, and understanding.

   C. anecdote or story, motivation, and overview.

Answer (A) is correct. (FAA-H-8083-9B Chap 5)
DISCUSSION: The basic introduction to a period of instruction consists of three elements: attention, motivation, and overview. By organizing the content in this manner, the instructor helps the learner obtain a firm grasp of the subject matter while minimizing the possibility of a rambling discussion.
    Answer (B) is incorrect. Application, correlation, and understanding are levels of learning, not the elements of an introduction to instruction. **Answer (C) is incorrect.** The introduction should be free of stories, jokes, or incidents that do not help the learners focus their attention on the lesson objective.

19. The known to unknown pattern helps the instructor lead the learner into new ideas and concepts by

   A. anxieties and insecurities.

   B. using something the learner already knows.

   C. previously held opinions, both valid and invalid.

Answer (B) is correct. (FAA-H-8083-9B Chap 5)
DISCUSSION: By using something the learner already knows as the point of departure, the instructor can lead into new ideas and concepts. For example, in developing a lesson on heading indicators, the instructor could begin with a discussion of the vacuum-driven heading indicator before proceeding to a description of the radio magnetic indicator (RMI).
    Answer (A) is incorrect. The known to unknown pattern helps the instructor lead the learner into new ideas and concepts by using something the learner already knows, not through anxieties and insecurities. **Answer (C) is incorrect.** By using something the learner already knows as the point of departure, the instructor can lead into new ideas and concepts, not through previously held opinions.

20. Examples of methods to gain learner attention include

   A. Jokes, video clips, questions.

   B. Lectures, guided discussions, demonstrations.

   C. Review problems, case studies, explanations.

Answer (A) is correct. (FAA-H-8083-9B Chap 5)
DISCUSSION: Stories, video clips, questions, or jokes can all be used to gain learner attention.
    Answer (B) is incorrect. Lectures do not prompt learner attention. Stories, video clips, questions, or jokes are all methods to gain learner attention. **Answer (C) is incorrect.** While case studies are a type of story, they are a type of problem-based learning and are used in the development stage of a lesson, not in the introduction.

21. Reinforcement of learner learning occurs primarily during which state of lesson organization?

   A. Introduction.

   B. Development.

   C. Conclusion.

Answer (C) is correct. (FAA-H-8083-9B Chap 5)
DISCUSSION: Conclusions retrace important elements of the lesson and relate them to the objective. This reinforces learning and improves retention.
    Answer (A) is incorrect. The introduction sets the stage for everything to come. **Answer (B) is incorrect.** The development is the main part of the lesson during which the instructor organizes the explanations and demonstrations in a manner that helps the learners achieve the desired learning outcomes.

5.3 Lesson Plan

22. Which statement is true regarding lesson plans?

   A. Lesson plans should not be directed toward the course objective; only to the lesson objective.

   B. A well-thought-out mental outline of a lesson may be used any time as long as the instructor is well prepared.

   C. Lesson plans help instructors keep a constant check on their own activity as well as that of their learners.

Answer (C) is correct. (FAA-H-8083-9B Chap 7)
DISCUSSION: Lesson plans help instructors keep a constant check on their own activity, as well as that of learners. The development of lesson plans by instructors signifies, in effect, that they have taught the lesson to themselves prior to attempting to teach the lesson to learners.
   Answer (A) is incorrect. A lesson plan should serve as a means of relating the lesson to the objectives of the course, as well as the lesson. **Answer (B) is incorrect.** A mental outline of a lesson is not a lesson plan. A lesson plan should be in written form regardless of an instructor's preparation.

23. When the instructor keeps the learner informed of lesson objectives and completion standards, it minimizes the learner's feelings of

   A. insecurity.

   B. resignation.

   C. aggressiveness.

Answer (A) is correct. (FAA-H-8083-9B Chap 8)
DISCUSSION: Learners feel insecure when they do not know the lesson objectives and the completion standards to which they will be held. Instructors can minimize such feelings of insecurity by telling learners what is expected of them and what to anticipate.
   Answer (B) is incorrect. Resignation occurs when a learner completes the early phase of training without understanding the fundamentals, not the objectives or completion standards, and becomes lost in the advanced phase. **Answer (C) is incorrect.** Aggression occurs when a learner becomes angry at something or someone. Aggression (or any other defense mechanism) may be used to defend a feeling of insecurity when a learner is not kept informed.

24. Which statement is true about lesson plans?

   A. Lesson plans should follow a prescribed format.

   B. Standard prepared lesson plans are effective for teaching all learners.

   C. The use of standard lesson plans may not be effective for learners requiring a different approach.

Answer (C) is correct. (FAA-H-8083-9B Chap 7)
DISCUSSION: A lesson plan for an instructional period should be appropriate to the background, experience, and ability of the particular learner(s). If the procedures outlined in the lesson plan are not leading to the desired results, the instructor should change the approach. Thus, the use of standard lesson plans may not be effective for learners requiring a different approach.
   Answer (A) is incorrect. Although lesson plans should all contain certain items, the format to be followed should be tailored to the particular learner(s). **Answer (B) is incorrect.** Lesson plans are only an outline of the lesson. An instructor may have to adapt the procedures in a standard prepared lesson plan so it will be effective with different learners.

25. A well developed lesson plan should

   A. promote uniformity of instruction regardless of the instructor teaching it.

   B. be a sketch of a program or teaching lecture.

   C. be a document that will not require changes or alterations.

Answer (A) is correct. (FAA-H-8083-9B Chap 7)
DISCUSSION: A well-developed lesson plan should

- Ensure the proper material is included and eliminate unimportant details.
- Make certain that due consideration is given to each part of the lesson.
- Aid the instructor in presenting the material in a suitable sequence for efficient learning.
- Provide an outline of the teaching procedure to be used.
- Serve as a means of relating the lesson to the objectives of the course of training.
- Give the inexperienced instructor confidence.
- Promote uniformity of instruction regardless of the instructor or the date on which the lesson is given.

   Answer (B) is incorrect. A well-developed lesson plan should be a well-written outline, not a vague sketch. **Answer (C) is incorrect.** A well-developed lesson plan should be a working document that can and should be revised as changes occur or are needed.

26. (Refer to Figure 1 on page 131.) Section A is titled:

    A. Overview.

    B. Objective.

    C. Introduction.

Answer (B) is correct. (FAA-H-8083-9B Chap 7)
    DISCUSSION: Section A of Fig. 1 is titled "Objective." The objective of the lesson is the reason for the lesson and should clearly state what the instructor expects the learner to know or do at the completion of the lesson.
    Answer (A) is incorrect. An overview is a subpart of an introduction to a lesson, not a titled section of a lesson plan.
    Answer (C) is incorrect. An introduction is part of an effective way to organize a lesson, not a titled section of a lesson plan.

27. (Refer to Figure 1 on page 131.) Section B is titled:

    A. Content.

    B. Elements.

    C. Course of Training.

Answer (A) is correct. (FAA-H-8083-9B Chap 7)
    DISCUSSION: Section B of Fig. 1 is titled "Content." This is a statement of the knowledge and skill necessary for the fulfillment of the lesson objective. This may include both elements previously learned and those to be introduced during this lesson.
    Answer (B) is incorrect. "Elements" is not a titled section of a lesson plan. **Answer (C) is incorrect.** The course of training is the overall objective of the instruction and is comprised of many different lesson plans, not a titled section of a lesson plan.

28. (Refer to Figure 1 on page 131.) Section C is titled:

    A. Schedule.

    B. Overview.

    C. Training Schedule.

Answer (A) is correct. (FAA-H-8083-9B Chap 7)
    DISCUSSION: Section C of Fig. 1 is titled "Schedule." The instructor should estimate the amount of time to be devoted to the presentation of the elements of that lesson.
    Answer (B) is incorrect. An overview is a subpart of an introduction to a lesson, not a titled section of a lesson plan.
    Answer (C) is incorrect. The correct title is "Schedule," not "Training Schedule."

29. (Refer to Figure 1 on page 131.) Section D is titled:

    A. Instructor's Actions.

    B. Equipment.

    C. Content.

Answer (B) is correct. (FAA-H-8083-9B Chap 7)
    DISCUSSION: Section D of Fig. 1 is titled "Equipment." This includes all instructional materials and training aids required to teach the lesson.
    Answer (A) is incorrect. "Instructor's Actions" is the title of the section of a lesson plan that contains a statement of the instructor's proposed procedures for presenting the elements of knowledge and performance involved in the lesson (Section E). **Answer (C) is incorrect.** "Content" is a statement of the knowledge and skill necessary for fulfillment of the lesson objective, not a list of instructional materials to be used in the lesson.

30. (Refer to Figure 1 on page 131.) Section E is titled:

    A. Content.

    B. Discussion.

    C. Instructor's Actions.

Answer (C) is correct. (FAA-H-8083-9B Chap 7)
    DISCUSSION: Section E of Fig. 1 is titled "Instructor's Actions." This is a statement of the instructor's proposed procedures for presenting the elements of knowledge and performance involved in the lesson.
    Answer (A) is incorrect. "Content" is a statement of the knowledge and skill necessary for fulfillment of the lesson objective, not a list of the instructor's actions. **Answer (B) is incorrect.** While this section states that a discussion will take place, it is specifically those actions taken by the instructor and not the learner.

31. (Refer to Figure 1 on page 131.) Section F is titled:

    A. Application.

    B. Understanding.

    C. Learner's Actions.

Answer (C) is correct. (FAA-H-8083-9B Chap 7)
    DISCUSSION: Section F of Fig. 1 is titled "Learner's Actions." This is a statement of desired learner responses to instruction.
    Answer (A) is incorrect. While this involves application of what the instructor has presented to the learner, this section is the instructor's desired learner's action during the lesson. **Answer (B) is incorrect.** Understanding is a level of learning, not a titled section of a lesson plan.

32. (Refer to Figure 1 below.) Section G is titled:

A. Summary.

B. Evaluation.

C. Completion Standards.

Answer (C) is correct. (FAA-H-8083-9B Chap 7)
    DISCUSSION: Section G of Fig. 1 is titled "Completion Standards." This is the evaluation basis for determining how well the learner has met the objective of the lesson in terms of knowledge and skill.
    Answer (A) is incorrect. A summary of a lesson would take place during the postflight discussion. **Answer (B) is incorrect.** Evaluation is part of the teaching process and would be used by the instructor to compare the learner's performance to the completion standards.

LESSON	Ground reference maneuvers	STUDENT		DATE	/ /

A _____ To develop the student's skill in planning and following a pattern over the ground compensating for wind drift at varying angles.

B _____ Use of ground references to control path
Observation and control of wind effect
Control of airplane attitude, altitude, and heading

C _____
Preflight discussion   :10
Instructor demonstrations   :25
Learner practice   :45
Postflight critique   :10

D _____ Chalkboard for preflight discussion
IFR visor for maneuvers reviewed

E _____ Preflight—discuss lesson objective. Diagram "S" turns, eight along a road, and rectangular course on a chalkboard.

Inflight—demonstrate elements.
Demonstrate following a road, "S" turns, eights along a road, and rectangular course, coach student practice.

Postflight—critique learner performance and make study assignment.

F _____ Preflight—discuss lesson objective and resolve questions.

Inflight—review previous maneuvers including power-off stalls and flight at minimum controllable airspeed.
Perform each new maneuver as directed.

Postflight—ask pertinent questions.

G _____ Student should demonstrate competency in maintaining orientation, airspeed within 10 knots, altitude within 100 feet, and headings within 10 degrees, and in making proper correction for wind drift.

Figure 1. Lesson Plan.

33. The main concern in developing a lesson plan is the

   A. format.

   B. content.

   C. learner.

Answer (C) is correct. (FAA-H-8083-9B Chap 7)
    DISCUSSION: The lesson plan must be appropriate for the particular learner. Because standard lesson plans may not be effective for learners who require a different approach, the main concern in developing a lesson plan is the learner.
    Answer (A) is incorrect. The format of the lesson plan will be developed based on the needs of the learner and the subject being taught. One lesson plan format does not work well for all learners; therefore, the format of a lesson plan is an ending point, not a starting point, in lesson plan development. **Answer (B) is incorrect.** While the content of a lesson plan is a concern in its development (e.g., how much time should be devoted to which subjects), the main concern in developing a lesson plan is the learner.

34. With regard to the characteristics of a well-planned lesson, each lesson should contain

   A. new material that is related to the lesson previously presented.

   B. one basic element of the principle, procedure, or skill appropriate to that lesson.

   C. every bit of information needed to reach the objective of the training syllabus.

Answer (A) is correct. (FAA-H-8083-9B Chap 7)
    DISCUSSION: One characteristic of a well-planned lesson is content, which means each lesson should contain new material. However, the new facts, principles, or skills should be related to the lesson previously presented. A short review of earlier lessons is usually necessary, especially in flight training.
    Answer (B) is incorrect. All of the elements, not only one, necessary to learn a simple procedure, principle, or skill should be presented. **Answer (C) is incorrect.** Each lesson should include all of the information needed to reach the objective of a particular lesson but not everything needed for the entire syllabus.

35. A primary consideration in planning for learner performance is the

   A. learner's motivational level.

   B. learner's intellectual level.

   C. length of the practice session.

Answer (C) is correct. (FAA-H-8083-9B Chap 3)
    DISCUSSION: In planning for learner performance, a primary consideration is the length of time devoted to practice. A beginning learner reaches a point where additional practice is not only unproductive but may even be harmful. When that point is reached, errors increase and motivation declines. As a learner gains experience, longer periods of practice are profitable.
    Answer (A) is incorrect. A learner's motivational level is important to an instructor since it directly relates to the learner's progress and ability to learn, not as a primary consideration in planning for learner performance. **Answer (B) is incorrect.** A primary consideration in learner performance is the length of time devoted to practice, not the learner's intellectual level.

36. A lesson plan, if constructed properly, will provide an outline for

   A. proceeding from the unknown to the known.

   B. the teaching procedure to be used in a single instructional period.

   C. establishing blocks of learning that become progressively larger in scope.

Answer (B) is correct. (FAA-H-8083-9B Chap 7)
    DISCUSSION: A properly constructed lesson plan is an organized outline or blueprint for a single instructional period. It is a necessary guide for the instructor in that it tells what to do, in what order to do it, and what procedure to use in teaching the material of the lesson.
    Answer (A) is incorrect. The lesson plan will usually proceed from the known to the unknown, not unknown to known. **Answer (C) is incorrect.** A syllabus, not a lesson plan, will provide an outline for establishing blocks of learning that become progressively larger in scope.

37. Each lesson of a training syllabus includes

   A. attention, motivation, and overview.

   B. introduction, development, and conclusion.

   C. objective, content, and completion standards.

Answer (C) is correct. (FAA-H-8083-9B Chap 7)
    DISCUSSION: Each lesson of a written training syllabus includes an objective, content, and completion standards.
    Answer (A) is incorrect. Attention, motivation, and overview are the parts of an introduction to a lesson. **Answer (B) is incorrect.** The structure of every lesson as it is being presented to a learner, not as found in a written syllabus, should be based on an introduction, a development, and a conclusion.

38. A primary consideration in planning for learner performance is the

- A. length of time devoted to practice.
- B. length of time devoted to evaluation.
- C. segmentation of the practice session.

Answer (A) is correct. (FAA-H-8083-9B Chap 3)
  DISCUSSION: In planning for learner performance, a primary consideration is the length of time devoted to practice. A beginning learner reaches a point where additional practice is not only unproductive, but may even be harmful. When this point is reached, errors increase, and motivation declines. As a learner gains experience, longer periods of practice are profitable.
  Answer (B) is incorrect. In the initial stages of learning, practical suggestions are more valuable to the learner than a grade. Early evaluation is usually teacher-oriented. It provides a check on teaching effectiveness; thus, it is not a primary consideration in learner performance planning. **Answer (C) is incorrect.** While the consideration of how to properly divide or segment a practice session is important, it is futile without first determining the appropriate length of the practice session itself.

39. Which of the following statements is true in regards to the properties of overlearning?

- A. Overlearning allows the learner to bypass the learning plateau phenomenon.
- B. Overlearning is the continued study of a skill after initial proficiency has been achieved.
- C. Targets the learner's deep memory.

Answer (B) is correct. (FAA-H-8083-9B Chap 3)
  DISCUSSION: Overlearning is the continued study of a skill after initial proficiency has been achieved. Practice proceeds beyond the point at which the act can be performed with the required degree of excellence. The phenomenon of overlearning sometimes occurs when knowledge used frequently begins to take on the properties of a skill.
  Answer (A) is incorrect. The learning plateau phenomenon can be present whether overlearning takes place or not. **Answer (C) is incorrect.** Overlearning does not pertain to the concept of deep memory.

40. Which is true regarding the overlearning of knowledge?

- A. Overlearning can result in automatic responses that are undesirable.
- B. Overlearning is helpful in increasing learner proficiency of a topic.
- C. Overlearning develops higher-order thinking skills.

Answer (A) is correct. (FAA-H-8083-9B Chap 3)
  DISCUSSION: Overlearning is the continued study of a skill after initial proficiency has been achieved. Practice proceeds beyond the point at which the act can be performed with the required degree of excellence. One common effect of overlearning is the development of automated routines rather than development of concept application skills.
  Answer (B) is incorrect. Overlearning generally degrades learner proficiency by creating automatic responses on the part of the learner, which limit the learner's understanding of a given topic. **Answer (C) is incorrect.** On the contrary, overlearning creates a barrier to the development of higher-order thinking skills by creating automated responses from the learner rather than actual concept mastery.

41. When teaching new material, the teaching process can be divided into which steps?

- A. Preparation, presentation, application, and review and evaluation.
- B. Preparation, demonstration, practice, and review.
- C. Explanation, demonstration, practice, and evaluation.

Answer (A) is correct. (FAA-H-8083-9B Chap 5)
  DISCUSSION: The four basic steps in the teaching process are preparation, presentation, application, and review and evaluation.
  Answer (B) is incorrect. Demonstration and practice are examples of teaching methods, not basic steps in the teaching process. **Answer (C) is incorrect.** Explanation, demonstration, and practice are examples of teaching methods, not basic steps in the teaching process.

42. Every lesson, when adequately developed, falls logically into the four steps of the teaching process -

- A. preparation, introduction, presentation, and review and evaluation.
- B. preparation, introduction, presentation, and review and application.
- C. preparation, presentation, application, and review and evaluation.

Answer (C) is correct. (FAA-H-8083-9B Chap 7)
  DISCUSSION: Every lesson, when developed adequately, falls logically into the four steps of the teaching process: preparation, presentation, application, and review/evaluation.
  Answer (A) is incorrect. The second basic step in the teaching process is presentation, not introduction, and the third basic step is application, not presentation. **Answer (B) is incorrect.** The second basic step in the teaching process is presentation, not introduction, the third basic step is application, not presentation, and the fourth basic step is review and evaluation, not review and application.

43. Which is not a step to ensuring a quality lesson?

    A. Instructor research.

    B. Assembling training aids.

    C. Determining the length of the practice session.

Answer (C) is correct. (FAA-H-8083-9B Chap 7)
    DISCUSSION: While a primary consideration in planning for learner performance, determining the length of the practice session is not a step to ensuring a quality lesson.
    Answer (A) is incorrect. Instructor research is a step to ensuring a quality lesson is provided to the learner. **Answer (B) is incorrect.** Assembling training aids is a step to ensuring a quality lesson is provided to the learner.

44. What are lesson plans designed to ensure?

    A. That each learner receive the best possible instruction under existing circumstances.

    B. To reinforce learning and retention of the stated objective.

    C. To provide a boost of self-confidence to each learner.

Answer (A) is correct. (FAA-H-8083-9B Chap 7)
    DISCUSSION: Lesson plans are designed to ensure that each learner receives the best possible instruction under existing circumstances.
    Answer (B) is incorrect. Conclusions reinforce learning and improve retention of what has been learned previously. **Answer (C) is incorrect.** Upon successful completion of a given block of learning, a learner's self-confidence should be boosted. Lesson plans are not designed to accomplish this.

45. How long should a flight lesson be?

    A. Shorter lessons for new learners.

    B. Longer lessons for new learners.

    C. Shorter lessons as learners gain experience.

Answer (A) is correct. (FAA-H-8083-9B Chap 3)
    DISCUSSION: In planning for learner skill acquisition, a primary consideration is the length of time devoted to practice. A beginning learner reaches a point where additional practice is not only unproductive but may even be harmful. As a learner gains experience, longer periods of practice become profitable.
    Answer (B) is incorrect. Lessons for new learners should be shorter, not longer, in length. **Answer (C) is incorrect.** As learners gain experience, the lesson length can be increased.

5.4   Instructional Aids and Training Technology

46. Which is a true statement concerning the use of instructional aids?

    A. Instructional aids ensure getting and holding the learner's attention.

    B. Instructional aids should be designed to cover the key points in a lesson.

    C. Instructional aids should not be used simply to cover a subject in less time.

Answer (B) is correct. (FAA-H-8083-9B Chap 5)
    DISCUSSION: Instructional aids are a good way to improve communication between the instructor and the learners. Instructional aids should be designed to cover the key points in a lesson.
    Answer (A) is incorrect. Appropriate instructional aids will help get the learner's attention, but they cannot ensure that it will hold the learner's attention. **Answer (C) is incorrect.** Instructional aids can help get a point across quickly and clearly, thus reducing the time spent on some subjects.

47. The use of instructional aids should be based on their ability to support a specific point in the lesson. What is the first step in determining if and where instructional aids are necessary?

    A. Organize subject material into an outline or a lesson plan.

    B. Determine what ideas should be supported with instructional aids.

    C. Clearly establish the lesson objective, being certain what must be communicated.

Answer (C) is correct. (FAA-H-8083-9B Chap 5)
    DISCUSSION: The first step in developing a lesson plan using instructional aids is, as in any lesson plan, to establish the lesson objective. Visual or other aids must help achieve the overall lesson objective. They should be strategically placed to recapture interest, shift to a new topic, or provide emphasis.
    Answer (A) is incorrect. Organizing the outline or lesson plan is the third, not first, step in the process. **Answer (B) is incorrect.** The final, not first, step in determining if and where instructional aids are necessary is to determine what ideas in the lesson should be supported with instructional aids.

48. Instructional aids used in the teaching/learning process should be

- A. self-supporting and require no explanation.
- B. compatible with the learning outcomes to be achieved.
- C. selected prior to developing and organizing the lesson plan.

Answer (B) is correct. (FAA-H-8083-9B Chap 5)
   DISCUSSION: After establishing lesson objectives, researching the subject, and organizing the material into a lesson plan, the instructor should determine what needs to be supported by visual or other instructional aids. The aids should be compatible with the learning outcomes to be achieved.
   Answer (A) is incorrect. Instructional aids are not self-supporting and will require explanation. **Answer (C) is incorrect.** Instructional aids should be compatible with the desired learning outcomes, which can best be done after, not prior to, developing and organizing the lesson plan.

49. Instructional aids used in the teaching/learning process should not be used

- A. as a crutch by the instructor.
- B. for teaching more in less time.
- C. to visualize relationships between abstracts.

Answer (A) is correct. (FAA-H-8083-9B Chap 5)
   DISCUSSION: Aids used in conjunction with oral presentation should emphasize, not distract from, the oral message. Also, the instructor should realize that such aids do not take the place of a sound lesson plan or instructor's input.
   Answer (B) is incorrect. Aids do help teach more in less time because they clarify and emphasize the lecture. The class can move to new material sooner. **Answer (C) is incorrect.** Instructional aids should be used to help learners to visualize relationships between abstracts.

50. What is one reason an instructor would use an instructional aid?

- A. To describe a desired outcome of training.
- B. To gain and hold learner attention.
- C. To describe the standards used to measure the objective.

Answer (B) is correct. (FAA-H-8083-9B Chap 5)
   DISCUSSION: A reason to use instructional aids in the teaching/learning process is that they will gain and hold the attention of learners.
   Answer (A) is incorrect. An element of a performance-based objective, the description of the skill or behavior describes a desired outcome of training in concrete terms that can be measured. **Answer (C) is incorrect.** Criteria describe the standards used to measure the accomplishment of the objective.

51. Instructional aids may be used

- A. to clarify the relationships between material objects and concepts.
- B. to cover broad subject areas.
- C. to add to the time it takes instructors to teach learners.

Answer (A) is correct. (FAA-H-8083-9B Chap 5)
   DISCUSSION: One use for instructional aids is to clarify the relationships between material objects and concepts. When relationships are presented visually, they often are much easier to understand.
   Answer (B) is incorrect. Ideally, instructional aids should be designed to cover the key points and concepts rather than broad subject areas or abstractions. **Answer (C) is incorrect.** Instructors are frequently asked to teach more and more in a smaller time frame. Instructional aids can help them do this. For example, instead of using many words to describe a sound, object, or function, the instructor plays a recording of the sound, shows a picture of the object, or presents a diagram of the function. Consequently, the learner learns faster and more accurately, and the instructor saves time in the process.

52. What kind of software responds quickly to a learner's choices and commands?

- A. Interactive video.
- B. Projected material.
- C. Programmed text.

Answer (A) is correct. (FAA-H-8083-9B Chap 5)
   DISCUSSION: Interactive video is a type of computer software that responds quickly to certain choices and commands by the user. The questions or directions are programmed using a branching technique, which provides several possible courses of action for the user to choose in order to move from one sequence to another.
   Answer (B) is incorrect. Projected learning involves lessons projected on a screen that are presented and paced by an instructor. This instructional aid is not a form of software that responds to a learner's choices and commands. **Answer (C) is incorrect.** Programmed text involves learning and assessment in small steps. The content is predetermined and does not give the learner the ability to make choices or commands.

STUDY UNIT SIX

CRITIQUE AND EVALUATION

(11 pages of outline)

6.1 THE INSTRUCTOR'S ASSESSMENT

1. No instructor skill is more important than the ability to analyze, appraise, and judge learner performance. Assessment is an essential and continuous component of the teaching and learning process.

   a. **Assessment** is the process of gathering measurable information to meet evaluation needs. It involves judgment by the instructor and collaboration with the learner during the evaluation stage.

   b. A learner looks to the instructor for guidance, suggestions for improvement, and encouragement.

   c. To enhance a learner's acceptance of further instruction, the instructor should keep the learner informed of the progress made.

      1) This will help minimize learner frustrations, which will keep the learner motivated to learn.

   d. Assessment helps the instructor see where more emphasis is needed and determine the readiness of the learner to move forward.

2. In order to provide direction and increase learner performance, assessments must be factual and must be aligned with the completion standards of the lesson.

3. An assessment should be **objective**.

   a. The effective assessment is focused on learner performance and should not reflect the personal opinions, likes, dislikes, and biases of the instructor.

   b. The assessment must be honest and based on the performance as it was, not as it could have been.

4. An assessment should be **flexible**.

   a. The instructor must fit the tone, technique, and content of the critique to the occasion and the learner.

   b. The instructor must evaluate the entire performance in the context it was accomplished and allow for variables, whether they occur on the part of the learner or from factors outside the learner's control.

5. An assessment should be **acceptable**.

    a. Before learners willingly accept their instructor's assessment, they must first willingly accept the instructor.

    b. The learners must have confidence in the instructor's qualifications, teaching ability, sincerity, competence, and authority.

        1) An instructor's manner, attitude, and familiarity with the subject at hand does much to serve this purpose.

    c. Instructors cannot rely solely on their position to make an assessment acceptable to their learners.

6. An assessment should be **comprehensive**.

    a. A comprehensive assessment is not necessarily long, nor must it treat every aspect of the performance in detail.

    b. The instructor must decide whether the greater benefit will come from a discussion of a few major points or a number of minor points.

    c. An effective assessment covers strengths as well as weaknesses.

7. An assessment should be **constructive**.

    a. An assessment is meaningless unless a learner profits from it.

    b. Praise for praise's sake is of no value if a learner is not taught how to capitalize on things that are done well and to improve in areas of lesser accomplishment.

    c. An instructor must give positive guidance when identifying a mistake or weakness.

        1) Negative comments that discourage should be omitted altogether.

8. An assessment must be **organized**.

    a. Almost any pattern is acceptable as long as it is logical and makes sense to the learner.

    b. An organizational pattern might be the sequence of the performance itself.

        1) EXAMPLE: A flight instructor may explain the sequence of events that lead to an undesirable performance on a given flight maneuver.

9. An assessment should be **thoughtful**.

    a. An effective assessment reflects an instructor's thoughtfulness toward the learner's need for self-esteem, recognition, and approval from others.

        1) The assessment must not minimize the inherent dignity and importance of the individual.

    b. Ridicule, anger, or fun at the expense of the learner has no place in the assessment.

        1) EXAMPLE: An instructor should try to deliver the assessment in private rather than in a group setting.

10. An assessment should be **specific**.

    a. The instructor's comments and recommendations should be specific, not so general that the learner can find nothing to hold onto.

        1) Learners cannot act on recommendations and strive to improve unless they know specifically what the recommendations are.

    b. Instructors should express ideas with firmness and authority in terms that cannot be misunderstood.

        1) Learners should have no doubt what they did well, what they did poorly, and specifically how they can improve.

6.2 TYPES OF ASSESSMENT

1. There are two categories of assessment: traditional assessment and authentic assessment.

    a. Assessments can be either formal or informal.

        1) Formal assessments usually involve documentation, e.g., quizzes or written exams.

        2) Informal assessments can include verbal critique and generally occur as needed.

2. **Traditional assessment** often involves written testing and is more likely to be used to evaluate a learner's progress at the rote level of learning.

    a. In a traditional assessment, one single answer will be correct (i.e., multiple choice, true/false, etc.).

        1) EXAMPLE: The FAA knowledge test for a given certificate or rating is a traditional assessment.

    b. Traditional assessments are formal in nature.

3. **Authentic assessment** requires the learner to demonstrate not only the rote and understanding levels, but also the application and correlation levels of learning. Authentic assessment generally requires the learner to perform real-world tasks.

    a. In an authentic assessment, specific standards are used to define acceptable performance on a task.

        1) EXAMPLE: The practical, or flight, portion of the FAA test is an authentic assessment.

    b. Learners must generate responses from skills and concepts previously learned.

    c. Authentic assessment focuses on the learning process, enhances the development of real-world skills, encourages higher order thinking skills (HOTS), and teaches learners to assess their own work and performance.

    d. Authentic assessment may not be as useful as traditional assessment in the early phases of training because the learner may not have enough information or knowledge about the concepts to participate fully.

4. Learner-centered assessment, an aspect of authentic assessment, is a form of learner-centered grading that uses open-ended questions to guide the learner through a self-assessment. The purpose of self-assessment is to stimulate growth in the learner's thought process and, in turn, behaviors. The four steps in this process include the following:

    a. **Replay** – Asking the learner to verbally replay the flight or procedure.

    b. **Reconstruct** – The learner identifies key things that (s)he should or could have done differently during the flight or maneuver.

    c. **Reflect** – Questions that require reflection on the event, often leading to insight.

        1) EXAMPLE: "Did you perform in accordance with the PTS?"

    d. **Redirect** – Helps the learner relate the lessons learned to other experiences and consider how they might help in future sessions.

        1) EXAMPLE: "Which aspects of this flight might apply to future situations, and how?"

5. Learner-centered assessment uses two broad grading rubrics: one that assesses proficiency in skill-focused maneuvers or procedures, and one that focuses on the decision-making aspect of flight training (referred to as Single-Pilot Resource Management, or SRM).

    a. Advantages of these forms of assessment include the following:

        1) It actively involves the learner,

        2) It establishes the habit of reflection and self-assessment, and

        3) These grades are not self-esteem related because they describe a level of performance. A learner cannot flunk a lesson.

6. The grading dimensions of maneuvers or procedures include the following:

   a. **Describe** – Learner is able to describe the elements of the scenario but needs assistance to execute the maneuver properly.

   b. **Explain** – Learner is able to describe the elements of the scenario and understands the concepts and principles that comprise the activity but needs assistance to execute the maneuver properly.

   c. **Practice** – Learner is able to plan and execute the scenario with some coaching.

   d. **Perform** – Learner is able to perform the activity without instructor assistance and identifies and makes corrections in a timely manner. Indicates satisfactory demonstration.

   e. **Not observed** – Any event not accomplished or required.

7. The grading dimensions of SRM include the following:

   a. **Explain** – Learner can verbally identify, describe, and understand risks but needs to be prompted to make decisions.

   b. **Practice** – Learner properly identifies, understands, and applies SRM principles and corrects minor deviations identified by the instructor.

   c. **Manage-Decide** – Learner correctly gathers information, identifies proper courses of action, evaluates risks for each course of action, and makes the appropriate decision without instructor input.

8. To choose an effective assessment method, flight instructors can use a four-step process.

   a. Determine Level-of-Learning Objectives

      1) The individual objectives are stated as general level-of-learning objectives.

      2) Because it defines the scope of the learning task, this is a good starting point for developing a test.

   b. List Indicators/Samples of Desired Behaviors

      1) List the indicators of behavior that give the best indication of the achievement of the objective.

      2) By carefully choosing these indicators of behavior, an instructor can obtain adequate evidence of learning.

   c. Establish Criterion Objectives

      1) Define criterion (performance-based) objectives that state the conditions under which the behavior is to be performed and the criteria that must be met.

      2) Criterion objectives provide the framework for developing test items that will measure the level of learning objectives.

         a) EXAMPLE: "The learner will demonstrate understanding of navigational charts and their symbols by completing a quiz with a minimum passing score of 70%."

   d. Develop Criterion-Referenced Assessment Items

      1) Criterion-referenced testing measures a learner's performance against a carefully written, measurable standard or criterion.

         a) Practical tests for pilot certification are an example of criterion-referenced testing because they are based on the predetermined Practical Test Standards (PTS)/Airman Certification Standards (ACS) as set forth by the FAA.

b)   The objective of the PTS/ACS is to ensure the certification of pilots at a high level of performance and proficiency, consistent with safety.

c)   The PTS/ACS should not be used merely to "teach the test;" rather, the document should be used as both a training tool and an assessment tool during flight training to ensure learners are adequately prepared for the practical test.

d)   The PTS/ACS is not a teaching tool. It is a testing tool. The overall focus of flight training should be on education, learning, and understanding why the standards are there and how they were set.

   i)   Instructors should not introduce the PTS/ACS until the last 3 hours of training prior to the practical test.

2)   Criterion-referenced tests feature performance-based objectives that can be reliably, rather than subjectively, measured. Performance testing is desirable for evaluating training that involves an operation, a procedure, or a process.

a)   EXAMPLE: A pretest constructed to measure knowledge and skills necessary to begin a course is a criterion-referenced test, as is a pre-solo aeronautical knowledge test.

3)   The results of the test (questions missed) identify areas that were not adequately covered.

9.   Airman Certification Standards (ACS) for Private Pilot – Airplane (PAR), Commercial Pilot – Airplane (CAX), and Instrument Rating – Airplane (IRA) recently became effective. Therefore, the Practical Test Standards (PTS) documents for PAR, CAX, and IRA have been canceled.

a.   Since September 2011, the FAA has worked closely with a diverse group of aviation community stakeholders to help the agency improve the testing and training standards, guidance, and test development and management components of the airman certification process.

1)   The industry participants in this effort developed the ACS framework to improve airman training and testing by providing an integrated, holistic system that clearly aligns airman testing with certification standards and guidance.

b.   Built on the existing PTS, which explicitly define the performance metrics and tolerances for each flight proficiency element listed in the Federal Aviation Regulations, the ACS enhances the PTS by defining the specific task elements for aeronautical knowledge, risk management, and skills needed to support each Area of Operation and Task.

1)   Simply, the ACS describes what an applicant must know, consider, and do to pass the knowledge and practical tests for a given airman certificate or rating. It is thus the single-source set of standards for both the knowledge test and practical test for a certificate or rating.

2)   By presenting the elements of knowledge, risk management, and skill in the integrated ACS format, the ACS approach better serves the applicant, the instructor, and the evaluator. In addition, the ACS approach enables the FAA to create and maintain a clear link among the regulations, knowledge and skill performance standards, guidance, and test materials.

NOTE: Most of the study questions for this subunit are based on known questions relevant to the PTS only and specific guidance from the FAA's *Aviation Instructor's Handbook*. If more questions specific to the ACS become available, an update will be published.

6.3 CRITIQUES AND ORAL ASSESSMENTS

1. A critique is an instructor-to-learner assessment.

   a. A critique is not necessarily negative in content. It considers the good along with the bad, the individual parts, the parts in relation to each other, and overall performance.

   b. It may be written, oral, or both.

   c. A critique should always be conducted immediately after the learner's performance while the details are easy to recall.

   d. The instructor may critique any activity that a learner performs or practices to improve skill, proficiency, and learning.

   e. A critique can and usually should be as varied in content as the performance being evaluated.

2. Types of Critiques

   a. **Instructor/Learner Critique**

      1) Group discussion in which members of the class are invited to offer criticism of a performance

      2) Should be carefully controlled and organized by the instructor

   b. **Learner-Led Critique**

      1) Learner-led assessment that, while generating learner interest, may not be effective because of learner inexperience

   c. **Small Group Critique**

      1) Small groups are assigned to analyze a specific area of performance.
      2) Once combined, a comprehensive assessment results.

   d. **Individual Learner Critique by Another Learner**

      1) This type of critique often allows the group to accept more ownership of the ideas expressed.

      2) Careful oversight should be maintained by the instructor to control the process.

   e. **Self-Critique**

   f. **Written Critique**

      1) Instructors can devote more time and thought to it than an oral assessment.
      2) Learners can refer to them as needed.
      3) Learner has a permanent record of suggestions, recommendations, and opinions.

3. The most common means of assessment is direct or indirect oral questioning of learners by the instructor. Questions may be loosely classified as fact questions and HOTS questions.

   a. The answer to a fact question is based on memory or recall (i.e., who, what, where, when, why).

   b. HOTS questions require the learner to combine a knowledge of facts with an ability to analyze situations, solve problems, and arrive at conclusions.

4. Proper quizzing by the instructor can have a number of desirable results. It can

    a. Reveal the effectiveness of the instructor's training methods,
    b. Check learner retention and comprehension of what has been learned,
    c. Review material already presented to the learner,
    d. Help retain learner interest and stimulate thinking,
    e. Emphasize the important points of training,
    f. Identify points that need more emphasis, and
    g. Promote active learner participation.

5. Characteristics of effective questions:

    a. Objective, or fact, questions have only one correct answer, while the answer to open-ended HOTS (higher order thinking skills) questions can be expressed in a variety of possible situations. Each question should call for a specific answer that can be readily evaluated by the instructor.

    b. Effective questions must

        1) Apply to the subject being taught
        2) Be brief and concise, but also clear and definite
        3) Be adapted to the ability, experience, and stage of training of the learner
        4) Center on only one idea (who, what, when, where, how, or why; not a combination)
        5) Present a challenge to the learner

            a) A question must be of suitable difficulty for the learners at that particular stage of training.

6. The following types of questions should be avoided:

    a. Yes/no questions. For example: "Do you understand?"

    b. Puzzling questions – ones that do not provide a clear, definite objective. For example: "Which of the airplane systems is the most responsive to pilot inputs?"

    c. Oversize questions – ones that are too broad in scope and could have multiple correct/incorrect responses. Again, no definite objective is stated. For example: "What is required before going flying?"

    d. Toss-up questions – more than one correct response is possible. For example: "In an emergency, should you squawk 7700 or pick a landing spot?"

    e. Bewilderment questions – questions that mentally confuse. For example: "In reading the altimeter, if you take temperature into account, as when flying from a cold air mass through a warm front, what precaution should you take when in mountainous areas?"

    f. Trick questions – questions that cause the learner to feel (s)he is engaged in a battle of wits with the instructor, thus changing learner focus from the message to the messenger. For example: Using double negatives. "What is not a characteristic of not relying solely on flight instruments during flight in IMC?"

    g. Irrelevant questions – diversions that introduce unrelated facts and thoughts and slow learner progress. For example: "How would the wing produce lift in outer space?"

7. When answering learner questions, the instructor needs to clearly understand the question before attempting an answer.

    a. The instructor should display interest in the learner's questions and give as direct and accurate an answer as possible.

    b. If a learner's question is too advanced for the particular lesson and confusion may result from a complete answer, the instructor may

        1) Carefully explain that the question was good and pertinent;

        2) Explain that to answer would unnecessarily complicate the learning task at hand; and

        3) Advise the learner to reintroduce the question later at the appropriate point in training or meet outside class for a more complete discussion.

8. Occasionally, a learner will ask a question the instructor cannot answer. The best course is to freely admit not knowing the answer.

    a. The instructor should then promise to find out or offer to help the learner look it up in appropriate references.

6.4 TYPES OF WRITTEN TEST QUESTIONS

1. Written test questions fall into two general categories:

    a. Supply-type and
    b. Selection-type.

2. Supply-type questions require the learner to furnish a response in the form of a word, sentence, or paragraph.

    a. Supply-type test items

        1) Require learners to organize their thoughts and ideas

        2) Demand the ability to express ideas

            a) This makes them valuable in measuring the learner's generalized understanding of a subject.

        3) Are subjective

            a) Thus, their main disadvantage is that they cannot be graded uniformly.

            b) The same test graded by different instructors probably would be assigned different scores.

        4) Take longer for learners to answer and for instructors to grade, which is a disadvantage

3. Selection-type questions include items for which two or more alternative responses are provided and there is only one single correct response.

    a. Selection-type test items

        1) Are highly objective.

            a) Thus, they are graded uniformly regardless of the learner or grader.

        2) Allow direct comparison of learners' accomplishments. For example, it is possible to compare learner performance

            a) Within the same class,
            b) Between classes, and
            c) Under different instructors.

    b. True/false, multiple-choice, and matching type questions are prime examples of selection-type questions.

4. The **true/false** test item is well adapted to the testing of knowledge of facts and detail, especially when there are only two possible answers.

    a. The chief disadvantage of the true/false test item is it creates the greatest probability of guessing because the learner always has a 50% chance of guessing correctly.

    b. Guidelines for effective use of true/false questions

        1) Include only one idea in each statement
        2) Make the statement either entirely true or entirely false
        3) Avoid the unnecessary use of negatives
        4) Avoid absolutes such as "all," "every," "only," "never," etc.

5. **Multiple-choice** test items may be used to determine learner achievement, ranging from acquisition of facts to understanding, reasoning, and ability to apply what has been learned.

    a. Multiple-choice test items consist of two parts: the stem and a list of possible responses.

        1) The **stem** includes the question, statement, or problem.
        2) Incorrect responses are called distractors.

    b. When multiple-choice items are intended to measure achievement at a higher level of learning, some or all of the alternatives should be acceptable, but one should be clearly better than the others.

    c. Multiple-choice test items should have all alternatives of approximately equal length.

        1) A common error made by instructors is to make the correct alternative longer than the incorrect ones.

    d. Three major challenges are common in the construction of multiple-choice test items.

        1) Developing a question or item stem that must be expressed clearly and without ambiguity
        2) Developing a statement or correct answer choice that cannot be refuted
        3) Writing distractors that are attractive to learners who do not possess the knowledge or understanding necessary to recognize the correct response

    e. The following are popular distractors:

        1) An incorrect response related to the situation that sounds convincing
        2) A common misconception
        3) A true statement that does not satisfy the requirements of the problem
        4) A statement that is too broad or too narrow for the requirements of the problem

6. **Matching** test items are particularly good for measuring the learner's ability to recognize relationships and to make associations between terms, parts, words, phrases, or symbols listed in one column with related items in another column.

    a. Matching reduces the probability of guessing correct responses compared to a series of multiple-choice items covering the same material.

6.5 CHARACTERISTICS OF A GOOD TEST

1. **Reliability**

    a.　The degree to which test results are consistent with repeated measurements.

    b.　The reliability of a written test is determined by whether it gives consistent measurement to a particular individual or group.

    c.　EXAMPLE: A written test that has reliability yields consistent results.

2. **Validity**

    a.　The extent to which a test measures what it is supposed to measure.

    b.　This is the most important consideration in test evaluation.

    c.　EXAMPLE: A written test has validity when it measures what it is supposed to measure and nothing else.

3. **Usability**

    a.　The functionality of a test.

    b.　EXAMPLE: A written test is usable when it is easy to give, easy to read, the wording is clear and concise, figures are appropriate to the test items and clearly drawn, and it is easily graded.

4. **Objectivity**

    a.　Describes singleness of scoring a test.

    b.　Selection-type test items (true/false, multiple-choice) are much easier to grade with objectivity.

    c.　EXAMPLE: In essay questions, it is nearly impossible to prevent an instructor's own biases from affecting the grade subject.

5. **Comprehensiveness**

    a.　The degree to which a test measures the overall objectives.

    b.　A written test must sample an appropriate cross-section of the objectives of instruction.

    c.　EXAMPLE: A written test is said to be comprehensive when it liberally samples whatever is being measured.

6. **Discrimination**

    a.　The degree to which a test distinguishes the differences between learners.

    b.　Three features of a test constructed to identify the difference in achievement of learners are

    　　1)　A wide range of scores,

    　　2)　All levels of difficulty, and

    　　3)　Items that distinguish between learners with differing levels of achievement of the course objectives.

    c.　EXAMPLE: A written test having the characteristic of discrimination will measure small differences in achievement between learners.

6.6 REVIEW AND EVALUATION

1. Review and evaluation of the learner's learning should be an integral part of each lesson.

    a. Evaluation of learner performance and accomplishment should be based on the objectives and goals established in the lesson plan.

2. Performance testing is desirable for evaluating training that involves an operation, procedure, or process.

    a. This method of evaluation is particularly suited to the measurement of a learner's ability in performing a task, either mental or physical.

3. Learners may perform a procedure or maneuver correctly but not fully understand the principles and objectives involved. If the instructor suspects this, learners should be required to vary the performance of the maneuver or procedure slightly.

    a. Learners who do not understand the principles involved will probably not be able to successfully complete the revised maneuver or procedure.

QUESTIONS AND ANSWER EXPLANATIONS: All of the Fundamentals of Instructing knowledge test questions chosen by the FAA for release as well as additional questions selected by Gleim relating to the material in the previous outlines are provided on the following pages. These questions have been organized into the same subunits as the outlines. To the immediate right of each question are the correct answer and answer explanations. You should cover these answers and answer explanations while responding to the questions. Refer to the general discussion in the Introduction on how to take the FAA knowledge test.

Remember that the questions from the FAA knowledge test bank have been reordered by topic and organized into a meaningful sequence. Also, the first line of the answer explanation gives the citation of the authoritative source for the answer.

QUESTIONS

6.1 The Instructor's Assessment

1. To be effective, an assessment should

    A. not contain negative remarks.

    B. treat every aspect of the performance in detail.

    C. be flexible enough to satisfy the requirements of the moment.

Answer (C) is correct. (FAA-H-8083-9B Chap 7)
    DISCUSSION: An effective assessment is one that is flexible enough to satisfy the requirements of the moment. The instructor must fit the tone, technique, and content of the assessment to the occasion and the learner. Thus, the instructor is faced with the problem of what to say, what to omit, and what to minimize. The challenge of the assessment is that the instructor must determine what to say at the proper moment.
    Answer (A) is incorrect. An assessment may contain negative remarks as long as they point toward improvement or a higher level of performance. **Answer (B) is incorrect.** A comprehensive assessment is not necessarily a long one, nor must it treat every aspect of the performance in detail. The instructor must decide whether the greater benefit will come from discussing a few major points or a number of minor points.

2. An instructor's assessment of a learner's performance should

    A. treat every aspect of the performance in detail.

    B. be conducted in private so that the learner is not embarrassed.

    C. provide direction and guidance to improve performance.

Answer (C) is correct. (FAA-H-8083-9B Chap 9)
    DISCUSSION: An assessment should improve a learner's performance and provide something constructive with which (s)he can work and advance. It should provide direction and guidance to improve performance.
    Answer (A) is incorrect. A comprehensive assessment is not necessarily a long one, nor must it treat every aspect of the performance in detail. The instructor must decide whether the greater benefit will come from discussing a few major points or a number of minor points. **Answer (B) is incorrect.** An assessment may be conducted in private or before the entire class. An assessment presented before the entire class can be beneficial to every learner in the classroom as well as to the learner who performed the exercise.

3. Which is true about an instructor's assessment of a learner's performance?

    A. Praise for praise's sake is of value.

    B. It should be constructive and objective.

    C. It should treat every aspect of the performance in detail.

Answer (B) is correct. (FAA-H-8083-9B Chap 6)
    DISCUSSION: An assessment must be constructive by explaining to the learner how to capitalize on things that are done well and to use them to compensate for lesser accomplishments. An assessment must also be objective by basing it on the performance as it was, not as it could have been.
    Answer (A) is incorrect. Praise for praise's sake is of no value if a learner is not taught how to capitalize on things that are done well and to use them to compensate for lesser accomplishments. **Answer (C) is incorrect.** A comprehensive assessment is not necessarily a long one, nor must it treat every aspect of the performance in detail. The instructor must decide whether the greater benefit will come from discussing a few major points or a number of minor points.

4. Which statement is true about instructors' assessment?

    A. Instructors should rely on their personality to make an assessment more acceptable.

    B. A comprehensive assessment should emphasize positive aspects of learner performance.

    C. Before learners willingly accept their instructor's assessment, they must first accept the instructor.

Answer (C) is correct. (FAA-H-8083-9B Chap 6)
    DISCUSSION: Learners must have confidence in the instructor's qualifications, teaching ability, sincerity, competence, and authority before they will willingly accept their instructor's assessment. An assessment holds little weight if the learner has no respect for the instructor.
    Answer (A) is incorrect. The effective assessment is focused on learner performance and should not reflect the personal opinions, likes, dislikes, and biases (i.e., personality) of the instructor. **Answer (B) is incorrect.** A comprehensive assessment means that good and bad points are covered adequately but not necessarily in exhaustive detail.

5. Which statement is true regarding an assessment that is constructive?

   A. An instructor's manner and attitude make an assessment constructive.

   B. Constructive assessments can inspire a learner to improve in areas of lesser accomplishment.

   C. A constructive assessment should express ideas with authority in terms that cannot be misunderstood.

Answer (B) is correct. (FAA-H-8083-9B Chap 6)
   DISCUSSION: Constructive assessments, including praise, can inspire a learner to improve in areas of lesser accomplishment.
   Answer (A) is incorrect. An instructor's manner and attitude make an assessment acceptable to the learner.
Answer (C) is incorrect. For an assessment to be specific, ideas should be expressed with firmness and in terms the learner cannot misunderstand.

6. What must an instructor do to ensure an assessment is thoughtful?

   A. The instructor must not minimize the importance and dignity of the individual.

   B. The instructor must give positive guidance when identifying a learner's mistakes.

   C. The instructor must limit negative comments that discourage.

Answer (A) is correct. (FAA-H-8083-9B Chap 6)
   DISCUSSION: The assessment given by the instructor must not minimize the inherent dignity and importance of the individual.
   Answer (B) is incorrect. Instructor guidance should be constructive, which will not necessarily contain only positive comments. **Answer (C) is incorrect.** Negative comments that discourage should be omitted altogether, not simply limited.

7. Which of the following statements is true?

   A. Instructor critiques should focus on only positive areas of the learner's performance.

   B. Instructor critiques should only focus on areas where the learner needs to improve.

   C. For an instructor's critique to be effective, the learner must first accept the instructor.

Answer (C) is correct. (FAA-H-8083-9B Chap 6)
   DISCUSSION: The learner must accept the instructor in order to accept his or her assessment willingly. Learners must have confidence in the instructor's qualifications, teaching ability, sincerity, competence, and authority.
   Answer (A) is incorrect. A proper critique should focus on both positive and negative aspects of the learner's performance. **Answer (B) is incorrect.** A proper critique should focus on both positive and negative aspects of the learner's performance.

8. The process of gathering measurable information to meet evaluation needs of a learner is known as what?

   A. Critique.

   B. Assessment.

   C. Appraisal.

Answer (B) is correct. (FAA-H-8083-9B Chap 6)
   DISCUSSION: Assessment is the process of gathering measurable information to meet evaluation needs.
   Answer (A) is incorrect. The critique is an instructor-to-learner assessment used in conjunction with either a traditional or an authentic assessment. **Answer (C) is incorrect.** While an assessment includes a combination of the ability to analyze, appraise, and judge learner performance, appraisal is not as all-encompassing a term as an assessment.

6.2 Types of Assessment

9. FAA Practical Test Standards are

    A.   criterion-referenced.

    B.   diagnostic-assessed.

    C.   formative-assessed.

Answer (A) is correct. (FAA-H-8083-9B Chap 6)
    DISCUSSION: Practical tests for maintenance technicians and pilots are criterion-referenced tests because the objective is for all successful applicants to meet the high standards of knowledge, skill, and safety required by one core standards document (the PTS) rather than other applicants seeking certification.
    Answer (B) is incorrect. Diagnostic assessments are used to assess learner knowledge or skills prior to a course of instruction. **Answer (C) is incorrect.** Formative assessments, which are not graded, are used as a wrap-up of the lesson and to set the stage for the next lesson. This type of assessment, which is limited to what transpired during that lesson, informs and guides the instructor on which areas to reinforce.

10. Practical tests for pilot certification are

    A.   evaluation-referenced.

    B.   selection type tests.

    C.   criterion-referenced.

Answer (C) is correct. (FAA-H-8083-9B Chap 6)
    DISCUSSION: Criterion-referenced tests measure an applicant's performance against carefully written, measurable standards or criteria. Practical tests for pilot certification are criterion-referenced. The PTS are the criteria.
    Answer (A) is incorrect. Practical tests are a form of evaluation, not evaluation-referenced. Evaluation-referenced is not a type of testing. **Answer (B) is incorrect.** Selection type tests require the learner to select an answer from two or more alternatives.

11. The Practical Test Standards should be used in

    A.   flight training and testing.

    B.   flight training only.

    C.   testing only.

Answer (A) is correct. (FAA-H-8083-9B Chap 6)
    DISCUSSION: Because the Practical Test Standards (PTS) documents are the primary evaluation tool of the FAA for the issuance of a pilot certificate, they obviously are testing documents. Because this information is publicly accessible, these documents absolutely should be used to train pilot applicants to ensure they meet the PTS requirements. This training should not be merely to "teach the test," but the PTS is a very valuable resource in evaluating a pilot applicant's eligibility to take the practical test.
    Answer (B) is incorrect. The PTS documents are the primary evaluation tool of the FAA for the issuance of a pilot certificate; therefore, they are to be used as testing documents in addition to their use as flight training skill standards. **Answer (C) is incorrect.** While the PTS documents are the primary evaluation tool of the FAA for the issuance of a pilot certificate, they are also a very valuable resource in evaluating a pilot applicant's eligibility to take the practical test.

12. To evaluate a learner's ability to use critical thinking skills in performing real-world tasks, which assessment method is most appropriate?

    A.   Authentic.

    B.   Supply-type.

    C.   Learner-centered.

Answer (A) is correct. (FAA-H-8083-9B Chap 6)
    DISCUSSION: Authentic assessment is a type of assessment in which the learner is asked to perform real-world tasks and demonstrate a meaningful application of skills and competencies. Authentic assessment lies at the heart of training today's aviation learners to use critical thinking skills.
    Answer (B) is incorrect. A supply-type test can be very helpful, for example, on a pre-solo knowledge test in determining whether the pilot in training has adequate knowledge of procedures, but it would not offer insight into a learner's critical thinking skills in performing real-world tasks. **Answer (C) is incorrect.** Learner-centered assessment is a component of authentic assessment, but it is not the same thing.

13. The objective of the Airman Certification Standards (ACS) is to ensure the certification of pilots at a high level of performance and proficiency, consistent with

   A. the time available.
   B. safety.
   C. their abilities.

Answer (B) is correct. (FAA-H-8083-9B Chap 6)
   DISCUSSION: The objective of the ACS is to ensure the certification of pilots at a high level of performance and proficiency, consistent with safety.
   Answer (A) is incorrect. The objective of the ACS is to ensure the certification of pilots at a high level of performance and proficiency, consistent with safety, not the time available.
   Answer (C) is incorrect. The objective of the ACS is to ensure the certification of pilots at a high level of performance and proficiency, consistent with safety, not their abilities.

14. Instructors must be aware of the fact that

   A. FAA Practical Test Standards (PTS) books are testing documents only.
   B. FAA Practical Test Standards (PTS) books should be introduced early in training and used as a measuring stick for learner performance and progress.
   C. FAA Practical Test Standards (PTS) books should be introduced 6 hours prior to the practical test.

Answer (A) is correct. (FAA-H-8083-9B Chap 6)
   DISCUSSION: The PTS is a testing tool, not a teaching tool. The overall focus of flight training should be on education, learning, and understanding why the standards are there and how they were set. The minimum standards to pass the checkride should not be introduced until the 3 hours of preparation for the checkride. To accommodate this, the FAA requires 3 hours of training in the 60 days preceding the Practical Test.
   Answer (B) is incorrect. The PTS should only be introduced in the last 3 hours of flight training prior to the checkride. **Answer (C) is incorrect.** The PTS should be introduced 3 hours, not 6 hours, prior to the checkride.

15. The FAA Practical Test Standards

   A. should be used as a primary training tool.
   B. contain tasks in addition to those presented in 14 CFR Part 61.
   C. contain testing standards only.

Answer (B) is correct. (FAA-H-8083-9B Chap 6)
   DISCUSSION: The PTS Areas of Operation for each pilot certificate and rating are listed in 14 CFR Part 61. The PTS documents list specific tasks that must be performed for each Area of Operation during an FAA Practical Test for a given certificate or rating.
   Answer (A) is incorrect. Instructors should avoid merely teaching from the PTS as this encourages learner pilots to aim for the minimum passing standard. While the PTS should obviously be a measuring standard, it should not be the primary teaching tool for a course of training. Instead, CFIs should use a training syllabus appropriate to the training that addresses the PTS tasks in a logical, productive way. **Answer (C) is incorrect.** In addition to testing standards, the PTS documents also contain important information on the conduct of the test, special emphasis items, pilot/instructor/examiner considerations, and test checklists.

16. A pretest constructed to measure knowledge and skills necessary to begin a course is referred to as a

   A. virtual-reality test.
   B. evaluation-referenced.
   C. criterion-referenced test.

Answer (C) is correct. (FAA-H-8083-9B Chap 6)
   DISCUSSION: A pretest is a criterion-referenced test constructed to measure the knowledge and skills that are necessary to begin a course. Criterion-referenced tests measure a learner's performance against carefully written, measurable standards or criteria.
   Answer (A) is incorrect. Virtual reality is a potential future method of computer-based training (CBT) that can simulate environments very realistically. It is not a type of test. **Answer (B) is incorrect.** Practical tests are a form of evaluation, not evaluation-referenced. Evaluation-referenced is not a type of testing.

17. Criterion-based assessment items would most likely be part of

    A. performance-based tests.

    B. multiple choice tests.

    C. oral quizzing.

Answer (A) is correct. (FAA-H-8083-9B Chap 6)
    DISCUSSION: Criterion-based tests are performance-based tests. In addition to the behavior expected, criterion objectives state the conditions under which the behavior is to be performed and the criteria that must be met. If the instructor developed performance-based objectives during the creation of lesson plans, criterion objectives have already been formulated. The criterion objective provides the framework for developing the test items used to measure the level of learning objectives.
    Answer (B) is incorrect. Criterion-based assessments are performance-based tests that may be administered through multiple formats. **Answer (C) is incorrect.** Criterion-based assessments are performance-based tests that may be administered through multiple formats.

18. Performance-based objectives are a distinguishable characteristic of

    A. formative assessments.

    B. subjective grading.

    C. criterion-referenced testing.

Answer (C) is correct. (FAA-H-8083-9B Chap 6)
    DISCUSSION: Performance-based objectives serve as a reference for the development of test items in criterion-referenced testing. Criterion-referenced tests evaluate based on carefully written, measurable standards or criteria.
    Answer (A) is incorrect. Formative assessments, which are not graded, are used as a wrap-up of the lesson and to set the stage for the next lesson. This type of assessment, which is limited to what transpired during that lesson, informs and guides the instructor on which areas to reinforce. **Answer (B) is incorrect.** Performance-based objectives provide carefully written, measurable standards or criteria for testing. They do not allow for subjective grading.

19. What is true of traditional assessments?

    A. They require the learner to demonstrate meaningful application of skills.

    B. They evaluate a learner's progress at a rote level of learning.

    C. There are multiple correct responses in traditional assessments.

Answer (B) is correct. (FAA-H-8083-9B Chap 6)
    DISCUSSION: Traditional assessments often involve written tests and are more likely to be used to evaluate a learner's progress at the rote level of learning.
    Answer (A) is incorrect. Authentic assessment, not traditional assessment, requires the learner to demonstrate meaningful application of skills and competencies. **Answer (C) is incorrect.** In a traditional assessment, only one single answer will be correct.

20. Which of the following assessment types focuses on real-world tasks?

    A. Traditional.

    B. Formal.

    C. Authentic.

Answer (C) is correct. (FAA-H-8083-9B Chap 6)
    DISCUSSION: Authentic assessment requires the learner to demonstrate not just the rote and understanding levels, but also the application and correlation levels of learning. Authentic assessment generally requires the learner to perform real-world tasks.
    Answer (A) is incorrect. During traditional assessment, the learner usually has a set amount of time to recognize or reproduce memorized terms, formulas, or data. There is a single answer that is correct. Consequently, the traditional assessment is more likely to be used to judge or evaluate the learner's progress at the rote and understanding levels of learning. **Answer (B) is incorrect.** Whether traditional or authentic, an assessment can be either formal or informal. Formal assessments usually involve documentation, such as a quiz or written examination. They are used periodically throughout a course, as well as at the end of a course, to measure and document whether or not the course objectives have been met.

21. Which type of assessment is more beneficial during the early stages of training?

   A. Learner-centered assessments.

   B. Traditional assessments.

   C. Authentic assessments.

Answer (B) is correct. (FAA-H-8083-9B Chap 6)
   DISCUSSION: Traditional assessments are generally more useful in the early phases of training, as the learner may not have enough information or knowledge about the concepts to participate fully.
   Answer (A) is incorrect. A learner-centered assessment, an aspect assessment, is a form of learner-centered grading that uses open-ended questions to guide the learner through a self-assessment. **Answer (C) is incorrect.** Authentic assessments may not be as useful as traditional assessments in the early phases of training, as the learner may not have enough information or knowledge about the concepts to participate fully.

22. What are the four steps in the learner-centered assessment process?

   A. Replay, reconstruct, redesign, redirect.

   B. Replay, reconstruct, reflect, redirect.

   C. Replay, repeat, reflect, redirect.

Answer (B) is correct. (FAA-H-8083-9B Chap 6)
   DISCUSSION: The four steps in the learner-centered assessment process are replay, reconstruct, reflect, redirect.
   Answer (A) is incorrect. Redesign is not a step in the learner-centered assessment process. The four steps in the learner-centered assessment process are replay, reconstruct, reflect, redirect. **Answer (C) is incorrect.** Repeat is not a step in the learner-centered assessment process and is the same as replay. The four steps in the learner-centered assessment process are replay, reconstruct, reflect, redirect.

23. What step in the learner-centered assessment process helps the learner relate the lessons learned to other experiences?

   A. Redirect.

   B. Replay.

   C. Reconstruct.

Answer (A) is correct. (FAA-H-8083-9B Chap 6)
   DISCUSSION: The last step, that of redirecting, helps the learner relate the lessons learned to other experiences and consider how they might help in future sessions.
   Answer (B) is incorrect. Replay occurs when a learner is asked to verbally replay or repeat the flight or procedure. **Answer (C) is incorrect.** Reconstruction occurs when the learner identifies key things that (s)he should or could have done differently during the flight or maneuver.

24. What grading dimension or level has a learner reached when they correctly gather information, identify proper courses of action, evaluate risk, and make an appropriate decision without instructor input?

   A. Explain.

   B. Practice.

   C. Manage-Decide.

Answer (C) is correct. (FAA-H-8083-9B Chap 6)
   DISCUSSION: A learner who correctly gathers information, identifies proper courses of action, evaluates risks for each course of action, and makes the appropriate decision without instructor input is at the "Manage-Decide" grading dimension of Single-Pilot Management.
   Answer (A) is incorrect. The grading dimension "Explain" describes when a learner can verbally identify, describe, and understand risks but needs to be prompted to make decisions. **Answer (B) is incorrect.** The grading dimension "Practice" describes a learner who properly identifies, understands, and applies SRM principles and corrects minor deviations identified by the instructor.

6.3 Critiques and Oral Assessments

25. Which is a valid reason for the use of proper oral quizzing during a lesson?

   A. Promotes active learner participation.

   B. Identifies points that need less emphasis.

   C. Helps the instructor determine the general intelligence level of the learners.

Answer (A) is correct. (FAA-H-8083-9B Chap 6)
   DISCUSSION: A valid reason for the use of proper oral quizzing during a lesson is to promote active learner participation, which is important to effective teaching.
   Answer (B) is incorrect. A valid reason for the use of proper oral quizzing during a lesson is that it identifies points that need more, not less, emphasis. **Answer (C) is incorrect.** A valid reason for the use of proper oral quizzing during a lesson is to check the learners' comprehension of what has been learned, not their general intelligence level.

26. Proper oral quizzing by the instructor during a lesson can have which result?

   A. Alerts the instructor to the level of learner motivation.

   B. Identifies points which need more emphasis.

   C. Can serve as a lead-in to introduce new material.

Answer (B) is correct. (FAA-H-8083-9B Chap 6)
   DISCUSSION: One desirable result of oral quizzing is that it helps the instructor identify points that need more emphasis. By noting learners' answers, the instructor can quickly spot weak points in understanding and give these extra attention.
   Answer (A) is incorrect. Learner performance on oral quizzes can indicate weak points in understanding but will not help the instructor gauge learner motivation. **Answer (C) is incorrect.** The introduction of new material is accomplished during the presentation, not evaluation, step of the teaching process.

27. One desirable result of proper oral quizzing by the instructor is to

   A. reveal the effectiveness of the instructor's training procedures.

   B. fulfill the requirements set forth in the overall objectives of the course.

   C. reveal the essential information from which the learner can determine progress.

Answer (A) is correct. (FAA-H-8083-9B Chap 6)
   DISCUSSION: One desirable result of proper oral quizzing by the instructor is that it reveals the effectiveness of the instructor's training procedures.
   Answer (B) is incorrect. Quizzing can only measure achievement, not fulfill the requirements, of the overall objectives of the course. **Answer (C) is incorrect.** An instructor should use the critique, not a quiz, to reveal the essential information from which the learner can determine progress.

28. During oral quizzing, which type of questions should an instructor expect a learner to answer based on memory or recall?

   A. Trick questions.

   B. Fact questions.

   C. HOTS (higher order thinking skills) questions.

Answer (B) is correct. (FAA-H-8083-9B Chap 6)
   DISCUSSION: The most common means of assessment is direct or indirect oral questioning of learners by the instructor. Questions may be loosely classified as fact questions and HOTS questions. The answer to a fact question is based on memory or recall. This type of question usually concerns who, what, when, and where. HOTS questions involve why or how, and they require the learner to combine knowledge of facts with an ability to analyze situations, solve problems, and arrive at conclusions.
   Answer (A) is incorrect. Trick questions should be avoided because they are a detriment to the learning process, but they can exist as either fact questions or HOTS questions. **Answer (C) is incorrect.** A HOTS question involves why or how, and it requires the learner to combine knowledge of facts with an ability to analyze situations, solve problems, and arrive at conclusions.

29. To be effective in oral quizzing during the conduct of a lesson, a question should

- A. be of suitable difficulty for that stage of training.
- B. include a combination of where, how, and why.
- C. divert the learner's thoughts to subjects covered in other lessons.

Answer (A) is correct. (FAA-H-8083-9B Chap 6)
DISCUSSION: During oral quizzing, an effective question must present a challenge to the learner. A question must be of suitable difficulty for the learner at that particular stage of training. These types of questions stimulate learning.
Answer (B) is incorrect. An effective question should be limited to who, what, when, where, how, or why, not a combination. **Answer (C) is incorrect.** An effective question must apply to the subject of instruction, not divert the learner's thoughts to subjects covered in other lessons.

30. During oral quizzing in a given lesson, effective questions should

- A. be brief and concise.
- B. provide answers that can be expressed in a variety of ways.
- C. divert the learner's thoughts to subjects covered in previous lessons.

Answer (A) is correct. (FAA-H-8083-9B Chap 6)
DISCUSSION: During oral quizzing, an effective question should be brief and concise but should also be clear and definite. Enough words must be used to establish the conditions or situations exactly so that instructor and learners will have the same mental picture.
Answer (B) is incorrect. All effective questions will have only one correct answer. **Answer (C) is incorrect.** An effective question must apply to the subject of instruction, not divert the learner's thoughts to subjects covered in previous lessons.

31. In all quizzing as a portion of the instruction process, the questions should

- A. include catch questions to develop the learner's perceptive power.
- B. call for specific answers and be readily evaluated by the instructor.
- C. include questions with more than one central idea to evaluate how completely a learner understands the subject.

Answer (B) is correct. (FAA-H-8083-9B Chap 6)
DISCUSSION: In any kind of testing, questions should have one specific answer so that the instructor can readily evaluate the learner's response. General questions tend to confuse rather than help, and unanswered questions serve no useful purpose at all.
Answer (A) is incorrect. Catch questions should be avoided at all times. The learners will feel they are engaged in a battle of wits with the instructor, and the whole significance of the subject of instruction will be lost. **Answer (C) is incorrect.** Effective questions used in quizzing should center on only one central idea.

32. To answer a learner's question, it is most important that the instructor

- A. clearly understand the question.
- B. have complete knowledge of the subject.
- C. introduce more complicated information to partially answer the question, if necessary.

Answer (A) is correct. (FAA-H-8083-9B Chap 6)
DISCUSSION: The answering of learners' questions can be an effective teaching method. To answer a learner's question, it is most important that the instructor clearly understands the question.
Answer (B) is incorrect. While an instructor may have knowledge of a subject, occasionally a learner will ask a question the instructor cannot answer. The instructor should admit not knowing the answer and should promise to get the answer or help the learner to find it. **Answer (C) is incorrect.** Introducing more complicated information to partially answer the question is normally unwise. Doing so would confuse the learner and complicate the learning task at hand.

33. With regards to oral quizzing, which type of question requires the learner to combine knowledge with the ability to analyze, solve problems, and arrive at conclusions?

- A. Fact questions.
- B. HOTS questions.
- C. Provocative questions.

Answer (B) is correct. (FAA-H-8083-9B Chap 6)
DISCUSSION: HOTS, or higher order thinking skills, questions usually involve why or how and require the learner to combine knowledge of facts with the ability to analyze situations, solve problems, and arrive at conclusions.
Answer (A) is incorrect. Fact questions involve answers that are based on memory or recall. This type of question usually concerns who, what, when, and where. **Answer (C) is incorrect.** Provocative, or controversial, questions are a type that should be avoided in oral quizzing.

34. For oral quizzing to be effective during a lesson, a question should

    A. be limited to who, what, when, where, why, or how, not a combination.

    B. include a combination of where, how, and why.

    C. be easy for the learner at that particular stage of training.

Answer (A) is correct. (FAA-H-8083-9B Chap 6)
    DISCUSSION: To be effective in oral quizzing, each question should center on only one idea, which is limited to who, what, where, when, how, or why, not a combination.
    Answer (B) is incorrect. A single question should be limited to who, what, when, where, how, or why, not a combination. **Answer (C) is incorrect.** Questions of suitable difficulty serve to stimulate learning. To be effective, questions must be adapted to the ability, experience, and stage of training of the learners and be of suitable difficulty.

35. When an instructor critiques a learner, it should always be

    A. done in private.

    B. subjective rather than objective.

    C. conducted immediately after the learner's performance.

Answer (C) is correct. (FAA-H-8083-9B Chap 6)
    DISCUSSION: The critique should always be conducted immediately after the learner's performance while the performance is still fresh in the learner's mind. Specific comments on "your third turn," for instance, would have little value a week after the maneuver was performed.
    Answer (A) is incorrect. A critique may be conducted in private or before the entire class. A critique presented before the entire class can be beneficial to every learner in the classroom as well as to the learner who performed the exercise. **Answer (B) is incorrect.** The critique should be objective rather than subjective.

36. Using double negatives is an example of which type of question that should be avoided?

    A. Irrelevant questions.

    B. Oversize questions.

    C. Trick questions.

Answer (C) is correct. (FAA-H-8083-9B Chap 6)
    DISCUSSION: Trick questions, such as double negatives, cause a learner to feel (s)he is engaged in a battle of wits with the instructor, thus changing learner focus from the message to the messenger.
    Answer (A) is incorrect. Irrelevant questions are diversions that introduce unrelated facts and thoughts and slow learner progress. **Answer (B) is incorrect.** Oversize questions are too broad in scope and could have multiple correct/incorrect responses. An example might be: "What is required before going flying?"

37. Which of the following is not a type of critique?

    A. Written critique.

    B. Instructor-absence critique.

    C. Individual learner critique by another learner.

Answer (B) is correct. (FAA-H-8083-9B Chap 6)
    DISCUSSION: Instructor-absence is not a type of critique. During all types of critiques, the instructor should be present to carefully control the process.
    Answer (A) is incorrect. The written critique is a type of critique. **Answer (C) is incorrect.** Individual learner critique by another learner is a type of critique.

38. What is a benefit of a written critique?

    A. The learner will have a permanent record of suggestions.

    B. Learners get to work together, thus sharing ideas.

    C. The written critique is always positive.

Answer (A) is correct. (FAA-H-8083-9B Chap 6)
    DISCUSSION: Learners will have a permanent record of suggestions, recommendations, and opinions to reference at a later date if needed.
    Answer (B) is incorrect. The sharing of ideas is a characteristic of the small group critique, not the written critique. **Answer (C) is incorrect.** All critiques, no matter what the format, can include both positive and negative comments.

39. What is true of irrelevant questions?

    A. They are too broad in scope and could have multiple correct responses.

    B. They change the learner's focus from the message to the messenger.

    C. They introduce unrelated facts and slow learner progress.

Answer (C) is correct. *(FAA-H-8083-9B Chap 6)*
    DISCUSSION: Irrelevant questions are diversions that introduce unrelated facts and thoughts and slow learner progress.
    Answer (A) is incorrect. Oversize questions, not irrelevant questions, are too broad in scope and could have multiple correct/incorrect responses. **Answer (B) is incorrect.** Trick questions are questions that cause the learner to feel (s)he is engaged in a battle of wits with the instructor, thus changing learner focus from the message to the messenger.

40. An instructor's critique of a learner's performance should be

    A. as varied in content as the performance being evaluated.

    B. an opportunity for an instructor to be critical of a learner's performance.

    C. always conducted in private.

Answer (A) is correct. *(FAA-H-8083-9B Chap 6)*
    DISCUSSION: An effective critique considers good as well as bad performance, the individual parts, relationships of the individual parts, and the overall performance. A critique can and usually should be as varied in content as the performance being evaluated.
    Answer (B) is incorrect. The word "critique" sometimes has a negative connotation, and the instructor needs to avoid using this method as an opportunity to be overly critical of learner performance. **Answer (C) is incorrect.** A critique may be conducted privately or before the entire class. A critique presented before the entire class can be beneficial to every learner in the classroom, as well as to the learner who performed the exercise or assignment. In this case, however, the instructor should avoid embarrassing the learner in front of the class.

41. The purpose of a critique is to

    A. identify only the learner's faults and weaknesses.

    B. give a delayed evaluation of the learner's performance.

    C. provide direction and guidance to raise the level of the learner's performance.

Answer (C) is correct. *(FAA-H-8083-9B Chap 6)*
    DISCUSSION: A critique provides the learner with constructive feedback (s)he can build upon. It should provide direction and guidance to raise the learner's level of performance.
    Answer (A) is incorrect. An effective critique considers good as well as bad performance. It is not necessarily negative in content. **Answer (B) is incorrect.** A critique is not the same thing as an evaluation, as it does not determine a learner's progress in a course. Even as part of an evaluation, a critique (guidance) should not be delayed.

6.4 Types of Written Test Questions

42. What is a characteristic of supply-type test items?

A. They are easily adapted to testing knowledge of facts and details.

B. Test results would be graded the same regardless of the learner or the grader.

C. The same test graded by different instructors would probably be given different scores.

Answer (C) is correct. (FAA-H-8083-9B Chap 6)
DISCUSSION: A characteristic of supply-type test items is that they cannot be graded with uniformity. The same test graded by different instructors would probably be assigned different scores. The same test graded by the same instructor on consecutive days might be assigned two different scores. There is no assurance that the grade assigned is the grade deserved.
Answer (A) is incorrect. True/false, not supply-type, test items are easily adapted to testing knowledge of facts and details. **Answer (B) is incorrect.** Selection-type, not supply-type, test items would be graded the same regardless of the learner or the grader.

43. Which is the main disadvantage of supply-type test items?

A. They cannot be graded with uniformity.

B. They are readily answered by guessing.

C. They are easily adapted to statistical analysis.

Answer (A) is correct. (FAA-H-8083-9B Chap 6)
DISCUSSION: The main disadvantage of supply-type test items is that they cannot be graded with uniformity. The same test graded by different instructors would probably be assigned different scores. The same test graded by the same instructor on consecutive days might be assigned two different scores. There is no assurance that the grade assigned is the grade deserved.
Answer (B) is incorrect. The main disadvantage of true/false, not supply-type, test items is they are readily answered by guessing. **Answer (C) is incorrect.** An advantage, not disadvantage, of selection-type, not supply-type, test items is that they are easily adapted to statistical analysis.

44. The primary advantage of supply-type testing is that

A. it can be graded quickly.

B. the learner is required to organize knowledge.

C. it can be graded with an answer key.

Answer (B) is correct. (FAA-H-8083-9A Appendix B)
DISCUSSION: Supply-type test items require the learner to furnish a response in the form of a word, sentence, or paragraph. The supply-type item requires the learner to organize knowledge. It demands an ability to express ideas and is thus valuable in measuring the learner's generalized understanding of a subject. For example, the supply-type item on a pre-solo knowledge test can be very helpful in determining whether the pilot in training has adequate knowledge of procedures.
Answer (A) is incorrect. Supply-type tests require more time for the learner to complete and more time for the instructor to grade. **Answer (C) is incorrect.** Supply-type tests cannot be effectively graded with an answer key. The same test graded by different instructors could be assigned different scores. Even the same test graded by the same instructor on consecutive days might be assigned altogether different scores.

45. Which statement is true relative to effective multiple-choice test items?

A. Negative words or phrases need not be emphasized.

B. Items should call for abstract background knowledge.

C. Keep all alternatives of approximately equal length.

Answer (C) is correct. (FAA-H-8083-9B Chap 6)
DISCUSSION: In preparing and reviewing the alternatives to a multiple-choice item, it is advisable to keep all alternatives approximately the same length. Research of instructor-made tests reveals that, in general, correct alternatives are longer than incorrect ones.
Answer (A) is incorrect. When negative words or phrases are used, they should be emphasized in order to be effective. **Answer (B) is incorrect.** Items should call for essential knowledge rather than for abstract background knowledge or unimportant facts.

46. Which type of test item creates the greatest probability of guessing?

A. True/false.

B. Supply-type.

C. Multiple-choice.

Answer (A) is correct. (FAA-H-8083-9B Chap 6)
DISCUSSION: The true/false test item creates the greatest probability of guessing because the learner always has a 50% chance of guessing correctly.
Answer (B) is incorrect. The true/false, not the supply-type, test item creates the greatest probability of guessing. **Answer (C) is incorrect.** The true/false, not the multiple-choice, test item creates the greatest probability of guessing.

47. One of the main advantages of selection-type test items over supply-type test items is that the selection-type

A. decreases discrimination between responses.

B. would be graded objectively regardless of the learner or the grader.

C. precludes comparison of learners under one instructor with those under another instructor.

Answer (B) is correct. *(FAA-H-8083-9B Chap 6)*
    DISCUSSION: One of the main advantages of selection-type test items over supply-type test items is that the selection-type are graded objectively regardless of the learner or grader.
    Answer (A) is incorrect. An advantage of the selection-type test item over the supply-type test item is that more areas of knowledge can be tested in a given time, thus increasing, not decreasing, comprehensiveness, validity, and discrimination.
    Answer (C) is incorrect. An advantage of the selection-type test item over supply-type test item is the ability to compare, not to preclude comparison of, learner performance under one instructor with those of another instructor.

48. Which statement is true about multiple-choice test items that are intended to measure achievement at a higher level of learning?

A. It is unethical to mislead learners into selecting an incorrect alternative.

B. Some or all of the alternatives should be acceptable, but only one should be clearly better than the others.

C. The use of common errors as distracting alternatives to divert the learner from the correct response is ineffective and invalid.

Answer (B) is correct. *(FAA-H-8083-9B Chap 6)*
    DISCUSSION: When multiple-choice test items are intended to measure achievement at a higher level of learning, some or all of the alternatives should be acceptable, but only one should be clearly better than the others. The instructions given should direct the learner to select the best alternative.
    Answer (A) is incorrect. When using multiple-choice test items, the learners are not supposed to guess the correct answer; they should select it only if they know it is correct. Thus, it is ethical, not unethical, to mislead learners into selecting an incorrect alternative. **Answer (C) is incorrect.** When using multiple-choice test items, the use of common errors as distracting alternatives to divert the learner from the correct response is effective, not ineffective, and valid, not invalid.

49. Which is one of the major difficulties encountered in the construction of multiple-choice test items?

A. Adapting the items to statistical item analysis.

B. Keeping all responses approximately equal in length.

C. Inventing distractors which will be attractive to learners lacking knowledge or understanding.

Answer (C) is correct. *(FAA-H-8083-9B Chap 6)*
    DISCUSSION: Three major difficulties are encountered in the construction of multiple-choice test items:

1. Development of a question or an item stem that can be expressed clearly without ambiguity.
2. Statement of an answer that cannot be refuted.
3. The invention of lures or distractors attractive to those learners who do not possess the knowledge or understanding necessary to recognize the correct answer.

    Answer (A) is incorrect. It is a major advantage, not difficulty, for a multiple-choice test item to be well adapted to statistical item analysis. **Answer (B) is incorrect.** A principle, not difficulty, of constructing a multiple-choice test item is to keep all responses approximately equal in length.

50. In a written test, which type of selection-type test items reduces the probability of guessing correct responses?

A. Essay.

B. Matching.

C. Multiple-choice.

Answer (B) is correct. *(FAA-H-8083-9B Chap 6)*
    DISCUSSION: In a written test, matching test items reduces the probability of guessing correct responses compared to a series of multiple-choice items covering the same material, especially if alternatives are used more than once.
    Answer (A) is incorrect. An essay question is a supply-type, not selection-type, test item. **Answer (C) is incorrect.** Matching, not multiple-choice, test items reduce the probability of guessing correct responses.

51. Which part of a multiple-choice test includes the question, statement, or problem?

A. The response.

B. The root.

C. The stem.

Answer (C) is correct. *(FAA-H-8083-9B Chap 6)*
    DISCUSSION: The stem includes the question, statement, or problem.
    Answer (A) is incorrect. The responses in a multiple-choice test are the combination of both the distractors and the one correct answer. **Answer (B) is incorrect.** The stem, not the root, of a question includes the question, statement, or problem.

6.5   Characteristics of a Good Test

52. A written test that has reliability

    A. yields consistent results.

    B. measures small differences in the achievement of learners.

    C. actually measures what it is supposed to measure and nothing else.

Answer (A) is correct. (FAA-H-8083-9B Chap 6)
DISCUSSION: A written test that has reliability is one that yields consistent results.
Answer (B) is incorrect. A written test that shows discrimination, not reliability, measures small differences in the achievement of learners. **Answer (C) is incorrect.** A written test that has validity, not reliability, actually measures what it is supposed to measure and nothing else.

53. A written test has validity when it

    A. yields consistent results.

    B. samples liberally whatever is being measured.

    C. measures what it is supposed to measure.

Answer (C) is correct. (FAA-H-8083-9B Chap 6)
DISCUSSION: A written test has validity when it measures what it is supposed to measure.
Answer (A) is incorrect. A written test has reliability, not validity, when it yields consistent results. **Answer (B) is incorrect.** A written test has comprehensiveness, not validity, when it samples liberally whatever is being measured.

54. Comprehensiveness is the degree to which a test

    A. measures the overall objectives.

    B. consists of an appropriate mix of easy, medium, and difficult questions.

    C. includes multiple-choice, essay, and true/false questions.

Answer (A) is correct. (FAA-H-8083-9B Chap 6)
DISCUSSION: Comprehensiveness is the degree to which a test measures the overall objectives. A written test must sample an appropriate cross-section of the objectives of instruction. The instructor has to make certain the evaluation includes a representative and comprehensive sampling of the objectives of the course.
Answer (B) is incorrect. Determining an "appropriate" mix of the difficulty level of questions is not necessary for a test to be comprehensive. **Answer (C) is incorrect.** The degree to which a test measures the overall objectives is not determined by the question type, but instead by the question content.

55. A written test is said to be comprehensive when it

    A. includes all levels of difficulty.

    B. samples liberally whatever is being measured.

    C. measures knowledge of the same topic in many different ways.

Answer (B) is correct. (FAA-H-8083-9B Chap 6)
DISCUSSION: A written test is said to be comprehensive when it samples liberally whatever is being measured.
Answer (A) is incorrect. A written test shows discrimination, not comprehensiveness, when it includes all levels of difficulty. **Answer (C) is incorrect.** A written test shows discrimination, not comprehensiveness, when it measures knowledge of the same topic in many different ways.

56. The characteristic of a written test, which measures small differences in achievement between learners, is its

   A. validity.

   B. reliability.

   C. discrimination.

Answer (C) is correct. *(FAA-H-8083-9B Chap 6)*
   DISCUSSION: The characteristic of a written test that measures small differences in achievement between learners is its discrimination.
   Answer (A) is incorrect. A written test has validity when it measures what it is supposed to and nothing else, not when it measures small differences in achievement between learners. **Answer (B) is incorrect.** A written test that has reliability is one that yields consistent results, not which measures small differences in achievement between learners.

57. A written test having the characteristic of discrimination will

   A. be easy to give and be easily graded.

   B. distinguish between learners both low and high in achievement.

   C. include a representative and comprehensive sampling of the course objectives.

Answer (B) is correct. *(FAA-H-8083-9B Chap 6)*
   DISCUSSION: When a written test has the characteristic of discrimination, each item will distinguish between learners who are low and learners who are high in achievement of the course objectives.
   Answer (A) is incorrect. A written test having the characteristic of usability, not discrimination, will be easy to give and be easily graded. **Answer (C) is incorrect.** A written test having the characteristic of comprehensiveness, not discrimination, will include a representative and comprehensive sampling of the course objectives.

58. A written test that is objective

   A. distinguishes the differences between learners.

   B. measures what is supposed to be measured.

   C. describes the singleness of scoring a test.

Answer (C) is correct. *(FAA-H-8083-9B Chap 6)*
   DISCUSSION: Objectivity describes singleness of scoring a test.
   Answer (A) is incorrect. Discrimination, not objectivity, distinguishes the differences between learners. **Answer (B) is incorrect.** Validity, not objectivity, measures what is supposed to be measured.

59. The most important consideration in test evaluation is what?

   A. Usability.

   B. Validity.

   C. Comprehensiveness.

Answer (B) is correct. *(FAA-H-8083-9B Chap 6)*
   DISCUSSION: Validity is the most important consideration in test evaluation.
   Answer (A) is incorrect. Validity, not usability, is the most important consideration in test evaluation. **Answer (C) is incorrect.** Validity, not comprehensiveness, is the most important consideration in test evaluation.

6.6 Review and Evaluation

60. Evaluation of learner performance and accomplishment during a lesson should be based on

    A. objectives and goals established in the lesson plan.

    B. performance of each learner compared to an objective standard.

    C. each learner's ability to make an objective evaluation of their own progress.

Answer (A) is correct. (FAA-H-8083-9B Chap 5)
    DISCUSSION: The evaluation of learner performance and accomplishment during a lesson should be based on the objectives and goals that were established in the instructor's lesson plan.
    Answer (B) is incorrect. A critique, not an evaluation, is based on comparing a learner's performance to an objective standard. **Answer (C) is incorrect.** A learner's own evaluation can only be subjective, not objective. Only the instructor can provide a realistic evaluation of performance and progress.

61. Which statement is true regarding learner evaluation?

    A. The learner's own evaluations can only be objective.

    B. Evaluation of the learner's learning should be an integral part of each lesson.

    C. If deficiencies or faults not associated with the present lesson are revealed, they should be corrected immediately.

Answer (B) is correct. (FAA-H-8083-9B Chap 5)
    DISCUSSION: Review and evaluation should be an integral part of each classroom or flight lesson. At the end of each class period, the instructor should review what has been covered during the lesson and require the learners to demonstrate the extent to which the lesson objectives have been met. Evaluation can be formal (performance, written tests) or informal (oral quiz or guided discussion).
    Answer (A) is incorrect. The learner's own evaluations can only be subjective, not objective. **Answer (C) is incorrect.** If deficiencies or faults not associated with the present lesson are revealed, they should be noted and pointed out. Corrective measures that are practicable at the time should be taken immediately, but more thorough remedial actions must be included in future lesson plans.

62. Which type test is desirable for evaluating training that involves an operation, procedure, or process?

    A. Oral.

    B. Performance.

    C. Proficiency.

Answer (B) is correct. (FAA-H-8083-9B Chap 6)
    DISCUSSION: Performance testing is desirable for evaluating training that involves an operation, procedure, or process. This method of evaluation is particularly suited to the measurement of a learner's ability in performing a task, either mental or physical.
    Answer (A) is incorrect. Performance, not oral, testing is desirable for evaluating training that involves an operation, procedure, or process. **Answer (C) is incorrect.** There is no proficiency-type test in evaluation, only oral, written, or performance.

63. When a learner performs a maneuver correctly but the instructor suspects the learner does not fully understand the principles and objectives involved, the instructor should

    A. defer on the matter to avoid lowering learner confidence.

    B. point out the suspected flaw to the learner.

    C. vary the performance of the maneuver slightly.

Answer (C) is correct. (FAA-H-8083-9B Chap 9)
    DISCUSSION: Learners may perform a procedure or maneuver correctly but not fully understand the principles and objectives involved. If the instructor suspects this, learners should be required to vary the performance of the maneuver or procedure slightly. Learners who do not understand the principles involved will probably not be able to successfully complete the revised maneuver or procedure.
    Answer (A) is incorrect. While it is important to prevent learner discouragement, it is more important to ensure that the learner possesses the required level of skill in each phase of training. Rather than ignoring the situation, an instructor can require that the learner repeat the maneuver in a slightly different way, thus evaluating the depth of the learner's mastery of the maneuver. **Answer (B) is incorrect.** Rather than projecting negativity onto the learner in a situation where the instructor could well be mistaken, it is best to have the learner perform the maneuver in a slightly different way, thus evaluating the depth of the learner's mastery of the maneuver.

APPENDIX A
FUNDAMENTALS OF INSTRUCTING PRACTICE TEST

The following 50 questions have been randomly selected from the fundamentals of instructing questions in our flight and ground instructor test bank. Topical coverage in this practice test is similar to that of the FAA pilot knowledge test. Use the correct answer listing on page 168 to grade your practice test.

1. To communicate effectively, instructors must

A — recognize the level of comprehension.
B — provide an atmosphere which encourages questioning.
C — reveal a positive attitude while delivering their message.

2. A communicator's words cannot communicate the desired meaning to another person unless the

A — words have meaningful referents.
B — words give the meaning that is in the mind of the receiver.
C — listener or reader has had some experience with the objects or concepts to which these words refer.

3. During integrated flight instruction, the instructor must be sure the learner

A — develops the habit of looking for other traffic.
B — is able to control the aircraft for extended periods under IMC.
C — can depend on the flight instruments when maneuvering by outside references.

4. Which statement is true regarding lesson plans?

A — Lesson plans should not be directed toward the course objective; only to the lesson objective.
B — A well-thought-out mental outline of a lesson may be used any time as long as the instructor is well prepared.
C — Lesson plans help instructors keep a constant check on their own activity as well as that of their learners.

5. (Refer to Figure 1 on page 131.) Section A is titled:

A — Overview.
B — Objective.
C — Introduction.

6. (Refer to Figure 1 on page 131.) Section C is titled:

A — Schedule.
B — Overview.
C — Training Schedule.

7. Which statement is true regarding true professionalism as an instructor?

A — Anything less than sincere performance destroys the effectiveness of the professional instructor.
B — To achieve professionalism, actions and decisions must be limited to standard patterns and practices.
C — A single definition of professionalism would encompass all of the qualifications and considerations which must be present.

8. Learner confidence tends to be destroyed if instructors

A — bluff whenever in doubt about some point.
B — continually identify learner errors and failures.
C — direct and control the learner's actions and behavior.

9. Learners quickly become apathetic when they

A — realize material is being withheld by the instructor.
B — understand the objectives toward which they are working.
C — recognize that the instructor is not adequately prepared.

10. In the learning process, fear or the element of threat will

A — narrow the learner's perceptual field.
B — decrease the rate of associative reactions.
C — cause a learner to focus on several areas of perception.

11. When under stress, normal individuals usually react

A — by showing excellent morale followed by deep depression.

B — by responding rapidly and exactly, often automatically, within the limits of their experience and training.

C — inappropriately such as extreme overcooperation, painstaking self-control, and inappropriate laughing or singing.

12. When learners display the defense mechanism called repression, they

A — refuse to accept reality.

B — place uncomfortable thoughts into inaccessible areas of the unconscious mind.

C — attempt to justify actions by asking numerous questions.

13. When a learner presents a belief opposite to what (s)he truly believes, it usually is an indication of the defense mechanism known as

A — fantasy.

B — reaction formation.

C — displacement.

14. Which of the learner's human needs offer the greatest challenge to an instructor?

A — Physiological.

B — Psychological.

C — Self-Actualization.

15. What should an instructor do with a learner who assumes that correction of errors is not important?

A — Divide complex flight maneuvers into elements.

B — Try to reduce the learner's overconfidence to reduce the chance of an accident.

C — Raise the standard of performance for each lesson, demanding greater effort.

16. By using abstractions in the communication process, the communicator will

A — bring forth specific items of experience in the minds of the receivers.

B — be using words which refer to objects or ideas that human beings can experience directly.

C — not evoke in the listener's or reader's mind the specific items of experience the communicator intends.

17. To ensure proper habits and correct techniques during training, an instructor should

A — use the building block technique of instruction.

B — repeat subject matter the learner has already learned.

C — introduce challenging material to continually motivate the learner.

18. During the flight portion of a practical test, the examiner simulates complete loss of engine power by closing the throttle and announcing "simulated engine failure." What level of learning is being tested?

A — Application.

B — Correlation.

C — Understanding.

19. According to one theory, some forgetting is due to the unconscious practice of submerging an unpleasant experience into the subconscious. This is called

A — suppression.

B — immersion.

C — repression.

20. Responses that produce a pleasurable return are called

A — reward.

B — praise.

C — positive feedback.

21. A change in behavior as a result of experience can be defined as

A — learning.

B — knowledge.

C — understanding.

22. Individuals make more progress learning if they have a clear objective. This is one feature of the principle of

A — primacy.

B — readiness.

C — willingness.

23. Things most often repeated are best remembered because of which principle of learning?

A — Principle of effect.

B — Principle of recency.

C — Principle of exercise.

24. Which principle of learning often creates a strong impression?

A — Principle of primacy.

B — Principle of intensity.

C — Principle of readiness.

25. The factor which contributes most to a learner's failure to remain receptive to new experiences and which creates a tendency to reject additional training is

A — basic needs.

B — element of threat.

C — negative self-concept.

26. Instruction, as opposed to the trial and error method of learning, is desirable because competent instruction speeds the learning process by

A — motivating the learner to a better performance.
B — emphasizing only the important points of training.
C — teaching the relationship of perceptions as they occur.

27. The best way to prepare a learner to perform a task is to

A — explain the purpose of the task.
B — provide a clear, step-by-step example.
C — give the learner an outline of the task.

28. To be effective, an assessment should

A — not contain negative remarks.
B — treat every aspect of the performance in detail.
C — be flexible enough to satisfy the requirements of the moment.

29. Which statement is true regarding an assessment that is constructive?

A — An instructor's manner and attitude make an assessment constructive.
B — Constructive assessments can inspire a learner to improve in areas of lesser accomplishment.
C — A constructive assessment should express ideas with authority in terms that cannot be misunderstood.

30. One desirable result of proper oral quizzing by the instructor is to

A — reveal the effectiveness of the instructor's training procedures.
B — fulfill the requirements set forth in the overall objectives of the course.
C — reveal the essential information from which the learner can determine progress.

31. To be effective in oral quizzing during the conduct of a lesson, a question should

A — be of suitable difficulty for that stage of training.
B — include a combination of where, how, and why.
C — divert the learner's thoughts to subjects covered in other lessons.

32. One of the main advantages of selection-type test items over supply-type test items is that the selection-type

A — decreases discrimination between responses.
B — would be graded objectively regardless of the learner or the grader.
C — precludes comparison of learners under one instructor with those under another instructor.

33. In a written test, which type of selection-type test items reduces the probability of guessing correct responses?

A — Essay.
B — Matching.
C — Multiple-choice.

34. A written test that has reliability

A — yields consistent results.
B — measures small differences in the achievement of learners.
C — actually measures what it is supposed to measure and nothing else.

35. A written test is said to be comprehensive when it

A — includes all levels of difficulty.
B — samples liberally whatever is being measured.
C — measures knowledge of the same topic in many different ways.

36. Which statement is true regarding learner evaluation?

A — The learner's own evaluations can only be objective.
B — Evaluation of the learner's learning should be an integral part of each lesson.
C — If deficiencies or faults not associated with the present lesson are revealed, they should be corrected immediately.

37. What is the last step in the demonstration/performance method?

A — Summary.
B — Evaluation.
C — Learner performance.

38. The basic demonstration/performance method of instruction consists of several steps in proper order. They are

A — instructor tells--learner does; learner tells--learner does; learner does--instructor evaluates.
B — instructor tells--instructor does; learner tells--instructor does; learner does--instructor evaluates.
C — instructor tells--instructor does; learner tells--instructor does; learner tells--learner does; learner does--instructor evaluates.

39. What is one advantage of a lecture?

A — A lecture is effective in showing relationships between theory and practice.
B — Excellent when additional research is required.
C — Allows for maximum attainment of certain types of learning outcomes.

40. Which teaching method is most economical in terms of the time required to present a given amount of material?

A — Briefing.
B — Teaching lecture.
C — Demonstration/performance.

41. The first step in preparing a lecture is to

A — research the subject.
B — develop the main ideas or key points.
C — establish the objective and desired outcome.

42. In a guided discussion, learning is achieved through the

A — skillful use of questions.
B — use of questions, each of which contains several ideas.
C — use of reverse questions directed to the class as a whole.

43. When it appears learners have adequately discussed the ideas presented during a guided discussion, one of the most valuable tools an instructor can use is

A — a session of verbal testing.
B — a written test on the subject discussed.
C — an interim summary of what the learners accomplished.

44. Which is generally the more effective way for an instructor to properly motivate learners?

A — Maintain pleasant personal relationships with learners.
B — Provide positive motivations by the promise or achievement of rewards.
C — Reinforce their self-confidence by requiring no tasks beyond their ability to perform.

45. Which statement is true concerning motivations?

A — Motivations must be tangible to be effective.
B — Motivations may be very subtle and difficult to identify.
C — Negative motivations often are as effective as positive motivations.

46. The overall learning objective of scenario-based training (SBT) is

A — that learners will improve their ability to recall previously learned information.
B — for the learner to be more prepared to make good decisions based on a variety of real world situations.
C — to promote situational awareness and opportunities for decision making.

47. What is a characteristic of an effective scenario?

A — It should not promote errors.
B — It should be in the form of a test.
C — It should include an account of a real world situation that contains an educational message.

48. Development and assembly of blocks of learning in their proper relationship will provide a means for

A — both the instructor and learner to easily correct faulty habit patterns.
B — challenging the learner by progressively increasing the units of learning.
C — allowing the learner to master the segments of the overall pilot performance requirements individually and combining these with other related segments.

49. The method of arranging lesson material from the simple to complex, past to present, and known to unknown, is one that

A — creates learner thought pattern departures.
B — shows the relationships of the main points of the lesson.
C — requires learners to actively participate in the lesson.

50. Instructional aids used in the teaching/learning process should not be used

A — as a crutch by the instructor.
B — for teaching more in less time.
C — to visualize relationships between abstracts.

Page Intentionally Left Blank

PRACTICE TEST LIST OF ANSWERS

The listing below gives the correct answers for your fundamentals of instructing practice knowledge test and the page number in this book on which you will find each question with the complete Gleim answer explanation.

Q. #	Answer	Page	Q. #	Answer	Page	Q. #	Answer	Page	Q. #	Answer	Page
1.	C	83	14.	C	75	27.	B	42	40.	B	104
2.	C	84	15.	C	58	28.	C	148	41.	C	104
3.	A	114	16.	C	85	29.	B	149	42.	A	106
4.	C	129	17.	A	35	30.	A	154	43.	C	107
5.	B	130	18.	B	37	31.	A	155	44.	B	76
6.	A	130	19.	C	34	32.	B	159	45.	B	77
7.	A	90	20.	B	34	33.	B	159	46.	B	110
8.	A	90	21.	A	27	34.	A	160	47.	A	110
9.	C	90	22.	B	28	35.	B	160	48.	C	125
10.	A	30	23.	C	28	36.	B	162	49.	B	127
11.	B	55	24.	A	28	37.	B	109	50.	A	135
12.	B	54	25.	C	52	38.	C	109			
13.	B	54	26.	C	31	39.	A	103			

APPENDIX B
REPRINT OF THE FAA'S
AVIATION INSTRUCTOR'S HANDBOOK

The FAA's *Aviation Instructor's Handbook* (FAA-H-8083-9B) consists of 10 chapters and 4 appendixes, which are briefly outlined in Study Units 1 through 6 of this book. The complete handbook is reprinted on pages 170-395 for your reference as you prepare for your FAA knowledge test and your FAA practical test. This handbook may also be useful to you whether you are already an active flight instructor or are becoming a flight instructor.

The complete *Aviation Instructor's Handbook* also can be found online at www.faa.gov/regulations_policies/handbooks_manuals/aviation/aviation_instructors_handbook/media/aviation_instructors_handbook.pdf.

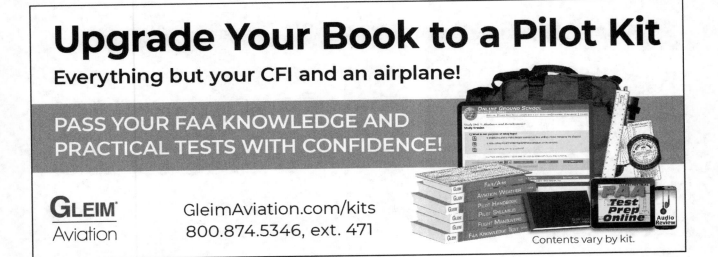

Aviation Instructor's Handbook (FAA-H-8083-9)
Preface

Designed for ground instructors, flight instructors, and aviation maintenance instructors, the Aviation Instructor's Handbook was developed by the Flight Standards Service, Airman Testing Standards Branch, in cooperation with aviation educators and industry to help beginning instructors understand and apply the fundamentals of instruction. This handbook provides aviation instructors with up-to-date information on learning and teaching, and how to relate this information to the task of teaching aeronautical knowledge and skills to learners. Experienced aviation instructors will also find the updated information useful for improving their effectiveness in training activities.

This handbook supersedes FAA-H-8083-9A, Aviation Instructor's Handbook, dated 2008.

This handbook is available for download, in PDF format, from www.faa.gov.

Comments regarding this publication should be emailed to AFS630comments@faa.gov.

The contents of this handbook do not have the force and effect of law and are not meant to bind the public in any way. This document is intended only to provide clarity to the public regarding existing requirements under the law or agency policies.

Aviation Instructor's Handbook (FAA-H-8083-9)

Acknowledgments

The Aviation Instructor's Handbook was produced by the Federal Aviation Administration (FAA). The FAA would like to extend its appreciation to several aviation industry organizations that provided assistance and input in the preparation of this handbook including: the General Aviation Manufacturers Association (GAMA), the Aircraft Owners and Pilots Association (AOPA), AOPA Air Safety Foundation (AOPA/ASF), the Experimental Aircraft Association (EAA), the National Association of Flight Instructors (NAFI), the National Air Transportation Association (NATA), the Small Aircraft Manufacturers Association (SAMA), the National Business Aviation Association (NBAA), members of the General Aviation Joint Steering Committee (GAJSC), Society of Aviation Educators (SAFE), and members of the Aviation Rulemaking Advisory Committee (ARAC) Airman Certification Standards Work Group.

Aviation Instructor's Handbook (FAA-H-8083-9)
Chapter 1: Risk Management and Single-Pilot Resource Management

Introduction

"Pull the throttle back!" Lenore, a flight instructor, ordered the learner, Jennifer, as the revolutions per minute (rpm) climbed past past 2,000 on engine start. "I did, I did!"

Both Jennifer and Lenore grabbed the mixture and pulled. The engine went from a deafening roar to silence. They looked at each other. "What happened?" asked Jennifer. "I don't know. Let's check the engine," Lenore said.

Ten minutes later, they had removed the cowling from the airplane. A quick engine check gave them the answer. The throttle rod-end was not connected to the carburetor arm—no bolt, no nut, just air between the rod-end and the arm. Jennifer looked at Lenore. "What if this had happened in flight?"

"What I want to know," Lenore said, "is how this happened at all. The annual inspection was signed off yesterday."

The previous day, the annual inspection had been signed off after a lengthy inspection by a local facility. Several mechanics had been involved in the inspection, including the owner/learner who had installed a headliner. The mechanic with the Inspection Authorization (IA) who signed off the annual was supervising several annuals, so most of the maintenance was performed by other mechanics.

After the inspection, the engine had been run-up according to the usual post-inspection procedures. The learner and instructor had flown the airplane for a half-hour familiarization flight. The next day's engine start resulted in a runaway engine with the apparent cause due to the lack of the throttle rod-end hardware being safetied.

Three deficient areas in this annual inspection were identified by a round-table discussion group of aircraft and powerplant (A&P) mechanics and the learner. These areas were:

- Lack of responsibility
- Checklist misuse
- Complacency

Lack of responsibility—no one took responsibility for the entire inspection. The chances of something being overlooked increase with an increase in the number of mechanics involved in an inspection. The responsible person is removed from the actual procedure. The learner remembers hearing the IA ask one of the engine mechanics about the throttle. However, the question was vague, the answer was vague, and the rod-end was not safetied.

Checklist misuse—Perhaps the throttle rod-end had been disconnected for maintenance after the IA had signed off the control inspection and marked that item as complete on the maintenance checklist. In that case, a discrepancy should have been entered onto the discrepancy sheet stating, "reconnect and safety throttle rod-end."

Complacency—an insidious and hard-to-identify attitude. Each of the mechanics involved in the incident thought someone else had inspected the throttle rod-end. The IA signed off the annual inspection after asking the mechanics about the items on the checklist, making frequent visits to the airplane, inspecting some of the various items, and deciding that was good enough. Complacency crippled the mechanics' quality of work by removing any thoughts of double-checking each other's work.

While a definite answer to the question of what happened remains a matter of speculation, professional mechanics heed warning signs of potential problems. The combination of a lengthy inspection, numerous technicians, an overworked supervisor, a poor checklist, and vague communication raise a red flag of caution.

This scenario underscores the need for safety risk management at all levels of aviation. Safety risk management, a formal system of hazard identification, assessment, and mitigation, is essential in keeping risk at acceptable levels. Part of this process is selecting the appropriate controls to mitigate the risk of the identified hazard. The primary objective of risk management is accident prevention, which is achieved by proactively identifying, assessing, and eliminating or mitigating safety-related hazards to acceptable levels.

This chapter discusses safety risk management in the aviation community, looking at it as preemptive, rather than reactive. The principles of risk management and the tools for teaching risk management in the flight training environment are addressed in Chapter 9, Techniques of Flight Instruction.

Defining Risk Management

Risk is defined as the probability and possible severity of accident or loss from exposure to various hazards, including injury to people and loss of resources. *[Figure 1-1]* All Federal Aviation Administration (FAA) operations in the United States involve risk and benefit from decisions that include risk assessment and risk management. Risk management, a formalized way of thinking about these topics, is the logical process of weighing the potential costs of risks against the possible benefits of allowing those risks to stand uncontrolled.

Types of Risk	
Total Risk	The sum of identified and unidentified risks.
Identified Risk	Risk which has been determined through various analysis techniques. The first task of system safety is to identify, within practical limitations, all possible risks.
Unidentified Risk	Risk not yet identified. Some unidentified risks are subsequently identified when a mishap occurs. Some risk is never known.
Unacceptable Risk	Risk which cannot be tolerated by the managing activity. It is a subset of identified risk that must be eliminated or controlled.
Acceptable Risk	Acceptable risk is the part of identified risk that is allowed to persist without further engineering or management action. Making this decision is a difficult yet necessary responsibility of the managing activity. This decision is made with full knowledge that it is the user who is exposed to this risk.
Residual Risk	Residual risk is the risk left over after system safety efforts have been fully employed. It is not necessarily the same as acceptable risk. Residual risk is the sum of acceptable risk and unidentified risk. This is the total risk passed on to the user.

Figure 1-1. *Types of risk.*

Risk management is a decision-making process designed to identify hazards systematically, assess the degree of risk, and determine the best course of action. Key terms are:

- Hazard—a present condition, event, object, or circumstance that could lead to or contribute to an unplanned or undesired event, such as an accident. It is a source of danger. For example, a nick in the propeller represents a hazard.

- Risk—the future impact of a hazard that is not controlled or eliminated. It is the possibility of loss or injury. The level of risk is measured by the number of people or resources affected (exposure); the extent of possible loss (severity); and likelihood of loss (probability).

- Safety—freedom from those conditions that can cause death, injury, occupational illness, or damage to or loss of equipment or property, or damage to the environment. Note that absolute safety is not possible because complete freedom from all hazardous conditions is not possible. Therefore, safety is a relative term that implies a level of risk that is both perceived and accepted.

Principles of Risk Management

The goal of risk management is to proactively identify safety-related hazards and mitigate the associated risks. Risk management is an important component of decision-making. When a pilot follows good decision-making practices, the inherent risk in a flight is reduced or even eliminated. The ability to make good decisions is based upon direct or indirect experience and education. It is important to remember the four fundamental principles of risk management:

Accept No Unnecessary Risk

Unnecessary risk is that which carries no commensurate return in terms of benefits or opportunities. Everything involves risk. The most logical choices for accomplishing a flight are those that meet all requirements with the minimum acceptable risk. The corollary to this axiom is "accept necessary risk" required to complete the flight or task successfully. Flying is impossible without risk, but unnecessary risk comes without a corresponding return. If flying a new airplane for the first time, a flight instructor might determine that the risk of making that flight in low instrument flight rules (IFR) conditions is unnecessary.

Make Risk Decisions at the Appropriate Level

Anyone can make a risk decision. However, risk decisions should be made by the person who can develop and implement risk controls. In a single-pilot situation, the pilot makes the decision to accept certain levels of risk, so why let anyone else—such as ATC or your passengers—make risk decisions for you? In the maintenance facility, an aviation maintenance technician (AMT) may need to elevate decisions to the next level in the chain of management upon determining that those controls available to him or her will not reduce residual risk to an acceptable level.

Accept Risk When Benefits Outweigh the Costs

All identified benefits should be compared against all identified costs. Even high-risk endeavors may be undertaken when there is clear knowledge that the sum of the benefits exceeds the sum of the costs. For example, in any flying activity, it is necessary to accept some degree of risk. A day with good weather, for example, is a much better time to fly an unfamiliar airplane for the first time than a day with low instrument flight rules (IFR) conditions.

Integrate Risk Management into Planning at All Levels

Risks are more easily assessed and managed in the early planning stages of a flight. Changes made later in the process of planning and executing may become more difficult, time consuming, and expensive. However, safety enhancement occurs at any time appropriate and effective risk management take place.

Risk Management Process

Risk management is a simple process which identifies operational hazards and takes reasonable measures to reduce risk to personnel, equipment, and the mission. During each flight, the pilot makes many decisions under hazardous conditions. To fly safely, the pilot needs to identify the risk, assess the degree of risk, and determine the best course of action to mitigate the risk.

Step 1: Identify the Hazard

A hazard is defined as any real or potential condition that can cause degradation, injury, illness, death, or damage to or loss of equipment or property. Experience, common sense, and specific analytical tools help identify risks. Once the pilot determines that a hazard poses a potential risk to the flight, it may be further analyzed.

Step 2: Assess the Risk

Each identified risk may be assessed in terms of its likelihood (probability) and its severity (consequences) that could result from the hazards based upon the exposure of humans or equipment to the hazards. An assessment of overall risk is then possible, typically by using a risk assessment matrix, such an online Flight Risk Awareness Tool (FRAT). This process defines the probability and severity of an accident.

Step 3: Mitigate the Risk

Investigate specific strategies and tools that reduce, mitigate, or eliminate the risk. High risks may be mitigated by taking action to lower likelihood and/or severity to lower levels. For serious risks, such actions may also be taken. Medium and low risks do not normally require mitigation. Effective control measures reduce or eliminate the most critical risks. The analysis may consider the overall costs and benefits of remedial actions, providing alternative choices when possible.

Implementing the Risk Management Process

The following principles allow for maximum benefit from series of steps described above that form a risk mitigation strategy:

- Apply the steps in sequence—each step is a building block for the next and should be completed before proceeding to the next. If a hazard identification step is interrupted to focus on the control of a particular hazard, more important hazards may be overlooked. Until all hazards are identified, the remainder of the process is not effective.

- Maintain a balance in the process—all steps are important. Allocate the time and resources to perform all.

- Apply the process in a cycle—the "supervise and review" step should include a brand-new look at the operation being analyzed to see whether new hazards can be identified.

- Involve people in the process—ensure that risk controls are mission supportive, and the people who do the work see them as positive actions. The people who are exposed to risks usually know best what works and what does not.

Identifying Risk

Hazards and their associated risks can either be obvious or harder to detect. You should methodically identify and classify risks to a proposed or ongoing flight by maintaining constant situational awareness. To assist this process, it is helpful to apply the simple acronym PAVE to your risk management process. The acronym stands for Pilot, Aircraft, Environment, External pressures. Use the following guidelines and questions to identify risk using the PAVE acronym.

The Pave Checklist

By incorporating the PAVE checklist into all stages of flight planning, the pilot divides the risks of flight into four categories: Pilot in command (PIC), Aircraft, enVironment, and External pressures (PAVE), which form part of a pilot's decision-making process.

With the PAVE checklist, pilots have a simple way to remember each category to examine for risk prior to each flight. Once a pilot identifies the risks of a flight, he or she needs to decide whether the risk or combination of risks can be managed safely and successfully. If not, the flight should be cancelled. If the pilot decides to continue with the flight, he or she should develop strategies to mitigate the risks. One way a pilot can control the risks is to set personal minimums for items in each risk category. These are limits unique to that individual pilot's current level of experience and proficiency.

For example, the aircraft may have a maximum crosswind component of 15 knots listed in the aircraft flight manual (AFM), and the pilot has experience with 10 knots of direct crosswind. It could be unsafe to exceed a 10 knot-crosswind component without additional training. Therefore, the 10 knots crosswind experience level should be that pilot's personal limitation until additional training with a flight instructor provides the pilot with additional experience for flying in crosswinds that exceed 10 knots.

One of the most important concepts that safe pilots understand is the difference between what is "legal" in terms of the regulations, and what is "smart" or "safe" in terms of pilot experience and proficiency.

P = Pilot in Command (PIC)

The pilot is one of the risk factors in a flight. When considering that risk, a pilot may ask, "Am I ready for this trip?" in terms of experience, currency, and physical and emotional condition. The IMSAFE checklist (described later in this chapter) combined with proficiency, recency, and currency helps provide the answer.

A = Aircraft

What limitations will the aircraft impose upon the trip? Ask the following questions:

- Is this the right aircraft for the flight?

- Am I familiar with and current in this aircraft? Aircraft performance figures and the AFM are based on a brand-new aircraft flown by a professional test pilot. Keep that in mind while assessing personal and aircraft performance.

- Is this aircraft equipped for the flight? Instruments? Lights? Navigation and communication equipment adequate?

- Can this aircraft use the runways available for the trip with an adequate margin of safety under the conditions to be flown?

- Can this aircraft carry the planned load?

- Can this aircraft operate at the altitudes needed for the trip?

- Does this aircraft have sufficient fuel capacity, with reserves, for trip legs planned?

- Does the fuel quantity delivered match the fuel quantity ordered?

V = EnVironment

Weather is a major environmental consideration. Earlier it was suggested pilots set their own personal minimums, especially when it comes to weather. As pilots evaluate the weather for a particular flight, they should consider the following:

- What are the current ceiling and visibility? In mountainous terrain, consider having higher minimums for ceiling and visibility, particularly if the terrain is unfamiliar.

- Consider the possibility that the weather may be different than forecast. Have alternative plans and be ready and willing to divert should an unexpected change occur.

- Consider the winds at the airports being used and the strength of the crosswind component.

- If flying in mountainous terrain, consider whether there are strong winds aloft. Strong winds in mountainous terrain can cause severe turbulence and downdrafts and can be very hazardous for aircraft even when there is no other significant weather.

- Are there any thunderstorms present or forecast?

- If there are clouds, is there any icing, current or forecast? What is the temperature-dew point spread and the current temperature at altitude? Can descent be made safely all along the route?

- If icing conditions are encountered, is the pilot experienced at operating the aircraft's deicing or anti-icing equipment? Is this equipment in good condition and functional? For what icing conditions is the aircraft rated, if any?

Evaluation of terrain is another important component of analyzing the flight environment. To avoid terrain and obstacles, especially at night or in low visibility, determine safe altitudes in advance by using the altitudes shown on VFR and IFR charts during preflight planning. Use maximum elevation figures (MEFs) and other easily obtainable data to minimize chances of an inflight collision with terrain or obstacles.

Airport considerations include:

- What lights are available at the destination and alternate airports? VASI/PAPI or ILS glideslope guidance? Is the terminal airport equipped with them? Are they working? Will the pilot need to use the radio to activate the airport lights?

- Check the Notices to Airmen (NOTAMs) for closed runways or airports. Look for runway or beacon lights out, nearby towers, etc.

- Choose the flight route wisely. An engine failure gives the nearby airports (and terrain) supreme importance.

- Are there shorter or obstructed fields at the destination and/or alternate airports?

Airspace considerations include:

- If the trip is over remote areas, are appropriate clothing, water, and survival gear onboard?

- If the trip includes flying over water or unpopulated areas might there be a loss of visual references?

- Will there be any airspace or temporary flight restrictions (TFRs) along the route of flight?

Night flying requires special consideration:

- Will the trip include flying over water or unpopulated areas?

- Will the flight conditions allow a safe emergency landing at night?

- Are the aircraft lights found to be operational during preflight and is a flashlight available that is appropriate for intended use before and during flight?

E = External Pressures

External pressures are influences external to the flight that create a sense of pressure to complete a flight—often at the expense of safety. Factors that can be external pressures include the following:

- Someone waiting at the airport for the flight's arrival.

- A passenger the pilot does not want to disappoint.

- The desire to demonstrate pilot qualifications.

- The desire to impress someone. (Probably the two most dangerous words in aviation are "Watch this!")

- The desire to satisfy a specific personal goal ("get-home-itis," "get-there-itis," and "let's-go-itis").

- The pilot's general goal-completion orientation.

- Emotional pressure associated with acknowledging that skill and experience levels may be lower than a pilot would like them to be. Pride can be a powerful external factor!

Management of external pressure is the single most important key to risk management because it is the one risk factor category that can cause a pilot to ignore all the other risk factors. External pressures put time-related pressure on the pilot and figure into a majority of accidents.

The use of personal standard operating procedures (SOPs) is one way to manage external pressures. The goal is to supply a release for the external pressures of a flight. These procedures include but are not limited to:

- Allow time on a trip for an extra fuel stop or to make an unexpected landing because of weather.

- Have alternate plans for a late arrival or make backup airline reservations for must-be-there trips.

- For important trips, plan to leave early enough so that there would still be time to drive to the destination.

- Advise those who are waiting at the destination that the arrival may be delayed. Know how to notify them when delays are encountered.

- Manage passengers' expectations. Make sure passengers know that they might not arrive on a firm schedule, but if they need to arrive by a certain time, they may make alternative plans.

- Eliminate pressure to return home, even on a casual day flight, by carrying a small overnight kit containing prescriptions, contact lens solutions, toiletries, or other necessities on every flight.

The key to managing external pressure is to be ready for and accept delays. Remember that people get delayed when traveling on airlines, driving a car, or taking a bus. The pilot's goal is to manage risk, not create hazards.

During each flight, decisions should be made regarding events involving interactions between the four risk elements—PIC, aircraft, environment, and external pressures. The decision-making process involves an evaluation of each of these risk elements to achieve an accurate perception of the flight situation. *[Figure 1-2]*

Figure 1-2. *One of the most important decisions that the pilot in command makes is the go/no-go decision. Evaluating each of these risk elements can help the pilot decide whether a flight should be conducted or continued.*

IMSAFE Checklist

As mentioned earlier, one of the best ways that single pilots can identify risk associated with physical and mental readiness for flying is to use the IMSAFE checklist acronym. *[Figure 1-3]*

Figure 1-3. *Prior to flight, pilots may use a checklist to assess their fitness, just as they evaluate the aircraft's airworthiness.*

1. **Illness**—Am I sick? Illness is an obvious pilot risk.

2. **Medication**—Am I taking any medicines that might affect my judgment or make me drowsy?

3. **Stress**—Am I under psychological pressure from the job? Do I have money, health, or family problems? Stress causes concentration and performance problems. While the regulations list medical conditions that require grounding, stress is not among them. A thorough evaluation of risk accounts for the effects of stress on performance.

4. **Alcohol**—Have I been drinking within 8 hours? Within 24 hours? A small amount of alcohol can impair flying skills. Alcohol also renders a pilot more susceptible to disorientation and hypoxia.

5. **Fatigue**—Am I tired and not adequately rested? Fatigue continues to be one of the most insidious hazards to flight safety, as it may not be apparent to a pilot until serious errors are made.

6. **Emotion**—Am I emotionally upset? The emotions of anger, depression, and anxiety from such events as a serious argument; death in the family; separation or divorce; loss of employment; and/or financial problems not only decrease alertness, but may also lead to taking risks that border on self-destruction. A pilot who experiences an emotionally upsetting event may choose to refrain from flying until the pilot has satisfactorily recovered.

Assessing Risk

Assessment of risk is an important part of good risk management. For example, the hazard of a nick in the propeller poses a risk only if the airplane is flown. If the damaged prop is exposed to the constant vibration of normal engine operation, there is a high risk is that it could fracture and cause catastrophic damage to the engine and/or airframe and the passengers.

Every flight has hazards and some level of risk associated with it. It is critical that pilots and especially learners can differentiate in advance between a low-risk flight and a high-risk flight, and then establish a review process and develop risk mitigation strategies to address flights throughout that range.

For the single pilot, assessing risk is not as simple as it sounds. For example, the pilot acts as his or her own quality control in making decisions. If a fatigued pilot who has flown 16 hours is asked if he or she is too tired to continue flying, the answer may be no. Most pilots are goal oriented and, when asked to accept a flight, there is a tendency to deny personal limitations while adding weight to issues not germane to the mission. For example, pilots of helicopter emergency services (EMS) have been known to make flight decisions that add significant weight to the patient's welfare. These pilots add weight to intangible factors (the patient in this case) and fail to appropriately quantify actual hazards such as fatigue or weather when making flight decisions. The single pilot deals with the intangible factors that may draw one into a hazardous position. Therefore, he or she has a greater vulnerability than a full crew.

Examining National Transportation Safety Board (NTSB) reports and other accident research can help a pilot learn to assess risk more effectively. For example, the accident rate during night VFR decreases by nearly 50 percent once a pilot obtains 100 hours and continues to decrease until the 1,000- hour level. The data suggest that for the first 500 hours, pilots flying VFR at night might want to establish higher personal limitations than are required by the regulations and, if applicable, apply instrument flying skills in this environment.

Several risk assessment models are available to assist in the process of assessing risk. The models, all taking slightly different approaches, seek a common goal of assessing risk in an objective manner.

The most basic tool is the risk matrix. *[Figure 1-4]* It assesses two items: the likelihood of an event occurring and the consequence of that event.

Figure 1-4. *This risk matrix can be used for almost any operation by assigning likelihood and severity. In the case presented, the pilot assigned the likelihood of occasional and the severity as catastrophic falls in the high-risk area.*

Likelihood of an Event

Likelihood is nothing more than taking a situation and determining the probability of its occurrence. It is rated as probable, occasional, remote, or improbable. For example, a pilot is flying from point A to point B (50 miles) in marginal visual flight rules (MVFR) conditions. The likelihood of encountering potential instrument meteorological conditions (IMC) is the first question the pilot needs to answer. The experiences of other pilots, coupled with the forecast, might cause the pilot to assign "occasional" to determine the probability of encountering IMC.

The following are guidelines for making assignments.

- Probable—an event will occur several times.
- Occasional—an event will probably occur sometime.
- Remote—an event is unlikely to occur but is possible.
- Improbable—an event is highly unlikely to occur.

Severity of an Event

The next element is the severity or consequence of a pilot's action(s). It can relate to injury and/or damage. If the individual in the example above is not an instrument flight rules (IFR) pilot, what are the consequences of encountering inadvertent IMC? In this case, because the pilot is not IFR rated, the consequences could be fatal. The following are guidelines for this assignment.

- Catastrophic—results in fatalities, total loss
- Critical—severe injury, major damage
- Marginal—minor injury, minor damage
- Negligible—less than minor injury, less than minor system damage

Assessing risk may be the most difficult part of risk management and applying the terms described above to specific risks takes some practice. Once you have assessed risk likelihood and severity for all identified risks, you can readily classify the overall risk level for that hazard. For example, simply connecting the two factors as shown in *Figure 1-4* indicates the risk is high and the pilot may consider whether to not fly or fly only after finding ways to mitigate, eliminate, or control the risk.

Risk

The final step in risk management is mitigation, which is the payoff for accomplishing the entire risk management process and will often allow for mission accomplishment (the reason most pilots fly). By effectively mitigating known risks to acceptable levels, pilots can complete their planned flights safely or ensure that alternate options are selected for those rare occasions when the planned or ongoing flight cannot be completed.

There are almost an infinite number of actions you can take, depending on the nature of the hazard or risk. For example, the pilot flying from point A to point B (50 miles) in MVFR conditions has several ways to reduce risk:

- Drive.
- Wait for the weather to improve to good visual flight rules (VFR) conditions.
- Take a pilot who is rated as an IFR pilot.
- Delay the flight.
- Cancel the flight.

Risk mitigation often begins days, sometimes weeks, before a planned flight. For example, a pilot flying a single-engine piston aircraft without ice protection lives in the Pacific Northwest and is planning a trip in January for a scheduled speech. While keeping the long-range weather forecast in mind, planning in advance gives the pilot several options to mitigate risk:

- Book commercial flight/transfer the risk to the airlines.
- Change the date of the event to accommodate weather.
- Cancel flight altogether.
- Depart a day early from the Pacific Northwest to avoid an incoming low-pressure area that will bring low IFR and certain icing conditions.

After all mitigating steps have been completed, you may confront the possibility that a flight cannot be made or continued for a variety of reasons not only for yourself but also for your passengers. Remember that many pilots have ignored or failed to mitigate serious and high-risk hazards, and a tragic fatal accident is all too often the result.

Flight Risk Assessment Tools

Because every flight has some level of risk, it is critical that pilots can differentiate, in advance, between a low risk flight and a high-risk flight, establish a review process, and develop risk mitigation strategies. A Flight Risk Analysis Tool (FRAT) enables proactive hazard identification, is easy to use, and can visually depict risk. It is a tool many pilots use to make better go/no-go decisions.

Why Should I Use a FRAT?

"In the thick" is no time to try to mitigate a potentially hazardous outcome. When preparing for a flight or maintenance task, pilots and maintenance technicians may set aside time to stop and think about the hazards involved.

Just thinking about this task may not consider the actual risk exposure. We may allow our personal desires to manipulate our risk assessment in order to meet personal goals. A formal process using pen and paper gives a perspective on the entire risk picture and is a good way to make a thorough analysis.

A risk assessment tool allows pilots to see the risk profile of a flight in its planning stages. Each pilot determines an acceptable level of risk for flight based on the type of operation, environment, aircraft used, training, and overall flight experience. When the risk for a flight exceeds the acceptable level, the hazards associated with that risk may be further evaluated and the risk reduced. A higher risk flight might not be operated if the hazards cannot be mitigated to an acceptable level.

What Do I Do with My Score?

When using a FRAT, the pilot creates numerical thresholds that trigger additional levels of scrutiny prior to a go/no-go decision for the flight. These thresholds help ensure that the safety standards of each individual flight are maintained. However, it is important that the pilot create realistic thresholds. If every flight is within the acceptable range under any condition, it is likely that the thresholds have not been set correctly.

An effective FRAT has at least three possible score ranges. These are often grouped into green, yellow and red sections.

- RED (HIGH): Risk likelihood and/or severity is normally reduced to lower levels before departure. Unless the risks involved in the flight can be mitigated (different crew/adding a copilot, better equipment, delayed launch time…) flight cancellation occurs.

- YELLOW (SERIOUS): Risk likelihood and/or severity needs reduction to lower levels before departure. Begin by mitigating some of the higher scoring items, and consider consulting with a flight instructor or mechanic if the score remains in the yellow.

- GREEN (MEDIUM): Flight can depart or continue, but risk severity and/or likelihood may be reduced.

No FRAT can anticipate all the hazards that may impact a particular flight but there are some common hazards that GA pilots encounter regularly. The National Business Aviation Association (NBAA) has developed a free online Flight Risk Awareness Tool (FRAT) to help flightcrews quickly assess threats to safety for a particular flight. Developed as part of a study, the FRAT presents operators with an easy-to-understand summary of the risks associated with each mission. No identifying data is collected to produce a risk analysis and pilots can try the tool before putting it to use on a live flight. This downloadable tool presents pilots with an easy-to-understand summary of the risks associated with each flight and can be found at https://nbaa.org/wp-content/uploads/2018/06/flight-risk-assessment-tool.pdf

Three-P Model for Pilots

As we have just learned with the Identify, Assess, & Mitigate model, risk management is a decision-making process designed to identify or perceive hazards systematically, assess the degree of risk associated with a hazard, and determine the best course of action to mitigate the risk. For example, the Perceive, Process, Perform (3P) model for aeronautical decision-making (ADM) offers a simple, practical, and structured way for pilots to manage risk. *[Figure 1-5]*

Figure 1-5. *3P Model (Perceive, Process, and Perform).*

To help understand the 3P model, it may be easier to relate this concept to the three steps of the Risk Management Process discussed earlier in this chapter. Recall that these three steps include identifying the risk, assessing the risk, and finally mitigating the risk. Imagine the 3P model in parallel to those three steps by perceiving (identifying the risk), processing (assessing the risk), and performing (mitigating the risk).

To use the 3P model, the pilot:

- Perceives the given set of circumstances for a flight.
- Processes by evaluating the impact of those circumstances on flight safety.
- Performs by implementing the best course of action.

In the first step, the goal is to develop situational awareness by perceiving hazards, which are present events, objects, or circumstances that could contribute to an undesired future event. In this step, the pilot systematically identifies and lists hazards associated with all aspects of the flight: pilot, aircraft, environment, and external pressures. It is important to consider how individual hazards might combine. Consider, for example, the hazard that arises when a new instrument pilot with no experience in actual instrument conditions wants to make a cross-country flight to an airport with low ceilings in order to attend an important business meeting.

In the second step, the goal is to process this information to determine whether the identified hazards constitute risk, which is defined as the future impact of a hazard that is not controlled or eliminated. The degree of risk posed by a given hazard can be measured in terms of exposure (number of people or resources affected), severity (extent of possible loss), and probability (the likelihood that a hazard will cause a loss). If the hazard is low ceilings, for example, the level of risk depends on a number of other factors, such as pilot training and experience, aircraft equipment, and fuel capacity.

In the third step, the goal is to perform by taking action to eliminate hazards or mitigate risk, and then continuously evaluate the outcome of this action. With the example of low ceilings at destination, for instance, the pilot can perform good ADM by selecting a suitable alternate, knowing where to find good weather, and carrying sufficient fuel to reach it. This course of action would mitigate the risk. The pilot also has the option to eliminate it entirely by waiting for better weather.

Once the pilot has completed the 3P decision process and selected a course of action, the process begins again because the set of circumstances brought about by the course of action requires analysis. The decision-making process is a continuous loop of perceiving, processing, and performing.

It is never too early to start teaching risk management. Using the 3P model gives flight instructors a tool to teach them a structured, efficient, and systematic way to identify hazards, assess risk, and implement effective risk controls. Practicing risk management needs to be as automatic in general aviation (GA) flying as basic aircraft control. Consider making the 3P discussion a standard feature of the preflight discussion. As is true for other flying skills, risk management habits are best developed through repetition and consistent adherence to specific procedures.

Hazard List for Aviation Technicians

AMTs should learn about risk management early in training. Instructors tasked with integrating risk management into instruction can turn to hazard assessments that identify the safety risks associated with the facility being used, the tools used in the procedure, and/or the job being performed.

The process for identifying hazards can be accomplished through the use of checklists, lessons learned, compliance inspections/audits, accidents/near misses, regulatory developments, and brainstorming sessions. For example, aviation accident reports from the National Transportation Safety Board (NTSB) can be used to generate discussions pertaining to faulty maintenance that led to aircraft accidents. All available sources should be used for identifying, characterizing, and controlling safety risks.

The 3P model can also be adapted for use in a nonflight environment, such as a maintenance facility. For example, the AMT perceives a hazard, processes its impact on shop or personnel safety, and then performs by implementing the best course of action to mitigate the perceived risk.

Pilot Self-Assessment

Setting personal minimums is an important step in mitigating risk, and safe pilots know how to properly self-assess. For example, in the opening scenario, the aircraft Mary plans to fly may have a maximum crosswind component of 15 knots listed in the aircraft flight manual (AFM), but she only has experience with 10 knots of direct crosswind. It could be unsafe to exceed a 10 knot-crosswind component without additional training. Therefore, the 10 knot-crosswind experience level should be Mary's personal limitation until additional training with Daniel provides her with additional experience for flying in crosswinds that exceed 10 knots.

Pilots in training should be taught that exercising good judgment begins prior to taking the controls of an aircraft. Often, pilots thoroughly check their aircraft to determine airworthiness, yet do not evaluate their own fitness for flight. Just as a checklist is used when preflighting an aircraft, a personal checklist based on such factors as experience, currency, and comfort level can help determine if a pilot is prepared for a particular flight. The FAA's "Personal Minimums Checklist" located in Appendix D is an excellent tool for pilots to use in self-assessment. This checklist reflects the PAVE approach to risk mitigation discussed in the previous paragraphs.

Worksheets for a more in-depth risk assessment are located in the "FAA/Industry Training Standards Personal and Weather Risk Assessment Guide" located online at www.faa.gov. This guide is designed to assist pilots in developing personal standardized procedures for accomplishing PIC responsibilities and in making better preflight and inflight weather decisions. Flight instructors should stress that frequent review of the personal guide keeps the information fresh and increases a pilot's ability to recognize the conditions in which a new risk assessment should be made, a key element in the decision-making process.

Situational Awareness

Situational awareness is the accurate perception and understanding of all the factors and conditions within the four fundamental risk elements that affect safety before, during, and after the flight. Maintaining situational awareness requires an understanding of the relative significance of these factors and their future impact on the flight. When situationally aware, the pilot has an overview of the total operation and is not fixated on one perceived significant factor. Some of the elements inside the aircraft to be considered are the status of aircraft systems, pilot, and passengers. In addition, an awareness of the environmental conditions of the flight, such as spatial orientation of the aircraft and its relationship to terrain, traffic, weather, and airspace should be maintained.

To maintain situational awareness, all of the skills involved in ADM are used. For example, an accurate perception of the pilot's fitness can be achieved through self-assessment and recognition of hazardous attitudes. A clear assessment of the status of navigation equipment can be obtained through workload management and establishing a productive relationship with ATC can be accomplished by effective resource use.

Obstacles to Maintaining Situational Awareness

Many obstacles exist that can interfere with a pilot's ability to maintain situational awareness. For example, fatigue, stress, or work overload can cause the pilot to fixate on a single perceived important item rather than maintaining an overall awareness of the flight situation. A contributing factor in many accidents is a distraction, which diverts the pilot's attention from monitoring the instruments or scanning outside the aircraft. Many flight deck distractions begin as a minor problem, such as a gauge that is not reading correctly, but result in accidents as the pilot diverts attention to the perceived problem and neglects to properly control the aircraft.

Fatigue, discussed as an obstacle to learning, is also an obstacle to maintaining situational awareness. It is a threat to aviation safety because it impairs alertness and performance. *[Figure 1-6]* The term is used to describe a range of experiences from sleepy, or tired, to exhausted. Two major physiological phenomena create fatigue: sleep loss and circadian rhythm disruption.

Figure 1-6. *Fatigue is a threat to aviation safety because it impairs alertness and performance.*

Fatigue is a normal response to many conditions common to flight operations because characteristics of the flight deck environment, such as low barometric pressure, humidity, noise, and vibration, make pilots susceptible to fatigue. The only effective treatment for fatigue is adequate sleep. As fatigue progresses, it is responsible for increased errors of omission, followed by errors of commission, and microsleeps, or involuntary sleep lapses lasting from a few seconds to a few minutes. For obvious reasons, errors caused by these short absences can have significant hazardous consequences in the aviation environment.

Sleep-deprived pilots may not notice sleepiness or other fatigue symptoms during preflight and departure flight operations. Once underway and established on altitude and heading, sleepiness and other fatigue symptoms tend to manifest themselves. Extreme fatigue can cause uncontrolled and involuntary shutdown of the brain. Regardless of motivation, professionalism, or training, an individual who is extremely sleepy can lapse into sleep at any time, despite the potential consequences of inattention. There are a number of countermeasures for coping with fatigue, as shown in *Figure 1-7*.

Figure 1-7. *Countermeasures for coping with fatigue.*

Complacency presents another obstacle to maintaining situational awareness. Defined as overconfidence from repeated experience on a specific activity, complacency has been implicated as a contributing factor in numerous aviation accidents and incidents. Like fatigue, complacency reduces the pilot's effectiveness in the flight deck. However, complacency is harder to recognize than fatigue, since everything is perceived to be progressing smoothly. Highly reliable automation has been shown to induce overconfidence and complacency. This can result in a pilot following the instructions of the automation even when common sense suggests otherwise. If the pilot assumes the autopilot is doing its job, he or she does not crosscheck the instruments or the aircraft's position frequently. If the autopilot fails, the pilot may not be mentally prepared to fly the aircraft manually. Instructors should be especially alert to complacency in learners with significant flight experience. For example, a pilot receiving a flight review in a familiar aircraft may be prone to complacency.

Advanced avionics have created a high degree of redundancy and dependability in modern aircraft systems, which can promote complacency and inattention. During flight training, the flight instructor should emphasize that routine flight operations may lead to a sense of complacency, which can threaten flight safety by reducing situational awareness.

By asking about positions of other aircraft in the traffic pattern, engine instrument indications, and the aircraft's location in relation to references on a chart, the flight instructor can determine if the learner is maintaining situational awareness. The flight instructor can also attempt to focus the learner's attention on an imaginary problem with the communication or navigation equipment. The flight instructor should point out that situational awareness is not being maintained if the learner diverts too much attention away from other tasks, such as controlling the aircraft or scanning for traffic. These are simple exercises that can be done throughout flight training, which help emphasize the importance of maintaining situational awareness.

Operational Pitfalls

There are numerous classic behavioral traps that can ensnare the unwary pilot. Pilots, particularly those with considerable experience, try to complete a flight as planned, please passengers, and meet schedules. This basic drive to demonstrate achievements can have an adverse effect on safety and can impose an unrealistic assessment of piloting skills under stressful conditions. These tendencies ultimately may bring about practices that are dangerous and sometimes illegal and may lead to a mishap. Learners develop awareness and learn to avoid many of these operational pitfalls through effective ADM training. The scenarios and examples provided by instructors during ADM instruction should involve these pitfalls. *[Figure 1-8]*

Single-Pilot Resource Management (SRM)

Single pilot resource management (SRM) is defined as the art and science of managing all the resources (both onboard the aircraft and from outside sources) available to a single pilot (prior to and during flight) to ensure the successful outcome of the flight. SRM includes the concepts of Aeronautical Decision-Making (ADM), Risk Management (RM), Task Management (TM), Automation Management (AM), Controlled Flight Into Terrain (CFIT) Awareness, and Situational Awareness (SA). SRM training helps the pilot maintain situational awareness by managing the automation and associated aircraft control and navigation tasks. This enables the pilot to accurately identify, assess, and manage risk and make accurate and timely decisions.

SRM is all about helping pilots learn how to gather information, analyze it, and make decisions. Although the flight is coordinated by a single person and not an onboard flightcrew, the use of available resources such as air traffic control (ATC) and Flight Service replicates the principles of CRM.

Operational Pitfalls
Peer Pressure
Poor decision-making may be based upon an emotional response to peers, rather than evaluating a situation objectively.
Mind Set
A pilot displays mind set through an inability to recognize and cope with changes in a given situation.
Get-There-Itis
This disposition impairs pilot judgment through a fixation on the original goal or destination, combined with a disregard for any alternative course of action.
Duck-Under Syndrome
A pilot may be tempted to make it into an airport by descending below minimums during an approach. There may be a belief that there is a built-in margin of error in every approach procedure, or a pilot may want to admit that the landing cannot be completed and a missed approach must be initiated.
Scud Running
This occurs when a pilot tries to maintain visual contact with the terrain at low altitudes while instrument conditions exist.
Continuing Visual Flight Rules (VFR) into Instrument Conditions
Spatial disorientation or collision with ground/obstacles may occur when a pilot continues VFR into instrument conditions. This can be even more dangerous if the pilot is not instrument rated or current.
Getting Behind the Aircraft
This pitfall can be caused by allowing events or the situation to control pilot actions. A constant state of surprise at what happens next may be exhibited when the pilot is getting behind the aircraft.
Loss of Positional or Situational Awareness
In extreme cases, when a pilot gets behind the aircraft, a loss of positional or situational awareness may result. The pilot may not know the aircraft's geographical location or may be unable to recognize deteriorating circumstances.
Operating Without Adequate Fuel Reserves
Ignoring minimum fuel reserve requirements is generally the result of overconfidence, lack of flight planning, or disregarding applicable regulations.
Descent Below the Minimum En Route Altitude
The duck-under syndrome, as mentioned above, can also occur during the en route portion of an IFR flight.
Flying Outside the Envelope
The assumed high-performance capability of a particular aircraft may cause a mistaken belief that it can meet the demands imposed by a pilot's overestimated flying skills.
Neglect of Flight Planning, Preflight Inspections, and Checklists
A pilot may rely on short- and long-term memory, regular flying skills, and familiar routes instead of established procedures and published checklists. This can be particularly true of experienced pilots.

Figure 1-8. *All experienced pilots have fallen prey to, or have been tempted by, one or more of these tendencies in their flying careers.*

SRM and the 5P Check

SRM is about gathering information, analyzing it, and making decisions. Learning how to identify problems, analyze the information, and make informed and timely decisions is not as straightforward as the training involved in learning specific maneuvers. Learning how to judge a situation and "how to think" in the endless variety of situations encountered while flying out in the "real world" is more difficult. There is no one right answer in ADM; rather, each pilot is expected to analyze each situation in light of experience level, personal minimums, and current physical and mental readiness level, and make his or her own decision.

SRM sounds good on paper, but it requires a way for pilots to understand and use it in their daily flights. One practical application is called the "Five Ps" (5 Ps). *[Figure 1-9]* The 5 Ps consist of "the Plan, the Plane, the Pilot, the Passengers, and the Programming." Each of these areas consists of a set of challenges and opportunities that face a single pilot. And each can substantially increase or decrease the risk of successfully completing the flight based on the pilot's ability to make informed and timely decisions. The 5 Ps are used to evaluate the pilot's current situation at key decision points during the flight, or when an emergency arises. These decision points include preflight, pretakeoff, hourly or at the midpoint of the flight, predescent, and just prior to the final approach fix or for visual flight rules (VFR) operations, just prior to entering the traffic pattern.

Figure 1-9. *The 5P checklist.*

The 5 Ps are based on the idea that the pilot has essentially five variables that impact his or her environment and that can cause the pilot to make a single critical decision, or several less critical decisions, that when added together can create a critical outcome. This concept stems from the belief that current decision-making models tend to be reactionary in nature. A change must occur and be detected to drive a risk management decision by the pilot. For instance, many pilots use risk management sheets that are filled out by the pilot prior to takeoff. These form a catalog of risks that may be encountered that day and turn them into numerical values. If the total exceeds a certain level, the flight is altered or canceled. Informal research shows that while these are useful documents for teaching risk factors, they are almost never used outside of formal training programs. The 5P concept is an attempt to take the information contained in those sheets and in the other available models and use it.

The 5P concept relies on the pilot to adopt a scheduled review of the critical variables at points in the flight where decisions are most likely to be effective. For instance, the easiest point to cancel a flight due to bad weather is before the pilot and passengers walk out the door to load the aircraft. So, the first decision point is preflight in the flight planning room, where all the information is readily available to make a sound decision, and where communication and Fixed Base Operator (FBO) services are readily available to make alternate travel plans.

The second easiest point in the flight to make a critical safety decision is just prior to takeoff. Few pilots have ever had to make an emergency takeoff. While the point of the 5P check is to help the pilot fly, the correct application of the 5P before takeoff is to assist in making a reasoned go/no-go decision based on all the information available. These two points in the process of flying are critical go/no-go points on each and every flight.

The third place to review the 5 Ps is at the midpoint of the flight. Often, pilots may wait until the Automated Terminal information Service (ATIS) is in range to check weather, yet at this point in the flight many good options have already passed behind the aircraft and pilot. Additionally, fatigue and low-altitude hypoxia serve to rob the pilot of much of his or her energy by the end of a long and tiring flight day. This leads to a transition from a decision-making mode to an acceptance mode on the part of the pilot. If the flight is longer than 2 hours, the 5P check should be conducted hourly.

The last two decision points are just prior to decent into the terminal area and just prior to the final approach fix, or if VFR just prior to entering the traffic pattern, as preparations for landing commence. Some pilots execute approaches with the expectation that they will land out of the approach every time. When using a risk management thought process, the pilot realizes that changing conditions (the 5 Ps again) may cause the pilot to divert or execute the missed approach on each approach. Let's look at a detailed discussion of each of the Five Ps.

The Plan

The plan can also be called the mission or the task. It contains the basic elements of cross-country planning, weather, route, fuel, publications currency, etc. The plan should be reviewed and updated several times during the course of the flight. A delayed takeoff due to maintenance, fast moving weather, and a short notice temporary flight restriction (TFR) may all radically alter the plan. The plan is not only about the flight plan, but also all the events that surround the flight and allow the pilot to accomplish the mission. The plan is always being updated and modified and is especially responsive to changes in the other four remaining Ps. If for no other reason, the 5P check reminds the pilot that the day's flight plan is real life and subject to change at any time.

Obviously, weather is a huge part of any plan. The addition of real time data link weather information gives the pilot a real advantage in inclement weather, but only if the pilot is trained to retrieve, and evaluate the weather in real time without sacrificing situational awareness. And of course, weather information should drive a decision, even if that decision is to continue on the current plan. Pilots of aircraft without data link weather should get updated weather in flight through Flight Service.

The Plane

Both the plan and the plane are fairly familiar to most pilots. The plane consists of the usual array of mechanical and cosmetic issues that every aircraft pilot, owner, or operator can identify. With the advent of advanced avionics, the plane has expanded to include database currency, automation status, and emergency backup systems that were unknown a few years ago. Much has been written about single-pilot IFR flight both with and without an autopilot. While this is a personal decision, it is just that—a decision. Low IFR in a non-autopilot equipped aircraft may depend on several of the other Ps to be discussed. Pilot proficiency, currency, and fatigue are among them.

The Pilot

Flying, especially when used for business transportation, can expose the pilot to high altitude flying, long distance and endurance, and more challenging weather.

The combination of late night, pilot fatigue, and the effects of sustained flight above 5,000 feet may cause pilots to become less discerning, less critical of information, less decisive, and more compliant and accepting. Just as the most critical portion of the flight approaches (for instance, a night instrument approach in the weather after a 4-hour flight), the pilot's guard is down the most. The 5P process helps a pilot recognize the physiological situation at the end of the flight before takeoff and continues to update personal conditions as the flight progresses. Once risks are identified, the pilot is in a better position to make alternate plans that lessen the effect of these factors and provide a safer solution.

The Passengers

One of the key differences between CRM and SRM may include the way passengers interact with the pilot. The pilot of a single-pilot aircraft may often interact with the passengers. In fact, the pilot and passengers may sit within arm's reach.

The desire of the passengers to make airline connections or important business meetings enters easily into this pilot's decision-making loop. Done in a healthy and open way, this can be a positive factor. Consider a flight to Dulles Airport and the passengers, both close friends and business partners, need to get to Washington, D.C., for an important meeting. The weather is VFR all the way to southern Virginia, then turns to low IFR as the pilot approaches Dulles. A pilot employing the 5P approach might consider reserving a rental car at an airport in northern North Carolina or southern Virginia to coincide with a refueling stop. Thus, the passengers have a way to get to Washington, and the pilot has an out to avoid being pressured into continuing the flight if the conditions do not improve.

Passengers can also be pilots. If no one is designated as pilot in command (PIC) and unplanned circumstances arise, the decision-making styles of several self-confident pilots may conflict.

Pilots also need to understand that non-pilots may not understand the level of risk involved in the flight. There is an element of risk in every flight. That is why SRM calls it risk management, not risk elimination. While a pilot may feel comfortable with the risk present in a night IFR flight, the passengers may not. A pilot employing SRM should ensure the passengers are involved in the decision-making and given tasks and duties to keep them busy and involved. If, upon a factual description of the risks present, the passengers decide to buy an airline ticket or rent a car, then a good decision has generally been made. This discussion also allows the pilot to move past what he or she *thinks* the passengers want to do and find out what they actually *want* to do. This removes self-induced pressure from the pilot.

The Programming

The electronic instrument displays, GPS, and autopilot reduce pilot workload and increase pilot situational awareness. While programming and operation of these devices are fairly simple and straightforward, unlike the analog instruments they replace, they tend to capture the pilot's attention and hold it for long periods of time. To avoid this phenomenon, the pilot should plan in advance when and where the programming for approaches, route changes, and airport information gathering should be accomplished as well as times it should not. Pilot familiarity with the equipment, the route, the local air traffic control environment, and personal capabilities vis-à-vis the automation should drive when, where, and how the automation is programmed and used.

The pilot should also consider what his or her capabilities are in response to last-minute changes of the approach (and the reprogramming required) and ability to make large-scale changes (a reroute for instance) while hand flying the aircraft. Since formats are not standardized, simply moving from one manufacturer's equipment to another should give the pilot pause and may require more conservative planning and decisions.

The SRM process is simple. At least five times before and during the flight, the pilot should review and consider the "Plan, the Plane, the Pilot, the Passengers, and the Programming" and make the appropriate decision required by the current situation. It is often said that failure to make a decision is a decision. Under SRM and the 5 Ps, even the decision to make no changes to the current plan is made through careful consideration of all the risk factors present.

Information Management

The volume of information presented in aviation training is enormous, but part of the process of good SRM is a continuous flow of information in and actions out. How a learner manages the flow of information definitely has an effect on the relative success or failure of each and every flight because proper information contributes to valid decisions. Scenario-based training (SBT) plays an important part in teaching the learner how to gather pertinent information from all available sources, make appropriate decisions, and assess the actions taken.

Some pilots who transition to an unfamiliar sophisticated aircraft, may be overwhelmed and unable to find a specific piece of information. The first critical information management skill includes understanding the systems and displays at a conceptual level. Remembering how the system is organized helps the pilot manage the available information. Simulation software and manuals on the specific system used are of great value in furthering understanding for both the flight instructor and the learner.

A good strategy for accessing and managing the available information from PFD to navigational charts is to stop, look, and analyze. The goal is for the learner to understand how to monitor, manage, and prioritize the information flow to accomplish specific tasks.

Task Management

Task management (TM), a significant factor in flight safety, is the process by which pilots manage the many, concurrent tasks that should be performed to safely and efficiently fly a modern aircraft. A task is a function performed by a human, as opposed to one performed by a machine (e.g., setting the target heading in the autopilot).

The flight deck is an environment in which important tasks compete for pilot attention at any given time. TM determines which tasks the pilot(s) should attend to. TM entails initiation of new tasks; monitoring of ongoing tasks to determine their status; prioritization of tasks based on their importance, status, urgency, and other factors; allocation of human and machine resources to high-priority tasks; interruption and subsequent resumption of lower priority tasks; and termination of tasks that are completed or no longer relevant.

When information flow exceeds a person's ability to mentally process the information, any additional information becomes unattended or displaces other tasks and information already being processed. Once the information flow reaches its limit, two alternatives exist: shed the unimportant tasks or perform all tasks at a less than optimal level. Like an electrical circuit being overloaded, either the consumption must be reduced, or a circuit failure is experienced. Once again, SBT helps the learner understand how to effectively manage tasks and properly prioritize them.

Automation Management

Automation management is the demonstrated ability to control and navigate an aircraft by means of the automated systems installed in the aircraft. One of the most important concepts of automation management is knowing when to use it and when not to use it. Ideally, the goal of the flight instructor is to train the learner until he or she understands how to operate the aircraft, using all the available automation. However, the flight instructor should ensure the learner also knows how and when to operate the aircraft without the benefit of the automation.

No one level of automation is appropriate for all flight situations, and the learner should know how to set the level of automation. It is important for a learner to know how to operate the particular automated system being used. This ensures the learner knows what to expect, how to monitor for proper operation, and promptly take appropriate action if the system does not perform as expected.

At the most basic level, managing the autopilot means knowing at all times which modes are engaged and which modes are armed to engage. The learner needs to verify that armed functions (e.g., navigation tracking or altitude capture) engage at the appropriate time. Automation management is a good place to practice the callout technique, especially after arming the system to make a change in course or altitude.

Aeronautical Decision-Making

Aviation training and flight operations are now seen as a system rather than individual concepts. The goal of system safety is for pilots to utilize all four concepts (ADM, risk management, situational awareness, and SRM) so that risk can be reduced to the lowest possible level.

ADM is a systematic approach to the mental process used by aircraft pilots to consistently determine the best course of action in response to a given set of circumstances. Risk management is a decision-making process designed to systematically identify hazards, assess the degree of risk, and determine the best course of action associated with each flight. Situational awareness is the accurate perception and understanding of all the factors and conditions within the four fundamental risk elements that affect safety before, during, and after the flight. SRM is the art and science of managing all resources (both onboard the aircraft and from outside sources) available to a single pilot (prior and during flight) to ensure the successful outcome of the flight.

These key principles are often collectively called ADM. The importance of teaching learners effective ADM skills cannot be overemphasized. While progress is continually being made in the advancement of pilot training methods, aircraft equipment and systems, and services for pilots, accidents still occur. Despite all the changes in technology to improve flight safety, one factor remains the same—the human factor. It is estimated that approximately 80 percent of all aviation accidents are human factors related.

By taking a system approach to aviation safety, flight instructors interweave aeronautical knowledge, aircraft control skills, ADM, risk management, situational awareness, and SRM into the training process.

Historically, the term "pilot error" has been used to describe the causes of these accidents. Pilot error means that an action or decision made by the pilot was the cause of, or contributing factor to, the accident. This definition also includes the pilot's failure to make a decision or take action. From a broader perspective, the phrase "human factors related" more aptly describes these accidents since it is usually not a single decision that leads to an accident, but a chain of events triggered by a number of factors.

The poor judgment chain, or the error chain, describes this concept of contributing factors in a human factors-related accident. Breaking one link in the chain is all that is usually necessary to change the outcome of the sequence of events. The best way to illustrate this concept to learners is to discuss specific situations that lead to aircraft accidents or incidents. The following is an example of the type of scenario that can be presented to illustrate the poor judgment chain.

A private pilot with 100 hours of flight time made a precautionary landing on a narrow dirt runway at a private airport. The pilot lost directional control during landing and swerved off the runway into the grass. A witness recalled later that the aircraft appeared to be too high and fast on final approach, and speculated the pilot was having difficulty controlling the aircraft in high winds. The weather at the time of the incident was reported as marginal VFR due to rain showers and thunderstorms. When the aircraft was fueled the following morning, 60 gallons of fuel were required to fill the 62-gallon capacity tanks.

By discussing the events that led to this incident, instructors can help learners understand how a series of   judgmental errors contributed to the final outcome of this flight.

- Weather decision—on the morning of the flight, the pilot was running late and, having acquired a computer printout of the forecast the night before, he did not self-brief or obtain a briefing from Flight Service before his departure.

- Flight planning decision/performance chart—the pilot calculated total fuel requirements for the trip based on a rule-of-thumb figure he had used previously for another airplane. He did not use the fuel tables printed in the pilot's operating handbook (POH) for the aircraft he was flying on this trip. After reaching his destination, the pilot did not request refueling. Based on his original calculations, he believed sufficient fuel remained for the flight home.

- Fatigue/failure to recognize personal limitations—in the presence of deteriorating weather, the pilot departed for the flight home at 5:00 p.m. He did not consider how fatigue and lack of extensive night flying experience could affect the flight.

- Fuel exhaustion—with the aircraft fuel supply almost exhausted, the pilot no longer had the option of diverting to avoid rapidly developing thunderstorms. He was forced to land at the nearest airfield available.

On numerous occasions during the flight, the pilot could have made decisions which may have prevented this incident. However, as the chain of events unfolded, each poor decision left him with fewer and fewer options. On the positive side, the pilot made a precautionary landing at a time and place of his choosing. VFR into IMC accidents often lead to fatalities. In this case, the pilot landed his aircraft without loss of life.

Teaching pilots to make sound decisions is the key to preventing accidents. Traditional pilot instruction has emphasized flying skills, knowledge of the aircraft, and familiarity with regulations. ADM training focuses on the decision-making process and the factors that affect a pilot's ability to make effective choices.

Timely decision-making is an important tool for any pilot. The learner who hesitates when prompt action is required, or who makes the decision to not decide, has made a wrong decision. Emergencies require the pilot to think—assess the situation, choose and execute the actions that assure safety.

It is important for flight instructors to teach learners that declaring an emergency when one occurs is an appropriate reaction. Once an emergency is declared, air traffic control (ATC) gives the pilot priority handling. 14 CFR Section 91.3, Responsibility and Authority of the Pilot in Command, states that "In an inflight emergency requiring immediate action, the pilot in command may deviate from any rule of this part to the extent required to meet that emergency."

Flight instructors should incorporate ADM, risk management, situational awareness, and SRM throughout the entire training course for all levels of learners. AC 60-22, Aeronautical Decision Making, provides background references, definitions, and other pertinent information about ADM training in the general aviation (GA) environment. *[Figure 1-10]*

The Decision-Making Process

An understanding of the decision-making process provides learners with a foundation for developing ADM skills. Some situations, such as engine failures, require a pilot to respond immediately using established procedures with little time for detailed analysis. Traditionally, pilots have been well trained to react to emergencies but are not as well prepared to make decisions, which require a more reflective response. Typically during a flight, the pilot has time to examine any changes that occur, gather information, and assess risk before reaching a decision. The steps leading to this conclusion constitute the decision-making process. When the decision-making process is presented to learners it is essential to discuss how the process applies to an actual flight situation. To explain the decision-making process, the instructor can introduce the following steps with the accompanying scenario that places the learners in the position of making a decision about a typical flight situation.

Defining the Problem

The first step in the decision-making process is to define the problem. This begins with recognizing that a change has occurred or that an expected change did not occur. A problem is perceived first by the senses, and then is distinguished through insight and experience. These same abilities, as well as an objective analysis of all available information, are used to determine the exact nature and severity of the problem.

One critical error that can be made during the decision-making process is incorrectly defining the problem. For example, failure of a landing-gear-extended light to illuminate could indicate that the gear is not down and locked into place or it could mean the bulb is burned out. The actions to be taken in each of these circumstances would be significantly different. Fixating on a problem that does not exist can divert the pilot's attention from important tasks. The pilot's failure to maintain an awareness of the circumstances regarding the flight now becomes the problem. This is why once an initial assumption is made regarding the problem, other sources should be used to verify that the pilot's conclusion is correct.

While on a cross-country flight, Brenda discovers her time en route between two checkpoints is significantly longer than the time she originally calculated. By noticing this discrepancy, she has recognized a change. Based on insight, cross-country flying experience, and knowledge of weather systems, she considers the possibility that she has an increased headwind. She verifies that the original calculations are correct and considers factors that may have lengthened the time between checkpoints, such as a climb or deviation off course. To determine if there is a change in the winds aloft forecast and to check recent pilot reports, she contacts Flight Service. After weighing each information source, she concludes that the headwind has increased. To determine the severity of the problem, she calculates a new groundspeed and reassesses fuel requirements.

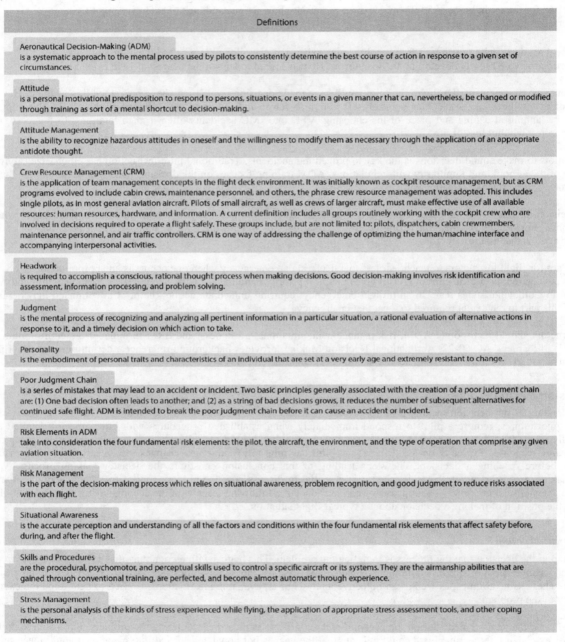

Figure 1-10. *Terms used in AC 60-22 to explain concepts used in ADM training.*

Choosing a Course of Action

After the problem has been identified, the pilot evaluates the need to react to it and determines the actions that may be taken to resolve the situation in the time available. The expected outcome of each possible action should be considered, and the risks assessed before the pilot decides on a response to the situation.

Brenda determines the fuel burn if she continues to her destination and considers other options: turning around and landing at a nearby airport, diverting off course, or landing prior to her destination at an airport en route. She considers the expected outcome of each possible action and assesses the risks involved. After studying the chart, she concludes an airport with fueling services is within a reasonable distance along her route. She can refuel there and continue to her destination without a significant loss of time.

Implementing the Decision and Evaluating the Outcome

Although a decision may be reached and a course of action implemented, the decision-making process is not complete. It is important to think ahead and determine how the decision could affect other phases of the flight. As the flight progresses, the pilot should continue to evaluate the outcome of the decision to ensure that it is producing the desired result.

To implement her decision, Brenda plots the course changes and calculates a new estimated time of arrival. She also amends her flight plan and checks weather conditions at the new destination. As she proceeds to the airport, she continues to monitor groundspeed, aircraft performance, and weather conditions to ensure no additional steps need to be taken to guarantee the safety of the flight.

Factors Affecting Decision-Making

It is important to stress to a learner that being familiar with the decision-making process does not ensure he or she has the good judgment to be a safe pilot. The ability to make effective decisions as PIC depends on a number of factors. Some circumstances, such as the time available to make a decision, may be beyond the pilot's control. However, a pilot can learn to recognize those factors that can be managed, and learn skills to improve decision-making ability and judgment.

Recognizing Hazardous Attitudes

While the ADM process does not eliminate errors, it helps the pilot recognize errors, and in turn enables the pilot to manage any errors to minimize their effects. In addition, two steps to improve flight safety are identifying personal attitudes hazardous to safe flight and learning behavior modification techniques.

Flight instructors should be able to spot hazardous attitudes in a learner because recognition of hazardous thoughts is the first step toward neutralizing them. Flight instructors should keep in mind that being fit to fly depends on more than just a pilot's physical condition and recency of experience. Hazardous attitudes contribute to poor pilot judgment and affect the quality of decisions.

Attitude can be defined as a personal motivational predisposition to respond to persons, situations, or events in a given manner. Studies have identified five hazardous attitudes that can affect a pilot's ability to make sound decisions and exercise authority properly. *[Figure 1-11]*

The Five Hazardous Attitudes
Anti-authority: "Don't tell me." This attitude is found in people who do not like anyone telling them what to do. In a sense, they are saying, "No one can tell me what to do." They may be resentful of having someone tell them what to do, or may regard rules, regulations, and procedures as silly or unnecessary. However, it is always pilot prerogative to question authority if it seems to be in error.
Impulsivity: "Do it quickly." This is the attitude of people who frequently feel the need to do something—anything—immediately. They do not stop to think about what they are about to do; they do not select the best alternative, and they do the first thing that comes to mind.
Invulnerability: "It won't happen to me." Many people believe that accidents happen to others, but never to them. They know accidents can happen, and they know that anyone can be affected. They never really feel or believe that they will be personally involved. Pilots who think this way are more likely to take chances and increase risk.
Macho: "I can do it." Pilots who are always trying to prove that they are better than anyone else are thinking, "I can do it, I'll show them." Pilots with this type of attitude will try to prove themselves by taking risks in order to impress others. While this pattern is thought to be a male characteristic, women are equally susceptible.
Resignation: "What's the use?" Pilots who think, "What's the use?" do not see themselves as being able to make a great deal of difference in what happens to them. When things go well, the pilot is apt to think that it is good luck. When things go badly, the pilot may feel that "someone is out to get me," or attribute it to bad luck. The pilot will leave the action to others, for better or worse. Sometimes, such pilots will even go along with unreasonable requests just to be a "nice guy."

Figure 1-11. *Pilots should examine their decisions carefully to ensure that their choices have not been influenced by a hazardous attitude*

In order for a learner to self-examine behaviors during flight, the learner should be taught the potential risks caused from hazardous attitudes and, more importantly, the antidote for each. *[Figure 1-12]* For example, if a learner has an easy time with flight training and seems to understand things very quickly, there may be a potential for that learner to develop a hazardous attitude regarding their ability. A successful flight instructor points out the potential for the behavior and teaches the learner the antidote for that attitude. Hazardous attitudes need to be noticed immediately and corrected with the proper antidote to minimize the potential for any flight hazard.

Hazardous Attitude	Antidotes
Macho Steve often brags to his friends about his skills as a pilot and how close to the ground he flies. During a local pleasure flight in his single-engine airplane, he decides to buzz some friends barbecuing at a nearby park.	Taking chances is foolish.
Anti-authority Although he knows that flying so low to the ground is prohibited by the regulations, he feels that the regulations are too restrictive in some circumstances.	Follow the rules. They are usually right.
Invulnerability Steve is not worried about an accident since he has flown this low many times before and he has not had any problems.	It could happen to me.
Impulsivity As he is buzzing the park, the airplane does not climb as well as Steve had anticipated and, without thinking, he pulls back hard on the yoke. The airspeed drops and the airplane is close to stalling as the wing brushes a power line.	Not so fast. Think first.
Resignation Although Steve manages to recover, the wing sustains minor damage. Steve thinks to himself, "It doesn't really matter how much effort I put in—the end result is the same whether I really try or not."	I'm not helpless. I can make a difference.

Figure 1-12. *Learners in training can be asked to identify hazardous attitudes and the corresponding antidotes when presented with flight scenarios.*

Stress Management

Learning how to recognize and cope with stress is another effective ADM tool. Stress is the body's response to demands placed upon it. These demands can be either pleasant or unpleasant in nature. The causes of stress for a pilot can range from unexpected weather or mechanical problems while in flight to personal issues unrelated to flying. Stress is an inevitable and necessary part of life; it adds motivation and heightens an individual's response to meet any challenge.

Everyone is stressed to some degree all the time. A certain amount of stress is good since it keeps a person alert and prevents complacency. However, the effects of stress are cumulative and, if not coped with adequately, they eventually add up to an intolerable burden. Performance generally increases with the onset of stress, peaks, and then begins to fall off rapidly as stress levels exceed a person's ability to cope. The ability to make effective decisions during flight can be impaired by stress. Factors, referred to as stressors, can increase a pilot's risk of error in the flight deck. *[Figure 1-13]*

Stressors
Physical Stress   Conditions associated with the environment, such as temperature and humidity extremes, noise, vibration, and lack of oxygen.
Physiological Stress   Physical conditions, such as fatigue, lack of physical fitness, sleep loss, missed meals (leading to low blood sugar levels), and illness.
Psychological Stress   Social or emotional factors, such as a death in the family, a divorce, a sick child, or a demotion at work. This type of stress may also be related to mental workload, such as analyzing a problem, navigating an aircraft, or making decisions.

Figure 1-13. *Three types of stressors that can affect pilot performance.*

One way of exploring the subject of stress with a learner is to recognize when stress is affecting performance. If a learner seems distracted, or has a particularly difficult time accomplishing the tasks of the lesson, the instructor can query the learner. Was the learner uncomfortable or tired during the flight? Is there some stress in another aspect of the learner's life that may be causing a distraction? This may prompt the learner to evaluate how these factors affect performance and judgment. The instructor should also try to determine if there are aspects of pilot training that are causing excessive amounts of stress for the learner. For example, if the learner consistently makes a decision not to fly, even though weather briefings indicate favorable conditions, it may be due to apprehension regarding the lesson content. Stalls, landings, or an impending solo flight may cause concern. By explaining a specific maneuver in greater detail or offering some additional encouragement, the instructor may be able to alleviate some of the learner's stress.

To help learners manage the accumulation of life stresses and prevent stress overload, instructors can recommend several techniques. For example, including relaxation time in a busy schedule and maintaining a program of physical fitness can help reduce stress levels. Learning to manage time more effectively can help pilots avoid heavy pressures imposed by getting behind schedule and not meeting deadlines. While these pressures may exist in the workplace, learners may also experience the same type of stress regarding their flight training schedule. Instructors can advise learners to self-assess to determine their capabilities and limitations and then set realistic goals. In addition, avoiding stressful situations and encounters can help pilots cope with stress.

Use of Resources

To make informed decisions during flight operations, learners should be familiar with the resources found both inside and outside the flight deck. Since useful tools and sources of information may not always be readily apparent, learning to recognize these resources is an essential part of ADM training. Resources should not only be identified, but learners should also develop the skills to evaluate whether they have the time to use a particular resource and the impact that its use would have upon the safety of flight. For example, the assistance of ATC may be very useful if a pilot is lost. However, in an emergency situation when action needs be taken quickly, time may not be available to contact ATC immediately. During training, flight instructors can routinely point out resources to learners.

Internal Resources

Internal resources are found in the flight deck during flight. However, some of the most valuable internal resources include ingenuity, knowledge, and skill. Pilots can enhance flight deck resources by improving their own capabilities. This can be accomplished by pursuing additional training and by frequently reviewing flight information publications including the Aeronautical Information Manual (AIM), instruction manuals for on board equipment, and safety journals.

With the advent of advanced avionics with glass displays, GPS, and autopilot, flying has become more complex. Avionics and automation systems are valuable resources, and flight instructors should teach learners how to use this equipment properly. If learners do not fully understand how to use the equipment, or if they rely on it so much that they become complacent, it can become a detriment to safe flight.

Checklists are essential flight deck resources for verifying that the aircraft instruments and systems are checked, set, and operating properly, as well as ensuring that the proper procedures are performed if there is a system malfunction or inflight emergency. Learners reluctant to use checklists can be reminded that pilots at all levels of experience refer to checklists, and that the more advanced the aircraft is, the more crucial checklists become. With the advent of electronic checklists, it has become easier to develop and maintain personal checklists from the manufacturer's checklist with additions for specific aircraft and operations.

In addition, the AFM/POH, which is required to be carried onboard the aircraft, is essential for accurate flight planning and for resolving inflight equipment malfunctions. Other valuable flight deck resources include current aeronautical charts and publications, such as the Chart Supplement (CS).

It should be pointed out to learners that passengers can also be a valuable resource. Passengers can help watch for traffic and may be able to provide information in an irregular situation, especially if they are familiar with flying. A strange smell or sound may alert a passenger to a potential problem. The PIC should brief passengers before the flight to make sure that they are comfortable voicing any concerns.

External Resources

Possibly the greatest external resources during flight are air traffic controllers. ATC can help decrease pilot workload by providing traffic advisories, radar vectors, and assistance in emergency situations. When learners use ATC during training, they develop the confidence to ask controllers to clarify instructions and to use ATC as a resource for assistance in unusual circumstances or emergencies. Fight Service specialists can provide updates on weather, answer questions about airport conditions, and may offer direction-finding assistance on frequencies used for flight plan communications. These services can be invaluable in enabling pilots to make informed inflight decisions.

Throughout training, learners can be asked to identify internal and external resources, which can be used in a variety of flight situations. For example, if a discrepancy is found during preflight, what resources can be used to determine its significance? In this case, the learner's knowledge of the aircraft, the POH, an instructor or other experienced pilot, or an AMT can be a resource which may help define the problem. During cross-country training, learners may be asked to consider the following situation. On a cross-country flight, you become disoriented. Although you are familiar with the area, you do not recognize any landmarks, and fuel is running low. What resources do you have to assist you? Learners should be able to identify their own skills and knowledge, aeronautical charts, ATC, Flight Service, and navigation equipment as some of the resources that can be used in this situation.

Workload Management

Effective workload management ensures that essential operations are accomplished by planning, prioritizing, and sequencing tasks to avoid work overload. As experience is gained, a pilot learns to recognize future workload requirements and can prepare for high workload periods during times of low workload. Instructors can teach this skill by prompting their learners to prepare for a high workload. For example, when en route, the learner can be asked to explain the actions that need to be taken during the approach to the airport. The learner should be able to describe the procedures for traffic pattern entry and landing preparation. Reviewing the appropriate chart and setting radio frequencies well in advance of need helps reduce workload as the flight nears the airport. In addition, the learner should listen to the Automatic Terminal Information Service (ATIS), Automated Surface Observing Systems (ASOS), or Automated Weather Observing System (AWOS), if available, and then monitor the tower frequency or Common Traffic Advisory Frequency (CTAF) to get a good idea of what traffic conditions to expect. Checklists should be performed well in advance so there is time to focus on traffic and ATC instructions. These procedures are especially important prior to entering a high-density traffic area, such as Class B airspace.

To manage workload, items should be prioritized. This concept should be emphasized to learners and reinforced when training procedures are performed. For example, during a go-around, adding power, gaining airspeed, and properly configuring the aircraft are priorities. Informing the tower of the balked landing should be accomplished only after these tasks are completed. learners should understand that priorities change as the situation changes. If fuel quantity is lower than expected on a cross-country flight, the priority can shift from making a scheduled arrival time at the destination, to locating a nearby airport to refuel. In an emergency situation, the first priority is to fly the aircraft and maintain a safe airspeed.

Another important part of managing workload is recognizing a work overload situation. The first effect of high workload is that the pilot begins to work faster. As workload increases, attention cannot be devoted to several tasks at one time, and the pilot may begin to focus on one item. When the pilot becomes task saturated, there is no awareness of inputs from various sources; decisions may be made on incomplete information, and the possibility of error increases. *[Figure 1-14]*

During a lesson, workload can be gradually increased as the instructor monitors the learner's management of tasks. The instructor should ensure that the learner has the ability to recognize a work overload situation. When becoming overloaded, the learner should stop, think, slow down, and prioritize. It is important that the learner understand options that may be available to decrease workload. For example, locating an item on a chart or setting a radio frequency may be delegated to another pilot or passenger, an autopilot (if available) may be used, or ATC may be enlisted to provide assistance.

Figure 1-14. *Accidents often occur when flying task requirements exceed pilot capabilities. The difference between these two factors is called the margin of safety. Note that in this idealized example, the margin of safety is minimal during the approach and landing. At this point, an emergency or distraction could overtax pilot capabilities, causing an accident.*

Teaching Decision-Making Skills

When instructor pilots discuss system safety, they generally worry about the loss of traditional stick-and-rudder skills. The fear is that emphasis on items such as risk management, ADM, SRM, and situational awareness detracts from the training necessary in developing safe pilots.

It is important to understand that system safety flight training occurs in three phases. First, there are the traditional stick and rudder maneuvers. In order to apply the critical thinking skills that are to follow, pilots should develop a high degree of confidence in their ability to fly the aircraft. Next, the tenets of system safety are introduced into the training environment as learners begin to understand how best to identify hazards, manage risk, and use all available resources to make each flight as safe as possible. This can be accomplished through scenarios that emphasize the skill sets being taught. Finally, the learner may be introduced to more complex scenarios that focus on several safety-of-flight issues. Thus, scenarios should start out rather simply, then progress in complexity and intensity as the learner becomes able to handle the increased workload.

A traditional stick-and-rudder maneuver such as short field landings can be used to illustrate how ADM and risk management can be incorporated into instruction. In phase 1 the initial focus is on developing the stick-and-rudder skills required to execute this operation safely. These include power and airspeed management, aircraft configuration, placement in the pattern, wind correction, determining the proper aim point and sight picture, etc. By emphasizing these points through repetition and practice, a learner eventually acquires the skills needed to execute a short field landing.

Phase II introduces the many factors that come into play when performing a short field landing, which include runway conditions, no-flap landings, airport obstructions, and rejected landings. The introduction of such items need not increase training times. In fact, all of the hazards or considerations referenced in the short field landing lesson plan may be discussed in detail during the ground portion of the instructional program. For example, if training has been conducted at an airport that enjoys an obstruction-free 6,000-foot runway, consider the implications of operating the same aircraft out of a 1,800-foot strip with an obstruction off the departure end. Add to that additional considerations, such as operating the aircraft at close to its maximum gross weight under conditions of high density altitude, and now a single training scenario has several layers of complexity. The ensuing discussion proves a valuable training exercise, and it comes with little additional ground and no added flight training.

Finally, phase III takes the previously discussed hazards, risks, and considerations, and incorporates them into a complex scenario. This forces a learner to consider not only a specific lesson item (in this case, short-field landings), but also requires that it be viewed in the greater context of the overall flight. For example, on a cross-country flight, the learner is presented with a realistic distraction, perhaps the illness of a passenger. This forces a diversion to an alternate for which the learner has not planned. The new destination airport has two runways, the longest of which is closed due to construction. The remaining runway is short, but while less than ideal, should prove suitable for landing. However, upon entering the pattern, the learner finds the electrically driven flaps do not extend. The learner should now consider whether to press on and attempt the landing or proceed to a secondary alternate.

If he or she decides to go forward and attempt the landing, this proves an excellent time to test the requisite stick and rudder skills. If the learner decides to proceed to a second alternate, this opens new training opportunities. Proceeding further tests cross-country skills, such as navigation, communication, management of a passenger in distress, as well as the other tasks associated with simply flying the aircraft. The outlined methodology simply takes a series of seemingly unrelated tasks and scripts them into a training exercise requiring both mechanical and cognitive skills to complete it successfully.

Scenario-based training (SBT) helps the flight instructor effectively teach ADM and risk management. The what, why, and how of SBT will be discussed extensively throughout this handbook. In teaching ADM, it is important to remember the learning objective is for the learner to exercise sound judgment and make good decisions. Thus, the flight instructor should be ready to turn the responsibility for planning and execution of the flight over to the learner as soon as possible. Although the flight instructor continues to demonstrate and instruct skill maneuvers, when the learner begins to make decisions, the flight instructor should revert to the role of mentor and/or learning facilitator.

The flight instructor is an integral part of the systems approach to training and is crucial to the implementation of an SBT program, which underlies the teaching of ADM. Remember, for SBT instruction to be effective, it is vital the flight instructor and learner establish the following information:

- Scenario destination(s)
- Desired learning outcome(s)
- Desired level of learner performance
- Possible inflight scenario changes

It is also important for the flight instructor to remember that a good scenario:

- Is not a test.
- Will not have a single correct answer.
- Does not offer an obvious answer.
- Engages all three learning domains.
- Is interactive.
- Should not promote errors.
- Should promote situational awareness and opportunities for decision-making.
- Requires time-pressured decisions.

The flight instructor should make the situation as realistic as possible. This means the learner knows where he or she is going and what transpires on the flight. While the actual flight may deviate from the original plan, it allows the learner to be placed in a realistic scenario. The learner should plan the flight to include:

- Route
- Destination(s)
- Weather
- NOTAMS
- Possible emergency procedures

Since the scenarios may have several good outcomes and a few poor ones, the flight instructor should understand in advance which outcomes are positive and/or negative and give the learner the freedom to make both good and poor decisions. This does not mean that the learner should be allowed to make an unsafe decision or commit an unsafe act. However, it does allow the learners to make decisions that fit their experience level and result in positive outcomes.

Teaching decision-making skills has become an integral part of flight training. The word "decision" is used several times in each ACS and applicants are judged on their ability to make a decision as well as their ability to perform a task. Thus, it is important for flight instructors to remember that decision-making is a component of the ACS.

Assessing SRM Skills

A learner's performance is often assessed only on a technical level. The instructor determines whether maneuvers are technically accurate and that procedures are performed in the right order. In SRM assessment, instructors should learn to assess on a different level. How did the learner arrive at a particular decision? What resources were used? Was risk assessed accurately when a go/no-go decision was made? Did the learner maintain situational awareness in the traffic pattern? Was workload managed effectively during a cross-country flight? How does the learner handle stress and fatigue?

Instructors should continually evaluate learner decision-making ability and offer suggestions for improvement. It is not always necessary to present complex situations, which require detailed analysis. By allowing learners to make decisions about typical issues that arise throughout the course of training, such as their fitness to fly, weather conditions, and equipment problems, instructors can address effective decision-making and allow learners to develop judgment skills. For example, when a discrepancy is found during preflight inspection, the learner should be allowed to initially determine the action to be taken. Then the effectiveness of the learner's choice and other options that may be available can be discussed.

Opportunities for improving decision-making abilities occur often during training. If the tower offers the learner a runway that requires landing with a tailwind in order to expedite traffic, the learner can be directed to assess the risks involved and asked to present alternative actions to be taken. Perhaps the most frequent choice that has to be made during flight training is the go/no-go decision based on weather. While the final choice to fly lies with the instructor, learners can be asked to assess the weather prior to each flight and make a go/no-go determination.

In addition, instructors should utilize SBT to create lessons that are specifically designed to test whether learners are applying SRM skills. Planning a flight lesson in which the learner is presented with simulated emergencies, a heavy workload, or other operational problems can be valuable in assessing the learner's judgment and decision-making skills. During the flight, learner performance can be evaluated for workload and/or stress management.

SRM grades are based on these four components:

- Explain—the learner can verbally identify, describe, and understand the risks inherent in the flight scenario. The learner needs to be prompted to identify risks and make decisions.

- Practice—the learner is able to identify, understand, and apply SRM principles to the actual flight situation. Coaching, instruction, and/or assistance from the flight instructor quickly corrects minor deviations and errors identified by the flight instructor. The learner is an active decision maker.

- Manage/Decide—the learner can correctly gather the most important data available both within and outside the flight deck, identify possible courses of action, evaluate the risk inherent in each course of action, and make the appropriate decision. Instructor intervention is not required for the safe completion of the flight.

- Not Observed—any event not accomplished or required.

Postflight, collaborative assessment or learner centered grading (LCG) also discussed in Chapter 6, Assessment, is a vital component of assessing a learner's SRM skills. As a reminder, collaborative assessment includes two parts: learner self-assessment and a detailed assessment by the flight instructor. The purpose of the self-assessment is to stimulate growth in the learner's thought processes and, in turn, behaviors. The self-assessment is followed by an in-depth discussion between the flight instructor and the learner, which compares the flight instructor's assessment to the learner's self-assessment.

An important element of SRM skills assessment is that the flight instructor provides a clear picture of the progress the learner is making during the training. Grading should also be progressive. During each flight, the learner should achieve a new level of learning. For flight one, the automation management area might be a "describe" item. By flight three, it would be a "practice" item, and by flight five, a "manage-decide" item.

Chapter Summary

This chapter introduced aviation instructors to the underlying concepts of safety risk management, which the FAA is integrating into all levels of the aviation community.

Aviation Instructor's Handbook (FAA-H-8083-9)
Chapter 2: Human Behavior

Introduction

Derek's learner, Jason, is very smart and able to retain a lot of information, but has a tendency to rush through the less exciting material and shows interest and attentiveness only when performing tasks that he finds to be interesting. This concerns Derek because he is worried that Jason will overlook many important details and rush through procedures. For a homework assignment Jason was told to take a very thorough look at Preflight Procedures and that for his next flight lesson they would discuss each step in detail. As Derek predicted, Jason found this assignment to be boring and was not prepared. Derek knows that Jason is a "thrill seeker" as he talks about his business, which is a wilderness adventure company. Derek wants to find a way to keep Jason focused and help him find excitement in all areas of learning so that he will understand the complex art of flying and aircraft safety.

Learning is the acquisition of knowledge or understanding of a subject or skill through education, experience, practice, or study. This chapter discusses behavior and how it affects the learning process. An instructor seeks to understand why people act the way they do and how people learn. An effective instructor uses knowledge of human behavior, basic human needs, the defense mechanisms humans use that prevent learning, and how adults learn in order to organize and conduct productive learning activities.

Definitions of Human Behavior

The study of human behavior is an attempt to explain how and why humans function the way they do. A complex topic, human behavior is a product both of innate human nature and of individual experience and environment. Definitions of human behavior abound, depending on the field of study. In the scientific world, human behavior is seen as the product of factors that cause people to act in predictable ways.

For example, speaking in public is very high on the list of fears many people have. While no two people react the same to any given fear, fear itself does trigger certain innate responses such as an increase in breathing rate. How a person handles that fear is a product of individual experiences. The person who has never spoken in public may be unable to fulfill the obligation. Another person, knowing his or her job requires public speaking, may choose to take a class on public speaking to learn how to cope with the fear.

Human behavior is also defined as the result of attempts to satisfy certain needs. These needs may be simple to understand and easy to identify, such as the need for food and water. They also may be complex, such as the need for respect and acceptance. A working knowledge of human behavior can help an instructor better understand a learner. It is also helpful to remember that to a large extent thoughts, feelings, and behavior are shared by all men or women, despite seemingly large cultural differences. For example, fear causes humans to either fight or flee. In the public speaking example above, one person may "flee" by not fulfilling the obligation. The other person may "fight" by learning techniques to deal with fear.

Another definition of human behavior focuses on the typical life course of humans. This approach emphasizes human development or the successive phases of growth in which human behavior is characterized by a distinct set of physical, physiological, and behavioral features. The thoughts, feelings, and behavior of an infant differ radically from those of a teen. Research shows that as an individual matures, his or her mode of action moves from dependency to self-direction. Therefore, the age of the learner impacts how the instructor designs the curriculum. Since the average age of a learner can vary, the instructor needs to offer a curriculum that addresses the varying learner tendency to self-direct. *[Figure 2-1]*

By observing human behavior, an instructor can gain the knowledge needed to better understand him or herself as an instructor as well as the learning needs of learners. Understanding human behavior leads to successful instruction.

Instructor and Learner Relationship

How does personality type testing affect instructors and learners? Research has led many educational psychologists to feel that based on personality type, everyone also has an individual style of learning. In this theory, working with that style, rather than against it, benefits both instructor and learner. Although controversy often swirls around the educational benefits of teaching learners according to personality types, it has gained a large following and been implemented at many levels of education. Today's learner can visit any number of websites, take a personality test, and discover what type of learner he or she is and how best to study.

In a continuing quest to figure out why humans do what they do, the mother-daughter team of Katharine Cook Briggs and Isabel Briggs Myers pioneered the Myers-Briggs Type Indicator (MBTI) test in 1962. The MBTI was based on Jungian theory, previous research into personality traits, and lengthy personal observations of human behavior by Myers and Briggs. They believed that much seemingly random variation in human behavior is actually quite orderly and consistent, being due to basic differences in the ways individuals prefer to use their perception and judgment.

They distilled human behavior into sixteen distinct personality types. Inspired by their research, clinical psychologist and author, Dr. David Keirsey condensed their sixteen types into four groups he calls Guardian, Artisan, Rational, and Idealist. Others have either contributed or continued to expand personality research and its influence on human behavior. Personality type testing now runs the gamut from helping people make career choices to helping people choose marriage partners.

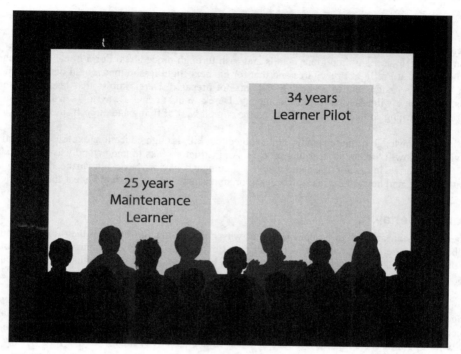

Figure 2-1. *The average age of a learner pilot is 34, while the average age of a maintenance learner is 25.*

Not only does personality type influence how one learns, it also influences how one teaches. Learning one's personality type helps an instructor recognize how he or she instructs. Why is it important to recognize personal instruction style? The match or mismatch between the way an instructor teaches and the way an individual learns contributes to instructional satisfaction or dissatisfaction. Learners whose styles are compatible with the teaching styles of an instructor tend to retain information longer, apply it more effectively, learn more, and have a more positive attitude toward the course in general. Although an instructor cannot change his or her preferred style of teaching to match a learning style, steps can be taken to actively bridge the differences.

Consider the Derek's dilemma with Jason described at the beginning of this chapter. Derek knows he is the type of instructor who provides a clear, precise syllabus and has a tendency to explain with step-by-step procedures. His teaching style relies on traditional techniques and he often finds himself teaching as he was taught. Observation leads Derek to believe Jason is the type of person who needs the action, excitement, and variation reflected in his career choice. In an effort to focus Jason on the need to learn all aspects of flight, Derek sets up a scenario for the day that features how to scout locations for future adventure tours.

By adjusting the flight scenario, Derek pushes himself out of his lock-step approach to teaching. He has also added an element of variation to the lesson that not only interests Jason, but is one of the reasons he wants to learn to fly.

Motivation

Motivation is the reason one acts or behaves in a certain way and lies at the heart of goals. A goal is the object of a person's effort. Motivation prompts learners to engage in hard work and affects learner success. Being smart or coordinated seldom guarantees success, but motivation routinely propels learners to the top. An important part of an aviation instructor's job is to discover what motivates each learner and to use this information to encourage him or her to work hard.

Motivation is probably the dominant force that governs the learner's progress and ability to understand and can be used to the advantage of the instructor. Motivation comes in many guises. It may be negative or positive. Negative motivation may engender fear, for example. While negative motivation may be useful in certain situations, characteristically it is not as effective in promoting efficient learning as positive motivation. *[Figure 2-2]* Positive motivation is provided by the promise or achievement of rewards. These rewards may be personal or social, they may involve financial gain, satisfaction of the self-concept, personal gain, or public recognition.

Figure 2-2. *Insecure and unpleasant training situations inhibit learning.*

Motivation may be tangible or intangible. Learners seeking intangible rewards are motivated by the desires for personal comfort and security, group approval, and the achievement of a favorable self-image. The desire for personal comfort and security is a form of motivation which instructors often forget. All learners want secure, pleasant conditions and a safe environment. If they recognize that what they are learning may promote these objectives, their attention is easier to attract and hold. Insecure and unpleasant training situations inhibit learning. Learners also want a tangible return for their efforts. For motivation to be effective on this level, learners know that their efforts are suitably rewarded. These rewards need to be constantly apparent to the learner during instruction, whether they are to be financial, self-esteem, or public recognition.

The tangible rewards of aviation are not always obvious during training. Traditional syllabi often contain lessons with objectives that are not immediately obvious to the learner.

These lessons may pay dividends during later instruction, a fact the learner may not appreciate and may result in less knowledge transfer than if the learner could relate all objectives to an operational need (law of readiness). The instructor should ensure that the learner is aware of those applications not immediately apparent. To reduce this issue, the instructor should develop appropriate scenarios that contain the elements to be practiced.

Everyone wants to avoid pain and injury. Learners normally are eager to identify operations or procedures that help prevent injury or loss of life. This is especially true when the learner knows that the ability to make timely decisions, or to act correctly in an emergency, is based on sound principles.

The attractive features of the activity to be learned also can be a strong motivational factor. Learners are anxious to gain skills that may be used to their advantage. If they understand that each task is useful in preparing for future activities, they are more willing to pursue it.

Another strong motivating force is group approval. Every person wants the approval of peers and superiors. Interest can be stimulated and maintained by building on this natural desire. Most learners enjoy the feeling of belonging to a group and are interested in accomplishment, which gives them prestige among their peers.

Every person seeks to establish a favorable self-image. In certain instances, this self-image may be submerged in feelings of insecurity or despondency. Fortunately, most people engaged in a task believe that success is possible under the right combination of circumstances and good fortune. This belief can be a powerful motivating force for learners. An instructor can effectively foster this motivation by the introduction of perceptions that are solidly based on previously learned factual information easily recognized. Each additional block of learning should help formulate insight, contributing to the ultimate training goals and promoting confidence in the overall training program. At the same time, it helps the learner develop a favorable self-image. As this confirmation progresses and confidence increases, advancement is more rapid and motivation is strengthened.

Positive motivation is essential to true learning. Negative motivation should be avoided with all but the most overconfident and impulsive learners. Slumps in learning are often due to declining motivation. Motivation does not remain at a uniformly high level. It may be affected by outside influences, such as physical or mental disturbances or inadequate instruction.

The instructor should strive to maintain motivation at the highest possible level. In addition, the instructor should be alert to detect and counter any lapses in motivation.

Where Does the Motivation to Learn Come From?

Motivation to learn can come from many sources. Some learners have a fundamental interest in aviation and experience sheer fascination with aircraft or with the experience of flight. Other learners may decide that aviation provides an opportunity to develop a wide variety of technical, physical, communication, and problem-solving abilities. Some see aviation as a way to boost their self-image or ego. Other learners are motivated by tradition and wish to follow in the footsteps of a relative or close friend. Some learners are motivated to pursue aviation training because it offers a promising career. To others, aviation offers prestige or acceptance within social groups. Some may think that aviation offers fun and excitement or simply a more convenient form of transportation. All of these sources of motivation have one thing in common: they all offer some type of reward in exchange for performing the hard work.

Aviation instructors should keep in mind that adult learners who are motivated to seek out an educational experience do so primarily because they have a use for the knowledge or skill being sought. Learning is a means to an end, not an end in itself. Based on this, it is important instructors determine why a learner enrolled in the course. Based on preference and/or class size, an instructor can conduct a brief personal interview with the learner or have them complete an information form. Asking questions such as "Why are you taking this course?" or "How do you plan to use the information you learn in this course?" may be all that is necessary.

Learner Questionnaire

A short questionnaire can be helpful in gathering additional background information. For example, it is helpful to know a learner's familiarity with the subject matter. Questions such as "Have you ever taken a course in aircraft maintenance?" or "Have you ever flown a small airplane?" or "Have you had any on-the-job training in avionics?" should garner the type of information needed.

A short questionnaire also offers an instructor the chance to discover how different learning styles may improve knowledge transfer (small groups, independent study, etc.). Another possible way to gather information about a learner is to have him or her write a brief autobiography which includes any experience with the subjects being taught. However an instructor gathers information about learners, the information helps the instructor allow for not only personal learning goals for the course, but also the goals and motivations of the learners, their background in aviation training, as well as their preferences. An instructor armed with this information can make the experience beneficial to all involved.

Maintaining Motivation

Motivation is generally not something that can be transferred from one person to another. Instructors should become skillful at recognizing problems with motivation and at encouraging learners to continue to do their best.

Rewarding Success

Positive feedback encourages learners. Practice positive feedback frequently by:

- Praising incremental successes during training.
- Relating daily accomplishments to lesson objectives.
- Commenting favorably on learner progress and level ability.

For example, as the learner progresses through training, remark on the milestones. When a learner first performs a task alone, congratulate him or her on having learned it.

When that same skill reaches an intermediate level, point out that the learner's performance is almost consistent with the requirements of the Airman Certification Standards (ACS), the set of standards detailing the knowledge and skills an airman needs to possess and demonstrate to obtain a pilot certificate. When performance is equal to the ACS requirements, comment favorably on the skill acquisition. When learner performance exceeds ACS requirements, point out what a benefit this will be when the learner performs under pressure during a practical test or on the job.

Presenting New Challenges

With each declaration of success, be sure to present learners with the next challenge. For example, when a learner begins to perform a skill consistently to ACS or PTS requirements, challenge him or her to continue to improve it such that the skill can be performed under pressure or when distracted. Instructors can also add new problems or situations to create a learning scenario.

Drops in Motivation

Instructors should be prepared to deal with a number of circumstances in which motivation levels drop. It is natural for motivation to wane somewhat after the initial excitement of the learner's first days of training, or between major training events such as solo, evaluations, or practical tests. Drops in motivation appear in several different ways. Learners may come to lessons unprepared or give the general sense that aviation training is no longer a priority. During these times, it is often helpful to remind learners of their own stated goals for seeking aviation training.

Learning plateaus are a common source of frustration, discouragement, and decreased learner motivation. A first line of defense against this situation is to explain that learning seldom proceeds at a constant pace—no one climbs the ladder of success by exactly one rung per day. Learners should be encouraged to continue to work hard and be reassured that results will follow.

Summary of Instructor Actions

To ensure that learners continue to work hard, the instructor should:

1. Ask new learners about their aviation training goals.
2. Reward incremental successes in learning.
3. Present new challenges.
4. Occasionally remind learners about their own stated goals for aviation training.
5. Assure learners that learning plateaus are normal and that improvement will resume with continued effort.

Human Needs and Motivation

Human needs are things all humans require for normal growth and development. These needs have been studied by psychologists and categorized in a number of ways. Henry A. Murray, one of the founders of personality psychology who was active in developing a theory of motivation, identified a list of core psychological needs in 1938. He described these needs as being either primary (based on biological needs, such as the need for food) or secondary (generally psychological, such as the need for independence). Murray believed the interplay of these needs produce distinct personality types and are internal influences on behavior.

Murray's research underpins the work of psychologist Abraham Maslow who also studied human needs, motivation, and personality. While working with monkeys during his early years of research, he noticed that some needs take precedence over others. For example, thirst is relieved before hunger because the need for water is a stronger need than the need for food. In 1954, Maslow published what has become known as Maslow's Hierarchy of Needs. *[Figure 2-3]* According to Maslow, human needs go beyond the obvious physical needs of food and shelter to include psychological needs, safety and security, love and belongingness, self-esteem, and self-actualization to achieve one's goals. Human needs are satisfied in order of importance. Once a need is satisfied, humans work to satisfy the next level of need. Need satisfaction is an ongoing behavior that determines everyday actions.

Since Maslow's findings, multiple psychological studies have proven that humans can experience higher levels of motivation while not having lower basic needs met. In a study from 2011, researchers at the University of Illinois found that Maslow's hierarchy was not universal and the order in which these needs were met did not have much impact on the satisfaction or happiness of an individual. Maslow's theory has little to no empirical data to support his findings on the five-need hierarchy (Whaba and Bridgewell, 1976).

Maslow's hierarchy states that each level has to be meet 100 percent before moving on to the next level of need. However, a person can still achieve what they were "born to do" while still being hungry.

What was apparent in multiple studies, however, was that humans have needs that affect their ability to focus on the task at hand. Learners tend to show little to no motivation or attention if most of their needs are not met. If a learner is hungry (physiological), their focus of perceptions (attention) will not be on the instructor and the subject being presented. Rather, it will be on satisfying the physiological need as soon as possible. The same can be said about an anxious learner attempting a fully-developed stall for the first time. If the learner feels unsafe (safety and security), their focus of perception is on their "flee" response and not the skill that the learner it trying to acquire. However, what is important here is the focus of perceptions, and the ability of the instructor to concentrate the learner's senses on the subject being presented.

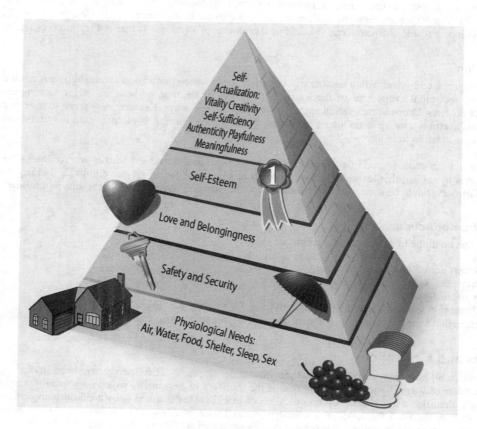

Figure 2-3. *Maslow's Hierarchy of Needs.*

Many learners are able to complete a maneuver or demonstrate knowledge while being hungry or thirsty, which means that for the most part, the entire need does not have to be fulfilled to 100 percent. What needs to be addressed is whether parts of each level have been met, which allows the focus of perception to be concentrated on the instruction given. It does not matter which order the needs are met, the order has little to no effect on the learner's learning ability. What matters is that the instructor verifies that most of the needs has been met (law of readiness) and is then able to focus the learner's senses (perception) on the lesson.

One of the main responsibilities of an aviation instructor is to help learners learn, which encompasses the law of readiness. To satisfy the law of readiness, an instructor can verify that a learner's needs have been met by conducting a thorough pre-assessment prior to beginning the lesson. The pre-assessment should verify whether the learner is physically and mentally ready to learn.

Meeting Human Needs to Encourage Learning

Physiological

These are biological needs. They consist of the need for air, food, water, and maintenance of the human body. If a learner is unwell, then little else matters. Unless the biological needs are met, a person cannot concentrate fully on learning, self-expression, or any other tasks. Instructors should monitor their learners to make sure that their basic physical needs have been met. A hungry or tired learner may not be able to perform as expected.

Security

Once the physiological needs are met, the need for security becomes active. All humans have a need to feel safe. Security needs are about keeping oneself from harm. If a learner does not feel safe, he or she cannot concentrate. The aviation instructor who stresses flight safety during training mitigates feelings of insecurity. A flight instructor should be aware of his learner's fear of certain flight regions and ease them into those situations carefully.

Belonging

When individuals are physically comfortable and do not feel threatened, they seek to satisfy their social needs of belonging. Maslow states that people seek to overcome feelings of loneliness and alienation. This involves both giving and receiving love, affection, and the sense of belonging. For example, aviation learners are usually out of their normal surroundings during training, and their need for association and belonging is more pronounced. Instructors should make every effort to help new learners feel at ease and to reinforce their decision to pursue a career or hobby in aviation.

Esteem

When the first three classes of needs are satisfied, the need for esteem can become dominant. Humans have a need for a stable, firmly based, high level of self-respect and respect from others. Esteem is about feeling good about one's self. Humans get esteem in two ways: internally or externally. Internally, a person judges himself or herself worthy by personally defined standards. High self-esteem results in self-confidence, independence, achievement, competence, and knowledge.

Most people, however, seek external esteem through social approval and esteem from other people, judging themselves by what others think of them. External self-esteem relates to one's reputation, such as status, recognition, appreciation, and respect of associates.

When esteem needs are satisfied, a person feels self-confident and valuable as a person in the world. When these needs are frustrated, the person feels inferior, weak, helpless, and worthless. Esteem needs not only have a strong influence on the instructor-learner relationship, but also may be the main reason for a learner's interest in aviation training.

Cognitive and Aesthetic

In later years, Maslow added cognitive (need to know and understand) and aesthetic (the emotional need of the artist) needs to the pyramid. He realized humans have a deep need to understand what is going on around them. If a person understands what is going on, he or she can either control the situation or make informed choices about what steps might be taken next. The brain even reinforces this need by giving humans a rush of dopamine whenever something is learned, which accounts for that satisfying "eureka!" moment. For example, a flight learner usually experiences a major "eureka!" moment upon completing the first solo flight.

Aesthetic needs connect directly with human emotions, which makes it a subtle factor in the domain of persuasion. When someone likes another person, a house, a painting, or a song, the reasons are not examined—he or she simply likes it. This need can factor into the learner-instructor relationship. If an instructor does not "like" a learner, this subtle feeling may affect the instructor's ability to teach.

Self-Actualization

When all of the foregoing needs are satisfied, then and only then are the needs for self-actualization activated. Maslow describes self-actualization as a person's need to be and do that which the person was "born to do." To paraphrase an old Army recruiting slogan, self-actualization is to "be all you can be."

Self-actualized people are characterized by:

- Being problem-focused.

- Incorporating an ongoing freshness of appreciation of life.

- A concern about personal growth.

- The ability to have peak experiences.

Helping a learner achieve his or her individual potential in aviation training offers the greatest challenge as well as reward to the instructor.

Instructors should help learners satisfy their human needs in a manner that creates a healthy learning environment. In this type of environment, learners experience fewer frustrations and, therefore, can devote more attention to their studies. Fulfillment of needs can be a powerful motivation in complex learning situations.

Human Nature and Motivation

Human nature refers to the general psychological characteristics, feelings, and behavioral traits shared by all humans. Consider Jason, who came to aviation because he wanted to participate more actively in another realm of his business. Derek needs to capitalize on this motivation to keep Jason interested in the step-by-step procedures that need to be learned in order to fly safely. There is a gap between Jason and his goal of earning a pilot certificate. It is Derek's job to close the gap. The successful instructor channels learner motivation and guides the learner toward the goal of obtaining aviation skills through education, experience, practice, and study.

The psychologist and Nobel Prize winner in Economics, Daniel Kahneman, summarized his findings of human behavior in his book titled, *Thinking, Fast and Slow*. Simply, he outlines that two systems of thought constantly compete for control over our behaviors that affect decision-making. The first system (fast) is the automatic reaction that individuals have developed through memory and experience. The second system (slow) relies on logic and reasoning to draw conclusions for the actions one takes. *[Figure 2-4]*

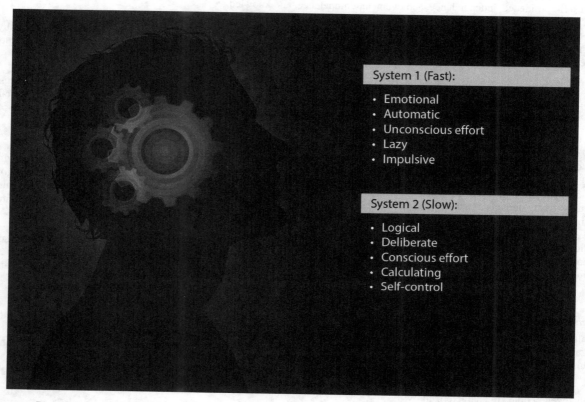

Figure 2-4. *Daniel Kahneman developed a two-system view of human behaviors that affect decision-making: System 1 (fast) represents the automatic responses, while System 2 (slow) represents the more logical and deliberate considerations used for decision-making.*

According to Kahneman's research, System 1 is primarily based in emotion and the unconscious mind. These are automatic "gut reactions" that require little thought or effort by the individual. For example, when presented with the simple math equation $2 + 2 = x$, the individual can easily solve the problem where $x = 4$. The response is instant and likely correct in this example. The inherent risk in using this thought system is that, as Kahneman explains, we are inherently lazy. It is exhausting to put forth the effort required to deliberately concentrate on a problem, especially one that appears to be so easy. This can lead to poor decision-making due to the assumption that the task at hand is as simple as past, similar, experiences suggest it to be.

In contrast, individuals rely on System 2 less frequently as it requires conscious effort to calculate and reason through a problem, and because of this System 2 is comparatively slower than System 1. While someone can easily solve the equation $2 + 2 = x$, the average person needs to pause and consider an answer if presented with a more difficult problem such as $48 \times 76 = y$. This system demands considerable effort and self-control of the individual and as a result, it is tempting to revert to the relative ease of System 1. In fact, once the immediate problem is solved, System 1 takes over again.

Understanding how these systems affect our decision-making can help instructors be more aware of learner pitfalls, such as assuming a complex problem is a simple one, or assuming that because a recent task led to a solution that the same solution can be used correctly for a similar task.

Since it is human nature to be motivated, the responsibility for discovering how to realize the potential of the learner lies with the instructor. How to mold a solid, healthy, productive relationship with a learner depends on the instructor's knowledge of human behavior and needs. Being able to recognize factors that inhibit the learning process also helps the instructor in this process.

Defense Mechanisms

Defense mechanisms can be biological or psychological. The biological defense mechanism is a physiological response that protects or preserves organisms. For example, when humans experience a danger or a threat, the "fight or flight" response kicks in. Adrenaline and other chemicals are activated and physical symptoms such as rapid heart rate and increased blood pressure occur.

For example, when an anxious learner pilot reacts to impending and full stalls during practice, the anxiety that the learner pilot may feel may resolve itself into a "fight or flight" response. There may be limited time to analyze the problem. Therefore, the learner needs the opportunity to experience and develop a comfort level that mitigates the anxiety.

The instructor needs to recognize the learner's apprehension about performing the recovery techniques and help them gain the necessary skill level to feel comfortable with the maneuver. In this case, the instructor could take the procedure apart and demonstrate each stage of an impending or full stall. Allowing the learner to then practice the stages in various realistic scenarios should instill the confidence needed to master the stall recovery.

Sigmund Freud introduced the psychological concept of the ego defense mechanism in 1894. The ego defense mechanism is an unconscious mental process to protect oneself from anxiety, unpleasant emotions, or to provide a refuge from a situation with which the individual cannot currently cope. For example, someone who blots out the memory of being physically assaulted is using a defense mechanism. People use these defenses to prevent unacceptable ideas or impulses from entering the conscious mind. Defense mechanisms soften feelings of failure, alleviate feelings of guilt, help an individual cope with reality, and protect one's self-image. [Figure 2-5]

When anxiety occurs, the mind tries to solve the problem or find an escape, but if these tactics do not work, defense mechanisms are triggered. Defense mechanisms share two common properties:

- They often appear unconsciously.

- They tend to distort, transform, or otherwise falsify reality.

Because reality is distorted, perception changes, which allows for a lessening of anxiety, with a corresponding reduction in tension. Repression and denial are two primary defense mechanisms.

Repression

Repression is the defense mechanism whereby a person places uncomfortable thoughts into inaccessible areas of the unconscious mind. Things a person is unable to cope with now are pushed away, to be dealt with at another time, or hopefully never because they faded away on their own accord. The level of repression can vary from temporarily forgetting an uncomfortable thought to amnesia, where the events that triggered the anxiety are deeply buried. Repressed memories do not disappear and may reappear in dreams or slips of the tongue ("Freudian slips"). For example, a learner pilot may have a repressed fear of flying that inhibits his or her ability to learn how to fly.

Denial

Denial is a refusal to accept external reality because it is too threatening. It is the refusal to acknowledge what has happened, is happening, or will happen. It is a form of repression through which stressful thoughts are banned from memory. Related to denial is minimization. When a person minimizes something, he or she accepts what happened, but in a diluted form.

For example, the instructor finds a water bottle under the rudder pedal of an aircraft the student took on a solo flight and explains the hazards of loose objects in the cabin. The learner, unwilling to accept the reality that his or her inattention could have caused an aircraft accident, denies having been inattentive on previous day. Or, the learner minimizes the incident, accepting he or she left the water bottle pointing out that nothing bad happened as a result of the action.

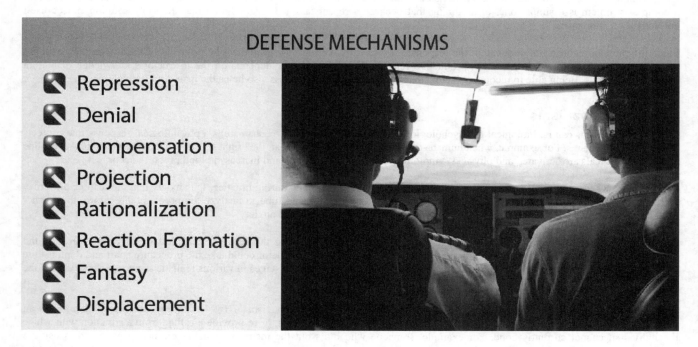

Figure 2-5. *Several common defense mechanisms may apply to aviation learners.*

Other defense mechanisms include but are not limited to the following:

Compensation

Compensation is a process of psychologically counterbalancing perceived weaknesses by emphasizing strength in other areas. Through compensation, learners often attempt to disguise the presence of a weak or undesirable quality by emphasizing a more positive one. The "I'm not a fighter, I'm a lover" philosophy can be an example of compensation. Compensation involves substituting success in a realm of life other than the realm in which the person suffers a weakness.

Projection

Through projection, an individual places his or her own unacceptable impulses onto someone else. A person relegates the blame for personal shortcomings, mistakes, and transgressions to others or attributes personal motives, desires, characteristics, and impulses to others. The learner pilot who fails a flight exam and says, "I failed because I had a poor examiner" believes the failure was not due to a lack of personal skill or knowledge. This learner projects blame onto an "unfair" examiner.

Learners who believe their instruction is inadequate, or that their efforts are not conscientiously considered and evaluated, do not learn well. In addition, their motivation suffers no matter how intent they are on learning to fly. Motivation also declines when a learner believes the instructor is making unreasonable demands for performance and progress. *[Figure 2-6]*

Assignment of difficult, but possible, goals usually provides a challenge and promotes learning. In a typical flight lesson, reasonable goals are listed in the lesson objectives and the desired levels of proficiency for the goals are included in statements that contain completion standards.

Rationalization

Rationalization is a subconscious technique for justifying actions that otherwise would be unacceptable. When true rationalization takes place, individuals sincerely believe in the plausible and acceptable excuses which seem real and justifiable. For example, a learner mechanic performs poorly on a test. He or she may justify the poor grade by claiming there was not enough time to learn the required information. The learner does not admit to failing to join the class study group or taking the computer quiz offered by the instructor.

Reaction Formation

In reaction formation a person fakes a belief opposite to the true belief because the true belief causes anxiety. The person feels an urge to do or say something and then actually does or says something that is the opposite of what he or she really wants. For example, a learner may develop a who-cares-how-other-people-feel attitude to cover up feelings of loneliness and a hunger for acceptance.

Figure 2-6. *The assignment of impossible or unreasonable goals discourages the learner, diminishes effort, and retards the learning process.*

Fantasy

Fantasy occurs when a learner engages in daydreams about how things should be rather than doing anything about how things are. The learner uses his or her imagination to escape from reality into a fictitious world—a world of success or pleasure. However, if a learner gets sufficient satisfaction from daydreaming, he or she may stop trying to achieve goals altogether. Perhaps the transitioning pilot is having trouble mastering a more complex aircraft, which jeopardizes his or her dream of becoming an airline pilot. It becomes easier to daydream about the career than to achieve the certification. Lost in the fantasy, the learner spends more time dreaming about being a successful airline pilot than working toward the goal. When carried to extremes, the worlds of fantasy and reality can become so confused that the dreamer cannot distinguish one from the other.

Displacement

This defense mechanism results in an unconscious shift of emotion, affect, or desire from the original object to a more acceptable, less threatening substitute. Displacement avoids the risk associated with feeling unpleasant emotions and puts them somewhere other than where they belong. For example, the avionics learner is angry with the instructor over a grade received but fears displaying the anger could antagonize the instructor. The learner might choose to direct the anger towards a different object without risking consequences related to the class.

Psychology textbooks or online references offer more in-depth information about defense mechanisms. While most defense mechanisms fall within the realm of normal behavior and serve a useful purpose, in some cases they may be associated with mental health problems. Defense mechanisms involve some degree of self-deception and distortion of reality. Thus, they alleviate the symptoms, not the causes, and do not solve problems. Moreover, because defense mechanisms operate on an unconscious level, they are not subject to normal conscious checks and balances. Once an individual realizes there is a conscious reliance on one of these devices, behavior ceases to be an unconscious adjustment mechanism and becomes, instead, an ineffective way of satisfying a need.

It may be difficult for an instructor to identify excessive reliance on defense mechanisms by a learner, but a personal crisis or other stressful event is usually the cause. For example, a death in the family, a divorce, or even a failing grade on an important test may trigger harmful defensive reactions. Physical symptoms such as a change in personality, angry outbursts, depression, or a general lack of interest may point to a problem. Drug or alcohol abuse also may become apparent. Less obvious indications may include social withdrawal, preoccupation with certain ideas, or an inability to concentrate.

An instructor needs to be familiar with typical defense mechanisms and have some knowledge of related behavioral problems. A perceptive instructor can help by using common sense and discussing the problem with the learner. The main objective should be to restore motivation and self-confidence. It should be noted that the human psyche is fragile and could be damaged by inept measures. Therefore, in severe cases involving the possibility of deep psychological problems, timely and skillful help is needed. In this event, the instructor should recommend that the learner use the services of a professional counselor.

Learner Emotional Reactions

While it is not necessary for a flight instructor to be a certified psychologist, it is helpful to learn how to analyze learner behavior before and during each flight lesson. This ability helps a flight instructor develop and use appropriate techniques for instruction yet to occur.

Anxiety

Anxiety is probably the most significant psychological factor affecting flight instruction. This is true because flying is a potentially threatening experience for those who are not accustomed to flying and the fear of falling is universal in human beings. While anxiety is a factor associated with aviation activities where lives depend on consistently doing the job right, the following paragraphs are primarily concerned with instruction and learner reactions.

Anxiety is a feeling of worry, nervousness, or unease, often about something that is going to happen, typically something with an uncertain outcome. It results from the fear of anything, real or imagined, which threatens the person who experiences it, and may have a potent effect on actions and the ability to learn from perceptions.

The responses to anxiety range from a hesitancy to act to the impulse to do something even if it's wrong. Some people affected by anxiety react appropriately, adequately, and more rapidly than they would in the absence of threat. Many, on the other hand, may freeze and be incapable of doing anything to correct the situation that has caused their anxiety. Others may do things without rational thought or reason.

Both normal and abnormal reactions to anxiety are of concern to the flight instructor. The normal reactions are significant because they indicate a need for special instruction to relieve the anxiety. The abnormal reactions are even more important because they may signify a deep-seated problem.

Anxiety can be countered by reinforcing the learners' enjoyment of flying and by teaching them to cope with their fears. An effective technique is to treat fears as a normal reaction, rather than ignoring them. Keep in mind that anxiety for learner pilots is usually associated with certain types of flight operations and maneuvers. Instructors should introduce these maneuvers with care, so that learners know what to expect and what their reactions should be. When introducing stalls, for example, instructors should first review the aerodynamic principles and explain how stalls affect flight characteristics. Then, carefully describe the physical sensations to be expected, as well as the recovery procedures.

Learner anxiety can be minimized throughout training by emphasizing the benefits and pleasurable experiences that can be derived from flying, rather than by continuously citing the unhappy consequences of faulty performances. Safe flying practices should be presented as conducive to satisfying, efficient, uninterrupted operations, rather than as necessary only to prevent catastrophe.

Impatience

Impatience is a greater deterrent to learning pilot skills than is generally recognized. For a learner, this may take the form of a desire to make an early solo flight, or to set out on cross-country flights before the basic elements of flight have been learned.

The impatient learner fails to understand the need for preliminary training and seeks only the ultimate objective without considering the means necessary to reach it. With every complex human endeavor, it is necessary to master the basics if the whole task is to be performed competently and safely. The instructor can correct learner impatience by presenting the necessary preliminary training one step at a time, with clearly stated goals for each step. The procedures and elements mastered in each step should be clearly identified when explaining or demonstrating the performance of the subsequent step.

Impatience can result from instruction keyed to the pace of a slow learner when it is applied to a motivated, fast learner. It is just as important that a learner be advanced to the subsequent step as soon as one goal has been attained, as it is to complete each step before the next one is undertaken. Disinterest grows rapidly when unnecessary repetition and drill are requested on operations that have already been adequately learned.

Worry or Lack of Interest

Worry or lack of interest has a detrimental effect on learning. Learners who are worried or emotionally upset are not ready to learn and derive little benefit from instruction. Worry or distraction may be due to learner concerns about progress in the training course, or may stem from circumstances completely unrelated to their instruction. Significant emotional upsets may be due to personal problems, emotional problems, or a dislike of the training program or the instructor.

The experiences of learners outside their training activities affect behavior and performance in training; the two cannot be separated. When learners begin flight training, they bring with them their interests, enthusiasms, fears, and troubles. The instructor cannot be responsible for these outside diversions, but cannot ignore them because they have a critical effect on the learning process. Instruction should be keyed to the utilization of the interests and enthusiasm learners bring with them, and to diverting their attention from their worries and troubles to learning the tasks at hand. This is admittedly difficult, but needs to be accomplished if learning is to proceed at a normal rate.

Worries and emotional upsets that result from a flight training course can be identified and addressed. These problems are often due to inadequacies of the course or of the instructor. The most effective cure is prevention. The instructor should be alert and ensure the learners understand the objectives of each step of their training, and that they know at the completion of each lesson exactly how well they have progressed and what deficiencies are apparent. Discouragement and emotional upsets are rare when learners feel that nothing is being withheld from them or is being neglected in their training.

Physical Discomfort, Illness, Fatigue, and Dehydration

Physical discomfort, illness, and fatigue will slow the rate of learning during both classroom instruction and flight training. Learners who are not completely at ease, and whose attention is diverted by discomforts such as the extremes of temperature, poor ventilation, inadequate lighting, or noise and confusion, cannot learn at a normal rate. This is true no matter how diligently they attempt to apply themselves to the learning task.

A minor illness such as a cold, or a major illness or injury interferes with the normal rate of learning. This is especially important for flight instruction. Most illnesses adversely affect the acuteness of vision, hearing, and feeling, all of which are essential to correct performance.

Airsickness can be a great deterrent to flight instruction. A learner who is airsick or bothered with incipient airsickness is incapable of learning at a normal rate. There is no sure cure for airsickness, but resistance or immunity usually can be developed in a relatively short period of time. An instructional flight should be terminated as soon as incipient sickness is experienced. As the learner develops immunity, flights can be increased in length until normal flight periods are practicable.

Keeping learners interested and occupied during flight is a deterrent to airsickness. They are much less apt to become airsick while operating the controls themselves. Blowing fresh air across the face also helps reduce symptoms of incipient sickness. Rough air and unexpected abrupt maneuvers tend to increase the chances of airsickness. Tension and apprehension contribute to airsickness and should be avoided.

Fatigue

Fatigue is one of the most treacherous hazards to flight safety as it may not be apparent to a pilot until serious errors are made. Fatigue can be either acute (short-term) or chronic (long-term). Acute fatigue, a normal occurrence of everyday living, is the tiredness felt after long periods of physical and mental strain, including strenuous muscular effort, immobility, heavy mental workload, strong emotional pressure, monotony, or lack of sleep.

Acute fatigue caused by training operations may be physical or mental, or both. It is not necessarily a function of physical strength or mental acuity. The amount of training any learner can absorb without incurring debilitating fatigue varies. Generally speaking, complex operations tend to induce fatigue more rapidly than simpler procedures do, regardless of the physical effort involved. Fatigue is the primary consideration in determining the length and frequency of flight instruction periods and flight instruction should be continued only as long as the learner is alert, receptive to instruction, and is performing at a level consistent with experience.

It is important for a flight instructor to be able to detect fatigue, both in assessing a learner's substandard performance early in a lesson, and also in recognizing the deterioration of performance. If fatigue occurs as a result of application to a learning task, the learner should be given a break in instruction and practice.

A flight instructor who is familiar with the signs indicative to acute fatigue will be more aware if the learner is experiencing them. The deficiencies listed below are apparent to others before the individual notices any physical signs of fatigue.

Acute fatigue is characterized by:

- Inattention

- Distractibility

- Errors in timing

- Neglect of secondary tasks

- Loss of accuracy and control

- Lack of awareness of error accumulation

- Irritability

Another form of fatigue is chronic fatigue which occurs when there is not enough time for a full recovery from repeated episodes of acute fatigue. Chronic fatigue's underlying cause is generally not "rest-related" and may have deeper points of origin. Therefore, rest alone may not resolve chronic fatigue.

Chronic fatigue is a combination of both physiological problems and psychological issues. Psychological problems such as financial, home life, or job-related stresses cause a lack of qualified rest that is only solved by mitigating the underlying problems before the fatigue is solved. Without resolution, human performance continues to deteriorate, and judgment becomes impaired so that unwarranted risks may be taken. Recovery from chronic fatigue requires a prolonged and deliberate solution. In either case, unless adequate precautions are taken, personal performance could be impaired and adversely affect pilot judgment and decision-making.

Dehydration and Heatstroke

Dehydration is the term given to a critical loss of water from the body. Dehydration reduces a pilot's level of alertness, producing a subsequent slowing of decision-making processes or even the inability to control the aircraft. The first noticeable effect of dehydration is fatigue, which in turn makes top physical and mental performance difficult, if not impossible. Flying for long periods in hot summer temperatures or at high altitudes increases susceptibility to dehydration. High altitude is an issue since dry air at high altitudes tends to increase the rate of water loss from the body. If this fluid is not replaced, fatigue progresses to dizziness, weakness, nausea, tingling of hands and feet, abdominal cramps, and extreme thirst.

Heatstroke is a condition caused by any inability of the body to control its temperature. Onset of this condition may be recognized by the symptoms of dehydration, but its recognition may occur too late if it results in a sudden complete collapse. To prevent these symptoms, it is recommended that an ample supply of water be carried and used at frequent intervals on any long flight, whether the pilot is thirsty or not. If the airplane has a canopy or roof window, wearing light-colored, porous clothing and a hat helps provide protection from the sun. Keeping the flight deck well ventilated aids in dissipating excess heat.

Apathy Due to Inadequate Instruction

Learners can become apathetic when they recognize that the instructor has made inadequate preparations for the instruction being given, or when the instruction appears to be deficient, contradictory, or insincere. To hold the learner's interest and to maintain the motivation necessary for efficient learning, instructors should provide well-planned, appropriate, and accurate instruction. Nothing destroys a learner's interest as quickly as a poorly organized period of instruction. Even an inexperienced learner realizes immediately when the instructor has failed to prepare a lesson. *[Figure 2-7]*

Instruction may be overly explicit and complicated, too elementary, or so general that it fails to evoke the interest necessary for effective learning. To be effective, the instructor teaches for the level of the learner. The presentation should be adjusted to be meaningful to the person for whom it is intended. For example, instruction in the preflight inspection of an aircraft should be presented quite differently for a learner who is a skilled aircraft maintenance technician (AMT) compared to the instruction on the same operation for a learner with no previous aeronautical experience. The instruction needed in each case is the same but a presentation meaningful to one of these learners might not be appropriate for the other.

Poor instructional presentations may result not only from poor preparation, but also from distracting mannerisms, personal untidiness, or the appearance of irritation with the learner. Creating the impression of talking down to the learner is one of the fastest ways for an instructor to lose learner confidence and attention. Once the instructor loses learner confidence, it is difficult to regain, and the learning rate is unnecessarily diminished.

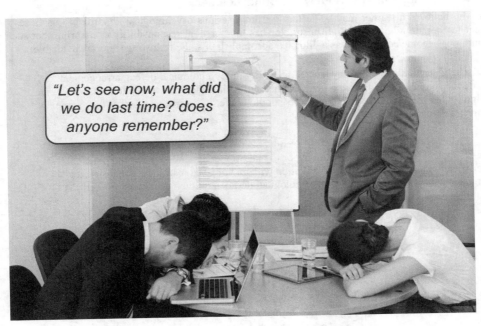

Figure 2-7. *Poor preparation leads to spotty coverage, misplaced emphasis, unnecessary repetition, and a lack of confidence on the part of the learner. The instructor should always have a plan.*

Normal Reactions to Stress

As mentioned earlier in the chapter, when a threat is recognized or imagined, the brain alerts the body. The adrenal gland activates hormones, which prepare the body to meet the threat or to retreat from it—the fight or flight syndrome.

Normal individuals begin to respond rapidly and exactly, within the limits of their experience and training. Many responses are automatic, highlighting the need for proper training in emergency operations prior to an actual emergency. The affected individual thinks rationally, acts rapidly, and is extremely sensitive to all aspects of the surroundings.

Abnormal Reactions to Stress

Reactions to stress may produce abnormal responses in some people. With them, response to anxiety or stress may be completely absent or at least inadequate. Their responses may be random or illogical, or they may do more than is called for by the situation.

During flight instruction, instructors are normally the only ones who can observe learners when they are under pressure. Instructors, therefore, are in a position to differentiate between safe and unsafe piloting actions. Instructors also may be able to detect potential psychological problems. The following learner reactions are indicative of abnormal reactions to stress. None of them provides an absolute indication, but the presence of any of them under conditions of stress is reason for careful instructor evaluation.

- Inappropriate reactions, such as extreme over-cooperation, painstaking self-control, inappropriate laughter or singing, and very rapid changes in emotions.

- Marked changes in mood on different lessons, such as excellent morale followed by deep depression.

- Severe anger directed toward the flight instructor, service personnel, and others.

In difficult situations, flight instructors should carefully examine learner responses and their own responses to the learners. These responses may be the normal products of a complex learning situation but they also can be indicative of psychological abnormalities that inhibit learning or are potentially very hazardous to future piloting operations. *[Figure 2-8]*

Flight Instructor Actions Regarding Seriously Abnormal Learners

A flight instructor who believes a learner may be suffering from a serious psychological abnormality has a responsibility to refrain from instructing that learner. In addition, a flight instructor has the personal responsibility of assuring that such a person does not continue flight training or become certificated as a pilot. To accomplish this, the following steps are available:

- If an instructor believes that a learner may have a disqualifying psychological defect, arrangements should be made for another instructor, who is not acquainted with the learner, to conduct an evaluation flight. After the flight, the two instructors should confer to determine whether they agree that further investigation or action is justified.

- The flight instructor's primary legal responsibility concerns the decision whether to endorse the learner to be competent for solo flight operations, or to make a recommendation for the practical test leading to certification as a pilot. If, after consultation with an unbiased instructor, the instructor believes that the learner may have a serious psychological deficiency, such endorsements and recommendations should be withheld.

Figure 2-8. *A learner with marked changes in mood during different lessons, such as excellent morale followed by deep depression, is indicative of an abnormal reaction to stress.*

AMTs and Flight Instructors as Learners

Both AMTs and flight instructors sometimes deal with new or unfamiliar technology. For instance, an instructor flying a different aircraft may have to manage a particular system or avionics suite for the first time. Likewise, the AMT who is accustomed to working with one type of aircraft has developed analytical processes that may not transfer to another aircraft as well as expected. In both cases, the instructors may be very highly experienced, but change and its associated stress may have risk consequences.

Technological advances in aircraft, powerplants, and systems can outpace the knowledge of flight instructors and AMTs if they don't ensure they remain adequately trained. This ongoing training may remind instructors of their own tendencies to become vulnerable and less objective. By understanding their own training, instructors gain the insight to direct learners to think rationally and overcome stress. Instructors should understand that their own actions and care for others during the training they provide can frame the way a learner responds well into the future.

Diminishing stress and strengthening a learner's confidence and decision-making skills can be achieved by incorporating a risk assessment tool into a training program. Risk assessment tools should always be used to help determine the level of risk involved with any flight so that the pilot or other support person maintains a margin of safety in the activity they are involved. Key to any risk assessment is the individual's objectivity to ensure safety during their flight.

Teaching the Adult Learner

While aviation instructors teach learners of all ages, the average aviation learner age is 30 years old. This means the aviation instructor needs to be versed in the needs of adult learners. The field of adult education is relatively young, having been established in the late twentieth century by Dr. Malcolm Knowles. His research revealed certain traits that need to be recognized when teaching adult learners as well as ways instructors can use these traits to teach older learners.

Adults as learners possess the following characteristics:

- Adults who are motivated to seek out a learning experience do so primarily because they have a use for the knowledge or skill being sought. Learning is a means to an end, not an end in itself.

- Adults seek out learning experiences in order to cope with specific life-changing events—marriage, divorce, a new job. They are ready to learn when they assume new roles.

- Adults are autonomous and self-directed; they need to be independent and exercise control.

- Adults have accumulated a foundation of life experiences and knowledge and draw upon this reservoir of experience for learning.

- Adults are goal-oriented.

- Adults are relevancy oriented. Their time perspective changes from one of postponed knowledge application to immediate application.

- Adults are practical, focusing on the aspects of a lesson most useful to them in their work.

- As do all learners, adults need to be shown respect.

- The need to increase or maintain a sense of self-esteem is a strong secondary motivator for adult learners

- Adults want to solve problems and apply new knowledge immediately.

Instructors should:

- Provide a training syllabus (see Chapter 7, Planning Instructional Activity) that is organized with clearly defined course objectives to show the learner how the training helps him or her attain specific goals.

- Help learners integrate new ideas with what they already know to ensure they keep and use the new information.

- Assume responsibility only for his or her own expectations, not for those of learners. It is important to clarify and articulate all learner expectations early on.

- Recognize the learner's need to control pace and start/stop time.

- Take advantage of the adult preference to self-direct and self-design learning projects by giving the learner frequent scenario based training (SBT) opportunities

- Remember that self-direction does not mean isolation. Studies of self-directed learning indicate self-directed projects involve other people as resources, guides, etc.

- Use books, programmed instruction, and computers which are popular with adult learners.

- Refrain from "spoon-feeding" the learner.

- Set a cooperative learning climate.

- Create opportunities for mutual planning.

An aviation learner may be the retired business executive who always wanted to learn how to fly, an Army helicopter pilot who wants to learn how to fly an airplane, or a former automobile mechanic who decides to pursue avionics. These learners may be financially stressed, or they may be financially secure. They may be healthy but they may be experiencing such age-related problems as diminished hearing or eyesight. Whatever the personal circumstances of the learner, he or she wants the learning experience to be problem-oriented, personalized, and the instructor to be accepting of the learner's need for self-direction and personal responsibility.

Chapter Summary

This chapter discussed how human behavior affects learning, the effect of human needs on learning, defense mechanisms learners use to prevent learning, how adults learn, and the flight instructor's role in determining a learner's future in the aviation community. For more information on these topics, it is recommended the instructor read a general educational psychology text or visit one of the many online sites devoted to education.

Aviation Instructor's Handbook (FAA-H-8083-9)
Chapter 3: The Learning Process

Introduction
The First Flight

When Beverly (learner) enthusiastically presents herself for her first day of flight instruction, Bill, her flight instructor, decides to spend some time in the classroom. Beverly knows a lot of facts about flying and shares her knowledge with Bill, but when he asks questions to test her understanding of the facts, she cannot answer them. During their first flight, Bill discovers Beverly has mastered a few basic skills but her performance is awkward, as if she were working from a list of memorized steps.

In the early stages of flight training, Beverly focuses all her attention on performing each skill. If Bill asks her a question or to perform two tasks at once, she loses her place and needs to restart. As she flies, she makes errors. When she catches herself making an error she becomes visibly frustrated. Then sometimes she does not notice an error and keeps moving ahead as if nothing were amiss. Since she is a beginner, Bill is patient.

The Check Ride

Months later, Bill is helping Beverly prepare for her practical test. Remembering her first days of instruction, Bill feels as if he were working with a different person. The breadth and depth of her classroom knowledge has grown. Beverly does not simply reiterate facts—she applies her knowledge to solve the problems Bill gives her. In addition to meeting all the elements listed in the Airmen Certification Standards (ACS), she also knows about her local environment, such as the nuances of local weather patterns.

In the aircraft, once awkward and tentative actions are now performed with a steady hand and confidence. Skills she struggled to learn in the past have become second nature. When asked to do several things simultaneously, she performs well. When Bill interrupts her, she mentally bookmarks where she is, contends with the interruption and then returns to the task at hand. She still makes errors, but they are small ones that she notices and corrects right away. She still gets frustrated when she makes an error, but she takes a deep breath, and continues on her way. She makes flying look easy and Bill is confident that tomorrow's meeting with the evaluator will go well.

Analysis of the First Flight and Check Ride

Between Beverly's first day of training and the day before her practical test, she has undergone some remarkable changes:

1. She has developed a collection of memorized facts into an in-depth understanding of how to fly and learned to apply this knowledge to problem-solving and decision-making.

2. Skills once performed awkwardly and deliberately are now performed smoothly and efficiently.

3. She comfortably performs several tasks at once, deals with distractions and interruptions, and maintains her focus in demanding situations. Knowledge and skills are now orchestrated.

4. She still makes errors, but they are less frequent, smaller in magnitude, and she quickly identifies and corrects them.

5. Her motivation and enthusiasm remain as high as they were on the first day of training.

6. She displays proficiency in all areas now: those at which she naturally excels as well as those she struggled to master in the past.

7. She deals with psychological obstacles, such as frustration, that initially got in the way of her learning.

8. She recognizes the importance of regular study and practice.

This scenario illustrates the goal of an aviation instructor: to teach each learner in such a way that he or she will become a competent pilot or aviation maintenance technician (AMT). In order to take a pilot or AMT from memorized facts to higher levels of knowledge and skill that include the ability to exercise judgment and solve problems, an instructor needs to know how people learn. Designed as a basic guide in applied educational psychology, this chapter addresses how people learn.

What is Learning?

Learning can be defined in many ways:

- A change in the behavior of the learner as a result of experience. The behavior can be physical and overt, or it can be intellectual or attitudinal.

- The process by which experience brings about a relatively permanent change in behavior.

- The change in behavior that results from experience and practice.

- Gaining knowledge or skills, or developing a behavior, through study, instruction, or experience.

- The process of acquiring knowledge or skill through study, experience, or teaching. It depends on experience and leads to long-term changes in behavior potential. Behavior potential describes the possible behavior of an individual (not actual behavior) in a given situation in order to achieve a goal.

- A relatively permanent change in cognition, resulting from experience and directly influencing behavior.

The effective instructor understands the subject being taught, the learner, the learning process, and the interrelationships that exist. An effective instructor also realizes learning is a complex procedure and assists each learner in reaching the desired outcomes while helping build self-esteem and confidence. *[Figure 3-1]*

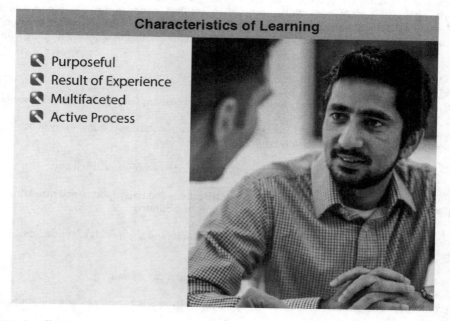

Figure 3-1. *An effective instructor understands the characteristics of learning and assists accordingly.*

The Framework for Learning

Research into how people learn gained momentum with the Swiss scientist and psychologist Jean Piaget, who studied the intellectual development of children in the early twentieth century. His studies influenced others to research not only how people learn, but also the best ways to teach them, leading eventually to the establishment of the field of educational psychology.

Learning Theory

Learning theory is a body of principles advocated by psychologists and educators to explain how people acquire skills, knowledge, and attitudes. Primary learning theories include classical and operant conditioning and social learning. *[Figure 3-2]*

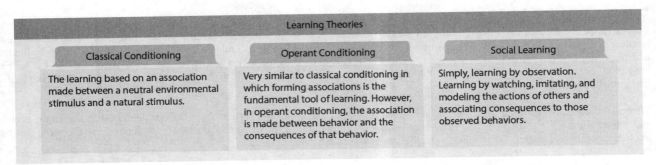

Figure 3-2. *Learning theories of psychology include classical conditioning, operant conditioning, and social learning.*

Classical conditioning is learning based on an association made between a neutral environmental stimulus and a natural stimulus. For example, the Russian psychologist Ivan Pavlov discovered that a dog could be trained to associate the sound of a beating metronome with being fed. Pavlov would start the metronome before presenting the dog with food. Over time, the dog learned to associate the unique sound with receiving food and, as a result, the dog would physically respond to only the sound of the metronome. Today, this experiment is commonly referred to as Pavlov's Dog.

Operant conditioning is very similar to classical conditioning in which forming associations is the fundamental tool of learning. However, in operant conditioning, the association is made between behavior and the consequences of that behavior. In this learning method, a positive behavior creates a positive consequence; a negative behavior creates a negative consequence. The learner then makes an association between behaviors and consequences and then predicts that future behaviors will result in similar consequences.

Social learning is simply learning by observation. Psychologist Albert Bandura's Social Learning Theory suggests, basically, that we all learn from each other. Learning occurs by observing the actions of those around us, imitating those actions, and finally modeling those actions ourselves that others around us may then observe, effectively perpetuating the learning process through continued social interactions. Bandura's theory states that there are four stages associated to social learning:

1. Attention—the ability of the observer to pay attention to others around him or her in order to learn.

2. Retention—the ability to remember an observed behavior to later repeat that behavior.

3. Reproduction—the act of producing a previously observed behavior. This may require additional skills beyond what was initially observed.

4. Motivation—the reason to reproduce an observed behavior.

Various branches of learning theory are used in formal training programs to improve and accelerate the learning process. Key concepts such as desired learning outcomes, objectives of the training, and depth of training also apply. When properly integrated, learning principles can be useful to aviation instructors and developers of instructional programs for both pilots and AMTs.

Many psychologists and educators have attempted to explain how people learn. While variations abound, modern learning theories grew out of two concepts of how people learn: behaviorism and cognitive theory.

Behaviorism

Behaviorism explains animal and human behavior entirely in terms of observable and measurable responses to stimuli. Behaviorism was introduced in the twentieth century and its followers believed all human behavior is conditioned more or less by events in the environment. Thus, human behavior can be predicted based on past rewards and punishments. Classic behaviorist theory in education stressed a system of rewards and punishment or the "carrot and stick" approach to learning. In modern education circles, behaviorism stresses the importance of having a particular form of behavior positively reinforced by someone (other than the learner) who shapes or controls what is learned. In aviation training, the instructor provides the reinforcement.

Today, behaviorism is now used more to break unwanted behaviors, such as smoking, than in teaching. The popularity of behaviorism has waned due to research that indicates learning is a much more complex process than a response to stimuli. Humans, far from being passive products of experience, are always actively interacting with the environment.

Cognitive Theory

Cognitive theory focuses on what is going on inside the mind. It is more concerned with cognition (the process of thinking and learning)—knowing, perceiving, problem-solving, decision-making, awareness, and related intellectual activities—than with stimulus and response. Learning is not just a change in behavior; it is a change in the way a learner thinks, understands, or feels. Theories based on cognition are concerned with the mental events of the learner. Much of the recent psychological thinking and experimentation in education includes some facets of the cognitive theory.

Theories of cognitive learning were established by psychologists and educators such as John Dewey, Jean Piaget, Benjamin Bloom, and Jerome Bruner. *[Figure 3-3]* There have been many interpretations of the research data dealing with cognitive theories. This has led to many different models for learning as well as some associated catch phrases.

Figure 3-3. *Psychologists and educators who established the theories of cognitive learning.*

For example, educator, psychologist, and philosopher, John Dewey introduced the concept "reflective thought." Dewey believed learning improves to the degree that it arises out of the process of reflection. Over the years, terminology describing reflection has spawned a host of synonyms, such as "critical thinking," "problem-solving," and "higher level thought."

For Dewey, the concept of reflective thought carried deep meaning. He saw reflection as a process that moves a learner from one experience into the next with deeper understanding of its relationships with and connections to other experiences and ideas. Thus, reflection leads the learner from the unclear to the clear.

Jean Piaget, who spent 50 years studying how children develop intellectually, became a major figure in the school of cognitive thought. His research led him to conclude there is always tension between assimilation (old ideas meeting new situations) and accommodation (changing the old ideas to meet the new situations). The resolution of this tension results in intellectual growth. Thus, humans develop cognitive skills through active interaction with the world (a basic premise of scenario-based training (SBT), discussed later in this chapter).

An American psychologist who studied with Piaget, Jerome Bruner became interested in how intellectual development related to the process of learning. His research led him to advocate learning from the known to the unknown, or from the concrete to the abstract, because humans best learn when relating new knowledge to existing knowledge. He introduced and developed the concept of the spiral curriculum, which revisits basic ideas repeatedly and builds on them in increasingly sophisticated ways as the learner matures and develops.

Consider the opening scenario with Bill and Beverly. Bill might effectively use this theory with Beverly because she arrived at her first class with a store of aviation facts. Building upon this knowledge, Bill can teach her how to keep the aircraft in straight and level flight while he reinforces what she knows about basic aerodynamics via demonstration and discussion. Since aerodynamics is a constant thread in the flight lessons, Bill is also able to employ the spiral curriculum concept in future lessons by repeatedly revisiting the basic concepts and building upon them as Beverly's skill and knowledge increase.

A group of educators led by Benjamin Bloom tried to classify the levels of thinking behaviors thought to be important in the processes of learning. *[Figure 3-4]* They wanted to classify education goals and objectives based on the assumption that abilities can be measured along a continuum from simple to complex. The result, which remains a popular framework for cognitive theory, was Bloom's Taxonomy of the Cognitive Domain. The taxonomy (a classification system according to presumed relationships) comprises six levels of intellectual behavior and progresses from the simplest to the most complex: knowledge, comprehension, application, analysis, synthesis, and evaluation. For more detailed information about the taxonomy, see Domains of Learning.

Figure 3-4. *Bloom's Taxonomy of the Cognitive Domain.*

Continued research into cognitive theory has led to theories such as information processing and constructivism. This is the basis of the organizing a lesson methods discussed in Chapter 5, The Teaching Process.

Information Processing Theory

Information processing theory uses a computer system as a model for human learning. The human brain processes incoming information, stores and retrieves it and generates responses to the information. This involves a number of cognitive processes: gathering and representing information (encoding), retaining of information, and retrieving the information when needed.

This learning system has limitations and needs to be operated properly. A computer gets input from a keyboard, mouse, etc., whereas the human brain gets input from the senses of sight, hearing, touch, taste, and smell. The amount of sensory input the brain receives per second ranges from thousands to millions of bits of information according to various theories. Regardless of the number, that is a lot of information for the brain to track and process.

One way the brain deals with all this information is to let many of the habitual and routine things go unnoticed. For example, a pilot who uses the rudder when entering a turn is usually unaware of pressing the pedal, even though it involves moving a leg, exerting pressure on the pedal, etc. The human unconscious takes charge, leaving conscious thought processes free to deal with issues that are not habitual.

Since information processing theorists approach learning primarily through a study of memory, this learning concept is revisited during the discussion of memory.

Constructivism

A derivative of cognitive theory, constructivism is a philosophy of learning that holds that learners do not acquire knowledge and skills passively but actively build or construct them based on their experiences. As implied by its name, constructivism emphasizes the constructing or building that goes on during the learning process. Therefore, it creates a learner-centered environment in which they assume responsibility for their own learning.

According to constructivism, humans construct a unique mental image by combining preexisting information with the information received from sense organs. Learning is the result of matching new information against this preexisting information and integrating it into meaningful connections. In constructivist thinking, learners are given more latitude to become effective problem solvers, identifying and evaluating problems, as well as deciphering ways in which to transfer their learning to these problems, all of which foster critical thinking skills. While the learner is at the center of the process, an experienced teacher is necessary to guide them through the information jungle. Constructivism techniques are good for some types of learning, some situations, and some individuals, but not all. This school of thought also encourages teaching learners how to use what are known as the higher order thinking skills (HOTS) from Bloom's Taxonomy and training based on problems or scenarios. Constructivism is the basis for several of the training delivery methods covered in Chapter 5, The Teaching Process.

Higher Order Thinking Skills (HOTS)

The constructivist theory of learning explains and supports the learning of HOTS, which is commonly called aeronautical decision-making (ADM) in aviation. HOTS lie in the last three levels on Bloom's Taxonomy of Learning: analysis, synthesis, and evaluation skills. Teaching the higher level thinking skills which are essential to judgment, decision-making, and critical thinking is important to aviation because a common thread in aviation accidents is the absence of higher order thinking skills (see Appendix E).

HOTS are taught like other cognitive skills, from simple to complex and from concrete to abstract. To teach HOTS effectively involves strategies and methods that include (1) using problem-based learning (PBL) instruction, (2) authentic problems, (3) real-world problems, (4) learner-centered learning, (5) active learning, (6) cooperative learning, and (7) customized instruction to meet the individual learner's needs. These strategies engage the learner in some form of mental activity, have the learner examine that mental activity and select the best solution, and challenge the learner to explore other ways to accomplish the task or the problem.

It should be remembered that critical thinking skills should be taught in the context of subject matter. Learners progress from simple to complex; therefore, they need some information before they can think about a subject beyond rote learning. For example, knowing that compliance with the weight and balance limits of any aircraft is critical to flight safety may not help an aviation learner interpret weight and balance charts unless he or she also knows something about the concept of a center of gravity.

If the learner does not yet have much subject matter knowledge, they can draw on past experiences to gain entry into complex concepts. For example, most learners probably played on a seesaw during their childhood. Thus, they have a basic experience of how weight and balance works around a center of gravity.

Additionally, HOTS should be emphasized throughout a program of study for best results. For aviation, this means HOTS should be taught in the initial pilot training program and in every subsequent pilot training program. Instructors need to teach the cognitive skills used in problem-solving until these techniques become automated and transferable to new situations or problems. Cognitive research has shown the learning of HOTS is not a change in observable behavior but the construction of meaning from experience.

Scenario-Based Training (SBT)

At the heart of HOTS lies scenario-based training (SBT) which is an example of the PBL instructional method and facilitates the enhancement of learning and the development and transference of thinking skills. SBT provides more realistic decision-making opportunities because it presents tasks in an operational environment; it correlates new information with previous knowledge, and introduces new information in a realistic context.

SBT is a training system that uses a structured script of "real-world" scenarios to address flight-training objectives in an operational environment. Such training can include initial training, transition training, upgrade training, recurrent training, and special training.

The instructor should adapt the scenarios to the aircraft, its specific flight characteristics and the likely flight environment, and should always require the learner to make real-time decisions in a realistic setting. The scenarios should always be planned and led by the learner (with the exception of the first flight or two or until the learner has developed the necessary skills).

SBT not only meets the challenge of teaching aeronautical knowledge to the application level of learning, but also enables the instructor to teach the underlying HOTS needed to improve ADM. The best use of scenarios draws the learner into formulating possible solutions, evaluating the possible solutions, deciding on a solution, judging the appropriateness of that decision and finally, reflecting on the mental process used in solving the problem. It causes the learner to consider whether the decision led to the best possible outcome and challenges the learner to consider other solutions.

SBT scenarios help learners better understand the decisions they have to make and also helps focus the learner on the decisions and consequences involved. It is being used to train people in everything from emergency response to hotel management. The strength of SBT lies in helping the learner gain a deeper understanding of the information and in the learner improving his or her ability to recall the information. This goal is reached when the material is presented as an authentic problem in a situated environment that allows the learner to "make meaning" of the information based on his or her past experience and personal interpretation.

SBT has become one of the primary methods to teach today's aviation learners how to make good aeronautical decisions which in turn enhances the safety of all aviation related activities. For information on how to create an SBT lesson, refer to Chapter 5, The Teaching Process, and for how to incorporate SBT into a training syllabus, refer to Chapter 7, Planning Instructional Activity.

Perceptions

Initially, all learning comes from perceptions, which are directed to the brain by one or more of the five senses: sight, hearing, touch, smell, and taste. Psychologists have also found that learning occurs most rapidly when information is received through more than one sense. *[Figure 3-5]*

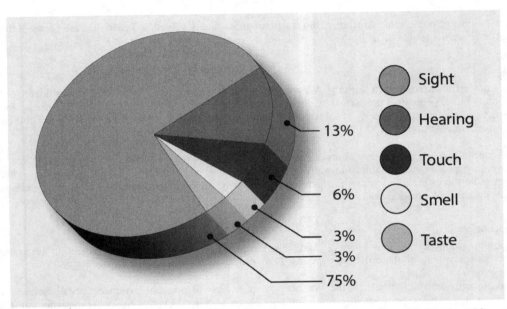

Figure 3-5. *Most learning occurs through sight, but the combination of sight and hearing accounts for about 88 percent of all perception.*

Perception involves more than the reception of stimuli from the five senses; it also involves a person giving meaning to sensations. People base their actions on the way they believe things to be. The experienced AMT, for example, perceives an engine malfunction quite differently than does an inexperienced learner. This occurs because the beginning aviation learner is overwhelmed by stimuli and often focuses on meaningless things, thus missing key information. It is important for the instructor to direct trainee's perceptions initially so that the learner detects and perceives relevant information.

Real meaning comes only from within a person, even though the perceptions, which evoke these meanings, result from external stimuli. The meanings, which are derived from perceptions, are influenced not only by the individual's experience, but also by many other factors. Knowledge of the factors that affect the perceptual process is very important to the aviation instructor because perceptions are the basis of all learning.

Factors that Affect Perception

Both internal and external factors affect an individual's ability to perceive:

- Physical organism

- Goals and values

- Self-concept

- Time and opportunity

- Element of threat

Physical Organization

The physical organism provides individuals with the perceptual apparatus for sensing the world around them. Pilots, for example, need to see, hear, feel, and respond adequately while they are in the air.

Goals and Values

Perceptions depend on one's values and goals. Every experience and sensation, which is funneled into one's central nervous system, is colored by the individual's own beliefs and value structures. Spectators at a ball game may see an infraction or foul differently depending on which team they support. The values of the learner are important for the instructor to know, because this knowledge assists in predicting how he or she interprets experiences and instructions.

Goals are also a product of one's value structure. Things that are more highly valued and cherished are pursued; those accorded less value and importance are not sought after.

Self-Concept

Self-concept is a powerful determinant in learning. A learner's self-image, described in such terms as "confident" or "insecure," has a great influence on the total perceptual process. If a learner's experiences tend to support a favorable self-image, the learner tends to remain receptive to subsequent experiences. If a learner has negative experiences, which tend to contradict self-concept, there is a tendency to reject additional training.

A negative self-concept inhibits the perceptual processes by introducing psychological barriers, which tend to keep the learner from perceiving. They may also inhibit the ability to properly implement what is perceived. That is, self-concept affects the ability to actually perform or do things. Learners who view themselves positively, on the other hand, are less defensive and more receptive to new experiences, instructions, and demonstrations.

Time and Opportunity

It takes time and opportunity to perceive. Learning some things depends on other past perceptions and on the availability of time to sense and relate these new things to the earlier perceptions. Thus, proper sequence and time are necessary.

A learner could probably stall an aircraft on the first attempt, regardless of previous experience. Stall recovery cannot really be learned, however, unless some experience in normal flight has been acquired. Even with such experience, time and practice are needed to relate the new sensations and experiences associated with stall recovery in order to develop a perception of the stall. In general, lengthening an experience and increasing its frequency are the most obvious ways to speed up learning, although this is not always effective. Many factors, in addition to the length and frequency of training periods, affect the rate of learning. The effectiveness of the use of a properly planned training syllabus is proportional to the consideration it gives to the time and opportunity factor in perception.

Element of Threat

The element of threat does not promote effective learning. In fact, fear adversely affects perception by narrowing the perceptual field. Confronted with threat, learners tend to limit their attention to the threatening object or condition. The field of vision is reduced, for example, when an individual is frightened and all the perceptual faculties are focused on the thing that has generated fear.

Flight instruction provides many clear examples of this. During the initial practice of steep turns, Beverly may focus her attention on the altimeter and completely disregard outside visual references. Anything Bill does that is interpreted as threatening makes Beverly less able to accept the experience Bill is trying to provide. It adversely affects all her physical, emotional, and mental faculties.

Learning is a psychological process, not necessarily a logical one. Trying to frighten a learner through threats of unsatisfactory reports or reprisals may seem logical, but is not effective psychologically. The effective instructor organizes teaching to fit the psychological needs of the learner. If a situation seems overwhelming, the learner feels unable to handle all of the factors involved; a threat exists. As long as the learner feels capable of coping with a situation, each new experience is viewed as a challenge.

A good instructor recognizes that behavior is directly influenced by the way a learner perceives, and perception is affected by all of these factors. Therefore, it is important for the instructor to facilitate the learning process by avoiding any actions which may inhibit or prevent the attainment of teaching goals. Teaching is consistently effective only when those factors that influence perception are recognized and taken into account.

Insight

Insight involves the grouping of perceptions into meaningful wholes. Creating insight is one of the instructor's major responsibilities. To ensure that this occurs, it is essential to keep each learner constantly receptive to new experiences and to help them understand how each piece relates to all other pieces of the total pattern of the task.

For example, during straight-and-level flight in an aircraft with a fixed-pitch propeller, the revolutions per minute (rpm) increase when the throttle is opened and decrease when it is closed. On the other hand, rpm changes can also result from changes in aircraft pitch attitude without changes in power setting. Obviously, engine speed, power setting, airspeed, and aircraft attitude are all related.

True learning requires an understanding of how each factor may affect all of the others and, at the same time, knowledge of how a change in any one of them may affect all of the others. This mental relating and grouping of associated perceptions is called insight.

Insight almost always occurs eventually, whether or not instruction is provided. For this reason, it is possible for a person to become an electrician by trial and error, just as one may become a lawyer by reading law. Instruction, however, speeds this learning process by teaching the relationship of perceptions as they occur, thus promoting the development of the learner's insight.

As perceptions increase in number, the learner develops insight by assembling them into larger blocks. As a result, learning becomes more meaningful and more permanent. Forgetting is less of a problem when there are more anchor points for tying insights together. It is a major responsibility of the instructor to organize demonstrations and explanations, and to direct practice so that the learner has better opportunities to understand the interrelationship of the many kinds of experiences that have been perceived. Pointing out the relationships as they occur, providing a secure and nonthreatening environment in which to learn, and helping the learner acquire and maintain a favorable self-concept are key steps in fostering the development of insight.

Acquiring Knowledge

Part of an aviation instructor's job is helping learners acquire knowledge. In this context, knowledge refers to information that humans are consciously aware of and can articulate. For example, knowledge of the fuel capacity of a particular aircraft, understanding how an internal combustion engine works, and the ability to determine the weight and balance of an aircraft are examples of knowledge.

Figure 3-6 shows the three phases of knowledge, a progression of how learners acquire knowledge. Some practical considerations about learning new knowledge and instructor actions that help learners acquire knowledge are summarized.

Memorization

A learner's first attempt to acquire knowledge about a new topic amounts to memorizing facts about steps in a procedure. For example, when Beverly is learning to use an altimeter, she may have memorized that the knob on the instrument is used to dial the current barometric pressure and that this number should be obtained from the recorded broadcast and set prior to flight.

Memorizing facts and steps has an advantage: it allows learners to get started quickly. For example, as soon as Beverly memorizes the purpose of the knob on the altimeter and the procedure for obtaining the current barometric pressure, she is able to properly configure the instrument for flight.

The limitations of memorization become apparent when a learner is asked to solve a problem or provide an explanation of something that is not covered by the newly acquired knowledge. For example, when asked whether she would rather have the altimeter mistakenly set too high or too low when flying in mountainous terrain, Beverly may not have an answer.

Understanding

A more experienced pilot can answer the altimeter question because she or he understands the ramifications of the question. Understanding, or the ability to notice similarities and make associations between the facts and procedural steps learned, is an important next stage in the knowledge acquisition process. At this stage, the learner begins to organize knowledge in useful ways and a collection of memorized facts gives way to understanding.

Understanding develops when learners begin to organize known facts and steps into coherent groups that come together to form an understanding of how a thing or a process works. For example, after learning to adjust the mixture control in cruise flight, Beverly learns that combustion requires a certain mixture of fuel and air, and that air becomes less dense as altitude increases.

Figure 3-6. *A learner acquires knowledge through memorization, understanding, and application.*

Combining these two ideas, she now understands the purpose of the mixture control is to keep these two quantities in balance as the aircraft changes altitude. "Mental model" or self-explanation is often used to refer to an organized collection of ideas that forms a learner's understanding of a thing or process.

The advantages of possessing this type of understanding include the following:

1. The learner is no longer limited to answering questions that match the memorized facts. For example, armed with the understanding of the mixture control, Beverly may now be able to produce answers to more challenging questions, such as what would happen if the mixture were set too rich or too lean.

2. Learners who understand a process have an easier time mastering variations of the processes, such as unfamiliar aircraft, new avionics systems, and unfamiliar airport procedures.

3. Understanding shared between people allows them to communicate more efficiently. For example, an experienced pilot might mention to an experienced mechanic that a magneto ran a bit rough during an engine run-up. This brief communication triggers access to a wealth of knowledge in the mind of the mechanic who instantly knows what to do.

4. Learners who understand the purpose behind procedure steps are better able to remember the procedure steps later, or reconstruct them when they are forgotten.

Mental models evolve as learners take in new information. For example, Bill could ask Beverly why flying with an inappropriate mixture setting is bad. A learner whose understanding includes knowledge about spark plugs and carbon deposits might answer correctly. If this same learner's understanding later extends to include knowledge about thermal efficiency and the stoichiometric equation for the combustion of gasoline, the explanations are likely to become much more sophisticated. No individual's understanding of anything is ever "complete."

Concept Learning

Concept learning is based on the assumption that humans tend to group objects, events, ideas, people, etc., that share one or more major attributes that set them apart. It also involves discrimination between types of things or ideas inside or outside of a concept set. By grouping information into concepts, humans reduce the complexities of life and create manageable categories. Although many theories about concept learning exist, categorization has always been a central aspect.

Concept learning enhances understanding when individuals formulate generalized concepts from particular facts or steps. Generalized concepts are more powerful than facts because instead of literally describing one thing, they describe many things at once.

For example, a new flight learner who sees several examples of weight-shift control (WSC) aircraft may formulate a category for WSC aircraft based on the wing, which is large and fabric covered. The power of the category becomes obvious when the learner sees a sport plane. Because of the similar wing, he or she immediately categorizes it as an ultralight and ascribes many of the properties of ultralight aircraft to the sport plane. In this way, the learner has used a generalized concept to begin understanding something new.

Most learners exhibit a natural tendency to categorize and become adept at recognizing members of most any category they create. If something is encountered that does not fit into a category, these learners formulate a new category or revise the definitions of existing categories. In the above example, the learner eventually needs to revise the category of ultralight to light-sport aircraft which encompasses both types of aircraft. Therefore, an important part of the learning process is continual revision of the categories used when learners encounter new things or exceptions to things previously catalogued.

Another type of generalization is a schema (the cognitive framework that helps people organize and interpret information). Schemas can be revised by any new information and are useful because they allow people to take shortcuts in interpreting a vast amount of information.

Humans form schemas when they notice reoccurring patterns in things frequently observed or done. Schemas help learners interpret things they observe by priming them to expect certain elements that match the schema. For example, schemas demonstrate why an experienced pilot is able to listen to and read back a lengthy departure clearance issued by air traffic control (ATC). Beginning flight learners often remember the controller's use of the words "the" and "and" and fail to note more important words that describe assigned altitudes or radio frequencies. The experienced pilot is successful because he or she possesses a schema for this type of event and knows in advance that the clearance contains five key pieces of information. While listening to the clearance, the pilot anticipates and is primed to capture those five things.

Similarly, learners create schemas for preflight inspection procedures and procedures required to operate advanced flight deck systems such as autopilots or multifunction displays. As with categories, humans continuously learn new schemas and revise old ones to accommodate new things as they continue to learn. While schemas help humans deal with information, they can also make it difficult to retain new information that does not conform to established schemas.

Thorndike and the Laws of Learning

One of the pioneers of educational psychology, E.L. Thorndike formulated three laws of learning in the early 20th century. *[Figure 3-7]* These laws are universally accepted and apply to all kinds of learning: the law of readiness, the law of exercise, and the law of effect. Since Thorndike set down his laws, three more have been added: the law of primacy, the law of intensity, and the law of recency.

Readiness

The basic needs of the learner need to be satisfied before he or she is ready or capable of learning (see Chapter 2, Human Behavior). The instructor can do little to motivate the learner if these needs have not been met. This means the individual should want to learn the task being presented and possesses the requisite knowledge and skill. In SBT, the instructor attempts to make the task as meaningful as possible and to keep it within the learner's capabilities.

Figure 3-7. *E. L. Thorndike (1874–1949).*

Learners best acquire new knowledge when they see a clear reason for doing so, often show a strong interest in learning what they believe they need to know next, and tend to set aside things for which they see no immediate need. For example, beginning flight learners commonly ignore the flight instructor's suggestion to use the trim control. These learners believe the control yoke is an adequate way to manipulate the aircraft's control surfaces. Later in training, when they need to divert their attention away from the controls to other tasks, they realize the importance of trim.

Instructors can take two steps to keep their learners in a state of readiness to learn. First, instructors should communicate a clear set of objectives to the learner and relate each new topic to those objectives. Second, instructors should introduce topics in a logical order and leave learners with a need to learn the next topic. The development and use of a well-designed curriculum accomplish this goal.

Readiness to learn also involves what is called the "teachable moment" or a moment of educational opportunity when a person is particularly responsive to being taught something. One of the most important skills to develop as an instructor is the ability to recognize and capitalize on "teachable moments" in aviation training. An instructor can find or create teachable moments in flight training activity whether it is pattern work, air work in the local practice area, cross-country, flight review, or instrument proficiency check.

Teachable moments present opportunities to convey information in a way that is relevant, effective, and memorable to the learner. They occur when a learner can clearly see how specific information or skills can be used in the real-world.

For example, while on final approach several deer cross the runway. Bill capitalizes on this teachable moment to stress the importance of always being ready to perform a go-around.

Effect

Learning involves the formation of connections, and connections are strengthened or weakened according to the law of effect. The law states that behaviors that lead to satisfying outcomes are likely to be repeated whereas behaviors that lead to undesired outcomes are less likely to recur. For example, if Bill teaches landings to Beverly during the first flight, she is likely to feel inferior and be frustrated, which weakens the intended learning connection.

The learner needs to have success in order to have more success in the future. It is important for the instructor to create situations designed to promote success. Positive training experiences are more apt to lead to success and motivate the learner, while negative training experiences might stimulate forgetfulness or avoidance. When presented correctly, SBT provides immediate positive experiences in terms of real-world applications.

To keep learning pleasant and to maintain motivation, an instructor should make positive comments about the learner's progress before discussing areas that need improving. Flight instructors have an opportunity to do this during the flight debriefing. For example, Bill praises Beverly on her aircraft control during all phases of flight but offers constructive comments on how to better maintain the runway centerline during landings.

Exercise

Connections are strengthened with practice and weakened when practice is discontinued, which reflects the adage "use it or lose it." The learner needs to practice what has been taught in order to understand and remember the learning. Practice strengthens the learning connection; disuse weakens it. Exercise is most meaningful and effective when a skill is learned within the context of a real-world application.

Primacy

When an error occurs pouring a concrete foundation for a building, undoing and correcting the job becomes much more difficult than doing it right the first time. Primacy in teaching and learning, what is learned first, often creates a strong, almost unshakable impression and underlies the reason an instructor needs to teach correctly the first time.

Also, if the task is learned in isolation, it is not initially applied to the overall performance, or if it needs to be relearned, the process can be confusing and time consuming. The first experience should be positive, functional, and lay the correct foundation for all that is to follow.

Intensity

Immediate, exciting, or dramatic learning connected to a real situation teaches a learner more than a routine or boring experience. Real-world applications (scenarios) that integrate procedures and tasks the learner is capable of understanding make a vivid impression, and he or she is least likely to forget the experience. For example, using realistic scenarios has been shown to be effective in the development of proficiency in flight maneuvers, tasks, and single-pilot resource management (SRM) skills.

Recency

The principle of recency states that things most recently learned are best remembered. Conversely, the further a learner is removed in time from a new fact or understanding, the more difficult it is to remember. For example, it is easy for a learner to recall a torque value used a few minutes earlier, but it is more difficult or even impossible to remember a value last studied or used further back in time.

Instructors recognize the principle of recency when they carefully plan a summary for a ground school lesson, a shop period, or a postflight critique. The instructor repeats, restates, or reemphasizes important points at the end of a lesson to help the learner remember them. The principle of recency often determines the sequence of lectures within a course of instruction.

In SBT, the closer the training or learning time is to the time of the actual scenario, the more apt the learner is to perform successfully. This law is most effectively addressed by making the training experience as much like the scenario as possible.

Domains of Learning

As mentioned during the discussion of Cognitive Theory, Dr. Bloom played a central role in transforming the field of educational psychology. Interested in what and how people learn, he proposed a framework to help understand the major areas of learning and thinking. He first classified them into three large groups *[Figure 3-8]* called the domains of learning:

- Cognitive (thinking)

- Affective (feeling)

- Psychomotor (doing)

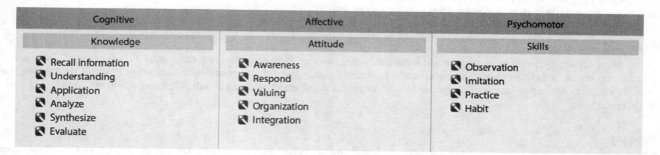

Figure 3-8. *An overview of the three learning domains.*

Cognitive Domain

The cognitive domain is one of the best known educational domains. It includes remembering specific facts (content knowledge) and concepts that help develop intellectual abilities and skills. There are six major categories, or levels, starting from the simplest behavior (recalling facts) to the most complex (evaluation). *[Figure 3-9]*

	Competence	Skills Demonstrated	Example
I	Knowledge: remembering information	Define, identify, label, state, list, match, select	1. State the standard temperature at sea level. 2. Define a logbook entry.
II	Comprehension: explaining the meaning of information	Describe, generalize, paraphrase, summarize, estimate, discuss	1. In one sentence explain why aviation uses a standard temperature. 2. Describe why a log entry is required by the FAA.
III	Application: using abstractions in concrete situation	Determine, chart, implement, prepare, solve, use, develop, explain, apply, relate, instruct, show, teaches	1. Using a standard lapse rate, determine what the temperature would be at a pressure altitude of 4000'. 2. Determine when a logbook entry is required.
IV	Analysis: breaking down a whole into component parts	Points out, differentiate distinguish, examine discriminate, compare, outline, prioritize, recognize, subdivide	1. Compare what the different temperatures would be at certain pressure altitudes based on the standard lapse rate. 2. Determine information required for logbook entry.
V	Synthesis: putting parts together to form a new and integrated whole	Create, design, plan, organize, generate, write, adapt, compare, formulate, devise, model, revise, incorporate	1. Generate a chart depicting temperatures for altitudes up to 12,000'. 2. Write a logbook entry for an oil change.
VI	Evaluation: making judgments about the merits of ideas, materials, or phenomena	Appraise, critique, judge, weigh, evaluate, select, compare and contrast, defend, interpret, support	1. Evaluate the importance of this information for a pilot. 2. Evaluate the necessity of keeping logbook entries.

Figure 3-9. *The six major levels of Bloom's Taxonomy of the Cognitive Domain with types of behavior with objectives.*

The four practical learning levels are rote, understanding, application, and correlation. *[Figure 3-10]* The lowest level is the ability to repeat something which one has been taught, without understanding or being able to apply what has been learned. This is referred to as rote learning. The fact level is a single concept. The key verbs which describe or measure this activity are words such as define, identify, and label. The comprehension or understanding level puts two or more concepts together and uses verbs such as describe, estimate, or explain. The application level puts two or more concepts together to form something new. Typical verbs at this level include "determine," "develop," and "solve."

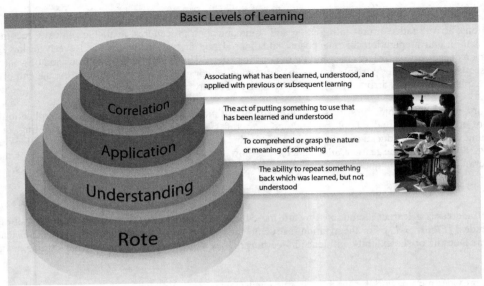

Figure 3-10. *Learning is progressive and occurs at several basic levels.*

For example, Bill may explain the procedure for entering a level, left turn to Beverly. The procedure includes several steps: (1) visually clear the area, (2) add a slight amount of power to maintain airspeed, (3) apply aileron control pressure to the left, (4) add sufficient rudder pressure in the direction of the turn to avoid slipping and skidding, and (5) increase back pressure to maintain altitude. When Beverly verbally repeats this instruction, she has learned the procedure by rote. This will not be very useful to her if there is never an opportunity to make a turn in flight, or if she has no knowledge of the function of aircraft controls.

With proper instruction on the effect and use of the flight controls, and experience in controlling the aircraft during straight-and-level flight, Beverly can consolidate old and new perceptions into an insight on how to make a turn. At this point, she has developed an understanding of the procedure for turning the aircraft in flight. This understanding is basic to effective learning, but may not necessarily enable her to make a correct turn on the first attempt.

When Beverly understands the procedure for entering a turn, has had turns demonstrated, and has practiced turn entries until consistency has been achieved, she has developed the skill to apply what has been learned. This is a major level of learning, and one at which the instructor is too often willing to stop. Discontinuing instruction on turn entries at this point and directing subsequent instruction exclusively to other elements of piloting performance is characteristic of piecemeal instruction, which is usually inefficient.

The correlation level of learning, which should be the objective of aviation instruction, is that level at which the individual becomes able to associate an element which has been taught with other segments or blocks of learning. The other segments may be items or skills previously learned or new tasks to be undertaken in the future. When Beverly has achieved this level of learning in turn entries, for example, she has developed the ability to correlate the elements of turn entries with the performance in traffic patterns.

The three higher levels of the cognitive domain include analysis, synthesis and evaluation (the HOTS level previously mentioned in the learning theory section). The analysis level involves breaking the information into its component parts, examining, and trying to understand the information in order to develop conclusions, make inferences, and/or find evidence to support generalizations. This level uses such verbs as points out, differentiate, distinguish, examine, discriminate, compare, outline, prioritize, recognize, or subdivide.

Synthesis involves putting parts together to form a new and integrated whole. Typical verbs for this level include create, design, plan, organize, generate, write, adapt, compare, formulate, devise, model, revise, or incorporate. The final level in the taxonomy is evaluation and involves making judgments about the merits of ideas, materials, or phenomena. The following example demonstrates the difference between learning on the first three levels versus learning critical thinking skills.

Bill provides a detailed explanation on how to control for wind drift. The explanation includes a thorough coverage of heading, speed, angle of bank, altitude, terrain, and wind direction plus velocity. The explanation is followed by a demonstration and repeated practice of a specific flight maneuver, such as turns around a point or S-turns across the road until the maneuver can be consistently accomplished in a safe and effective manner within a specified limit of heading, altitude, and airspeed. At the end of this lesson, Beverly is only capable of performing the maneuver.

Then Bill asks Beverly to plan for the arrival at a specific nontowered airport. The planning should take into consideration the possible wind conditions, arrival paths, airport information and communication procedures, available runways, recommended traffic patterns, courses of action, and preparation for unexpected situations. Upon arrival at the airport, Beverly makes decisions (with guidance and feedback as necessary) to safely enter and fly the traffic pattern. This is followed by a discussion of what was done, why it was done, the consequences, and other possible courses of action and how it applies to other airports. At the end of this lesson the learner is capable of explaining the safe arrival at any nontowered airport in any wind condition.

For aviation instructors, educational objectives for the first three levels (knowledge, comprehension, and application) are generally gained as the result of attending a ground school, reading about aircraft systems, listening to a preflight briefing, or taking part in computer-based training. The highest educational objective levels in this domain (analysis, synthesis, and evaluation) can be acquired through SBT training. For example, the learner pilot understands how to correctly evaluate a flight maneuver or the maintenance learner repairs an aircraft engine. Sample questions for each level of the cognitive domain are provided in Figure 3-9.

Affective Domain

The affective domain addresses a learner's emotions toward the educational experience. It includes feelings, values, enthusiasms, motivations, and attitudes. *[Figure 3-11]* For the aviation instructor, this may mean how the individual approaches learning. Is he or she motivated to learn? Does he or she exhibit confidence in learning? Does the learner display a positive attitude towards safety and risk mitigation?

The affective domain provides a framework for teaching in five levels: awareness, response, value, organizing, and integration. In this taxonomy, the learner begins on the awareness level and is open to learning, willing to listen to the instructor. As the learner traverses the taxonomy, he or she responds by participating actively in the training, decides the value of the training, organizes the training into his or her personal belief system, and finally internalizes it.

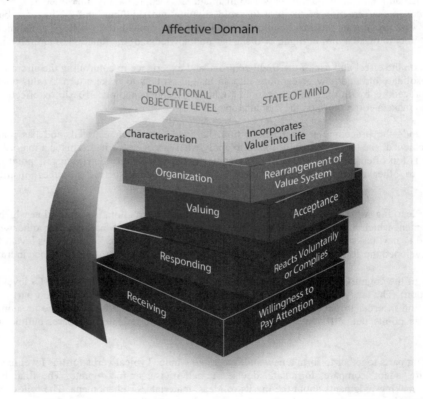

Figure 3-11. *The affective domain (attitudes, beliefs, and values) contains five educational objective levels.*

The affective domain is more difficult to measure, but motivation and enthusiasm are important components of any learning. Therefore, the aviation instructor should be acquainted with this facet of learning. Motivation is discussed in depth later in the chapter.

Psychomotor Domain

The psychomotor domain is skill based and includes physical movement, coordination, and use of the motor-skill areas. *[Figure 3-12]* Development of these skills utilizes repetitive practice and is measured in terms of speed, precision, distance, and techniques. While various examples of the psychomotor domain exist, the practical instructional levels for aviation training purposes include the following:

- Observation
- Imitation
- Practice
- Habit

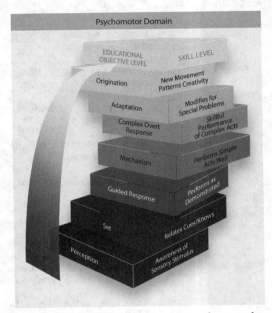

Figure 3-12. *The psychomotor domain (physical skills) consists of seven educational objective levels.*

These basic levels make up the broad instructional process, independent of the specific domain chosen and are important components of instruction when aviation instructors prepare learners for the practical test.

At the first level, the learner observes a more experienced person perform the skill. The instructor has the learner observe sequences and relationships that lead to the finished product. Observation may be supplemented by reading, watching a DVD, or computer-based training. The second level is imitation in which the learner attempts to copy the skill under the watchful eye of the instructor.

The practice level is a proficiency building experience in which the learner tries a specific activity over and over. It may be conducted by the learner without direct oversight of the instructor, such as touch-and-go landings for the flight learner who has flown a successful solo flight. The habit level is reached when the learner can perform the skill in twice the time that it takes the instructor or an expert to perform. The evaluation of ability is a performance or skill test. If a person continues to perfect a skill, it eventually becomes a skill performed at the expert level.

Skills involving the psychomotor domain include learning to fly a precision instrument approach procedure, programming a global positioning system (GPS) receiver, or using sophisticated maintenance equipment. As physical tasks and equipment become more complex, the requirement for integration of cognitive and physical skills increases.

Summary of Instructor Actions

To help learners acquire knowledge, the instructor should:

- Ask learners to recite or practice newly acquired knowledge.
- Ask questions that probe learner understanding and prompt them to think about what they have learned in different ways.
- Present opportunities for learners to apply what they know to solving problems or making decisions.
- Present learners with problems and decisions that test the limits of their knowledge.
- Demonstrate the benefits of understanding and being able to apply knowledge.
- Introduce new topics as they support the objectives of the lesson, whenever possible.

These additional levels of learning are the basis of the knowledge, attitude, and skill learning objectives commonly used in advanced qualification programs for airline training. They also can be tied to the ACS to show the level of knowledge or skill required for a particular task. A list of action verbs for the three domains shows appropriate behavioral objectives at each level. [Figure 3-13] Instructors who are familiar with curriculum development recognize that the action verbs are examples of performance-based objectives.

	Objective Level	Action Verbs for Each Level
COGNITIVE DOMAIN	Evaluation	Assess, evaluate, interpret, judge, rate, score, or write
	Synthesis	Compile, compose, design, reconstruct, or formulate
	Analysis	Compare, discriminate, distinguish, or separate
	Application	Compute, demonstrate, employ, operate, or solve
	Comprehension	Convert, explain, locate, report, restate, or select
	Knowledge	Describe, identify, name, point to, recognize, or recall
AFFECTIVE DOMAIN	Characterization	Assess, delegate, practice, influence, revise, and maintain
	Organization	Accept responsibility, adhere, defend, and formulate
	Valuing	Appreciate, follow, join, justify, show concern, or share
	Responding	Conform, greet, help, perform, recite, or write
	Receiving	Ask, choose, give, locate, select, rely, or use
PSYCHOMOTOR DOMAIN	Origination	Combine, compose, construct, design, or originate
	Adaptation	Adapt, alter, change, rearrange, reorganize, or revise
	Complex Overt Response	Same as guided response except more highly coordinated
	Mechanism	Same as guided response except with greater proficiency
	Guided Response	Assemble, build, calibrate, fix, grind, or mend
	Set	Begin, move, react, respond, start, or select
	Perception	Choose, detect, identify, isolate, or compare

Figure 3-13. *A listing such as the one shown here is useful for development of almost any training program.*

Characteristics of Learning

The ability to learn is one of the most outstanding human characteristics. Learning occurs continuously throughout a person's lifetime. To understand how people learn, it is necessary to understand what happens to the individual during the process. In spite of numerous theories and contrasting views, psychologists generally agree there are many characteristics of learning.

Knowledge of the general characteristics of learning help an aviation instructor use them in a learning situation. If learning is a change in behavior as a result of experience, then instruction needs to include a careful and systematic creation of those experiences that promote learning. This process can be quite complex because, among other things, an individual's background strongly influences the way that person learns. To be effective, the learning situation also should be purposeful, based on experience, multifaceted, and involve an active process.

Learning Is Purposeful

Each learner sees a learning situation from a different viewpoint. Each learner is a unique individual whose past experiences affect readiness to learn and understanding of the requirements involved. For example, an instructor may give two aviation maintenance learners the assignment of learning certain inspection procedures. One learner may catch on quickly and be able to competently present the assigned material. The combination of an aviation background and future goals may enable that learner to realize the need and value of learning the procedures. A second learner's goal may only be to comply with the instructor's assignment, and may result in only minimum preparation. The responses differ because each learner acts in accordance with what he or she sees in the situation.

Most people have fairly definite ideas about what they want to do and achieve. Their goals sometimes are short term, involving a matter of days or weeks. On the other hand, their goals may be carefully planned for a career or a lifetime. Each learner has specific intentions and goals. Some may be shared by other learners. Learners learn from any activity that tends to further their goals. Their individual needs and attitudes may determine what they learn as much as what the instructor is trying to teach. In the process of learning, the goals are of paramount significance. To be effective, aviation instructors need to find ways to relate new learning to the learner's goals.

Learning Is a Result of Experience

Since learning is an individual process, the instructor cannot do it for the learner. The learner can learn only from personal experiences; therefore, learning and knowledge cannot exist apart from a person. A person's knowledge is a result of experience, and no two people have had identical experiences. Even when observing the same event, two people react differently; they learn different things from it, according to the manner in which the situation affects their individual needs. Previous experience conditions a person to respond to some things and to ignore others.

All learning is by experience, but learning takes place in different forms and in varying degrees of richness and depth. For instance, some experiences involve the whole person while others may be based only on hearing and memory. Aviation instructors are faced with the problem of providing learning experiences that are meaningful, varied, and appropriate. As an example, learners can learn to say a list of words through repeated drill, or they can learn to recite certain principles of flight by rote. However, they can make them meaningful only if they understand them well enough to apply them correctly to real situations. If an experience challenges the learners, requires involvement with feelings, thoughts, memory of past experiences, and physical activity, it is more effective than a learning experience in which all the learners have to do is commit something to memory.

It seems clear enough that the learning of a physical skill requires actual experience in performing that skill. Pilots in training learn to fly aircraft only if their experiences include flying an aircraft; AMTs in training learn to overhaul power plants only by actually performing that task. Mental habits are also learned through practice. If learners are to use sound judgment and develop decision-making skills, they need experiences that involve knowledge of general principles and require the use of judgment in solving realistic problems.

Learning Is Multifaceted

If instructors see their objective as being only to train their learners' memory and muscles, they are underestimating the potential of the teaching situation. Individuals learn much more than expected if they fully exercise their minds and feelings. The fact that these items were not included in the instructor's plan does not prevent them from influencing the learning situation.

Psychologists sometimes classify learning by types, such as verbal, conceptual, perceptual, motor, problem-solving, and emotional. Other classifications refer to intellectual skills, cognitive strategies, and attitudinal changes, along with descriptive terms like surface or deep learning. However useful these divisions may be, they are somewhat artificial. For example, a class learning to apply the scientific method of problem-solving may learn the method by trying to solve real problems. But in doing so, the class also engages in verbal learning and sensory perception at the same time. Each learner approaches the task with preconceived ideas and feelings, and for many learners, these ideas change as a result of experience. Therefore, the learning process may include verbal elements, conceptual elements, perceptual elements, emotional elements, and problem-solving elements all taking place at once. This aspect of learning will become more evident later in this handbook when lesson planning is discussed.

Learning is multifaceted in still another way. While learning the subject at hand, individuals may be learning other things as well. They may be developing attitudes about aviation—good or bad—depending on what they experience. Under a skillful instructor, they may learn self-reliance. The list is seemingly endless. This type of learning is sometimes referred to as incidental, but it may have a great impact on the total development of the learner.

Learning Is an Active Process

Learners do not soak up knowledge like a sponge absorbs water. The instructor cannot assume that learners remember something just because they were in the classroom, shop, or aircraft when the instructor presented the material. Neither can the instructor assume the learners can apply what they know because they can quote the correct answer verbatim. For effective knowledge transfer, learners need to react and respond, perhaps outwardly, perhaps only inwardly, emotionally, or intellectually.

Learning Styles

Learning styles are simply different approaches or ways of learning based on the fact that people absorb and process information in different ways. Learning style is an individual's preference for understanding experiences and changing them into knowledge. It denotes the typical strategy a learner adopts in a learning situation. For example, information may be learned in a variety of ways: by seeing or hearing, by reflecting or acting, analyzing or visualizing, or it may be learned piecemeal or steadily. Just as people learn differently, they also have different teaching methods. Some instructors rely on lectures, others demonstrate, and others may prefer computer simulation training. Everyone has a mixture of strengths and preferences, not a single style or preference to the complete exclusion of any other. Please bear this in mind when using these ideas.

As mentioned in Chapter 2, Human Behavior, and the discussion of personality types and learning, underpinning the idea of learning style is the theory that everyone has an individual style of learning. According to this approach, if the learner and instructor work with that style, rather than against it, both benefit. Currently, 71 different theories of learning styles have been identified. These theories run from simple to complex, usually reflecting scientific research about how the brain processes information. While the scientific community may be surprised at how the research has been used, many educators and school systems have become advocates of applying learning style to teaching methods.

Another model for learning, the Approaches to Learning model, bases its theory on the learner's intentions. For example, is the learner interested in short-term memorization of the material or long-term knowledge? Does the learner want a passing grade on a pop quiz or the ability to use the material to repair an engine? One feature of the Approaches to Learning is that the approach to learning depends on an individual's reasons for learning. This theory reflects the Chapter 2, Human Behavior, discussion of adult learners who come to aviation training with definite reasons.

While controversy exists over the scientific value of learning styles as well as approaches to learning, many educational psychologists advocate their use in the learning process. Knowledge of learning styles and approaches can help an instructor make adjustments in how material is presented if his or her learning/teaching style differs from the way an individual learns. Since a learner's information processing technique, personality, social interaction tendencies, and the instructional methods used are all significant factors, training programs should be sensitive to different learning styles.

Right Brain/Left Brain

According to research on the human brain, people have a preferred side of the brain to use for understanding and storing information. While both sides of the brain are involved in nearly every human activity, it has been shown that those with right-brain dominance are characterized as being spatially oriented, creative, intuitive, and emotional. Those with left-brain dominance are more verbal, analytical, and objective. Generally, the brain functions as a whole. For example, the right hemisphere may recognize a face, while the left associates a name to go with the face.

While most people seem to have a dominant side, it is a preference, not an absolute. On the other hand, when learning is new, difficult, or stressful, the brain seems to go on autopilot to the preferred side. Recognizing a learner's dominant brain hemisphere gives the instructor a guide for ways to teach and reinforce material. There are also some people who use both sides of the brain equally well for understanding and storing information. *[Figure 3-14]*

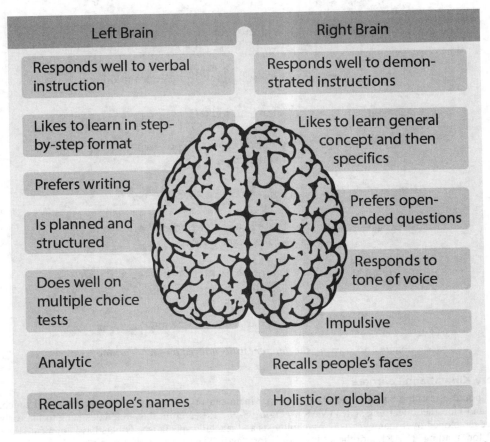

Figure 3-14. *The importance of recognizing a dominant brain hemisphere gives the instructor a guide for ways to teach and reinforce learning.*

Holistic/Serialistic Theory

As seen in *Figure 3-14,* right and left brain learners have preferences for how they process information. Based on information processing theory, left brain learners or serialistic learners have an analytic approach to learning. Because they gain understanding in linear steps, with each step logically following the previous one, these learners need well-defined, sequential steps where the overall picture is developed slowly, thoroughly, and logically. This is a bottom-up strategy.

Right brain or holistic learners favor the holistic strategy and prefer a big picture or global perspective. This is a top-down strategy and learners tend to learn in large jumps, absorbing material almost randomly without seeing connections, until suddenly "it" clicks and they get it. Global learners solve complex problems rapidly once they have grasped the big picture, but they often have difficulty explaining how they did it. This type of learner seeks overall comprehension; analogies help this individual.

Index of Learning Styles

In 1988, Richard Felder and Linda Silverman designed a learning style model with parallel learning styles that classified individuals as having learning preferences in sensing or intuitive, visual or verbal, active or reflective, sequential or global (discussed under holistic/serialistic learning style). A questionnaire developed by Felder and Solomon that offers learners the opportunity to assess learning preferences at no cost for noncommercial purposes is available at www.webtools.ncsu.edu/learningstyles/. [Figure 3-15]

Learning Style	Traits
Active	Tends to retain and understand information by doing something with it
Reflective	Prefers to think about information quietly
Sensing	Likes learning facts
Intuitive	Prefers discovering possibilities and relationships
Visual	Remembers best what is seen
Verbal	Learns more from words–written and spoken explanations
Sequential	Learns best with step-by-step explanations
Global	Tends to learn in large jumps

Figure 3-15. *Some of the different traits utilized by each learning style.*

Visual, Auditory Kinesthetic Learners

One of the most popular learning styles is based on the three main sensory receptors: vision, hearing, and touch. These are called visual, auditory, and kinesthetic learning styles (VAK). *[Figure 3-16]* Research in this area dates back to the early 20th century and the concepts were developed over many years by psychologists and teaching specialists. Others have augmented the VAK model with the addition of R for "reading" (VARK), or the addition of T for "tactile" (VAKT), or even a combination of the terms for VARKT.

Learning Style	Traits	Teaching Tips
Visual	Seeing, reading	Use graphs, charts, videos.
Auditory	Hearing, speaking	Have learner verbalize questions.
Kinesthetic	Touching, doing	Use demonstrations of skills.

Figure 3-16. *Visual, auditory, and kinesthetic learning styles (VAK).*

Learners generally use all three styles to receive information, but one of these three ways of receiving information is dominant. Once again, the dominant style of receiving information is the best way for a person to learn new information, but this style may not be the same for every task. The learner may use one style of learning or a combination of styles depending on the task.

Visual learners rely on seeing information. They learn best if a major component of the lesson is something they can see, and work best with printed and graphic materials, visual displays including diagrams, illustrated text books, overhead presentations, videos, flip charts, and hand-outs. They store information in their brains as pictures or images. They like to take extensive notes. Statistically, most people are visual learners.

Auditory learners transfer knowledge through listening and speaking. These learners need an oral component to the lesson such as verbal instructions. These learners have excellent listening skills and remember what was discussed over what was seen. They are better at verbally explaining than at writing. Since auditory learners prefer to listen to material, they are not good note takers.

Kinesthetic learners process and store information through physical experience such as touching, manipulating, using, or doing. They like to move around while trying to solve a problem and learn best when the material being taught involves hands-on practical experiences. Their concentration tends to wander when there is no external stimulation. They also learn from demonstration by watching carefully, then imagining or mirroring the demonstrator's movements.

Learners may prefer one of these three learning styles over another, but most employ all three depending on the material being taught. For example, when Beverly makes her first landing with Bill guiding her attempt, she employs visual, auditory, and kinesthetic learning. As the aircraft enters downwind, Beverly uses visual cues to recognize the airport and landing strip as she lines the aircraft up to land. As Bill talks her through the procedures, Beverly is using her auditory learning skills to learn how to land the aircraft. Finally, she needs to use kinesthetic skills to perform the actual landing.

Remember, good learners are capable of processing information in a variety of ways. The key to meeting individual needs is to ensure a variety of learning styles are addressed in every lesson.

Superlinks

In a theory proposed by Ricki Linksman, the learning style ideas discussed in the preceding paragraphs have been melded into a concept based on the VAKT learning styles plus brain hemisphere preference. This "superlink," as she calls it, is the easiest way for a learner to process information in order to understand, remember, and retain it. Matching visual, auditory, kinesthetic, and tactile with right- and left-brain research, Linksman created eight superlinks: visual left-brain, visual right-brain, auditory left-brain, auditory right-brain, tactile left-brain, tactile right-brain, kinesthetic left-brain, and kinesthetic right-brain. These superlinks accelerate learning by targeting the best way a person learns.

Summary

As mentioned earlier, there are many models of how people learn. Some models identify styles or approaches that are easily recognized such as collaborative, sharing learners who enjoy working with others, versus competitive learners who are grade conscious and feel they should do better than their peers. Participant learners normally have a desire to learn and enjoy attending class, and avoidant learners do not take part in class activities and have little interest in learning.

The environment also influences learning style. In real life, most learners find it necessary to adapt to a traditional style-learning environment provided by a school, university, or other educational/training establishment. Sometimes, the learner's way of learning may or may not be compatible with his or her environment.

Instructors who recognize either the learning style or learning approach and problems associated with them are more effective teachers than those who do not. Also, these instructors are prepared to develop appropriate lesson plans and provide guidance, counseling, or other advisory services, as required.

Acquiring Skill Knowledge

An aviation instructor also helps a learner acquire skill knowledge, which is knowledge reflected in motor or manual skills and in cognitive or mental skills, that manifests itself in the doing of something. Thus, skill knowledge differs from declarative knowledge because the learner is not usually aware of it consciously or able to articulate the skill. Evidence of skill knowledge is gained through observations of performance. This knowledge of how to do things is based on extensive practice, which leads to the storage of skill knowledge. An everyday example of skill knowledge is the ability to ride a bicycle.

Skill knowledge is acquired slowly through related experience. For example, a maintenance individual in training who is learning to weld typically burns or cracks the metal being welded while an expert welder's work is free of such imperfections. What does the experienced welder "know" that the beginner does not? The expert welder has had many hours of practice and a knowing-is-in-the-doing ability the inexperienced welder lacks. It isn't always possible to reduce to mere words that which one knows or knows how to do.

Stages of Skill Acquisition

Individuals make their way from beginner to expert via three characteristic stages for skill acquisition (or the learning process) as follows: cognitive, associative, and automaticity. An instructor needs to recognize each stage in learner performance in order to assess progress.

Cognitive Stage

Cognitive learning has a basis in factual knowledge. Since the learner has no prior knowledge of flying, the instructor first introduces him or her to a basic skill. The learner then memorizes the steps required to perform the skill. As the learner carries out these memorized steps, he or she is often unaware of progress, or may fixate on one aspect of performance. Performing the skill at this stage typically requires all the learner's attention; distractions introduced by an instructor often cause performance to deteriorate or stop.

The best way to prepare the learner to perform a task is to provide a clear, step-by-step example. Having a model to follow permits learners to get a clear picture of each step in the sequence so they understand what is required and how to do it. In flight or maintenance training, the instructor provides the demonstration, emphasizing the steps and techniques. During classroom instruction, an outside expert may be used, either in person or in a video presentation. In any case, learners need to have a clear impression of what they are to do.

For example, Beverly enters a steep turn after increasing power by a prescribed amount and adjusting the pitch trim. She fixates on the attitude indicator as she attempts to achieve the desired bank angle. The bank angle exceeds tolerances as she struggles to correct it, making many abrupt control inputs.

Associative Stage

Even demonstrating how to do something does not result in the learner learning the skill. Practice is necessary in order for the learner to learn how to coordinate muscles with visual and tactile senses. Learning to perform various aircraft maintenance skills or flight maneuvers requires practice. Another benefit of practice is that as the learner gains proficiency in a skill, verbal instructions become more meaningful. A long, detailed explanation is confusing before the learner begins performing, whereas specific comments are more meaningful and useful after the skill has been partially mastered.

As the storage of a skill via practice continues, the learner understands how to associate individual steps in performance with likely outcomes. The learner no longer performs a series of memorized steps, but is able to assess his or her progress along the way and make adjustments in performance. Performing the skill still requires deliberate attention, but the learner is better able to deal with distractions.

For example, Beverly enters the steep turn and again struggles to achieve the desired bank angle. Still working on the bank angle, she remembers the persistent altitude control problem and glances at the altimeter. Noticing that the aircraft has descended almost 100 feet, she increases back pressure on the control and adjusts the trim slightly. She goes back to a continuing struggle with the bank angle, keeping it under control with some effort, and completes the turn 80 feet higher than started.

Automatic Response Stage

Automaticity is one of the by-products of practice. As procedures become automatic, less attention is required to carry them out, so it is possible to do other things simultaneously, or at least do other things more comfortably. By this stage, learner performance of the skill is rapid and smooth. The learner devotes much less deliberate attention to performance, and may be able to carry on a conversation or perform other tasks while performing the skill. The learner makes far fewer adjustments during his or her performance and these adjustments tend to be small. The learner may no longer be able to remember the individual steps in the procedure, or explain how to perform the skill.

For example, the learner smoothly increases power, adds back pressure on the yoke, and trims the aircraft as a turn is entered. During the turn, the instructor questions the learner on an unrelated topic. The learner answers the questions, while making two small adjustments in pitch and trim, and then rolls out of the turn with the altimeter centered on the target altitude. Noting the dramatically improved performance, the instructor asks "What are you doing differently?" The learner seems unsure and says, "I have developed a feel for it."

Knowledge of Results

In some simple skills, learners can discover their own errors quite easily. In other cases, such as learning complex aircraft maintenance skills, flight maneuvers, or flight crew duties, mistakes are not always apparent. A learner may know that something is wrong, but not know how to correct it. In any case, the instructor provides a helpful and often critical function in making certain that the learners are aware of their progress. It is perhaps as important for learners to know when they are right as when they are wrong. They should be told as soon after the performance as possible, and should not be allowed to practice mistakes. It is more difficult to unlearn a mistake, and then learn the skill correctly, than to learn correctly in the first place. One way to make learners aware of their progress is to repeat a demonstration or example and to show them the standards their performance should ultimately meet.

How to Develop Skills

Theories about how a skill evolves from the awkward and deliberate performance associated with the cognitive stage to the smooth and steady-handed performance of the automatic response stage have one thing in common: progress appears to depend on repeated practice. Making progress toward automating a skill seems to be largely a matter of performing the skill over and over again. In skill learning, the first trials are slow and coordination is lacking. Mistakes are frequent but each trial provides clues for improvement in subsequent trials. The learner modifies different aspects of the skill such as how to hold the yoke or how to weld.

How long does it take to become proficient at a skill? Studies of skill learning have demonstrated that progress tends to follow what is known as a power law of practice. This law simply states that the speed of performance of a task improves as a power of the number of times that the task is performed. The logarithm of the reaction time for a particular task decreases linearly with the logarithm of the number of practice trials taken. Qualitatively, the law simply says that practice improves performance.

The graph in *Figure 3-17* shows how the power law of practice relates the time required to perform a skill to the number of times the skill has been practiced. While it is impossible to predict how many practice trials a learner will require to develop a skill to maturity, the general shape of the power law of practice offers some clues. Learning progress proceeds at a fast pace in the beginning (when there is ample room for improvement) and tends to slow down as performance becomes more skilled. In later stages of learning, improvement is more gradual. Once the curve levels off, it may stay level for a significant period of time. Further improvement may even seem unlikely. This is called a learning plateau.

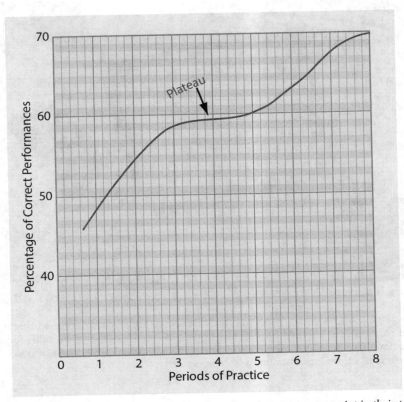

Figure 3-17. *Learners will probably experience a learning plateau at some point in their training.*

Learning Plateaus

A learning plateau may signify any number of conditions. For example, the learner may have reached capability limits, may be consolidating levels of skill, interest may have waned, or the learner may need a more efficient method for increasing progress. Keep in mind that the apparent lack of increasing proficiency does not necessarily mean that learning has ceased. When learning motor skills, a plateau, is normal and should be expected after an initial period of rapid improvement.

The instructor should prepare the learner for this situation to avert discouragement by explaining that the plateau is normal and temporary. Instructors can help learners who fall into a plateau by moving the learner to a different place in the curriculum and giving the current task a break. Instructors should also be aware that they can bring on a learning plateau by over-practice. Learning plateau problems can sometimes be alleviated also by the instructor better explaining the lesson, the reason for the lesson, and how it applies to the learner.

Types of Practice

Once a learner learns the skill, it is important to continue some practice to improve retention, but the power law of practice raises the question of whether or not there is a point at which continued practice no longer leads to improvement. Since athletic coaches, among others, are very interested in maximizing performance, much research has been done on the subject. Within the last few years, research has shown that how practice is structured makes an important impact on how well people retain what they have learned.

There are three types of practice, each of which yields particular results in acquiring skills: deliberate, blocked, and random.

Deliberate Practice

In order for a learner to gain skill knowledge on how to perform the skill automatically, he or she needs to engage in deliberate practice. This practice is aimed at a particular goal. During deliberate practice, the learner practices specific areas for improvement and receives specific feedback after practice. The feedback points out discrepancies between the actual performance and the performance goal sought. During deliberate practice, a learner focuses on eliminating these discrepancies. *[Figure 3-18]*

Figure 3-18. *A learner exhibits deliberate practice by plotting courses for his next training flight.*

Studies of skill learning suggest a learner achieves better results if distractions are avoided during deliberate practice. When feedback is needed to correct learner performance, it should be brief and explicit. Examples of individual skills for pilots are landings, stalls, steep turns, and procedure flows. Examples for maintenance technicians are correct installation of piston rings on a reciprocating engine, setting timing on an aircraft engine, and installing a tach generator.

Unlike the acquisition of knowledge, skill learning does not benefit from the instructor introducing the learner to new ideas or prompting the learner to think about old ones in different ways. On the other hand, instructors should not confuse distractions during skill learning with the legitimate use of distractions to help a learner learn how to manage his or her attention while coordinating several tasks that have been mastered to some degree.

Blocked Practice

Blocked practice is practicing the same drill until the movement becomes automatic. Doing the same task over and over leads to better short-term performance, but poorer long-term learning. It tends to fool not only the learner but the instructor into thinking the skills have been well learned. While blocked practice enhances current performance, it does not improve either concept learning or retrieval from long-term memory. *[Figure 3-19]*

Figure 3-19. *Pilot practices cross-wind landings repeatedly to improve performance.*

Random Practice

Random practice mixes up the skills to be acquired throughout the practice session. This type of practice leads to better retention because by performing a series of separate skills in a random order, the learner starts to recognize the similarities and differences of each skill which makes it more meaningful. The learner also is able to store the skill more effectively in the long-term memory. Learners get to retrieve steps and parameters from long-term memory which helps learners recognize patterns between tasks.

Blocked practice performance scores well during the actual practice when compared to random practice performance. But on a test given the next day, random practice does better than blocked practice. For long-term retention of aviation knowledge, the instructor who uses well-written SBT which encourages random practice and leads to better retention of information.

How much practice is needed to attain proficiency? In planning for learner skill acquisition, a primary consideration is the length of time devoted to practice. A beginning learner reaches a point where additional practice is not only unproductive, but may even be harmful. When this point is reached, errors increase, and motivation declines. As a learner gains experience, longer periods of practice are profitable.

Another consideration is the problem of whether to divide the practice period. Perhaps even the related instruction should be broken down into segments, or it may be advantageous to plan one continuous, integrated sequence. The answer depends on the nature of the skill. Some skills are composed of closely related steps, each dependent on the preceding one. Learning to pack a parachute is a good example. Other skills are composed of related subgroups of skills. Learning to overhaul an aircraft engine is a good example.

One way to structure practice to get the most from learning is to expose the learner to the same knowledge and skill in different contexts. For example, after practicing the short field landing in the aircraft, return to the classroom and rehearse the procedure using the toy airplane. Then, watch a video that shows a variety of back-to-back landings and have the learner describe what went right and what went wrong. Each of these methods gives the learner the chance practice the maneuver while adding new perceptions and insights to his or her skill base.

Evaluation Versus Critique

In the initial stages of skill acquisition, practical suggestions are more valuable to the learner than a grade. Early evaluation is usually teacher oriented. It provides a check on teaching effectiveness, can be used to predict learner outcomes, and can help the teacher locate special problem areas. The observations on which the evaluations are based also can identify the learner's strengths and weaknesses, a prerequisite for making constructive criticism. For additional information, refer to Chapter 6, Assessment.

As a learner practices a skill, it is important he or she perform the skill correctly and that the skill being practiced is one that needs to be developed to maturity. An instructor ensures a skill is practiced correctly by monitoring the practice and providing feedback about the skill development. The learner profits by having someone watch the performance and provide constructive criticism to help eliminate errors. Providing compliments on aspects of the skill that were performed correctly help keep the evaluation positive. Allowing the learner to critique his or her performance enhances learner-centered training.

Instructors should note learners can develop deviations from the intended method of performance at any stage of skill acquisition.

Overlearning of Knowledge

Overlearning is the continued study of a skill after initial proficiency has been achieved. Practice proceeds beyond the point at which the act can be performed with the required degree of excellence. The phenomenon of overlearning sometimes occurs when knowledge used frequently begins to take on the properties of a skill. For example, a learner's everyday knowledge about weight and balance concepts tends to center on the routine use of familiar charts found in the aircraft. Eventually, the learner's performance is characterized less by an understanding of weight and balance concepts, and more by an automatic process in which rows and columns of familiar charts give desired numbers.

In some cases, the overlearning of knowledge has the advantage of making application of knowledge more streamlined and efficient. In other cases, the development of automated routines can lead to problems. For example, a verbal checklist procedure becomes so automatic that a streamlined recitation of checklist items becomes decoupled from the thoughts and actions the checklist items are intended to trigger. In this case, the pilot or mechanic may not stop to consider each item.

The development of automated skills can impede further learning or lead to forgetting general knowledge. In one study, learner pilots and flight instructors were asked to solve weight and balance problems using charts taken from two different aircraft: (1) a small single-engine airplane they flew on a daily basis and (2) a different small single-engine airplane in which they had no experience. Test scores were surprisingly low when the charts for the unfamiliar airplane were used, and this was as true for instructors as it was for learners. The results suggest pilots had focused on developing streamlined, automatic procedures tuned to the details of the familiar aircraft charts while their ability to use their understanding of overall weight and balance concepts seemed to have diminished.

Instructors should remain aware of skills learners develop as a result of overlearning and help make sure that their actions continue to be accompanied by a use of their underlying knowledge. As a learner progresses, the key difference between knowledge and skill becomes apparent. Memorized facts about a topic that once supported the beginner's awkward performance of the skill tend to develop into deeper understanding. Skill acquisition involves learning many individual steps that eventually meld into a seemingly continuous automated process, at which point the learner has entered the procedural knowledge realm, and may no longer be consciously aware of the individual steps.

Application of Skill

The final and critical question is "Can the learner use the information received?" It is not uncommon to find that learners devote weeks and months in school learning new abilities, and then fail to apply these abilities on the job. To solve this problem, two conditions need to be present. First, the learner needs to understand the skill so well that it becomes easy, even habitual. Second, the learner should be able to recognize the types of situations where it is appropriate to use the skill. This second condition involves the question of transfer of learning, which is discussed later in this chapter.

Summary of Instructor Actions

To help learners acquire skills, the instructor should:

- Explain that the key to acquiring and improving any skill is continued practice.
- Monitor learner practice of skills and provide immediate feedback.
- Avoid conversation and other distractions when learners are practicing individual skills.
- Explain that learning plateaus are common and that continued practice leads to continued improvement.

Putting It All Together

Many skills are taught before a learner can fly an airplane or a maintenance learner can rebuild an aircraft engine. Just as practicing scales is a fundamental part of learning to play the piano, the learner does not "make music" until the ability to combine the notes in a variety of ways is acquired. For the learner pilot or technician, practicing specific skills is essential, but flying a cross-country trip or repairing a collapsed landing gear requires "putting it all together" in the right way to achieve success.

The following section looks at the challenge of learning to perform several tasks at once, dealing with distractions and interruptions, overcoming problems with fixation and inattention. It also describes the benefits of using realistic training scenarios to develop these abilities.

The Multitasking Mistake

The term multitasking is often taken for granted to mean handling several tasks at the same time. For example, when a pilot is on approach for a landing it is easy to assume that the experienced pilot is performing tasks in concurrence such as ATC communications, scanning instrumentation, and adjusting for minor deviations through the flight controls. We assume that, due to experience and practiced refinement, such skills at some point become automatic and somewhat instinctive. This belief can lead to a false sense of confidence that the routine procedure at hand is *only* routine and therefore does not require the added attention to question one's assumption that there will be no deviation in that task. *[Figure 3-20]*

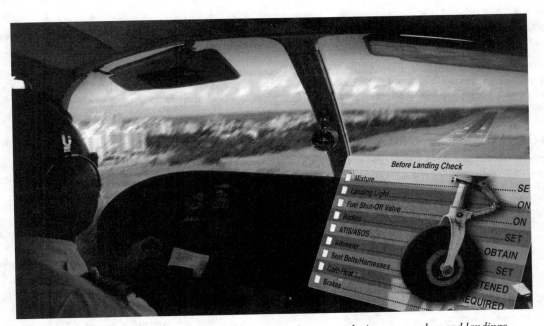

Figure 3-20. *A pilot is required to perform several tasks at once during approaches and landings.*

Priorities of Task Management

It is generally impossible to look at two different things at the same time. The area of focused vision (called the fovea) is only a few degrees in span and can only be directed to one location at a time. Similarly, people cannot listen to two conversations at the same time. While both conversations fall upon the ears at once, people need to devote their attention to the comprehension of one, to the exclusion of the other.

In the flight deck, a pilot is encumbered with any number competing events, tasks, and actions that each demand the attention of the pilot. While the pilot may believe that he or she is successfully managing these many tasks at the same time, in actuality, it is difficult to process more than one thought in congruence. This is especially true when one or more tasks go beyond perceived automation and require cognitive effort. To help reduce the risk of information-processing bottlenecks, it may be necessary for the pilot to employ attention switching.

Continuously switching attention back and forth between two or more tasks is attention switching. For example, when Beverly uses a checklist to perform a preflight inspection, she continuously switches her attention between the checklist and the equipment she is inspecting. She looks at the checklist to retrieve the next step in the procedure, and then looks at the equipment to perform the step.

There is a danger in task switching. The individual may decide that one task is less of a priority than another and choose to postpone resolution of that task. In doing so, it is very easy to simply forget the deferred task completely. Or, should the pilot become momentarily distracted, then effort should be made to remember what task to return to and at what stage of resolution that task was left in. Even the act of managing such tasks is in and of itself a task.

Increased Workload, Diminished Quality

A common response to an overwhelming workload is to reduce the level of standards for quality and achievement. Preemptively evaluating an impending task list to then choose to reduce (or even remove) relatively unimportant tasks can be a safe and effective action against the stresses that often comes with overburdened workload. However, it is not always the case that individuals have the time (or cognitive discipline as referenced in Chapter 2, Human Behavior) to accurately predict what tasks should instead be focused on. Sometimes the individual (especially those inexperienced or under high stress) reverts to a reaction-based response process. This can create a negative environment that may actually induce more stress as the individual continually tries to respond to each task without an overall plan.

Learning to Task Manage

Before learners are asked to perform several tasks at once, instructors should ensure that the learner has devoted enough time to study and practice such that the individual tasks can be performed reasonably well in isolation.

Inexperience with an individual task can often hinder attempts to combine it with other tasks. For example, a learner distracted by trying to interpret unfamiliar symbols on a sectional chart inadvertently deviates from assigned attitude or heading. An instructor recognizes the need to spend more time with these skills in isolation. In this case, there is nothing about the experience of controlling the aircraft that helps learners better understand chart symbols.

Distractions and Interruptions

A distraction is an unexpected event that causes the learner's attention to be momentarily diverted. Learners need to decide whether or not a distraction warrants further attention or action on their part. Once this has been decided, the learners either turn their attention back to what they were doing, or act on the distraction.

An interruption is an unexpected event for which the learner voluntarily suspends performance of one task in order to complete a different one. Interruptions are a significant source of errors and learners need to be aware of the potential for errors caused by interruptions and develop procedures for dealing with them. A classic example is an interruption that occurs while a learner is following the steps in a written procedure or checklist. The learner puts down the checklist, deals with the interruption, and then returns to the procedure—but erroneously picks up at a later point in the procedure, omitting one or more steps.

Fixation and Inattention

Since human attention is limited in focus and highly prone to distraction, people are vulnerable to two other types of problems: fixation and inattention.

Fixation occurs when a learner becomes absorbed in performing one task to the exclusion of other tasks. Instructors see many examples of this in learner performance. Beginning instrument pilots characteristically fixate on particular instruments, attempting to control one aspect of their performance while other aspects deteriorate. Fixation on a task is often a sign that the task has not received enough practice in isolation. That is, the learner has not yet mastered the task well enough to perform it in addition to other tasks. Fixation can happen even when individual skills have been reasonably mastered, when learners have not yet learned the importance of managing their own limited attentional resources.

Inattention occurs when a learner fails to pay attention to a task that is important. Inattention is sometimes a natural by-product of fixation. Learners fixate on one task and become too busy to attend to other tasks. Inattention also happens when learners are not busy: attention may drift when they become bored or think that a task does not deserve their attention. In some cases, this type of inattention is difficult to eliminate through training and practice. For example, it is well known that humans perform poorly when placed in the role of passive monitor. Many studies have shown how performance rapidly deteriorates when humans are asked to passively monitor gauges or the progress of an automated system such as a GPS navigation computer or autopilot. Furthermore, it seems that the more reliable the system becomes, the poorer the human performance becomes at the monitoring task. The first line of defense against this type of inattention is to alert the learner to the problem, and to help develop habits that keep their attention focused.

How to Identify Fixation or Inattention Problems

One way for instructors to identify problems with fixation and inattention is to try and follow where learners look. To accomplish this, instructors can glance at a learner's eyes to try to determine where they are looking. Learners who appear to look at one instrument for an extended period of time might have a problem with fixation. Learners whose gaze is never directed toward engine instruments might have a problem with inattention.

The technique of following learner eye movements is useful, but has limitations since looking in the same direction is not the same as "seeing" what the learner sees.

Scenario-Based Training (SBT)

Research and practical experience have demonstrated the usefulness of practicing in realistic scenarios—ones that resemble the environment in which knowledge and skills are later used. Instructors should devise scenarios that allow learners to practice what they have learned. This is challenging because different learners need to practice different things at different times, and because different working environments present different practice opportunities.

What makes a good scenario? A good scenario:

- Has a clear set of objectives.
- Is tailored to the needs of the learner.
- Capitalizes on the nuances of the local environment.

For example, Bill is introducing Beverly to a low-fuel emergency. His objective at this early stage is to simply enable Beverly to recall the sorts of actions that are appropriate for a low-fuel emergency. He decides to use the classroom environment as a first practice scenario. He asks Beverly about what sorts of actions she might take if such an event would occur. She has some good ideas but he asks her to think more about before her next lesson. On her next lesson he gives her the same exercise. This time her answers are consistent and insightful. Bill decides that this scenario has served its purpose and moves on.

During their next flight, Bill's objective is having Beverly recall and carry out the steps that she was able to cite in the classroom. As they arrive at their home airport, he presents Beverly with a low-fuel scenario. He notes that she remembers much of what she was able to recall in the classroom, but amidst the excitement, has forgotten a few things. He uses the same scenario at a different airport on their next flight, and she performs admirably.

Later in her training, Bill's next objective is to enable her to recall and perform the emergency steps in concert with other piloting duties. They depart on a cross-country flight from a populated area to a remote area. While en route, Bill presents Beverly with a low-fuel emergency scenario knowing that there is only one airport nearby and that it is not easy to spot. She successfully uses her available navigational resources to locate and arrive at the airport. Upon returning home, Bill attempts to generalize her new abilities and put yet a different spin on the same problem. He presents the low-fuel scenario, taking advantage of the fact that there are eight nearby airports. All of the airports are in plain view, and she can choose one.

Each of these scenarios taught Beverly something she needed to learn next, and made good use of the surroundings and available circumstances. As these examples illustrate, there is no list of "canned" scenarios that can be used for all learners. Instructors should devise their own scenarios by considering what each learner needs to practice, and exploiting features of the local environment that allow them to do it.

The Learning Route to Expertise

What does it take to successfully orchestrate all of the knowledge and skills the learner has learned into what instructors, evaluators, and other pilots and mechanics would regard as true expertise? All evidence seems to point once again to the idea of practice. Just as the perfection of an individual skill seems to rely on repeated practice, so does the combination of knowledge and skills that make up our abilities to do the real-world job of pilot or mechanic.

How much practice does it take to become a true expert? In a study of expert performers in fields ranging from science to music to chess, one psychologist found that no performer had reached true expertise without having invested at least ten years of practice in his or her field. Experts have been found to use two tools to help them gain expertise in their field: cognitive strategies and problem-solving tactics.

Cognitive Strategies

The idea of cognitive strategies emerged over 50 years ago in the context of human information processing theory. Cognitive strategies refer to the knowledge of procedures or knowledge about how to do something in contrast with the knowledge of facts. They use the mind to solve a problem or complete a task and provide a structure for learning that actively promotes the comprehension and retention of knowledge. A cognitive strategy helps the learner develop internal procedures that enable him or her to perform higher level operations.

As learners acquire experience, they develop their own strategies for dealing with problems that arise frequently. For example, a learner develops the following strategy for avoiding inadvertent flight into instrument meteorological conditions (IMC) at night. He or she checks the weather prior to departure, obtains updates on the weather every hour, and plans to divert to an alternate destination at the first suspicion of unexpected weather ahead.

One approach to helping develop cognitive strategies is to study and identify the strategies that experts use and then teach these strategies to the learners. Expert strategies were identified by researchers who presented experts with problems to solve and asked them to think aloud as they attempted to solve the problems. These cognitive strategies can be taught to learners, usually with successful results.

Problem-Solving Tactics

Problem-solving tactics are specific actions intended to get a particular result, and this type of knowledge represents the most targeted knowledge in the expert's arsenal. For example, a learner notices how easy it is to make a mistake with a takeoff distance chart after using it several times. She notices her finger drifts upward or downward when sliding it across a row of numbers on the chart, sometimes landing on the wrong number. The learner formulates several tactics to ensure she obtains the correct figures: (1) work slowly and deliberately, (2) use a ruler, and (3) double-check the work.

But even the experts had to practice. In a study of violinists at a music academy in Berlin, researchers compared the "best" learners to those who were regarded as merely "very good." Using estimates of how many total hours each learner had spent practicing during his or her lifetime, the researchers found that the best violinists had spent an average of 7,000 hours practicing, while the very good violinists had logged about 5,000 hours. The scientific study of expertise reiterates the adage: "Practice makes perfect."

Awareness of Existence of Unknowns

An important aspect of an expert's knowledge is an awareness of what he or she does not know. This is not always the case with a learner. It's important that an instructor be aware of situations in which learners have acquired "book" knowledge, but not yet acquired the more in-depth understanding that comes from association and experience. For example, after acquiring substantial knowledge of a single-engine, two-seat training aircraft, learners should understand that a four-seat aircraft by the same manufacturer should be approached with caution and not overconfidence.

Summary of Instructor Actions

To help learners exercise their knowledge and skills in a concerted fashion, the instructor should:

- Explain the difference between normal task switching and interruption multitasking and give examples of each.
- Ensure that individual skills are reasonably well-practiced before asking learners to perform several tasks at once.
- Teach learners how to deal with distractions and interruptions and provide them with opportunities to practice.
- Point out fixation and inattention when it occurs.
- Devise scenarios that allow learners to use their knowledge and skill to solve realistic problems and make decisions.
- Explain to the learner that continued practice with the goal of improving leads to continued improvement.

Errors

Errors are a natural part of human performance. Beginners, as well as the most highly skilled experts, are vulnerable to error, and this is perhaps the most important thing to understand about error. To believe people can eliminate errors from their performance is to commit the biggest error of all. Instructors and learners alike should be prepared for occasional errors by learning about common kinds of errors, how errors can be minimized, how to learn from errors, and how to recover from errors when they are made.

Kinds of Errors

There are two kinds of errors: slips and mistakes.

Slip

A slip occurs when a person plans to do one thing, but then inadvertently does something else. Slips are errors of action. Slips can take on a variety of different forms. One of the most common forms of slips is to simply neglect to do something. Other forms of slips occur when people confuse two things that are similar. Accidentally using a manual that is similar to the one really needed is an example of this type of slip.

Other forms of slips happen when someone is asked to perform a routine procedure in a slightly different way. For example, Beverly has been assigned runway 30 for many days in a row. This morning she approaches to land and ATC assigns runway 12 instead. As she approaches the traffic pattern, she turns to enter the pattern for runway 30 out of habit.

Time pressure is another common source of slips. Studies of people performing a variety of tasks demonstrated a phenomenon called the speed-accuracy tradeoff. The more hurried one's work becomes the more slips one is likely to make.

Mistake

A mistake occurs when a person plans to do the wrong thing and is successful. Mistakes are errors of thought. Mistakes are sometimes the result of gaps or misconceptions in the learner's understanding. One type of mistake happens when a learner formulates an understanding of a phenomenon and then later encounters a situation that shows how this understanding was incorrect or incomplete. For example, overly simplistic understanding of weather frequently leads inexperienced learners into situations that are unexpected.

Experts are not immune to making mistakes, which sometimes arise from the way an expert draws upon knowledge of familiar problems and responds to them using familiar solutions. *[Figure 3-21]* Mistakes can occur when the expert categorizes a particular case incorrectly. For example, an experienced pilot may become accustomed to ignoring nuisance alerts issued by his traffic alerting system when approaching his home airport, as many aircraft on the ground turn on their transponders prior to takeoff. One night, he ignores an alert that was generated not by an aircraft on the ground, but rather by another aircraft that has turned in front of him on final approach.

Reducing Error

Although it is impossible to eliminate errors entirely, there are ways to reduce them, as described in the following paragraphs.

Learning and Practicing

The first line of defense against errors is learning and practice. Higher levels of knowledge and skill are associated with a lower frequency and magnitude of error.

Taking Time

Errors can often be reduced by working deliberately at a comfortable pace. Hurrying does not achieve the same results as faster performance that is gained by increasing one's skill through continued practice.

Checking for Errors

Another way to help avoid errors is to look actively for evidence of them. Many tasks in aviation offer a means of checking work. Learners should be encouraged to look for new ways of checking their work.

Figure 3-21. *Other mistakes arise under pressure. For example, a technician or pilot might perform a cursory inspection of an aircraft to save time, only to have a problem manifest itself later.*

Using Reminders

Errors are reduced when visible reminders are present and actively used. Checklists and other published procedures are examples of reminders. Many aircraft instruments such as heading indicators offer bugs that can be used to remind the pilot about assigned headings and courses and some may also prompt altitudes and airspeeds. Mechanics and pilots alike can use notepads to jot down reminders or information that should otherwise be committed to memory.

Developing Routines

The use of standardized procedures for routine tasks is widely known to help reduce error. Even when a checklist procedure is unavailable or impractical, learners can help reduce the occurrence of error by adopting standardized procedures.

Raising Awareness

Another line of defense against errors is to raise one's awareness when operating in conditions under which errors are known to happen (e.g., changes in routine, time pressure), or in conditions under which defenses against errors have been compromised (e.g., fatigue, lack of recent practice).

Error Recovery

Given that the occasional error is inevitable, it is a worthwhile exercise to practice recovering from commonly made errors, or those that pose serious consequences. All flight learners need to learn and practice a lost procedure to ensure that they can recover from the situation in which they have lost their way. It is useful to devote the same sort of preparation to other common learner errors.

Learning from Error

Error can be a valuable learning resource. Learners naturally make errors, which instructors can utilize in training to help while being careful not to let the individual practice doing the wrong thing. When a learner makes an error, it is useful to ask them to consider why the error happened, and what could be done differently to prevent the error from happening again in the future. In some cases, errors are slips that simply reveal the need for more practice. In other cases, errors point to aspects of learner methods or habits that might be improved. For example, beginning instrument flight learners commonly make errors when managing two communications radios, each with an active and standby frequency. When the same learners understand each radio's specific purpose (e.g., ATIS, ground, tower frequencies), error rates often drop quickly.

Instructors and learners should be aware of a natural human tendency to resist learning from errors. That is, there is a tendency to "explain away" errors, dismissing them as one-time events that will likely never happen again. The same phenomenon occurs when observing errors made by others. Reading an accident or incident report, it is easy to spot where a pilot or mechanic made an error and regard the error as something that could never happen to the reader. It is important to note that this type of bias is not necessarily the result of ego or overconfidence; rather, it is something to which we are all susceptible. Psychologist Baruch Fischoff studied hindsight explanations given by people who were presented with descriptions of situations and their ultimate outcomes. When asked to provide explanations for events that had already occurred and for which the outcome was known, people explained that the outcomes were "obvious" and "predictable." When the same events without the outcomes were presented to a second group, peoples' prediction of the outcome was no better than chance guessing. The study nicely illustrates the popular adage that "hindsight is 20/20."

Summary of Instructor Actions

To help learners learn from errors they make and be prepared for them in the future, an instructor should:

- Explain that pilots and mechanics at all levels of skill and experience make occasional errors.

- Explain that the magnitude and frequency of errors tend to decrease as skill and experience increases.

- Explain the difference between slips and mistakes and provide examples of each.

- Explain ways in which the learner can help minimize errors.

- Allow the learner to practice recovering from common errors.

- Point out errors when they occur and ask the learner to explain why they occurred.

Memory

Memory is the vital link between the learner learning/retaining information and the cognitive process of applying what is learned. It is the ability of people and other organisms to encode (initial perception and registration of information), store (retention of encoded information over time), and retrieve (processes involved in using stored information) information. *[Figure 3-22]* When a person successfully recalls a past experience (or skill), information about the experience has been encoded, stored, and retrieved.

Figure 3-22. *Information processing within the sensory register, working on short-term memory, and long-term memory includes complex coding, sorting, storing, and recall functions.*

Although there is no universal agreement of how memory works, a widely accepted model has three components: sensory memory, short-term memory (STM), and long-term memory (LTM).

Sensory Memory

Sensory memory is the part of the memory system that receives initial stimuli from the environment and processes them according to the individual's preconceived concept of what is important. Other factors can influence the reception of information by sensory memory. For example, if the input is dramatic and impacts more than one of the five senses, that information is more likely to make an impression. The sensory memory processes stimuli from the environment within seconds, discards what is considered extraneous, and processes what is determined by the individual to be relevant. This is a selective process where the sensory register is set to recognize certain stimuli and immediately transmit them to the STM for action. The process is called precoding. An example of sensory precoding is recognition of a fire alarm. No matter what is happening at the time, when the sensory register detects a fire alarm, the working memory is immediately made aware of the alarm and preset responses begin to take place. Sensory memory is capable of retaining information for only a very short period of time and within seconds the relevant information is passed to the STM.

Short-Term Memory (STM)

Short-term memory is the part of the memory system where information is stored for roughly 30 seconds, after which it may rapidly fade or be consolidated into long-term memory, depending on the individual's priorities. Several common steps help retention in STM. These include rehearsal or repetition of the information and sorting or categorization into systematic chunks. The sorting process is usually called coding or chunking. A key limitation of STM is that it takes 5–10 seconds to properly code information and if the coding process is interrupted, that information is easily lost since it is stored for only 30 seconds. The goal of the STM is to put the information to immediate use.

STM is not only time-limited, it also has limited capacity, usually about seven bits or chunks of information. A seven-digit telephone number is an example. As indicated, the time limitation may be overcome by rehearsal. This means learning the information by a rote memorization process. Of course, rote memorization is subject to imperfections in both the duration of recall and in its accuracy. The coding process is more useful in a learning situation. In addition, the coding process may involve recoding to adjust the information to individual experiences. This is when actual learning begins to take place. Therefore, recoding may be described as a process of relating incoming information to concepts or knowledge already in memory.

Brain research has led to the conclusion that STM resembles the control tower of a major airport and is responsible for scheduling and coordinating all incoming and outgoing flights. STM has three basic operations: iconic memory, acoustic memory, and working memory. Iconic memory is the brief sensory memory of visual images. Acoustic memory is the encoded memory of a brief sound memory or the ability to hold sounds in STM. Of the two, acoustic memory can be held longer than iconic memory. Working memory is an active process to keep information until it is put to use (think of a phone number repeated until used). It is useful in remembering a spoken sentence or a string of digits.

Also called "scratch-pad" memory, working memory is of short duration and has limited capacity. It simultaneously stores and manipulates information. The goal of the working memory is not really to move the information from STM to LTM, but merely put the information to immediate use.

STM retention makes information available long enough for it to be rehearsed. For example, if the learner repeats the number to himself, it can be transferred to some sort of longer term storage. To retain information for extended periods of time, it needs to be transferred from STM to LTM. This process involves encoding or consolidation of information into LTM where it can then be retrieved.

Long-Term Memory (LTM)

LTM is relatively permanent storage of unlimited information, and it is possible for memories in LTM to remain there for a lifetime. What is stored in LTM affects a person's perceptions of the world and affects what information in the environment is noticed. Information that passes from STM to LTM typically has some significance attached to it. For example, imagine how difficult it would be for a pilot to forget the first day he or she soloed. This is a significant day in any pilot's training, so when the information was processed, significance was attached to it, the information was deemed important, and it was transferred into LTM.

There appear to be other reasons information is transferred to LTM because the average human brain stores numerous insignificant facts. One explanation is repetition; people tend to remember things the more they are rehearsed. Information also ends up in LTM because it is somehow attached to something significant. A person may remember the color of the clothing of the recipient of a wedding proposal. The color of the clothing plays no important role, but is attached to the memory of the experience.

For the stored information to be useful, some special effort was expended during the encoding or consolidation of information in STM. The encoding should provide meaning and connections between old and new information. If initial encoding is not properly accomplished, recall is distorted and it may be impossible. The more effective the encoding process, the easier the recall. However, it should be noted that the LTM is a reconstruction, not a pure recall of information or events. It is also subject to limitations, such as time, biases, and, in many cases, personal inaccuracies. This is one reason why two people who view the same event often have totally different recollections. Memory also applies to psychomotor skills. For example, with practice, a tennis player may be able to serve a tennis ball at a high rate of speed and with accuracy. This may be accomplished with very little thought. For a pilot, the ability to instinctively perform certain maneuvers or tasks that require manual dexterity and precision, provides obvious benefits. For example, it allows the pilot more time to concentrate on other essential duties such as navigation, communications with ATC facilities, and visual scanning for other aircraft.

Information in LTM is stored in interrelated networks of schemas which are the cognitive frameworks that help people organize and interpret information. Schemas guide recognition and understanding of new information by providing expectations about what should occur. Since LTM is organized into schemas, instructors should consciously look for ways to make training relevant and meaningful enough for the learner to transfer new information to LTM. This can be accomplished by activating existing schemas before presenting new information. For example, a brief review of the previous lesson via discussion, video, questions, etc.

Remembering What Has Been Learned

The moment people learn something new and add it to their repertoire of knowledge and skill, they are confronted with a second task: the task of remembering it. Remembering is a challenge because of a natural feature of human memory-forgetting. Forgetting is such an apparent part of human memory that it is often the first thing that people think of when they bring up the topic of memory.

The following section discusses how remembering and forgetting happens in predictable ways that help keep human memories tuned to the demands of everyday life. Memories help people keep fresh precisely those things needed next, and let slip those things that have outlived their usefulness. Understanding the factors that determine what is remembered and what is forgotten helps instructor and learner get the most from memory.

How Usage Affects Memory

The ability to retrieve knowledge or skills from memory is primarily related to two things: (1) how often that knowledge has been used in the past; and (2) how recently the knowledge has been used. These two factors are called frequency and recency of use. Frequency and recency can be present individually or in combination.

Frequency and recency—knowledge that enjoys both frequency and recency is likely to be retrieved easily and quickly. This is knowledge much used in the past that continues to be used in the present. This is the ideal situation for knowledge and skills that need to be used.

Frequency only—knowledge that has been used much in the past but that has not been used recently is vulnerable to being forgotten. This type of knowledge is likely to be retrieved slowly or not at all. To retrieve this knowledge and skill, some recent rehearsal or practice needs to be added in order to refresh the memory.

Recency only—knowledge that has been recently used but has not been used in the past is knowledge that has been recently acquired. This type of knowledge is particularly vulnerable to being forgotten since there is little to distinguish it from "throw away" knowledge, such as an hourly weather broadcast. To remember this knowledge requires a program of regular rehearsal to build up its frequency.

Forgetting

Forgetting, which refers to loss of a memory, typically involves a failure in memory retrieval. The failure may be due to the decay or overwriting of information which has been temporarily stored in STM, but generally forgetting refers to loss of information from LTM. The information is not lost, per se, it is somewhere in the person's LTM, but he or she is not able to retrieve and remember it.

Why do people forget? Why don't we remember everything? Do we need to remember everything? Most of the information people are exposed to each day has a short period of usefulness with little need to retain it. For example, why would anyone need to remember the details of an hourly weather broadcast ten years ago?

Thus, forgetting knowledge is not always a bad thing. For example, forgetting old information keeps new information up to date. Many theories on why people forget have been offered to explain the phenomenon, among them retrieval failure, fading, interference, and repression or suppression.

Retrieval Failure

Retrieval failure is simply the inability to retrieve information, that tip-of-the-tongue phenomenon when a person knows the meaning of a word, or the answer to a question, but cannot retrieve it. It is also caused by the fact that sometimes people simply do not encode information well and the information never makes it to LTM or is lost before it can attach itself to the LTM. This is sometimes referred to as failure to store.

Fading

The theory of fading or decay suggests that a person forgets information that is not used for an extended period of time, that it fades away or decays. It had been suggested that humans are physiologically preprogrammed to eventually erase data that no longer appears pertinent.

On the other hand, experimental studies show that a hypnotized person can describe specific details of an event, which normally is beyond recall. Apparently the memory is there, locked in the recesses of the mind. The difficulty is summoning the memory to consciousness or retrieving the link that leads to it.

Interference

Interference theory suggests that people forget something because a certain experience has overshadowed it, or that the learning of similar things has intervened. This theory might explain how the range of experiences after graduation from school causes a person to forget or to lose knowledge. In other words, new events displace many things that had been learned. From experiments, at least two conclusions about interference may be drawn. First, similar material seems to interfere with memory more than dissimilar material; and second, material not well learned suffers most from interference.

Repression or Suppression

Freudian psychology advances the view that some forgetting is caused by repression or suppression. In repression or suppression, a memory is pushed out of reach because the individual does not want to remember the feelings associated with it. Repression is an unconscious form of forgetting while suppression is a conscious form.

Forgetting information does not mean it is gone forever. Sometimes it is still there, just inaccessible.

Retention of Learning

Each of the theories of forgetting implies that when a person forgets something, it is not actually lost. Rather, it is simply unavailable for recall. The instructor's problem is how to make certain that the learner's learning is readily available for recall. The following suggestions can help.

Teach thoroughly and with meaning. Material thoroughly learned is highly resistant to forgetting. This is suggested by experimental studies and it also was pointed out in the sections on skill learning. Meaningful learning builds patterns of relationships in the learner's consciousness, which is one reason to conduct SBT. In contrast, rote learning is superficial and is not easily retained. Meaningful learning goes deep because it involves principles and concepts anchored in the learner's own experiences. The following discussion emphasizes five principles, which are generally accepted as having a direct application to remembering.

Praise Stimulates Remembering

Responses that give a pleasurable return tend to be repeated. Absence of praise or recognition tends to discourage, and any form of negativism in the acceptance of a response tends to make its recall less likely.

Recall Is Promoted by Association

As discussed earlier, each bit of information or action, which is associated with something to be learned, tends to facilitate its later recall by the learner. Unique or disassociated facts tend to be forgotten unless they are of special interest or application.

Favorable Attitudes Aid Retention

People learn and remember only what they wish to know. Without motivation there is little chance for recall. The most effective motivation is based on positive or rewarding objectives.

Learning with All Senses Is Most Effective

Although people generally receive what is learned through the eyes and ears, other senses also contribute to most perceptions. When several senses respond together, a fuller understanding and greater chance of recall is achieved.

Meaningful Repetition Aids Recall

Each repetition gives the learner an opportunity to gain a clearer and more accurate perception of the subject to be learned, but mere repetition does not guarantee retention. Practice provides an opportunity for learning, but does not cause it. Further, some research indicates that three or four repetitions provide the maximum effect, after which the rate of learning and probability of retention fall off rapidly.

Along with these five principles, there is a considerable amount of additional literature on retention of learning during a typical academic lesson. After the first 10–15 minutes, the rate of retention drops significantly until about the last 5–10 minutes when learners wake up again. Learners passively listening to a lecture have roughly a five percent retention rate over a 24-hour period, but individuals actively engaged in the learning process have a much higher retention. This clearly reiterates the point that active learning is superior to just listening.

Mnemonics

A mnemonic uses a pattern of letters, ideas, visual images, or associations to assist in remembering information. It is a memory enhancing strategy that involves teaching learners to link new information to information they already know. Its chief value lies in helping learners recall information that needs to be recalled in a particular order by encoding difficult-to-remember information in a way that makes it easier to remember. Research shows that providing learners with memorization techniques improves their ability to recall information. Mnemonics include but are not limited to acronyms, acrostics, rhymes, or chaining.

Acronyms form a word from the first letters of other words. For example, "AIM" is the acronym for Aeronautical Information Manual.

An acrostic is a poem, word puzzle, or other composition in which the first letter of each line or word is a cue to the idea the learner wishes to remember. For example, Every Good Boy Does Fine is used to remember the order of the G-clef notes in music. An example of a useful aviation acrostic is the memory aid for one of the magnetic compass errors. The letters "ANDS" indicate:

- Accelerate
- North
- Decelerate
- South

Rhymes and melody are another way to remember information. Rhymes such as "In 1492, Columbus sailed the ocean blue." Most children learn the alphabet using a familiar melody "Twinkle, Twinkle, Little Star." A well-known mnemonic rhyme for remembering the days of the month is the familiar, "30 days hath September, April, June, and November..."

Chaining is used for ordered or unordered lists and consists of creating a story in which each word or idea that needs to be remembered cues the next idea.

Variations of the encoding process are practically endless. Developing a logical strategy for encoding information is a significant step in the learning process.

Transfer of Learning

Transfer of learning is broadly defined as the ability to apply knowledge or procedures learned in one context to new contexts. Learning occurs more quickly and he or she develops a deeper understanding of the task if he or she brings some knowledge or skills from previous learning. A positive transfer of learning occurs when the individual practices under a variety of conditions, underscoring again the value of SBT.

A distinction is commonly made between near and far transfer. Near transfer consists of transfer from initial learning that is situated in a given setting to ones that are closely related. Far transfer refers both to the ability to use what was learned in one setting to a different one as well as the ability to solve novel problems that share a common structure with the knowledge initially acquired. There is a third way to talk about transfer called generativity. In this context it means learners have the ability on their own to come up with novel solutions.

During a learning experience, previous knowledge usually aids the learner, but sometimes interferes with the current task. Consider the learning of two skills. If the learning of skill A helps to learn skill B, positive transfer occurs. If learning skill A hinders the learning of skill B, negative transfer occurs. For example, the practice of slow flight (skill A) helps Beverly learn short-field landings (skill B). However, practice in making a landing approach in an airplane (skill A) may hinder learning to make an approach in a helicopter (skill B). It should be noted that the learning of skill B might affect the retention or proficiency of skill A, either positively or negatively. While these processes may help substantiate the interference theory of forgetting, they are still concerned with the transfer of learning.

It is clear that some degree of transfer is involved in all learning. This is true because, except for certain inherent responses, all new learning is based upon previous experience. People interpret new things in terms of what they already know.

Many aspects of teaching profit by this type of transfer, perhaps explaining why learners of apparently equal ability have differing success in certain areas. Negative transfer may hinder the learning of some; positive transfer may help others. This points to a need to know the learner's past experience and current knowledge. In lesson and syllabus development, instructors can plan for transfer by organizing course materials and individual lesson materials in a meaningful sequence. Each phase should help the learner understand what is to follow.

The cause of transfer and exactly how it occurs is difficult to determine, but no one disputes the fact that transfer occurs. For the instructor, the significance of transference lies in the fact that the learners can be helped to achieve it. The following suggestions are representative of what educational psychologists believe should be done:

- Plan for transfer as a primary objective. As in all areas of teaching, the chance for success is increased if the instructor deliberately plans to achieve it.

- Ensure that the learners understand that information can be applied to other situations. Prepare them to seek other applications.

- Maintain high-order learning standards. Overlearning may be appropriate. The more thoroughly the learners understand the material, the more likely they are to see its relationship to new situations.

- Avoid unnecessary rote learning, since it does not foster transfer.

- Provide meaningful learning experiences that build confidence in their ability to transfer knowledge. This suggests activities that challenge them to exercise their imagination and ingenuity in applying their knowledge and skills.

- Use instructional material that helps form valid concepts and generalizations. Use materials that make relationships clear.

Habit Formation

The formation of correct habit patterns from the beginning of any learning process is essential to further learning and for correct performance after the completion of training. Remember, primacy is one of the fundamental principles of learning. Therefore, it is the instructor's responsibility to insist on correct techniques and procedures from the outset of training to provide proper habit patterns. It is much easier to foster proper habits from the beginning of training than to correct faulty ones later.

Due to the high level of knowledge and skill required in aviation for both pilots and maintenance technicians, training has traditionally followed a building block concept. This means new learning and habit patterns are based on a solid foundation of experience and/or old learning. Everything from intricate cognitive processes to simple motor skills depends on what the learner already knows and how that knowledge can be applied in the present. As knowledge and skill increase, there is an expanding base upon which to build for the future.

How Understanding Affects Memory

The ability to remember is greatly affected by the level of understanding of what has been learned. Many studies have demonstrated a depth-of-processing effect on memory: the more deeply humans think about what they have learned, the more likely they are able to retrieve that knowledge later. Depth-of-processing is the natural result of the kinds of learning activities described earlier: beginning with memorized information and then elaborating upon it, making associations, constructing explanations, all in pursuit of furthering understanding.

The effects of depth of processing on memory are quite powerful and result from even the simplest attempts to elaborate on what has been learned. One study asked participants to memorize sentences such as "The pilot arrived late." Half of the participants simply memorized the sentences as they were. The other participants were asked to develop an elaboration for the sentence such as "because of the bad weather."

When put to a test, participants who created elaborations were significantly better able to recall the sentences. When memories for sentences had decayed, it seems that remembered words from the elaborations helped people recall them.

Remembering during Training

Remembering what is learned on a day-to-day basis is the first challenge learners need to meet. As learners are presented with new knowledge each day, they should work to maintain that new knowledge plus all the knowledge they learned on previous days. Indeed, remembering during training is a challenge that increases in magnitude each day.

The first threat to newly acquired knowledge is a lack of frequent usage in the past. To address this threat, the learner needs to engage in regular practice of what they have learned. Learners often put off daily studying in favor of "cramming" the night before an evaluation. These learners should be made aware that shorter and regularly spaced study sessions produce memory results that far exceed those obtained from cramming.

A second threat to newly acquired knowledge exists if a learner lacks the degree of understanding that may assist with the recall of that knowledge. Study practices that combine repetition of knowledge along with efforts to increase one's understanding of the knowledge lead to best results. The idea of reading with "study questions" in mind is one that has received much attention by memory researchers.

Experiments have found that not only does answering study questions lead to better memory, but so does the very act of creating study questions. In one experiment in which learners read a text and were then tested on their comprehension, learners who wrote their own study questions and then discarded them unanswered exhibited better recall than learners who simply read the text.

Remembering after Training

Learners should leave the training environment with a sound understanding that a certificate is in no sense a guarantee that they will remember anything that they have learned. It seems that no one is exempt from the process of forgetting. Continued practice of their knowledge and skill is the only means of retaining what they learned, and practice is important after they become certificated pilots and mechanics as it is during their training.

One study of pilots' retention of aeronautical knowledge showed that learners' retention of some topics was superior to that of their own instructors. It seems that the learners' active use and recent rehearsal of these knowledge topics in preparation for knowledge and practical tests outweighed the effects of the more frequent (but less recent) usage on the part of the instructors. This finding nicely demonstrates that an instructor's knowledge is just as vulnerable to forgetting when it has not been recently practiced.

In the same study, the ability of certificated pilots to remember details about regulations was related to the number of months since each pilot's last flight review. This suggests that pilots may take steps to sharpen their knowledge before a flight review and allow it to decay between reviews. Even skills that become automatic during training may not remain automatic after a period of disuse.

Sources of Knowledge

Aviation learners obtain knowledge from a variety of sources while training to be pilots or mechanics. The aviation instructor is the learner's primary source of knowledge, but an instructor also recommends other sources of knowledge. These include books, photographs, videos, diagrams and charts, and other instructional materials. These sources are important for the learner because they allow information to be archived and easily transferred from one person to another. They also allow the reader to self-pace the acquisition of information and permit the reader to pause, think, formulate, and reformulate his or her understanding.

The instructor also encourages the learner to gain experience in the real-world of aviation. These experiences enhance the learner's incidental learning: observation of other pilots or mechanics, thinking about what has been learned, formulation of schemas, and ability to make correlations about what has been learned. Interactive computer-based instruction programs, another excellent source of knowledge, often go hand-in-hand with the flight training syllabus, assuring academics are delivered just-in-time to complement lessons.

Summary of Instructor Actions

To help learners remember what they have learned, the instructor should:

- Discuss the difference between short-term memory and long-term memory.
- Explain the effect of frequent and recent usage of knowledge on remembering and forgetting.
- Explain the effect of depth of understanding on remembering and forgetting.
- Encourage learner use of mnemonic devices while studying.
- Explain the benefits of studying at regularly spaced intervals, and the disadvantages of "cramming."

Chapter Summary

Learning theory has caused instruction to move from basic skills and pure facts to linking new information with prior knowledge, from relying on a single authority to recognizing multiple sources of knowledge, and from novice-like to expert-like problem-solving. While educational theories facilitate learning, no one learning theory is good for all learning situations and all learners. Instruction in aviation should utilize a combination of learning theories.

Aviation Instructor's Handbook (FAA-H-8083-9)
Chapter 4: Effective Communication

Introduction

Carol, a flight instructor, has planned the first tailwheel flight with Jacob, her learner pilot. She begins the preflight briefing with an explanation of the tendency of tailwheel aircraft to yaw in normal takeoff. This yawing tendency gives the illusion that the tailwheel aircraft is unstable during the takeoff. Since this yawing tendency occurs on every takeoff, it is predictable and the pilot is able to compensate for it. Carol then discusses the precession, which causes the noticeable yaw when the tail is raised from a three-point attitude to a level flight attitude. This change of attitude tilts the horizontal axis of the propeller, and the resulting precession produces a forward force on the right side (90° ahead in the direction of rotation), yawing the aircraft's nose to the left. To demonstrate the yawing tendency, she places a model aircraft prop under a desk lamp. *[Figure 4-1]* By moving the prop, the shadow it casts illustrates the pitch change of the propeller when the aircraft is on its tailwheel and when the aircraft is raised to a level flight attitude.

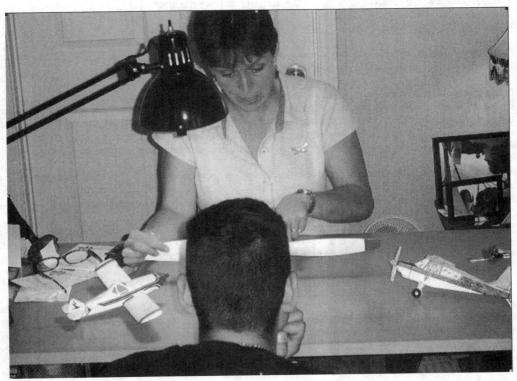

Figure 4-1. *An aviation instructor communicates with her learner using model airplanes to ensure the learner's understanding of the principles discussed.*

Effective communication is an essential element of instruction. An aviation instructor may possess a high level of technical knowledge, but he or she needs to cultivate the ability to communicate effectively in order to share this knowledge with learners. Although communication is a complex process, aviation instructors need to develop a comfortable style of communication that meets the goal of passing on desired information to learners.

Communicating effectively is based on similarity of the idea transmitted by the source and received by the receiver. Similarly, as the source, instructors have communicated effectively if the learner has understood the idea/concept/action transmitted in the manner in which it was intended to be understood.

It is also important to recognize that communication is a two-way process. Each instructor and learner may have a unique communication style, and bridging the gap between these styles is an important aspect of providing instruction. The elements of effective communication, the barriers to communication, and the development of communication skills are discussed in this chapter.

Basic Elements of Communication

Communication takes place when one person transmits ideas or feelings to another person or group of people. The effectiveness of the communication is measured by the similarity between the idea transmitted and the idea received. The process of communication is composed of three elements:

- Source (sender, speaker, writer, encoder, transmitter, or instructor)

- Symbols used in composing and transmitting the message (words or signs [model prop/desk lamp in *Figure 4-1])*

- Receiver (listener, reader, decoder, or learner)

The three elements are dynamically interrelated since each element is dependent on the others for effective communication to take place. The relationship between the source and the receiver is also dynamic and depends on the two-way flow of symbols between the source and the receiver. The source depends on feedback from the receiver to properly tailor the communication to the situation. The source also provides feedback to the receiver to reinforce the desired receiver responses.

Source

As indicated, the source in communication is the sender, speaker, writer, encoder, transmitter, or instructor. The effectiveness of persons acting in the role of communicators is related to at least three basic factors.

First, their ability to select and use language is essential for transmitting symbols that are meaningful to listeners and readers. It is the responsibility of the speaker or writer, as the source of communication, to realize that the effectiveness of the communication is dependent on the receiver's understanding of the symbols or words being used. For example, if an aviation maintenance instructor were to use aviation acronyms like ADs, TCDS or STCs or a flight instructor were to use aviation acronyms like ILS, TCAS, or TAWS with a new maintenance learner or learner pilot respectively, effective communication would be difficult if not impossible.

Second, communicators consciously or unconsciously reveal information about themselves. This includes their self-image, their view of the ideas being communicated, and their feelings toward the receivers. Communicators need to be confident; they should illustrate that the message is important, and that the receivers have a need to know the ideas presented.

Third, successful communicators speak or write from accurate, up-to-date, and stimulating material. Communicators should convey the most current and interesting information available. Doing so holds the receiver's interest. Out-of-date information causes the instructor to lose credibility, and uninteresting information may cause the receiver's attention to be lost.

Symbols

At its basic level, all communication is achieved through symbols, which are simple oral, visual, or tactile codes. The words in the vocabulary constitute a basic code. Common gestures and facial expressions form another, but codes and symbols alone do not communicate complex concepts. These are communicated only when symbols are combined in meaningful wholes as ideas, sentences, paragraphs, speeches, or chapters that mean something to the receiver. When symbols are combined into these units, each portion becomes important to effective communication.

On a higher level, communication with symbols relies upon different perceptions, sometimes referred to as channels. While many theories have been proposed, one popular theory indicates that the symbols are perceived through one of three sensory channels: visual, auditory, or kinesthetic. As discussed in Chapter 3, visual learners rely on seeing, auditory learners prefer listening and speaking, while kinesthetic learners process and store information through physical experience such as touching, manipulating, using, or doing.

The instructor may gain and retain the learner's attention by using a variety of channels. As an example, instead of telling a learner to adjust the trim, the instructor can move the trim wheel while the learner tries to maintain a given aircraft attitude. The learner experiences by feel that the trim wheel affects the amount of control pressure needed to maintain the attitude. At the same time, the instructor can explain to the learner that what is felt is forward or back pressure on the controls. After that, the learner begins to understand the correct meaning of control pressure and trim, and when told to adjust the trim to relieve control pressure, the learner responds in the manner desired by the instructor. Instructors commonly rely on the hearing and seeing channels of communication. However, using all channels may improve the learning process. For teaching motor skills, the sense of touch, or kinesthetic learning, is added as the learner practices the skill.

An instructor should constantly monitor feedback from the learner in order to identify misunderstandings and tailor the presentation of information. Periodically asking the learner to explain his or her understanding of new information while it is being conveyed is one way to obtain such feedback. The instructor may then modify the symbols he or she uses, as appropriate, to optimize communication. *[Figure 4-2]* In addition to feedback received by the instructor, learners also need feedback from the instructor on how they are doing. The feedback not only informs the learners of their performance, but can also serve as a valuable source of motivation. An instructor's praise builds the learner's self-confidence and reinforces favorable behavior. On the other hand, negative feedback should be used carefully. To avoid embarrassing a learner, use negative feedback only in private. This information should be delivered as a description of actual performance and given in a nonjudgmental manner.

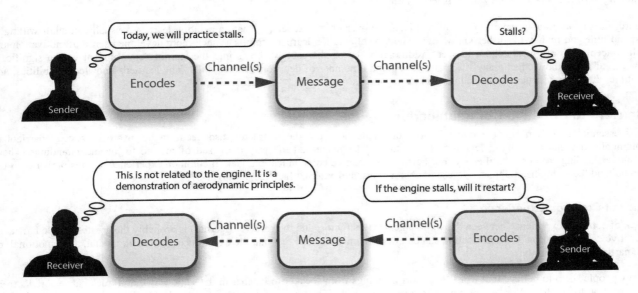

Figure 4-2. *The instructor realizes from the response of the learner that "stall" has been interpreted by the learner to have something to do with the engine quitting. Recognizing that the learner has misunderstood, the instructor is able to clarify the information and help the learner to obtain the desired outcome.*

For example, it would be appropriate to tell a maintenance learner that a safety wire installation is not satisfactory. To refer to the work as careless would not be good and could do harm to the learner's feeling of self-worth.

The parts of the total idea should be analyzed to determine which are most suited to starting or ending the communication, and which are best for the purpose of explaining, clarifying, or emphasizing. All of these functions are required for effective transmission of ideas. The process finally culminates in the determination of the medium best suited for their transmission.

Receiver

The receiver is the listener, reader, decoder, or learner—the individual or individuals to whom the message is directed. Effective communicators should always keep in mind that communication succeeds only in relation to the reaction of their receivers. When the receiver reacts with understanding and changes his or her behavior according to the intent of the source, effective communication has taken place.

In order to understand the process of communication, three characteristics of receivers need to be understood: abilities, attitudes, and experiences.

First, an instructor needs to determine the abilities of the learner in order to properly communicate. One factor that can have an effect on learner ability is his or her background. For example, consider how familiar the learner may be with aviation. The familiarity may range from having grown up around aviation to absolutely no familiarity at all. Some learners may have highly developed motor skills, and others have not had opportunities to develop these skills. These factors should be taken into consideration when presenting information to a learner.

The instructor should also understand that the viewpoint and background of people may vary because of cultural differences. The instructor should be aware of possible differences, but not overreact or make assumptions because of these differences. For example, just because a learner is a college graduate does not guarantee rapid advancement in aviation training. A learner's education certainly affects the instructor's style of presentation, but that style should be based on the evaluation of the learner's knowledge of the aviation subject being taught.

Second, the attitudes learners exhibit may indicate resistance, willingness, or passive neutrality. To gain and hold learner attention, attitudes should be molded into forms that promote reception of information. A varied communicative approach works best in reaching most learners since they have different attitudes.

Third, instructors in aviation enjoy a unique advantage over other teachers, in that an aviation learner is usually an adult willing to expend time and money to further knowledge. The typical aviation learner exhibits a much more developed sense of motivation and self-concept than a typical school learner. Additionally, he or she usually comes into the learning environment with a significant amount of prior knowledge, many life experiences, and a number of decision-making skills. The learner's knowledge, abilities, and attitudes affect the instructor's communication strategy.

Barriers to Effective Communication

It is essential to understand the dynamics of communication, but the instructor also needs to be aware of several barriers to communication that can inhibit learning. The nature of language and the way it is used often lead to misunderstandings. These misunderstandings can be identified by four barriers to effective communication: lack of common experience, confusion between the symbol and the symbolized object, overuse of abstractions, and external factors. *[Figure 4-3]*

Lack of Common Experience

Lack of common experience between the communicator (instructor) and the receiver (learner) is probably the greatest single barrier to effective communication. Communication can be effective only to the extent that the experiences (physical, mental, and emotional) of the participants are similar.

Many people seem to believe that words transport meanings from speaker to listener in the same way that a truck carries bricks from one location to another. Words, however, rarely carry precisely the same meaning from the mind of the instructor to the mind of the learner. In fact, words, in themselves, do not transfer meanings at all. Whether spoken or written, words are merely stimuli used to arouse a response in the learner.

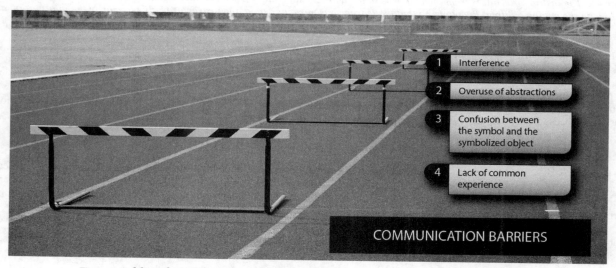

Figure 4-3. *Misunderstandings stem primarily from four barriers to effective communication.*

The learner's past experience with the words and things to which they refer determines how the learner responds to what the instructor says. An instructor's words cannot communicate the desired meaning to another person unless the learner has had some experience with the objects or concepts to which these words refer. Since it is the learners' experience that forms vocabulary, it is also essential that instructors speak the same language as the learners. When the instructor's terminology is necessary to convey the idea, some time needs to be spent making certain the learners understand that terminology.

For example, a maintenance instructor tells a learner to time the magnetos. A learner new to the maintenance field might think a stopwatch or clock would be necessary to do the requested task. Instruction would be necessary for the learner to understand that the procedure has nothing to do with the usual concept of time.

The English language abounds in words that mean different things to different people. To a farmer, the word "tractor" means the machine that pulls the implements to cultivate the soil; to a trucker, it is the vehicle used to pull a semitrailer; in aviation, a tractor propeller is the opposite of a pusher propeller. Each technical field has its own vocabulary. Technical words might mean something entirely different to a person outside that field, or perhaps mean nothing at all. In order for communication to be effective, the learners' understanding of the meaning of the words needs to be the same as the instructor's understanding.

When either the instructor, the learner, or both utilize English as a second language, the instructor notes whether this creates a significant barrier to communication. Except in cases of special accommodation for a medical disability, any learner seeking a pilot certificate or a maintenance learner seeking to become an AMT with operating privileges in the United States demonstrates the ability to communicate in English before certification or exercise of privilege. If reasonable doubt exists as to the ability of an aviation learner to communicate in English at an appropriate level, the instructor should refer to Advisory Circular (AC) 60-28, *FAA English Language Standard for an FAA Certificate Issued Under 14 CFR Parts 61, 63, 65, and 107*, for further guidance.

Confusion Between the Symbol and the Symbolized Object

Confusion between the symbol and the symbolized object results when a word is confused with what it is meant to represent. Although it is obvious that words and the connotations they carry can be different, people sometimes fail to make the distinction. An aviation maintenance technician (AMT) might be introduced as a mechanic. To many people, the term mechanic conjures up images of a person laboring over an automobile. Being referred to as an aircraft mechanic might be an improvement in some people's minds, but neither really portrays the training and skill of the AMT. Words and symbols do not always represent the same thing to every person. To communicate effectively, speakers and writers should account for possible misinterpretation. Words and symbols can then be chosen to represent what the speaker or writer intends.

Overuse of Abstractions

Abstractions are words that are general rather than specific. Concrete words or terms refer to objects people can relate directly to their own experiences. These words or terms specify an idea that can be perceived or a thing that can be visualized. Abstract words, on the other hand, stand for ideas that cannot be directly experienced, things that do not call forth mental images in the minds of the learners. The word aircraft is an abstract word. It does not call to mind a specific aircraft. One learner may visualize an airplane, while another might visualize a helicopter, and still another learner might visualize an airship. *[Figure 4-4]* Although the word airplane is more specific, various learners might envision anything from a Boeing 777 to a Piper Cub.

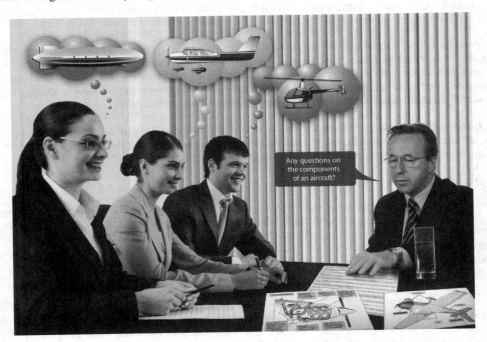

Figure 4-4. *Overuse of abstract terms can interfere with effective communication.*

Aircraft engines represent another example of abstractions. When an instructor refers to aircraft engines in general, some learners might think of jet engines, while others would think of reciprocating engines. Even reciprocating engine is too abstract since it could be a radial engine, an inline engine, a V-type engine, or an opposed type engine. Use of the technical language of engines, as in Lycoming IO-360, would narrow the engine type, but would only be understood by learners who understand the terminology particular to aircraft engines.

Abstractions should be avoided in most cases, but there are times when abstractions are necessary and useful. Aerodynamics is applicable to all aircraft and is an example of an abstraction that can lead to understanding aircraft flight characteristics. The danger of abstractions is that they do not evoke the same specific items of experience in the minds of the learners that the instructor intends. When such terms are used, they should be linked with specific experiences through examples and illustrations.

For instance, when an approach to landing is going badly, telling a learner to take appropriate measures might not result in the desired action. It would be better to tell the learner to conduct a go-around since this is an action that has the same meaning. When maintenance learners are being taught to torque the bolts on an engine, it would be better to tell them to torque the bolts in accordance with the maintenance manual for that engine rather than simply to torque the bolts to the proper values. Whenever possible, the level of abstraction should be reduced by using concrete, specific terms. This better defines and gains control of images produced in the minds of the learners.

External Factors

Some barriers to effective communication can be controlled by the instructor. Others are external factors outside of the instructor's control that prevent a process or activity from being carried out properly. These factors may include physiological, environmental, and psychological elements. To communicate effectively, the instructor should consider the effects of these factors and mitigate them where possible.

Physiological external factors include biological conditions such as hearing loss, injury, physical illness, or other congenital condition. These physiological factors may cause learner discomfort and inhibit communication. The instructor should adapt the presentation to allow the learner to feel better about the situation and be more receptive to new ideas. Adaptation could be as simple as putting off a lesson until the learner is over an illness. Another accommodation could be the use of a seat cushion to allow a learner to sit properly in the airplane.

With the advent of more sophisticated technology, multitasking has become a form of physiological external factors. The term multitask comes from a computer's ability to simultaneously execute more than one program or task at a time. Although it now refers to humans performing multiple tasks simultaneously, humans are not computers. Research shows that although human comprehension can handle two simple, low-level cognitive tasks at once, a higher level cognitive task takes brain function and concentration to perform optimally. Adding even a simple activity diminishes the comprehension and recall of both. Research shows that multitasking is just a series of constant micro-interruptions and "stop-go" decisions, all of which tend to reduce mental and motor performance.

Environmental external factors are caused by external physical conditions. One example of this is the noise level found in many light aircraft. Noise not only impairs the communication process, but also can result in long-term damage to hearing. One solution to this problem is the use of headphones and an intercom system. If an intercom system is not available, a good solution is the use of earplugs. It has been shown that in addition to protecting hearing, use of earplugs actually clarifies speaker output. Vibration is another possible example of environmental external factors, applicable to rotary wing aircraft.

A psychological external factor is a product of how the instructor and learner feel at the time the communication process is occurring. If either instructor or learner is not committed to the communication process, communication is impaired. Fear of the situation or mistrust between the instructor and learner disrupts communication and severely inhibits the flow of information.

Interference

Interference occurs when the message gets disrupted, truncated, or added to somewhere in the communication sequence. While the instructor or learner may believe that an intact message has been sent and received, the assumption may be inaccurate. Noise and other factors may distort the message. Psychological factors also interfere with the receipt of a message. Instructors and learners confirm the message and its proper communication when observing the effect of a message. Additional feedback and confirmation reduce potential harmful effects from interference.

Developing Communication Skills

Communication skills need to be developed; they do not occur automatically. The ability to effectively communicate stems from experience. The experience of instructional communication begins with role playing during training to be an instructor, continues during the actual instruction, and is enhanced by additional training.

Role Playing

Role playing is a method of learning in which learners perform a particular role. In role playing, the learner is provided with a general description of a situation and then applies a new skill or knowledge to perform the role. Experience in instructional communication comes from actually doing it and is learned in the beginning by role playing during the instructor's initial training. For example, a flight instructor applicant can fly with a flight instructor who assumes the role of a learner pilot. In this role, the flight instructor can duplicate known learner responses and then critique the applicant's role as instructor. A mentor or supervisor can play the learner AMT for a maintenance instructor applicant.

It is essential for the flight instructor to develop good ground instruction skills, as well as flight instruction skills to prepare learners for what is to transpire in the air. Likewise, the maintenance instructor develops classroom teaching skills to prepare the maintenance learner for practical, hands-on tasks. In both cases, effective communication is necessary to reinforce the skills that have been attempted and to assess or critique the results. This development continues as an instructor progresses in experience. What worked early on might be refined or replaced by some other technique as the instructor gains more experience.

A new instructor is more likely to find a comfortable style of communication in an environment that is not threatening. For a prospective maintenance instructor, this might take the form of conducting a class on welding while under the supervision of a maintenance supervisor; the flight instructor applicant usually flies with a flight instructor who role plays as the learner.

Current Federal Aviation Administration (FAA) training emphasis has moved from a maneuvers-based training standard to what is called scenario-based training (SBT). SBT is a highly effective approach that allows learners to understand, then apply their knowledge as they participate in realistic scenarios. This method of instruction and learning allows learners to move from theory to practical application of skills during their training. Instructor applicants, flight or maintenance, need to think in terms of SBT while they are learners. Not only does it prepare them to react appropriately in the situations they encounter in the workplace, it also helps them as instructors when they are responsible for creating scenarios for their learners.

For example, James (the flight instructor applicant) designs a scenario in which Ray (the flight instructor playing the role of learner) is performing stalls to Airman Certification Standards (ACS). James briefs Ray on the maneuver before the flight, demonstrates the stall, and then talks Ray through the maneuver. Ray pretends to be an anxious learner pilot, replicating reactions he himself has experienced with flight learners. After the flight, James critiques their instruction period. As increased emphasis is placed on SBT, there will be a corresponding increase in the importance of role playing.

Instructional Communication

Instruction has taken place when the instructor explains a particular procedure and subsequently determines that the learner exhibits the desired response. Even so, the instructor can improve communication by adhering to techniques of good communication.

One of the basic principles used in public speaking courses is to encourage participants to make presentations about something they understand. It would not be good if an instructor without a maintenance background tried to teach a course for aviation maintenance. Instructors perform better when speaking of something they know very well and for which they have a high level of confidence.

The instructor should not be afraid to use examples of past experiences to illustrate particular points. When teaching the procedures to be used for transitioning from instrument meteorological conditions (IMC) to visual cues during an approach, it would be helpful to be able to tell the learner about encountering these same conditions. An instructor's personal experiences make instruction more valuable than reading the same information in a textbook. The instructor should be cautioned, however, to exercise restraint with this technique of illustration, as these types of discussions frequently degrade into a "war story" or "there I was" discussion.

The instructor needs some way of determining results, and the method used should be related to the expected outcome. In the case of flight training, the instructor can judge the actual performance of a maneuver. For a maintenance learner, the instructor can judge the level of accomplishment of a maintenance procedure. In both cases, the instructor determines whether the learner has actually received and retained the knowledge or if acceptable performance was a one-time event.

The aviation learner should know how and why something should be done. For example, a maintenance learner may know how to tighten a particular fastener to a specified torque, but it is more important to know that the security and integrity of any fastener depends on proper torque. In this way, the learner would be more likely to torque all fasteners properly in the future. For a flight learner, simply knowing the different airspeeds for takeoffs and landings is not enough. It is essential to know the reasons for different airspeeds in specific situations to fully understand the importance of proper airspeed control. Normally, the instructor determines the level of understanding by use of some type of evaluation. See Chapter 6, Assessment, for more information.

Listening

Instructors should know something about their learners in order to communicate effectively. As discussed earlier, an instructor needs to determine the abilities of the learners and properly communicate, and one way of becoming better acquainted with learners is to be a good listener. Good instructors work to master listening ability and frequently self-evaluate in this area. Instructors can use a number of techniques to become better at listening. *[Figure 4-5]*

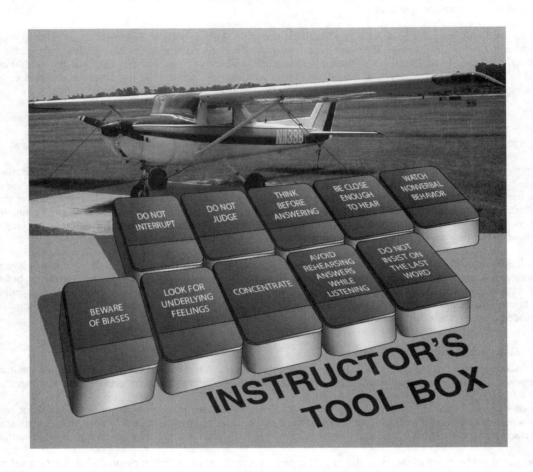

Figure 4-5. *Instructors can use a number of tools to become better at listening.*

Just as it is important for instructors to want to listen in order to be effective listeners, it is necessary for learners to want to listen. Wanting to listen is just one of several techniques that allow a learner to listen effectively. Instructors can improve the percentage of information transfer by teaching learners how to listen. *[Figure 4-6]*

Listening is more than hearing. Most instructors are familiar with the concept that listening is "hearing with comprehension." When the learner hears something being communicated, he or she may or may not comprehend what is being transmitted. On the other hand, when the learner truly hears the communication, he or she then interprets the communication based on their knowledge to that point, processes the information to a level of understanding, and attempts to make a correlation of that communicated information to the task at hand. The increased level of motivation of typical flight and aviation maintenance learners makes this process much easier.

Remind learners that certain emotions interfere with how they listen. For example, an instrument learner pilot anticipating drastic changes in requested routing becomes anxious. In this frame of mind, it is very difficult for the learner to listen and process the new route. If a learner who is terrified of the prospect of spins attempts to listen to a lesson on spins, the emotions felt might overwhelm the attempt to listen. This requires a means to allay the anxiety and fear. If the instructor or learner knows that certain areas arouse emotion, they may consider additional conditioning that prepares the learner to listen.

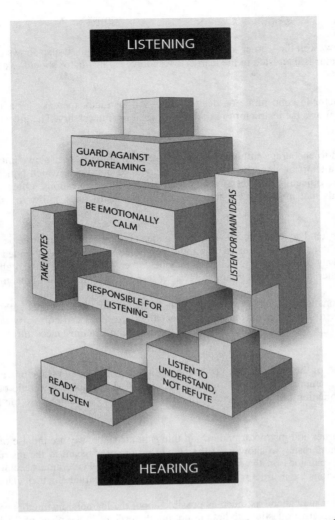

Figure 4-6. *Learners can improve their listening skills by applying the steps to effective listening.*

Listening for main ideas is another listening technique. Primarily a technique for listening to a lecture or formal lesson presentation, it sometimes applies to hands-on situations as well. People who concentrate on remembering or recording facts might very well miss the message because they have not picked up on the big picture. A listener should always ask, what is the purpose of what I am listening to? By doing this, the listener can relate the words to the overall concept.

The instructor should ensure that the learner is aware of the danger of daydreaming. Most people can listen much faster than even the fastest talker can speak. This leaves room for the mind to get off onto some other subject. The listener who is aware of this problem can concentrate on repeating, paraphrasing, or summarizing the speaker's words. Doing so uses the extra time to reinforce the speaker's words, allowing the learner to retain more of the information.

Nobody can remember everything. Note taking allows the learner to use an organized system to reconstruct what was said during the lesson. Every learner has a slightly different system, but no attempt to record the lecture verbatim should be made.

In most cases, a shorthand or abbreviated system of the learner's choosing should be encouraged. Notetaking is merely a method of allowing the learner to recreate the lecture so that it can be studied. The same notetaking skills can be used outside the classroom any time information needs to be retained. For example, copying an instrument clearance word for word is very difficult. By knowing the format of a typical clearance, learner instrument pilots can develop their own system of abbreviations. This allows them to copy the clearance in a useful form for read back and for flying the clearance. By incorporating all or some of these techniques, learners retain more information. Instructors can vastly improve retention of information by making certain their learners have the best possible listening skills.

Questioning

Good questioning can determine how well the learner understands what is being taught. It also shows the learner that the instructor is paying attention and that the instructor is interested in the learner's response. An instructor should ask focused, open-ended questions and avoid closed-ended questions.

Focused questions allow the instructor to concentrate on desired areas. An instructor may ask for additional details, examples, and impressions from the learner. This allows the instructor to ask further questions if necessary. The presentation can then be modified to fit the understanding of the learner.

Open-ended questions are designed to encourage full, meaningful answers using the learner's own knowledge and perceptions while closed-ended questions encourage a short or single-word answer. Open-ended questions, which typically begin with words such as "why" and "how" tend to be more objective and less leading than closed-ended questions. Often open-ended questions are not technically questions, but statements that implicitly ask for completion. An instructor's ability to ask open-ended questions is an important skill to develop.

In contrast, closed-ended questions tend to evaluate the learner's understanding only at the rote level of learning. Closed-ended questions can be answered by "yes" or "no." When used in a multiple choice scenario, closed-ended questions have a finite set of answers from which the respondent chooses. One of the choices may be "other." It is a good idea to allow respondents to write in an optional response if they choose "other" because developing the learner response may lead to insights into the learning process.

One benefit of closed-ended questions is that they are relatively easy to standardize and the data gathered easily lend themselves to statistical analysis. The down side to closed-ended questions is that they are more difficult to write than open-ended questions, generally lead the learner towards the desired answer, and may under certain circumstances direct the conversation toward the instructor's own agenda.

To be effective, questions, regardless of the type, are adapted to the ability, experience, and stage of training of the learner. Effective questions and, therefore, effective communications center on only one idea. A single question should be limited to who, what, when, where, why, or how and not a combination of these. Effective questioning presents a challenge to the learner. Questions of suitable difficulty serve to stimulate learning.

Two ways of confirming that the learner and instructor understand things in the same way are the use of paraphrasing and perception checking. The instructor can use paraphrasing to show what the learner's statement meant to the instructor. In this way, the learner can then make any corrections or expansions on the statement in order to clarify. Perception checking gets to the feelings of the learner, again by stating what perceptions the instructor has of the behavior that the learner can then clarify as necessary.

Since it is important that the instructor understand as much as possible about the learners, instructors can be much more effective by using improved listening skills and effective questions to help in putting themselves in the place of the learners. Questions should be phrased to focus the learner on the decision-making process and the exercise of good judgment.

Knowledge of the subject material and skill at instructional communication are necessary to be an instructor. Increasing the depth of knowledge in either area makes the instructor more effective.

Instructional Enhancement

An instructor never stops learning. While professional development is discussed in greater detail in Chapter 8, the more an instructor knows about a subject, the better the instructor is at conveying that information. For example, a maintenance instructor teaching basic electricity might be able to teach at a minimally satisfactory level if the instructor had only the same training level as that being taught. If asked a question that exceeded the instructor's knowledge, the instructor could research the answer and get back to the learner. It would be much better if the instructor, through experience or additional training, was prepared to answer the question initially. Additional knowledge and training would also bolster the instructor's confidence and give the instructional presentation more depth. Technically qualified instructors, however, consider the level of the learner and present relevant information to enhance understanding or to stimulate the interest of the learner.

Chapter Summary

An awareness of the basic elements of the communicative process (source, symbols, and receiver) is the foundation for a successful communicator. Recognizing the various barriers to communication further enhances the flow of ideas between an instructor and the learner. Instructors develop communications skills in order to convey desired information to the learners. They also recognize that communication is a two-way process. In the end, successful communication has taken place if the desired results have been achieved.

Aviation Instructor's Handbook (FAA-H-8083-9)

Chapter 5: The Teaching Process

Introduction

Bob, an aviation maintenance instructor, arrives thirty minutes before a scheduled class to prepare for the lesson he plans to present that day. A quick visual scan tells him the classroom has good lighting, the desks are in order, and the room presents a neat overall appearance. He places his lecture notes on the podium, checking to make sure they are all there and in the correct order. Then, he turns on the computer to ensure the components are working correctly. A quick run of his visual presentation reassures him this portion of his lecture is ready. Next, he counts the handouts he plans to distribute to the class. By now, learners are beginning to filter into the classroom. With his preparations complete, Bob is free to greet the learners, chat with them socially, or answer any questions they might have about the previous class.

Today's class is Bob's introductory lecture on aircraft weight and balance. Using a software program, he has created a presentation featuring examples of safety problems caused by out-of-balance aircraft. He uses these images to introduce the class to the importance of aircraft weight and balance in safe flying. Then, Bob teaches the class how to compute weight and balance for a generic aircraft. To reinforce the lecture, Bob divides the class into small groups and distributes handouts which contain sample weight and balance problems. Working as a group, the learners solve the first weight and balance problem. During this time, Bob and the learners freely discuss how to figure weight and balance for that particular aircraft. Once the problem is solved, Bob reiterates the steps used to calculate weight and balance. Now Bob assigns another problem to the learners to be solved independently in class. After each learner completes this assignment, Bob is confident they will be able to successfully complete the remaining three weight and balance problems as homework for the next class.

By using a combination of teaching methods and instructional aids, Bob achieves his instructional objective, which is for the learners to compute weight and balance. In order to present this lesson, Bob has taken the theoretical information presented in previous chapters—concepts and principles pertinent to human behavior, how people learn, and effective communication—into the classroom. He has turned this knowledge into practical methodology for teaching purposes. Drawing on previously discussed theoretical knowledge, this chapter discusses specific recommendations on how to teach aviation learners.

What is Teaching?

Teaching is to instruct or train. Teachers often complete some type of formal training, have specialized knowledge, have been certified or validated in some way, and adhere to a set of standards of performance. Defining a "good instructor" has proven more elusive, but in *The Essence of Good Teaching* (1985), psychologist Stanford C. Ericksen wrote "good teachers select and organize worthwhile course material, lead learners to encode and integrate this material in memorable form, ensure competence in the procedures and methods of a discipline, sustain intellectual curiosity, and promote how to learn independently."

Process

The teaching process organizes the material an instructor wishes to teach in such a way that the learner can understand   it. The teaching process consists of four steps: preparation, presentation, application, and assessment. Regardless of the teaching or training delivery method used, the overall sequence remains the same. Much research has been devoted to trying to discover what makes an effective instructor. This research has revealed that effective instructors come in many forms, but they know how to process four essential teaching steps mentioned above. *[Figure 5-1]*

The remainder of this chapter explores the qualities of effective teachers and the methods used for preparing, presenting applying, and assessing lesson material and covers various delivery methods in depth.

Essential Teaching Skills

Four essential skills good teachers have include:

1. People skills
2. Subject matter expertise
3. Assessment skills
4. Management skills

People Skills

Effective instructors relate well to people. Effective communication, discussed in Chapter 4, underlies people skills. It is important for instructors to remember:

- Technical knowledge is useless if the instructor fails to communicate it effectively.

- The two-way process of effective communication includes actively listening to the learner.

Figure 5-1. *Aviation instructors organize course material and use procedures and methods that promote learning.*

In the previous scenario, Bob uses the guided group discussion period to listen to his learners discuss the weight and balance problem. By listening to their discussion and questions, he can pinpoint problem areas and explain them more fully during the review of the solved problem.

People skills also include the ability to interact respectfully, pick up when learners are not following along, provide motivation, and adapt to the needs of the learner when necessary. Another important people skill used by effective instructors is to challenge learners intellectually while supporting their efforts. Effective instructors also display enthusiasm for their subject matter and express themselves clearly.

Subject Matter Expertise

A subject matter expert (SME) is a person who possesses a high level of expertise, knowledge, or skill in a particular area. For example, the instructor in the opening scenario is an aviation maintenance SME.

Effective instructors have a sincere interest in learning and professional growth. There are a number of professional development opportunities for aviation instructors, such as Federal Aviation Administration (FAA) seminars, industry conventions, professional organizations, and online classes. Networking with and observing other instructors and seeking mentoring from an experienced instructor to learn new strategies is also helpful. By being a lifelong learner, the aviation professional remains current in both aviation and education. This topic is explored more thoroughly in the section titled Professional Development found within Chapter 8 of this handbook: Instructor Responsibilities and Professionalism

Management Skills

Management skills generally include the ability to plan, organize, lead, and supervise. For the effective instructor, this translates into being able to plan, organize, and carry out a lesson. A well-planned lesson means the instructor is also practicing time management skills and ensures the time allocated for the lesson is used effectively.

To manage time well, it is important that an instructor plans how to use the time to achieve the lesson goals. This includes time for what needs to be done as well as time to handle the unexpected. It minimizes stress by not planning too much for the allotted time.

Time management also come into play for the aviation instructor who is teaching a class. Consider the opening scenario in which Bob arrived early for the class and ensured the classroom was ready by completing a series of tasks.

Another management skill that enhances the effectiveness of aviation instructors is supervision of the learners. For the flight instructor, this may entail overseeing the preflight procedures. For the maintenance instructor, this may mean monitoring a maintenance procedure. While it is important to provide hands-on tasks in the lesson plan to engage learners, it is also important to ensure the learners complete the tasks correctly.

Assessment Skills

In Chapter 3, The Learning Process, learning was defined as a change in the behavior as a result of experience. The behavior can be physical and overt, or it can be intellectual or attitudinal. This change is measurable and therefore can be assessed.

Assessment of learning is a complex process, and it is important to be clear about the purposes of the assessment. There are several points at which assessments can be made: before training, during training, and after training. Assessment of learning is another important skill of an effective instructor. *[Figure 5-2]* This topic is discussed in detail in Chapter 6, Assessment.

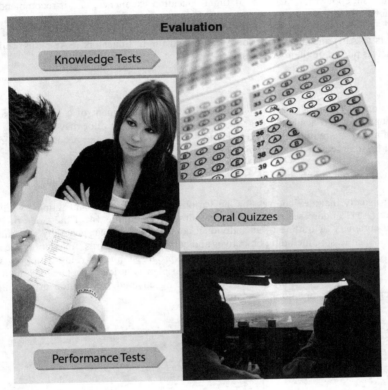

Figure 5-2. *An effective instructor uses a variety of tools to evaluate how learners learn, as well as what they know.*

Instructor's Code of Ethics

While many of the characteristics of effective instructors discussed in the previous paragraphs hold true for any instructor, the aviation instructor has the added responsibility of molding an aviation citizen—a pilot or maintenance technician who will be an asset to the rest of the aviation community. The following code describes the concept of a good aviation citizen.

An aviation instructor needs to remember he or she is teaching a pilot or technician who should:

1. Make safety the number one priority,
2. Develop and exercise good judgment in making decisions,
3. Recognize and manage risk effectively,
4. Be accountable for his or her actions,
5. Act with responsibility and courtesy,
6. Adhere to prudent operating practices and personal operating parameters, and
7. Adhere to applicable laws and regulations.

In addition, an aviation instructor needs to remember he or she is teaching a pilot who should:

1. Seek proficiency in control of the aircraft,
2. Use flight deck technology in a safe and appropriate way,
3. Be confident in a wide variety of flight situations, and
4. Be respectful of the privilege of flight.

These concepts are also part of the Flight Instructors Model Code of Conduct (FIMCC), designed to enhance flight and ground instructor safety and professionalism. Developed by a diverse team of aviation professionals and extensively peer-reviewed within the aviation community, the FIMCC offers a vision of excellence to help flight and ground instructors build professional relationships with their learners.

A formal code of conduct/ethics serves as a tool to promote safety, good judgment, ethical behavior, and personal responsibility—all components of professionalism. The code offers a vision of flight education excellence, and it recommends operating practices to improve the quality and safety of flight instruction. The FIMCC is one of several similar codes that can be found at www.secureav.com. such as the Aviator's Model Code of Conduct and a Student Pilot's Model Code of Conduct. The National Association of Flight Instructors (NAFI) and the Society of Aviation and Flight Educators (SAFE), as well as similar groups, also have a code of ethics for instructors posted on their websites.

Course of Training

In education, a course of training is a complete series of studies leading to attainment of a specific goal. The goal might be a certificate of completion, graduation, or an academic degree. For example, a learner pilot may enroll in a private pilot certificate course, and upon completion of all course requirements, be awarded a graduation certificate. A course of training also may be limited to something like the additional training required for operating high-performance airplanes.

Other terms closely associated with a course of training include curriculum, syllabus, and lesson plan.

A curriculum for pilot training usually includes courses for the various pilot certificates and ratings, while the curriculum for an aviation maintenance technician (AMT) addresses the subject areas described in Title 14 of the Code of Federal Regulations (14 CFR) part 147. A syllabus is a summary or outline of an individual course of study that generally contains multiple lessons. The syllabus contains a description of each lesson, including objectives and completion standards. In aviation, the term "training syllabus" is commonly used and in this context it is a step-by-step, building block progression of learning with provisions for regular review and assessments at prescribed stages of learning. *[Figure 5-3]* A lesson plan is a detailed plan for how a specific lesson will be conducted. It includes the lesson objectives, organization of material being covered, description of teaching aids, instruction and learner actions, and evaluation criteria and completions standards.

Figure 5-3. *The syllabus defines the unit of training, states by objective what the learner is expected to accomplish during the unit of training, shows an organized plan for instruction, and dictates the assessment process for either the unit or stages of learning.*

Preparation of a Lesson

A determination of objectives and standards precedes instruction. Although some schools and independent instructors may develop their own syllabus, in practice, many instructors use a commercially-developed syllabus. For the aviation instructor, the objectives listed in the syllabus are a beginning point for instruction.

Training Objectives and Standards

Aviation training involves two types of objectives: performance-based and decision-based. Performance-based objectives help define exactly what needs to be done and how it is done during each lesson. As the learner progresses through higher levels of performance and understanding, the instructor should shift the training focus to decision-based training objectives. Decision-based training objectives rely on a more dynamic training environment and are ideally suited to scenario-based training and teach aviation learners critical thinking skills, such as risk management and aeronautical decision-making (ADM).

As indicated in Chapter 3, The Learning Process, training objectives apply to all three domains of learning—cognitive (knowledge), affective (attitudes, beliefs, values), and psychomotor (physical skills). Objectives should incorporate the desired level of learning, and these level of learning objectives may apply to one or more of the three domains of learning. Since each domain includes several educational or skill levels, the instructor adapts training objectives to a specific performance level of knowledge or skill. Clearly defined training objectives that the learner understands are essential to the teaching process regardless of the teaching technique used.

Standards are closely tied to objectives since they include a description of the desired knowledge, behavior, or skill stated in specific terms, along with conditions and criteria. When a learner performs according to well-defined standards, evidence of learning is apparent. Standards should contain comprehensive examples of the desired learning outcomes, or behaviors. As indicated in Chapter 3, The Learning Process, standards for the level of learning in the cognitive and psychomotor domains are easily established. However, the design of standards to evaluate a learner's level of understanding or overt behavior in the affective domain (attitudes, beliefs, and values) is more difficult.

The overall objective of an aviation training course is usually well established, and the general standards are included in various rules and related publications. For example, eligibility, knowledge, proficiency, and experience requirements for pilots and AMT learners are stipulated in the regulations, and the standards are published in the applicable Airman Certification Standards (ACS)/Practical Test Standards (PTS) or oral and practical tests (O&Ps). It should be noted that ACS/PTS and O&P standards are limited to the most critical job tasks. Certification tests do not represent an entire training syllabus.

A broad, overall objective of any pilot training course is to qualify the learner to be a competent, efficient, safe pilot for the operation of specific aircraft types under stated conditions. Similar objectives and standards are established for AMT learners. While the established criteria or standards to determine whether the training has been adequate use the 14 CFR certification requirements, professional instructors should not limit their objectives to meeting the minimum published requirements for pilot or AMT certification.

Successful instructors teach their learners not only how, but also why and when. By incorporating ADM and risk management into each lesson, the aviation instructor helps the learner understand, develop, and reinforce the decision-making process which ultimately leads to sound judgment and good decision-making skills.

Performance-Based Objectives

Performance-based objectives set measurable, reasonable standards describing the learner's desired performance, and may be referred to as a behavioral, performance, instructional, or educational objective. All refer to the same thing, the behavior of the learner.

These objectives provide a way of stating the level of performance a learner needs to demonstrate before he or she progresses to the next stage of instruction. Again, the objectives should be clear, measurable, and repeatable and mean the same thing to any knowledgeable reader. The objectives should be written to avoid the fallibility of recall, interpretation, or loss of specificity with time.

Performance-based objectives consist of three elements: description of the skill or behavior, the conditions, and the criteria. Each part should be stated in a way that leaves every reader with the same picture of the objective, how it is performed, and at the level of performance. *[Figure 5-4]*

Description of the Skill or Behavior

The description of the skill or behavior explains the desired outcome of the instruction as a change in knowledge, skill, or attitude. The skill or behavior should be in concrete and measurable terms. Phrases such as "knowledge of ..." and "awareness of ..." cannot be measured very well and should be avoided. Phrases like "able to select from a list of ..." or "able to repeat the steps to ..." are better because they describe something measurable.

Figure 5-4. *Performance-based objectives are made up of a description of the skill or behavior, conditions, and criteria.*

Conditions

Conditions explain the rules for demonstration of the skill. If the desired objective is to navigate from point A to point B, the objective, as stated, is not specific enough for all learners to do it in the same way. Information such as equipment, tools, reference material, and limiting parameters should be included. For example, inserting several conditions narrows the objective as follows: "Using appropriate charts, a prepared flight log, and training aircraft, navigate from point A to point B while maintaining standard hemispheric altitudes." Sometimes, in the process of reading the objective, someone might say, "But, what if ...?" This is a good indication that the conditions are confusing and need clarification.

Criteria

Criteria are the standards that measure the accomplishment of the objective. Good criteria define performance so there can be no question whether or not the performance meets the objective. In the previous example, the criteria may include that navigation from point A to point B be accomplished within 5 minutes of the preplanned flight time and that en route altitude be maintained within 200 feet. The revised performance-based objective may now also include arrival at point B within 5 minutes of planned arrival time and cruise altitude should be maintained within 200 feet during the en route phase of the flight." The alert reader has already noted that the conditions and criteria changed slightly during the development of these objectives. In real-world objective development, that is exactly the way it will occur. Conditions and criteria may be refined as necessary.

The Importance of the ACS in Aviation Training Curricula

ACS documents hold an important position in aviation training curricula because they supply the instructor with specific performance objectives based on the standards for the issuance of a particular aviation certificate or rating. *[Figure 5-5]* The FAA frequently reviews the ACS test Areas of Operation and Tasks to maintain their relevance to the current aviation environment. Test items included as part of a test or evaluation should be both content valid and criterion valid. Content validity means that a particular maneuver or procedure closely mimics what is required in actual flying. Criterion validity means that the completion standards for the test are reflective of acceptable standards.

For example, in flight training, content validity is reflected by a particular maneuver closely mimicking a maneuver required in actual flight, such as the learner pilot being able to recover from a power-off stall. Criterion validity means that the completion standards for the test are reflective of acceptable standards in actual flight. Thus, the learner pilot exhibits knowledge of all the elements involved in a power-off stall as listed in the ACS.

Figure 5-5. *Examples of Airman Certification Standards.*

As discussed in Chapter 3, The Learning Process, humans develop cognitive skills through active interaction with the world. This concept has led to the adoption of scenario-based training in many fields, including aviation. An effective aviation instructor uses the maneuver-based approach of the ACS but presents the objectives in a scenario situation.

It has been found that flight learners using SBT methods demonstrate flying skills equal to or better than those trained under the maneuver-based approach only. Of even more significance is that the same data also suggest that SBT learners demonstrate better decision-making skills than maneuver-based learners—most likely because their training occurred while performing realistic flight maneuvers and not artificial maneuvers designed only for teaching that maneuver.

The incorporation of SBT as part of the lesson is discussed in more detail later in this chapter, as well as in Chapter 7, Planning Instructional Activity.

Decision-Based Objectives

The design and use of decision-based objectives specifically develops pilot judgment and ADM skills. Improper pilot decisions cause a significant percentage of all accidents, and the majority of fatal accidents in aircraft. Decision-based objectives facilitate a higher level of learning and application. By using dynamic and meaningful scenarios, the instructor teaches the learner how to gather information and make informed, safe, and timely decisions.

Decision-based training is not a new concept. Experienced instructors have been using scenarios that require dynamic problem solving to teach cross-country operations, emergency procedures, and other flight skills for years.

Decision-based learning objectives and the use of flight training scenarios do not preclude traditional maneuver-based training. Rather, flight maneuvers are integrated into the flight training scenarios and conducted as they would occur in the real-world. Those maneuvers requiring repetition may still be taught during concentrated settings. However, once they are learned, they are integrated into realistic and dynamic flight situations.

Decision-based objectives are also important for the aviation instructor planning AMT training. An AMT uses ADM and risk management skills during the repair and maintenance of aircraft.

Other Uses of Training Objectives

Performance-based and decision-based objectives help an instructor design a complete lesson plan. An instructor can use the standards of assessment, objectives, conditions, and criteria to fashion many of the details on the lesson plan. For example, many of the objective components may be used to determine the elements of the lesson and the schedule of events. The equipment necessary and the instructor and learner actions anticipated during the lesson have also been specified. By listing the criteria for the training objectives, the instructor has already established the completion standards normally included as part of the lesson plan.

Use of training objectives also provides the learner with a better understanding of the big picture, as well as knowledge of what is expected. This overview can alleviate a significant source of uncertainty and frustration on the part of the learner.

Presentation of a Lesson

How does an instructor keep the attention of a class? The steps in *Figure 5-6* form a guideline for lesson presentation. Many of them can be combined during the actual presentation. For example, consider a video presentation given during the weight and balance lecture. The video adds a multimedia element to the lecture, is a good attention getter, and can visually demonstrate the learning objective.

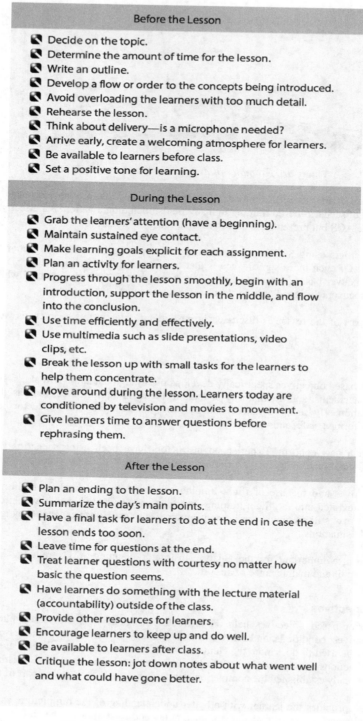

Before the Lesson

- Decide on the topic.
- Determine the amount of time for the lesson.
- Write an outline.
- Develop a flow or order to the concepts being introduced.
- Avoid overloading the learners with too much detail.
- Rehearse the lesson.
- Think about delivery—is a microphone needed?
- Arrive early, create a welcoming atmosphere for learners.
- Be available to learners before class.
- Set a positive tone for learning.

During the Lesson

- Grab the learners' attention (have a beginning).
- Maintain sustained eye contact.
- Make learning goals explicit for each assignment.
- Plan an activity for learners.
- Progress through the lesson smoothly, begin with an introduction, support the lesson in the middle, and flow into the conclusion.
- Use time efficiently and effectively.
- Use multimedia such as slide presentations, video clips, etc.
- Break the lesson up with small tasks for the learners to help them concentrate.
- Move around during the lesson. Learners today are conditioned by television and movies to movement.
- Give learners time to answer questions before rephrasing them.

After the Lesson

- Plan an ending to the lesson.
- Summarize the day's main points.
- Have a final task for learners to do at the end in case the lesson ends too soon.
- Leave time for questions at the end.
- Treat learner questions with courtesy no matter how basic the question seems.
- Have learners do something with the lecture material (accountability) outside of the class.
- Provide other resources for learners.
- Encourage learners to keep up and do well.
- Be available to learners after class.
- Critique the lesson: jot down notes about what went well and what could have gone better.

Figure 5-6. *Guidelines for presenting lessons.*

Organization of Material

After determining objectives and standards, an instructor formulates a plan of action to lead learners through the course in a logical manner toward the desired goal. Usually, the goal for learners is a certificate or rating. It could be a private pilot certificate, an instrument rating, an AMT certificate or, other rating. In all cases, a systematic plan of action requires the use of an appropriate training syllabus. Generally, the syllabus contains a description of each lesson, including objectives and completion standards.

The main concern of the instructor is usually organizing a block of training with integrated lesson plans. The traditional organization of a lesson plan is introduction, development, and conclusion.

Lesson Introduction

The introduction sets the stage for everything to come. Efforts in this area pay great dividends in terms of quality of instruction. In brief, the introduction is made up of three elements: attention, motivation, and an overview.

Attention

The purpose of the attention element is to focus each learner's attention on the lesson. The instructor begins by telling a story, showing a video clip, asking a question, or telling a joke. Any of these may be appropriate at one time or another. Regardless of which is used, it should relate to the subject and establish a background for developing the learning outcomes. Telling a story or a joke unrelated in some way to the subject distracts from the lesson. The main concern is to focus everyone's attention on the subject. *[Figure 5-7]*

Figure 5-7. *The attention element causes learners to focus on the upcoming lesson.*

Motivation

The motivation element offers the learners specific reasons why the lesson content is important to know, understand, apply, or perform and thus ensures readiness (Thorndike's Law of Readiness). The instructor may provide examples where someone applied the knowledge or remind the learners of an upcoming assessment. The motivation should appeal to each learner personally and engender a desire to understand the material.

Overview

Every lesson introduction should contain an overview that tells the group what is to be covered during the period. A clear, concise presentation of the objective and the key ideas gives the learners a road map of the route to be followed. A good visual aid can help the instructor show the learners the path that they are to travel.

Development

Development is the main part of the lesson. Here, the instructor develops the subject matter in a manner that helps the learners achieve the desired outcomes. The instructor organizes the material logically to show the relationships of the main points. The instructor may show these primary relationships by developing the main points in one of the following ways: from past to present, simple to complex, known to unknown, and most frequently used to least used.

Past to Present

In this pattern of development, the subject matter is arranged chronologically, from the present to the past or from the past to the present. Time relationships are most suitable when history is an important consideration, as in tracing the development of radio navigation systems.

Simple-to-Complex

The simple-to-complex pattern helps the instructor lead the learner from simple facts or ideas to an understanding of the phenomena or concepts involved. When beginning a study of jet propulsion the learner might start by considering the forces involved when releasing air from a toy balloon and finish by taking part in a discussion of a complex gas turbine engine.

Do not be afraid to omit less important information at first in order to simplify the learning process. If Class D, E, and G airspace are the only airspace types being utilized by a learner, save the discussion of A, B, and C airspace until they have operating familiarity with the other types. Less information at first is easier to absorb.

Known to Unknown

By using something the learner already knows as the point of departure, the instructor can lead into new ideas and concepts. For example, when developing a lesson on heading indicators, the instructor could begin with a discussion of the magnetic compass before proceeding to a description of gyroscopic indicators.

Most Frequently Used to Least Used

In some subjects, certain information or concepts are common to all who use the material. This fourth organizational pattern starts with common usage before progressing to the rarer ones. Even though some aircraft are equipped with a computerized navigational system, instructors should begin by teaching learners the basics of navigation since all pilots use the basic skills.

Under each main point in a lesson, the subordinate points should lead naturally from one to another. With this arrangement, each point leads logically to and serves as a reminder of the next. Meaningful transition from one main point to another keeps the learners oriented, aware of where they have been, and where they are going. This permits learners to sort or categorize information in their working or short-term memory and allows them to process and remember what they have been taught.

Conclusion

An effective conclusion retraces the important elements of the lesson and relates them to the objective. This review and wrap-up of ideas reinforces learning and improves retention. New ideas should not be introduced in the conclusion because they are likely to confuse the learners

By organizing the lesson material into a logical format, the instructor maximizes the opportunity for learners to retain the desired information. Since each teaching situation is unique, the setting and purpose of the lesson determines which teaching method is used.

Training Delivery Methods

Today's instructor can choose from a wealth of ways to present instructional material: lecture, discussion, guided discussion, problem based, group learning, demonstration-performance, or e-learning. In a typical lesson, an effective instructor normally uses a combination of methods. The instructor determines which teaching method best conveys the information and when to use it. For example, Bob lectures in the opening scenario, but after teaching how to compute weight and balance, he uses group learning to reinforce the lecture.

Lecture Method

In the lecture method, the instructor delivers knowledge via lectures to learners who are more or less silent participants. Lectures are best used when an instructor wishes to convey a general understanding of a subject. In general, lectures begin with an introduction of the topic to be discussed. The body of the lecture follows with a summary of the lecture's main points at the end.

Lectures may introduce new subjects, summarize ideas, show relationships between theory and practice, and reemphasize main points. Thus, the lecture method is adaptable to many different settings, including small or large groups. Finally, lectures may be combined with other teaching methods to give added meaning and direction.

There are different varieties of lectures. During the illustrated talk, the speaker relies heavily on visual aids to convey ideas to the listeners. When using a briefing, the speaker presents a concise array of facts to the listeners who normally do not expect elaboration of supporting material. During a formal lecture, the speaker's purpose is to inform, to persuade, or to entertain with little or no verbal participation by the learners. When using a teaching lecture, the instructor plans and delivers an oral presentation in a manner that allows some participation by the learners and helps direct them toward the desired learning outcomes.

Teaching Lecture

The teaching lecture is favored by aviation instructors because it allows some active participation by the learners. In other methods of teaching such as demonstration-performance or guided discussion, the instructor receives direct reaction from the learners, either verbally or by some form of body language. However in the teaching lecture, the feedback is not nearly as obvious and is much harder to interpret. An effective instructor develops a keen perception for subtle responses from the class—facial expressions, manner of taking notes, and apparent interest or disinterest in the lesson. The effective instructor is able to interpret the meaning of these reactions and adjust the lesson accordingly.

Preparing the Teaching Lecture

The following four steps should be followed in the planning phase of preparation:

1. Establishing the objective and desired outcomes
2. Researching the subject
3. Organizing the material
4. Planning productive classroom activities

While developing the lesson, the instructor also should strongly consider the use of examples and personal experiences related to the subject of the lesson. The instructor may support any point with meaningful examples, comparisons, statistics, or testimony.

After completing the preliminary planning and writing of the lesson plan, the instructor should rehearse the lecture to build self-confidence. Rehearsals, or dry runs, help smooth out the mechanics of using notes, visual aids, and other instructional devices. If possible, the instructor should have another knowledgeable person or another instructor observe the practice sessions and act as a critic. This critique helps the instructor judge the adequacy of supporting materials and visual aids, as well as the overall presentation. [Figure 5-8]

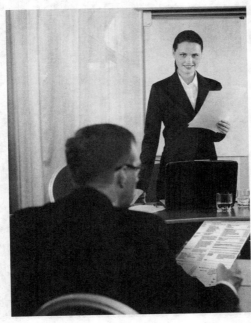

Figure 5-8. *Instructors should try a dry run with another instructor to get a feel for the lecture presentation.*

Suitable Language

In the teaching lecture, simple rather than complex words should be used whenever possible. The instructor should not, use substandard English or errors in grammar.

If the subject matter includes technical terms, the instructor should clearly define each one so that no learner is in doubt about its meaning. Whenever possible, the instructor should use specific rather than general words. For example, the specific words, "a leak in the fuel line" tell more than the general term "discrepancy."

Another way the instructor can add life to the lecture is to vary his or her tone of voice and pace of speaking. In addition, using sentences of different length helps, since consistent use of short sentences results in a choppy style. On the other hand, poorly constructed long sentences are difficult to follow and can easily become tangled. To ensure clarity and variety, the instructor should normally use sentences of short and medium length.

Types of Delivery

A good teaching lecture utilizes an extemporaneous technique. The instructor speaks from a mental or written outline, but does not read or memorize the material to be presented. Because the exact words to express an idea are spontaneous, the lecture is more personalized than one that is read or spoken from memory.

If the instructor realizes from puzzled expressions that a number of learners fail to grasp an idea, that point can be further elaborated until the reactions indicate they understand. The extemporaneous presentation reflects the instructor's personal enthusiasm and is more flexible than other methods. For these reasons, it is likely to hold the interest of the learners.

Notes used wisely can ensure accuracy, jog the memory, and dispel the fear of forgetting. They are essential for   reporting complicated information, and they may help keep the lecture on track. The instructor who requires notes should use them sparingly and unobtrusively but at the same time should make no effort to hide them from the learners. *[Figure 5-9]*

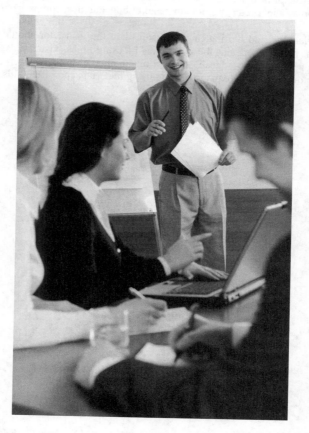

Figure 5-9. *Notes allow the accurate dissemination of complicated information.*

An informal lecture includes active learner participation. Learning is best achieved if learners participate actively in a friendly, relaxed atmosphere. The use of questions achieves active learner participation. In this way, the learners are encouraged to make contributions that supplement the lecture. However, it is the instructor's responsibility to plan, organize, develop, and present the major portion of a lesson.

Advantages and Disadvantages of the Lecture

A lecture is a convenient way to instruct large groups. If necessary, a public address system can be used to amplify the speaker's voice. Lectures can be used to present information that would be difficult for the learners to get in other ways, particularly if they do not have the time required for research, or if they do not have access to reference material. Lectures supplement other teaching devices and methods. A brief introductory lecture can give direction and purpose to a demonstration or prepare learners for a discussion by telling them something about the subject matter to be covered.

In a lecture, the instructor can present many ideas in a relatively short time. Logically organized tasks and ideas can be presented concisely and in rapid sequence.

The lecture is particularly suitable for explaining any necessary background information. By using a lecture in this way, the instructor can offer learners with varied backgrounds a common understanding of essential principles and facts. However, lectures do not allow an instructor a precise measure of learner understanding of the material covered.

To achieve desired learning outcomes through the lecture method, an instructor needs considerable skill in speaking. As indicated in Chapter 3, The Learning Process, a learner's rate of retention drops off significantly after the first 10-15 minutes of a lecture and improves at the end. Research has shown that learning is an active process—the more involved learners are in the process, the more they retain.

The lecture does not foster attainment of certain types of learning outcomes, such as motor skills, which need to be perfected via hands-on practice. Thus, an instructor who introduces some form of active learner participation in the middle of a lecture greatly increases retention.

Discussion Method

The discussion method modifies the pure lecture form by using lecture and then discussion to actively integrate the learner into the process. In the discussion method, the instructor provides a short lecture, which gives basic knowledge to the learners. This short lecture is followed by instructor-learner and learner- learner discussion.

This method relies on discussion and the exchange of ideas. Everyone has the opportunity to comment, listen, think, and participate. By being actively engaged in discussing the lecture, learners improve their recall and ability to use the information.

It is important for the instructor to keep the discussion focused on the subject matter. The instructor may need to initiate leading questions, comment on any disagreements, ensure that all learners participate, and summarize what has been learned.

Tying the discussion method into the lecture method not only provides active participation, it also allows learners to develop higher order thinking skills (HOTS). The give and take of the discussion method also helps learners evaluate ideas, concepts, and principles. When using this method, instructors should keep their own discussion to a minimum since the goal is learner participation.

Guided Discussion Method

Instructors can also use another form of discussion, the guided discussion method, to ensure the learner has correctly received and interpreted subject information. The learner needs a level of knowledge about the topic to be discussed, either through reading prior to class or a short lecture to set up the topic to be discussed. This training method employs instructor-guided discussion with the instructor maintains control of the discussion. It can be used during classroom periods and preflight and postflight briefings. The discussions reflect whatever level of knowledge and experience the learners have gained.

The goal of guided discussions is to draw out the knowledge of the learner. The greater the participation becomes, the more effective the learning will be. All members of the group should follow the discussion. The instructor should treat everyone impartially, encourage questions, exercise patience and tact, and comment on all responses with the goal of reinforcing a learning objective related to the lesson. The instructor acts as a facilitator to encourage discussion between learners without sarcasm.

Use of Questions in a Guided Discussion

In the guided discussion, learning is achieved through the skillful use of questions. Questions can be categorized by function and characteristics.

The instructor often uses a lead-off question to open up an area for discussion. After the discussion develops, the instructor may ask a follow-up question to guide the discussion. The reasons for using a follow-up question may vary. The instructor may want a learner to explain something more thoroughly, or may need to bring the discussion back to a point from which it has strayed. An instructor may answer a question with a question and direct that question back to the person posing the question or other participant.

Questions are so much a part of teaching that they are often taken for granted. Effective use of questions may result in more learning than any other single technique used by instructors. Instructors should avoid questions that can be answered by short factual statements or yes or no responses and ask open-ended questions that are thought provoking and require more mental activity. Since most aviation training is at the understanding level or higher, questions should require learners to grasp concepts, explain similarities and differences, and to infer cause-and-effect relationships. *[Figure 5-10]*

Characteristics of an Effective Question

- Applies to the subject of instruction
- Is brief and concise, but also clear and definite
- Is adapted to the learners' ability, experience, and stage of training
- Centers on only one idea
- Presents a challenge to the learners

Figure 5-10. *If the objectives of a lesson are clearly established in advance, instructors will find it much easier to ask appropriate questions that keep the discussion moving in the planned direction.*

Planning a Guided Discussion

Planning a guided discussion is similar to planning a lecture. (Note that the following suggestions include many that are appropriate for planning cooperative learning, to be discussed later in the chapter.)

- Select an appropriate topic. Unless the learners have some knowledge to exchange with each other, they cannot reach the desired learning outcomes. If necessary, make assignments that give the learners an adequate background for discussing the lesson topic.

- State the specific lesson objective at the understanding level of learning. Through discussion, the learners develop an understanding of the subject by sharing knowledge, experiences, and backgrounds. The desired learning outcomes should stem from the objective.

- Conduct adequate research to become familiar with the topic. The instructor should always be alert for ideas that will enhance a lesson for a particular group of learners. Similarly, the instructor can consider any prediscussion assignment while conducting research for the classroom period. During this research process, the instructor should also earmark reading material that appears to be appropriate as background material for learners. Such material should be well organized and based on fundamentals.

- Organize the main and subordinate points of the lesson in a logical sequence. The guided discussion has three main parts: introduction, discussion, and conclusion. The introduction consists of three elements: attention, motivation, and overview. During the discussion, the instructor should be certain that the main points discussed build logically with the objective. The conclusion consists of the summary of the main points. By organizing in this manner, the instructor phrases the questions to help the learners obtain a firm grasp of the subject matter and to minimize the possibility of a rambling discussion.

- Plan at least one lead-off question for each desired learning outcome. While preparing questions, the instructor should remember that the purpose is to stimulate discussion, not merely to get answers. Lead-off questions should usually begin with how or why. For example, it is better to ask "Why does an aircraft normally require a longer takeoff run at Denver than at New Orleans?" instead of "Would you expect an aircraft to require a longer takeoff run at Denver or at New Orleans?" Learners can answer the second question by merely saying "Denver," but the first question is likely to start a discussion of air density, engine efficiency, and the effect of temperature on performance.

Learner Preparation for a Guided Discussion

It is the instructor's responsibility to help learners prepare themselves for the discussion. Each learner should be encouraged to accept responsibility for contributing to the discussion and benefiting from it. Throughout the time the instructor prepares the learners for their discussion, they should be made aware of the lesson objective(s). In certain instances, the instructor has no opportunity to assign preliminary work. In such cases, it is practical and advisable to give the learners a brief general survey of the topic during the introduction. Normally, learners should not be asked to discuss a subject without some background in that subject.

Guiding a Discussion—Instructor Technique

The techniques used to guide a discussion require practice and experience. The instructor needs to keep up with the discussion and know when to intervene with questions or redirect the group's focus. The following information provides a framework for successfully conducting the guided discussion.

Introduction

The introduction should include an attention element, a motivation element, and an overview of key points. To encourage enthusiasm and stimulate discussion, the instructor should create a relaxed, informal atmosphere. Each learner should be given the opportunity to discuss the various aspects of the subject, and feel free to do so. Moreover, the learner should feel a personal responsibility to contribute. The instructor should try to make the learners feel that their ideas and active participation are wanted and needed.

Discussion

The instructor opens the discussion by asking one of the prepared lead-off questions. Discussion questions should be easy for learners to understand and put forth decisively. While the instructor should have the answer in mind before asking the question, the learners need to think about the question before answering. It takes time for learners to recall data, determine how to answer, or to think of an example.

The more difficult the question, the more time the learners need to answer. If the instructor sees puzzled expressions, denoting that the learners do not understand the question, it should be rephrased in a slightly different form. The nature of the questions should be determined by the lesson objective and desired learning outcomes.

Once the discussion is underway, the instructor should listen attentively to the ideas, experiences, and examples contributed by the learners during the discussion. Remember that during the preparation, the instructor listed some of the anticipated responses that would, if discussed by the learners, indicate that they had a firm grasp of the subject. By using "how" and "why" follow- up questions, the instructor should be able to guide the discussion toward the objective of helping learners understand the subject.

After the learners discuss the ideas that support this particular part of the lesson, the instructor should summarize what they have accomplished using an interim summary. This usually occurs after the discussion of each learning outcome to bring ideas together and help in transition, showing how the discussion by the group related to and supported the objective. An interim summary reinforces learning in relation to a specific learning outcome. The interim summary may also be used to keep the group on the subject or to divert the discussion to another member.

Conclusion

A guided discussion closes by summarizing the material covered. The instructor ties together the various points or topics discussed, and shows the relationships between the facts brought forth and the practical application of these facts. For example, while concluding a discussion on density altitude, an instructor might describe an accident, which occurred due to a pilot attempting to take off at a high-altitude airport with a fully loaded aircraft on a hot day.

The summary should be succinct, but not incomplete. If the discussion has revealed that certain areas are not understood by one or more members of the group, the instructor should clarify or cover this material again.

Advantages

Training methods involving discussion encourage learners to listen to and learn from their instructor and each other. Open-ended questions during guided discussion leads to concepts of risk management and ADM. The use of "What If?" during the discussion calls for high order thinking skills and exposes the learner to the decision-making process.

From the description of guided discussion, it is obvious this method works well in a group situation, but it can be modified for an interactive one-on-one learning situation. *[Figure 5-11]*

Figure 5-11. *As the learner grows in flight knowledge, he or she should be able to lead the postflight review while the instructor guides the discussion with targeted questions.*

Problem-Based Learning

In 1966, the McMaster University School of Medicine in Canada pioneered a new approach to teaching and curriculum design called problem-based learning (PBL). In the intervening years, PBL has helped shift the focus of learning from an instructor-centered approach to a learner-centered approach. There are many definitions for PBL, but this handbook defines it as a learning environment where lessons involve learners with problems encountered in real life and that ask them to find real-world solutions.

PBL starts with a carefully constructed problem to which there is no single solution. The benefit of PBL lies in helping the learner gain a deeper understanding of the information and in improving his or her ability to recall the information.

When presenting material as an authentic problem in a situated environment, the learner may "make meaning" of the information based on past experience and personal interpretation. This problem type encourages the development of HOTS, which include cognitive processes such as problem solving and decision-making, as well as the cognitive skills of analysis, synthesis and evaluation.

Developing good problems that motivate, focus, and initiate learning are an important component of PBL. Effective problems:

1. Relate to the real-world so learners want to solve them.
2. Require learners to make decisions.
3. Are open-ended and not limited to one correct answer.
4. Are connected to previously learned knowledge as well as new knowledge.
5. Reflect lesson objective(s).
6. Challenge learners to think critically.

Teaching Higher Order Thinking Skills (HOTS)

To teach the cognitive skills needed in making decisions and judgments effectively, an instructor should incorporate analysis, synthesis, and evaluation into lessons using PBL. HOTS should be taught throughout the curriculum from simple to complex and from concrete to abstract.

Basic approach to teaching HOTS:

1. Set up the problem.
2. Determine learning outcomes for the problem.
3. Solve the problem or task.
4. Reflect on problem-solving process.
5. Consider additional solutions through guided discovery.
6. Reevaluate solution with additional options.
7. Reflect on this solution and why it could be the best solution.
8. Consider what "best" means (Is it situational?).

Types of Problem-Based Instruction

A problem-based lesson usually involves an incentive or need to solve the problem. It includes a decision on how to find a solution, a possible solution, an explanation for the reasons used to reach that solution, and then reflection on the solution. A discussion of three types of problem-based instruction follow: scenario-based, collaborative problem-solving, and case study.

Scenario-Based Training Method (SBT)

SBT uses a highly structured script of real-world experiences to address aviation training objectives in an operational environment. It presents realistic situations that allow learners to rehearse mentally and explore practical application of various bits of knowledge. Pilot decisions cause a significant percentage of all accidents and the majority of fatal accidents, and SBT challenges the learner or transitioning pilot using a variety of flight scenarios with the goal of avoiding accidents. These scenarios require the pilot to manage the available resources, exercise sound judgment, and make timely decisions. Such training can include initial training, transition training, upgrade training, recurrent training, and special training. Since it has been documented that learners gain more knowledge when actively involved in the learning process, SBT is also used to train AMTs.

The scenario may not have one right or one wrong answer, which reflects situations faced in the real-world. It is important for the instructor to understand in advance which outcomes are positive and/or negative and give the learner freedom to make both good and poor decisions without jeopardizing safety. This allows the learner to make decisions that fit his or her experience level and result in positive outcomes.

Once the class has mastered the ability to compute weight and balance, Bob decides to give them a real-world scenario. A customer wants a tail strobe light installed on his Piper Cherokee 180. How will this installation affect the weight and balance of the aircraft?

The learners need to plan to remove the position light, install a power supply, and also install the tail strobe light. Then they need to consider all the actions and procedures that affect the final weight and balance of the aircraft. What if part of the assembly does not fit properly? The real-world problem forces the learner to analyze, evaluate, and make decisions about the procedures required.

For the flight instructor, a good scenario tells a story that begins with a reason to fly because a pilot's decisions differ depending on the motivation to fly. For example, Mark and his college fraternity brothers bought tickets for a playoff game at their alma mater. Mark volunteered to fly all of them to the game in an airplane he rented. Another friend is planning to meet them at the airport and drive everyone to the game and back.

Mark has strong motivation to fly his friends to the game, so he checks the weather for College Airport which is reported as clear and unrestricted visibility. His flight is a go, yet, 15 miles from College Airport he descends to 1,000 feet to stay below the lowering clouds and encounters rain and lowering visibility to 3 miles. The terrain is flat farmland with no published obstacles. What will he do now?

Remember, a good inflight scenario is a learning experience. SBT is a powerful tool because the future is unpredictable and there is no way to train a pilot for every combination of events that may happen in the future. A good scenario:

1. Is not a test;
2. Will not have one right answer;
3. Does not offer an obvious answer;
4. Should not promote errors; and
5. Should promote situational awareness and opportunities for decision-making.

Collaborative Problem-Solving Method

When using the collaborative problem-solving method, the instructor provides a problem to a group who then solves it. The instructor provides assistance when needed, but understands that learning to solve the problem without assistance is part of the learning process. This method can be modified for an interactive one-on-one learning situation such as an independent aviation instructor might encounter. The instructor provides the problem to the learner and participates in finding solutions by offering limited assistance as the learner solves it. Once again, open-ended "what if" problems encourage the learners an opportunity to develop HOTS.

Case Study Method

An increasingly popular form of teaching, the case study, contains a story relative to the learner that forces him or her to deal with situations encountered in real life. The instructor presents the case to the learners who then analyze it, come to conclusions, and offer possible solutions. Effective case studies require the learner to use critical thinking skills.

The National Transportation Safety Board (NTSB) descriptions of aviation accidents provide an excellent source of real-world case studies for flight instructors. By removing the NTSB determination of probable cause, a flight instructor can use the description as a case study and allow the learners to discuss probable cause without bias. The learners analyze the information and suggest possible reasons for the accident. The instructor then shares the NTSB's determination of probable cause, which can lead to further discussions of how to avoid this type of accident.

Electronic Learning (E-Learning)

Electronic learning or e-learning has become an umbrella term for any type of education that involves an electronic component. *[Figure 5-12]* E-learning comes in many formats. It can be a stand-alone software program that takes a learner from lecture to exam or it can be an interactive web-based course.

Time flexible, cost competitive, learner-centered, easily updated, accessible anytime and anywhere; e-learning has many advantages that make it a popular addition to the field of education.

E-learning is now used for training at many different levels. For example, technology flight training devices and flight simulators are used by everyone from flight schools to major airlines, as well as the military. Flight Schools of all types may offer training using a variety of computer-based desk top Basic Aviation Training Devices (BATDs), stand-alone, personal computer based advanced aviation training devices (AATDs) and even more advance Flight Training Devices (FTDs) for a portion of the time a pilot needs for various certificates and ratings. Major airlines have high-level flight simulators that are so realistic that transitioning crews meet all qualifications in the flight simulator. Likewise, military pilots use flight training devices or flight simulators to prepare for flying aircraft, such as the A-10, for which there are no two-seat training versions. With e-learning, sophisticated databases can organize vast amounts of information that can be quickly sorted, searched, found, and cross-indexed.

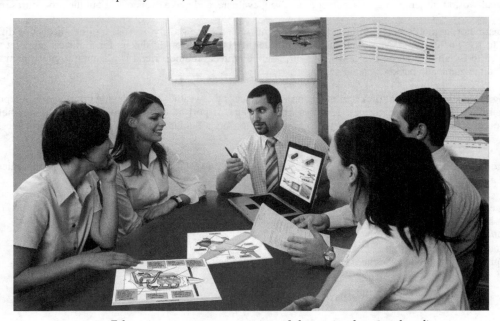

Figure 5-12. *E-learning encompasses a variety of electronic educational media.*

The active nature of e-learning enhances the overall learning process several ways. Well-designed programs allow learners to feel more in control of the content and how fast they learn it. They can explore areas of interest and discover more about a subject on their own. In addition, e-learning often seems more enjoyable than learning from a classroom lecture. Main advantages include less time spent on instruction compared to traditional classroom training, and a higher level of mastery and retention.

Distance learning, or the use of electronic media to deliver instruction when the instructor and learner are separated, is another advantage to e-learning. Participants in a class may be located on different continents, yet share the same teaching experience. Distance learning also may be defined as a system and process that connects learners with resources for learning. As sources for access to information expand, the possibilities for distance learning increase.

While e-learning has many training advantages, it also has limitations which can include the lack of peer interaction and personal feedback, depending on what method of e-learning is used. For the instructor, maintaining control of the learning situation may be difficult. It also may be difficult to find good programs for certain subject areas, and the expense associated with the equipment, software, and facilities need to be considered. In addition, instructors and learners may lack sufficient experience with specific programs to take full advantage of the software that is available.

Improper or excessive use of e-learning should be avoided. For example, a flight instructor should not rely exclusively on a software program on traffic patterns and landings to do the ground instruction for a learner pilot, and then expect the learner to demonstrate patterns and landings in the aircraft. Likewise, it would be unfair to expect a maintenance learner to safely and properly perform a compression check on an aircraft engine if he or she received only e-learning training.

Along with the many types of e-learning, there are a variety of terms used to describe the educational use of the computer. This handbook will use the term "computer-assisted learning" in the following discussion.

Computer-Assisted Learning (CAL) Method

Computer-assisted learning (CAL) couples the personal computer (PC) with multimedia software to create a training device. For example, major aircraft manufacturers have developed CAL programs to teach aircraft systems and maintenance procedures to their employees, reducing the amount of instructor time necessary to train aircrews and maintenance technicians on the new equipment. End users of the aircraft, such as the major airlines, can purchase the training materials with the aircraft in order to accomplish both initial and recurrent training of their personnel. Major advantages of CAL are that learners can progress at a rate which is comfortable for them and are often able to access the CAL at their own convenience.

Another benefit of CAL is an FAA test prep study guide, useful for preparation for the FAA knowledge tests. These programs typically allow the learners to select a test, complete the questions, and find out how they did on the test. The learner may then conduct a review of questions missed.

Some of the more advanced CAL applications allow learners to progress through a series of interactive segments where the presentation varies as a result of their responses. They can focus on the area they either need to study or want to study. For example, a maintenance learner who wants to find information on the refueling of a specific aircraft could use a CAL program to access the refueling section, and study the entire procedure. If the learner wishes to repeat a section or a portion of the section, it can be done at any time.

CAL programs can be used by the instructor as another type of study reference. Just as a learner can reread a section in a text, the learner may review portions of a CAL program. The instructor should continue to monitor and evaluate the progress of the learner as usual. This is necessary to be certain a learner is on track with the training syllabus. When using CAL, instructors may do more one-on-one instruction than in a normal classroom setting, since repetitive forms of teaching may be accomplished by computer. Remember, the computer has no way of knowing when a learner is having difficulty, and it will always be the responsibility of the instructor to provide monitoring and oversight of learner progress. *[Figure 5-13]*

Real interactivity with CAL means the learner is fully engaged with the instruction by doing something meaningful which makes the subject of study come alive. For example, the learner controls the pace of instruction, reviews previous material, jumps forward, and receives instant feedback. With advanced tracking features, CAL also can be used to test the learner's achievement, compare the results with past performance, and indicate weak or strong areas.

For most aviation training, the computer should be thought of as a valuable instructional aid, and CAL is a useful tool for aviation instructors. For example, in teaching aircraft maintenance, CAL programs produced by various aircraft manufacturers can be used to expose learners to equipment not normally found at a maintenance school. Another use of computers would allow learners to review procedures at their own pace while the instructor is involved in hands-on training with others. The major advantage of CAL is that it is interactive—the computer responds in different ways, depending on learner input. When using CAL, the instructor should remain actively involved with the learners by using close supervision, questions, examinations, quizzes, or guided discussions on the subject matter to constantly assess progress.

Figure 5-13. *The instructor continually monitors learner performance when using CAL, as with all instructional aids.*

Simulation, Role-Playing, and Video Gaming

Simulation (the appearance of real life), role-playing (playing a specific role in the context of a real-world situation), and video gaming have taken e-learning in new directions. *[Figure 5-14]* The popularity of simulation games that provide players with complex situations and opportunities to learn have drawn educators into the gaming field as they seek interactive educational games that help retain subject matter learning.

The advantages of simulation/role-playing games come as the learner obtains new information, develops skills, connects and manipulates information. A game gives the learner a stake in the outcome by putting them into the shoes of a character (role-playing) who needs to overcome a real-world scenario. Learning evolves as a result of the interactions with the game, and these games usually promote the development of critical thinking skills.

Not every aviation learning objective can be delivered via this teaching method, but it should prove to be a useful tool in the instructor's tool box as the number and content of educational games increase.

Figure 5-14. *Flight simulator.*

Cooperative or Group Learning Method

Cooperative or group learning organizes learners into small groups who can work together to maximize understanding. Research indicates that learners completing cooperative learning group tasks tend to have better test scores, higher self-esteem, improved social skills, and greater comprehension of the subjects they are studying. Perhaps the most significant characteristic of group learning is that it continually requires active participation in the learning process.

Conditions and Controls

In spite of its advantages, success with cooperative or group learning depends on conditions and controls. First of all, instructors need to begin planning early to determine what the group is expected to learn and to be able to do on their own. The group task may emphasize academic achievement, cognitive abilities, or physical skills, but the instructor should use clear and specific objectives to describe the knowledge and/or abilities the learners are to acquire and then demonstrate on their own.

The following conditions and controls are useful for cooperative learning:

- Small, heterogeneous groups

- Clear, complete instructions of what learners are to do, in what order, with what materials, and when appropriate—what learners are to do as evidence of their mastery of targeted content and skills

- Learner perception of targeted objectives as their own, personal objectives

- The opportunity for learner success

- Learner access to and comprehension of required information

- Sufficient time for learning

- Individual accountability

- Recognition and rewards for group success

- Time after completion of group tasks for learners to systematically reflect upon how they worked together as a team

In practice, collaborative, learner-led, instructor-led, or working group strategies are types of group learning. In these examples, the leader or the instructor serves as a coach or facilitator who interacts with the group, as necessary, to keep it on track or to encourage everyone in the group to participate.

Demonstration-Performance Method

Best used for the mastery of mental or physical skills that require practice, the demonstration-performance method is based on the principle that people learn by doing. In this method, learners observe the skill and then try to reproduce it. It is well suited for the aircraft maintenance instructor who uses it in the shop to teach welding, and the flight instructor who uses it in teaching piloting skills.

Every instructor should recognize the importance of learner performance in the process. Early in demonstration and performance lesson, the instructor should identify the most important learning outcomes. Next, explain and demonstrate the steps involved in performing the skill being taught. Then, allow learners time to practice each step, so they can increase their ability to perform the skill.

The demonstration-performance method is divided into five phases: explanation, demonstration, learner performance, instructor supervision, and evaluation. *[Figure 5-15]*

Explanation Phase

Explanations need to be clear, pertinent to the objectives of the particular lesson to be presented, and based on the known experience and knowledge of the learners. In teaching a skill, the instructor conveys to the learners the precise actions they are to perform. In addition to the necessary steps, the instructor should describe the end result of these efforts. Before leaving this phase, the instructor should encourage learners to ask questions about any step of the procedure that they do not understand.

Demonstration-Performance Method

- ◤ Explanation
- ◤ Demonstration
- ◤ Learner Performance
- ◤ Instructor Supervision
- ◤ Evaluation

Figure 5-15. *The demonstration-performance method of teaching has five essential phases.*

Demonstration Phase

The instructor shows learners the actions necessary to perform a skill. Extraneous activity should be excluded from the demonstration so that learners clearly understand the desired actions. If the demonstration deviates from the explanation, this deviation should be immediately acknowledged and explained.

Learner Performance and Instruction Supervision Phases

While they involve separate actions, the learner's performance of the physical or mental skills that and the instructor's supervision occur at the same time.

The instructor needs to allot enough time for meaningful activity. Through doing, learners learn to follow correct procedures and to reach established standards. It is important that learners be given an opportunity to perform the skill as soon as possible after a demonstration. In flight training, the instructor may allow the learner to follow along on the controls during the demonstration of a maneuver. Immediately thereafter, the instructor should have the learner attempt to perform the maneuver, coaching as necessary. In the opening scenario, learners performed a task (weight and balance computation) as a group, and prior to terminating the performance phase, they were allowed to independently complete the task at least once with supervision and coaching as necessary.

Evaluation Phase

In this phase, the instructor judges learner performance. The learner displays whatever competence has been attained, and the instructor identifies how well the skill has been mastered. To test performance ability, the instructor requires learners to work independently throughout this phase and makes some comment about how each performed the skill relative to the way it was taught. From this measurement of learner achievement, the instructor determines the effectiveness of the instruction.

Drill and Practice Method

Drill and practice, based on Thorndike's law of exercise discussed in Chapter 3, The Learning Process, predicts that connections are strengthened with practice. The human mind rarely retains, evaluates, and applies new concepts or practices after one exposure. Learners do not master welding during one shop period or perform crosswind landings during one instructional flight. They learn by practicing and applying what they have been told and shown. Every time practice occurs, learning continues. Effective use of drill and practice revolves around what skill is being developed. The instructor provides opportunities for learners to practice and while directing the process toward an objective.

Conclusion

A successful instructor needs to be various teaching methods. Although lecture and demonstration-performance methods usually work well, awareness of other methods and teaching tools such as guided discussion, cooperative learning, and computer-assisted learning better prepares an instructor for a wide variety of teaching situations.

Obviously, the aviation instructor is the key to effective teaching. The instructor's tools are different teaching methods. Just as the technician uses some tools more than others, the instructor uses some methods more often than others. As is the case with the technician, there are times when a less used tool is the exact tool needed for a particular situation. The instructor's success is determined to a large degree by the ability to organize material and to select and utilize a teaching method appropriate to a particular lesson.

Application of the Lesson

Application is the learner's use of the presented material. If it is a classroom presentation, the learner may be asked to explain the new material. If it is a new flight maneuver, the learner may be asked to perform the maneuver just been demonstrated. In most instructional situations, the instructor's explanation and demonstration activities alternate with learner performance efforts. Usually the instructor offers corrections and further demonstrations. This is necessary because each learner needs to perform the maneuver or operation the right way the first few times to establish a good habit. Faulty habits are difficult to correct and need to be addressed as soon as possible. Flight instructors should know about this issue since learners often practice without an instructor. Periodic review and assessment by the instructor is necessary to ensure that the learner has not acquired any bad habits, and learners should practice maneuvers on solo flights only after demonstrating reasonable competence.

As the learner becomes proficient with the fundamentals of flight and aircraft maneuvers or maintenance procedures, the instructor should increasingly emphasize ADM as a means of applying what has been previously learned. For example, the flight learner may be asked to plan for the arrival at a specific nontowered airport. The planning should take into consideration the wind conditions, arrival paths, communication procedures, available runways, recommended traffic patterns, and courses of action in the event the unexpected occurs. Upon arrival at the airport the learner makes decisions (with guidance and feedback as necessary) to safely enter and fly the traffic pattern.

Assessment of the Lesson

Before the end of the instructional period, the instructor should review what has been covered during the lesson and ask the learners to demonstrate how well the lesson objectives have been met. Review and assessment are integral parts of each classroom, or flight lesson. The instructor's assessment may be informal and recorded only for the instructor's own use in planning the next lesson, or it may be formal. Often, the assessment is formal and results recorded to certify the learner's progress in the course. Assessment is explored in more detail in Chapter 6.

Instructional Aids and Training Technologies

Instructional aids are devices that assist an instructor in the teaching-learning process. Instructional aids are not self-supporting; they support, supplement, or reinforce what is being taught. In contrast, training media are generally described as any physical means that communicates an instructional message to learners. For example, the instructor's voice, printed text, video cassettes, interactive computer programs, part-task trainers, flight training devices, or flight simulators, and numerous other types of training devices are considered training media.

In school settings, instructors may be involved in the selection and preparation of instructional aids, but they often are already in place. An independent instructor may select or prepare instructional aids. Whatever the setting, instructors need to know how to use them effectively.

Instructional Aid Theory

There is general agreement about certain factors that seem pertinent to understanding the use of instructional aids.

- Carefully selected charts, graphs, pictures, or other well-organized visual aids are examples of items that help the learner understand, as well as retain, essential information.

- Ideally, instructional aids cover the key points and concepts.

- The coverage should be straightforward and factual so it is easy for learners to remember and recall.

- Generally, instructional aids that are relatively simple are best.

Reasons for Use of Instructional Aids

Properly used instructional aids help gain and hold the attention of learners. Audio or visual aids can be very useful in supporting a topic, and the combination of both audio and visual stimuli is particularly effective since the two most important senses are involved. One caution—the instructional aid should keep learner attention on the subject; it should not be a distracting gimmick.

Clearly, a major goal of all instruction is for the learner to be able to retain as much knowledge of the subject as possible, especially the key points. Numerous studies have attempted to determine how well instructional aids serve this purpose. Indications from the studies vary greatly—from modest results, which show a 10 to 15 percent increase in retention, to more optimistic results in which retention is increased by as much as 80 percent. *[Figure 5-16]*

Figure 5-16. *Studies generally agree that measurable improvement in learner retention of information occurs when instruction is supported by appropriate instructional aids.*

Good instructional aids also can help solve certain language barrier problems. Consider the continued expansion of technical terminology in everyday usage. This, coupled with culturally diverse backgrounds of today's learners, makes it necessary for instructors to be precise in their choice of terminology. Words or terms used in an instructional aid should be carefully selected to convey the same meaning for the learner as they do for the instructor. They should provide an accurate visual image and make learning easier.

Another use for instructional aids is to clarify the relationships between material objects and concepts. When relationships are presented visually, they often are much easier to understand. For example, the subsystems within a physical unit are relatively easy to relate to each other through the use of schematics or diagrams. Symbols, graphs, and diagrams can also show relationships of location, size, time, frequency, and value. By symbolizing the factors involved, it is even possible to visualize abstract relationships.

Instructors are frequently asked to teach more and more in a smaller time frame. Instructional aids can help them do this. For example, instead of using many words to describe a sound, object, or function, the instructor plays a recording of the sound, shows a picture of the object, or presents a diagram of the function. Consequently, the learner gains knowledge faster and more accurately, and the instructor saves time in the process.

Guidelines for Use of Instructional Aids

The use of any instructional aid should be planned, based on its ability to support a specific point in a lesson. The following process can be used to determine if and where instructional aids are necessary:

- Clearly establish the lesson objective. Be certain of what is to be communicated.

- Gather the necessary data by researching for support material.

- Organize the material into an outline or a lesson plan. The plan should include all key points that need to be covered. This may include important safety considerations.

- Select the ideas to be supported with instructional aids. The aids should be concentrated on the key points. Aids are often appropriate when long segments of technical description are necessary, when a point is complex and difficult to put into words, when instructors find themselves forming visual images, or when learners are puzzled by an explanation or description.

Aids should be simple and compatible with the learning outcomes to be achieved. Obviously, an explanation of elaborate equipment may require detailed schematics or mock-ups, but less complex equipment may lend itself to only basic shapes or figures. Since aids are normally used in conjunction with a verbal presentation, words on the aid should be kept to a minimum. In many cases, visual symbols and slogans can replace in-depth explanations. The instructor should avoid the temptation to use the aids as a crutch. The tendency toward unnecessarily distracting artwork should be avoided.

Instructional aids should appeal to the learner and be based on sound principles of instructional design. When practical, they should encourage learner participation. They also should be meaningful to the learner, lead to the desired behavioral objectives, and provide appropriate reinforcement. Aids that involve mastering a physical skill should guide learners toward mastery of the skill or task specified in the lesson objective.

Instructional aids have no value in the learning process if they cannot be heard or seen. Recordings of sounds and speeches should be tested for correct volume and quality in the actual environment in which they will be used. Visual aids should be visible to the entire class. All lettering and illustrations need to be large enough to be seen easily by the learners farthest from the aids. Colors should provide clear contrast.

While many instructional aids come with purchased material, the effectiveness of instructor-produced aids and the ease of their preparation can be increased by initially planning them in rough draft form. The rough draft should be carefully checked for technical accuracy, proper terminology, grammar, spelling, basic balance, clarity, and simplicity. Instructional aids should also be reviewed to determine whether their use is feasible in the training environment and whether they are appropriate for the learners. See the figure for a summary of the desired qualities of instructional aids. *[Figure 5-17]*

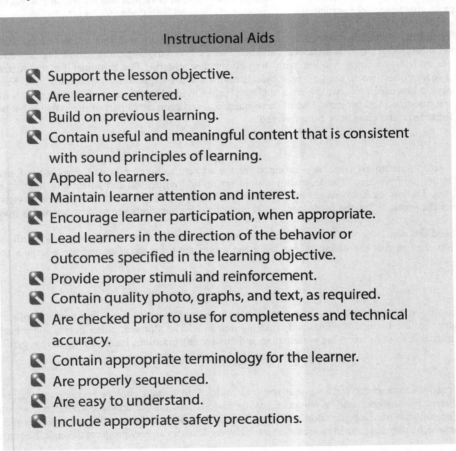

Instructional Aids

- Support the lesson objective.
- Are learner centered.
- Build on previous learning.
- Contain useful and meaningful content that is consistent with sound principles of learning.
- Appeal to learners.
- Maintain learner attention and interest.
- Encourage learner participation, when appropriate.
- Lead learners in the direction of the behavior or outcomes specified in the learning objective.
- Provide proper stimuli and reinforcement.
- Contain quality photo, graphs, and text, as required.
- Are checked prior to use for completeness and technical accuracy.
- Contain appropriate terminology for the learner.
- Are properly sequenced.
- Are easy to understand.
- Include appropriate safety precautions.

Figure 5-17. *Guidelines for effective instructional aids.*

Types of Instructional Aids

Some of the most common and economical aids are marker boards and supplemental print materials, including charts, diagrams, and graphs. Other aids include projected material, video, computer-based programs, and models, mock-ups, or cut-aways.

Marker Board

The marker board is a classroom tool for instructors. Its versatility and effectiveness provide several advantages for most types of instruction. First, the material presented can be erased, allowing the surface to be used again and again; and second, the boards serve as an excellent medium for joint learner-instructor activity in the classroom.

Supplemental Print Material

Print media, including photographs, reproductions of pictures, drawings, murals, cartoons, and other print materials are valuable supplemental aids. Charts, diagrams, and graphs are also in this category. Many of these items are suitable for long-term use on bulletin boards and in briefing areas. Pictures, drawings, and photographs are especially effective because they provide common visual imagery for both instructors and learners. In addition, they also provide realistic details necessary for visual recognition of important subject material. In many cases, this type of supplemental training media may be reproduced in a format for projection on a screen or other clear surface.

Enhanced Training Materials

Training syllabi represent enhanced training material and contain provisions for instructor endorsements and recordkeeping. Such syllabi not only present the course of training in a logical step-by-step, building block sequence, they contain provisions to remind both learners and instructors of critical regulatory training benchmarks which are approaching. When required endorsements and recordkeeping provisions are designed into training syllabi, it is much easier, from the instructor's standpoint, to conduct required training, track learner progress, and certify records. The training record can be reviewed and the training status easily assessed in case the learner transfers to another school or instructor.

Another example of enhanced, instructor-oriented material for pilot training is a maneuvers guide or handbook which includes the ACS as an integral part of the description of maneuvers and procedures. From the beginning learners understand how to perform the maneuver or procedure and also become familiar with the performance criteria. The examiner for the Airframe and Powerplant (A&P) is required to ask four questions in each of the subject areas, which are required by the regulations to be taught. The examiner also is required to assign a practical project from each subject area. Individual maintenance instructors, as well as publishers, have compiled lists of typical questions and projects. Use of these questions and projects as part of the syllabus helps an instructor ensure that all subject areas for a particular class have been covered.

Projected Material

Whatever type of projected training aid used, it is essential for the content to be current and support the lesson. Use of projected materials requires planning and practice. The instructor should set up and adjust the equipment and lighting beforehand and then preview the presentation. During a classroom session, the instructor should provide learners with an overview of the presentation before showing it. After the presentation, the instructor should allow time for questions and a summary of key points.

Computers have changed the way information is presented to today's learner. A laptop computer may be all that is needed for the one-on-one presentation. For groups, the instructor can tailor the presentation for the class and use a large screen or other viewing system.

Video

Instructors need to follow some basic guidelines when using video. The presentation is not designed to replace the instructor. Prior planning will help determine the important points and concepts that should be stressed, either during the presentation or summary. Instructors should be available to summarize the presentation and answer any questions learners may have regarding content.

Interactive Systems

"Interactive" refers broadly to computer software that responds quickly to certain choices and commands by the user. A typical system consists of interactive material and a computer. With search-and-find features incorporated, the system is a powerful information source. The software may include additional features such as image banks with full color photos and graphics, as well as questions or directions which are programmed to create interactivity for learners as they progress through the course.

The questions or directions are programmed using a branching technique, which provides several possible courses of action for the user to choose in order to move from one sequence to another. For example, a program may indicate, "That was incorrect. Go back to … and try again."

Computer-Assisted Learning (CAL)

As mentioned earlier, CAL has become a popular training delivery method. In its basic form, CAL is a combination of more than one instructional media, such as audio, text, graphics, and video (or film) usually shown on a PC.

With CAL, the roles of both learner and instructor change. Learners become more involved and instructors may no longer occupy a center-stage position in a typical classroom setting. Instead, instructors become supportive facilitators. As such, they serve as guides or resource experts and circulate among learners who are working individually or in small groups. This results in considerable one-on-one instructor-learner interaction. Thus, the instructor provides assistance, reinforcement, and answers for those who need it most.

In this situation, the CAL should still be considered as an add-on instructional aid to improve traditional classroom instruction. The instructor, although no longer the center of attention, continues to maintain adequate control over the learning environment to ensure learning objectives are being achieved. *[Figure 5-18]*

A more advanced application of computer-based training may involve less instructor control. For example, a laboratory-type environment may be configured with separate study areas for each learner. With this setup, the physical facility is usually referred to as a learning center or training center.

Learners in these centers are often monitored by a teacher's aide or other trained personnel who can provide guidance, answer questions, and act as a conduit to the instructor who is responsible for the training. In this case, the responsible instructor needs to establish procedures to make sure the required training is accomplished, since he or she certifies learner competency at the end of the course.

Figure 5-18. *In a computer-assisted learning environment, the instructor still ensures that learning objectives are being achieved.*

Models, Mock-ups, and Cut-Aways

Models, mock-ups, and cut-aways are additional instructional aids. A model is a copy of a real object. It can be an enlargement, a reduction, or the same size as the original. The scale model represents an exact reproduction of the original, while simplified models do not represent reality in all details. Some models are solid and show only the outline of the object they portray, while others can be manipulated or operated.

Although a model may not be a realistic copy of an actual piece of equipment, it can be used effectively in explaining operating principles of various types of equipment. Models are especially adaptable to small group discussions in which learners are encouraged to ask questions. A model is even more effective if it works like the original, and if it can be taken apart and reassembled. With the display of an operating model, the learners can observe how each part works in relation to the other parts. When the instructor points to each part of the model while explaining these relationships, the learners can better understand the mechanical principles involved. As instructional aids, models are usually more practical than originals because they are lightweight and easy to manipulate.

A mock-up is a three-dimensional or specialized type of working model made from real or synthetic materials. It is used for study, training, or testing in place of the real object, which is too costly or too dangerous, or which is impossible to obtain. The mock-up may emphasize or highlight elements or components for learning and eliminate nonessential elements.

Cut-aways, another type of model, are built in sections and can be taken apart to reveal the internal structure. Whenever possible, the various parts should be labeled or colored to clarify relationships.

Production and equipment costs are limiting factors to consider in developing and using models, mock-ups, and cut-aways. Depending on the nature of the representation, cost can vary. For instance, scale replicas are often very expensive. In general, if a two-dimensional representation will satisfy the instructor's requirement, it should be used.

Test Preparation Material

Test preparation material applies to an array of paper, video, and computer software products that are designed by commercial publishers to help learner applicants prepare for FAA tests. While test preparation materials may be effective in preparing for FAA tests, the danger is that learners may be able to pass a given test, but fail to learn other critical information essential to safe piloting and maintenance practices. FAA inspectors and designated examiners report that learner applicants sometimes exhibit a lack of knowledge during oral questioning, even though many have easily passed the FAA knowledge test. A major shortcoming of test preparation materials is that the emphasis is on rote learning, which is the lowest of all levels of learning.

Test preparation materials, as well as instructors, that dwell on teaching the test are shortchanging learner applicants. All instructors who use test preparation publications should stress that these materials are not designed as stand-alone learning tools. They should be considered as a supplement to instructor-led training.

Future Developments

Electronic communications, including use of computer databases, voice mail, e-mail, Internet, World Wide Web, and satellite-based, wireless communications, are routine and this explosion of information access affects aviation training. It will be even more significant in the future.

Computer technology continues to advance in quantum leaps, challenging traditional ways of teaching. For example, voice-recognition technology, which lets computers accept spoken rather than keyed input, is highly effective for technical training.

Miniature electro-optical devices allow computer-aided information to be projected electronically on sunglass-style eye wear which is connected to a lightweight, belt mounted computer. Computer-aided information is particularly useful for aviation maintenance activities. For example, it would be possible for a technician's eyes to easily move back and forth from computer-generated technical data to the actual hardware while diagnosing and correcting a maintenance problem.

Trends in training indicate a shift from the typical classroom to more extensive use of a lab-type environment with computer work or study stations. Using simulation devices, computer networks, and multimedia programs, learners become more actively involved and responsible for their own training. Aviation-related learning centers are usually associated with colleges, universities, and research centers. The airlines, as well as aeronautical programs at some colleges and universities, have used similar facilities for many years.

Another type of computer-based technology, virtual reality (VR), creates a sensory experience that allows a participant to believe and barely distinguish a virtual experience from a real one. VR uses graphics with animation systems, sounds, and images to reproduce electronic versions of real-life experience. Despite enormous potential, VR is expensive.

For those engaged in aviation training, the challenge is staying abreast of technological changes that apply to training and adopting those that are the most useful and cost effective. Since much of the new technology is based on computer technology, instructors with well-developed computer skills are in demand.

While evaluating new teaching methods and technology, instructors should remember their main teaching goals. Electronic information on computer networks and bulletin boards may come from reputable publishers, as well as community, state, and national government agencies. There is, however, no guarantee that all of this information is current or even accurate.

Chapter Summary

As indicated by this discussion, the teaching process organizes the material an instructor wishes to teach in such a way that the learner understands what is being taught. An effective instructor uses a combination of teaching methods as well as instructional aids to achieve this goal.

By being well prepared, an effective instructor presents and applies lesson material, and also periodically assesses learning. An effective instructor never stops learning. He or she maintains currency in the subject matter being taught, as well as how to teach it by reading professional journals and other aviation publications, many of which can be viewed or purchased via the Internet, another source of valuable aviation information for professional instructors.

Aviation Instructor's Handbook (FAA-H-8083-9)
Chapter 6: Assessment

Introduction

Assessment is an essential component of teaching and learning, and it provides the instructor with immediate feedback on the quality of instruction. Instructors continuously evaluate a learner's performance in order to provide guidance, suggestions for improvement, and positive reinforcement.

This chapter examines the instructor's role when assessing levels of learning, it describes methods of assessment, and it discusses how instructors may construct and conduct effective assessments. Since learners are different and each situation is unique, instructors individualize an assessment as needed. Aviation instructors can use the techniques and methods described in this chapter as appropriate.

Assessment Terminology

This chapter presents two broad categories of assessment. The first is traditional assessment, which often involves the kind of written testing (e.g., multiple choice, matching) and grading that is most familiar to instructors and learners. To achieve a passing score on a traditional assessment, the learner usually has a set amount of time to recognize or reproduce memorized terms, formulas, or data. There is a single answer that is correct. Consequently, the traditional assessment usually assesses the learner's progress at the rote and understanding levels of learning. However, carefully crafted scenario questions can assess higher levels of learning.

The second category of assessment is authentic assessment. Authentic assessment requires the learner to demonstrate not just rote and understanding, but also the application and correlation levels of learning. Authentic assessment generally requires the learner to perform real-world tasks and demonstrate a meaningful application of skills and competencies. In other words, the authentic assessment requires the learner to exhibit in-depth knowledge by generating a solution instead of merely choosing a response.

In authentic assessment, there are specific performance criteria, or standards, that learners know in advance of the actual assessment. The terms "criteria/criterion" and "standard" are often used interchangeably. They refer to the characteristics that define acceptable performance on a task. Another term used in association with authentic assessment is "rubric." A rubric is a guide used to score performance assessments in a reliable, fair, and valid manner. It is generally composed of dimensions for judging learner performance, a scale for rating performances on each dimension, and standards of excellence for specified performance levels.

Whether knowledge or skill, an assessment can be either formal or informal. Formal assessments usually involve documentation, such as a quiz or written examination. They are used periodically throughout a course, as well as at the end of a course, to measure and document whether or not the course objectives have been met. Informal assessments, which can include verbal critique, generally occur as needed and are not part of the final grade.

Other terms associated with assessment include diagnostic, formative, and summative.

- Diagnostic assessments assess learner knowledge or skills prior to a course of instruction.

- Formative assessments, which are not graded, provide a wrap-up of the lesson and set the stage for the next lesson. This type of assessment, limited to what transpired during that lesson, informs the instructor what to reinforce.

- Summative assessments, used periodically throughout the training, measure how well learning has progressed to that point. For example, a stage-check, a chapter quiz, or an end-of-course test can measure the learner's overall mastery of the training. These assessments are an integral part of the lesson, as well as the course of training.

Purpose of Assessment

An effective assessment provides critical information to both the instructor and the learner. Both instructor and learner need to know how well the learner is progressing. A good assessment provides practical and specific feedback to learners. This includes direction and guidance indicating how they may raise their level of performance. Most importantly, a well-designed and effective assessment provides an opportunity for self-evaluation that enhances the learner's aeronautical decision-making and judgment skills.

A well-designed assessment highlights the areas in which a learner's performance is incorrect or inadequate, it helps the instructor see where more emphasis is needed. If, for example, several learners falter when they reach the same step in a weight-and-balance problem, the instructor should recognize the need for a more detailed explanation, another demonstration of the step, or special emphasis in the assessment of subsequent performance.

General Characteristics of Effective Assessment

In order to provide direction and raise the learner's level of performance, assessment needs to be factual, and it should align with the completion standards of the lesson. An effective assessment displays the characteristics shown in *Figure 6-1*.

- Objective
- Flexible
- Acceptable
- Comprehensive
- Constructive
- Organized
- Thoughtful
- Specific

Figure 6-1. *Effective assessments share a number of characteristics.*

Objective

The personal opinions, likes, dislikes, or biases of the instructor might affect an assessment. A conflict of personalities can alter an opinion. Sympathy or over-identification with a learner, to such a degree that it influences objectivity, is known as "halo error." To what extent does effective assessment need to focus on objectivity and actual learner performance? If an assessment is to be effective, it needs to be honest; and it must be based on the facts of the performance as they were, not as they could have been.

Flexible

The instructor should evaluate the entire performance of a learner in the context in which it is accomplished. Sometimes a good learner turns in a poor performance, and a poor learner turns in a good one. A friendly learner may suddenly become hostile, or a hostile learner may suddenly become friendly and cooperative. The instructor fits the tone, technique, and content of the assessment to the occasion, as well as to the learner. An assessment should be designed and executed so that the instructor can allow for variables. The ongoing challenge for the instructor is deciding what to say, what to omit, what to stress, and what to minimize at the proper moment.

Acceptable

Consider that learners do not like negative feedback. What makes an honest assessment acceptable to the learner? A certificate or credential alone rarely suffices. Learners need to have confidence in the instructor's qualifications, teaching ability, sincerity, competence, and authority. Usually, instructors have the opportunity to establish themselves with learners before the formal assessment arises. If not, however, the instructor's manner, attitude, and familiarity with the subject at hand serves this purpose. Assessments presented fairly, with authority, conviction, sincerity, and from a position of recognizable competence tend to work well.

Comprehensive

A comprehensive assessment is not necessarily a long one, nor need it treat every aspect of the performance in detail. While it includes strengths as well as weaknesses, the degree of coverage of each should fit the situation. The instructor might report what most needs improvement, or only what the learner can reasonably be expected to improve. The instructor decides whether the greater benefit comes from a discussion of a few major points or a number of minor points.

Constructive

An assessment is pointless unless the learner benefits from it. Praise can capitalize on things that are done well and inspire the learner to improve in areas of lesser accomplishment. When identifying a mistake or weakness, the instructor needs to give positive guidance for correction. Praise for its own sake or negative comments that do not point toward improvement or a higher level of performance should be omitted from an assessment altogether.

Organized

An assessment must be organized. Almost any pattern is acceptable, as long as it is logical and makes sense to the learner. An effective organizational pattern might be the sequence of the performance itself. Sometimes an assessment can begin at the point at which a demonstration failed, and work backward through the steps that led to the failure. A success can be analyzed in similar fashion. Alternatively, a glaring deficiency can serve as the core of an assessment. Breaking the whole into parts, or building the parts into a whole, is another possible organizational approach.

Thoughtful

An effective assessment reflects the instructor's thoughtfulness toward the learner's need for self-esteem, recognition, and approval. The instructor refrains from minimizing the inherent dignity and importance of the individual. Ridicule, anger, or fun at the expense of the learner has no place in assessment. While being straightforward and honest, the instructor should always respect the learner's personal feelings. For example, the instructor should try to deliver criticism in private.

Specific

The instructor's comments and recommendations should be specific. Learners cannot act on recommendations unless they know specifically what the recommendations are. A statement such as, "Your second weld wasn't as good as your first," has little constructive value. Instead, the instructor should say why it was not as good and offer suggestions on how to improve the weld. If the instructor has a clear, well-founded, and supportable idea in mind, it should be expressed with firmness and authority, and in terms that cannot be misunderstood. At the conclusion of an assessment, learners should have no doubt about what they did well and what they did poorly and, most importantly, specifically how they can improve.

Traditional Assessment

As defined earlier, traditional assessment generally refers to written testing, such as multiple choice, matching, true/false, fill in the blank, etc. Learners typically complete written assessments within a specified time. There is a single, correct response for each item. The assessment, or test, assumes that all learners should learn the same thing, and relies on rote memorization of facts. Responses are often machine scored and offer little opportunity for a demonstration of the thought processes characteristic of critical thinking skills.

Traditional assessment lends itself to instructor centered teaching styles. The instructor teaches the material at a low level, and the measure of performance is limited. In traditional assessment, fairly simple grading matrices such as shown in *Figure 6-2* are used. Due to this approach, a satisfactory grade for one lesson may not reflect a learner's ability to apply knowledge in a different situation.

Still, tests of this nature do have a place in the assessment hierarchy. Multiple choice, supply type, and other such tests are useful in assessing the learner's grasp of information, concepts, terms, processes, and rules—factual knowledge that forms the foundation needed for the learner to advance to higher levels of learning.

Characteristics of a Good Written Assessment (Test)

Whether or not an instructor designs his or her own tests or uses commercially available test banks, it is important to know the components of an effective test. *(Note: This section is intended to introduce basic concepts of written-test design. Please see Appendix A for testing and test-writing publications.)*

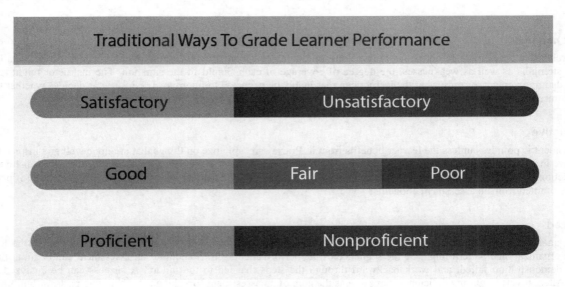

Figure 6-2. *Traditional grading.*

A test is a set of questions, problems, or exercises intended to determine whether the learner possesses a particular knowledge or skill. A test can consist of just one test item, but it usually consists of a number of test items. A test item measures a single objective and calls for a single response. The test could be as simple as the correct answer to an essay question or as complex as completing a knowledge or practical test. Regardless of the underlying purpose, effective tests share certain characteristics. *[Figure 6-3]*

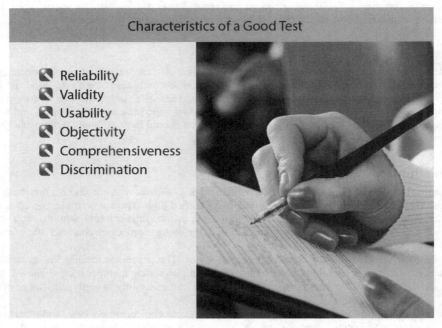

Figure 6-3. *Effective tests have six primary characteristics.*

Reliability is the degree to which test results are consistent with repeated measurements. If identical measurements are obtained every time a certain instrument is applied to a certain dimension, the instrument is considered reliable. The reliability of a written test is judged by whether it gives consistent measurement to a particular individual or group. Keep in mind, though, that knowledge, skills, and understanding can improve with subsequent attempts at taking the same test, because the first test serves as a learning device.

Validity is the extent to which a test measures what it is supposed to measure, and it is the most important consideration in test evaluation. The instructor must carefully consider whether the test actually measures what it is supposed to measure. To estimate validity, several instructors read the test critically and consider its content relative to the stated objectives of the instruction. Items that do not pertain directly to the objectives of the course should be modified or eliminated.

Usability refers to the functionality of tests. A usable written test is easy to give if it is printed in a type size large enough for learners to read easily. The wording of both the directions for taking the test and of the test items needs to be clear and concise. Graphics, charts, and illustrations appropriate to the test items must be clearly drawn, and the test should be easily graded.

Objectivity describes singleness of scoring of a test. Essay questions provide an example of this principle. It is nearly impossible to prevent an instructor's own knowledge and experience in the subject area, writing style, or grammar from affecting the grade awarded. Selection-type test items, such as true/false or multiple choice, are much easier to grade objectively.

Comprehensiveness is the degree to which a test measures the overall objectives. Suppose, for example, an AMT wants to measure the compression of an aircraft engine. Measuring compression on a single cylinder would not provide an indication of the entire engine. Similarly, a written test must sample an appropriate cross-section of the objectives of instruction. The instructor makes certain the evaluation includes a representative and comprehensive sampling of the objectives of the course.

Discrimination is the degree to which a test distinguishes the difference between learners and may be appropriate for assessment of academic achievement. However, minimum standards are far more important in assessments leading to pilot certification. If necessary for classroom evaluation of academic achievement, a test must measure small differences in achievement in relation to the objectives of the course. A test designed for discrimination contains:

1. A wide range of scores
2. All levels of difficulty
3. Items that distinguish between learners with differing levels of achievement of the course objectives

Please see Appendix B for information on the advantages and disadvantages of multiple choice, supply type, and other written assessment instruments, as well as guidance on creating effective test items.

Authentic Assessment

Authentic assessment asks the learner to perform real-world tasks and demonstrate a meaningful application of skills and competencies. Authentic assessment lies at the heart of training today's aviation learner to use critical thinking skills. Rather than selecting from predetermined responses, learners must generate responses from skills and concepts they have learned. By using open-ended questions and established performance criteria, authentic assessment focuses on the learning process, enhances the development of real-world skills, encourages higher order thinking skills, and teaches learners to assess their own work and performance.

Learner-Centered Assessment

There are several aspects of effective authentic assessment. The first is the use of open-ended questions in what might be called a "collaborative critique," which is a form of learner-centered grading. As described in the scenario that introduced this chapter, the instructor begins by using a four-step series of open-ended questions to guide the learner through a complete self-assessment.

Replay—the instructor asks the learner to verbally replay the flight or procedure. While the learner speaks, the instructor listens for areas where the account does not seem accurate. At the right moment, the instructor discusses any discrepancy with the learner. This approach gives the learner a chance to validate his or her own perceptions, and it gives the instructor critical insight into the learner's judgment abilities.

Reconstruct—the reconstruction stage encourages learning by identifying the key things that the learner would have, could have, or should have done differently during the flight or procedure.

Reflect—insights come from investing perceptions and experiences with meaning, requiring reflection on the events. For example:

1. What was the most important thing you learned today?
2. What part of the session was easiest for you? What part was hardest?
3. Did anything make you uncomfortable? If so, when did it occur?
4. How would you assess your performance and your decisions?
5. How did your performance compare to the standards in the ACS?

Redirect—the final step is to help the learner relate lessons learned in this session to other experiences and consider how they might help in future sessions. Questions might include:

- How does this experience relate to previous lessons?

- What might be done to mitigate a similar risk in a future situation?

- Which aspects of this experience might apply to future situations, and how?

- What personal minimums should be established, and what additional proficiency flying and/or training might be useful?

Any self-assessment stimulates growth in the learner's thought processes and, in turn, behaviors. An in-depth discussion between the instructor and the learner may follow, which compares the instructor's assessment to the learner's self-assessment. Through this discussion, the instructor and the learner jointly determine the learner's progress. The progress may be recorded on a rubric as part of a training program. As explained earlier, a rubric is a guide for scoring performance assessments in a reliable, fair, and valid manner. It is generally composed of dimensions for judging learner performance, a scale for rating performances on each dimension, and standards of excellence for specified performance levels.

The collaborative assessment process in learner-centered grading uses two broad rubrics: one that assesses the learner's level of proficiency on skill-focused maneuvers or procedures, and one that assesses the learner's level of proficiency on single-pilot resource management (SRM), which is the cognitive or decision-making aspect of flight training.

The performance assessment dimensions for each type of rubric are as follows:

Maneuver or Procedure "Grades"

- Describe—at the completion of the scenario, the learner is able to describe the physical characteristics and cognitive elements of the scenario activities but needs assistance to execute the maneuver or procedure successfully.

- Explain—at the completion of the scenario, the learner is able to describe the scenario activity and understand the underlying concepts, principles, and procedures that comprise the activity, but needs assistance to execute the maneuver or procedure successfully.

- Practice—at the completion of the scenario, the learner is able to plan and execute the scenario. Coaching, instruction, and/or assistance will correct deviations and errors identified by the instructor.

- Perform—at the completion of the scenario, the learner is able to perform the activity without instructor assistance. The learner will identify and correct errors and deviations in an expeditious manner. At no time will the successful completion of the activity be in doubt. ("Perform" is used to signify that the learner is satisfactorily demonstrating proficiency in traditional piloting and systems operation skills).

- Not observed—any event not accomplished or required.

For example, a learner can describe a landing and can tell the flight instructor about the physical characteristics and appearance of the landing. On a good day, with the wind straight down the runway, the learner may be able to practice landings with some success while still functioning at the rote level of learning. However, on a gusty crosswind day the learner needs a deeper level of understanding to adapt to the different conditions. If a learner can explain all the basic physics associated with lift/drag and crosswind correction, he or she is more likely to practice successfully and eventually perform a landing under a wide variety of conditions.

Assessing Risk Management Skills

- Explain—the learner can verbally identify, describe, and understand the risks inherent in the flight scenario, but needs to be prompted to identify risks and make decisions.

- Practice—the learner is able to identify, understand, and apply SRM principles to the actual flight situation. Coaching, instruction, and/or assistance quickly corrects minor deviations and errors identified by the instructor. The learner is an active decision maker.

- Manage-Decide—the learner can correctly gather the most important data available both inside and outside the flight deck, identify possible courses of action, evaluate the risk inherent in each course of action, and make the appropriate decision. Instructor intervention is not required for the safe completion of the flight.

In SRM, the learner may be able to describe basic SRM principles during the first flight. Later, he or she is able to explain how SRM applies to different scenarios that are presented on the ground and in the air. When the learner actually begins to make quality decisions based on good SRM techniques, he or she earns a grade of manage-decide. The advantage of this type of grading is that both flight instructor and learner know exactly where the learning has progressed.

Let's look at how the rubric in *Figure 6-4* might be used in a flight training scenario. During the postflight debriefing, flight instructor Linda asks her learner, Brian, to assess his performance for the day using the Replay, Reconstruct, Reflect, and Redirect guided discussion questions described in the Learner-Centered Assessment section presented earlier in this chapter. Based on this assessment, she and Brian discuss where Brian's performance falls in the rubrics for maneuvers/procedures and SRM. This part of the assessment may be verbally discussed or, alternatively, Brian and Linda separately create an assessment sheet for each element of the flight.

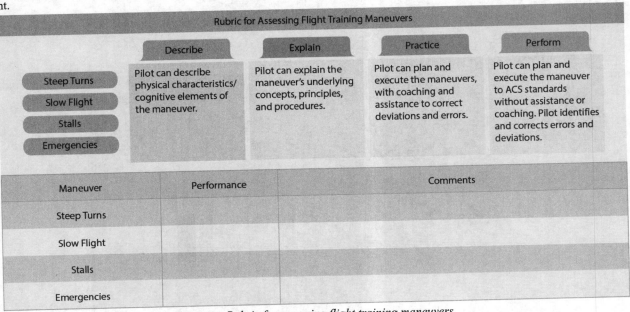

Figure 6-4. *Rubric for assessing flight training maneuvers.*

When Brian studies the performance levels, he decides he was at the "Perform" level since he had not made any mistakes. Where he had rated the item as "Perform," Linda had rated it as "Practice." During the ensuing discussion, Brian understands where he needs more practice before his performance is at the "Perform" level.

This approach to assessment has several key advantages. One is that it actively involves the learner in the assessment process and establishes the habit of healthy reflection and self-assessment that is critical to being a safe pilot. Another is that these grades are not self-esteem related, since they do not describe a recognized level of prestige (such as A+ or "Outstanding"), but rather a level of performance. The learner cannot flunk a lesson. Instead, he or she demonstrates a particular level of flight and SRM skills.

Both instructors and learners may initially be reluctant to use this method of assessment. Instructors may think it requires more time, when in fact it is merely a more structured, effective, and collaborative version of a traditional postflight critique. Also, instructors who learned in the more traditional assessment structure must be careful not to equate or force the dimensions of the rubric into the traditional grading mold of A through F. One way to avoid this temptation is to remember that evaluation should be progressive: the learner may achieve a new level of learning during each lesson. For example, in flight one, a task might be a "describe" item. By flight three, it is a "practice" item, and by flight five, it is a "manage-decide" item.

The learner may be reluctant to self-assess if he or she has not had the chance to participate in such a process before. Therefore, the instructor may need to teach the learner how to become an active participant in the collaborative assessment.

Choosing an Effective Assessment Method

When deciding how to assess learner progress, aviation instructors can follow a four-step process.

1. Determine level-of-learning objectives.
2. List indicators of desired behaviors.
3. Establish criterion objectives.
4. Develop criterion-referenced test items.

This process is useful for tests that apply to the cognitive and affective domains of learning, and also can be used for skill testing in the psychomotor domain. The development process for criterion-referenced tests follows a general-to-specific pattern. *[Figure 6-5]*

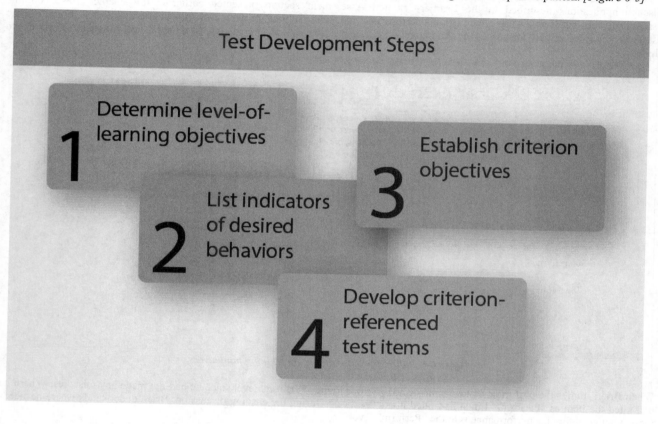

Figure 6-5. *The development process for criterion-referenced tests follows a general-to-specific pattern.*

Instructors should be aware that authentic assessment may not be as useful as traditional assessment in the early phases of training, because the learner does not have enough information about the concepts or knowledge to participate fully. As discussed in Chapter 3, The Learning Process, when exposed to a new topic, learners first tend to acquire and memorize facts. As learning progresses, they begin to organize their knowledge to formulate an understanding of the things they have memorized. When learners possess the knowledge needed to analyze, synthesize, and evaluate (i.e., application and correlation levels of learning), they can participate more fully in the assessment process.

Determine Level-of-Learning Objectives

The first step in developing an appropriate assessment is to state the individual objectives as general, level-of-learning objectives. The objectives should measure one of the learning levels of the cognitive, affective, or psychomotor domains described in Chapter 3. The levels of cognitive learning include knowledge, comprehension, application, analysis, synthesis, and evaluation.

For the understanding level, an objective could be stated as, "Describe how to perform a compression test on an aircraft reciprocating engine." This objective requires a learner to explain how to do a compression test, but not necessarily perform a compression test (application level). Further, the learner would not be expected to compare the results of compression tests on different engines (application level), design a compression test for a different type of engine (correlation level), or interpret the results of the compression test (correlation level). A general level-of-learning objective is a good starting point for developing a test because it defines the scope of the learning task.

List Indicators/Samples of Desired Behaviors

The second step is to list the indicators or samples of behavior that give the best indication of the achievement of the objective. The instructor selects behaviors that can be measured and which give the best evidence of learning. For example, if the instructor expects the learner to display the understanding level of learning on compression testing, some of the specific test question answers should describe appropriate tools and equipment, the proper equipment setup, appropriate safety procedures, and the steps used to obtain compression readings. The overall test must be comprehensive enough to give a true representation of the learning to be measured. It is not usually feasible to measure every aspect of a level of learning objective, but by carefully choosing samples of behavior, the instructor can obtain adequate evidence of learning.

Establish Criterion Objectives

The next step in the test development process is to define criterion (performance-based) objectives. In addition to the behavior expected, criterion objectives state the conditions under which the behavior is to be performed, and the criteria that must be met. If the instructor developed performance-based objectives during the creation of lesson plans, criterion objectives have already been formulated. The criterion objective provides the framework for developing the test items used to measure the level of learning objectives. In the compression test example, a criterion objective to measure the understanding level of learning might be stated as, "The learner will demonstrate understanding of compression test procedures for reciprocating aircraft engines by completing a quiz with a minimum passing score of 70 percent."

Develop Criterion-Referenced Assessment Items

The last step is to develop criterion-referenced assessment items. The development of written test questions is covered in the reference section. While developing written test questions, the instructor should attempt to measure the behaviors described in the criterion objective(s). The questions in the exam for the compression test example should cover all of the areas necessary to give evidence of understanding the procedure. The results of the test (questions missed) identify areas that were not adequately covered.

Performance-based objectives serve as a reference for the development of test items. If the test is the pre-solo knowledge test, the objectives are for the learner to understand the regulations, the local area, the aircraft type, and the procedures to be used. The test should measure the learner's knowledge in these specific areas. Individual instructors should develop their own tests to measure the progress of their learners. If the test is to measure the readiness of a learner to take a knowledge test, it should be based on the objectives of all the lessons the learner has received.

Aviation training also involves performance tests for maneuvers or procedures. The flight instructor does not administer the practical test for a pilot certificate, nor does the aviation maintenance instructor administer the oral and practical exam for certification as an aviation maintenance technician (AMT). However, aviation instructors do get involved with the same skill or performance testing that is measured in these tests. Performance testing is desirable for evaluating training that involves an operation, a procedure, or a process. The job of the instructor is to prepare the learner to take these tests. Therefore, each element of the practical test should be evaluated prior to sending an applicant for the practical exam.

Practical tests for maintenance technicians and pilots are criterion-referenced tests. The practical tests, defined in the Airman Certification Standards and Practical Test Standards (ACS/PTS), are criterion referenced because the objective is for all successful applicants to meet the high standards of knowledge, skill, and safety required by the regulations. The purpose of the ACS/PTS is to delineate the standards by which FAA inspectors, designated pilot examiners (DPEs), and designated maintenance examiners (DMEs) conduct tests for ratings and certificates. The standards reflect the requirements of Title 14 of the Code of Federal Regulations (14 CFR) parts 61, 65, 91, and other FAA publications, including the Aeronautical Information Manual (AIM) and pertinent advisory circulars and handbooks.

The objectives in the ACS/PTS ensure the certification of pilots and maintenance technicians at a high level of performance and proficiency, consistent with safety. The ACS/PTS for aeronautical certificates and ratings include areas of operation and tasks that reflect the requirements of the FAA publications mentioned above. Areas of operation define phases of the practical test arranged in a logical sequence within each standard. They usually begin with preflight preparation and end with postflight procedures. Tasks are titles of knowledge areas, flight procedures, or maneuvers appropriate to an area of operation. Included are references to the applicable regulations or publications. Private pilot applicants are evaluated in all tasks of each area of operation. Flight instructor applicants are evaluated on one or more tasks in each area of operation. In addition, certain tasks are required to be covered and are identified by notes immediately following the area of operation titles.

Since evaluators may cover every task in the ACS/PTS on the practical test, the instructor should evaluate all of the tasks before recommending the maintenance technician or pilot applicant for the practical test. While this evaluation is not necessarily formal, it should adhere to criterion-referenced testing.

Critiques and Oral Assessments

Used in conjunction with either traditional or authentic assessment, the critique is an instructor-to-learner assessment. These methods can also be used either individually, or in a classroom setting.

The word critique sometimes has a negative connotation, and the instructor needs to avoid using this method as an opportunity to be overly critical of learner performance. An effective critique considers good as well as bad performance, the individual parts, relationships of the individual parts, and the overall performance. A critique can and usually should be as varied in content as the performance being evaluated.

A critique may be oral, written, or both. It should come immediately after a learner's performance, while the details of the performance are easy to recall. An instructor may critique any activity a learner performs or practices to improve skill, proficiency, and learning. A critique may be conducted privately or before the entire class. A critique presented before the entire class can be beneficial to every learner in the classroom, as well as to the learner who performed the exercise or assignment. In this case, however, the instructor should avoid embarrassing the learner in front of the class.

There are several useful ways to conduct a critique.

Instructor/Learner Critique

The instructor leads a group discussion in an instructor/learner critique in which members of the class are invited to offer criticism of a performance. This method should be controlled carefully and directed with a clear purpose. It should be organized, and not allowed to degenerate into a random free-for-all.

Learner-Led Critique

The instructor asks a learner to lead the assessment in a learner-led critique. The instructor can specify the pattern of organization and the techniques or can leave it to the discretion of the chosen leader. Because of the inexperience of the participants in the lesson area, learner-led assessments may not be efficient, but they can generate learner interest and learning.

Small Group Critique

For the small group critique, the class is divided into small groups, each assigned a specific area to analyze. Each group presents its findings to the class. It is desirable for the instructor to furnish the criteria and guidelines. The combined reports from the groups can result in a comprehensive assessment.

Individual Learner Critique by Another Learner

The instructor may require another learner to present the entire assessment. A variation is for the instructor to ask a number of learners questions about the manner and quality of performance. Discussion of the performance and of the assessment can often allow the group to accept more ownership of the ideas expressed. As with all assessments incorporating learner participation, it is important that the instructor maintain firm control over the process.

Self-Critique

A learner critiques personal performance in a self-critique. Like all other methods, a self-critique receives control and supervision from the instructor.

Written Critique

A written critique has three advantages. First, the instructor can devote more time and thought to it than to an oral assessment in the classroom. Second, learners can keep written assessments and refer to them whenever they wish. Third, when the instructor asks all learners to write an assessment of a performance, the learner-performer has the permanent record of the suggestions, recommendations, and opinions of all the other learners. The disadvantage of a written assessment is that other members of the class do not benefit.

Whatever the type of critique, the instructor should resolve disagreements and correct erroneous impressions. The instructor also makes allowances for the learners' relative inexperience. Normally, the instructor should reserve time at the end of the learner assessment to cover those areas that might have been omitted, not emphasized sufficiently, or considered worth repeating.

Oral Assessment

The most common means of assessment is direct or indirect oral questioning of learners by the instructor. Questions may be loosely classified as fact questions and HOTS questions. The answer to a fact question is based on memory or recall. This type of question usually concerns who, what, when, and where. HOTS questions involve why or how and require the learner to combine knowledge of facts with an ability to analyze situations, solve problems, and arrive at conclusions.

Proper quizzing by the instructor can have a number of desirable results, such as:

1. Reveals the effectiveness of the instructor's training methods
2. Checks learner retention of what has been learned
3. Reviews material already presented to the learner
4. Can be used to retain learner interest and stimulate thinking
5. Emphasizes the important points of training
6. Identifies points that need more emphasis
7. Checks comprehension of what has been learned
8. Promotes active learner participation, which is important to effective learning

Characteristics of Effective Questions

The instructor should devise and write pertinent questions in advance. One method is to place them in the lesson plan. Prepared questions merely serve as a framework, and as the lesson progresses, should be supplemented by such impromptu questions as the instructor considers appropriate. Objective questions have only one correct answer, while the answer to an open-ended HOTS question can be expressed in a variety of possible solutions.

To be effective, questions must:

1. Apply to the subject of instruction.
2. Be brief and concise, but also clear and definite.
3. Be adapted to the ability, experience, and stage of training of the learners.
4. Center on only one idea (limited to who, what, when, where, how, or why, not a combination).
5. Present a challenge to the learners.

Types of Questions to Avoid

Effective quizzing does not include yes/no questions such as "Do you understand?" or "Do you have any questions?" Instructors should also avoid the following types of questions:

- Puzzle—"What is the first action you should take if a conventional gear airplane with a weak right brake is swerving left in a right crosswind during a full flap, power-on wheel landing?"

- Oversize—"What do you do before beginning an engine overhaul?"

- Toss-up—"In an emergency, should you squawk 7700 or pick a landing spot?"

- Bewilderment—"In reading the altimeter—you know you set a sensitive altimeter for the nearest station pressure—if you take temperature into account, as when flying from a cold air mass through a warm front, what precaution should you take when in a mountainous area?"

- Trick questions—these questions cause the learners to develop the feeling that they are engaged in a battle of wits with the instructor, and the whole significance of the subject of the instruction involved is lost. An example of a trick question would be one in which the response options are 1, 2, 3, and 4, but they are placed in the following form:

  A. 4
  B. 3
  C. 2
  D. 1

- Irrelevant questions—diversions that introduce only unrelated facts and thoughts and slow the learner's progress. Questions unrelated to the test topics are not helpful in evaluating the learner's knowledge of the subject at hand. An example of an irrelevant question would be to ask a question about tire inflation during a test on the timing of magnetos.

Answering Learner Questions

Tips for responding effectively to learner questions, especially in a classroom setting:

1. Be sure that you clearly understand the question before attempting to answer.
2. Display interest in the learner's question and frame an answer that is as direct and accurate as possible.
3. After responding, determine whether or not the learner is satisfied with the answer.

Sometimes it is unwise to introduce considerations more complicated or advanced than necessary to completely answer a learner's question at the current point in training. In this case, the instructor should carefully explain to the learner that the question was good and pertinent, but that a detailed answer would, at this time, unnecessarily complicate the learning tasks. The instructor should invite the learner to reintroduce the question later at the appropriate point in training.

Occasionally, a learner asks a question that the instructor cannot answer. In such cases, the instructor should freely admit not knowing the answer, but should promise to get the answer or, if practicable, offer to help the learner look it up in available references.

Scenario-Based Training

Since flying has become more complex, the focus of training needs to address pilot decision-making and risk management, a concept the authors call Single Pilot Resource Management (SRM). Since SRM training requires practicing the decision-making process in real time and in real situations, a new form of GA training that goes beyond the traditional task and maneuver-based training is recommended. The FITS program emphasizes combining traditional task and maneuver training with Scenario Based Training (SBT) to teach the advanced pilot judgment and risk management skills required in the SRM environment.

In many respects, scenario-based training is not a new concept. Experienced flight instructors have been using scenarios to teach cross country operations, emergency procedures, and other flight skills for years. Scenario-based training puts the learner pilot into the normal cross-country environment much earlier than traditional flight training programs. The goal is to begin training the pilot, through meaningful repetition, how to gather information and make informed and timely decisions. We routinely refer to this process as "experience." Scenario-based learning does not preclude traditional maneuver-based training. Rather, flight maneuvers are integrated into the flight scenarios and conducted, as they would occur in the real world. Those maneuvers requiring repetition may still be taught during concentrated settings. However, once they are learned, they are then integrated into realistic flight situations.

The flight instructor is crucial to the implementation of a scenario-based training program. In this capacity, an instructor serves in the learning environment as an advisor and guide for the learner. The duties, responsibilities, and authority of the flight instructor include the following:

- Orient new learners to the scenario-based training system.

- Help the learner become a confident planner and in-flight manager of each flight and a critical evaluator of their own performance.

- Help the learner understand the knowledge requirements present in real world applications.

- Diagnose learning difficulties and help the individual overcome them.

- Be able to evaluate learner progress and maintain appropriate records.

- Provide continuous review of learning.

The flight instructor is the key to success, and different instructional techniques are required for successful SBT. Remembering that the learning objective is for the learner to be more ready to exercise sound judgment and make good decisions; the flight instructor turns the responsibility for planning and execution of the flight over to the learner as soon as possible. The flight instructor will continue to demonstrate and instruct skill maneuvers in the traditional manner, however, when the learner begins to make decisions the flight instructor should revert to the role of mentor and/or learning facilitator.

Each situation a learner faces may not have one right, and one wrong answer. Instead, learners will encounter situations in training that may have several "good" outcomes as well as the potential for some "poor" ones. While the flight instructor should understand in advance which outcomes are positive or negative, the instructor allows the learner to make both good and poor decisions. This does not mean that the learner should be allowed to make an unsafe decision or commit an unsafe act. However, it does allow the learner to make decisions that fit their experience level and result in positive outcomes.

Chapter Summary

This chapter described the methods and techniques aviation instructors use to assess learner progress. A well-designed and timely assessment defines what is worth knowing, enhances motivation, and improves learning. Today's learners want to know the criteria by which they are assessed, and they want practical and specific feedback. Aviation instructors familiar with different types of assessments know how and when to use them to promote a productive learning environment.

Aviation Instructor's Handbook (FAA-H-8083-9)
Chapter 7: Planning Instructional Activity

Introduction

Susan (learner) and Bill (flight instructor) are flying a lesson scenario which consists of a short cross-country leg to a local airport for some practice landings followed by a return to the home airport located in Class C airspace. While practicing landings at the nontowered airport, Susan notes that the ceiling is lowering, and the crosswind is beginning to increase. In his own mind, Bill is convinced that they can practice landings for another 30 minutes to an hour and still return to home base. However, instead of telling Susan this, while taxiing back after a full stop landing, he first asks her several questions.

- Has the flight situation changed since they left the home field?

- What does she think of the weather situation?

- How can we gain more information?
    - Check with Flight Service by cell phone or on the radio?
    - Stop at the local Fixed Based Operator (FBO) and call back to the home FBO to check on weather?

- Are there other issues?
    - Fuel?
    - Schedule?

- Aircraft equipment (instrument flight rules (IFR)/visual flight rules (VFR)) and pilot capability?

Susan decides that she would be more comfortable returning to the home airport and practicing landings there to stay out of the weather. Although not his plan, it is a good plan based on accurate situational awareness and good risk management skills, so Bill agrees. Susan is now beginning to gain confidence by practicing her judgment and decision-making skills. In the postflight critique, Susan leads a discussion of this and other decisions she has made in order to learn more about understanding hazards and mitigating risk.

In the past, the aviation instructor was a capable pilot or aviation technician with a general understanding of basic teaching methods and techniques. Currently, the Federal Aviation Administration (FAA) places greater emphasis on the instructor's role and skill as a teacher and mentor. The instructor should understand how to create and use lesson objectives and lesson plans. The instructor should know how to assess learning and motivate learners through proper feedback and by setting a good example. The learning that takes place is a direct result of the instructor's active lesson preparation, delivery, observation, and assessment.

Historically, aviation instruction focused on the performance of specific procedures and/or maneuvers, and measured learning with objective standards. Changing technology and innovations in learning provide today's aviation instructors with the opportunity to use new methods and teach to new standards. One of these methods, introduced in Chapter 5, The Teaching Process, is scenario-based training (SBT). While SBT is an integral component of today's aviation training, the instructor is crucial to its implementation. By emphasizing SBT, the instructor functions in the learning environment as an advisor and guide for the learner.

This chapter reviews the planning required by the professional aviation instructor as it relates to four key topics—course of training, blocks of learning, training syllabus, and lesson plans. It also explains how to integrate SBT, aeronautical decision-making (ADM), and risk management into the aviation training lesson.

Course of Training

Whatever the method of teaching, the key to developing well-planned and organized aviation instruction includes using lesson plans and a training syllabus that meet all regulatory certification requirements. Much of the basic planning necessary for the flight instructor and maintenance instructor is provided by the knowledge and proficiency requirements published in Title 14 of the Code of Federal Regulations (14 CFR) parts 61 and 65, approved school syllabi, and the various texts, manuals, and training courses available.

As discussed in Chapter 5, The Teaching Process, a course of training is a series of studies leading to attainment of a specific goal such as a certificate of completion, graduation, or an academic degree. An instructor plans instructional content around the course of training by determining the objectives and standards, which in turn determine individual lesson plans, test items, and levels of learning. For a complete discussion of these items, see Chapter 5.

Blocks of Learning

After the overall training objectives have been established, the next step is the identification of the blocks of learning which constitute the necessary parts of the total objective. Just as in building a pyramid, some blocks are submerged in the structure and never appear on the surface, but each is an integral and necessary part of the structure. Thus, the various blocks are not isolated subjects, but essential parts of the whole. During the process of identifying the blocks of learning to be assembled for the proposed training activity, the instructor should also examine each block to ensure it is an integral part of the structure. Extraneous blocks of instruction are expensive frills, especially in-flight instruction, and detract from, rather than assist in, the completion of the final objective.

While determining the overall training objectives is a necessary first step in the planning process, early identification of the foundation blocks of learning is also essential. Training for any such complicated and involved task as piloting or maintaining an aircraft requires the development and assembly of many segments or blocks of learning in their proper relationships. In this way, a learner can master the segments or blocks individually and can progressively combine these with other related segments until their sum meets the overall training objectives.

The blocks of learning identified during the planning and management of a training activity should be fairly consistent in scope. They should represent units of learning which can be measured and evaluated—not a sequence of periods of instruction. For example, the flight training of a private pilot might be divided into the following major blocks: achievement of the knowledge and skills necessary for solo, the knowledge and skills necessary for solo cross-country flight, and the knowledge and skills appropriate for obtaining a private pilot certificate. *[Figure 7-1]*

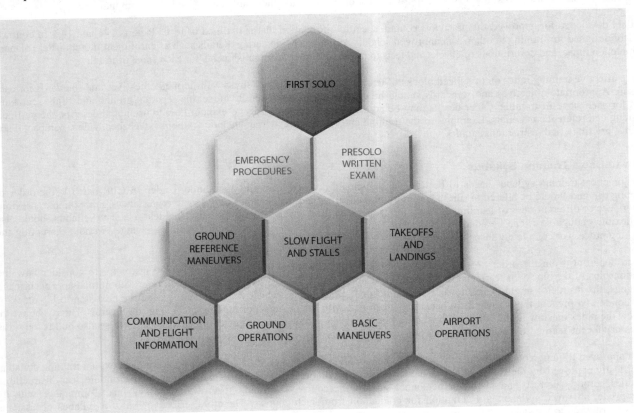

Figure 7-1. *The presolo stage or phase of private pilot training is comprised of several basic building blocks. These blocks of learning, which should include coordinated ground and flight training, lead up to the first solo.*

Use of the building block approach provides the learner with a boost in self-confidence. This normally occurs each time a block is completed. Otherwise, an overall goal, such as earning a mechanic's certificate, may seem unobtainable. If the larger blocks are broken down into smaller blocks of instruction, each on its own is more manageable. Humans learn from the simple to the complex. For example, a learner pilot should understand and master the technique of a normal landing prior to being introduced to short-field and soft-field landings. A helicopter pilot should be proficient in running landings before the instructor introduces a no hydraulics approach and landing.

By becoming familiar with the learner's aviation background, an instructor can plan the sequence of instruction blocks. Does the applicant have previous aeronautical experience or possess a pilot certificate in another category? This information will help the instructor design appropriate training blocks. For example, if the learner is a helicopter pilot who is transitioning to an airplane, he or she will understand speed control, but not necessarily know how to achieve it in an airplane. The instructor can plan blocks of instruction that build on what the learner already knows.

Training Syllabus

Instructors need a practical guide to help them make sure the training is accomplished in a logical sequence and that all of the requirements are completed and properly documented. A well organized, comprehensive syllabus can fulfill these needs.

Syllabus Format and Content

The format and organization of the syllabus may vary, but it always should be in the form of an abstract or digest of the course of training. It should contain blocks of learning to be completed in the most efficient order. Since a syllabus is intended to be a summary of a course of training, it should be fairly brief, yet comprehensive enough to cover essential information. This information is usually presented in an outline format with lesson-by-lesson coverage. Some syllabi include tables to show recommended training time for each lesson, as well as the overall minimum time requirements. *[Figure 7-2]*

While many instructors may develop their own training syllabi, there are many well-designed commercial products that may be used. These are found in various training manuals, approved school syllabi, and other publications available from industry.

Syllabi developed for approved flight schools contain specific information that is outlined in 14 CFR parts 141 and 142. In contrast, syllabi designed for training in other than approved schools may not provide certain details such as enrollment prerequisites, planned completion times, and descriptions of checks and tests to measure learner accomplishments for each stage of training.

Since effective training relies on organized blocks of learning, all syllabi should stress well-defined objectives and standards for each lesson. Appropriate objectives and standards should be established for the overall course, the separate ground and flight segments, and for each stage of training. Other details may be added to a syllabus in order to explain how to use it and describe the pertinent training and reference materials. Examples of the training and reference materials include textbooks, websites, video, compact discs, exams, briefings, and instructional guides.

How to Use a Training Syllabus

Any practical training syllabus needs to be flexible and should be used primarily as a guide. Under 14 CFR part 61, the order of training can and should be altered to suit the progress of the learner and the demands of special circumstances. For example, previous experience or different rates of learning often require some alteration or repetition to fit individual learners. The syllabus should also be flexible enough so it can be adapted to weather variations, aircraft availability, and scheduling changes without disrupting the teaching process or completely suspending training.

When departing from the order prescribed by the syllabus, however, it is the responsibility of the instructor to consider how the relationships of the blocks of learning are affected. For example, if the learner is having a difficult time with normal approaches and landings, the instructor might decide to delay adding short-field landings, which were originally to be the next step in his block of instruction. To prevent the learner from becoming frustrated with his or her poor landing technique, the instructor may choose to review the block on slow flight, which offers the learner a chance to do well and regain confidence. This exercise also builds the skills necessary for the learner to master approaches and normal landings.

Each approved training course provided by a certificated aviation school should be conducted in accordance with a training syllabus specifically approved by the FAA. At certificated schools, the syllabus is a key part of the training course outline. The instructional facilities, airport, aircraft, and instructor personnel support the course of training specified in the syllabus. Compliance with the appropriate, approved syllabus is a condition for graduation from such courses. Therefore, effective use of a syllabus necessitates that it be referred to throughout the entire course of training. Both the instructor and the learner should have a copy of the approved syllabus. However, as previously mentioned, adherence to a syllabus should not be so stringent that it becomes inflexible or unchangeable. It should be flexible enough to adapt to the special needs of individual learners.

Ground training lessons and classroom lectures concentrate on the cognitive domain of learning. A typical lesson might include defining, labeling, or listing what the learner understands so far. Many of the knowledge areas are directly or indirectly concerned with safety, ADM, and judgment. Since these subjects are associated with the affective domain of learning (emotion), instructors who find a way to stress safety, ADM, and judgment, along with the traditional aviation subjects, can favorably influence a learner's attitude, beliefs, and values.

STAGE 1 | GROUND LESSON 2

LESSON OBJECTIVES

- Learn important safety of flight considerations.
- Become thoroughly familiar with airports, including marking and lighting aids.
- Learn the significance of airspace divisions and how to use the radio for communications.
- Understand the capabilities and use of radar and other ATC services.

CONTENT

Introduce:

Section A—Safety of Flight
- ☐ Visual Scanning
- ☐ Collision Avoidance Precautions
- ☐ Blind Spots and Aircraft Design
- ☐ Right-of-Way Rules
- ☐ Minimum Safe Altitudes
- ☐ VFR Cruising Altitudes
- ☐ Special Safety Considerations

Section B—Airports
- ☐ Towered and Nontowered Airports
- ☐ Runway and Taxiway Markings
- ☐ Airport Signs
- ☐ Wind Direction Indicators
- ☐ Segmented Circle
- ☐ Noise Abatement Procedures
- ☐ Airport Lighting

Section C—Airspace
- ☐ Cloud Clearance and Visibility
- ☐ Special Use and Other Airspace Areas

Section D—Radio Communications
- ☐ VHF Communications Equipment
- ☐ Coordinated Universal Time
- ☐ Radio Procedures
- ☐ Common Traffic Advisory Frequency
- ☐ Flight Service Stations

Section E—Radar and ATC Services
- ☐ Radar
- ☐ Transponder
- ☐ FAA Radar Systems

COMPLETION STANDARDS

The learner will complete Private Pilot Exercises 2A, 2B, 2C, 2D, and 2E with a minimum passing score of 80%. The instructor will review each incorrect response to ensure understanding before the learner progresses to Ground Lesson 3.

Figure 7-2. *This excerpt of a ground lesson shows a unit of ground instruction. In this example, neither the time nor the number of ground training periods to be devoted to the lesson is specified. The lesson should include three parts—objective, content, and completion standards.*

Flight training lessons or aviation technical lab sessions also include knowledge areas, but they generally emphasize the psychomotor domain of learning because the learner is "doing" something. The lesson plan shown in *Figure 7-3* shows the main elements of a ground lesson for a flight learner. The affective domain of learning is also important in this type of training; a learner's attitude toward safety, ADM, and judgment, should be a major concern of the instructor.

STAGE 1	FLIGHT LESSON 4

Dual—Local (1.0)

Note: A view-limiting device is required for 0.2 hours of dual instrument time allocated to Flight Lesson 4.

LESSON OBJECTIVES

- Practice the maneuvers listed for review to gain additional proficiency and demonstrate the ability to recognize and recover from stalls.
- The learner will also receive instruction and practice in the maneuvers and procedures listed for introduction, including emergency operations and additional practice of airplane control by instrument reference (IR).
- Instructor may demonstrate secondary, accelerated maneuver, crossed control, and elevator trim stalls.
- Emphasis will be on procedures related to airport operations, steep turns, slow flight, stalls, and stall recovery.

CONTENT

Introduce:

- ❑ Systems and Equipment Malfunctions
- ❑ Emergency Procedures
- ❑ Emergency Descent
- ❑ Emergency Approach and Landing
- ❑ Emergency Equipment and Survival Gear
- ❑ Climbing and Descending Turns (VR)(IR)

Review:

- ❑ Airport and Runway Markings and Lighting
- ❑ Airspeed and Configuration Changes
- ❑ Flight at Approach Speed
- ❑ Flight at Various Airspeeds From Cruise to Slow Flight
- ❑ Maneuvering During Slow Flight
- ❑ Power-Off Stalls
- ❑ Power-On Stalls
- ❑ Normal Takeoffs and Landings
- ❑ Collision Avoidance Precautions
- ❑ Traffic Patterns

COMPLETION STANDARDS

- Displays increased proficiency in coordinated airplane attitude control during basic maneuvers.
- Performs unassisted takeoffs.
- Demonstrates correct communications and traffic pattern procedures.
- Completes landings with instructor assistance.
- Demonstrates basic understanding of steep turns, slow flight, stalls, stall recovery, and emergency operations.
- Completes demonstrated stalls.
- Indicates basic understanding of airplane control by use of the flight instruments.

Figure 7-3. *A flight training lesson, like a ground training lesson, should include an objective, content, and completion standards. More than one objective could, and often does, apply to a single flight lesson.*

The flight training syllabus should include Risk Management instruction unique to each stage, phase, or training element to help the learner identify the risks involved and employ strategies to mitigate them. Throughout the learner's training scenarios the instructor should include increasingly more subtle risks so that the learner becomes more skilled in identifying them and able to develop effective mitigation strategies. The aviation technician syllabus should also emphasize what constitutes unsafe practices, such as the ease of introducing foreign object damage (FOD) to an aircraft when the location of tools is not monitored.

A syllabus may include several other items that add to or clarify the objective, content, or standards. A lesson may specify the recommended class time, reference or study materials, recommended sequence of training, and study assignment for the next lesson. Both ground and flight lessons may have explanatory information notes added to specific lessons. *[Figure 7-4]*

Typical syllabus notes

- Learners should read Chapter 1 of the textbook prior to Ground Lesson 1.

- All preflight duties and procedures will be performed and evaluated prior to each flight. Therefore, they will not appear in the content outlines.

- The notation "VR" or "IR" is used to indicate maneuvers which should be performed by both visual references and instrument references during the conduct of integrated flight instruction.

- A view-limiting device is required for the 0.2 hours of dual instrument time allocated to Flight Lesson 4.

- The demonstrated stalls are not a proficiency requirement for private pilot certification. The purpose of the demonstrations is to help the learner learn how to recognize, prevent, and if necessary, recover before the stall develops into a spin. These stalls should not be practiced without a qualified flight instructor. In addition, some stalls may be prohibited in some airplanes.

Figure 7-4. *Information in the form of notes may be added to individual ground or flight lessons in a syllabus when they are necessary.*

While a syllabus is designed to provide a road map showing how to accomplish the overall objective of a course of training, it may be useful for other purposes. As already mentioned, it can be used as a checklist to ensure that required training has successfully been completed. Thus, a syllabus can be an effective tool for recordkeeping. Enhanced syllabi, which also are designed for recordkeeping, can be very beneficial to the independent instructor.

This recordkeeping function is usually facilitated by boxes or blank spaces adjacent to the knowledge areas, procedures, or maneuvers in a lesson. Most syllabi introduce each procedure or maneuver in one lesson and review them in subsequent lessons. Some syllabi also include provisions for grading learner performance and recording both ground and flight training time. Accurate recordkeeping is necessary to keep both the learner and the instructor informed on the status of training. These records also serve as a basis for endorsements and recommendations for knowledge and practical tests. Some training syllabi or records may include coded numbers or letters for other instructors to record their evaluation of a learner's progress and knowledge or skill level. *[Figure 7-5]*

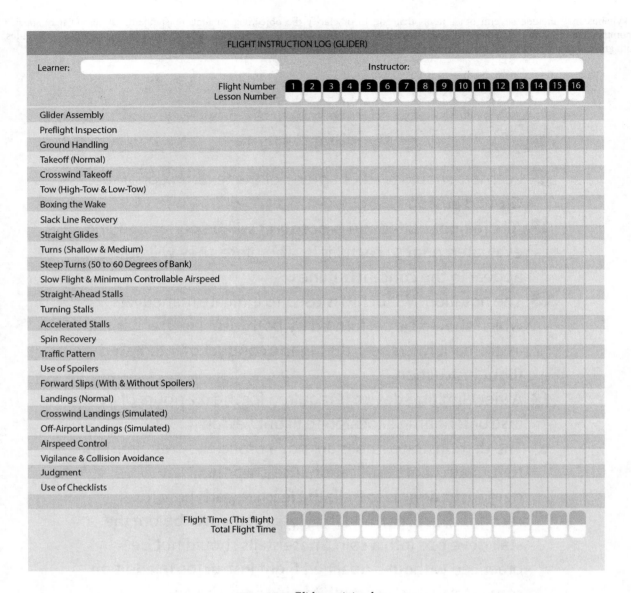

Figure 7-5. *Glider training log.*

Another benefit of using a syllabus is that it helps in the development of lesson plans. A well-constructed syllabus already contains much of the essential information that is required in a lesson plan, including objectives, content, and completion standards.

Lesson Plans

A lesson plan is an organized outline for a single instructional period. It is a necessary guide for the instructor because it tells what to do, in what order to do it, and what procedure to use in teaching the material of a lesson. Lesson plans should be prepared for each training period and be developed to show specific knowledge and/or skills to be taught.

A mental outline of a lesson is not a lesson plan. A lesson plan should be put into writing. Another instructor should be able to take the lesson plan and know what to do in conducting the same period of instruction. Written out, the lesson plan can be analyzed for adequacy and completeness.

Lesson plans make excellent recordkeeping forms that can become a permanent part of a pilot's training record. They can be formatted for the instructor to carry in the aircraft and include a checklist for indicating what portions of the lesson were completed, date of completion, the flight instructor's signature, and time flown. The lesson plan can also have a notation section for flight instructor comments.

A training folder for each learner helps an instructor keep all pertinent data in one place. The folder should include items such as lesson plans, training requirements, flight or ground instruction received, 14 CFR part 61 requirements met, solo endorsements, and any other training information. Many training records are now recorded and maintained electronically. These records should be kept for at least 3 years. Good recordkeeping also provides each instructor with the number of learners he or she has trained, which is helpful information for an instructor who needs to renew his or her certificate.

Purpose of the Lesson Plan

Lesson plans are designed to assure that each learner receives the best possible instruction under the existing conditions. Lesson plans help instructors keep a constant check on their own activity, as well as that of their learners. The development of lesson plans by instructors signifies, in effect, that they have taught the lessons to themselves prior to attempting to teach the lessons to learners. An adequate lesson plan, when properly used, should:

- Assure a wise selection of material and the elimination of unimportant details.

- Make certain that due consideration is given to each part of the lesson.

- Aid the instructor in presenting the material in a suitable sequence for efficient learning.

- Provide an outline of the teaching procedure to be used.

- Serve as a means of relating the lesson to the objectives of the course of training.

- Give the inexperienced instructor confidence.

- Promote uniformity of instruction regardless of the instructor or the date on which the lesson is given.

Characteristics of a Well-Planned Lesson

The quality of planning affects the quality of results. Successful professionals understand that the price of excellence is hard work and thorough preparation. The effective instructor realizes that the time and energy spent in planning and preparing each lesson is well worth the effort in the long run.

A complete cycle of planning usually includes several steps. After the objective is determined, the instructor researches the subject as it is defined by the objective. Once the research is complete, the instructor determines the method of instruction and identifies a useful lesson planning format. The decision of how to organize the lesson and the selection of suitable support material come next. The final steps include assembling training aids and writing the lesson plan outline. One technique for writing the lesson plan outline is to prepare the beginning and ending first. Then, complete the outline and revise as required. A lesson plan should be a working document that can and should be revised as changes occur or are needed.

The following are some of the important characteristics that should be reflected in all well-planned lessons.

Unity—each lesson should be a unified segment of instruction. A lesson is concerned with certain limited objectives, which are stated in terms of desired learning outcomes. All teaching procedures and materials should be selected to attain these objectives.

Content—each lesson should contain new material. However, the new facts, principles, procedures, or skills should be related to the lesson previously presented. A short review of earlier lessons is usually necessary, particularly in-flight training.

Scope—each lesson should be reasonable in scope. A person can master only a few principles or skills at a time, the number depending on complexity. Presenting too much material in a lesson results in confusion; presenting too little material results in inefficiency.

Practicality—each lesson should be planned in terms of the conditions under which the training is to be conducted. Lesson plans conducted in an airplane or ground trainer will differ from those conducted in a classroom. Also, the kinds and quantities of instructional aids available have a great influence on lesson planning and instructional procedures.

Flexibility—although the lesson plan provides an outline and sequence for the training to be conducted, a degree of flexibility should be incorporated. For example, the outline of content may include blank spaces for add-on material, if required.

Relation to course of training—each lesson should be planned and taught so that its relation to the course objectives is clear to each learner. For example, a lesson on short-field takeoffs and landings should be related to both the certification and safety objectives of the course of training.

Instructional steps—every lesson, when adequately developed, falls logically into the four steps of the teaching process: preparation, presentation, application, and review and evaluation.

How to Use a Lesson Plan Properly

Be familiar with the lesson plan. The instructor should study each step of the plan and should be thoroughly familiar with as much information related to the subject as possible.

Use the lesson plan as a guide. The lesson plan is an outline for conducting an instructional period. It assures that pertinent materials are at hand and that the presentation is accomplished with order and unity. Having a plan prevents the instructor from getting off track, omitting essential points, and introducing irrelevant material. Learners have a right to expect an instructor to give the same attention to teaching that they give to learning. The most certain means of achieving teaching success is to have a carefully reviewed lesson plan.

Adapt the lesson plan to the class or learner. In teaching a class, the instructor may find that the procedures outlined in the lesson plan are not leading to the desired results. In this situation, the instructor should change the approach. There is no certain way of predicting the reactions of different groups of learners. An approach that has been successful with one group may not be equally successful with another.

A lesson plan for an instructional flight period should be appropriate to the background, flight experience, and ability of the particular learner. A lesson plan may have to be modified considerably during flight, due to deficiencies in the learner's knowledge or poor mastery of elements essential to the effective completion of the lesson. In some cases, the entire lesson plan may have to be abandoned in favor of review.

Revise the lesson plan periodically. After a lesson plan has been prepared for a training period, a continuous revision may be necessary. This is true for a number of reasons such as availability or non-availability of instructional aids, changes in regulations, or new manuals and textbooks.

Lesson Plan Formats

The format and style of a lesson plan depends on several factors. Certainly, the subject matter helps determine how a lesson is presented and what teaching method is used. Individual lesson plans may be quite simple for one-on-one training, or they may be elaborate and complicated for large, structured classroom lessons. Preferably, each lesson should have somewhat limited objectives that are achievable within a reasonable period of time. This principle should apply to both ground and flight training. However, as previously noted, aviation training is not simple. It involves all three domains of learning, and the objectives usually include the higher levels of learning, at least at the application level.

In spite of need for varied subject coverage, diverse teaching methods, and relatively high-level learning objectives, most aviation lesson plans have the common characteristics already discussed. All should include objectives, content to support the objectives, and completion standards. Various authorities often divide the main headings into several subheadings; terminology, even for the main headings, varies extensively. For example, completion standards may be called assessment, review and feedback, performance evaluation, or some other related term.

Commercially developed lesson plans are acceptable for most training situations, including use by flight instructor applicants during their practical tests. However, all instructors should recognize that even well-designed preprinted lesson plans may need to be modified. Therefore, instructors are encouraged to use creativity when adapting preprinted lesson plans or when developing their own lesson plans for specific learners or training circumstances.

In the traditional lesson plan illustrated by *Figure 7-6*, the objective is "The learner will learn to control for wind drift." According to the plan, the instructor reviews topics already covered including heading, speed, angle of bank, altitude, terrain, and wind direction plus velocity. This explanation is followed by a demonstration and repeated practice of a specific flight maneuver, such as turns around a point or S-turns across the road until the maneuver can be consistently accomplished in a safe and effective manner within a specified limit of heading, altitude, and airspeed. At the end of this lesson, the learner is only capable of practicing the maneuver with assistance from the instructor.

The traditional type of training lesson plan with its focus on the task and maneuver or procedure continues to meet many aviation learning requirements, but as discussed earlier in the chapter, it is being augmented by more realistic and fluid forms of problem-based learning such as SBT. For the flight instructor, this type of training does not preclude traditional maneuver-based training. Rather, flight maneuvers are integrated into the flight scenarios and conducted as they would occur in the real world. Those maneuvers requiring repetition are still taught during concentrated settings; once learned, they are then integrated into realistic flight situations.

For the aviation technician instructor, SBT enhances traditional classroom instruction. By integrating SBT into the lesson, learners are required to deal with problems they will encounter in the real world.

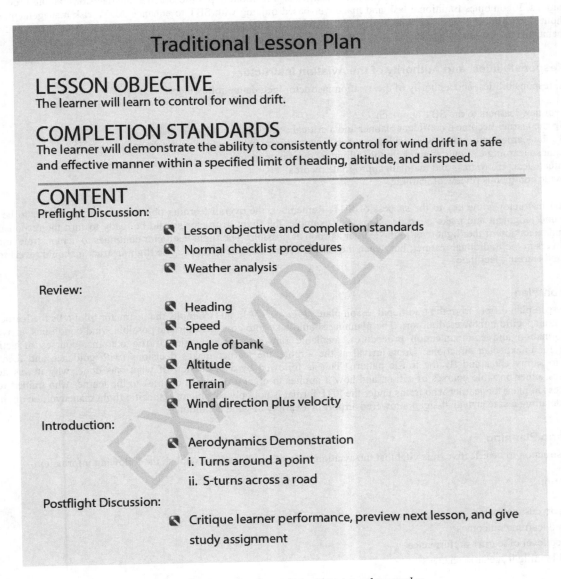

Traditional Lesson Plan

LESSON OBJECTIVE
The learner will learn to control for wind drift.

COMPLETION STANDARDS
The learner will demonstrate the ability to consistently control for wind drift in a safe and effective manner within a specified limit of heading, altitude, and airspeed.

CONTENT
Preflight Discussion:
- Lesson objective and completion standards
- Normal checklist procedures
- Weather analysis

Review:
- Heading
- Speed
- Angle of bank
- Altitude
- Terrain
- Wind direction plus velocity

Introduction:
- Aerodynamics Demonstration
  - i. Turns around a point
  - ii. S-turns across a road

Postflight Discussion:
- Critique learner performance, preview next lesson, and give study assignment

Figure 7-6. *Example of a traditional training lesson plan.*

Scenario-Based Training (SBT)

Improper pilot decisions cause a significant percentage of all accidents and the majority of fatal accidents in light single- and twin-engine aircraft. The goal of SBT is to challenge the learner or transitioning pilot with a variety of flight scenarios to improve decision-making skills. These scenarios train the pilot to manage the resources available in the flight deck, consider hazards, exercise sound judgment, and make timely decisions that promote safety.

As defined in Chapter 5, SBT is a training method that uses a highly structured script of real world experiences to address aviation training objectives in an operational environment. Such training can include initial training, transition training, upgrade training, recurrent training, and special training. Since humans develop cognitive skills through active interaction with the world, an effective aviation instructor uses the maneuver- or procedure-based approach but presents the objectives in a scenario situation.

Although some flight instructors have used the SBT approach as a teaching method for many years, the current emphasis on SBT in aviation training reflects education research that shows learning is more effective when participants are actively involved in the learning process.

Single-Pilot Resource Management (SRM) requires the learner or transitioning pilot to practice the decision-making process in real-world situations, It combines traditional task and maneuver-based training with SBT to enhance ADM, risk management, and SRM skills without compromising basic aeronautical skills. Instead of training pilots to pass practical tests, this program focuses on expertly managed real-world challenges.

Duties, Responsibilities, and Authority of the Aviation Instructor

The duties, responsibilities, and authority of the aviation instructor include the following:

1. Orient new learners to the SBT approach.
2. Help the learner become a confident planner and a critical self-evaluator of performance.
3. Help the learner understand the knowledge requirements present in real world applications.
4. Diagnose learning difficulties and help the individual overcome them.
5. Evaluate learner progress and maintain appropriate records.
6. Provide continuous review of learning.

The aviation instructor is the key to the success of SBT. Remember, the overall learning objective is for the learner to be ready to exercise sound judgment and make good decisions. For example, the flight instructor should be ready to turn the responsibility for planning and execution of the flight over to the learner as soon as possible. The flight instructor continues to demonstrate and instruct skill maneuvers in the traditional manner; but, when the learner begins to make decisions, the flight instructor should revert to the role of mentor and learning facilitator.

SBT Lesson Plan

The SBT lesson plan differs from the traditional lesson plan. *[Figure 7-7]* In this example, the instructor pilot tells the learner to plan for arrival at a specific nontowered airport. The planning should take into consideration the possible wind conditions, arrival paths, airport information and communication procedures, available runways, recommended traffic patterns, courses of action, and preparation for unexpected situations. Upon arrival at the airport, the learner makes decisions (with guidance and feedback, as necessary) to safely enter and fly the traffic pattern. This is followed by a discussion of what was done, why it was done, the consequences, other possible courses of action, and how it applies to other airports. In contrast to the learner who trained under the traditional lesson plan, the learner who trains under the SBT format is not only capable of a specific flight maneuver, he or she is now capable of detailing a safe arrival at any nontowered airport in a variety of wind condition.

Pre-Scenario Planning

For SBT instruction to be effective, it is vital that the aviation instructor and learner establish the following information:

Flight scenario:

- Scenario destination(s)
- Desired learning outcomes
- Desired level of learner performance
- Possible inflight scenario changes

Nonflight scenario:

- Narrative of the task goal
- Desired learning outcomes
- Desired level of learner performance
- Possible scenario changes

Scenario-Based Training Lesson Plan

Type of Training

Initial

Maneuver or Training Objective

Plan for arrival at a specific nontowered airport.

Scenario

Prepare to fly to the Enterprise Municipal Airport (EDN) in order to visit the Army Aviation Museum at Fort Rucker.

Completion Standards

The learner is capable of explaining the safe arrival at any nontowered airport in any wind condition.

Possible Hazards or Considerations

- ⚑ Ground-based obstructions/hazards
- ⚑ Wind conditions
- ⚑ Visibility/ceiling
- ⚑ Engine-out procedures
- ⚑ Airport traffic

Mitigation Strategies and Resources

(Every hazard or consideration should be addressed through the use of some mitigating strategy or resource. Those provided below serve only as an example to illustrate the system safety methodology.)

Ground-based obstructions/hazards:
The instructor and learner will review all available resources, including sectional/terminal area charts, A/FD, and Notices To Airmen (NOTAMs). Using aircraft performance data found in the POH/FM, the potential impact of any obstructions or hazards during departure, en route, and arrival will be assessed and a strategy developed to address any concerns.

Wind conditions:
The instructor and learner will use the aircraft POH/FM and assess the runway environment prior to making a determination. This would also be an excellent catalyst for a discussion of personal minimums and any additional training requirements.

Visibility/ceiling:
The instructor and learner will discuss the impact of visibility/ceiling as it relates to departure, en route, and landing at an nontowered airport in various wind conditions. For example, if circumstances demand the conduct of a circling approach under marginal VFR conditions, does the learner have the confidence and proficiency to fly a tight pattern while managing airspeed, aircraft coordination, etc? Under such circumstances, would it be more desirable to conduct a straight-in approach with a slight tailwind (if that is even an option)? How much wind would be too much? What other variables/options should be considered (perhaps a diversion to a more suitable airport)?

Engine-out procedures:
Should an engine fail or partial loss of power occur, the learner and instructor should discuss and simulate in a manner consistent with safety, engine-out procedures as part of a comprehensive training program.

Airport traffic:
Traffic at both towered and nontowered airports often necessitates wide variations in landing patterns. While issues stemming from airport traffic may largely be addressed through sound flying technique, the instructor can take an otherwise routine lesson and introduce other risk elements, thus promoting the learner's development of critical decision-making skills.

Fly the Scenario

Postflight Review

This review should include a dialogue between the instructor pilot and the learner or transitioning pilot encompassing the flight scenario. Generally, the instructor pilot should lead the discussion with questions that generate reflective thinking on how the overall flight went. The instructor pilot should use this to assist in evaluating the learner or transitioning pilot's assessment skills, judgment, and decision-making skills. Typically, the discussion should begin with learner self-critique; the instructor pilot enables the learner to solve the problems and draw conclusions. Based on this analysis, the learner and instructor pilot should discuss methods for improvement, even on those items that were considered successful.

Figure 7-7. *SBT lesson plan.*

The aviation industry is moving from traditional knowledge-related learning outcomes to an emphasis on increased internalized learning in which learners assess situations and react appropriately. Enhancement of knowledge and understanding usually accompanies a dynamic learning experience.

Reality is the ultimate learning situation and SBT attempts to get as close as possible to this ideal. It addresses learning that occurs in a context or situation. It is based on the concept of situated cognition, which is the idea that knowledge cannot be known and fully understood independent of its context. In other words, humans learn better from realistic situations where they are counted on to perform.

For example, realistic cross-country flight scenarios planned and executed by the pilot in training with assistance from the flight instructor begin the early development of flight deck management skills, situational awareness, and ADM. Continued engagement by the learner in the planning, executing, and assessment of each scenario reinforces development throughout the training. It is important to remember the learner is responsible for planning the flight scenario from a menu of short cross-country flights developed by the training provider. While the flight instructor will certainly assist the learner in aircraft performance data, weight and balance, and general aircraft layout prior to the first lesson, the sooner the learner assumes these responsibilities, the better the learning environment. The scenario descriptions offered in the FAA generic syllabi are a starting point for the training provider. Scenarios can be tailored for the local weather and terrain conditions and are most effective when they replicate the environment most likely encountered by the learners.

SBT is a compilation of basic learning theory, adult learning concepts, and the best of the traditional aviation training procedures. Above all, it is about learning complex tasks in a realistic environment at a pace and in a structure the individual learner can comprehend and process. *[Figure 7-8]* Good teaching techniques are still important, but only if they aid in learning. More detailed information about SBT can be found at www.faa.gov/training_testing/training/fits/more/.

The Main Points To Remember About Scenario-Based Training

◙ SBT is situated in a real context and is based on the idea that knowledge cannot be gained and fully integrated independent of its context.

◙ SBT accords with a performance improvement and behavior change philosophy of the learning function.

◙ SBT is different from traditional instructional design; one must be aware of the differences to successfully employ SBT.

◙ Most learning solutions should employ both traditional training and SBT.

◙ Traditional learning elements should enhance the SBT elements.

◙ It is essential to place boundaries around scenarios to make the transitions between scenarios and traditional learning as efficient as possible.

◙ Open-ended qualitative learner feedback is key to successful scenario revision, but revisions should not further complicate the scenario unless highly justified.

Figure 7-8. *Points to remember about scenario-based training.*

Single-Pilot Resource Management

SRM is the art and science of managing all the resources (both on-board the aircraft and from outside sources) available to a single pilot (prior and during flight) to ensure that the successful outcome of the flight is never in doubt.

The emergence of very light jet (VLJ) aircraft may also affect air travel. *[Figure 7-9]* Central to their economic success is the concept of single-pilot operations. Since the aircraft is heavily automated, the pilot's workload may actually be less than the current workload in some high performance single-engine aircraft. This allows more time for the pilot to gather and analyze information about weather, winds, landing conditions, fuel state, pilot physical condition, and passenger desires.

Figure 7-9. *Very light jet aircraft in flight.*

However, unless the pilot is trained to manage all of these factors and to let the aircraft automation assist, the workload may be very high. SRM training helps the pilot maintain situational awareness by managing the automation and associated aircraft control and navigation tasks. This enables the pilot to accurately assess, manage risk, and make accurate and timely decisions. SBT enhances SRM because SBT helps pilots learn how to gather information, analyze it, and make decisions.

Chapter Summary

As indicated by this chapter, it is possible to develop well-planned and organized instruction by using a training syllabus and lesson plans that meet all regulatory certification requirements. By identifying and incorporating "blocks of learning" into the teaching of objectives, the instructor can plan lessons that build on prior knowledge. Maneuver and/or procedure training coupled with SBT will help the aviation instructor train professional aviators and technicians who are able to gather and analyze information to aid in making good aeronautical decisions and decrease risk factors, leading to a successful flight or maintenance outcome.

As this training program evolves and new resources are introduced, aviation instructors may access web-based documents such as the generic transition syllabus at www.faa.gov/.

Aviation Instructor's Handbook (FAA-H-8083-9)
Chapter 8: Aviation Instructor Responsibilities and Professionalism

Introduction

Since learners look to aviation instructors as role models, it is important that instructors not only know how to teach, but that they project a knowledgeable and professional image. This chapter addresses the responsibilities of aviation instructors as trainers and as safety advocates. It explains how aviation instructors can enhance their professional image, and offers suggestions and sources of information to assist in professional development.

Aviation Instructor Responsibilities

The job of an aviation instructor is to transfer knowledge. Previous chapters have discussed how people learn, the teaching process, and teaching methods. To summarize in brief, instructors help learners meet and exceed established standards. Instructors measure learner performance against those standards and give positive reinforcement along the way. *[Figure 8-1]*

Responsibilities of All Aviation Instructors

- Helping learners learn
- Providing adequate instruction
- Demanding appropiate standards of performance
- Emphasizing the positive
- Ensuring aviation safety

Figure 8-1. *There are five main responsibilities of aviation instructors.*

Helping Learners

Learning should be an enjoyable experience. By making each lesson a pleasurable experience, the instructor helps the learner maintain a high level of motivation. This does not mean the instructor sacrifices standards of performance to make things easy. The learner experiences satisfaction by doing a good job or by meeting the challenge of a difficult task.

The idea that people need to be led to learning by making it easy is a fallacy. Though learners might initially be drawn to less difficult tasks, they ultimately devote more effort to activities that bring rewards. The use of standards, and measurement against standards, is key to helping learners. Meeting standards holds its own satisfaction for learners. People want to feel capable; they are proud of the successful achievement of difficult goals.

Learning should be interesting. Knowing the objective of each period of instruction gives meaning and interest to the learner, as well as the instructor. Not knowing lesson objectives often leads to confusion, disinterest, and uneasiness on the part of the learner.

Providing Adequate Instruction

To tailor his or her teaching technique to the learner, the flight instructor analyzes the learner's personality, thinking, and ability. No two learners are alike, and a particular method of instruction may not be equally effective for all learners. The instructor talks with a learner at some length to learn about their background, interests, temperament, and way of thinking, and should be prepared to change his or her methods of instruction as the learner advances through successive stages of training.

An instructor who incorrectly analyzes a learner may find the instruction does not produce the desired results. For example, the instructor at first thinks the individual is not a quick learner because that learner is quiet and reserved. Such a learner may fail to act at the proper time due to lack of self-confidence, even though the situation is correctly understood. In this case, instruction is directed toward developing learner self-confidence, rather than drill on flight fundamentals. In another case, too much criticism may discourage a timid person, whereas brisk instruction may force a more diligent application to the learning task. A learner requiring more time to learn also requires instructional methods that combine tact, keen perception, and delicate handling. If such a learner receives too much help and encouragement, a feeling of incompetence may develop.

For learners who exhibit slow progress due to discouragement or lack of confidence, instructors should assign more easily attained goals. Before attempting a complex task, the instructor separates it into discrete elements, and the learner practices and becomes good at each element. For example, instruction in S-turns may begin with consideration for headings only. Elements of altitude control, drift correction, and coordination can be introduced one at a time. As the learner gains confidence and ability, goals are increased in difficulty.

Conversely, fast learners can also create challenges for the instructor. Because these learners make few mistakes, they may assume that the correction of errors is unimportant. Overconfidence may result, which leads to faulty performance. For these learners, the instructor constantly raises the standard of performance for each lesson, demanding greater effort. Individuals learn only if aware of their errors, and better retention of skills exists for learners who focus their attention on an analysis of their performance. On the other hand, deficiencies should not be invented solely for the learners' benefit. Unfair criticism immediately destroys a learner's confidence in the instructor.

In some ways, an aviation instructor serves as a practical psychologist. As discussed in Chapters 2, Human Behavior, and 3, The Learning Process, an instructor can meet this responsibility by becoming familiar and conversant in the fundamentals of instructing and through a careful analysis of and continuing interest in learners.

Most new instructors tend to adopt the teaching methods used by their own instructors or the methods by which they themselves learn best. The fact that one has learned under a certain system of instruction does not mean that the best and most efficient learning occurred. The new instructor needs to remain open-minded and seek other resources and information to develop enhanced teaching ability.

Standards of Performance

An aviation instructor is responsible for training an applicant to established standards in all subject matter areas, procedures, and maneuvers included in the tasks within each area of operation in the appropriate Airman Certification (ACS)/Airman Practical Test Standards (PTS). It should be emphasized that the ACS/PTS book is a testing document, not a teaching document. *[Figure 8-2]*

Figure 8-2. *Acceptable standards in all subject matter areas, procedures, and maneuvers are included in the appropriate Airman Certification Standards (ACS)/Practical Test Standards (PTS).*

Emphasizing the Positive

The way instructors conduct themselves and the attitudes they display make an impression on learners. An aviation instructor's ability to teach in a manner that gives learners a positive image of aviation contributes to the instructor's success. *[Figure 8-3]*

Figure 8-3. *Learners learn more when instruction is presented in a positive and professional manner.*

Chapter 3, The Learning Process, emphasized that a negative self-concept inhibits the perceptual process, that fear adversely affects learner perceptions, that the feeling of being threatened limits the ability to perceive, and that negative motivation is not as effective as positive motivation. Merely knowing about these factors is not enough. Instructors need to detect these factors in their learners and strive to prevent negative feelings from undermining the instructional process.

Consider how the following negative scenarios conducted during the first lesson might adversely influence and turn off a new learner pilot who has limited or no aviation experience:

- An indoctrination in preflight procedures with emphasis on the critical precautions taken before every flight because "…emergencies in flight can be caused by an improper preflight and are often disastrous."

- Instruction and hands-on training in the care taken in taxiing an airplane because "…if you go too fast, you lose directional control of the aircraft."

- Introduction and demonstration of stalls, because "… this is how so many people lose their lives in airplanes."

- Illustrating and demonstrating forced landings during the first lesson, because "…one should always be prepared to cope with a rope break in a glider."

These new experiences might make the new learner wonder if learning to fly is a good idea.

In contrast, consider a first flight lesson in which the preflight inspection is presented to familiarize the learner with the aircraft and its components, and the flight is a perfectly normal one to a nearby airport, with return. Following the flight, the instructor can call the learner's attention to the ease with which the trip was made in comparison with other modes of transportation, and the fact that no critical incidents were encountered or expected.

This does not mean stalls and emergency procedures should be omitted from training. It only illustrates the positive approach in which the learner does not receive overwhelming information. Using a syllabus that considers the learner's ability to comprehend new information means a foundation exists for that information. The introduction of emergency procedures after the learner has developed an acquaintance with normal operations is less likely to be discouraging and frightening, or to inhibit learning by the imposition of fear.

Nothing in aviation that demands that learners suffer as part of their instruction. Every effort should be made to ensure instruction is given under positive conditions that reinforce training. Instructors may provide flexible training and modify the method of instruction when learners have difficulty grasping a task. In essence, a learner's failure to perform often results from an instructor's inability to transfer the required information.

Emphasize the positive because positive instruction results in positive learning.

Minimizing Learner Frustration

Minimizing learner frustrations in the classroom, shop, or during flight training is an instructor's responsibility. Instructors can encourage rather than discourage learning by following some basic rules.

For example, lesson plans used as part of an organized curriculum help the learner pilot measure training progress. Since most pilots don't want to be learners, the ability to measure their progress or "see an end in sight" reduces frustration and increases pilot motivation. *[Figure 8-4]*

Minimizing Learner Frustration

- Motivate learners
- Keep learners informed
- Approach learners as individuals
- Give credit when due
- Criticize constructively
- Be consistent
- Admit errors

Figure 8-4. *These are practical ways to minimize learner frustration.*

Motivate learners—more can be gained from wanting to learn than from being forced to learn. Too often, learners do not realize how a particular lesson or course can help them reach an important goal. When learners can see the benefits and purpose of the lesson or course, their enjoyment and their efforts increase.

Keep learners informed—learners feel insecure when they do not know what is expected of them or what is going to happen to them. Instructors can minimize feelings of insecurity by telling learners what is expected of them and what they can expect in return. Instructors keep learners informed in various ways, including giving them an overview of the course, keeping them posted on their progress, and giving them adequate notice of examinations, assignments, or other requirements.

Approach learners as individuals—when instructors limit their thinking to the whole group without considering the individuals who make up that group, their efforts are directed at an average personality that really fits no one. Each group has its own personality that stems from the characteristics and interactions of its members. Each individual within the group has a unique personality.

Give credit when due—when learners do something extremely well, they normally expect their abilities and efforts to be noticed. Otherwise, they may become frustrated. Praise or credit from the instructor is usually ample reward and provides an incentive to do even better. Praise pays dividends in learner effort and achievement when deserved, but when given too freely, it becomes valueless.

Criticize constructively—although it is important to give praise and credit when deserved, it is equally important to identify mistakes and failures. It does not help to tell learners they have made errors and not provide explanations. If a learner has made an earnest effort but is told that the work is unsatisfactory, with no other explanation, frustration occurs. Errors cannot be corrected if they are not identified, and if they are not identified, they will probably be perpetuated through faulty practice. On the other hand, if the learner is briefed on the errors and is told how to correct them, progress can be made.

Be consistent—learners want to please their instructor. This is the same desire that influences much of the behavior of subordinates toward their superiors in industry and business. Naturally, learners have a keen interest in knowing what is required to please the instructor. If the same thing is acceptable one day and unacceptable the next, the learner becomes confused. The instructor's philosophy and actions need to be consistent.

Admit errors—who expects an instructor to be perfect? The instructor can win the respect of learners by honestly acknowledging mistakes. If the instructor tries to cover up or bluff, learners sense it quickly. Such behavior tends to destroy learner confidence in the instructor. If in doubt about something, the instructor should admit it.

Flight Instructor Responsibilities

Learning to fly should provide learners with an opportunity for exploration and experimentation. It should be a habit-building period during which learners devote their attention, memory, and judgment to the development of correct habit patterns. All aviation instructors shoulder an enormous responsibility because their learners will ultimately be flying, servicing, or repairing aircraft. Flight instructors may have the additional responsibility regarding evaluation of learner pilots and deciding when they are ready to solo. The flight instructor's job is to "mold" the learner pilot into a safe pilot who takes a professional approach to flying. Other flight instructor responsibilities can be found in Title 14 of the Code of Federal Regulations (14 CFR) part 61 and FAA advisory circulars (ACs). *[Figure 8-5]*

Additional Responsibilities of Flight Instructors

- Evaluation of learner piloting ability
- Pilot supervision
- Practical test recommendations
- Flight instructor endorsements
- Additional training and endorsements
- Pilot proficiency
- See and avoid responsibility
- Learner's pre-solo flight thought process

Figure 8-5. *The flight instructor has many additional responsibilities.*

Instructors should be current and proficient in the aircraft they use and encourage each pilot to learn as much as possible and to continually "raise the bar." Flight instructors teach other pilots to remain focused on safety of flight and to use risk mitigation. It is also important to provide an understanding of why pilots are trained to standards, how these standards are set, and that meeting the standard provides a limited margin of safety.

Physiological Obstacles for Flight Learners

Although most learner pilots have been exposed to air travel, they may not have flown in light, training aircraft. Consequently, learners may react to unfamiliar noises or vibrations, or experience unfamiliar sensations due to G-force, or an uncomfortable feeling in the stomach. To teach effectively, instructors cannot ignore the existence of these negative factors, nor should they ridicule learners who are adversely affected. These negative sensations can usually be overcome by understanding the nature of their causes. Remember, a sick learner is preoccupied and may not have the mental or physical capacity to learn.

Ensuring Learner Skill Set

Flight instructors ensure learner pilots develop the required skills and knowledge prior to solo flight. The learner pilot needs to show consistency in the required solo tasks: takeoffs and landings, ability to prioritize maintaining control of the aircraft, proficiency in flight, traffic pattern operation, proper navigation skills, and proper radio procedure and communication skills. Learner pilots should receive instruction to ask for assistance or help from the ATC system when needed.

Mastery of the skill set includes consistent use as well as increased accuracy of performance. The decision to determine when a learner is ready for solo flight should be a joint decision between learner and instructor. Generally, this determination is made when the instructor observes the learner from preflight to engine start to engine shutdown and the learner performs consistently, without need of instructor assistance.

Flight instructors need to provide adequate flight and ground instruction for each item included in the applicable ACS/ PTS. The ACS integrates risk management and safety throughout and with supplementary appendix information. PTS lists special emphasis items. Some common items include:

1. Positive aircraft control
2. Procedures for positive exchange of flight controls
3. Stall and spin awareness
4. Collision avoidance
5. Wake turbulence and low-level wind turbulence and wind shear avoidance
6. Runway incursion avoidance
7. Controlled flight into terrain (CFIT)
8. Aeronautical decision-making (ADM)/risk management
9. Checklist usage
10. Spatial disorientation
11. Temporary flight restrictions (TFR)
12. Special use airspace (SUA)
13. Aviation security
14. Wire strike avoidance

Flight instructors should be current on the latest procedures regarding pilot training, certification, and safety. It is the flight instructor's responsibility to maintain a current library of information. These sources are listed in the appropriate ACS/PTS, and other sources can be located on the Internet at www.faa.gov and www.faasafety.gov. The FAA websites provide comprehensive information to pilots and instructors. Other aviation organizations also have excellent information. However, an instructor should follow procedures in the manner prescribed by the FAA. If an instructor needs any assistance, he or she should contact a more experienced instructor, an FAA Designated Pilot Examiner (DPE), or the local Flight Standards District Office (FSDO).

Aviator's Model Code of Conduct

The Aviator's Model Code of Conduct presents broad guidance and recommendations for General Aviation (GA) pilots to improve airmanship, flight safety, and to sustain and improve the GA community. The Code of Conduct presents a vision of excellence in GA aviation. Its principles both complement and supplement what is merely legal. The Code of Conduct is not a "standard" and is not intended to be implemented as such. The code of conduct consists of the following seven sections:

1. General Responsibilities of Aviators
2. Passengers and People on the Surface
3. Training and Proficiency
4. Security
5. Environmental Issues
6. Use of Technology
7. Advancement and Promotion of General Aviation

Each section provides flight instructors a list of principles and sample recommended practices. Successful instructor pilots continue to self-evaluate and find ways to make themselves safer and more productive. The Aviator's Model Code of Conduct provides guidance and principles instructors should integrate into their own practices. More information about the Aviator's Model Code of Conduct can be found at www.secureav.com.

Safety Practices and Accident Prevention

Aviation instructors are on the front line of efforts to improve the safety record of the aviation industry. Safety, one of the most fundamental considerations in aviation training, is paramount. Comprehensive FAA regulations promote safety by eliminating or mitigating conditions that can cause death, injury, or damage, but even the strictest compliance with regulations may not guarantee safety. Rules and regulations are designed to address known or suspected conditions detrimental to safety, but there is always a chance that some new combination of circumstances not contemplated by the regulations will arise. It is important for aviation instructors to be proactive to ensure the safety of flight or maintenance training activities.

The safety practices aviation instructors emphasize have a long-lasting effect on learners. Generally, learners consider their instructor to be a role model whose habits they attempt to imitate, whether consciously or unconsciously. The instructor's advocacy and description of safety practices mean little to a learner if the instructor does not demonstrate them consistently. For example, if a maintenance learner observes the instructor violating safety practices by not wearing safety glasses around hazardous equipment, the learner probably will not be conscientious about using safety equipment when the instructor is not around. One of the best actions a flight or maintenance instructor can take to enhance aviation safety is to emphasize safety by example.

Another way for the instructor to advocate safety is to partner with the FAA Safety Team (FAASTeam). The FAASTeam is dedicated to improving the aviation safety record by conveying safety principles and practices through training, outreach, and education. More information is available at <u>FAASafety.gov</u>.

Flight Instructor Qualifications

A flight instructor needs to be thoroughly familiar with the functions, characteristics, and proper use of all flight instruments, avionics, and other aircraft systems being used for training. This is especially important due to the wide variety in global positioning systems (GPS) and glass panel displays.

Each flight instructor should maintain familiarity with current pilot training techniques and certification requirements. Frequent review of new periodicals and technical publications, personal contacts with FAA inspectors and designated pilot examiners (DPE), and participation in pilot and flight instructor clinics such as the FAASTeam/SAFE quarterly series of Flight Instructor Open Forums facilitate awareness of current requirements. Additional information can be obtained from veteran flight instructors. *[Figure 8-6]* The continued use of outmoded instructional procedures or the preparation of learners using obsolete certification requirements usually involves rationalization.

Teaching Tips from Veteran Flight Instructors

1. Use a video device to rehearse preflight briefings until delivery is polished.
2. Find a mentor to provide a second opinion on how well a learner is performing during critical phases of flight training (such as first solo) for the first few pilot trainings.
3. Encourage a high standard of performance.
4. Just because it's legal, doesn't make it safe. Maintain a high level of supervision of pilot training operations.
5. Develop a safety-culture environment.
6. Assign organized, specific, appropriate homework after each flight session.
7. Use all available tools to supplement teaching and assignments: online sources, seminars, flight simulators, etc.
8. Know the background, credentials, security issues, medications, etc., of the learner before climbing into the cockpit with him or her.
9. Thoroughly and carefully document all training events as though the National Transportation Safety Board (NTSB) were going to read them.
10. Postflight debriefing after an FAA checkride is an excellent opportunity for additional learning.
11. Encourage each learner to establish personal minimums.
12. Include a review of NTSB accident reports during advanced instructional activity.

Figure 8-6. *Teaching tips from veteran flight instructors.*

Professionalism

The aviation instructor is the central figure in aviation training and bears responsibility for all phases of required training. The instructor, either pilot or aircraft maintenance technician, needs to be a professional. As professionals, aviation instructors strive to maintain the highest level of knowledge, training, and currency in the field of aviation. To achieve this goal, instructors need to commit themselves to continuous, lifelong learning and professional development through study, service, and membership in professional organizations such as the Society of Aviation and Flight Educators (SAFE), the National Association of Flight Instructors (NAFI) and Professional Aviation Mechanics Association (PAMA). Professionals build a library of resources that keeps them informed of the most current procedures, publications, and educational opportunities. Being a professional also means behaving in a professional manner. *[Figure 8-7]* An aviation instructor should strive to practice the characteristics on the Instructor Do's list when teaching a learner.

Instructor Do's

- Be professional at all times.
- Be sincere.
- Present a professional appearance and personal habits.
- Maintain a calm demeanor.
- Practice safety and accident prevention at all times.
- Avoid profanity.
- Define common terms.
- Continue professional development.
- Minimize learner frustration.
- Motivate the learner.
- Keep the learner informed.
- Approach each learner as an individual.
- Give credit when due.
- Criticize constructively.
- Be consistent.
- Admit errors.

Instructor Don'ts

- Ridicule the learner's performance.
- Use profanity.
- Model irresponsible flight behaviors.
- Say one thing but do another.
- Forget personal hygiene.
- Disrespect the learner.
- Demand unreasonable progress.
- Forget the learner is new to aviation jargon.
- Set the learner up for failure.
- Correct errors without an explanation of what went wrong.

Figure 8-7. *Guidelines for an aviation instructor.*

Sincerity

An aviation learner normally accepts a competent instructor as a teacher. However, the aviation instructor should be straightforward and honest at all times. Attempting to hide inadequacy behind a smokescreen of unrelated instruction makes it impossible for the instructor to command the respect and full attention of a learner. Any facade of instructor pretentiousness, whether it is real or mistakenly presumed, causes the learner to lose confidence in the instructor and adversely affects learning.

Acceptance of the Learner

The instructor needs to accept learners as they are, including all their faults and problems. The learner is a person who wants to learn, and the instructor is a person who is available to help in the learning process. The professional relationship between the instructor and learner should be based on a mutual acknowledgement that the learner and the instructor are important to each other, and that both are working toward the same objective.

Under no circumstance should the instructor do anything which implies degrading the learner. Acceptance (rather than ridicule) and support (rather than reproof) encourage learning. Learners need to be treated with respect, regardless of whether they are quick to learn or require more time to absorb certain concepts. Criticizing a learner who does not learn rapidly is similar to a doctor reprimanding a patient who does not get well as rapidly as predicted.

Personal Appearance and Habits

Personal appearance has an important effect on the professional image of the instructor. Today's aviation customer expects an instructor to be neat, clean, and appropriately dressed. Since the instructor is engaged in a learning situation, the attire worn should be appropriate to professional status. *[Figure 8-8]*

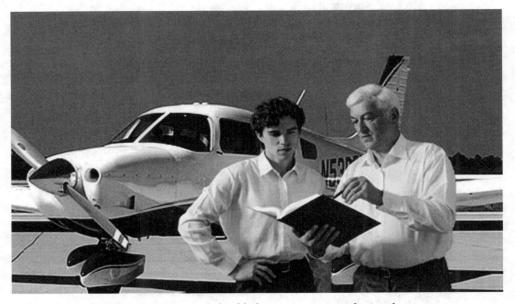

Figure 8-8. *The aviation instructor should always present a professional appearance.*

Personal habits have a significant effect on the professional image. The exercise of common courtesy is perhaps the most important of these. An instructor who is rude, thoughtless, and inattentive cannot hold the respect of a learner, regardless of the instructor's ability as a pilot or aviation maintenance technician. Personal cleanliness is important to aviation instruction. Frequently, an instructor and a learner work in close proximity, and even little annoyances such as body odor or bad breath can cause serious distractions from learning the tasks at hand.

Demeanor

The attitude and behavior of the instructor can contribute much to a professional image. The instructor should avoid erratic movements, distracting speech habits, and capricious changes in mood. The professional image requires development of a calm, thoughtful, and disciplined demeanor.

The successful instructor avoids contradictory directions, reacting differently to similar or identical errors at different times, demanding unreasonable performance or progress, criticizing a learner unfairly, or presenting an overbearing manner or air of flippancy. Effective instruction is best conducted in a calm, pleasant, thoughtful manner that puts the learner at ease. The instructor should constantly demonstrate competence in the subject matter and genuine interest in the learner's well-being.

Proper Language

In aviation instruction, as in other professional activities, the use of profanity and obscene language leads to distrust or, at best, to a lack of complete confidence in the instructor. Many people object to such language. The professional instructor speaks normally, without inhibitions, and speaks positively and descriptively, without profanity.

Evaluation of Learner Ability

Evaluation of a learner's ability is an important element of instruction. Used in this context, evaluation refers to judging a learner's ability to perform a maneuver or procedure.

Demonstrated Ability

Evaluation of demonstrated ability during flight or maintenance instruction is based upon established standards of performance, suitably modified to apply to the learner's experience and stage of development as a pilot or mechanic. The evaluation considers the learner's mastery of the elements involved in the maneuver or procedure, rather than merely the overall performance. For example, qualification of learner pilots for solo and solo cross-country privileges depends upon demonstrations of performance.

Keeping the Learner Informed

When evaluating learner demonstrations of ability, the aviation instructor should keep the learner informed of progress. This may be done as each procedure or maneuver is completed or summarized during a postflight or class critique. These critiques should be in a written format, such as notes, to aid the instructor in covering all areas that were noticed during the flight or lesson. When explaining errors in performance, instructors point out the elements in which the deficiencies are believed to have originated and, if possible, suggest appropriate corrective measures.

Professional Development

Aviation is changing rapidly, and aviation instructors need to continue to develop their knowledge and skills in order to teach successfully in this environment. The aviation instructor is well respected by other technicians and pilots because instructors have trained extensively to be certificated. Flight instructors undergo comprehensive evaluations and a practical test to obtain a flight instructor certificate. 14 CFR part 147 requires all instructors teaching maintenance subjects to hold an FAA certificate as an aircraft maintenance technician.

Successful, professional aviation instructors do not become complacent or satisfied with their own qualifications and abilities and are constantly alert for ways to improve their qualifications, effectiveness, and the services they provide to learners. Considered by their learners to be a source of up-to-date information, instructors have the opportunity and responsibility to introduce new procedures and techniques both to their learners and to other aviation professionals with whom they come in contact.

Continuing Education

A professional aviation instructor continually updates his or her knowledge and skills. This goal is attained in a variety of ways, such as reading an article in a technical publication or taking a course at a technical school. There are many different sources of information the aviation instructor can use in order to remain current in aviation knowledge and teaching.

Government

One of the first educational sources for the instructor is the FAA and other governmental agencies. The FAA either sponsors or collaborates in sponsoring aviation programs, seminars, and workshops for the public. For example, the FAA conducts safety seminars around the country in conjunction with the aviation industry. These seminars, although directed at pilots, can be a useful source of knowledge for aviation instructors.

The FAA is a rich source of information that can be used to enhance an instructor's knowledge. Regulations, advisory circulars, airworthiness directives, orders, and notices are some of the documents that can be downloaded from the FAA website at www.faa.gov.

Participation in the Pilot Proficiency Awards Program is a good way for a flight instructor to improve proficiency and to serve as an example to learners. Another way is to work toward the Gold Seal Flight Instructor Certificate. Accomplishing the requirements of the certificate is evidence the instructor has performed at a very high level as a flight instructor. See AC 61-65, Certification: Pilots and Flight and Ground Instructors, for a list of requirements for earning this certificate.

Similarly, the Aviation Maintenance Awards Program affords the aviation maintenance instructor the opportunity for increased education through attendance at FAA or industry maintenance training seminars. Details for the awarding of bronze through diamond pins can be found in AC 65-25, Aviation Maintenance Technician Awards Program.

The FAA approves the providers who conduct Flight Instructor Refresher Courses (FIRCs) in accordance with AC 61-83, Nationally Scheduled FAA-Approved Industry-Conducted Flight Instructor Refresher Course. These courses are available for flight instructors to complete the training requirements for renewal of flight instructor certificates.

The FAA cosponsors Inspection Authorization (IA) seminars. These seminars are open to all maintenance technicians and are a good source of additional training and education for maintenance instructors.

Educational/Training Institutions

Professional aviation instructors can further increase their knowledge and skill in aviation specialties by attending classes at local community colleges, technical schools, or universities. These schools may offer complete degree programs in aviation subjects as well as single-subject courses of benefit to instructors.

Commercial Organizations

Commercial organizations are another important source of education/training for the aviation instructor. Some may be publishers or online suppliers of training materials while others may provide complete ground and flight training programs for professional pilots and instructors. These companies often provide a wide variety of study programs including videos, computer-based training, and printed publications. Many offer training that can be attended either at the home base of the company, at classes or seminars around the country, or through internet sites.

There are numerous organizations around the country that offer courses of training for aviation instructors. These are generally courses that are available to all pilots and technicians but are especially useful for instructors to improve their abilities. Examples of such courses include workshops for maintenance technicians to enhance their skills in subjects such as composites, sheet metal fabrication, and fabric covering. For pilots, there are courses in mountain flying, spin training, upset prevention and recovery, and tail wheel qualification to name a few. Flight instructors also may increase their aviation knowledge and experience by adding additional category and class ratings to their certificates.

Industry Organizations

Other significant sources of ongoing education for aviation instructors are aviation organizations. These organizations not only provide educational articles in their publications, but also present training programs or cosponsor such programs.

Many industry organizations have local affiliated chapters that make it easy to meet other pilots, technicians, and instructors. These meetings frequently include presentations by industry experts, as well as formal training sessions. Some aviation industry organizations conduct their own training sessions on areas such as the flight instructor refresher course and Inspection Authorization (IA) seminars. Properly organized safety symposiums and training clinics are valuable sources of refresher training. They are also an excellent opportunity to exchange information with other instructors.

Sources of Material

An aviation instructor should maintain access to current flight publications or maintenance publications. For the flight instructor, this includes current copies of regulations pertinent to pilot qualification and certification, Aeronautical Information Manual (AIM), ACS/PTS, and pilot training manuals. The aviation maintenance instructor should have copies of applicable regulations, current knowledge and ACS/PTS, and maintenance training manuals. Aviation instructors should be thoroughly familiar with current certification and rating requirements in order to provide competent instruction. Many of the advisory circulars should be considered by the aviation instructor as references. The www.faa.gov website maintains current advisory circulars under the Regulations and Policies tab.

In addition to government publications, a number of excellent handbooks and other reference materials are available from commercial publishers through print and online media. Aviation periodicals and technical journals from the aviation industry are other sources of valuable information for instructors. Many public and institutional libraries have excellent resource material on educational psychology, teaching methods, testing, and other aviation related subjects.

The aviation instructor has two reasons to maintain a source of current information and publications. First, the instructor needs a steady supply of fresh material to make instruction interesting and up to date. Second, instructors should keep themselves well informed by maintaining familiarity with what is being written in current aviation publications. Many of these publications are in printed form, but increasingly, information is available through electronic means. *[Figure 8-9]*

Printed Material

In aviation, documentation in the form of flight publications or maintenance data needs to be immediately available for referral while flying or conducting maintenance. While the portability of printed material meets this need for immediate availability, printed material has two disadvantages. First, it takes up space for storage and second, it can be time consuming to keep printed material current. Many publishers of printed material now make their information available in electronic format. For example, most FAA regulations, standards, and guides are available either in electronic form or as hard copy.

Non-FAA publications are available through the GPO and from the National Technical Information Service (NTIS). Publications not printed by the U.S. Government Printing Office are available from the many publishers and suppliers of books. Commercial publishers usually provide catalogues and toll-free numbers or websites for ordering their products.

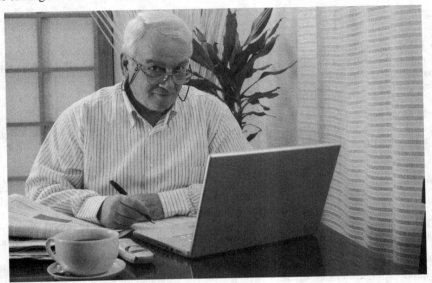

Figure 8-9. *Aviation instructors can improve their knowledge by becoming familiar with information on the internet.*

Electronic Sources

Access to the internet via personal computers, tablets, and smartphones has opened up a vast storehouse of information for the aviation instructor at the FAA website, www.faa.gov and many, many other websites and apps.

Professional aviation instructors should continue to expand their knowledge and skills in order to remain competent. The field of aviation is advancing, and the instructor also needs to advance. Instructors can best do this by taking advantage of the wide variety of materials available from the FAA, other government agencies, commercial publishers and vendors, and from industry trade groups. These materials are available at training sessions and seminars, from printed books, papers, magazines, and from the internet and other electronic sources. Instructors who commit to continuing education are able to provide the highest quality instruction to their learners.

Chapter Summary

This chapter discussed the responsibilities of aviation instructors to the learner, the public, and the FAA in the training process. The additional responsibilities of flight instructors who teach new learner pilots as well as rated pilots seeking add-on certification, the role of aviation instructors as safety advocates, and ways in which aviation instructors can enhance their professional image and development were explored.

Aviation Instructor's Handbook (FAA-H-8083-9)
Chapter 9: Techniques of Flight Instruction

Introduction

Flight instructor Daniel decides his learner, Mary, has gained enough confidence and experience that it is time for her to develop personal weather minimums. While researching the subject at the Federal Aviation Administration (FAA) website, he locates several sources that provide background information indicating that weather often poses some of the greatest risks to general aviation (GA) pilots, regardless of their experience level. He also finds charts and a lesson plan he can use.

Daniel's decision to help Mary develop personal weather minimums reflects a key component of the flight instructor's job: providing the learner with the tools to ensure safety during a flight. What does "safety" really mean? How can a flight instructor ensure the safety of flight training activities, and also train clients to operate their aircraft safely after they leave the relatively protected flight training environment?

According to one definition, safety is the freedom from conditions that can cause death, injury, or illness; damage to loss of equipment or property, or damage to the environment. FAA regulations are intended to promote safety by eliminating or mitigating conditions that can cause death, injury, or damage. These regulations are comprehensive but instructors recognize that even the strictest compliance with regulations may not guarantee safety. Rules and regulations are designed to address known or suspected conditions detrimental to safety, but there is always the possibility that a combination of hazardous circumstances will arise.

The recognition of aviation training and flight operations as a system led to a "system approach" to aviation safety. This chapter discusses some of the practices found to make flight safer on a systemic basis including—aeronautical decision-making (ADM), risk management, situational awareness, and single-pilot resource management (SRM). These components should be included in a modern flight training program.

Practical Flight Instructor Strategies

During all phases of flight training, instructors should remember that individuals learn through observing others; therefore, the instructor needs to model safe and professional behavior. The flight instructor should demonstrate good operational sense at all times:

- Before the flight—discuss safety and the importance of a proper preflight and use of the checklist.

- During flight—prioritize the tasks of aviating, navigating, and communicating. Instill importance of aircraft control, "see and avoid," situational awareness, and workload management in the learner.

- During landing—conduct stabilized approaches, maintain desired airspeed on final, demonstrate good judgment for go-arounds, wake turbulence, traffic, and terrain avoidance. Correct faulty approaches and landings. Make touchdowns on the centerline in the first third of the runway.

- After the flight—review or discuss flight events and choices using ADM principles. Plan a remediation if trends indicate an inadequate skill, a hazardous attitude, or inadequate knowledge of risk mitigation.

Flight instructors should produce safe pilots. For that reason, instructors should encourage each learner to learn as much as possible. When introducing lesson tasks, flight instructors should not focus on the minimum acceptable standards for passing the checkride. The ACS/PTS is not a teaching tool. It is a testing tool. The overall focus of flight training should be on education, learning, and understanding why the standards are there and how they were set. The completion standards for each lesson should gradually reach or exceed those in the ACS/PTS before final preparation for the checkride.

Integrating Instruction Techniques

A flight instructor uses many instructional techniques during ground instruction, when using simulation, and during hands-on aircraft training. Since flight training costs are high and new aircraft are more complex than in the past, the total training experience should provide a solid base of knowledge and maximize the learner's time without sacrificing the quality of the end product. This section looks at teaching techniques in greater detail.

Ground Instruction

Ground instruction can be highly effective if it follows an overall plan designed to prepare the learner for flight. In Chapter 7, Planning Instructional Activity, *Figure 7-2* shows a ground lesson that includes clear objectives. However, ground training objectives should be related to flight training objectives whenever possible. When elements are taught on the ground (as theory), their practice and application is also experienced in the air. The instructor should point out the connection between the theory and practice to maximize the benefit from integrated ground and flight instruction. *[Figure 9-1]*

Additionally, ground instruction need not be in the classroom for maximum effectiveness. For example, conduct a preflight using an actual aircraft although initially taught in an academic setting. Additionally, when airspace is being taught an invaluable reinforcement of training includes taking the learners to ATC facilities where they can see management of the National Airspace System (NAS) from another perspective.

Figure 9-1. *The learner prepares to execute a power-off stall maneuver in-flight that was taught in ground school.*

Studies have shown that a mix of instructional elements provides the best balance during ground instruction. Learners who use electronic media extensively are generally not as well trained as those who receive a balanced mix of ground teaching methods that include e-learning, class, and one-on-one instruction integrated with technological tools that support the instruction versus replacing it.

Ground instruction is a key element that sets the foundation and is critical to learner pilots becoming well educated and successfully transitioning into the flight environment. It should be deliberative, supportive of the learner's interwoven flight education, and highly rewarding to both the learner and instructor(s) alike.

Use of Flight Simulation Training Devices

The FAA separates flight simulation trainers into three specific categories:

- Full Flight Simulator (FFS)

- Flight Training Device (FTD)

- Aviation Training Device (ATD)

The National Simulator Program located in Atlanta, GA provides for the evaluation and qualification of FFSs and FTDs. 14 CFR part 60 provides the criteria for the qualification of FFSs *[Figure 9-2]* and FTDs *[Figures 9-3 and 9-4]* and further divides these qualifications as FFS Level A-D and FTD Level 4-7. A qualification letter is provided annually by the FAA to the operator and identifies the level of qualification. The level of approval affects what maneuvers or tasks may be accomplished in an FFS or FTD. These FAA-qualified trainers are collectively described in part 60 as Flight Simulation Training Devices (FSTD). Each device requires sponsorship by a part 119 certificate holder (part 135/121 operators), or a part 141/142 Pilot School/Training Center, and are most often used by the airlines or aviation colleges/universities. All training accomplished in FFSs and FTDs is part of an FAA-approved training program.

Figure 9-2. *A Level C simulator.*

The General Aviation and Commercial Division located in Washington, DC provides for the evaluation and approval of ATDs. Advisory Circular AC 61-136, *FAA Approval of Aviation Training Devices and Their Use for Training and Experience* provides the criteria for ATD approvals and use, and further divides them into two categories; Basic or Advanced ATD approvals (BATD/AATD). The letter of authorization provided by the FAA to the manufacturer specifies the training credits or experience requirements that can be acquired using that model trainer. These training devices are predominately used by general aviation flight schools providing flight training under 14 CFR part 61 or part 141 regulations. ATDs cannot be used for airman practical tests or type rating training requirements.

Figure 9-3. *An example of a Level 6 Flight Training Device (FTD).*

Integrated Training Curricula

An integrated training curriculum can use an FFS, FTD, or ATD to provide seamless training from the classroom to the aircraft. An instructor initially provides the required knowledge in a classroom environment and then follows with procedural training in the simulator. For example, when utilizing an integrated ground and flight-training program, an authorized instructor would initially teach the required knowledge specific to instrument landing system (ILS) design, and the associated flight operations through ground and classroom training. The instructor then provides instruction on aircraft flight procedures and details specific to operations in national airspace system. After the learner has gained the required knowledge and understands the procedures, the instructor then adds practicing the psychomotor skills of the task in the simulator. The instructor would then demonstrate and teach the instrument approach task to the learner simulating the flight environment in a FAA-qualified trainer. When the student becomes proficient with the instrument procedure in the simulator, the instruction would then transition to the aircraft to verify proficiency and reinforce the airman certification standards. Most operational tasks and procedures for private pilot certificates, instrument ratings, commercial pilot certificates, and airline transport pilot certificates can be initially taught in an FFS, FTD, or ATD.

Logging Training Time and Experience

Instructors or pilots logging time in an FFS or FTD should log and record the FAA ID number or serial number of the device being used for training. FSTDs are re-qualified on an annual basis and users should verify the qualification is current and valid. When logging training time in an ATD, pilot time is logged as a basic aviation training device (BATD) or advanced aviation training device (AATD) time, and the pilot record should identify the manufacturer and model of the ATD trainer. Letters of authorization (LOAs) for ATD's are valid for five years and a copy of the LOA should be retained by the pilot in training.

Pilot time logged in an FFS, FFS, or ATD must be recorded as prescribed in 14 CFR part 61, section 61.51(h). The maximum credit permitted for certificates and ratings is identified in part 61 and 141. However, there is no limit on how much time can be logged in an FFS, FTD, or ATD. The FAA recommends that training should continue in the simulator until the required tasks are accomplished successfully, before attempting the same tasks in an aircraft.

Figure 9-4. *A level 4 FTD used for procedure training.*

On-Aircraft Training

On-aircraft training is the continuation of work that is initiated on the ground and part of the integrated training process. As indicated in Chapter 7, Planning Instructional Activity, the instructor must plan the flight given to the learner to the same extent as the learner who prepares for it. Just as it is important to have objectives for ground instruction, it is equally important that the flight instruction have objectives and a syllabus paired with previous instruction given on the ground (to include academic training). Flight training is not a one size fits all and often must be tailored for the individual. For example, satisfactory progress in learning stalls through flight instruction "only" would be diminished as compared to discussing them on the ground; inclusive of the types, stalls, and their aerodynamic basis. Just because the learner has received ground school instruction on a particular aspect, the instructor should always review that same task with the learner before flight to reinforce the learning process as necessary. *[Figure 9-5]*

Figure 9-5. *Reinforcing what the learner was taught on the ground is critical to learner knowledge.*

On-aircraft training is integrated with ground instruction and not autonomously separate and distinct. By pairing flight and ground instruction together, the learner will advance further, faster, and attain more of the educational goals the instructor tries to impart.

Demonstration-Performance Training Delivery Method

The demonstration-performance training delivery method was discussed briefly in Chapter 5, The Teaching Process, but the following in-depth discussion is geared to the flight instructor. This training method has been in use for a long time and is very effective in teaching kinesthetic skills so flight instructors find it valuable in teaching procedures and maneuvers. The demonstration-performance method is divided into four phases: explanation, demonstration, learner performance with instructor supervision, and evaluation. *[Figure 9-6]*

Explanation Phase

The flight instructor needs to be well prepared and highly organized to teach complex maneuvers and procedures effectively. The learner should be intellectually and psychologically ready for the learning activity. The explanation phase is accomplished prior to the flight lesson with a discussion of lesson objectives and completion standards, as well as a thorough preflight briefing. The instructor presents clear and pertinent objectives of the particular lesson to be presented, based on the known experience and knowledge of the learner. Instructors need to provide details on the lesson content, performance expectations and evaluation measures. When teaching a skill, the instructor conveys the precise actions the learner will perform. In addition to the necessary steps, the instructor should describe the end result of these efforts. The explanation phase also should include coverage of appropriate safety procedures. Before leaving this phase, the instructor should encourage learners to ask questions about any step of the procedure that they do not understand.

Demonstration Phase

The instructor demonstrates the actions necessary to perform a skill and may describe the actions simultaneously. The instructor avoids extraneous activity as much as possible so that learners get a clear understanding of the task. If, due to some unanticipated circumstances, the demonstration does not closely conform to the explanation, this deviation should be immediately acknowledged and explained.

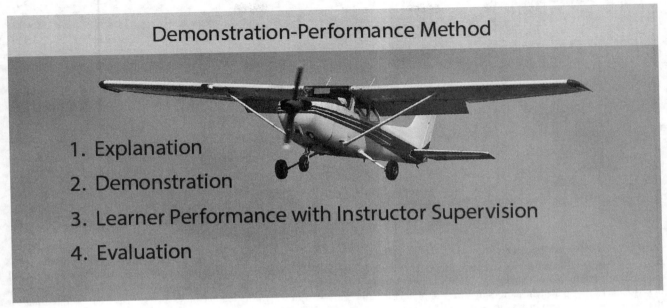

Figure 9-6. *The demonstration-performance method of teaching has four essential phases.*

Learner Performance and Instruction Supervision Phases

As discussed in Chapter 5, The Teaching Process, these two phases involve separate actions that are performed concurrently. The first of these phases is the learner's performance of the physical or mental skills that have been explained and demonstrated. The second activity is the instructor's supervision.

Learner performance requires learners to act and do. To gain skills, learners must practice. The instructor must, therefore, allot enough time for meaningful activity. Through doing, learners can follow correct procedures and reach established standards. It is important that learners be given an opportunity to perform the skill as soon as possible after a demonstration.

Then, the instructor reviews what has been covered during the instructional flight and determines to what extent the learner has met the objectives outlined during the preflight discussion. The instructor should be satisfied that the learner is well prepared and understands the task before starting. The instructor observes as the learner performs, and then makes appropriate comments.

Evaluation Phase

In this phase, the instructor traditionally evaluates learner performance, records the learner's performance, and verbally advises the learner of the progress made toward the objectives. Regardless of how well a skill is taught, there may still be performance deficiencies. When pointing out areas that need improvement, offer concrete suggestions that help. If possible, avoid ending the evaluation on a negative note.

As discussed in Chapter 6, Assessment, collaborative assessment (or learner centered grading (LCG)) is a form of authentic assessment currently used in aviation training with problem-based learning (PBL). PBL structures the lessons to confront learners with problems that are encountered in real life and forces them to reach real-world solutions. Scenario-based training (SBT), a type of PBL, uses a highly structured script of real-world experiences to address aviation training objectives in an operational environment. Collaborative assessment is used to evaluate whether certain learning criteria were met during the SBT.

Collaborative assessment includes two parts—learner self-assessment and a detailed assessment by the flight instructor. The purpose of the self-assessment is to stimulate growth in the learner's thought processes and, in turn, behaviors. The self-assessment is followed by an in-depth discussion between the instructor and the learner which compares the instructor's assessment to the learner's self-assessment.

The Telling-and-Doing Technique

The demonstration-performance method can be applied to the telling-and-doing technique of flight instruction in three steps. However, the telling-and-doing technique includes specific variations for flight instruction. *[Figure 9-7]*

Traditional Teaching Process	Demonstration-Performance Method	Telling-and-Doing Technique
Preparation	Explanation	Preparation
Presentation	Demonstration	Instructor tells Instructor does
		Learner tells Instructor does
Application	Learner performance supervision	Learner tells Learner does
Review and Evaluation	Evaluation	Learner does Instructor evaluates

Figure 9-7. *This comparison of steps in the teaching process, the demonstration-performance method, and the telling-and-doing technique highlights similarities as well as differences. The main difference in the telling-and-doing technique is the important transition, learner tells—instructor does, which occurs between the second and third step.*

Instructor Tells—Instructor Does

First, the flight instructor gives a carefully planned demonstration of the procedure or maneuver with accompanying verbal explanation. While demonstrating inflight maneuvers, the instructor should explain the required power settings, aircraft attitudes, and describe any other pertinent factors that may apply. This is the only step in which the learner plays a passive role. It is important for the demonstration to conform to the explanation as closely as possible. In addition, it should be demonstrated in the same sequence in which it was explained so as to avoid confusion and provide reinforcement. Since learners generally imitate the instructor's performance, the instructor needs to demonstrate the skill exactly the way the learners are expected to practice it, including all safety procedures that should be followed. As previously explained, if the demonstration does not closely conform to the explanation, this deviation should be immediately acknowledged and explained.

Most physical skills lend themselves to a sequential pattern where the skill is explained in the same step-by-step order normally used to perform it. When the skill being taught relates to previously learned procedures or maneuvers, the known to unknown strategy may be effective. When teaching more than one skill at the same time, the simple-to-complex strategy works well. By starting with the simplest skill, a learner gains confidence and is less likely to become frustrated when building skills that are more complex.

Another consideration in this phase is the language used. Instructors should attempt to avoid unnecessary jargon and technical terms that their learners do not know. Instructors should also take care to clearly describe the actions learners are expected to perform. Communication is the key. It is neither appropriate nor effective for instructors to try to impress learners with their expertise by using language that is unnecessarily complicated.

As an example, a level turn might be demonstrated and described by the instructor in the following way:

- Use outside visual references and monitor the flight instruments.

- After clearing the airspace around the aircraft, add power slightly, turn the aircraft in the desired direction, and apply a slight amount of back pressure on the yoke to maintain altitude. Maintain coordinated flight by applying rudder in the direction of the turn.

- Remember, the ailerons control the roll rate, as well as the angle of bank. The rate at which the aircraft rolls depends on how much aileron deflection is used. How far the aircraft rolls (steepness of the bank) depends on how long the ailerons are deflected, since the aircraft continues to roll as long as the ailerons are deflected. When the desired angle of bank is reached, neutralize the ailerons, and trim as appropriate.

- Lead the roll-out by approximately one-half the number of degrees of the angle of bank. Use coordinated aileron and rudder control pressures. Simultaneously begin releasing the back pressure so aileron, rudder, and elevator pressures are neutralized when the aircraft reaches the wings-level position.

- Leading the roll-out heading by one-half the bank angle is a good rule of thumb for initial training. However, keep in mind that the required amount of lead really depends on the type of turn, turn rate, and roll-out rate. As a pilot gains experience, he or she will develop a consistent roll-in and roll-out technique for various types of turns. Upon reaching a wings-level attitude, reduce power and trim to remove control pressures.

Learner Tells—Instructor Does

Second, the learner tells as the instructor does. In this step, the learner actually plays the role of instructor, telling the instructor what to do and how to do it. Two benefits accrue from this step: the learner, being freed from the need to concentrate on performance of the maneuver and from concern about its outcome, is able to organize his or her thoughts regarding the steps involved and the techniques to be used. In the process of explaining the maneuver as the instructor performs it, perceptions begin to develop into insights. Mental habits begin to form with repetition of the instructions previously received. Plus, the instructor is able to evaluate the learner's understanding of the factors involved in performance of the maneuver.

According to the principle of primacy, it is important for the instructor to make sure the learner gets it right the first time. The learner should also understand the correct sequence and be aware of safety precautions for each procedure or maneuver. If a misunderstanding exists, it can be corrected before the learner becomes absorbed in controlling the aircraft.

Learner Tells—Learner Does

Application is the third step in this method. This is where learning takes place and where performance habits are formed. If the learner has been adequately prepared and the procedure or maneuver fully explained and demonstrated, meaningful learning occurs. The instructor should be alert during the learner's practice to detect any errors in technique and to prevent the formation of faulty

At the same time, the learner should be encouraged to think about what to do during the performance of a maneuver, until it becomes habitual. In this step, the thinking is done verbally. This focuses concentration on the task to be accomplished, so that total involvement in the maneuver is fostered. All of the learner's physical and mental faculties are brought into play. The instructor should be aware of the learner's thought processes. It is easy to determine whether an error is induced by a misconception or by a simple lack of motor skills. Therefore, in addition to forcing total concentration on the part of the learner, this method provides a means for keeping the instructor aware of what the learner is thinking. The learner is not only learning to do something, but he or she is also learning a self-teaching process that is highly desirable in development of a skill.

The exact procedures that the instructor should use during learner practice depend on factors such as the learner's proficiency level, the type of maneuver, and the stage of training. The instructor should exercise good judgment to decide how much control to use. With potentially hazardous or difficult maneuvers, the instructor should be alert and ready to take control at any time. This is especially true during a learner's first attempt at a particular maneuver. On the other hand, if a learner is progressing normally, the instructor should avoid unnecessary interruptions or too much assistance.

A typical test of how much control is needed often occurs during a learner's first few attempts to land an aircraft. The instructor must quickly evaluate the learner's need for help, and not hesitate to take control, if required. At the same time, the learner should be allowed to practice the entire maneuver often enough to achieve the level of proficiency established in the lesson objectives. Since this is a learning phase rather than an evaluation phase of the training, errors or unsafe practices should be identified and corrected in a positive and timely way. In some cases, the learner is not able to meet the proficiency level specified in the lesson objectives within the allotted time. When this occurs, the instructor should be prepared to schedule additional training.

Positive Exchange of Flight Controls

Positive exchange of flight controls is an integral part of flight training. It is especially critical during the demonstration-performance method of flight instruction. Due to the importance of this subject, the following discussion provides guidance on the recommended procedure to use for the positive exchange of flight controls between pilots when operating an aircraft.

Background

Incident/accident statistics indicate a need to place additional emphasis on the exchange of control of an aircraft by pilots. Numerous accidents have occurred due to a lack of communication or misunderstanding regarding who had actual control of the aircraft, particularly between learners and flight instructors. Establishing the following procedure during initial training will ensure the formation of a habit pattern that should stay with learners throughout their flying careers.

Procedure

During flight training, there should always be a clear understanding between learners and flight instructors about who has control of the aircraft. The preflight briefing should include procedures for the exchange of flight controls. A positive three-step process in the exchange of flight controls between pilots is a proven procedure and one that is strongly recommended. When an instructor is teaching a maneuver to a learner, the instructor normally demonstrates the maneuver first, then has the learner follow along on the controls during a demonstration and, finally, the learner performs the maneuver with the instructor following along on the controls. [Figure 9-8]

Flight instructors should always guard the controls and be prepared to take control of the aircraft. When necessary, the instructor should take the controls and calmly announce, "I have the flight controls." If an instructor allows a learner to remain on the controls, the instructor may not have full and effective control of the aircraft. Anxious learners can be incredibly strong and usually exhibit reactions inappropriate to the situation. If a recovery is necessary, there is absolutely nothing to be gained by having the learner on the controls and having to fight for control of the aircraft. Learners should never be allowed to exceed the flight instructor's limits. Flight instructors should not exceed their own ability to perceive a problem, decide upon a course of action, and physically react within their ability to fly the aircraft.

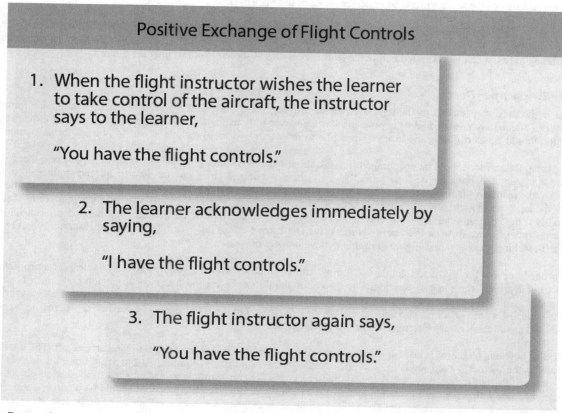

Positive Exchange of Flight Controls

1. When the flight instructor wishes the learner to take control of the aircraft, the instructor says to the learner,

   "You have the flight controls."

2. The learner acknowledges immediately by saying,

   "I have the flight controls."

3. The flight instructor again says,

   "You have the flight controls."

Figure 9-8. *During this procedure, a visual check is recommended to see that the other person actually has the flight controls. When returning the controls to the instructor, the learner should follow the same procedure the instructor used when giving control to the learner. The learner should stay on the controls and keep flying the aircraft until the instructor says, "I have the flight controls." There should never be any doubt about who is flying the aircraft.*

Sterile Flight Deck Rule

Commonly known as the "sterile flight deck rule," Title 14 of the Code of Federal Regulations (14 CFR) part 121, section 121.542 requires airline flight crewmembers to refrain from nonessential activities during critical phases of flight. As defined in the regulation, critical phases of flight are all ground operations involving taxi, takeoff, and landing, and all other flight operations below 10,000 feet except cruise flight. Nonessential activities include such activities as eating, reading a newspaper, or chatting. A series of aircraft accidents caused by flight crews who were distracted from their flight duties during critical phases of the flight caused the FAA to propose the rule. While the regulation grew out of accidents in the airline industry, it holds true for the entire aviation community. Pilots can improve flight safety significantly by reducing distractions during critical phases of flight. It is important the flight instructor not only teach the concept of a sterile flight deck but also model such behavior during flight instruction.

Use of Distractions

National Transportation Safety Board (NTSB) statistics reveal that most stall/spin accidents occurred when the pilot's attention was diverted from the primary task of flying the aircraft. Sixty percent of stall/spin accidents occurred during takeoff and landing, and twenty percent were preceded by engine failure. Preoccupation inside or outside the flight deck while changing aircraft configuration or trim, maneuvering to avoid other traffic, or clearing hazardous obstacles during takeoff and climb could create a potential stall/spin situation. The intentional practice of stalls and spins seldom resulted in an accident. The real danger was inadvertent stalls induced by distractions during routine flight situations.

Pilots at all skill levels should be aware of the increased risk of entering into an inadvertent stall or spin or the possibility of an upset while performing tasks that are secondary to controlling the aircraft. The FAA has established a policy for use of certain distractions on practical tests for pilot certification. The purpose is to determine that applicants possess the skills required to cope with distractions while maintaining the degree of aircraft control required for safe flight. The most effective training is the simulation of scenarios that can lead to inadvertent stalls by creating distractions while the learner is practicing certain maneuvers.

Instructor responsibilities include teaching the learner to divide his or her attention between the distracting task and maintaining control of the aircraft. The following are examples of distractions that can be used for this training:

- Drop a pencil. Ask the learner to pick it up.
- Ask the learner to determine a heading to an airport using a chart.
- Ask the learner to reset the clock.
- Ask the learner to get something from the back seat.
- Ask the learner to read the outside air temperature.
- Ask the learner to compute true airspeed with a flight computer.
- Ask the learner to identify terrain or objects on the ground.
- Ask the learner to identify a field suitable for a forced landing.
- Have the learner climb 200 feet and maintain altitude, then descend 200 feet and maintain altitude.
- Have the learner reverse course after a series of S-turns.

It is a flight instructor's responsibility to teach the learner how to take charge during a flight. A pilot in command (PIC) must know when to tell any passengers, even a Designated Pilot Examiner (DPE), when the PIC finds actions in the aircraft that distract and interfere with the safe conduct of the flight.

Integrated Flight Instruction

Integrated flight instruction is flight instruction during which learners are taught to perform flight maneuvers both by outside visual references and by reference to flight instruments. For this type of instruction to be fully effective, the use of instrument references should begin the first time each new maneuver is introduced. No distinction in the pilot's operation of the flight controls is permitted, regardless of whether outside references or instrument indications are used for the performance of the maneuver. When this training technique is used, instruction in the control of an aircraft by outside visual references is integrated with instruction in the use of flight instrument indications for the same operations.

Development of Habit Patterns

It important for the learner to establish the habit of observing and relying on flight instruments from the beginning of flight training. It is equally important for the learner to learn the feel and sounds of the airplane while conducting maneuvers, such as being able to sense when the airplane is out of trim or in a nose-high or nose-low attitude. Learners who have performed all normal flight maneuvers by reference to instruments, as well as by outside references, develop the habit of continuously monitoring their own and the aircraft's performance. The early establishment of the habits of instrument cross-check, instrument interpretation, and aircraft control is highly useful to the learner. The habitual attention to instrument indications leads to improved landings because of more precise airspeed control. Effective use of instruments also results in superior cross-country navigation, better coordination, and generally, a better overall pilot competency level.

General aviation accident reports provide ample support for the belief that reference to flight instruments is important to safety. The safety record of pilots who hold instrument ratings is significantly better than that of pilots with comparable flight time who have never received formal flight training for an instrument rating. Pilots in training who are asked to perform all normal flight maneuvers by reference to instruments, as well as by outside references, will develop the habit of continuously monitoring their own and the aircraft's performance. . The habits formed at this time also give the learner a firm foundation for later training for an instrument rating.

Operating Efficiency

As learners become more proficient in monitoring and correcting their own flight technique by reference to flight instruments, the performance obtained from an aircraft increases noticeably. This is particularly true of modern, complex, or high-performance aircraft, which are responsive to the use of correct operating airspeeds.

The use of correct power settings and climb speeds and the accurate control of headings during climbs result in a measurable increase in climb performance. Holding precise headings and altitudes in cruising flight definitely increases average cruising performance.

The use of integrated flight instruction provides the learner with the ability to control an aircraft in flight for limited periods if outside references are lost. In an emergency, this ability could save the pilot's life and those of the passengers.

During the conduct of integrated flight training, the flight instructor needs to impress on the learners and ascertain they understand that the introduction to the use of flight instruments does not prepare them for operations in marginal weather or instrument meteorological conditions (IMC). According to NTSB accident data, inflight encounters with weather (attempting VFR flight into IMC) is one of the most common causes of fatalities.

Procedures

Integrated flight instruction begins with the first briefing on the function of the flight controls. This briefing includes the instrument indications to be expected, as well as the outside references to be used to control the attitude of the aircraft.

Each new flight maneuver is introduced using both outside and instrument references with learners developing the ability to maneuver an aircraft equally as well by instrument or outside references. They naturally accept the fact that the manipulation of the flight controls is identical, regardless of which references are used to determine the attitude of the aircraft. This practice should continue throughout the flight instruction for all maneuvers. To fully achieve the demonstrated benefits of this type of training, the use of visual and instrument references must be constantly integrated throughout the training. Failure to do so lengthens the flight instruction necessary for the learner to achieve the competency required for a private pilot certificate.

See and Avoid

From the start of flight training, the instructor ensures learners develop the habit of looking for other air traffic at all times. If learners believe the instructor assumes all responsibility for scanning and collision avoidance procedures, they do not develop the habit of maintaining a constant vigilance, which is essential to safety. Any observed tendency of a learner to enter flight maneuvers without first making a careful check for other air traffic needs to be corrected immediately. Recent studies of midair collisions determined that:

- Flight instructors were onboard the aircraft in 37 percent of the accidents in the study.

- Most of the aircraft involved in collisions are engaged in recreational flying not on any type of flight plan.

- Most midair collisions occur in VFR weather conditions during weekend daylight hours.

- The vast majority of accidents occurred at or near nontowered airports and at altitudes below 1,000 feet.

- Pilots of all experience levels were involved in midair collisions, from pilots on their first solo, to 20,000 hour veterans.

- Most collisions occur in daylight with visibility greater than 3 miles.

It is imperative to introduce 14 CFR part 91, section 91.113 "right-of-way" rules to the learner. Practice the "see and avoid" concept at all times regardless of whether the training is conducted under VFR or instrument flight rules (IFR). For more information on how to reduce the odds of becoming involved in a midair collision, see Advisory Circular 90-48 (as amended).

Assessment of Piloting Ability

Assessment is an essential component of the teaching process and determines how, what, and how well a learner is learning. A well-designed assessment provides a learner with something constructive upon which he or she can work or build. An assessment should provide direction and guidance to raise the level of performance. Learners must understand the purpose of the assessment; otherwise, they will be unlikely to accept the evaluation offered and little improvement will result. There are many types of assessment but the flight instructor generally uses the review, collaborative assessment (LCG), written tests, and performance-based tests to ascertain knowledge or practical skill levels. Refer to Chapter 6 for an in-depth discussion of the types of assessment available to the flight instructor.

An assessment can also be used as a tool for reteaching. Although not all assessments lend themselves to reteaching, the instructor should be alert to the possibility and take advantage of the opportunity when it arises. If the instructor observes a deficiency and determines a task needs reteaching, the instructor demonstrates the maneuver, allows the learner to practice the maneuver under direction, and finally evaluates learner accomplishment by observing the performance.

Demonstrated Ability

Assessment of demonstrated ability during flight instruction must be based upon established standards of performance, suitably modified to apply to the learner's experience and stage of development as a pilot. The assessment must consider the learner's mastery of the elements involved in the maneuver, rather than merely the overall performance.

In order for a learner to be signed off for a solo flight, the instructor needs to determine that the learner is qualified and proficient in the flight tasks necessary for the flight. The instructor bases this assessment on the learner's ability to demonstrate consistent proficiency on a number of flight maneuvers. Pilot skill evaluations occur during the conduct of courses at FAA-approved schools, and teaching instructors should verify that learners meet the proficiency requirements prior to sending them for any stage check.

Postflight Evaluation

In assessing piloting ability, it is important for the flight instructor to keep the learner informed of progress. This may be done as each procedure or maneuver is completed or summarized during postflight critiques. Postflight critiques should be in a written format, such as notes to aid the flight instructor in covering all areas that were noticed during the flight or lesson. Traditionally, flight instructors explained errors in performance, pointed out elements in which the deficiencies were believed to have originated and, if possible, suggested appropriate corrective measures. Traditional assessment depends on a grading scale of "excellent, good, fair, poor" or "exceeds standards, meets standards, needs more training" which often meets the instructor's needs but not the needs of the learner.

With the advent of SBT, collaborative assessment is used whenever the learner has completed a scenario. As discussed in Chapters 5, The Teaching Process, and Chapter 6, Assessment, SBT uses a highly structured script of real-world experiences to address aviation training objectives in an operational environment. During the postflight evaluation, collaborative assessment is used to evaluate whether certain learning criteria were met during the SBT.

Collaborative assessment includes learner self-assessment and a detailed assessment by the aviation instructor. The purpose of the self-assessment is to stimulate growth in the learner's thought processes and, in turn, behaviors. The self-assessment is followed by an in-depth discussion between the instructor and the learner which compares the instructor's assessment to the learner's self-assessment.

First Solo Flight

During the learner's first solo flight, the instructor needs to be present to assist in answering questions or resolving any issues that arise during the flight. To ensure the solo flight is a positive, confidence-building experience for the learner, the flight instructor needs to consider time of day when scheduling the flight. Time of day is a factor in traffic congestion, possible winds, sun angles, and reflection.

If possible, the flight instructor needs access to a portable radio during any supervised solo operations. A radio enables the instructor to terminate the solo operation if he or she observes a situation developing. The flight instructor needs should use good judgment when communicating with a solo learner. Keep all radio communications to a minimum. Do not talk to the learner on short final of the landing approach.

Post-Solo Debriefing

During a post-solo debriefing, the flight instructor discusses what took place during the learner's solo flight. It is important for the flight instructor to answer any questions the learner may have as result of a solo flight. Instructors need to be involved in all aspects of the flight to ensure the learner utilizes correct flight procedures. It is very important for the flight instructor to debrief a learner immediately after a solo flight. With the flight vividly etched in the learner's memory, questions about the flight will come quickly.

Correction of Learner Errors

Correction of learner errors does not include the practice of taking over from learners immediately when a mistake is made. Safety permitting, it is frequently better to let learners progress part of the way into the mistake and find a way out. For example, in a weight-shift control aircraft the bar is moved right to turn left. A learner may show an initial tendency to move the bar in the direction of the desired turn. This tendency dissipates with time, but allowing the learner to see the effect of his or her control input is a valuable aid in illustrating the stability of the aircraft. It is difficult for learners to learn a maneuver properly if they seldom have the opportunity to correct an error.

On the other hand, learners may perform a procedure or maneuver correctly and not fully understand the principles and objectives involved. When the instructor suspects this, learners should be required to vary the performance of the maneuver slightly, combine it with other operations, or apply the same elements to the performance of other maneuvers. Learners who do not understand the principles involved will probably not be able to do this successfully.

Pilot Supervision

Flight instructors have the responsibility to provide guidance and restraint with respect to the solo operations of their learners. This is by far the most important flight instructor responsibility. The flight instructor is the only person in a position to make the determination a learner is ready for solo operations. Before endorsing a learner for solo flight, the instructor should require the learner to demonstrate consistent ability to perform all of the fundamental maneuvers.

Dealing with Normal Challenges

Instructors should teach learners how to solve ordinary problems encountered during flight. Traffic pattern congestion, change in active runway, or unexpected crosswinds are challenges the learner masters individually before being able to perform them collectively.

Visualization

SBT lends itself well to visualization techniques. For example, have a learner visualize how the flight may occur under normal circumstances, with the learner describing the progress of the flight. Then, the instructor adds unforeseen circumstances such as a sudden change in weather that brings excessive winds during final approach. Other examples of SBT can have the instructor adding undesired landing sites for balloon learner pilots, rope breaks for glider learners, and radio outages for instrument airplane learners. Now, the learner gets to visualize how to handle the unexpected change.

During this visualization, the flight instructor can ask questions to check the learner's thought processes. The job of the instructor is to challenge the learner with realistic flying situations without creating an overburdening unrealistic scenarios.

Practice Landings

Aircraft speed and control take precedence over other actions during landings and takeoffs. Full stop landings help the learner develop aircraft control, allow for careful checklist use, and allow time for detailed instruction.

Instructors should stress touching down in the first third of the runway to ensure stopping before the end of the runway. This means teaching learners to go-around if they do not touch down within that distance. Instructors should also stress the need for a go-around if the landing develops an oscillation or results in a significant bounce. These techniques equip a learner for safe solo. Furthermore, requiring the learner to make full stop landings during the first solo gives the instructor the opportunity to stop the flight if necessary.

When instructing in a glider (other than a motor glider), a go-around will not be possible. Instructors should teach learners to make low energy landings based on current weather and wind conditions. This technique prepares learners to make an off-field landing if or when necessary.

Practical Test Recommendations

Provision is made on the airman certificate or rating application form for the written recommendation of the flight instructor who has prepared the applicant for the practical test involved. Signing this recommendation imposes a serious responsibility on the flight instructor. A flight instructor who makes a practical test recommendation for an applicant seeking a certificate or rating should require the applicant to thoroughly demonstrate the knowledge and skill level required for that certificate or rating. This demonstration should in no instance be less than the complete procedure prescribed in the applicable ACS/PTS.

When the instructor endorses the applicant for the practical test, his or her signature on the FAA Form 8710-1, Airman Certificate and/or Rating Application, is valid for 60 days. This is also true with the flight proficiency endorsement that is placed in the applicant's logbook or training record (Advisory Circular (AC) 61-65). These two dates should be the same.

Instructors need to document completion of prerequisites for a practical test. Examples of all common endorsements can be found in the current issue of AC 61-65, Appendix A. The appendix in the AC also includes references to 14 CFR part 61 for more details concerning the respective endorsements. The examples shown contain the essential elements of each endorsement. It is not necessary for all endorsements to be worded exactly as those in the AC. For example, changes to regulatory requirements may affect the wording, or the instructor may customize the endorsement to accommodate any special circumstances concerning the applicant. However, at a minimum, the instructor needs to cite the appropriate 14 CFR part 61 section that has been completed.

FAA inspectors and DPEs rely on flight instructor recommendations as evidence of qualification for certification, and proof that a review has been given of the subject areas found to be deficient on the appropriate knowledge test. Recommendations also provide assurance that the applicant has had a thorough briefing on the ACS/PTS and the associated knowledge areas, maneuvers, and procedures. If the flight instructor has trained and prepared the applicant competently, the applicant should have no problem passing the practical test.

If a flight instructor fails to ensure a learner pilot or additional rating pilot meets the requirements of regulations prior to making endorsements to allow solo flight or additional rating, that instructor is exhibiting a serious deficiency in performance. The FAA may hold that instructor accountable. Providing a solo endorsement for a learner pilot who is not proficient for solo flight operations, or providing an endorsement for an additional rating for a pilot not meeting the appropriate regulatory requirements also represents a breach of faith with the learner or applicant.

Chapter Summary

This chapter discussed the demonstration-performance and telling-and-doing training delivery methods of flight instruction, SBT techniques, practical strategies flight instructors can use to enhance their instruction, integrated flight instruction, positive exchange of flight controls, use of distractions, simulators and flight training devices, obstacles to learning encountered during flight training, and how to evaluate learners. Additional information on recommendations and endorsements can be found in Appendix C, Certificates, Ratings, and Endorsements.

Aviation Instructor's Handbook (FAA-H-8083-9)
Chapter 10: Teaching Practical Risk Management during Flight Instruction

Introduction

Examination of accident data leads to the inevitable conclusion that many aviation accidents involve poor risk management decisions. Therefore, effective risk management is one of the most important skills a pilot needs to learn, understand, and practice as a habit. Since flight instructors continually deal with risk, they quickly become subject matter experts.

Instructors know to increase the scope of risk management while teaching. For example, risk management during flight instruction includes a consideration of the dangers from maneuvers performed incorrectly by the learner close to the ground, in addition to all the other risks associated with the flight.

Chapter 1, Risk Management and Single-Pilot Resource Management, discussed the foundations of effective risk management, as well as other critical skills that are a part of single-pilot resource management (SRM). Flight instructors, however, may want additional practical guidance on teaching risk management to pilots of various experience levels and applying risk management to instructional flights. This chapter provides such practical guidance.

Poor Risk Management and Accident Causality
Traditional Accident Investigation Taxonomy

Aviation accidents are investigated by both the National Transportation Safety Board (NTSB) and the Federal Aviation Administration (FAA). The role of the NTSB is to determine the probable cause of accidents and make recommendations, while the FAA seeks to determine if the accident revealed deficiencies in pilot training, aircraft certification, air traffic control or another area of FAA responsibility. The two government entities are often assisted by other interested parties, such as aircraft and/or engine manufacturers, in an effort to determine the facts.

The NTSB role can be illustrated by looking at a typical accident report. [*Figure 10-1*] While this accident occurred several decades ago and the pilot had LORAN navigation, the lack of risk assessment by the pilot is typical. Pilots have confronted the same type of scenario and many have repeated similar behavior when faced with a significant and potentially lethal hazard.

National Transportation Safety Board
Aviation Accident Final Report

Location:	Seekonk, MA	**Accident Number:**	BFO94FA008
Date & Time:	11/14/1993, 0026 EST	**Registration:**	N4224H
Aircraft:	MOONEY MO-20J	**Aircraft Damage:**	Destroyed
Defining Event:		**Injuries:**	2 Fatal
Flight Conducted Under:	Part 91: General Aviation - Business		

Analysis

During a four hour IFR cross country flight, in cruise, the engine's dry air vacuum pump failed. The pilot elected to continue to his final destination, about 180 miles away, navigating by his LORAN. The pilot was notified by air traffic control personnel that in order to continue to his destination, IMC could not be avoided. The pilot stated that IMC was not a problem and he continued the flight. During a no gyro vector approach to the localizer in IMC, at an altitude of about 1,900 feet MSL, the pilot became spatially disoriented and lost control of the airplane. The airplane impacted the terrain and the pilot and passenger were fatally injured. The dry air vacuum pump was examined. The examination revealed that the input shaft of the pump was fractured prior to impact.

Probable Cause and Findings

The National Transportation Safety Board determines the probable cause(s) of this accident to be:
The pilot's inadequate in-flight planning/decision to continue flight into known adverse weather conditions after the engine's dry air vacuum pump failed and the pilot's failure to maintain airplane control during approach. A factor in the accident was the dry air vacuum pump failure.

Figure 10-1. *NTSB Accident Report.*

Key findings of the NTSB final report of the Mooney accident, highlighted in yellow, emphasized the pilot's loss of control of the aircraft and inadequate in-flight planning. These facts accurately described the final events of the flight leading to the loss of control. In fact, conventional accident analysis classifies accidents such as this one as pilot error due to loss of control.

Risk Analysis Using the PAVE Checklist

The NTSB report on the Mooney accident reviews the accident facts to arrive at its probable-cause finding. Yet, there is more to learn about the root causality of the accident by examining the pilot's reaction to events during the flight using the PAVE acronym from Chapter 1.

The pilot knew about the vacuum pump failure and the instrument meteorological conditions (IMC) ahead of him. The faulty equipment generated an aircraft, or "A" hazard and IMC generated an environment or "V" hazard. The combination of those two hazards created an unacceptable risk once the pilot decided to penetrate the weather. In addition, it is possible that the pilot's desire to get to his destination created an external pressure, or "E" hazard. Finally, the pilot's assumption that he could control the aircraft with critical instruments inoperative created a pilot, or "P" hazard. The risk assessment matrix [*Figure 10-2*], indicates catastrophic consequences were possible from loss of control in IMC, and the likelihood of loss of control after a vacuum pump failure, was at least occasional or even probable. Thus, the overall risk presented was high or red and needed mitigation of some kind.

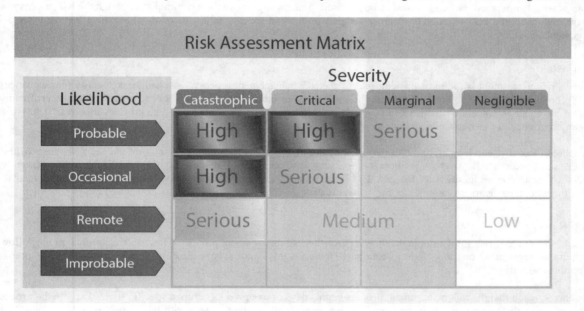

Figure 10-2. *This risk matrix can be used for almost any operation by assigning likelihood and severity. In the case presented, the likelihood of occasional and the severity as catastrophic falls in the high-risk area.*

The pilot's most effective mitigation may have been to divert and land while still in visual meteorological conditions (VMC). Why was the pilot unable to practice effective risk management on this flight? Lack of risk management training may have created an inability to cope with a difficult situation.

Instructors have a role and a responsibility to help pilots obtain the necessary risk management training and to adopt a safety culture that embraces risk management and mitigation of risk. The instructor's role in risk management should be incorporated at all levels of training, from a new pilot with little experience to a multi-thousand-hour pilot taking recurrent training.

When to Teach Risk Management

The importance of risk management suggests that it should be taught at the very start of flight training and should be integrated into any actual flight training, rather than taught as a separate subject. However, it will be even more effective if the learner receives ground instruction on this topic prior to the first flight lesson. This preliminary instruction should also be part of any formal ground school.

Risk management activity and discussion should be included in all preflight and postflight briefings. Learners should be encouraged to participate and even lead such discussions as their experience increases.

Risk management training should not be confined to initial training. Recurrent, transition, flight reviews, instrument proficiency checks, and other training and currency events should also include risk management.

Identifying Risk

As described in Chapter 1, the PAVE checklist is an effective and accepted means for identifying risk. Its four categories capture broad areas of risk and provide the learner with convenient "buckets" for risk identification. Instructors should coach learners, as required, to ensure they use the PAVE checklist methodically and consider all the sub-elements in each bucket. For example, the "P" applies to both the learner pilot and the instructor pilot, and has two major sub-elements. The first includes pilot qualification, currency and proficiency. The second "P" sub-element covers aeromedical hazards and risks and, as described in Chapter 1, the acronym IMSAFE can be used to identify those hazards and risks.

Instructors should identify common hazards that generate flight risks. The PAVE checklist can be used to analyze each hazard for its level of risk. For example, the instructor can show that certain weather hazards are almost always "red" and create a need for mitigation when encountered. Examples include a solid line of thunderstorms ahead, or IMC before takeoff if the pilot is not instrument rated and current or the aircraft is not suitably IFR equipped.

The instructor should emphasize that risk can be effectively managed, and learners should acquire the necessary skills to accomplish this. In many cases, learners will be professionals who are used to managing risk in their workplace, although the hazards may be very different. Instructors should acknowledge the learner's expertise in those areas. The instructor should involve the learner in aviation risk management decisions.

Assessing Risk

In some ways, risk assessment is the most difficult part of the risk management process. Assessing risk severity (consequences) and likelihood (probability) can be subjective during flight operations. In other aviation applications, such as aircraft certification, the likelihood of an event is calculated mathematically, and consequences are also precisely defined. Nevertheless, risk assessment accuracy can improve with practice and experience.

Instructors should initially lead learners through the assessment phase of each risk identified and provide examples that will help the learner gain confidence in risk assessment. For example, the instructor could suggest an event with a low but generally fixed likelihood, such as an engine failure after takeoff. The learner should consider the outcomes from various responses to that event. A review of the outcomes identifies the severity for the risk matrix.

Mitigating Risk

As explained in Chapter 1, risk mitigation is the "payoff" for the risk management process. Effective risk mitigation may allow for a proposed flight to begin or an ongoing flight to continue. However, this is not always the case, and the pilot should be prepared to delay or terminate any flight.

Instructors should teach that the risk management process begins days or even weeks before a specific flight. Early in the process, if a pilot identifies a risk that cannot be easily mitigated, such as a forecast weather system with widespread icing conditions, then the pilot can transfer the risk by getting an airline ticket. Alternatively, if the flight's purpose is just recreational, then the pilot can eliminate the risk by cancelling the flight. Other examples of risk elimination include not flying if the crosswind exceeds a limit or not practicing stalls if the ceiling is below a set value.

Whenever a flight is contemplated, the process to mitigate each identified risk assessed as high (red) or serious (yellow) can begin. Instructors should emphasize to learners that medium (green) risks may be mitigated, if possible, following the principle of not accepting unnecessary risk.

Instructors should emphasize that even though risk management may begin days before a flight, it continues into the immediate pre-flight planning and throughout the flight itself. Instructors can plan to introduce scenarios in-flight that simulate hazards and ask the learner to practice how to identify, assess, and mitigate.

The final step in risk mitigation is to consider whether or not to accept the remaining risk. A pilot accomplishes this step consciously and on behalf of any passengers. During flight instruction, the instructor mitigates the risk associated with a learner's actions by operating at a safe altitude and by guarding the controls. The instructor consciously accepts the risk that remains. Although the mitigation process completes, the instructor is vigilant for any hazard that needs consideration.

The acronym TEAM describes the steps in the mitigation process. TEAM represents transfer, eliminate, accept, and mitigate. These steps describe actions pilots take to deal with risk appropriately. During flight instruction, the instructor takes steps to ensure safety through risk mitigation and then operates with lower risk when the learner flies. Note that an unprepared learner constitutes a serious hazard. Prudent risk mitigation includes using a syllabus, providing quality ground instruction, and conducting a thorough briefing before each training flight.

Risk Management Tools

The risk management process is largely intuitive, but as with many new concepts, it can be daunting to the learner, especially at the beginning of training. Accordingly, the instructor should use available tools to simplify or make the process more orderly and effective.

The TEAM acronym and the risk assessment matrix discussed previously should be considered as primary tools for teaching risk management. Learners should be encouraged to use these simple tools as a basis for conducting risk management during and after their flight training.

On many flights, the risk management process can be more complex, and a more sophisticated risk management tool is needed. As discussed in Chapter 1, a flight risk assessment tool (FRAT) can serve this purpose.

There are a variety of FRATs available from various sources. Many of these FRATs have numerical scoring systems. A fixed list of hazards and associated risks are presented and assigned "scores" based on the severity of the hazard. Typically, if the total score is below a certain number, the pilot can begin the flight. If the score is above a certain number then some sort of mitigating action is required.

Numerical FRATs should be used with caution. A low score can still have one or more hazards and associated risks that, if not properly mitigated, can create unacceptable levels of risk. This can happen because a risk on a particular flight is not included in the FRAT's list, or there is only one risk, but it is extreme. As an example, a line of embedded thunderstorms may block your route. If that is the only item identified as a risk then the "score" may suggest a "go" decision without requiring mitigation.

Risk Management Teaching Techniques by Phase of Instruction

Instructors should teach risk management using a building block approach. This method will be effective with both new pilots as well as existing pilots who have not previously been exposed to formal risk management training.

Risk Management Training through the Private Pilot Level

A new learner's exposure to risk management should begin before the first flight and become part of a routine that continues throughout initial training. Instructors should emphasize both practical risk management techniques and skills needed to comply with the Airman Certification Standards (ACS).

Pre-Solo

Instructor-led and guided risk management training should occur during pre-solo instruction. Risk management should be part of every preflight and postflight brief. To assist in structuring the risk management process, the learner should be introduced to a non-numerical FRAT, and its use should be demonstrated by the instructor during the first few flights. By the first solo, the learner should be able to conduct a basic risk management analysis.

Post-Solo Prior to Cross-Country Training

During the initial solo and dual flights following the first solo, the learner should be able to perform a risk analysis of the planned flight, with occasional coaching from the instructor. The instructor should review the learner's risk analysis for all solo flights and provide any required feedback. At the completion of solo flights, the learner should de-brief the instructor on the risk management aspects of the flight.

Cross-Country Training

During the cross-country phase of training, learners should master risk management techniques commensurate with the complexity of flights and the terrain along the route to the destination(s). This could include, for a private certificate, flights at night, flights in complex airspace, or to unfamiliar airports. Instructors should ask the learner to accomplish a full risk analysis for every dual and solo cross-country flight. The process should include use of a FRAT or other method of analysis. The instructor should review and approve the risk analysis, just as would be done for other aspects of the learner's preflight preparation and calculations.

Risk Management Training for Experienced Pilots

Risk management is not a task confined solely to the initial training environment. Instructors should ensure that risk management is part of all training events for all certificated pilots. This is especially important for pilots who have not been exposed to risk management standards now contained in the ACS.

Instrument Training

Risk management training is vital during instruction for the instrument rating because of the potential hazards related to IMC. Instructors should emphasize broad risk management techniques and strategies that will allow a pilot to analyze and evaluate complex weather and other elements that generate risk. For example, an instructor might suggest that a pilot consider the risk management aspects of flight in:

- single-engine aircraft or over terrain higher than the single-engine service ceiling of a multiengine aircraft

- aircraft with a single alternator or a single radio and navigation system

- night conditions

- low IMC

- icing conditions or at altitudes above the freezing level

Transition Training

Pilots transitioning to more advanced aircraft will encounter additional types of risk associated with such aircraft. These include more complex systems and avionics, enhanced performance, and expanded abnormal and emergency procedures. Pilots transitioning to lighter, slower aircraft will also encounter additional risk due to less performance capability than the pilot has come to expect.

Before teaching in advanced aircraft, instructors should ensure that they have familiarity with the aircraft and equipment. Instructors should employ scenarios that emphasize risk management aspects of operating advanced aircraft in the National Airspace System. In addition to risk management, other SRM skills such as automation management, task and workload management, and maintaining situational awareness should be emphasized. In most instances, the pilot seeking training will be instrument rated and the instructor should evaluate the pilot's risk management and other SRM proficiency under an IFR scenario.

Recurrent Training, Flight Reviews, and Instrument Proficiency Checks

Instructors should particularly emphasize risk management during any kind of recurrent training or proficiency event. Many pilots who held certificates prior to the introduction of the ACS may not have been exposed to formal risk management training or evaluation.

Instructors should consider using scenarios to evaluate pilot risk management proficiency. The scenario should be constructed in a way that mirrors the pilot's typical operating profile. However, if the pilot plans to change that operating profile, the instructor should discuss or evaluate the pilot's ability to address any potential new risk management issues. For example, a pilot usually operates flights between rural airports in Class E airspace, but is soon planning to begin flying regularly to a location in Class B airspace. In this case, the instructor should address the operating requirements, such as Mode "C" and ADS-B, and the environmental risk factors related to Class B operation.

Risk Management during Operational Flights

Pilots who are already certificated conduct most of their flights without an instructor present. As an instructor, you should encourage them to practice effective risk management on all their flights.

Realistically, pilots will not always follow the risk management procedures discussed in this chapter. Instructors should encourage pilots to scale their risk management procedures to match the complexity of the flight. For example, for a local flight, it is acceptable to use an abbreviated risk management protocol using the PAVE acronym to briefly review the major elements of potential risk. However, for longer or more complex flights it may be desirable to complete a FRAT. A key objective for instructors is to provide risk management guidance that will allow pilots to think of risk management intuitively, as a part of the preparation for every flight and continuously while the flight progresses.

Risk Management Training for Professional Pilots

Instructors may encounter pilots who fly professionally. Many professional pilots operate as a crew and receive ongoing and recurrent training at a Part 142 training center. Instructors who work in classrooms or simulators at such a facility will likely be proficient in subjects such as crew resource management (CRM). They may also be exposed to other training and operating concepts, such as threat and error management (TEM), which has similar elements to risk management.

Instructors may encounter professional pilots who own their own aircraft and fly them outside of their professional environment. An instructor who provides transition or other flight instruction services to professional pilots should emphasize risk management as part of the training. Pilots who operate professionally as a crew may not be used to operating as a single-pilot, without the support infrastructure of their professional employer. Their risk management responsibilities may need adaptation to flying their own aircraft.

Managing Risk during Flight Instruction

Instructors know the need to manage risk during flight instruction. The risk management techniques are the same as taught to learners, however, there are a few hazards that are unique to flight instruction. The resulting risk can be identified, assessed, and mitigated. For example:

- Ask the learner to fly specific maneuvers after giving appropriate training.

- Choose practice locations that provide safe options.

- Perform maneuvers with sufficient altitude.

- Stay alert for the unexpected either from the learner or external elements.

- Be prepared to take over the control of the aircraft.

In flight, instructors can manage risk by constantly being aware of potential risk elements and managing them in real time. To do this, the instructor needs to maintain situational awareness of pertinent information, not only of the state of the aircraft, the surrounding traffic, the weather, the airspace, and the surrounding area; but also what the learner is doing and planning to do.

Common Flight Instruction Risks

The best process for analyzing flight instruction risks is to identify them as you would on any other flight, using the PAVE acronym. There may be many potential risks to conducting flight instruction. The examples below are only meant to be representative. Instructors should always conduct a risk analysis prior to providing instruction.

Pilot Risks

This category involves both qualification and aeromedical risks. From a qualification perspective, instructors know that the learner will generally be less proficient than the instructor. Instructors may also have qualification, currency, and proficiency issues. Instructors should be familiar with aircraft, avionics, and procedures. Any unfamiliarity creates a hazard. The aeromedical risks require the instructor to be tuned in to not only his own aeromedical state, but that of the learner.

During flight instruction, pilot risk includes both the learner pilot and the instructor pilot. The instructor needs to be prepared for the learner to make mistakes such as those listed in the Airplane Flying Handbook. The risks of these mistakes can be mitigated by being proactive in planning activities based on current conditions, and by allowing enough time and space both to allow the learner to practice and to allow the instructor to take over control of the aircraft before the situation deteriorates beyond the instructor's ability to fly the aircraft.

Aircraft Risks

Aircraft used in flight instruction may not always be under the direct control and maintenance supervision of the instructor, resulting in the instructor not being aware of inoperative systems and equipment or overdue inspections. For two-place trainer aircraft, payload is often limited, requiring a reduction in the amount of fuel carried. Performance may also be marginal in high density-altitude situations.

Environmental Risks

The airspace used for flight training and practice may be crowded, creating a potential collision hazard. Many areas of the country where flight instruction is conducted often have restricted visibility due to haze, pollution, or other factors that aggravate a potential collision hazard. Airspace in these areas may also be complex and subject to restrictions. Conducting certain maneuvers can also create hazards and potential risks. For example, practicing full stalls can result in inadvertent spins. Simulated engine failures, if performed incorrectly, can and have created real emergencies and caused accidents. Practice approaches without ATC surveillance can concentrate aircraft along the same path.

External Pressure Risks

Learners often experience scheduling problems, and this can be aggravated by aircraft problems, weather issues, and other unpredictable events. Learners are also subject to other external pressures involving work, family, finance, and other issues. All of these can create distractions, anxiety, and other responses that can degrade learner performance.

Best Practices for Managing Risk during Flight Instruction

Instructors can best assess and mitigate identified risks by following the risk management procedures outlined in this chapter. In all cases, the instructor should include the learner in the risk management during dual instruction. For example, the instructor should emphasize that they are both responsible for maintaining a lookout to see and avoid other air traffic. The learner should also be instructed on how to assist resolving items such as aircraft airworthiness status and issues involving the training environment, such as airspace, NOTAMs, or TFRs.

Specific mitigations for the instructional hazards and risks identified in previous paragraphs include, but are not limited to, the following procedures.

Pilot Risks

The instructor's qualifications are paramount in mitigating currency and proficiency issues. Instructors should familiarize themselves with aircraft models and avionics before instructing. This could be as simple as reviewing the pilot operating handbook (POH) or avionics manuals or as extensive as acquiring flight time in such equipment before giving instruction.

Instructor aeromedical risks should be constantly monitored using the IMSAFE model. Similarly, the instructor should communicate with the learner to establish a confidence level that will encourage learners to come forward to disclose their own aeromedical issues well in advance of scheduled flights, so that they may be rescheduled if necessary.

Aircraft Risks

The instructor should determine the aircraft's official airworthiness status before scheduled flights and before conducting the actual preflight. Unless instructing in their own aircraft, instructors should be familiar with the aircraft operator's procedures for reporting and correcting discrepancies and review the current discrepancy report. Any questions regarding airworthiness status should be resolved with maintenance personnel before conducting the preflight inspection. The instructor should consider involving the learner in this process and should emphasize that it is intended to manage risk by reducing the likelihood and/or severity of potential hazards and risks arising from failed equipment.

Environmental Risks

Environmental risks are one of the most frequent causes of accidents. These notably include risks generated by weather, terrain, and night operation hazards and additionally include airports, airspace, and other environmental factors. All these hazards and risks will likely come into play at some point during the instruction process. Accordingly, instructors should emphasize accurate assessment and mitigation of such risks when providing instruction.

The instructor should involve the learner in every step of the assessment and mitigation process. For example, the weather may be marginal VFR. If the scheduled dual instruction called for practicing stalls and slow flight, the instructor should coach the learner to identify the risks involved in conducting stall practice under such conditions, such as inadvertently entering IMC or practicing stalls at too low an altitude. The instructor and learner can discuss ways to mitigate the risk, such as changing the lesson plan to stay in the traffic pattern, conducting a lesson in a flight simulation training device or ground school, or rescheduling the lesson altogether.

External Pressure Risks

External pressures can create the most insidious of hazards and risks. Instructors should ease learner concerns about schedule conflicts with events in their professional and personal lives. Instructors should be conscious of each learner's schedule limitations and other external factors that could affect their performance. Instructors should also emphasize the ability to make schedule changes as needed, change training from an airplane to classroom instruction, or terminate a lesson early if the learner appears apprehensive about time pressures or other external concerns.

Notes on Instructional Risk Management in the Flight Deck

The instructor is involved with risk management on multiple levels, which include not only managing the risk of a particular phase of flight or maneuver, but also teaching risk management and managing the risks of providing in-flight instruction. Some concepts an instructor should bear in mind while teaching most maneuvers include:

- Identify relevant hazards systematically and keep track of hazards during maneuvering (the learner manipulating controls may be a significant hazard).

- Avoid creating a hazard by attempting to teach something at an inappropriate time (e.g., discussing takeoff technique while entering the runway, when attention should be devoted to aircraft control and ensuring that the runway is clear) or at an inappropriate altitude (e.g., teaching stalls below a cloud layer, which does not allow an adequate amount of altitude to recover).

- Discuss hazards and risk mitigation in detail during preflight and postflight.

- Prompt the learner to identify hazards in flight and on their own and to verbalize thought processes and risk mitigations (e.g., while preparing to execute a ground reference maneuver, ask the learner to identify potential collision hazards and a safe place to make an emergency landing).

The following discussion contains examples of instructor considerations while providing in-flight instruction on various maneuvers. Among other things, the examples demonstrate the extent to which instructional techniques and instructional risk management are interconnected, and why a systematic, integrated approach to risk management provides safety.

Managing Risk while Teaching Takeoffs

The time it takes for an aircraft to begin its takeoff and initiate a climb is only a matter of seconds. There may not be time to teach effectively during the takeoff. Apart from introducing unnecessary hazards (e.g., missing a radio transmission from tower), the learner's attention is placed almost entirely on trying to safely maneuver the aircraft. Any information an instructor is trying to convey during the takeoff may not be heard or processed by the learner. The instructor should conduct the majority of their teaching (e.g. airspeeds, pitch attitudes, visual references, flight control inputs, engine parameters) prior to contacting tower or announcing their intentions on the CTAF at a non-towered airport. This will avoid over-stimulating the learner's senses, help maintain a sterile flight deck, and support situational awareness and collision avoidance.

When teaching a learner to take off, it is imperative that the instructor create realistic scenarios of takeoff types. The scenario should not create hazards that result in the learner attempting to maintain an unsafe climb rate or excessive pitch attitude. An effective scenario should mimic what a learner will encounter outside of flight training. For example, if the instructor wants to prompt the learner to conduct a confined or obstacle clearance takeoff, the instructor could specify where an (imaginary) obstacle exists. The point where the obstacle exists should be realistic. During soft-field takeoffs in an airplane, the instructor should monitor aircraft drift while the learner is trying to remain in ground effect. The instructor should not let the drift escalate beyond the learner's control and should pay close attention to pitch attitude and airspeed throughout the maneuver.

Insufficient spacing from preceding aircraft during takeoffs also creates various hazards. Some hazards include wake turbulence, insufficient in-trail spacing, and insufficient separation from an aircraft approaching to land. The instructor ensures that there is sufficient spacing from landing and departing aircraft prior to entering any space being used for departures and arrivals. This will also help teach the learner sound decision making and risk management skills.

Managing Risk while Teaching Landings

Many complex decisions are made during the landing phase. Novice learner pilots have little experience to rely on. Instructors sometimes fall prey to teaching landings mechanically. Instead, it is necessary to convey problems and solutions (power, control, and configuration changes) based on what is actually happening on that specific approach. When an instructor teaches mechanically, they cause the learner to be ill-equipped to identify or manage constantly changing conditions. This teaching method may result in unstable approaches and faulty landings. The instructor should prompt the learner on the current conditions and how to correct the situation to maintain a stabilized approach. The decision on choosing aiming points and touchdown points should not be made mechanically either. It is the instructor's responsibility to teach the learner how to pick appropriate aiming and touchdown points based on the type of aircraft, the landing being attempted, the environment and conditions present, and the expected landing performance.

Some of the same hazards associated while teaching takeoffs are also present while teaching landings. The instructor may want to convey a lot of information while simultaneously verifying that the aircraft is being flown safely. This may cause a decrease in attention to collision avoidance or loss of situational awareness. Excessive teaching and coaching on final approach may cause missed radio transmissions from air traffic control or aircraft in the pattern. To avoid this, the instructor should only use concise prompting on approach to landings with the learner.

Certain landings present unique risks. The instructor teaches the appropriate pre-landing reconnaissance for unfamiliar landing areas or uncontrolled fields. During landings in strong winds, the instructor should have the skill sufficient to deal with the wind conditions. During a short-field or confined area landing, certain aircraft may fly at a slower approach speed. The instructor should be aware of any risk associated with flight at slow speeds or any other condition that reduces safety margins. During all types of approaches to landing, instructors need to remain aware of risks associated with a variety of learner errors. For example, if an airplane pilot makes a 180° power-off accuracy approach and landing, the instructor should anticipate potential landing errors. Learners may understand not to sacrifice a stable approach and a safe landing for the sake of accuracy, but they might not be ready to apply that knowledge.

Chapter Summary

Poor risk management contributes to many fatal accidents. Accordingly, instructors should emphasize and practice risk management in all types of instruction, from primary to advanced training. Instructors should use accepted risk management tools to make training more effective and consistent. Instructors should also use a building block approach to teaching risk management. Risks encountered while giving instruction are similar to those that learners will encounter on operational flights, giving instructors the opportunity to highlight risk management as a tool to be used for safe and enjoyable flying.

Aviation Instructor's Handbook (FAA-H-8083-9)

Appendix A: References

Ashcraft, M.H., 1994: *Human Memory and Cognition.*
New York: Harper Collins.

Bloom, B.S. (Ed.), 1956: *Taxonomy of Educational Objectives: The Classification of Educational Goals, Handbook I: Cognitive Domain.* New York: David McKay.

Bloom, B.S., and others, 1971: *Handbook on Formative and Summative Evaluation of Student Learning.* New York: McGraw-Hill.

Brookfield, S.D., 1991: *Understanding and Facilitating Adult Learning.* San Francisco: Jossey-Bass.

Claxton, C.S., & Murrell, P.H., 1987: *Learning Styles: Implications for Improving Instructional Practices.* ASHE-ERIC Higher Education Report No. 4, Association for the Study of Higher Education.

Council of Aviation Accreditation, 1995: *Accreditation Standards Manual.* Auburn: Council of Aviation Accreditation.

Davis, J.R., 1993: *Better Teaching, More Learning: Strategies for Success in Postsecondary Settings.* Phoenix: Oryx Press.

Dick, W., & Carey, L., 2000: *The Systematic Design of Instruction.* New York: Harper Collins.

Driscoll, M.P., 1999: Psychology of Learning for Instruction. Boston: Allyn & Bacon.

Duncan, P.A., 1998, 1999: Surfing the Aviation Web, Parts 1, 2, and 3, *FAA Aviation News,* Nov/Dec, Jan/Feb, Mar. Washington: U.S. Department of Transportation, Federal Aviation Administration.

ERIC (Educational Resources Information Center), 1992-1997: *ERIC Digests.* Washington: U.S. Department of Education, Office of Educational Research and Improvement.

FAA, 2009: *Risk Management Handbook.* FAA-H-8083-2. Washington: U.S. Department of Transportation, Federal Aviation Administration.

FAA, 2018: *Certification: Pilots and Flight Instructors.* AC 61-65. Washington: U.S. Department of Transportation, Federal Aviation Administration.

FAA, 2000: *Stall and Spin Awareness Training.* AC 61-67. Washington: U.S. Department of Transportation, Federal Aviation Administration.

FAA, 2018: *Nationally Scheduled, FAA-Approved, Industry-Conducted Flight Instructor Refresher Course.* AC 61-83. Washington: U.S. Department of Transportation, Federal Aviation Administration.

FAA, 2000: *Pilot Certificates: Aircraft Type Ratings.* AC 61-89. Washington: U.S. Department of Transportation, Federal Aviation Administration.

FAA, 2011: *WINGS - Pilot Proficiency Programs* . AC 61-91. Washington: U.S. Department of Transportation, Federal Aviation Administration.

FAA, 2018: *Currency and Additional Qualification Requirements for Certificated Pilots.* AC 61-98. Washington: U.S. Department of Transportation, Federal Aviation Administration.

FAA, 1989: *Announcement of Availability: Industry-Developed Transition Training Guidelines for High Performance Aircraft.* AC 61-103. Washington: U.S. Department of Transportation, Federal Aviation Administration.

FAA, 2003: *Operations of Aircraft at Altitudes Above 25,000 Feet MSL and/or MACH Numbers (Mmo) Greater than .75.* AC 61-107. Washington: U.S. Department of Transportation, Federal Aviation Administration.

FAA, 2007: Aviation Maintenance Technician Awards Program. AC 65-25. Washington: U.S. Department of Transportation, Federal Aviation Administration.

FAA, 2004: *Crew Resource Management Training.* AC 120-51. Washington: U.S. Department of Transportation, Federal Aviation Administration.

FAA, 2015: *Transition to Unfamiliar Aircraft*, AC 90-109. Washington: U.S. Department of Transportation, Federal Aviation Administration.

FAA, 2018: *FAA Approval if Aviation Training Devices and Their Use for Training and Experience*, AC 61-136. Washington: U.S. Department of Transportation, Federal Aviation Administration.

FAA, 2017: *FAA English Language Standard for an FA Certificate Issued Under 14 CFR Parts 61, 63, 65, and 107*, AC 61-28. Washington: U.S. Department of Transportation, Federal Aviation Administration.

FAA, 2018: *Flight Instructors as Certifying Officials for Student Pilot and Remote Pilot Certificates, AC 61-141*. Washington: U.S. Department of Transportation, Federal Aviation Administration.

FAA, 2017: *Airline Transport Pilot Certification Training Program, AC 61-138*. Washington: U.S. Department of Transportation, Federal Aviation Administration.

FAA, 1987: *Aeronautical Decision Making for Students and Private Pilots*. DOT/FAA/PM-86/41. Springfield, VA: National Technical Information Service.

FAA, 1988: *Aeronautical Decision Making for Commercial Pilots*. DOT/FAA/PM-86/42. Springfield, VA: National Technical Information Service.

FAA, 1987: *Aeronautical Decision Making for Instrument Pilots*. DOT/FAA/PM-86/43. Springfield, VA: National Technical Information Service.

FAA, 1987: *Aeronautical Decision Making for Instructor Pilots*. DOT/FAA/PM-86/44. Springfield, VA: National Technical Information Service.

FAA, 1987: *Aeronautical Decision Making for Helicopter Pilots*. DOT/FAA/PM-86/45. Springfield, VA: National Technical Information Service.

FAA, 1989: *Aeronautical Decision Making/Cockpit Resource Management*. DOT/FAA/PM-86/46. Springfield, VA: National Technical Information Service.

FAA, 2018: *Private Pilot - Airplane Airman Certification Standards*. FAA-S-ACS-6. Washington: U.S. Department of Transportation, Federal Aviation Administration.

FAA, 1995: *Aviation Safety Program Manager's Handbook*. FAA-H-8740.1. Washington: U.S. Department of Transportation, Federal Aviation Administration.

FAA, 1996: *Aviation Safety Counselor Manual*. FAAM-8740.3. Washington: U.S. Department of Transportation, Federal Aviation Administration.

Gagne, R.M., & Briggs, L.J., 2004: *Principles of Instructional Design*. New York: Holt, Reinhart and Winston.

Garland, Daniel J., Will, John A., & Hopkins, V. David, 1999: *Handbook of Aviation Human Factors*. Mahwak, NJ: Lawrence Erlbaum Associates.

Gredler, M.E., 2004: *Learning and Instruction: Theory into Practice*. Upper Saddle River, NJ: Prentice-Hall.

Hawkins, F.H., 1993: *Human Factors in Flight*. Brookfield, VA: Ashgate.

Hunt, G.J.F. (Ed.), 1997: *Designing Instruction for Human Factors Training*. Brookfield, VT: Ashgate.

Jacobs, L.C., & Chase, C.I., 1992: *Developing and Using Tests Effectively*. San Francisco: Jossey-Bass.

Jeppesen Sanderson, 1990-1999: *CFI Renewal Program, Volumes 1 through 6*. Englewood, CO: Jeppesen Sanderson.

Johnston, N., Fuller, R., & McDonald, N. (Eds.), 1995: *Aviation Psychology: Training and Selection*. Brookfield, VT: Ashgate.

Kahneman, Daniel, 2011: *Thinking, Fast and Slow*. New York: Farrar, Straus and Giroux.

Kemp, J.E., 1985: *The Instructional Design Process*. New York: Harper & Row.

Krathwohl, D.R., and others, 2000: *Taxonomy of Educational Objectives: The Classification of Educational Goals, Handbook II: Affective Domain*. New York: David McKay.

Loukopoulos, Loukia D., Dismukes, R. Key, and Barshi, Immanuel, 2016: *The Multitasking Myth*. New York, NY: Routledge.

Mager, R.F., 1997: *Making Instruction Work*. Belmont, CA: David S. Lake Publishers.

Mager, R.F., 1997: *Preparing Instructional Objectives*. Belmont, CA: David S. Lake Publishers.

Mazur, J.E., 2005: Learning and Behavior. (4th ed.) Upper Saddle River, NJ: Prentice-Hall.

Meyers, C., & Jones, T.B., 1993: *Promoting Active Learning*. San Francisco: Jossey-Bass.

Rothwell, W.J., & Kazanas, H.F., 2003: *Mastering the Instructional Design Process: A Systematic Approach*. San Francisco: Jossey-Bass.

Sarasin, L.C., 2006: *Learning Style Perspectives: Impact in the Classroom*. Madison: Atwood.

Taylor, R.L., 1991: *Human Factors,* Volume 6. Greenwich: Belvoir Publications.

Telfer, R.A. (Ed.), 1997: *Aviation Instruction and Training*. Brookfield: Ashgate.

Telfer, R.A. & Biggs, J.,1988: The Psychology of Flight Training. Ames: Iowa State University Press.

Telfer, R.A., & Moore, P.J. (Eds.), 1997: *Aviation Training; Learners, Instruction and Organization*. Brookfield: Ashgate.

Thorndike, R.L., (Ed.), 1971: *Educational Measurement,* 2d Edition. Washington: American Council on Education.

Trollip, S.R., & Jensen, R.S., 1991: *Human Factors for General Aviation*. Englewood, CO: Jeppesen Sanderson.

USAF, 2003: *Guidebook for Air Force Instructors,* AF Manual 36-2236. Washington: Department of Defense, United States Air Force.

Wickens, C.D., 1999: *Engineering Psychology and Human Performance*. New York: Harper Collins.

Wiener, E.L. & Nagel, D.C., 1989: *Human Factors in Aviation*. San Diego: Academic Press.

Aviation Instructor's Handbook (FAA-H-8083-9)

Appendix B: Developing a Test Item Bank

Developing a bank of test questions is difficult and time consuming. This task demands a mastery of the subject, an ability to write clearly, and an ability to visualize realistic situations for use in developing problems. Because it is so difficult to develop good test items, many instructors rely on commercially-prepared test materials. However, there are a few instructors who write their own questions and maintain them in a database or a system of folders. *[Figure B-1]*

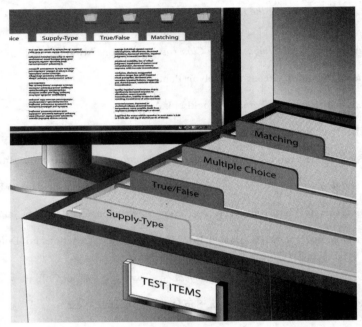

Figure B-1. *A bank of test items makes it easier to construct new tests.*

Written Test Items
Supply Type

Supply type test items ask the learner to furnish a response in the form of a word, sentence, or paragraph. The supply-type item allows the learner to organize knowledge. It shows an ability to express ideas and measures the learner's generalized understanding of a subject. For example, the supply type item on a pre-solo knowledge test can be very helpful in determining whether the pilot-in-training has adequate knowledge of procedures.

There are several disadvantages of supply-type items. First, they cannot be graded with reliability. The same test graded by different instructors could be assigned different scores. Even the same test graded by the same instructor on consecutive days might be assigned a different score. Second, supply-type items require more time for the learner to complete and more time for the instructor to grade.

Selection Type

Selection type test items require the learner to select from two or more alternatives. There is a single correct response for each item. It assumes all learners should learn the same thing, and relies on rote memorization of facts. Written tests made up of selection type items are highly reliable, meaning that the results would be graded the same regardless of the learner taking the test or the person grading it. In fact, this type of test item lends itself very well to machine scoring.

Also, selection type items make it possible to directly compare learner accomplishment. For example, it is possible to compare the performance of learners within one class to learners in a different class, or learners under one instructor with those under another instructor. By using selection type items, the instructor can test on many more areas of knowledge in a given time than could be done by requiring the learner to supply written responses. This increase in comprehensiveness can be expected to increase validity and discrimination. Selection type tests are well adapted to statistical item analysis.

True-False

The true-false test item consists of a statement followed by an opportunity for the learner to choose whether the statement is true or false. This item type has a wide range of usage. It is well adapted for testing knowledge of facts and details, especially when there are only two possible answers.

The chief disadvantage is that true-false questions create the greatest probability of guessing. Also, true-false questions are more likely to utilize rote memory than knowledge of the subject. In general, therefore, true-false questions are not considered valid (i.e., they do not measure what they are intended to measure).

To use true-false questions, consider the following guidelines for effective test items:

- Include only one idea in each statement.

- Use original statements rather than verbatim text.

- Make the statement entirely true or entirely false.

- Avoid the unnecessary use of negatives, which tend to confuse the reader.

- Underline or otherwise emphasize the negative word(s) if they must be used.

- Keep wording and sentence structure as simple as possible.

- Make statements both definite and clear.

- Avoid the use of ambiguous words and terms (some, any, generally, most times, etc.)

- Use terms which mean the same thing to all learners whenever possible.

- Avoid absolutes (all, every, only, no, never, etc.). These words are known as determiners because they provide clues to the correct answer.

- Avoid patterns in the sequence of correct responses because learners can often identify the patterns.

- Make statements brief and approximately same length.

- State the source of a statement if it is controversial (sources have differing information).

Multiple Choice

A multiple choice test item consists of two parts: the stem, which includes the question, statement, or problem; and a list of possible responses. Incorrect answers are called distractors. When properly devised and constructed, multiple choice items offer several advantages that make this type more widely used and versatile than either the matching or the true-false items. *[Figure B-2]*

Multiple choice test questions can help determine learner achievement, ranging from acquisition of facts to understanding, reasoning, and ability to apply what has been learned. It is appropriate to use multiple choice when the question, statement, or problem has the following characteristics:

- Built-in and unique solution, such as a specific application of laws or principles.

- Wording of the item is clearly limiting, so that the learner must choose the best of several offered solutions rather than a universal solution.

- Several options that are plausible or even scientifically accurate.

- Several pertinent solutions, with the learner asked to identify the most appropriate solution.

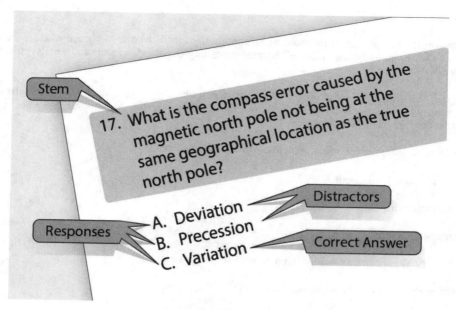

Figure B-2. *Sample multiple choice test item.*

Three major challenges are common in the construction of multiple choice test items. One is the development of a question or an item stem that must be expressed clearly and without ambiguity. A second is that the statement of an answer or correct response cannot be refuted. Finally, the distractors must be written in such a way that they are attractive to those learners who do not possess the knowledge or understanding necessary to recognize the keyed response.

A multiple choice item stem may take one of several basic forms:

• A direct question followed by several possible answers.

• An incomplete sentence followed by several possible phrases that complete the sentence.

• A stated problem based on an accompanying graph, diagram, or other artwork followed by the correct response and the distractors.

The learner may be asked to select the one correct choice or completion, the one choice that is an incorrect answer or completion, or the one choice that is the best answer option presented in the test item.

Beginning test writers find it easier to write items in the question form. In general, the form with the options as answers to a question is preferable to the form that uses an incomplete statement as the stem. It is more easily phrased and is more natural for the learner to read. Less likely to contain ambiguities, it usually results in more similarity between the options and gives fewer clues to the correct response.

When multiple choice questions are used, three or four alternatives are generally provided. It is usually difficult to construct more than four convincing responses; that is, responses which appear to be correct to a person who has not mastered the subject matter. Learners are not supposed to guess the correct option; they should select an alternative only if they know it is correct. An effective means of diverting the learner from the correct response is to use common learner errors as distractors. For example, if writing a question on the conversion of degrees Celsius to degrees Fahrenheit, providing alternatives derived by using incorrect formulas would be logical, since using the wrong formula is a common learner error.

Items intended to measure the rote level of learning should have only one correct alternative; all other alternatives should be clearly incorrect. When items are to measure achievement at a higher level of learning, some or all of the alternatives should be acceptable responses—but one should be clearly better than the others. In either case, the instructions given should direct the learner to select the best alternative.

To use multiple choice questions, consider the following guidelines for construction of effective test items:

- Make each item independent of every other item in the test. Do not permit one question to reveal, or depend on, the correct answer to another question.

- Design questions that call for essential knowledge rather than for abstract background knowledge or unimportant facts.

- State each question in language appropriate to the learners.

- Include sketches, diagrams, or pictures when they can present a situation more vividly than words. They generally speed the testing process, add interest, and help to avoid reading difficulties and technical language.

- When a negative is used, emphasize the negative word or phrase by underlining, bold facing, italicizing, or printing in a different color.

- Avoid questions containing double negatives, which invariably cause confusion.

- Avoid trick questions, unimportant details, ambiguities, and leading questions that confuse and antagonize the learner. If attention to detail is an objective, detailed construction of alternatives is preferable to trick questions.

Stems

When developing the stem of a multiple choice item, the following general principles should be utilized. *[Figure B-3]*

- The stem should clearly present the central problem or idea. The function of the stem is to set the stage for the alternatives that follow.

- The stem should contain only material relevant to its solution, unless the selection of what is relevant is part of the problem.

- The stem should be worded in such a way that it does not give away the correct response. Avoid the use of determiners, such as clue words or phrases.

- Put everything that pertains to all alternatives in the stem of the item. This helps to avoid repetitious alternatives and saves time.

- Generally avoid using "a" or "an" at the end of the stem. They may give away the correct choice. Every alternative should grammatically fit with the stem of the item.

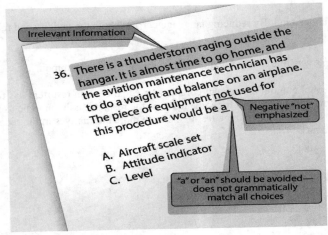

Figure B-3. *This is an example of a multiple choice question with a poorly written stem.*

Alternatives

The alternatives in a multiple choice test item are as important as the stem. They should be formulated with care; simply being incorrect should not be the only criterion for the distracting alternatives.

Popular distractors are:

- An incorrect response related to the situation and which sounds convincing.

- A common misconception.

- A statement which is true, but which does not satisfy the requirements of the problem.

- A statement that is either too broad or too narrow for the requirements of the problem.

Research of instructor-made tests reveals that, in general, correct alternatives are longer than incorrect ones. When alternatives are numbers, they should generally be listed in ascending or descending order of magnitude or length.

Matching

A matching test item consists of two lists, which may include a combination of words, terms, illustrations, phrases, or sentences. The learner matches alternatives in one list with related alternatives in a second list.

In reality, a matching exercise is a collection of related multiple choice items. In a given period of time, more samples of a learner's knowledge usually can be measured with matching rather than multiple choice items. The matching item is particularly good for measuring a learner's ability to recognize relationships and to make associations between terms, parts, words, phrases, clauses, or symbols listed in one column with related items in another column. Matching reduces the probability of guessing correct responses, especially if alternatives may be used more than once. The testing time can also be used more efficiently.

The following guidelines help in the construction of effective matching test items:

- Give specific and complete instructions. Do not make the learner guess what is required.

- Test only essential information; never test unimportant details.

- Use closely related materials throughout an item. If learners can divide the alternatives into distinct groups, the item is reduced to several multiple choice items with few alternatives, and the possibility of guessing is distinctly increased.

- Make all alternatives credible responses to each element in the first column, wherever possible, to minimize guessing by elimination.

- Use language the learner can understand. By reducing language barriers, both the validity and reliability of the test is improved.

- Arrange the alternatives in some sensible order. An alphabetical arrangement is common.

Matching-type test items are either equal column or unequal column. An equal column test item has the same number of alternatives in each column. When using this form, always provide for some items in the response column to be used more than once, or not at all, to preclude guessing by elimination. Unequal column type test items have more alternatives in the second column than in the first and are generally preferable to equal columns.

Aviation Instructor's Handbook (FAA-H-8083-9)
Appendix C: Certificates, Ratings, and Endorsements

Flight Instructor Endorsements

The authority and responsibility for flight instructors to endorse initial learner certificates, logbooks for solo and solo cross-country, additional aircraft ratings, and flight privileges are outlined in Title 14 of the Code of Federal Regulations (14 CFR) part 61. In addition, Advisory Circular (AC) 61-65, *Certification: Pilots and Flight and Ground Instructors*, provides guidance for pilots, flight instructors, ground instructors, and examiners on the certification standards, knowledge test procedures, and other requirements of 14 CFR part 61. By utilizing AC 61-65, the flight instructor does not omit any required endorsement for the rating sought, which ensures standardization. It is important for the flight instructor to understand and use AC 61-65 in the certification process.

Instructors should note that evaluations include an English language component. If the instructor doubts that a learner meets the FAA English Language Standard (AELS), the instructor should not endorse the review or check as complete. The instructor may also reach out to their local FSDO for assistance if the learner's continued operation could affect safety of the NAS. For further guidance on this subject refer to FAA AC 60-28, *FAA English Language Standard for an FAA Certificate Issued Under 14 CFR parts 61, 63, 65, and 107.*

The regulatory requirements for recording and logging time come from several different regulations that should be viewed together.

- 14 CFR part 61, section 61.189 requires flight instructors to sign the logbook of each person to whom that instructor has given flight training or ground training. That section also contains instructor requirements for maintaining a record of endorsements given to the applicant.

- 14 CFR part 61, section 61.193 authorizes instructors to make endorsements applicants need for various certificates or ratings.

- Subparts of 14 CFR part 61 detail the training an applicant needs to log in order to qualify for a rating or privilege. For example, 14 CFR part 61, subpart C, section 61.87(c)(1) requires a student pilot to receive and log flight training in specific maneuvers and procedures.

- 14 CFR part 61, section 61.51 details the information required for logbook entries.

Flight instructors may also provide training and make logbook endorsements for pilots who are already certificated such as sport, recreational, private, commercial, and instrument rated pilots, as well as for other flight instructors. Typical endorsements include but are not limited to flight reviews, instrument proficiency checks, the additional training required for high performance, high altitude, and tail wheel aircraft, and types of glider launches.

Additional rating applicants (e.g., multiengine add-on, seaplane add-on, glider add-on, helicopter add-on) are rated pilots and not considered student pilots nor do they need a student pilot certificate.

- In accordance with 14 CFR part 61, section 61.31(d)(2), applicants without the appropriate rating require an instructor's logbook endorsement prior to solo flight.

- 14 CFR part 61, section 61.63 contains the requirement for an endorsement for an applicant prior to testing for an added rating.

Sample practical test endorsements are listed in AC 61-65. Any requirement for an applicant to receive and log a practical test endorsement is cited in the relevant 14 CFR subpart for each rating. For example, 14 CFR part 61, subpart F, section 61.123(c) requires an endorsement from an authorized instructor for an applicant for a commercial pilot certificate. Note that when giving an endorsement, there is no rule that prevents an instructor from adding a requirement.

The flight instructor may need to customize the endorsement due to an applicant's special circumstances or changes in regulatory requirements, but it is recommended all endorsements be worded as closely as possible to those in AC 61-65. At a minimum, the flight instructor needs to cite the appropriate 14 CFR part 61 section that has been completed. *[Figure C-1]*

Federal Aviation Administration (FAA) inspectors and designated pilot examiners (DPEs) rely on flight instructor recommendations for learner or pilot applicant testing. These recommendations are accepted as evidence of qualification for certification and proof that a review of the subject areas found to be deficient on the appropriate knowledge test has been given by the flight instructor. Recommendations also provide assurance the applicant has had a thorough briefing on the Practical Test Standards (PTS), Airman Certification Standards (ACS), and the associated knowledge areas, maneuvers, and procedures. If the flight instructor has trained and prepared the applicant competently, the applicant should have no difficulty in passing the written and practical tests.

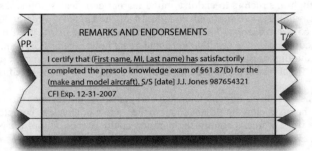

Figure C-1. *This is a sample logbook endorsement for pre-solo aeronautical knowledge.*

Sport Pilot

Many consider the advent of the sport pilot certification to be one of the most significant changes to the airman certification structure to have occurred in over 50 years. Because of the growing cost to acquire the private pilot certification, more and more aviation enthusiasts are considering the sport pilot as an alternative. Many aircraft already meet the light sport aircraft criteria, and many manufacturers are now producing modern light sport aircraft. Flight instructors should review 14 CFR part 61, subparts J and K, for the requirements for, and privileges and limitations of, the sport pilot certifications.

14 CFR part 61, subparts J and K, also describe the process for sport pilots and flight instructors with a sport pilot rating to add additional category/class privileges. Light sport aircraft meet certain criteria, and a well-informed flight instructor should be acquainted with the basic requirements.

FAA Forms 8710-1, 8610-2, and 8710-11

Forms 8710-1, 8610-2, and 8710-11 are versions of the Airman Certificate and/or Rating Application. The instructor should ensure the applicant is prepared for the test and has met all the regulatory requirements, including knowledge, proficiency, required endorsements, and experience requirements before the application process. The applicant then either completes the 8710 or 8610 paper form by hand or uses the Integrated Airman Certification and Rating Application (IACRA) electronic application system available at iacra.faa.gov/IACRA/Default.aspx.

Whenever possible, applicants should use the IACRA system to make their application. The system provides internal checking, and reduces the error rate. Any mistake or omission on a paper application form may cause a significant delay in the issuance of an FAA certificate.

Instructor Records

14 CFR part 61, section 61.189 requires the flight instructor to maintain a record that includes information on the type of endorsement, the name of the person receiving the endorsement, and the date of the endorsement. This information may be kept in a logbook or a separate document. For a knowledge or practical test endorsement, the record must include the kind of test, the date, and the results. Records of endorsements must be maintained for at least 3 years.

Knowledge Tests

14 CFR part 61, section 61.39(a)(1) requires that the applicant pass a knowledge test. When preparing an applicant for certification (e.g., recreational, private, commercial or instrument), the flight instructor may provide the learner with an endorsement to certify he or she has the required knowledge in accordance with 14 CFR part 61, section 61.35. Bear in mind that some additional ratings do not require a knowledge test. For information concerning additional aircraft certifications not requiring knowledge tests, refer to AC 61-65. Flight instructors (not including sport pilot instructors) take an FOI knowledge test or an aircraft subject matter test as required by 14 CFR part 61, sections 61.183(e) and 61.183(f). Added flight instructor ratings require a knowledge test on subject matter (part 61, section 61.183(f)), but the current added rating tests are shorter than the original flight instructor certification test under part 61, section 61.183(f).

Sport pilot applicants take a knowledge test required by 14 CFR part 61, section 61.307(a). The regulation requires a logbook endorsement from an authorized instructor in order to be able to take the knowledge test. 14 CFR part 61, section 61.405(a) requires a logbook endorsement from an authorized instructor for sport pilot instructor applicants. A Fundamentals of Instructing test may also apply in accordance with part 61, section 61.405(a)(1).

If the applicant fails a knowledge test, the applicant needs an endorsement from an authorized instructor who gave additional training in accordance with 14 CFR part 61, section 61.49(a) in order to retake the test. There is an unsigned endorsement provided on the knowledge test report that may be utilized by the instructor.

Additional Training and Endorsements

Flight instructors may provide training and endorsements for certificated pilots. AC 61-98, Currency Requirement and Guidance for the Flight Review and Instrument Proficiency Check, contains relevant information for certificated pilots and flight instructors for flight review required by 14 CFR part 61, section 61.56 or meeting recent flight experience requirements of section 61.57.

The AC includes general guidance in each of these areas, references to other related documents, and sample training plans that are pertinent to this type of training.

Flight Reviews

The requirements for a flight review are contained in 14 CFR part 61, section 61.56. The flight review is the aeronautical equivalent of a regular medical checkup and ongoing health improvement program.

Effective pilot refresher training should be based on specific objectives and standards. The objectives should include a thorough checkout appropriate to the pilot certificate and aircraft ratings held, and the standards should be at least those required for the issuance of that pilot certificate. Before beginning any training, the pilot and the instructor should agree fully on these objectives and standards, and, as training progresses, the pilot should be kept appraised of progress toward achieving those goals.

A flight review is an excellent opportunity for a flight instructor to review pilot decision-making (ADM) skills. To get the information needed to evaluate ADM skills, including risk management, give the pilot multiple opportunities to make decisions and ask questions about those decisions. For example, ask the pilot to explain why the alternate airport selected for a diversion exercise is a safe and appropriate choice. What are the possible hazards, and what can the pilot do to mitigate them? Be alert to the pilot's information and automation management skills as well. For example, does the pilot perform regular "common sense crosschecks?" For more ideas on generating scenarios that teach risk management, visit www.faa.gov/regulations_policies/ handbooks_manuals/aviation/pilot_risk/.

AC 61-98, *Currency Requirement and Guidance for the Flight Review and Instrument Proficiency Check*, provides guidance for conducting a flight review. An appendix in the AC includes a sample flight review checklist, which contains portions of 14 CFR part 61, section 61.56 and a sample endorsement. At the conclusion of a successful flight review, the logbook of the pilot should be endorsed, as recommended. *[Figure C-2]*

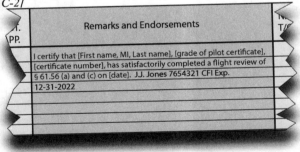

Figure C-2. *This sample logbook endorsement is for completion of a flight review.*

Instrument Proficiency Checks

Instrument rated pilots who fail to meet instrument currency requirements of 14 CFR part 61, section 61.57(c) for more than 6 calendar months are required by 14 CFR part 61, section 61.57(d) to complete an instrument proficiency check (IPC) in order to regain their instrument flying privileges. This does not apply to pilots meeting certain exceptions outlined in section 61.57(e).

14 CFR part 61, section 61.57(d) contains the requirements for an IPC. AC 61-98 contains guidance for the conduct of an (IPC). The Instrument Rating Airman Certification Standards (ACS) provides additional IPC information.

Aircraft and instrument ratings appropriate to the aircraft being flown need to be listed on the flight instructor's instructor certificate as indicated in 14 CFR part 61, section 61.57(d)(2).

Instructors as Certifying Officials for Student and Remote Certificates

14 CFR part 61, section 61.85(b) and part 107, section 107.63(b)(1) allow instructors to accept a Student Pilot or Remote Pilot Application. AC 61-141, *Flight Instructors as Certifying Officials for Student Pilot and Remote Pilot Applicants*, has process details for instructors and applicants.

Aircraft Checkouts/Transitions

Certificated pilots depend on flight instructors for aircraft checkouts and transition training including high performance airplanes, tail wheel airplanes, motor gliders, and aircraft capable of flight at high altitudes. The flight instructor who checks out and certifies the competency of a pilot in an aircraft for which a type rating is not required by regulation accepts major responsibility for the safety of future passengers. Many newer light airplanes are comparable in performance and complexity to transport airplanes. For these, the flight instructor's checkout should be at least as thorough as an official type rating practical test. Other considerations include:

- AC 90-109, Transition to Unfamiliar Aircraft, contains information help plan the transition to any unfamiliar fixed-wing airplanes, including type-certificated (TC) and/or experimental airplanes.

For the conduct of an aircraft checkout, it is essential the flight instructor is fully qualified in the aircraft used and thoroughly familiar with its operating procedures, AFM, and operating limitations. An instructor who does not meet the recent flight experience prescribed by regulations for the aircraft concerned should not attempt to check out another pilot.

The flight instructor should utilize a plan of action and a written training syllabus based on the appropriate ACS/PTS, and record in the pilot's logbook the exact extent of any checkout conducted. This record serves a twofold purpose: it benefits the pilot concerned and it protects the flight instructor if questions arise later. In the event the instructor finds a pilot's performance to be insufficient to allow sign-off, the pilot should be thoroughly debriefed on all problem areas and further instruction scheduled. In some cases, a referral to another instructor may be appropriate.

Pilot Proficiency

Professional flight instructors maintain knowledge and skill as instructors and as pilots. The flight instructor is at the leading edge of the aviation industry's efforts to improve aviation safety through additional training.

Instructors planning to take the ATP multiengine airplane knowledge test may refer to AC 61-138, *Airline Transport Pilot Certification Training Program*, for further guidance.

Aviation Instructor's Handbook (FAA-H-8083-9)

Appendix D: Personal Minimums Checklist

Pilot:_____

Date Revised: _____

Reviewed with: _____, (if applicable)

Your Personal Minimums Checklist—

- Is an easy-to-use, personal tool tailored to your level of skill, knowledge, and ability.
- Helps you control and manage risk by identifying even subtle risk factors.
- Allows you to fly with less stress and less risk. Practice "Conservatism Without Guilt."

Each item provides you with either a space to complete a personal minimum or a checklist item to think about. Spend some quiet time completing each blank and consider other items that apply to your personal minimums. Give yourself permission to choose higher minimums than those specified in the regulations, aircraft flight manuals, or other rules.

How To Use Your Checklist

Use this checklist just as you would use one for your aircraft. Carry the checklist in your flight kit. Use it at home as you start planning a flight and again just before you make your final decision to fly. Be wary if you have an item that's marginal in any single risk factor category. But if you have items in more than one category, you may be headed for trouble. If you have marginal items in two or more risk factors/categories, do not go!

Periodically review and revise your checklist as your personal circumstances change, such as your proficiency, recency, or training. You should never make your minimums less restrictive unless a significant positive event has occurred. However, it is okay to make your minimums more restrictive at any time. And never make your minimums less restrictive when you are planning a specific flight, or else external pressures will influence you.

Have a fun and safe flight!

Pilot

Takeoffs/landings	_____ in the last _____ days
Hours in make/model	_____ in the last _____ days
Instrument approaches	_____ (simulated or actual) in the last _____ days
Instrument flight hours	_____ (simulated or actual) in the last _____ days
Terrain and airspace	familiar

Physical Condition

Sleep	_____ hours in the last 24 hours
Food and water	in the last _____ hours
Alcohol	None in the last _____ hours
Drugs or medication	None in the last _____ hours
Stressful events	None in the last _____ days
Illnesses	None in the last _____ days

Aircraft

Fuel Reserves (Cross-Country)

VFR day	_____	hours
VFR Night	_____	hours
IFR day	_____	hours
IFR Night	_____	hours

Experience in Type

Takeoffs/landings	_____ in the last _____ days	
Takeoffs/landings	_____ in aircraft type	

Aircraft Performance

Establish that you have additional performance available over that required. Consider the following:

- Gross weight
- Load distribution
- Density altitude
- Performance charts

Aircraft Equipment

Avionics	familiar with equipment (including autopilot and GPS systems)
COM/NAV	equipment appropriate to flight
Charts	current
Clothing	suitable for preflight and flight
Survival gear	appropriate for flight/terrain

Environment

Airport Conditions

Crosswind	_____ % of max POH
Runway length	_____ % more than POH

Weather

Reports and forecasts	not more than _____ hours old
Icing conditions	within aircraft/pilot capabilities

Weather for VFR

Ceiling day	_____ feet
Ceiling Night	_____ feet
Visibility day	_____ miles
Visibility Night	_____ miles

Weather for IFR
Precision Approaches

Ceiling	_____ feet above min.
Visibility	_____ mile(s) above min.

Non-Precision Approaches
Ceiling   _____ feet above min.

Visibility   _____ mile(s) above min.

Missed Approaches
No more than   _____ before diverting

Takeoff Minimums
Ceiling   _____ feet

Visibility   _____ mile(s)

External Pressures
Trip Planning
Allowance for delays   _____ minutes

Alternate Plans for Diversion or Cancellation

- Notification of person(s) you are meeting
- Passengers briefed on diversion or cancellation plans and alternatives
- Modification or cancellation of car rental, restaurant, or hotel reservations
- Arrangement of alternative transportation (airline, car, etc.)

Personal Equipment

- Credit card and telephone numbers available for alternate plans
- Appropriate clothing or personal needs (eyewear, medication, etc.) in the event of unexpected stay

Importance of Trip

The more important the trip, the more tendency there is to compromise personal minimums, and the more important it becomes to have alternate plans.

Aviation Instructor's Handbook (FAA-H-8083-9)
Glossary

A

Abstractions. Words that are general rather than specific. Aircraft is an abstraction; airplane is less abstract; jet is more specific; and jet airliner is still more specific.

Aeronautical decision-making (ADM). A systematic approach to the mental process used by aircraft pilots to consistently determine the best course of action in response to a given set of circumstances.

Affective domain. A grouping of levels of learning associated with a person's attitudes, personal beliefs, and values which range from receiving through responding, valuing, and organization to characterization.

Air traffic control (ATC). A service provided by the FAA to promote the safe, orderly, and expeditious flow of air traffic.

Aircraft checkouts. An instructional program designed to familiarize and qualify a pilot to act as pilot in command of a particular aircraft type.

Airman Certification Standards (ACS). An FAA published list of standards which must be met for the issuance of a particular pilot certificate or rating. FAA inspectors and designated pilot examiners use these standards when conducting pilot practical tests and flight instructors should use the ACS while preparing applicants for practical tests.

Anxiety. Mental discomfort that arises from the fear of anything, real or imagined. May have a potent effect on actions and the ability to learn from perceptions.

Application. A basic level of learning at which the individual puts something to use that has been learned and understood.

Application step. The third step of the teaching process, where the learner performs the procedure or demonstrates the knowledge required in the lesson. In the telling-and-doing technique of flight instruction, this step consists of the learner doing the procedure while explaining it.

Area of operation. A phase of the practical test within the Airman Certification Standards (ACS) or the Practical Test Standards (PTS).

ATC. See air traffic control.

Attitude. A personal motivational predisposition to respond to persons, situations, or events in a given manner that can, nevertheless, be changed or modified through training as a sort of mental shortcut to decision-making.

Attitude management. The ability to recognize one's own hazardous attitudes and the willingness to modify them as necessary through the application of appropriate antidotal thoughts.

Authentic assessment. An assessment in which the learner is asked to perform real-world tasks, and demonstrate a meaningful application of skills and competencies.

B

Basic need. A perception factor that describes a person's ability to maintain and enhance the organized self.

Behaviorism. Theory of learning that stresses the importance of having a particular form of behavior reinforced by someone other than the learner to shape or control what is learned.

Bookmark. A means of saving addresses on the World Wide Web (WWW) for easy future access. Usually done by selecting a button on the web browser screen, it saves the current web address so it does not have to be input again in a lengthy series of characters.

Branching. A programming technique which allows users of interactive video, multimedia courseware, or online training to choose from several courses of action in moving from one sequence to another.

Briefing. An oral presentation where the speaker presents a concise array of facts without inclusion of extensive supporting material.

Building block concept. Concept of learning that new knowledge and skills are best based on a solid foundation of previous experience and/or old learning. As knowledge and skills increase, the base expands, supporting further learning.

C

CBI. See computer-based instruction.

CBT. See computer-based training.

CD. See compact disk.

Cognitive domain. A grouping of levels of learning associated with mental activity. In order of increasing complexity, the domains are knowledge, comprehension, application, analysis, synthesis, and evaluation.

Compact disk (CD). A small plastic optical disk which contains recorded music or computer data. Also, a popular format for storing information digitally. The major advantage of a CD is its capability to store enormous amounts of information.

Comprehensiveness. The degree to which a test measures the overall objective.

Computer-assisted instruction. Instruction in which the instructor is responsible for the class and uses the computer to assist in the instruction.

Computer-based training (CBT). The use of the computer as a training device. CBT is sometimes called computer-based instruction (CBI); the terms and acronyms are synonymous and may be used interchangeably.

Condition. The second part of a performance-based objective which describes the framework under which the skill or behavior will be demonstrated.

Confusion between the symbol and the symbolized object. Results when a word is confused with what it is meant to represent. Words and symbols create confusion when they mean different things to different people.

Cooperative or group learning. An instructional strategy which organizes learners into small groups so that they can work together to maximize their own and each other's learning.

Correlation. A basic level of learning where the learner can associate what has been learned, understood, and applied with previous or subsequent learning.

Course of training. A complete series of studies leading to attainment of a specific goal, such as a certificate of completion, graduation, or an academic degree.

Crew resource management (CRM). The application of team management concepts in the flight deck environment. It was initially known as cockpit resource management, but as CRM programs evolved to include cabin crews, maintenance personnel and others, the phrase "crew resource management" has been adopted. This includes single pilots, as in most general aviation aircraft. Pilots of small aircraft, as well as crews of larger aircraft, must make effective use of all available resources; human resources, hardware, and information. A current definition includes all groups routinely working with the cockpit crew who are involved in decisions required to operate a flight safely. These groups include, but are not limited to: pilots, dispatchers, cabin crewmembers, maintenance personnel, and air traffic controllers. CRM is one way of addressing the challenge of optimizing the human/ machine interface and accompanying interpersonal activities.

Criteria. The third part of a performance-based objective, descriptions of standards that will be used to measure the accomplishment of the objective.

Criterion-referenced testing. System of testing where learners are graded against a carefully written, measurable standard or criterion rather than against each other.

CRM. See crew resource management.

Curriculum. A set of courses in an area of specialization offered by an educational institution. A curriculum for a pilot school usually includes courses for the various pilot certificates and ratings.

Cut-away. Model of an object that is built in sections so it can be taken apart to reveal the inner structure.

D

Defense mechanisms. Subconscious ego-protecting reactions to unpleasant situations.

Demonstration-performance method. An educational presentation where an instructor first shows the learner the correct way to perform an activity and then has the learner attempt the same activity.

Description of the skill or behavior. The first part of a performance-based objective which explains the desired outcome of instruction in concrete terms that can be measured.

Determiners. In test items, words which give a clue to the answer. Words such as "always" and "never" are determiners in true-false questions. Since absolutes are rare, such words usually make the statement false.

Direct question. A question used for follow-up purposes, but directed at a specific individual.

Discrimination. The degree to which a test distinguishes the differences between learners.

Distractors. Incorrect responses to a multiple-choice test item.

Disuse. A theory of forgetting that suggests a person forgets those things that are not used.

Drill and practice method. A time-honored training delivery method based on the learning principle that connections are strengthened with practice.

E

Effect. A principle of learning that learning is strengthened when accompanied by a pleasant or satisfying feeling, and that learning is weakened when associated with an unpleasant feeling.

Electronic learning (e-learning). Any type of education that involves an electronic component such as the Internet, a network, a stand-alone computer, CD/DVDs, video conferencing, websites, or e-mail in its delivery.

Element of threat. A perception factor that describes how a person is unlikely to easily comprehend an event if that person is feeling threatened since most of a person's effort is focused on whatever is threatening them.

Exercise. A principle of learning emphasizing that those things most often repeated are best remembered.

F

FAASTeam. See Federal Aviation Administration Safety Team.

FAASTeam Program Manager. The person who designs, implements, and evaluates the FAASTeam within the FAA Flight Standards District Office (FSDO) area of responsibility.

FAASTeam Representative. A volunteer within the aviation community who shares technical expertise and professional knowledge as a part of the FAASTeam.

Federal Aviation Administration Safety Team (FAASTeam). An organization promoting safety standards and the reduction of aircraft related accidents. Each of the eight FAA Flight Standards regions have a dedicated FAASTeam office.

Flight review. A 14 CFR part 61.56 requirement designed to assess and update a pilot's knowledge and skills.

Flight training devices (FTDs). A full-size replica of the instruments, equipment, panels, and controls of an aircraft, or set of aircraft, in an open flight deck area or in an enclosed cockpit. A force (motion) cueing system or visual system is not required.

Follow-up question. In the guided discussion method, a question used by an instructor to get the discussion back on track or to get the learners to explain something more thoroughly.

Formal lecture. An oral presentation where the purpose is to inform, persuade, or entertain with little or no verbal participation by the listeners.

FTD. See flight training device.

G

Goals and values. A perception factor that describes how a person's perception of an event depends on beliefs. Motivation toward learning is affected by how much value a person puts on education. Instructors who have some idea of the goals and values of their learners will be more successful in teaching them.

Guided discussion method. An educational presentation typically used in the classroom where the topic to be covered by a group is introduced and the instructor participates only as necessary to keep the group focused on the subject.

H

Hierarchy of human needs. A listing by Abraham Maslow of needs from the most basic to the most fulfilling: physiological, security, belonging, esteem, cognitive and aesthetic, and self-actualization.

Human factors. A multidisciplinary field devoted to optimizing human performance and reducing human error. It incorporates the methods and principles of the behavioral and social sciences, engineering, and physiology. It may be described as the applied science which studies people working together in concert with machines. Human factors involve variables that influence individual performance, as well as team or crew performance.

Human nature. The general psychological characteristics, feelings, and behavioral traits shared by all humans.

I

Illustrated talk. An oral presentation where the speaker relies heavily on visual aids to convey ideas to the listeners.

Insight. The grouping of perceptions into meaningful wholes. Creating insight is one of the instructor's major responsibilities.

Instructional aids. Devices that assist an instructor in the teaching-learning process. They are supplementary training devices, and are not self-supporting.

Instrument proficiency check. An evaluation ride based on the instrument rating practical test standard which is required to regain instrument flying privileges when the privileges have expired due to lack of currency.

Integrated flight instruction. A technique of flight instruction in which learners are taught to perform flight maneuvers by reference to both the flight instruments and to outside visual references from the time the maneuver is first introduced. Handling of the controls is the same regardless of whether flight instruments or outside references are being used.

Intensity. A principle of learning in which a dramatic or exciting learning experience is likely to be remembered longer than a boring experience. Learners experiencing the real thing will learn understand more than when they are merely told about the real thing.

Interactive video. Software that responds quickly to certain choices and commands by the user. A typical system consists of a compact disk, computer, and video technology.

Interference. (1) A theory of forgetting proposing that a person forgets something because a certain experience overshadows it, or the learning of similar things has intervened. (2) Barriers to effective communication that are caused by physiological, environmental, and psychological factors outside the direct control of the instructor. The instructor must take these factors into account in order to communicate effectively.

Internet. An electronic network that connects computers around the world.

J

Judgment. The mental process of recognizing and analyzing all pertinent information in a particular situation, a rational evaluation of alternative actions in response to it, and a timely decision on which action to take.

K

Knowledge. Information that humans are consciously aware of and can articulate.

L

Lack of common experience. In communication, a difficulty which arises because words have different meanings for the source and the receiver of information due to their differing backgrounds.

Lead-off question. In the guided discussion method, a question used by an instructor to open up an area for discussion and get the discussion started.

Learning. A change in behavior as a result of experience.

Learning plateau. A learning phenomenon where progress appears to cease or slow down for a significant period of time before once again increasing.

Learning style. Preferred way(s) by which people learn. Common learning styles include visual, auditory, and kinesthetic, or tactile (hands on). Learning skills can be loosely grouped into physical and cognitive styles.

Learning theory. A body of principles advocated by psychologists and educators to explain how people acquire skills, knowledge, and attitudes.

Lecture method. An educational presentation usually delivered by an instructor to a group of learners with the use of instructional aids and training devices. Lectures are useful for the presentation of new material, summarizing ideas, and showing relationships between theory and practice.

Lesson plan. An organized outline for a single instructional period. It is a necessary guide for the instructor in that it tells what to do, in what order to do it, and what procedure to use in teaching the material of a lesson.

Link. On a website, an external web location that can be accessed by merely clicking on words identifying the new site. They are usually identified by a different color type, underlining, or a button (picture or icon) indicating access to a new site.

Long-term memory. The portion of the brain that stores information that has been determined to be of sufficient value to be retained. In order for it to be retained in long-term memory, it must have been processed or coded in the working memory.

M

Matching-type test item. A test item in which the learner is asked to match alternatives on one list to related alternatives on a second list. The lists may include words, terms, illustrations, phrases, or sentences.

Memory. The ability of people and other organisms to encode (initial perception and registration of information), store (retention of encoded information over time), and retrieve (processes involved in using stored information) information.

Mock-up. A three-dimensional working model used in which the actual object is either unavailable or too expensive to use. Mock-ups may emphasize some elements while eliminating nonessential elements.

Model. A copy of a real object which can be life-size, smaller, or larger than the original.

Motivation. A need or desire that causes a person to act. Motivation can be positive or negative, tangible or intangible, subtle or obvious.

Multimedia. A combination of more than one instructional medium. This format can include audio, text, graphics, animations, and video. Recently, multimedia implies a computer-based presentation.

Multiple choice-type test item. A test item consisting of a question or statement followed by a list of alternative answers or responses.

N

Navigate. To move between websites on the internet. Navigation is often accomplished by means of links or connections between sites.

Norm-referenced testing. System of testing in which learners are ranked against the performance of other learners.

O

Objectivity. The singleness of scoring of a test; it does not reflect the biases of the person grading the test.

Overhead question. In the guided discussion method, a question directed to the entire group in order to stimulate thought and discussion from the entire group. An overhead question may be used by an instructor as the lead-off question.

P

Perceptions. The basis of all learning, perceptions result when a person gives meaning to external stimuli or sensations. Meaning derived from perception is influenced by an individual's experience and many other factors.

Performance-based objectives. A statement of purpose for a lesson or instructional period that includes three elements: a description of the skill or behavior desired of the learner, a set of conditions under which the measurement will be taken, and a set of criteria describing the standard used to measure accomplishment of the objective.

Personal computer-based aviation training device (PCATD). A device which uses software which can be displayed on a personal computer to replicate the instrument panel of an airplane. A PCATD must replicate a type of airplane or family of airplanes and meet the virtual control requirements specified in Advisory Circular (AC) 61-126.

Personality. The embodiment of personal traits and characteristics of an individual that are set at a very early age and are extremely resistant to change.

Physical organism. A perception factor that describes a person's ability to sense the world around them.

Pilot error. Pilot action/inaction or decision/indecision causing or contributing to an accident or incident.

Poor judgment chain. A series of mistakes that may lead to an accident or incident. Two basic principles generally associated with the creation of a poor judgment chain are: (1) one bad decision often leads to another; and (2) as a string of bad decisions grows, it reduces the number of subsequent alternatives for continued safe flight. Aeronautical decision-making is intended to break the poor judgment chain before it can cause an accident or incident.

Practical Test Standards (PTS). An FAA published list of standards which must be met for the issuance of a particular pilot certificate or rating. FAA inspectors and designated pilot examiners use these standards when conducting pilot practical tests and flight instructors should use the PTS while preparing applicants for practical tests.

Preparation. The first step of the teaching process, which consists of determining the scope of the lesson, the objectives, and the goals to be attained. This portion also includes making certain all necessary supplies are on hand. When using the telling-and-doing technique of flight instruction, this step is accomplished prior to the flight lesson.

Presentation. The second step of the teaching process, which consists of delivering information or demonstrating the skills that make up the lesson. The delivery could be by either the lecture method or demonstration-performance method. In the telling-and-doing technique of flight instruction, this is the segment in which the instructor both talks about and performs the procedure.

Pretest. A test used to determine whether a learner has the necessary qualifications to begin a course of study. Also used to determine the level of knowledge a learner has in relation to the material that will be presented in the course.

Primacy. A principle of learning in which the first experience of something often creates a strong, almost unshakable impression. The importance to an instructor is that the first time something is demonstrated, it must be shown correctly since that experience is the one most likely to be remembered by the learner.

Problem-based learning. Lessons in such a way as to confront learners with problems that are encountered in real life which force them to reach real-world solutions.

Psychomotor domain. A grouping of levels of learning associated with physical skill levels which range from perception through set, guided response, mechanism, complex overt response, and adaptation to origination.

PTS. See Practical Test Standards.

R

Readiness. A principle of learning where the eagerness and single-mindedness of a person toward learning affect the outcome of the learning experience.

Receiver. In communication, the listener, reader, or learner who takes in a message containing information from a source, processes it, reacts with understanding, and changes behavior in accordance with the message.

Recency. Principle of learning stating that things learned recently are remembered better than things learned some time ago. As time passes, less is remembered. Instructors use this principle when summarizing the important points at the end of a lecture in order for learners to better remember them.

Relay question. Used in response to a learner's question, the question is redirected to another individual.

Reliability. The degree to which test results are consistent with repeated measurements.

Repression. Theory of forgetting proposing that a person is more likely to forget information which is unpleasant or produces anxiety.

Response. Possible answer to a multiple choice test item. The correct response is often called the keyed response, and incorrect responses are called distractors.

Reverse question. Used in response to a learner's question. Rather than give a direct answer to the learner's query, the instructor returns the question to the same individual to provide the answer.

Review and evaluation. The fourth and last step in the teaching process, which consists of a review of all material and an evaluation of the learners. In the telling-and-doing technique of flight instruction, this step consists of the instructor evaluating the performance while the learner performs the required procedure.

Rhetorical question. Generally, a question asked for a purpose other than to obtain the information the question asks. For this handbook's purpose, a question asked to stimulate group thought. Normally answered by the instructor, it is more commonly used in lecturing rather than in guided discussions.

Risk elements in ADM. Take into consideration the four fundamental risk elements: the pilot, the aircraft, the environment, and external pressures.

Risk management. The part of the decision-making process which relies on situational awareness, problem recognition, and good judgment to reduce risks associated with each flight.

Rote learning. A basic level of learning in which the learner has the ability to repeat back something learned, with no understanding or ability to apply what was learned.

S

Scenario-based training (SBT). Training method that uses a highly structured script of real-world experiences to address aviation training objectives in an operational environment.

Selection-type test items. Test items requiring the learner to choose from two or more alternatives provided. True-false, matching, and multiple choice type questions are examples of selection type test items.

Self-concept. A perception factor that ties together how people feel about themselves with how well they receive experiences.

Sensory register. That portion of the brain which receives input from the five senses. The individual's preconceived concept of what is important determines how the register prioritizes the information for passing it on to the rest of the brain for action.

Single-Pilot Resource Management (SRM). The art/science of managing all the resources (both onboard the aircraft and from outside sources) available to a single pilot (prior and during flight) to ensure that the successful outcome of the flight is never in doubt.

Sites. Internet addresses which provide information and often are linked to other similar sites

Situational awareness. The accurate perception and understanding of all the factors and conditions within the four fundamental risk elements that affect safety before, during, and after the flight.

Skill knowledge. Knowledge reflected in motor or manual skills and in cognitive or mental skills that manifests itself in the doing of something.

Skills and procedures. The procedural, psychomotor, and perceptual skills used to control a specific aircraft or its systems. They are the stick and rudder or airmanship abilities that are gained through conventional training, are perfected, and become almost automatic through experience.

Source. In communication, the sender, speaker, transmitter, or instructor who composes and transmits a message made up of symbols which are meaningful to listeners and readers.

Stem. The part of a multiple choice test item consisting of the question, statement, or problem.

Stress management. The personal analysis of the kinds of stress experienced while flying, the application of appropriate stress assessment tools, and other coping mechanisms.

Supply-type test item. Question in which the learner supplies answers as opposed to selecting from choices provided. Essay or fill-in-the-blank-type questions are examples of supply-type test items.

Symbols. In communication, simple oral and visual codes such as words, gestures, and facial expressions which are formed into sentences, paragraphs, lectures, or chapters to compose and transmit a message that means something to the receiver of the information.

T

Task. Knowledge area, flight procedure, or maneuver within an area of operation in a practical test standard.

Taxonomy of educational objectives. A systematic classification scheme for sorting learning outcomes into three broad categories (cognitive, affective, and psychomotor) and ranking the desired outcomes in a developmental hierarchy from least complex to most complex.

Teaching. Instructing, training, or imparting knowledge or skill; the profession of someone who teaches.

Teaching lecture. An oral presentation that is directed toward desired learning outcomes. Some learner participation is allowed.

Telling-and-doing technique. A technique of flight instruction that consists of the instructor first telling the learner about a new procedure and then demonstrating it. This is followed by the learner telling and the instructor doing. Third, the learner explains the new procedure while doing it. Last, the instructor evaluates while the learner performs the procedure.

Test. A set of questions, problems, or exercises for determining whether a person has a particular knowledge or skill.

Test item. A question, problem, or exercise that measures a single objective and requires a single response.

Time and opportunity. A perception factor in which learning something is dependent on the individual having the time to sense and relate current experiences in context with previous events.

Traditional assessment. Written testing, such as multiple choice, matching, true-false, or fill-in-the-blank.

Training course outline. Within a curriculum, describes the content of a particular course by statement of objectives, descriptions of teaching aids, definition of evaluation criteria, and indication of desired outcome.

Training media. Any physical means that communicates an instructional message to learners.

Training syllabus. A step-by-step, building block progression of learning with provisions for regular review and evaluations at prescribed stages of learning. The syllabus defines the unit of training, states by objective what the learner is expected to accomplish during the unit of training, shows an organized plan for instruction, and dictates the evaluation process for either the unit or stages of learning.

Transfer of learning. The ability to apply knowledge or procedures learned in one context to new contexts

Transition training. An instructional program designed to familiarize and qualify a pilot to fly types of aircraft not previously flown, such as tail wheel aircraft, high performance aircraft, and aircraft capable of flying at high altitudes.

True-false test item. A test item consisting of a statement followed by an opportunity for the learner to determine whether the statement is true or false.

U

Understanding. A basic level of learning at which a learner comprehends or grasps the nature or meaning of something.

Usability. The functionality of tests.

V

Validity. The extent to which a test measures what it is supposed to measure.

Virtual reality (VR). A form of computer-based technology that creates a sensory experience allowing a participant to believe and barely distinguish a virtual experience from a real one. VR uses graphics with animation systems, sounds, and images to reproduce electronic versions of real-life experience.

W

Working or short-term memory. The portion of the brain that receives information from the sensory register. This portion of the brain can store information in memory for only a short period of time. If the information is determined by an individual to be important enough to remember, it must be coded in some way for transmittal to long-term memory.

Aviation Instructor's Handbook (FAA-H-8083-9)
Index

D

APPENDIX C
GROUND SCHOOL COURSE SUGGESTIONS

The purpose of this appendix is to suggest ideas concerning marketing, organization, and presentation of ground schools for pilot knowledge tests. We would appreciate any comments or suggestions you may have after reading this material, as will other aviation professionals when we incorporate this information into subsequent editions. Please send feedback to us at your convenience at www.GleimAviation.com/questions. Thank you.

RATIONALE FOR CONDUCTING A GROUND SCHOOL

1. **Aid to the industry.** General aviation (including flight instruction), while more financially sound than it has been in years past, is still not normally a high-profit enterprise.

    a. A ground school is the first step into aviation for many learners who will one day become aircraft renters and owners--the people who sustain GA. While it will not generate large profits for a business on its own, a ground school sets the stage for a lasting relationship between a flight school/FBO and its learners.

2. **Maintaining a professional level of currency and familiarity with aviation subjects.** Obtaining your flight and/or ground instructor certificate will keep you up to date on the Federal Aviation Regulations and all other academic areas of flight. Additionally, teaching will challenge you to learn and understand a wide variety of material.

3. **Finding new customers.** Many flight instructors use ground schools as a source of new pilots.

4. **Public service.** Many flight and/or ground instructors provide ground schools to Civil Air Patrol (CAP) chapters, high school classes, etc., as a public service to young people.

5. **Personal employment.** Obtaining your flight and/or ground instructor certificate can lead to opportunities for part-time work at FBOs, community colleges, and adult education programs.

POTENTIAL SPONSORS OF GROUND SCHOOLS

1. **Community colleges.** Call your local junior college and ask if a ground school is offered. Ask what division it is in and call the dean or director to indicate your interest in teaching the ground school. While talking to the dean or director, you should obtain a course outline, as well as information on the cost and class schedule. The college may already have an instructor, but you should make known your interest in teaching in case there should be an opening.

   a. Send us the dean or director's name and address and your own name and address. We will send him or her a complimentary copy of *Private Pilot FAA Knowledge Test Prep* or *Sport Pilot FAA Knowledge Test Prep* and explain that it was at your suggestion. We will reiterate your interest in presenting a ground school.

2. **Local high school adult education centers.** Call all local high schools for more information.

3. **FBOs.** Inquire at your local airport, or search on the Internet (e.g., www.airnav.com).

4. **Civil Air Patrol units.** Inquire at your local armed forces recruiting or training station for the name and telephone number of local CAP unit commanders (see the U.S. Government section of your telephone book).

   a. You can also find information about the CAP's aerospace education program at the Civil Air Patrol National Headquarters website (www.gocivilairpatrol.com).

MARKETING GROUND SCHOOLS

The objective of marketing a ground school is to contact interested learners if you are beginning a new ground school and to increase enrollment if you are associated with an existing ground school. The following are only a few suggestions.

1. **Internet.** Create a simple website or have one built for you to advertise your services, schedule, location, etc. Gleim can provide you with buttons leading directly to our products in our aviation store.

2. **Social media.** Advertise your services on various social media platforms, such as Facebook, Twitter, and Instagram. Participate in forums where you can connect with prospective learners and fellow instructors. Create videos introducing yourself and your services to share on hosts, such as YouTube, and share links to these videos on social media.

3. **Radio ads.** Call your local radio station and pay for an advertisement or, preferably, have it broadcast as a public service announcement.

4. **Posters.** Prepare posters and provide a telephone number. Post them at your local community college, university, airport, stores, etc.

GROUND SCHOOL COURSE ORGANIZATION

We hope you will use *Pilot Handbook*, as well as *Private Pilot FAA Knowledge Test Prep*, **FAA Test Prep Online**, and/or **Gleim Online Ground School** for your ground school. Based on that presumption, it is probably easiest to follow our study unit organization, which is the same in both *Pilot Handbook* and *Private Pilot FAA Knowledge Test Prep*.

We recommend that you incorporate a Sport Pilot ground school with your Private Pilot ground school to help you maximize the number of learners interested in the course. Sport pilots need to know approximately 70% of the required material for Private Pilot to pass their FAA knowledge test. It is beneficial for them to learn more than what is required for them to pass the FAA knowledge test; therefore, we include additional study units in *Sport Pilot FAA Knowledge Test Prep*.

Make sure that you are aware of the differences between Sport Pilot and Private Pilot and make it clear to your learners which information they may omit for Sport Pilot.

Private Pilot FAA Knowledge Test Prep

Study Unit   1 • Airplanes and Aerodynamics
Study Unit   2 • Airplane Instruments, Engines, and Systems
Study Unit   3 • Airports, Air Traffic Control, and Airspace
Study Unit   4 • Federal Aviation Regulations
Study Unit   5 • Airplane Performance and Weight and Balance
Study Unit   6 • Aeromedical Factors and Aeronautical Decision Making (ADM)
Study Unit   7 • Aviation Weather
Study Unit   8 • Aviation Weather Services
Study Unit   9 • Navigation: Charts and Publications
Study Unit 10 • Navigation Systems
Study Unit 11 • Cross-Country Flight Planning

Sport Pilot FAA Knowledge Test Prep

Study Unit   1 • Airports
Study Unit   2 • Airspace
Study Unit   3 • Federal Aviation Regulations – 14 CFR Parts 1 through 61
Study Unit   4 • Federal Aviation Regulations – 14 CFR Parts 91.3 through 91.123
Study Unit   5 • Federal Aviation Regulations – 14 CFR Parts 91.159 through 91.421 and
                         NTSB Part 830
Study Unit   6 • Aeromedical Factors and Aeronautical Decision Making (ADM)
Study Unit   7 • Aviation Weather
Study Unit   8 • Weather Services
Study Unit   9 • Sectional Charts and Airspace
Study Unit 10 • Navigation and Preflight Preparation
Study Unit 11 • Airplanes and Aerodynamics
Study Unit 12 • Airplane Instruments
Study Unit 13 • Airplane Engines and Systems
Study Unit 14 • Airplane Performance and Weight and Balance

You will probably not have exactly 11 class sessions, which may necessitate combining study units for various classes. Approximately 12 sessions of 2 hours each should be adequate if your course objective is to get your learners ready for their pilot knowledge test. Even if you have 11 sessions, you may still want to combine certain study units and spend more time on other units. As an example of how study units might be combined for Private Pilot, if you have a 5-week program that meets for 10 sessions, you might want to combine Study Units 9, 10, and 11. You could easily cover the Introduction in Session 1 and still use a good part of the session to get into Study Unit 1. Then spend another entire meeting to finish Study Unit 1.

If your course objective is to cover all the subjects in the amount of detail needed by proficient pilots (rather than simply to "teach the test"), 16 to 18 2-hour sessions should be adequate. More time is needed for this comprehensive course because the FAA does not test every topic that your learners need to know in order to be safe, capable pilots. Having 16 to 18 sessions will allow you to spend more than one session on the largest and most important study units in *Pilot Handbook* (Study Units 1 through 4) and will allow you to spend extra time on challenging concepts like airspace and radio navigation. A comprehensive course outline for Private Pilot might entail two sessions for the Introduction and Study Unit 1, two sessions for Study Unit 2, two sessions for Study Unit 3, one to two sessions for Study Unit 4 (depending on how detailed you wish to get), one to two sessions for Study Unit 5, and one session each for Study Units 6 through 11. Any extra time left in the course can be spent reviewing difficult topics and engaging in test-specific preparation.

Regardless of your course objective, you may wish to reserve 5 or 10 minutes at the end of each session for an overview and introduction of the material to be covered in the next session. That will help your learners study for the next session and help them understand it. Remember to always assign additional study at home to keep your learners engaged and prepared.

COURSE SYLLABUS AND HANDOUTS

1. At the beginning of the course, you should distribute an outline of the material to be covered in the course. It should show the meeting times, quiz schedule, and reading assignments for each session.

2. A suggested syllabus for a 9-week class (whose objective is to prepare learners for the test) that meets for 3 hours one night per week is presented on the following page.

    a. Undoubtedly, you will have to change the scheduling of topics. The topics have been overlapped so that you can talk about the same topic during two periods; i.e., you can provide double exposure. Introducing the topic the week before provides 3 weeks' coverage, which may be useful to your learners.

3. Of course, the six study units in this book will be helpful to you as general background in preparing and presenting your ground school.

GLEIM PILOT KITS

The Gleim **Private Pilot Kit** and **Sport Pilot Kit** are designed to simplify and facilitate your learners' flight and ground training. There are different levels of each kit available. The Pilot Kits may include

- *FAA Knowledge Test Prep*
- *Flight Maneuvers and Practical Test Prep*
- *Pilot Handbook*
- *FAR/AIM*
- *Syllabus*
- *ACS and Oral Exam Guide* (Private Pilot only)
- Logbook (hard cover)
- Training Record

- Online Ground School
- FAA Test Prep Online
- Audio Review (Private Pilot only)
- Online Communication Course
- Security-Related Airspace Course
- Navigational plotter
- Flight computer
- Flight bag

For ground training, your learners will need to have at least a textbook *(Pilot Handbook)*, a *FAR/AIM*, a means of test preparation (*Private Pilot FAA Knowledge Test Prep* or *Sport Pilot FAA Knowledge Test Prep*, **FAA Test Prep Online**, and/or Gleim **Online Ground School**), a navigational plotter, and a flight computer. These items make up most of the Pilot Kits; the remaining items are primarily concerned with flight training. Because most people who take ground school courses intend to undertake flight training, it makes sense for your learners to go ahead and obtain everything they will need at one time (at substantial savings) by purchasing the Pilot Kit.

SAMPLE COURSE SYLLABUS

COURSE SYLLABUS

Jonesville Community College
Evening Education Course 1121

Tuesday evenings, 7:00 - 10:00 p.m.
North Campus, Building C, Room 171

PRIVATE PILOT/SPORT PILOT GROUND SCHOOL
Summer Term A, 20XX
June 1 - July 27

INSTRUCTOR: Mr. Harold Gray, AGI
Office: (111) 555-5252
Home: (111) 555-2525

COURSE OBJECTIVE: Learn the material required by the FAA for the private pilot knowledge test (airplane) and sport pilot knowledge test with the objective of each learner passing the test.

CLASSROOM PROCEDURE: Lecture and guided discussion.

1. Each class will begin with a review and questions from the last class (approximately 5-15 minutes).

2. Next, there will be a brief overview and core concepts for the current evening's assignment, followed by class discussion and questions.

3. When appropriate, after the class break, an in-class quiz will be administered, self-graded, and analyzed through class discussion.

4. The last 15-30 minutes of each class session will be directed toward an overview and discussion of the next class's assignment.

5. Visual aids and handouts will be used as appropriate.

REQUIRED TEXT: *Private Pilot FAA Knowledge Test Prep*, by Irvin N. Gleim and Garrett W. Gleim, or *Sport Pilot FAA Knowledge Test Prep*, by Irvin N. Gleim and Garrett W. Gleim

RECOMMENDED TEXT: *Pilot Handbook*, by Irvin N. Gleim and Garrett W. Gleim

These texts are available in the College Bookstore on the North Campus, which is open until 8:00 p.m. each Tuesday.

SCHEDULE

Class	Date	PPKT* Study Units	SPKT** Study Units	Topic
1	June 1	Introduction, 1	Introduction, 11	Introduction, Aerodynamic Theory
2	June 8	1, 2	11, 13	Aerodynamics and Airplane Systems
3	June 15	2, 3	1, 2, 13	Airplane Systems, Airports, ATC
4	June 22	3, 4	2-5	Airspace, 14 CFR
5	June 29	4, 5	3-5, 14	14 CFR, Airplane Performance
6	July 6	5, 6	6, 14	Weight and Balance, Aeromedical Factors
7	July 13	7, 8	7, 8	Aviation Weather and Weather Services
8	July 20	9, 10, 11	9, 10	Navigation, Cross-Country Flight
9	July 27			Review for pilot knowledge test

* PPKT = *Private Pilot FAA Knowledge Test Prep*
** SPKT = *Sport Pilot FAA Knowledge Test Prep*

You may photocopy this syllabus and change it in any way you like.

ENROLLMENT PROCEDURES

1. You should make a list of the learners and their contact information so you can contact them in the event the classes need to be changed, rescheduled, etc.

    a. Note the form and date of their payment.

2. As each learner enrolls, you can sell (or give, if the materials are included in the cost of the ground school course) him or her book(s), software, and/or online course access.

3. If you have a syllabus ready, distribute copies to your learners and encourage them to do some study in advance.

4. With respect to requiring or recommending *Pilot Handbook* and *Aviation Weather and Weather Services*, you may proceed as follows:

    a. For each learner, put one copy of each title on reserve in the bookstore of your choice.

    b. Get one copy of each book and pass them around to the class; indicate learners can purchase another one from you, a local FBO, or the bookstore you are using.

    c. Alternatively, have them order the materials by calling us at (800) 874-5346 or ordering online at www.GleimAviation.com.

5. Note that you may wish to encourage each person who enrolls or even inquires about the program to invite friends to take the course with him or her. The idea is to build enrollment through enthusiasm for and interest in aviation.

THE FIRST CLASS SESSION

1. Preliminaries

    a. Arrive early with a supply of books, handouts, and your lecture notes for the first lecture.

    b. Begin by enrolling any learners who show up at the first class without having already enrolled.

    c. Go over the roll and pass out the syllabus.

    d. Introduce yourself.

2. Learner-Instructor Interaction

    a. Tell the learners about your background, the origin of the course, your reasons for teaching, and any other relevant personal things.

    b. Tell the class that you need to learn more about them in order to teach effectively.

        1) Ask people to introduce themselves.

        2) Unless the class is too large, make notes on your roster to individualize participants and help you learn their names.

        3) Ask them why they are taking the course, if they have any flying experience, if they know anyone else who flies, if they have ever flown before in a small aircraft, etc.

    c. Such interaction is an ice-breaker, allowing you to get to know your learners and allowing them to get to know you and one another.

3. Discussion of Course Objective (FAA Pilot Knowledge Test)

   a. Display ***Private Pilot FAA Knowledge Test Prep*** and ***Sport Pilot FAA Knowledge Test Prep***.

   b. Point out that the textbooks have sample FAA questions reorganized by topic with answer explanations next to them.

   c. Indicate that the areas tested on the exams will be the topics specified on your syllabus (course outline), that the test will be only 60 questions for private and 40 questions for sport, and that the learners need to get at least 42 questions correct for private and 28 questions correct for sport in order to pass.

      1) This will be very easy because they will have gone over many possible test questions during your course (all of which appear in ***Private Pilot FAA Knowledge Test Prep*** and ***Sport Pilot FAA Knowledge Test Prep***), as well as additional material to help them learn how to fly safely.

   d. Explain the content of ***Private Pilot FAA Knowledge Test Prep*** and/or ***Sport Pilot FAA Knowledge Test Prep***.

      1) Explain that the Introduction is the current topic of discussion.

      2) Show them the organization of Study Units 1 through 11 for Private Pilot and Study Units 1 through 14 for Sport Pilot.

         a) Each study unit begins with an outline, subunit by subunit (topic by topic).

         b) Following the outlines are questions and answer explanations organized in the same subunits and presented in the same order.

         c) Thus, the learners are able to study and try to learn the material before they answer the questions. This format provides an extra level of reinforcement as they study the material.

4. Discussion of Course Objective (Comprehensive Coverage)

   a. Display ***Pilot Handbook*** and ***Private Pilot FAA Knowledge Test Prep*** or ***Sport Pilot FAA Knowledge Test Prep***.

   b. Explain that both ***Pilot Handbook*** and ***Private Pilot FAA Knowledge Test Prep*** have the same study unit numbers and titles, which means that the content of each study unit number in both books will correspond (for ***Sport Pilot FAA Knowledge Test Prep***, they will need to refer to the index).

      1) Explain that, because the study units of these books are complementary, Study Units 1 through 4 of ***Pilot Handbook*** are disproportionately larger than their counterparts in ***Private Pilot FAA Knowledge Test Prep*** and ***Sport Pilot FAA Knowledge Test Prep***. Explain that this is because there is a lot of material that the FAA does not test, but with which a pilot must be familiar in order to fly safely (much of this untested material happens to fit into the first four study units).

      2) Explain that more time will therefore be spent on Study Units 1 through 4 of ***Pilot Handbook***.

   c. Explain that, while your learners will be well prepared for their pilot knowledge test at the completion of this course, it is not your goal to simply "teach the test" and that you plan to give them a solid background in aviation topics.

      1) Explain that they will be expected to follow the progress of the course in ***Private Pilot FAA Knowledge Test Prep*** or ***Sport Pilot FAA Knowledge Test Prep*** on their own and that you will primarily be teaching out of ***Pilot Handbook***.

      2) Provide additional background about how to use ***Private Pilot FAA Knowledge Test Prep*** or ***Sport Pilot FAA Knowledge Test Prep*** based on item 3. of this list.

LECTURE PRESENTATION

1. There are many ways to present a lecture, and you should use the method with which you feel most comfortable. The best method for you will be the best method for your learners because you will perform better.

2. One approach to keep in mind is the idea of hitting the high points or key concepts.

    a. What are the basic or major concepts within any topic? These are generally outlined at the opening of each study unit in ***Private Pilot FAA Knowledge Test Prep*** and ***Sport Pilot FAA Knowledge Test Prep***.

    b. To amplify these concepts and provide additional discussion, consult ***Pilot Handbook***, after which you can use additional examples from other textbooks, including the FAA/government textbooks.

3. A major objective of your lecture presentation is to make it interactive: The learners must respond to you and participate.

    a. Learning is **not** a one-way communication from you to your learners.

    b. You need to ask questions of individual learners and of the class as a whole so that they can react and commit to an answer (silently or orally) and then get immediate feedback about the accuracy of their responses.

4. Have them work examples, e.g., provide them with a calculation and ask them to determine the answer.

    a. You could present a series of sample questions, take away the alternative answers, and have them work through a couple of exercises.

    b. You might also put these on overhead projectors.

5. Your preparation before class is very important. You should consult the lesson plan discussed in Study Unit 5, Subunit 3, "Lesson Plan," beginning on page 120 and review Study Unit 4, "Teaching Methods," beginning on page 93.

VISUAL AIDS

1. Visual aids include small model airplanes, videos, slides, blackboard presentations, overhead projector pictures, etc.

2. Visual aids are most helpful in explaining ideas that are abstract when presented verbally (e.g., airspace).

3. You can bring items to class and pass them around, such as navigation tools/charts and operating manuals from airplanes.

4. Experiment with visual aids. Use them as attention-getters or to break the pace of the normal presentation.

5. If using presentation software (such as Microsoft PowerPoint), avoid reading from slides. Use this tool to present important (i.e., tested) concepts as well as images, animations, and/or video.

COURSE EVALUATIONS

1. At the end of the course, but before the session set aside for the FAA knowledge test, you should administer a course evaluation.

    a. Your objective is to obtain feedback from your learners about how the course can be improved in several aspects, including

        1) Course organization
        2) Textbook(s)
        3) Lecture presentation
        4) Physical facilities

    b. Let the learners know that you are seeking constructive criticism across many areas.

    c. Tell them that you do not want to make them ill at ease, so you are going to ask one member (tell them who) to hold the evaluations until the course is over.

    d. If the course is for grade credit, the evaluations should be held until after you have turned in the grades.

2. Please feel free to photocopy and modify the course evaluation illustrated below. Note that you should leave the back blank for additional written comments.

3. Remember that, at the conclusion of the last class session prior to your learners taking the FAA pilot knowledge test, you need to complete the Instructor Certification Form at the back of ***Private Pilot FAA Knowledge Test Prep*** or ***Sport Pilot FAA Knowledge Test Prep*** for each learner.

Date _____

(NAME OF COURSE)
GROUND SCHOOL EVALUATION FORM

This Ground School is being presented to aid you in your preparation for the FAA knowledge test. Please help us by answering the following questions, keeping in mind our objective: to help you prepare for the FAA knowledge test. Please check one response for each line. Return the completed form to the person designated to hold the evaluations until the completion of the last class (or after grades have been turned in).

Instructor	Excellent	Good	Adequate	Poor
1. Instructor presentation of material	——	——	——	——
2. Instructor knowledge of subject	——	——	——	——
3. Allocation of time to topics	——	——	——	——
4. Use of slides, boards, visual aids, etc.	——	——	——	——
5. Use of handouts, problems, etc.	——	——	——	——
Other questions				
6. Overall rating of instructor	——	——	——	——
7. Classroom comfort	——	——	——	——
8. Progress of class as a whole	——	——	——	——
9. Outlines in *FAA Knowledge Test Prep*	——	——	——	——
10. Answer explanations in *FAA Knowledge Test Prep*	——	——	——	——
11. Overall rating of *FAA Knowledge Test Prep*	——	——	——	——

12. **Other comments.** Please explain poor responses and make any other suggestions you feel may be relevant in the space provided below and on the back of this sheet. **Thank you.**

HELPING YOUR LEARNERS SELECT A COMPUTER TESTING CENTER

1. Since most computer testing centers have limited seating, it is unlikely that you will be able to have all of your learners take the test at the same time and place.

    a. Thus, you will need to help your learners in the selection of a computer testing center.

2. Call each testing service to determine if any discounts are being offered and the payment policy. Explain your class situation (number of learners, etc.).

    a. Some learners may not have a credit card, so they need to select a computer testing center that will accept a check or cash at the time of the test.

        1) Some computer testing services may require that a check or money order be sent before the learner can take the test.

    b. Make yourself available to assist your learners as necessary.

3. Provide your learners with the contact information for the following PSI computer testing service and the results of your inquiries.

    PSI   (800) 211-2754 or www.psiexams.com

4. Discuss the examination process and demonstrate testing procedures by using Gleim **FAA Test Prep Online**.

5. You, as a flight instructor, are required to maintain a record of each person for whom you sign a certification for a pilot knowledge test, including the kind of test, date of test, and the test result (14 CFR 61.189).

    a. An efficient way of obtaining test results is to pre-address and stamp one postcard for each learner (include the learner's name on the card) and explain why you need these returned.

        1) Hand them out on the exam day.
        2) Ask learners to mail their numerical scores to you.
        3) List the learner scores on your roster as they come in the mail.
        4) Call any individuals who have not submitted cards.

    b. Email is another simple method for obtaining this information.

    c. You can use these pass rates in future advertising.

AN ALTERNATIVE APPROACH: EXPANDING YOUR MARKET

1. You may wish to broaden your ground school course so that it appeals to aviation enthusiasts interested in doing more than passing the FAA private pilot (airplane) or sport pilot knowledge test. If so, you need to

    a. Diversify your marketing plan and advertisements.
    b. Edit the suggested syllabus (make it more general).
    c. Prepare fewer class assignments focused on the FAA pilot knowledge test.

2. Can you prepare learner pilots for the FAA pilot knowledge test **and** provide a general-interest aviation course?

    a. Many ground schools are so directed, especially at community colleges where a considerable number of enrollees do not take the FAA pilot knowledge test.

    b. One approach is to emphasize discussion of sample FAA test questions at the end (optional part) of each class, e.g., in a 100-minute class.

        1) The last 30 minutes might be restricted to discussion of sample FAA questions in *Private Pilot FAA Knowledge Test Prep* and/or *Sport Pilot FAA Knowledge Test Prep*.

        2) The first 70 minutes would involve lecture discussion.

    c. Occasional questions might be discussed, but the emphasis would be on learning about airplanes, weather, and navigation rather than passing the FAA pilot knowledge test.

    d. In such a course, *Pilot Handbook* would be the required text instead of *Private Pilot FAA Knowledge Test Prep* or *Sport Pilot FAA Knowledge Test Prep*, which can be optional.

3. With these general guidelines, we trust you will take the plunge and **start your class** (or at least begin to prepare for it) **right now**! It is fun, and it provides a valuable service -- teaching new aviation enthusiasts to **ENJOY FLYING -- SAFELY!**

408

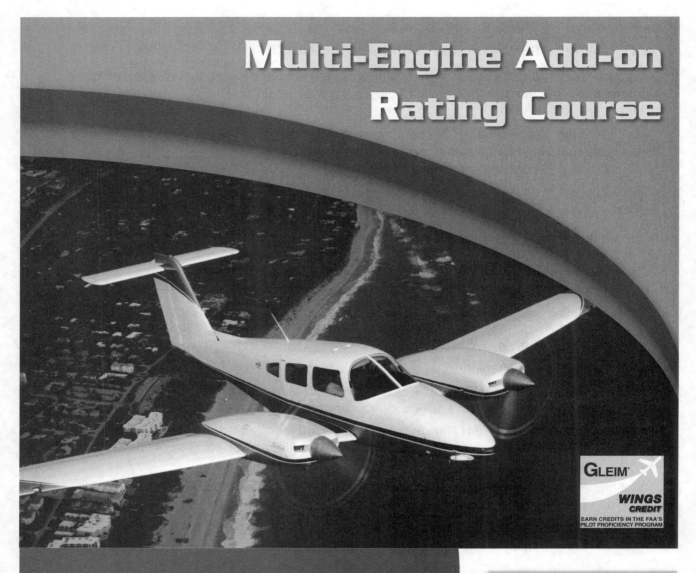

CROSS-REFERENCES TO
THE FAA LEARNING STATEMENT CODES

Pages 409 through 412 contain a listing of all of the questions from our fundamentals of instructing knowledge test bank. The questions are in FAA learning statement code (LSC) sequence. (Refer to page 14 in the Introduction for a complete listing and description of each.) To the right of each LSC, we present our study unit/question number and our answer. For example, note below that PLT022 is cross-referenced to 3-17, which represents our Study Unit 3, question 17; the correct answer is B.

The first line of each of our answer explanations in Study Units 1 through 6 contains

1. The correct answer and
2. A reference for the answer explanation, e.g., *FAA-H-8083-9B Chap 1*. If this reference is not useful, use the following chart to identify the learning statement code to determine the specific reference appropriate for the question.

FAA Learning Code	Gleim SU/ Q. No.	Gleim Answer	FAA Learning Code	Gleim SU/ Q. No.	Gleim Answer	FAA Learning Code	Gleim SU/ Q. No.	Gleim Answer
PLT022	3–17	B	PLT211	6–58	C	PLT229	3–78	C
PLT022	3–20	C	PLT211	6–59	B	PLT229	3–79	B
PLT022	3–24	A	PLT227	4–45	A	PLT229	3–80	B
PLT103	3–21	B	PLT227	4–46	A	PLT229	6–7	C
PLT103	3–23	A	PLT227	4–47	C	PLT230	2–38	A
PLT103	3–29	A	PLT227	4–48	B	PLT230	3–18	B
PLT103	3–32	B	PLT227	4–49	A	PLT230	3–65	C
PLT204	3–37	B	PLT227	4–50	B	PLT230	3–66	B
PLT204	3–38	B	PLT227	4–51	A	PLT230	3–67	B
PLT204	3–39	A	PLT228	5–22	C	PLT230	3–68	A
PLT204	3–40	C	PLT228	5–24	C	PLT230	3–69	B
PLT204	3–41	C	PLT228	5–26	B	PLT230	3–70	C
PLT204	3–42	B	PLT228	5–27	A	PLT230	3–71	B
PLT204	3–43	A	PLT228	5–28	A	PLT230	4–53	B
PLT204	3–44	B	PLT228	5–29	B	PLT231	1–16	A
PLT204	3–45	C	PLT228	5–30	C	PLT231	1–17	A
PLT204	3–46	C	PLT228	5–31	C	PLT231	1–21	A
PLT204	3–47	C	PLT228	5–32	C	PLT231	2–17	B
PLT204	3–48	C	PLT228	5–33	C	PLT231	2–18	C
PLT204	3–52	B	PLT228	5–36	B	PLT231	2–19	B
PLT204	3–53	B	PLT228	5–37	C	PLT231	2–20	B
PLT204	3–54	C	PLT228	5–43	C	PLT231	2–21	A
PLT204	3–55	A	PLT228	5–44	A	PLT231	2–22	A
PLT204	3–56	C	PLT228	5–52	A	PLT231	2–23	C
PLT204	3–57	A	PLT229	3–73	A	PLT231	2–25	A
PLT204	3–58	B	PLT229	3–74	B	PLT231	2–27	A
PLT211	6–11	A	PLT229	3–75	A	PLT231	2–29	C
PLT211	6–15	B	PLT229	3–76	C	PLT231	2–30	A
PLT211	6–18	C	PLT229	3–77	A	PLT231	2–31	C

FAA Learning Code	Gleim SU/ Q. No.	Gleim Answer	FAA Learning Code	Gleim SU/ Q. No.	Gleim Answer	FAA Learning Code	Gleim SU/ Q. No.	Gleim Answer
PLT231	2–32	C	PLT295	2–36	C	PLT307	1–37	B
PLT231	3–6	A	PLT295	3–50	C	PLT307	1–38	C
PLT232	2–26	C	PLT295	3–51	C	PLT307	5–39	B
PLT232	2–28	B	PLT295	4–54	B	PLT307	5–40	A
PLT232	2–34	B	PLT295	5–1	A	PLT308	1–1	A
PLT232	2–35	B	PLT295	5–6	A	PLT308	1–4	B
PLT232	2–37	B	PLT295	5–11	A	PLT308	1–5	C
PLT232	3–31	B	PLT295	5–25	A	PLT308	1–6	A
PLT232	3–34	A	PLT295	5–35	C	PLT308	1–7	A
PLT232	3–36	A	PLT295	5–38	A	PLT308	1–8	A
PLT233	2–5	C	PLT295	5–45	A	PLT308	1–9	C
PLT233	2–6	C	PLT306	1–3	C	PLT308	1–10	B
PLT233	2–7	B	PLT306	1–19	B	PLT308	1–11	A
PLT233	2–8	C	PLT306	1–27	B	PLT308	1–12	A
PLT233	2–9	A	PLT306	1–31	B	PLT308	1–15	B
PLT233	2–10	B	PLT306	1–39	B	PLT308	1–18	A
PLT233	2–11	B	PLT306	1–40	C	PLT308	1–24	B
PLT233	2–12	B	PLT306	1–41	A	PLT308	1–28	A
PLT233	2–13	B	PLT306	1–42	A	PLT308	1–50	B
PLT233	2–14	B	PLT306	1–43	A	PLT308	1–51	C
PLT233	2–15	B	PLT306	1–47	B	PLT308	1–52	C
PLT233	2–16	B	PLT306	1–48	C	PLT308	1–53	B
PLT270	3–1	B	PLT306	1–49	A	PLT308	1–54	A
PLT270	3–2	C	PLT306	1–55	A	PLT308	1–56	C
PLT270	3–3	C	PLT306	1–57	A	PLT308	1–58	A
PLT270	3–4	C	PLT306	1–67	A	PLT308	1–59	B
PLT270	3–22	B	PLT306	1–71	A	PLT308	1–60	C
PLT271	3–19	C	PLT306	1–72	C	PLT308	1–61	A
PLT271	3–26	C	PLT306	1–73	B	PLT308	1–62	C
PLT271	3–27	A	PLT307	1–2	C	PLT308	1–63	B
PLT271	3–28	A	PLT307	1–22	B	PLT308	1–64	A
PLT271	3–30	C	PLT307	1–23	C	PLT308	1–65	B
PLT272	2–24	A	PLT307	1–25	A	PLT308	1–74	A
PLT272	3–25	C	PLT307	1–26	A	PLT308	1–75	B
PLT272	3–33	C	PLT307	1–29	C	PLT308	2–1	C
PLT272	3–35	C	PLT307	1–30	C	PLT308	2–2	A
PLT295	1–69	B	PLT307	1–32	A	PLT481	1–20	C
PLT295	1–70	C	PLT307	1–33	B	PLT481	1–66	B
PLT295	1–76	A	PLT307	1–34	C	PLT481	1–68	B
PLT295	1–77	B	PLT307	1–35	C	PLT481	1–78	A
PLT295	2–33	B	PLT307	1–36	B	PLT481	1–79	B

FAA Learning Code	Gleim SU/ Q. No.	Gleim Answer	FAA Learning Code	Gleim SU/ Q. No.	Gleim Answer	FAA Learning Code	Gleim SU/ Q. No.	Gleim Answer
PLT481	3–59	C	PLT482	6–39	C	PLT488	4–10	C
PLT481	3–60	C	PLT482	6–40	A	PLT488	4–11	A
PLT481	3–62	B	PLT482	6–42	C	PLT488	4–12	B
PLT481	3–64	A	PLT482	6–43	A	PLT488	4–13	B
PLT481	6–13	B	PLT482	6–44	B	PLT488	4–14	B
PLT481	6–41	C	PLT482	6–45	C	PLT488	4–15	A
PLT481	6–63	C	PLT482	6–46	A	PLT488	4–16	B
PLT482	1–45	C	PLT482	6–47	B	PLT488	4–17	A
PLT482	1–46	C	PLT482	6–48	B	PLT488	4–18	C
PLT482	4–55	C	PLT482	6–49	C	PLT488	4–19	B
PLT482	6–1	C	PLT482	6–50	B	PLT488	4–20	C
PLT482	6–2	C	PLT482	6–51	C	PLT488	4–21	C
PLT482	6–3	B	PLT482	6–52	A	PLT489	5–16	B
PLT482	6–4	C	PLT482	6–53	C	PLT489	5–19	B
PLT482	6–5	B	PLT482	6–54	A	PLT490	1–13	A
PLT482	6–6	A	PLT482	6–55	B	PLT490	1–14	A
PLT482	6–8	B	PLT482	6–56	C	PLT490	2–3	A
PLT482	6–10	C	PLT482	6–57	B	PLT490	2–4	C
PLT482	6–12	A	PLT482	6–60	A	PLT490	2–39	A
PLT482	6–16	C	PLT482	6–61	B	PLT490	2–40	B
PLT482	6–17	A	PLT482	6–62	B	PLT490	3–5	B
PLT482	6–19	B	PLT487	3–72	B	PLT490	3–7	A
PLT482	6–20	C	PLT487	4–22	C	PLT490	3–8	B
PLT482	6–21	B	PLT487	4–23	C	PLT490	3–9	B
PLT482	6–22	B	PLT487	4–24	C	PLT490	3–10	B
PLT482	6–23	A	PLT487	4–25	C	PLT490	3–11	A
PLT482	6–24	C	PLT487	4–26	B	PLT490	3–12	B
PLT482	6–25	A	PLT487	4–27	C	PLT490	3–13	C
PLT482	6–26	B	PLT487	4–28	B	PLT490	3–14	A
PLT482	6–27	A	PLT487	4–29	B	PLT490	3–15	A
PLT482	6–28	B	PLT487	4–30	B	PLT490	3–16	C
PLT482	6–29	A	PLT488	3–49	A	PLT490	3–61	A
PLT482	6–30	A	PLT488	4–1	A	PLT490	3–63	A
PLT482	6–31	B	PLT488	4–2	A	PLT490	4–52	B
PLT482	6–32	A	PLT488	4–3	B	PLT490	5–23	A
PLT482	6–33	B	PLT488	4–4	B	PLT491	4–31	B
PLT482	6–34	A	PLT488	4–5	B	PLT491	4–32	A
PLT482	6–35	C	PLT488	4–6	C	PLT491	4–33	A
PLT482	6–36	C	PLT488	4–7	C	PLT491	4–34	A
PLT482	6–37	B	PLT488	4–8	B	PLT491	4–35	A
PLT482	6–38	A	PLT488	4–9	A	PLT491	4–36	C

FAA Learning Code	Gleim SU/ Q. No.	Gleim Answer
PLT491	4–37	C
PLT491	4–38	B
PLT491	4–42	B
PLT491	4–43	C
PLT491	4–44	B
PLT491	5–2	B
PLT491	5–3	C
PLT491	5–4	C
PLT491	5–5	C
PLT491	5–7	B
PLT491	5–8	C
PLT491	5–9	C
PLT491	5–10	C
PLT491	5–12	B
PLT491	5–13	B
PLT491	5–14	C
PLT491	5–15	A
PLT491	5–17	A
PLT491	5–18	A
PLT491	5–20	A
PLT491	5–21	C
PLT491	5–34	A
PLT491	5–41	A
PLT491	5–42	C
PLT504	5–46	B
PLT504	5–49	A
PLT504	5–50	B
PLT504	6–9	A
PLT504	6–14	A
PLT505	1–44	A
PLT505	4–39	A
PLT505	4–40	C
PLT505	4–41	C
PLT505	5–47	C
PLT505	5–48	B
PLT505	5–51	A

LESSON:

LEARNER: _____ **DATE:** _____

OBJECTIVE

CONTENT

SCHEDULE

EQUIPMENT

INSTRUCTOR'S ACTIONS

LEARNER'S ACTIONS

COMPLETION STANDARDS

ABBREVIATIONS AND ACRONYMS IN
FUNDAMENTALS OF INSTRUCTING FAA KNOWLEDGE TEST PREP

14 CFR	Code of Federal Regulations	MH	magnetic heading
AC	Advisory Circular	MOA	Military Operations Area
ACS	Airman Certification Standards	MSL	mean sea level
AD	Airworthiness Directive	MTR	military training route
ADM	aeronautical decision making	MVFR	marginal VFR
AFSS	Automated Flight Service Station	NFCT	nonfederal control tower
AGL	above ground level	NM	nautical mile
AIM	*Aeronautical Information Manual*	NPRM	Notice of Proposed Rulemaking
AIRMET	Airman's Meteorological Information	NTSB	National Transportation Safety Board
AME	aviation medical examiner	OAT	outside air temperature
ANDS	accelerate north, decelerate south	OBS	omnibearing selector
AOE	airport of entry	PAPI	precision approach path indicator
ARTS	Automated Radar Terminal System	PBL	problem-based learning
ASEL	airplane single-engine land	PCL	pilot-controlled lighting
ATA	actual time of arrival	PIC	pilot in command
ATC	Air Traffic Control	PIREP	pilot weather report
ATIS	Automatic Terminal Information Service	POH	Pilot's Operating Handbook
AWOS	Automated Weather Observing System	PTS	Practical Test Standards
CAL	computer-assisted learning	RB	relative bearing
CDI	course deviation indicator	SBT	scenario-based training
CDT	central daylight time	SFC	surface
CFI	certificated flight instructor	SIGMET	Significant Meteorological Information
CG	center of gravity	SM	statute mile
CH	compass heading	SRM	single-pilot resource management
CT	control tower	STC	supplemental type certificate
CTAF	Common Traffic Advisory Frequency	SVFR	special VFR
DME	distance measuring equipment	TACAN	Tactical Air Navigation
DT	daylight time	TAF	terminal aerodrome forecast
DVFR	defense VFR	TAS	true airspeed
ELT	emergency locator transmitter	TC	true course
ETA	estimated time of arrival	TH	true heading
ETD	estimated time of departure	UHF	ultra high frequency
FAA	Federal Aviation Administration	UTC	Coordinated Universal Time
FAA-H-8083-9B	*Aviation Instructor's Handbook*	V_A	maneuvering speed
FAR	Federal Aviation Regulation	VASI	visual approach slope indicator
FBO	fixed-base operator	V_{FE}	maximum flap extended speed
FCC	Federal Communications Commission	VFR	visual flight rules
FD	winds and temperatures aloft forecast	VHF	very high frequency
FL	flight level	VHF/DF	VHF direction finder
FSS	Flight Service Station	VIP	video integrated processor
GPH	gallons per hour	V_{LE}	maximum landing gear extended speed
Hg	mercury	V_{NE}	never-exceed speed
HOTS	higher order thinking skills	V_{NO}	maximum structural cruising speed
HP	horsepower	VOR	VHF omnidirectional range
IAS	indicated airspeed	VORTAC	collocated VOR and TACAN
ICAO	International Civil Aviation Organization	VOT	VOR test facility
IFR	instrument flight rules	VR	visual route
IMC	instrument meteorological conditions	V_{S0}	stalling speed or the minimum steady flight speed in the landing configuration
IR	instrument route		
ISA	International Standard Atmosphere	V_{S1}	stalling speed or the minimum steady flight speed obtained in a specific configuration
LLWAS	low-level wind-shear alert system		
mb	millibar		
MB	magnetic bearing	V_X	speed for best angle of climb
MC	magnetic course	V_Y	speed for best rate of climb
MEF	maximum elevation figure	WCA	wind correction angle
METAR	aviation routine weather report	Z	Zulu or UTC time

AUTHORS' RECOMMENDATIONS

Gleim cooperates with and supports all aspects of the flight training industry, particularly organizations that focus on aviation recruitment and flight training. Below are some of the top organizations for anyone interested in aviation.

EXPERIMENTAL AIRCRAFT ASSOCIATION: YOUNG EAGLES PROGRAM

The Experimental Aircraft Association's (EAA) Young Eagles Program has provided free introductory flights to over 1 million young people ages 8 to 17. This program helps young people understand the important role aviation plays in our daily lives and provides insight into how an airplane flies, what it takes to become a pilot, and the high standards flying demands in terms of safety and quality.

NOTE: The Gleim *Learn to Fly* booklet (available for free at www.GleimAviation.com/learn-to-fly) is used as "ground school" training for Young Eagles programs. For more information about the Young Eagles Program, visit www.youngeagles.org or call 1-800-564-6322.

AIRCRAFT OWNERS AND PILOTS ASSOCIATION

The Aircraft Owners and Pilots Association (AOPA) hosts an informational web page on getting started in aviation for those still dreaming about flying, those who are ready to begin, and those who are already making the journey. Interested individuals can order a FREE subscription to Flight Training Magazine, which explains how amazing it is to be a pilot. Other resources are available, such as a flight school finder, a guide on what to expect throughout training, an explanation of pilot certification options, a FREE flight training newsletter, and much more. To learn more, visit www.aopa.org.

CIVIL AIR PATROL: CADET ORIENTATION FLIGHT PROGRAM

The Civil Air Patrol (CAP) Cadet Orientation Flight Program is designed to introduce CAP cadets to flying. The program is voluntary and primarily motivational, and it is designed to stimulate cadets' interest in and knowledge of aviation.

Each orientation flight is approximately 1 hour, follows a prescribed syllabus, and is usually in the local area of the airport. Except for takeoff, landing, and a few other portions of the flight, cadets are encouraged to handle the controls. For information about the CAP cadet program nearest you, visit www.gocivilairpatrol.com.

WOMEN IN AVIATION INTERNATIONAL

Women in Aviation International (WAI) is a nonprofit organization dedicated to the encouragement and advancement of women in all aviation career fields and interests. Its diverse membership includes astronauts, corporate pilots, maintenance technicians, air traffic controllers, business owners, educators and students, journalists, flight attendants, air show performers, airport managers, and many others.

WAI provides year-round resources to assist women in aviation and encourage young women to consider aviation as a career. WAI also offers educational outreach programs to educators, aviation industry members, and young people nationally and internationally. An annual Girls in Aviation Day was recently initiated for girls ages 8 to 17. Learn more at www.wai.org.

NINETY-NINES

The Ninety-Nines (99s) is an international organization of women pilots with thousands of members from over 40 countries. Its goal is to promote advancement of aviation through education, scholarships, and mutual support. The 99s have co-sponsored over 75% of FAA pilot safety programs in the U.S. and annually sponsor hundreds of educational programs, such as aerospace workshops for teachers, airport tours for school children, fear-of-flying clinics for airline passengers, and flight instructor revalidation seminars. Learn more at www.ninety-nines.org.

INDEX